Public Policy Theories, Models, and Concepts

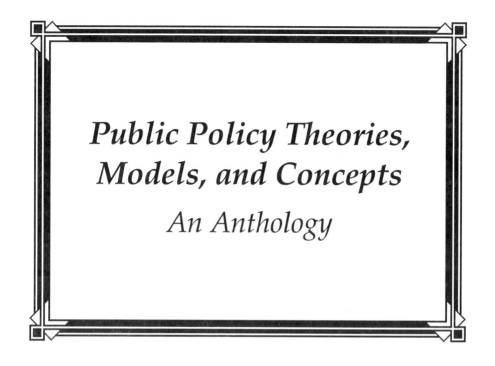

Public Policy Theories, Models, and Concepts

An Anthology

Daniel C. McCool
University of Utah

PRENTICE HALL, Englewood Cliffs, New Jersey 07632

Library of Congress Cataloging-in-Publication Data

Public policy theories, models, and concepts: an anthology/Daniel
    C. McCool [editor].
        p.   cm.
    Includes bibliographical references.
    ISBN 0-13-737867-X
    1. Policy sciences.   2. Political planning.   I. McCool, Daniel,
    H97.P835   1995
    320'.6—dc20   94-22744
                                                            CIP

Editorial/production supervision: Judy Hartman
Editorial director: Charlyce Jones Owen
Cover design: DeLuca Design
Buyer: Bob Anderson

© 1995 by Prentice-Hall, Inc.
A Simon & Schuster Company
Englewood Cliffs, New Jersey 07632

Printed in the United States of America
10   9   8   7   6   5   4   3   2   1

ISBN 0-13-737867-X

PRENTICE-HALL INTERNATIONAL (UK) LIMITED, *London*
PRENTICE-HALL OF AUSTRALIA PTY. LIMITED, *Sydney*
PRENTICE-HALL CANADA INC., *Toronto*
PRENTICE-HALL HISPANOAMERICANA, S.A., *Mexico*
PRENTICE-HALL OF INDIA PRIVATE LIMITED, *New Delhi*
PRENTICE-HALL OF JAPAN, INC., *Tokyo*
SIMON & SCHUSTER ASIA PTE. LTD., *Singapore*
EDITORA PRENTICE-HALL DO BRASIL, LTDA., *Rio de Janeiro*

I dedicate this book to my parents,
Jack W. McCool and Olivia Grace McCool.

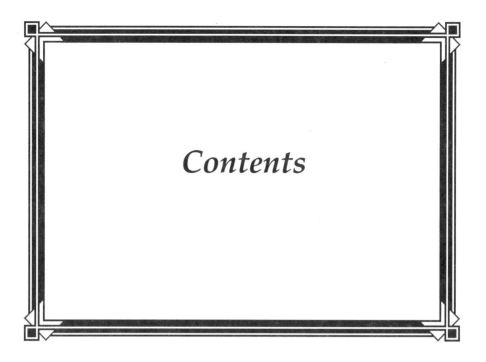

Contents

Section 3   The Process of Public
Policy Making   105

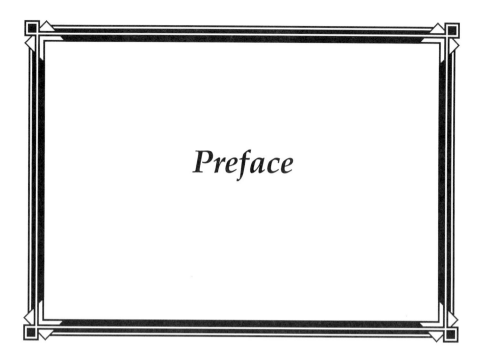

Preface

On the first day of my policy theory class, I pull a toy car out of my brief-case—a two-inch-long replica of a fancy Italian sports car. "Those of you who know something about cars: What is this?" The students study it. Some look puzzled, but a few are quick to demonstrate their expertise.

"It's a Lamborghini," one of them says.

"No," I reply. They all furrow their brows, squinting. A few other guesses are offered.

"A Ferrari?"

"Nope."

Finally I reveal the answer to the trick question: "It's a *model* of a Lamborghini, right?" They all nod, knowing that they've been had, but already realizing that the difference between a car and a model of a car is, after all, a significant distinction.

Next, without realizing it, we begin discussing theoretical validity. "How do you know this is a model of a Lamborghini? It has no engine, the steering wheel doesn't turn, and you certainly can't drive it. In fact this model has only six parts, but a real Lamborghini has 20,000 parts." After some discussion we conclude that a model need only represent the general outline of the reality it represents in order to have some degree of accuracy or meaning.

Then I bring out another toy car, but this one is a very simple model of carved wood. "Is this a model of a Lamborghini?" I ask. Some say yes, others say no, still others say that it could be. "What is the difference between these two models?" Many answers are offered, usually in reference to specific parts of each car. I then place the two model cars side by side. "The differences between these two toys provides a lesson in theoretical validity, economy, replication, and generalization. If you are thinking about these models and what they represent, then you are already beginning to theorize." To use a phrase coined by my students, they are beginning to "think theoretically."

Using toys is an unusual way to begin a class in policy theory. But students are often intimidated by theory, and starting with a lesson that is visually verifiable informs them immediately that it really does make sense—there is no magic—and they are quite capable of conceptualization. The first lesson of theory is to convince students that they engage in abstraction on an almost daily basis—that they have been thinking theoretically all along. Ball notes that, "Even our most 'direct' observations are impregnated with expectations; thus there is no natural dividing line between 'basic' or 'observational' propositions and 'theoretical' ones."[1] Every generalization, every notation of patterned response, every analogy, is a form of theory. As Duncan MacRae points out, "Any public argument for a policy in terms of its expected results implies at least an intuitive causal model. . . ."[2]

By definition theory is abstract. But that does not mean it is irrelevant, other worldly, or too arcane for practical use. Thus the second lesson of theory building is that, if the theory has no relevance or usefulness, and cannot be understood, then it is not much of a theory. As Frankfort-Nachmias and Nachmias point out, ". . . theory is of practice, and in this sense it will be accepted or rejected. . . . In principle there is no contrast between theory and practice" (1992, 37).

Theory has gotten a bad rap, and an important task in any theory course is to convince students that much of what they have heard about theory is not true. The popular misconception of theory is fed by common phrases such as, "Well, that's how it's supposed to work in theory, but in reality. . . ." It seems that in the popular mind all theory is bad theory.

This is especially true in the social sciences. Students with a well-developed need for exactitude quickly become frustrated with social science theory. They want correlations of 99.5 percent, not moderate levels of probability; they can always think of exceptions to any theory offered; they can cite many examples of theories that appear to be lacking in "common sense," or that merely belabor the obvious. They do, of course, have a point.

---

[1]Ball, Terence (1976). "From Paradigms to Research Programs: Toward a Post-Kuhnian Political Science." *American Journal of Political Science*. XX (Feb.): 151–75.

[2]MacRae, Duncan (1976). *The Social Function of Social Science*. New Haven: Yale University Press.

Thus, in any theory class, it is best to start not with theory, but with the students' antagonism to theory—a "theory anxiety" akin to math anxiety. Talking with students about this, one quickly discovers they do not like theory because, to phrase it bluntly, it is too theoretical; they prefer policy substance—something that is "real." The task, then, is to convince students that theory *is* real—an abstraction of real.

This book exposes students to a wide variety of real theories and concepts of public policy. It begins by providing students with the criteria for evaluating theory. The goal is to help them study theory without intimidation, so they will ultimately discover that theory, even social science theory, can serve as a guide rather than an impediment to reasoned inquiry.

ACKNOWLEDGMENTS

This book is a direct result of my interaction with graduate students in the Executive Master of Public Administration Program at the University of Utah. These students taught me a great deal about teaching theory and about the theories themselves. Once they got the hang of it, they could quickly discern any weaknesses in the theories presented in this book, and they often conceived of revisions to the theories that were insightful and constructive. I am especially grateful for the contribution made by the first executive cohort: Frank Bell, Kathy Hobby, Sheldon Elman, John Harbert, Joanne Milner, Dan Parker, Rosiland McGee, Debbie Wynkoop-Green, June Skollingsberg, Alan Nichols, Terry Holzworth, Ron Daniels, Pat Fleming, and Rayce Tucker. This book is much improved as a result of their suggestions. I also received helpful feedback from colleagues Peter Diamond, Susan Olson, F. Ted Hebert, Ibrahim Karawan, and Peri Schwartz-Shea, and from Ira Sharkansky and Donna Gelfand and the following reviewers: Michael E. Kraft, *University of Wisconsin*–Green Bay; and John F. Whitney, Jr., *Lincoln Land Community College*. I also want to thank Jolaine Randall and the Center for Public Policy and Administration at the University of Utah. And finally, I am very appreciative of the authors whose work appears in this book. They have, in a very real sense, given us a lot to think about.

D.C.M

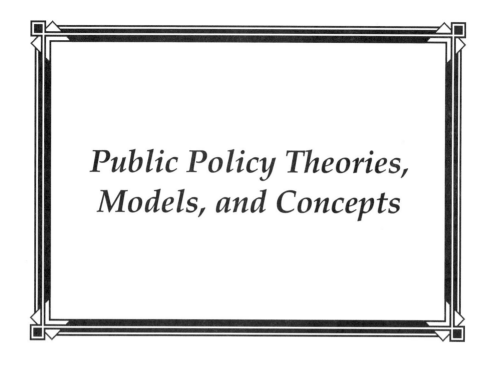

Public Policy Theories, Models, and Concepts

1

The Theoretical Foundation of Policy Studies

It could be argued that the study of public policy is as old as Plato's concern for The Republic (or older; see Dunn 1981, 8–19. Also see Levy 1988, 1–2), but the systematic analysis of the "output" of government is of quite recent origin. Indeed, all of the selections in this volume were written in the last forty years. The study of public policy did not suddenly spring into existence in the fifties and sixties, however. In 1921 Charles Merriam argued for the "cross fertilization of politics with science, so called, or more strictly with modern methods of inquiry and investigation. . . " (1921, 181). Two years later Merriam helped found the Social Science Research Council, which was dedicated to encouraging interdisciplinary research on diverse sociopolitical problems.

During and immediately after World War II, the need for applied research became more evident. The development of operations research and advancements in the study of economics and social psychology helped point the way to a more systematic and empirical investigation of policy making. It was not until 1951, however, that the concept of a "policy science" was clearly enunciated by Harold Lasswell. Lasswell's seminal work identified six basic characteristics of an emerging field of study "concerned with explaining the policy-making and policy-executing process" (1951, 14).

1

1. *Interdisciplinary.* Taking a cue from his mentor, Charles Merriam, Lasswell argued that policy science includes "the results of the social, psychological, and natural sciences in so far as they have a bearing on the policy needs of a given period" (1951, 4).

2. *Empirical.* Again following Merriam, Lasswell stressed the need for appropriate quantitative methodologies, which would produce "authentic information and responsible interpretations" (1951, 4). Lasswell was enamored with the intellectual traditions of logical positivism, but he still maintained a healthy skepticism of "brute empiricism" (see Malecha 1989, 4–5). He was aware of the limitations of empirical measurement when applied to policy: "The richness of the context in the study of interpersonal relations is such that it can be expressed only in part in quantitative terms" (1951, 8).

3. *Megapolicy.* Lasswell argued that policy science should focus on the big questions: "The basic emphasis. . . is upon the fundamental problems of man in society, rather than upon the topical issues of the moment" (1951, 8). He felt this focus on larger concerns would help the policy scientist rise above the querulous and trivial problems of low-level government functionaries.

4. *Theoretical Complexity.* Lasswell was acutely aware of the problems created when simple models are indiscriminately applied to the intricacies of human behavior. He noted that the "most fruitful hypotheses" are often derived from "rather complicated models" (1951, 9).

5. *Applied.* The emphasis was on research that would be of direct and immediate value to policy makers. Lasswell wanted the policy sciences to improve "the concrete content of the information and the interpretations available to policymakers" (1951, 3).

6. *Normative/Prescriptive.* It was Lasswell's hope that policy science could be used to buttress democratic government. Writing during the tense, formative years of the Cold War, he predicted that policy research would ultimately evolve into the "policy sciences of democracy" (1951, 10). This does not mean, however, that he was promoting some kind of prodemocratic propaganda effort. Rather, he viewed policy science as a way of protecting democracy from the politicization of information. This would be accomplished through "the development of social institutions which, devoted to inquiry, would help to counter the subtle influences of ideology as well as the obvious threats and temptations of power in the policy domain" (Torgerson 1992, 227).

Lasswell's call for the policy sciences was a significant milestone in the study of public policy, but at the time it was largely unheeded. There are a number of reasons for this. First, there were virtually no specialists trained in policy analysis. The work that had been done up to that time had truly been a pioneering effort, with scholars creating methodology and concepts as they were needed. Second, the computers necessary to handle huge data sets had not yet been developed. The technological capacity to do large-scale applied empirical research did not exist until the 1960s (see Putt and Springer 1989, 10–13). Third, the "behavioralist revolution,"[1] which was

---

[1]The term *behavioralism* refers to the movement in social science to abandon an institutional approach in favor of a rigid empiricism like that found in the physical sciences. The emphasis on quantitative methodology was congruent with Lasswell's concept of a policy science, but the behavioralists rejected outright any sort of applied, substantive policy research, especially if it was prescriptive in nature (see Ripley 1985, 15–16).

gaining credence in the early fifties, rejected applied substantive research, especially prescriptive studies. Fourth, policy science violated the disciplinary boundary lines of the day, falling victim to turf battles and jurisdictional squabbles. Writing about policy analysis, Jenkins-Smith points out that it "must take the analyst wherever the policy issue leads, making analysis the multidisciplinary activity par excellence" (1990, 11). And last, the prevailing scholarly ethos lead to a number of methodological and theoretical constrictions, even for those who were interested in pursuing Lasswell's goals.

> Lasswell's own unique emphasis on how macroproblems set the stage for the policy sciences was missed by the "new social science" advocates and descendants for whom he blazed trails. Social and psychological perspectives were providing ever narrowing definitions of both scientific method and appropriate ontology for the social sciences. The objectivity norms discredited the "useful knowledge" focus, while the micropolitics focus of most empirical theory made the growing literature more useful for explaining action than for forecasting policy needs and suggesting problem resolution (Graham 1988, 153).

These restrictive scholarly traditions had a particularly acute impact on policy science because it was such an unprecedented departure from past scientific endeavor. Throughout the tradition-bound fifties, policy science remained on the fringe. As Hugh Heclo noted, it was "historically a period of unusual barrenness in policy studies" (1972, 86).

It was not until the late 1960s that the study of public policy began to blossom and gain credibility. The Great Society programs of the Johnson administration created a need for a better understanding of expanded government activity. Robertson and Judd point out that "the explicit study of policy processes and outcomes evolved because of the proliferation of government programs in the 1960s and early 1970s" (1989, vii). This was not just a matter of orchestrating numerous new programs; the problems that government was attempting to solve presented an unprecedented challenge. Ham and Hill note that "the scale and apparent intractability of the problems facing government in western industrialized societies led policymakers to seek help in the solution of those problems" (1984, 1). This "help" came in the form of social science research that attempted to assess the impact of various programs, and in some cases, to suggest alternatives.

The demand for improved policy analysis made it evident that much of the traditional academic work in the social sciences was unsuitable for applied policy research. Hogwood and Gunn explain:

> . . . there has been over the past twenty-five years a spasmodic dissatisfaction in some academic circles with the very limited practical contribution to problem-solving made by the social sciences. Research and teaching have often been seen as "over-academic," inward-looking, concerned with methodology rather than substance, and irrelevant to real social problems (1984, 34).

This discontent with existing scholarly approaches created additional impetus to follow Lasswell's advice and construct new approaches both within and among various academic disciplines.

As the potential uses of policy research gained recognition, public and private funding became more accessible. This in turn led to improvements in theory, methodology, and research design. Policy science had become a "growth industry" (Doron 1992, 306). This growth and maturation of the policy studies field is reflected in the literature. In the late sixties two edited books helped set the tone for a new era that Randall Ripley called the "policy analysis and evaluation alternative," which followed and to some extent displaced the "behavioralist" and "new left" eras (1985, 14–18). *The Study of Policy Formation* (1968), edited by Raymond A. Bauer and Kenneth J. Gergen, was a collection of theoretical, methodological, and substantive policy research. In the introductory chapter Bauer explains that policy research is inherently difficult because of the "open system" and "transactional" nature of policy: "One of our major objectives is to think through the question of how the notion of anything being possibly related to everything else can be made tractable for the empirical researcher" (1968, 20). In other words, policy does not exist in discrete units; it is part of a complex system without clear demarcations. How does one study a subject without a beginning or an end, without parameters?

Also published in 1968 was Austin Ranney's influential edited volume, *Political Science and Public Policy* (which was partially sponsored by the Social Science Research Council). Ranney asked: "should political scientists in their research and teaching pay substantially more attention to policy contents than they have in recent years?" (1968, 3). He noted two reasons why the behavioralists concentrated on policy process to the exclusion of policy content.

> First, many behavioral political scientists evidently feel that focusing on content is likely to lead to evaluations of present policies and exhortations for new ones; and evaluations and exhortations, they feel, not only have no place in scientific enterprise, but are likely to divert scholarly attention and energy away from true scholarship. Second, many behavioral political scientists are concerned that the discipline may spread itself too thin by trying to do too much (1968, 12).

Ranney offered a spirited response to the behavioralists and echoed Lasswell's call to improve popular government through policy research; the study of policy content will "improve our understanding of policy processes and policy outcomes. . . [and] enable us to evaluate past and present policies more objectively, and/or advise policy-makers, with high technical skill and reliability, about the effectiveness of means and the interrelations of goals" (1968, 19).

Other landmark studies appeared in the late sixties and early seventies. Yehezkel Dror's *Public Policy making Reexamined* (1968) offered an "optimal model" of policy making that combined many of the best policy concepts in use at that time. He followed this with *Design for Policy Sciences* (1971), which argued that the existing scientific paradigms were totally inadequate for policy research and proposed a new policy science paradigm. In the same year Lasswell published a book that updated and refined his notion of the policy sciences (*A Pre-View of Policy Sciences*, 1971). At about the same time a book edited by Ira Sharkansky (1970) made a pioneering effort to identify the appropriate roles and uses of empirically based policy analysis. And two years later Thomas Dye published the first edition of his widely read text, *Understanding Public Policy* (1972).

By the late 1970s a wide variety of texts were available, as well as countless case studies, conceptual works, and empirical studies. Also, a number of journals devoted exclusively to policy emerged, including the *Policy Studies Journal* and the *Policy Studies Review* (both published by the Policy Studies Organization), *Policy Science*, and the *Journal of Policy Analysis and Management*. By the eighties, policy science had come into its own: "Policy sciences is not a simple, incremental modification of any of the standard disciplinary or professional approaches. It is a fundamental change in outlook, orientation, methods, procedures, and attitudes" (Brewer and deLeon 1983, 6). Ripley views "policy analysis and evaluation" as a new era quite distinct from the behavioralism of earlier years: "they [policy analysts] are concerned with reaching normatively based conclusions and making prescriptions as well as doing solid empirical work based on longitudinal data, appropriate quantification, and methodological rigor. . . they deny that a concern with prescription is prohibited by a concern with rigor or 'science'" (1985, 17–18).

During this era of growth and maturation, policy analysis as a professional endeavor discovered its limits. The failure of many government programs to live up to their promise, the rise and fall of program budgeting, and the backlash against central planning created a heightened awareness of what can—and cannot—be accomplished by government-via-analysis. It also focused attention on the implications of large-scale policy analysis for democracy.

> The presumption that scientific analysis alone could dictate optimum policy conjured up visions of an Orwellian society in which technocrats operating under the cloak of science invade individual privacy and manipulate society for their purposes (Putt and Springer 1989, 15).

Additional questions were raised concerning the quality of published research on policy. A burgeoning literature had developed, but there were some obvious inadequacies. Much of the early (i.e., sixties and seventies) policy literature can be classified into two groups. At one extreme, many studies of policy were descriptive and atheoretical. In many cases the ideological bias of the author was much in evidence. Far from being the policy *science* envisioned by Lasswell, this literature had more in common with political journalism or history. At the other extreme a very technical literature, with an exclusive emphasis on empirical methodology, developed under the rubric of policy analysis. The former was as broad and undefined as the latter was narrow and overly specialized. Neither made great contributions to policy theory. Yet despite these trends, an amorphous theoretical tradition began to emerge. Conceptually this literature grew more sophisticated over time, and it is only in recent years that a sufficient theoretical literature has accumulated to justify a book devoted to public policy theory.

POLICY THEORY TODAY

Despite the difficulties associated with policy theory building, a rudimentary foundation is beginning to take shape. William Dunn recently noted that "In the past twenty years we have made considerable progress in developing new and more appropriate theories, models, and methods for public policy analysis" (1988, 720). However, this progress does not mean that some kind of scientific threshold has been achieved; according to Stephen Linder and B. Guy Peters,

> . . . there appears to be a loose consensus on several features of policy inquiry including its problem orientation, contextuality, and multiple methodologies. . . . While we in the policy sciences are by no means at the stage of doing *normal science,* certain habits and modes of thinking have become more or less institutionalized (1988, 738).

The refinement of policy theory has been a process of recognizing the special challenges of building theories that can encompass such disparate and complex phenomena. Peter House writes that "At this stage in the development of policy modeling. . . our theoretical underpinnings (at least in the rather broadly defined area of the social or policy sciences) are becoming better, because we now realize that in our social system, actions can and do engender secondary impacts and that there is real interest in making these impacts known" (1982, 111). MacRae is also cognizant of the unique challenges that confront the policy theorist: "In the face of these problems—the risk of politicization, the multiplicity of methods, and the weakness of evidence—we require special safeguards to maintain common concerns and common standards in the development of policy models within technical communities" (1985, 150. Also see May 1986, 109).

These views of theory and model building in the policy sciences are among the more optimistic interpretations. A less sanguine view is more typical, as follows:

> "the new public policy is an intellectual jungle swallowing up with unbounded voracity almost anything, but which it cannot give disciplined—by which I mean theoretically enlightened—attention" (Eulau 1977, 421).

"policy studies are regarded by many political scientists, economists, and sociologists as second-best research. . . the field of inquiry is too broad and varied to fit within a single theoretical framework or set of methodologies. Policy inquiry is not considered a science" (Dresang 1983, ix).

"the study of public policy, as it is conveyed in much of the political science literature, is remarkably devoid of theory" (Stone 1988, 3).

"A review of previous research. . . suggests that a unifying paradigm is lacking; a common theoretical base and consistent findings are absent" (Rogers 1988, 21).

"unlike the older and well-established academic disciplines, a theoretical tradition has not yet emerged to guide policy analysis" (Robertson and Judd 1989).

"in the eyes of many political scientists, policy scholars have made only very modest contributions to the development of reasonably clear, generalizable, and empirically-verified theories of the policy process" (Sabatier 1989, 5).

It is undoubtedly true that a dominant theoretical tradition has yet to develop.[2] On the other hand, it may be unnecessary, and unwise, to attempt to place all policy science on the Procrustean bed of a single theoretical construct. Jenkins notes that "there is no one best way. The nature of the policy problem is such that a variety of approaches are required to deal with the complexity of the process" (1978, 20. Also see Anderson 1988). Policy studies is indeed "remarkably devoid" of *a theory*, yet there is a diverse literature that is theoretically instructive. Indeed, some argue there may be too many theories.

One of the salient characteristics of policy studies is not the dearth, but the plethora of theories. This assertion may seem peculiar since the study of politics is often attacked as being "atheoretical." Yet a close (empirical) analysis of the literature will demonstrate the frequency of theoretical explanations. The lack of satisfaction stems from the ad hoc nature of policy theory. A new theory with its own set of assumptions tends to be generated to explain almost *every* new phenomenon; alternatively, the same phenomenon occasionally is explained by several theories with no basis for choice among them. Thus, the dissatisfaction in policy analysis is with the lack of a general theory that provides predictive models applicable to diverse situations with only slight modification or extension of the fundamental assumptions (Blair and Maser 1977, 282).

[2]The absence of a dominant paradigm is not unique to policy studies; it is a condition common to many disciplines in the social sciences, especially political science, which Lane recently characterized as being in a "era of eclecticism" (1990: 927). The book edited by William T. Bluhm, *The Paradigm Problem in Political Science* (1982) illuminates this problem. Also relevant is Paul Roth's argument for "methodological pluralism" in the philosophy of science (1987). From an entirely different perspective, James Miller explains how, in the early fifties, an interdisciplinary group of social scientists developed a theory for *all* of the behavioral sciences, which they called the "general behavior systems theory" (1956, 31).

Mazmanian and Sabatier concur in this assessment: "Today, researchers are faced with an embarrassment of riches; they must choose which theoretical perspective to adopt and which specific hypotheses to test" (1980, 439. Also see: Jennings 1983, 3–4). In short, the problem is not the absence of policy theory, but the comprehensiveness and generalizability of that theory (see Muzzio and De Maio 1988, 127).

There are two possible explanations for this situation. First, as suggested above, it may be inappropriate to attempt to construct a universal theory of policy; the subject is simply too diverse, the number of variables too immense, and the relationships too complex to be explained by a single theoretical approach (we will return to this topic in the final chapter). As Bobrow and Dryzek point out, twenty years of research has made it evident that "the reductionist dream of a unified social science under a single theoretical banner is dead" (1987, 5).

A second explanation concerns the propensity of policy scholars to isolate themselves in a single theoretical or substantive specialty. As a result, there has been little effort to discover commonalities and combinations among the various theoretical contributions. One way to begin resolving this problem is to examine the leading theories, models, and concepts together, in a single collection, in an effort to incite integrative analysis and possibly reveal the existence of valid theoretical generalizations. Hence the reason for this book.

DEFINITIONS

One of the first steps in the development of any scientific enterprise is to develop a specialized vocabulary. Unfortunately, in the area of policy studies there is a bewildering array of terms, many of which are conceptually indistinct. Bobrow and Dryzek are quite correct when they characterize the field as a "babel of tongues in which participants talk past rather than to one another" (1987, 4). Given these difficulties it is worth reviewing some of the basic terms in an effort to clarify them.

The term *public policy* is a good place to start. There are innumerable definitions, but most of them have some common elements. Lasswell defined policy as simply "the most important choices" (1951, 5). Austin Ranney (1968, 7), another early writer in the policy field, offered a more complex definition of policy that included the following elements:

    A particular object or goal
    A desired course of events
    A selected line of action
    A declaration of intent
    An implementation of intent

In contrast, Thomas Dye says that public policy is "whatever governments choose to do or not to do" (1987, 1). It would appear safe to assume that the term implies some course of government action toward some goal, however broadly defined.

The definitional thicket becomes even more impenetrable when we attempt to distinguish among four commonly used terms: policy science, policy studies, policy evaluation, and policy analysis.

Policy Science

1. "the application of knowledge and rationality to perceived social problems" (Dror 1971, 49).
2. "systematic, empirical studies of how policies are made and put into effect. . ." (Lasswell 1971, 1).
3. "an umbrella term describing a broad-gauge intellectual approach applied to the examination of societally critical problems" (deLeon 1988, 7).

Policy Studies

1. "any research that relates to or promotes the public interest" (Palumbo 1981, 8).
2. "the study of the nature, causes, and effects of governmental decisions for dealing with social problems" (Nagel 1987, 219).

Policy Evaluation

1. "is not so much a set of analytical techniques as it is a mode of thinking about relationships among elements of the policy process" (Hofferbert 1986, 513).
2. "policy evaluators organize their research efforts around an existing program and ask how well it is achieving its intended objectives. . ." (Greenberger, Crenson, and Crissey 1976, 30).
3. "is the broad title given to judging the consequences of what governments do and say" (Dubnick and Bardes 1983, 203).

Policy Analysis

1. "is a form of applied research carried out to acquire a deeper understanding of sociotechnical issues and to bring about better solutions" (Quade 1989, 4).
2. "is an applied social science discipline which uses multiple methods of inquiry and argument to produce and transform policy-relevant information that may be utilized in political settings to resolve policy problems" (Dunn 1981, 35).
3. "is principally concerned with describing and investigating how and why particular policies are proposed, adopted, and implemented. It focuses on explanation rather than prescription, on searching scientifically for the causes and consequences of policy, and on general explanatory propositions" (Cochran et. al 1986, 3).
4. "a set of techniques and criteria with which to evaluate public policy options and select among them. . ." (Jenkins-Smith 1990, 1).

Obviously the conceptual distinction between these terms is rather indistinct.[3] It would appear that, when the word *policy* appears as a prefix to the words *science, studies, evaluation,* and *analysis,* we are talking about activity that investigates some form of government problem or output. This includes studies that examine the policy-making process to determine how it affects the output of that process. Hogwood and Gunn note that these terms "are used by various authors in different ways, at times interchangeably, at times in an attempt to impose a particular meaning on a specific term" (1984, 26). In an effort to clarify the terminology, they have suggested a scheme for delineating the relationships between these terms. In Figure 1-1 they make a basic distinction between policy studies and policy analysis, with policy evaluation occupying the common area.

Randall Ripley helps to clarify some of these terms, especially as they relate to political science, by using a continuum based on "specific policy issue focus" and the degree to which the research can be applied immediately. In Figure 1-2 he places multidisciplinary policy studies at the low end of focus/utility and the policy sciences at the other end (1985, 5. Also see Weimer and Vining 1992: 1–14).

Although the terminology is confusing, there is a common strain. George Graham writes of a "policy orientation" that succinctly summarizes the lofty goals of this genre of research: "The policy orientation provides a means for dealing with humane purposes in the best scientific framework possible to aid those who will make social choices. The instrumental end is better intelligence" (1988, 152).

Terminological confusion is not unique to policy science; there are also unclear distinctions between some of the general terms of science. For example, Rudner writes that "there are few terms of the scientific lexicon whose use. . . has remained for so long in so anarchic a state as has the term 'theory.' Like the term 'model,'. . . 'theory' is used in various ways—many

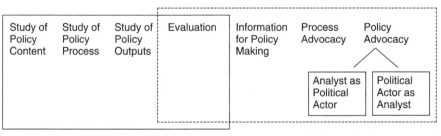

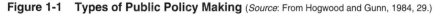

Figure 1-1   Types of Public Policy Making (*Source*: From Hogwood and Gunn, 1984, 29.)

[3]The differences between these terms are discussed in the first volume of the *Policy Evaluation Newsletter-Journal* (Summer 1992): 4–6.

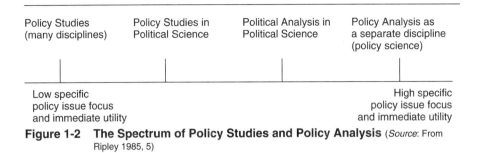

Figure 1-2   **The Spectrum of Policy Studies and Policy Analysis** (*Source*: From Ripley 1985, 5)

of them inane" (1966, 10). Singleton, Straits, and Straits write that "'Theory' is one of the most elusive and misunderstood terms in science" (1993, 23). The title of this book makes reference to theories, models, and concepts. Hence it is worthwhile to offer some definitions of these terms:

Theory

1. "A formulation of apparent relationships or underlying principles of certain observed phenomena which has been verified to some degree" (Webster's New World Dictionary).
2. ". . . a closed system from which are generated predictions about the nature of man's world—predictions that, when made, the theorist agrees must be open to some kind of empirical test" (Dubin 1969, 8).
3. ". . . a coding scheme for the storage and retrieval of information. Theory organizes. . . by arranging information in such a way that it is not completely chaotic, can be easily stored, and, what is more important, easily retrieved" (Deutsch 1972, 19).
4. "A theory is a systematically related set of statements, including some lawlike generalizations, that is empirically testable" (Rudner 1966, 10).
5. "All theories are analogies, and all analogies are theories" (Simon and Newell 1956, 82).

Model

1. "A model. . . is a representation of reality; it delineates certain aspects of the real world as being relevant to the problem under investigation, it makes explicit the significant relationships among the aspects, and it enables the formulation of empirically testable propositions regarding the nature of these relationships" (Frankfort-Nachmias, and Nachmias 1992, 44).
2. ". . . models are analogies which problem-solvers use to clarify their thinking about a relatively complex presentation" (Lippitt 1973, 2).
3. "A model is simply an attempt to represent reality by abstracting out of a confusing welter of events and observations the essential elements of an object or situation: to make some preliminary guesses as to what is relevant and what is not, and how things fit together" (Hayes 1992, 6).
4. "A policy model shows how, and to what extent, public policy alternatives cause outcomes that can be described by one or more value concepts" (MacRae 1985, 82).

Concept

1. "Concepts are abstractions communicated by words or other signs that refer to common properties among phenomena" (Singleton, Straits, and Straits 1993, 20).
2. "an underlying variable, not necessarily in operational form, entering into theory, models, or public discussion" (MacRae 1985, 34).
3. "A concept, or a series of interrelated concepts (which we refer to as a *model*), should suggest relationships in the real world that can be tested and verified" (Dye 1992, 45).
4. "The terms designating the things about which a science tries to make sense are its concepts" (Dubin 1969, 27).

The confusion in terminology is exacerbated by the changing meaning of these terms. In 1956 Simon and Newell noted that the word *model* was considered synonymous with mathematical theory (1956, 66). In the sixties Dubin considered *theory* and *model* to be interchangeable, but Rudner noted that *model* was often used "to refer to any theoretical formulation other than a theory" (1966, 23. Also see Frohock, 1967, 4–7). Forcese and Richer defined a theory as "a model that has been tested" (1973, 44). At about the same time, Lave and March defined *model* "as a generic term for any systematic set of conjectures about real world observations" (1975, 4). House and Shull write that "in current bureaucratic parlance, the term *model* usually refers to a computer program that uses extensive data and analyzes several variables and relationships" (1988, 12).

Furthermore, it is important to understand that there are specific relationships among these terms; they are associated with each other in the larger scheme of science. For example, Neil Smelser offers an explanation of the relationship between three critically important scientific terms: (1) *hypotheses* are "statements of the conditions under which dependent variables may be expected to vary in certain ways"; (2) *models* are where "a number of hypotheses are combined and organized into a system," and (3) *theories* are where a "number of models are embedded in definitions, assumptions, and postulates" (1968, 5–6).

To a certain extent, the definitions of these various terms is contextual. Like the theories themselves, the terminology must maintain sufficient flexibility to accommodate the incredible diversity of the subject matter. This makes research and theory building more difficult, but it is a necessary sacrifice to the multifarious nature of public policy.

CRITERIA FOR A GOOD THEORY

In order to examine a variety of theoretical thinking, we need a yardstick by which to evaluate the utility—the strengths and weaknesses—of the various contributions in this volume. The criteria offered as follows have been culled from a variety of sources and can be applied to both theories and models. Three caveats are in order. First, some of the criteria are readily applicable to physical science, but less helpful as a gauge for social science theory. Nevertheless they are crucial elements in terms of general scientific standards. It is important to recognize that many of the selections in this book are thought-pieces; their purpose is to provoke a new line of inquiry, not to present a fully matured theoretical treatise.

Second, no policy theory can fully satisfy all the criteria; our expectations, especially in the social sciences, must be realistic. There is no corollary to the law of gravity in the social sciences. In their "how to" book on policy analysis, Stokey and Zeckhauser caution their readers: "Many of the policy decisions you will encounter will not fit neatly and automatically into the models presented here, for the real world is rich and complex. Policy analysis is not an assembly line process, where a single-purpose tool can be applied repeatedly to whatever problem comes along" (1978, 6–7).

The third caveat concerns the relationship between the criteria. It is not possible to establish an interval ranking among them; there is no way to individually weight each criteria according to its importance. In some cases the criteria are interactive; a theory that meets one of them will also meet another. But in some cases there may be an inverse relationship between them. For example, a theory might be made more testable by making it less powerful. Thus, the criteria must be viewed as a collective entity; consider them together rather than as a check-off list where each one scores a certain number of points.

Having said that, it is still true that some of the criteria are more difficult to achieve than others, and as a result, are often given more emphasis. Validity is perhaps the most important because, if a theory lacks validity, it does not really matter if it meets the other criteria. Once validity is established, the greatest difficulty is to construct theory that provides causal explanations and is predictive. This does not mean the other criteria are unimportant. Rather, a theory that is valid, explains causation, and can predict often has a greater potential to satisfy some of the other criteria. Again, the point is that there are important relationships between the criteria.

Validity

A theory is valid if it is an accurate representation of the reality it attempts to explain. Quade points out that validation "is the process of determining that the outputs of a model conform to reality" (1989, 155). In other words, does the model or theory explain what it purports to explain? Absolute validation is not possible in a technical sense; we can never "prove" a theory is totally valid because we can never test all potential disproofs (i.e., falsifications of the theory). It is important to distinguish validity from *verification*, which determines whether the functions of the model have been ex-

ecuted properly: "verification is a test of whether the model has been synthesized exactly as intended. Verification of a model indicates that it has
been faithful to its conception, irrespective of whether or not it and its conception are valid" (Greenberger et al., 1976, 70).

Economy

A theory or model must be simpler than the phenomena being studied: "A model is supposed to make a complex world more manageable for
the problem solver; so the ultimate objective is to develop a model that ful-
fills its objective by applying the simplest possible form" (Dubnick and
Bardes 1983, 48). This process of simplification involves two tasks. First, a
balance must be struck between complexity and inclusiveness on one hand,
and simplicity and clarity on the other. And second, since only some of the
relevant variables can be included to achieve this balance, the theorist must
assign a priority of importance to these variables and then decide which can
be safely omitted. This is a critical step in theory building; if done poorly, it
may "contribute to the selective distortion of reality" (Dunn 1981, 111).

Testability

A theory that cannot be tested to see if it is accurate is less useful in
a scientific sense (it may still be interesting, provocative, and insightful,
however). To be testable in the scientific sense means that the theory must
relate to "observable features of the universe" (Rudner 1966, 21), or in other
words, we can test a theory only if we can measure or at least confirm the
existence of the phenomenon to which the theory refers. A theory of public
policy that can be tested permits us to examine the results, and validate,
modify, or reject the theory. In terms of methodology this test can be *quantitative* or *qualitative*. Quantitative tests involve the use of empirical methodologies—statistics such as correlation coefficients, regression analysis,
causal path analysis, and so forth. Empirical tests require that the concepts
and variables used in the theory be *operationalized*, meaning there must be a
way to assign numerical values to them. Not all tests of theory must be statistical; qualitative methodology uses a combination of language and numbers (see Van Maanen 1983; Marshall and Rossman 1989; Frankfort-Nachmias and Nachmias 1992, 271–90; King, Keohane, and Verba 1994). In some
situations this approach may reveal more information than statistical operations.

Organization/Understanding

The purpose of science is to help us understand the world around us.
Good theory brings order out of chaos; it explains what otherwise would
not be explicable (this assumes, of course, that the phenomenon being stud-

ied is potentially explicable). Karl Deutsch points out that theory serves as an instrument "for dissociating and recombining information" (1972, 20). In this fashion theory helps us to systematically structure our knowledge.

Heuristic

Good theory acts as a catalyst to induce and guide further research. Science is cumulative; it proceeds in small increments of knowledge acquisition, each based upon prior work. Newton is reputed to have said, If I have seen farther, it is by standing on the shoulders of giants, referring to how previous scholars had led him to his discoveries. Deutsch calls theory "a search instrument" for "sensitizing our research course and our information intake" (1972, 19). Thus theory helps us learn and discover (which is the meaning of the greek root for this word). This points to the essential building block nature of the scientific process; as we learn, we accept, modify, or reject our theories. As Hayes points out, ". . . all models are subject to revision or replacement in light of experience and hard evidence. Faulty models are discarded. Promising but incomplete models are modifed" (1992, 7).

Causal Explanation

Randall Ripley writes that the "question of cause-and-effect is central no matter what the specific subject matter is. . . policy analysis . . . must always pose the question, Why? It must always seek explanations" (1985, 9). Good theory will uncover causal relationships that we would have overlooked otherwise. Indeed, some of the most useful research is counterintuitive; it surprises us by discovering causal relationships that we never expected to exist.

Predictive

Prediction is risky business, especially in the social sciences. Nevertheless the best theories are those that identify causal relationships and project them into the future. Lave and March note that "models are evaluated in terms of their ability to predict correctly other new facts" (1975, 19). Goodin argues that a theory is useful if there is "a tight fit between predictions of the theoretical model and the empirical data" (1976, 6).

Relevance/Usefulness

Some theories provide clear explanations of phenomena that are of no interest to us. The best policy theory helps us solve important problems. Dubnick and Bardes write that "a model must be assessed in terms of its ability to provide us with a useful understanding of the world" (1983, 38). Some students will undoubtedly ask: Why do we need theory at all? Goodin provides a succinct answer.

> We choose policies hoping to produce certain kinds of results, and we must know how the system is wired in order to know which lever to pull. But this understanding must be theoretical, not just the product of accumulated practical experience or random hunches, if we are to be able to anticipate all the side effects of the policy and say how the system will respond under altered conditions or in the long term, of which we have no experience. (1982, 4–5)

Thus useful theory provides insights and understanding that cannot be obtained otherwise. It serves as a guide to phenomena that are crucially important to us.

Powerful

A powerful theory explains a lot, or in Quade's words, it "offers a large number of nontrivial inferences" (1989, 155). Lave and March note that "models become rich through their implications. It is necessary to devise models that yield significant derivations. . ." (1975, 4). Goodin states flatly, "The wider the range of phenomena explained the better the theory." (1976, 6). Theory is most helpful if it can be applied to many different cases, or in other words, the theory is *generalizable* (Singleton, Straits, and Straits 1993, 22). Powerful theory also forcefully concentrates our scientific inquiry. Dubin notes that "an essential characteristic of a powerful model is that it distinguishes a realm of phenomena and focuses analytical attention only upon that realm" (1969, 19).

Reliability

Also known as "replication," this refers to whether repeated tests of the same research procedure yield similar results. Hoover explains how replication helps maintain accuracy and objectivity: "Replication constitutes a very strong test of a good study because it can reveal the errors that might have crept in through the procedures and evaluative judgments contained in the principal study" (1992, 33). Forcese and Richer argue that replication, "the successive examination and reexamination" of findings (1973, 10), enables researchers to ferret out, not only errors, but bias in the research (1973, 24).

In the physical sciences the process of testing for reliability is rather straightforward; the scientist merely repeats the laboratory procedures described in the literature to determine if the same results are achieved. If they are not, it could be that the description of the procedure is technically faulty, or that the basic premise or theory upon which the research is based is incorrect. In contrast, social phenomena seldom provide opportunities for exact replication; we must often settle for approximations. Or, a single phenomenon is studied—a case study, which offers a feasible way to do research, but is always subject to the criticism that it can never be exactly replicated.

Objectivity

The role of values in theory building is an area of contentious debate. This debate is beyond the scope of this book, but we still need to recognize its importance. The ideal of positivist science assumes objectivity—that theoretically based inquiry can be achieved without the intrusion of the researcher's personal bias. Some argue that, while the ideal of total objectivity may be illusive, we should aspire to it, and we can approximate it. Others argue that bias is inevitable, especially in the social sciences.[4] Putt and Springer note that "Policy research can clarify ideas and provide empirical evidence, but it cannot erase value differences or make them irrelevant" (1989, 20). Good theory does not determine values, but it can clarify the relationship between specific values and reality. We may possess a set of values that are quite clear to us, but still be unsure of how these values—and associated behaviors—affect the world around us. Policy science may help to explain that relationship (see Shils and Finch 1949, on Max Weber).

Honest Theory

Unfortunately, science has a great potential for abuse. Good theory should make it obvious to us how the values of the theoretician affected the formulation of the theory; it should not be used as a ruse to disguise ulterior goals. Nor should scientific theory be used to legitimize certain policy prescriptions by "lend[ing] the dignity of science" to increase popular support (Greenberger, Crenson, and Crissey 1976, 46). This has long been a problem in the social sciences. Thirty-seven years ago Kimpton claimed that

---

[4]Many political theorists and philosophers argue that objective, value-free empirical social science is impossible. Indeed, some talk of a "post-empiricist" philosophy of science designed to fill the void left by "the general collapse of positivism" (Roth 1987, 1, 2). Also relevant is the critique of empirical theory and the "excessive scientism of orthodox positivism" offered by Richard Bernstein (1976, 1986). Of interest here is "Mannheim's Paradox," which reasons that social science has demonstrated that social and political thought is always influenced by the values and experiences of the thinker, and therefore, the thought of all social scientists must also be influenced by their values and experiences (see Noble 1982). But for most scientists, the term objectivity merely indicates that diverse researchers have agreed on certain methodologies for generating and interpreting data; you don't have to be a robot, but you must be competent in standardized technique.

Some overzealous critics of positivism attack an exaggerated parody: "Positivism promises that technically sophisticated, apolitical engineers can use value-free criteria and methods to find ideal solutions to an array of medical, social, and political problems" (Mitchell 1988, 215). For a different perspective see Rudner (1966, 73–83) or Simon (1985, 293–304).

"the largest single problem in the social sciences comes from the fact that the field is overpopulated with propounders of partisan theses disguised as theories. . . " (1956, 352). More recently, Hoover notes that "Much damage has been done to the cause of good social science by those who pretend disinterest to the point where their research conceals opinions that covertly structure their conclusions" (1992, 9). Values and preferences should not be presented as neutral facts; normative theory masquerading as empirical theory is deceptive and dangerous. Dubnick and Bardes point out how theories and policy models are sometimes abused in order to further someone's political goals.

> The fact that policy models are merely potential tools in our effort to understand the world of public policy is sometimes ignored by those who use them. This can have dire consequences. These tools often become 'creeds' in the hands of those who fail to comprehend the instrumental nature of their use. . . . Once elevated to the level of ideologies, problem-solving tools can become dangerous implements. They lose their identity as instruments for analytic understanding and instead become unchallengeable grounds for policy actions (1983, 15–16).

The purpose of scholarly theory is to inform, not to prejudice.

With a little imagination, and some modification, these criteria can be applied to most of the policy theory literature, including the selections in this volume. You will find that much of the work in the field falls far short of the theoretical ideal. To a certain extent this is due to the nature of the social sciences. It can also be attributed to the relative youth of the field. For the aspiring policy theorist, the future is wide open, the potential for significant contribution is enormous, and the effort is sorely needed.

THINKING THEORETICALLY

There is a lot of misunderstanding—perhaps even prejudice—against theory in the popular mind. Therefore, it is a good idea to establish a foundation of understanding theory before we begin actually reading, and trying to comprehend, theory. The misunderstandings of theory are many, but they can be grouped into five basic areas.

First, students often confuse the theorist with the theory, or confuse the substance of the theory with the theory itself. The fact is, a good theorist can develop a good theory about an evil phenomenon. When we speak of a "good" theory, we are not making a *normative* evaluation (i.e., a moral judgment). A theory is good if it meets our previous criteria. A theory of the Holocaust may provide an insightful and unique causal explanation of why Nazi guards pulled the lever to begin gassing prisoners. To evaluate such a theory, we must separate our revulsion of the phenomenon from our ability to judge objectively the extent to which the theory meets the criteria for a "good' theory. Perhaps "good" is not an entirely appropriate word in this context, but the only accurate replacement would be "theoretical," which leaves us with the tautology of "theoretical theory."

This is an important point in policy theory, because students are asked to evaluate theory that may be threatening to long-held political values. Students often state that elitism is a bad theory because it usurps popular control of government and threatens democracy. Of course, the theory itself usurps nothing; it holds that elites rule—not elite theorists and their ideas. Elitism may be a threat to democracy, but that does not mean it is bad theory; if it is a more valid explanation of political power than traditional democracy, then it is a better theory than our cherished concept of rule by, of, and for the people.

The student of theory must distinguish between *normative* theory, which is a conceptualization of a preference—what ought to be, as opposed to *empirical* theory—which attempts to conceive of what actually exists. In theory, as in life, what we want and what we get are often two different things. In this book the reader will encounter both of these kinds of theories; often the difference is not easily discernible, as theorists often find it difficult to separate their own preferences from their conceptualizations of reality.

A second reason students have difficulty understanding theory is because there are many different kinds of theory. For example, Fred Frohock, in the first few pages of *The Nature of Political Inquiry* (1967), mentions formal theory, descriptive theory, instrumental theory, historical theory, causal theory, classical theory, and modern theory. The different kinds of models identified in the literature are even more numerous. Greenberger, Crenson, and Crissey discuss descriptive, prescriptive, normative, optimization, and simulation models (1976, 59–63); Lippitt identifies five kinds of models: graphic, pictorial, schematic, mathematical, and simulation (1973, 33). Quade uses four kinds of models: analytic, simulation, gaming, and judgmental (1989, 148–52). The first step in evaluating a theory or model is to figure out what kind it is. Only then can we determine the extent to which it serves its purpose.

A third point that must be understood concerns the nature of theory itself; is it a means or an end? We must ask: What are we trying to achieve by concocting all these theories? Fischer writes that "The development of causal theory is the dominant concern of mainstream political science" (1980, 20). In a similar vein Forcese and Richer argue that theory "is the object or goal of science, and therefore theory is the output and the result of cumulative research" (1973, 47). Singleton, Straits, and Straits make the same assumption (1993, 28). I believe these viewpoints are mistaken, because they assume that theory is an end, rather than a means. Quite the contrary, theory is nothing more than a tool—a strategic device—to increase understanding. Policy theory is a servant to our thoughts, a guide to the universe of human behavior in a political setting. Mary Douglas calls it "an advantage for thinking" that "gives support to ideas"(1989, 855).

When we assume that theory is our goal, we ascribe to it powers it cannot possess; we assume social science research based on theory is making decisions for us. "The influence of social science. . . depends on its ability to discover general laws of social processes which will eventually enable man to control his social environment" (Rein 1976, 39). Of course theory does not "control" anything; good theory will enable us to better *understand* our social environment; control is a function of politics and culture, not theory. Theory does not make good public policy—only good policy makers make good public policy. But theory can guide our inquiry so that those policy makers can make better-informed decisions.

If theory is only a means to an end, then what is the goal? We can return to Lasswell for the answer: Policy theory, and the research based upon it, should lead to a "fuller realization of human dignity" (1951, 10). In a similar vein Ronald Brunner writes that the purpose of policy science is to achieve "freedom through insight" (1992, 311). In other words, the grand purpose of policy theory is to enhance the quality of social life. The ultimate measure of a good theory, then, is the extent to which it leads us to this goal.

A fourth aspect of theory that troubles students is what they view as verbose, overly complex language. Students often ask: Why do they make it so complicated and hard to understand? Or they respond to a particular reading with: "He could have said that in a page or two." These reactions are no doubt exacerbated by the tendency of academics to develop their own argot, which often appears to the uninitiated to be designed to maximize obtuseness rather than theoretical clarity. No doubt we invent terms with excessive zeal,[5] but specificity in terms is an absolute necessity in theory building. If it appears to the student that the authors in this book have gone overboard in defining their subject, it is because they want to make sure they are communicating a difficult concept with some degree of precision.

Because theory is abstract, we cannot point to something and say: "There it is, that's what I mean." We must depend on word descriptions for everything. When theories, and their consequent hypotheses, are tested, the researcher must operationalize the variables or terms. This requires an exacting degree of specificity. For example, if a theory posits that budget deficits are caused by shifts in economic power, the theorist would have to define explicitly what constitutes a "shift," and "economic power." Even the relatively straightforward term, *budget deficit*, would require explanation; does the theorist mean deficits as small as 0.05% of the total? Does off-budget spending count? As you can see, things get complicated very fast.

---

[5] We shall call this tendency *compulsive terminologicalism.*

A final point concerns the misconception that theory building, because it is so abstract, is some sort of mechanical, robotic activity carried on by large computers that digest linear data patterns and then emit arcane formulations. Although such a description could be applied to the analysis of data generated by theories, the construction of theory itself is a demonstrably creative endeavor. The first vestige of theory is nothing less than a flight of the imagination. It is common to think of a dichotomy between science and art, but this is inaccurate; the creative process of theory building has a lot in common with art (the true dichotomy is between science and faith). Hoover writes that science is "not a system for frustrating [the] exercise of intuition and imagination; rather it is a set of procedures for making such ideas as fruitful and productive as human ingenuity allows. . . " (1992, 10). Marshall and Rossman compare it to "the detective work of Sherlock Holmes or the best tradition of investigative reporting. . . " (1989, 21). The theorist is not the computer "nerd" with a dozen well-sharpened pencils; instead, the theorist is Rodin's *Thinker*, sitting on a stump observing, intuiting, reasoning, trying to figure out why things happen as they do.

THE PLAN OF THE BOOK

Two decades ago Robert Dubin drew a sharp contrast between natural science and social science. His characterization of social science theory as "a history of ideas" is a particularly appropriate description of the policy theory that has accumulated in the years since Dubin wrote:

> The natural scientist is an inveterate fact gatherer, exceptionally skilled at developing more and more accurate and subtle means for accumulating experimental facts. By way of contrast, social scientists have tended to accumulate theories and theoretical models. The social scientist funds theory and not data. It is not unusual for courses in the area of theory in a social science discipline to be a recital of what each notable historical figure in the field believed or said. The student typically learns a history of ideas about the empirical world that falls within the range of his particular social-science discipline. But he may be singularly ignorant of the descriptive and factual character of that domain. The behavioral scientist tends to accumulate belief systems and call this the *theory* of his field. (1969, 238–39)

In the last twenty years, much has been done to reduce our ignorance of the "descriptive and factual character" of policy to which Dubin alludes. This is primarily due to the efforts of empirical policy analysis. The focus of this book, however, is on *ideas*, loosely characterized as theories, models, and concepts. Much of what is included is less than full-blown theory; this is not unusual in the social sciences: "A striking feature of the literature of social science is that it is copiously salted with nontheoretical formulations. They occur under a dizzying variety of names: 'typology,' 'typologi-

cal schema,' 'conceptual schema,' 'conceptual model,' 'classificational system,' 'definitional system,' and many others" (Rudner 1966, 28). Nevertheless these ideas still constitute an important contribution to theory building
in the policy sciences. The goal is to provide the student of public policy with
an overview of the most influential and promising work in policy theory.

This book includes previously published works, either book chapters
(some of which are edited) or journal articles, that have had a significant
impact—or potential impact—on the study of public policy and the effort to
develop a theoretical foundation. In deciding which works to include, I
used the following criteria:

> Its use by scholars, including the successful application of the author's ideas
> to substantive policy studies, and its use as a building block by other formula-
> tors of policy theory.
>
> The frequency of citation in policy texts, books from other subfields within
> political science, and introductory political science textbooks.
>
> The nature and extent of critiques and revisions of the work.
>
> The value of the work as an addition to existing conceptualizations. Some of
> the works included are not widely cited, but nevertheless provide a crucial
> addition to the development of a particular concept. These works are cri-
> tiques, tests, and revisions. They are not as prominent as the original work,
> but are important to our contemporary understanding of seminal concepts.
>
> The potential of the work to have an impact on policy theory. It is important
> to include recent work in this volume. I looked for published work that pre-
> sents new ideas and interpretations, or provides an insightful critique of pre-
> vailing concepts.

It is worth noting that a vast array of conceptual work has been done,
but not all of it could be included. I did not poll other policy scholars to get
a consensus as to what to include. If such a poll were conducted, there
would no doubt be considerable disparity in their responses. That disparity
is in part a testament to the infancy of the field, but it is also indicative of
the volume and breadth of the literature. This book will expose the student
to an eclectic set of ideas that represents much of the current thinking in
public policy theory.

The book is organized into four conceptual categories. Some of these
are self-defining, such as the section on subsystems and the material on typologies. On the other hand, Section 3, "The Process of Public Policy Making," consists of a less homogeneous assortment of work. And some of the
selections, especially those in Section 2, "The Scope of Participation in Public Policy Making," could also be labeled as contemporary political theory.
It is appropriate that they be included in this volume because of their relevance to public policy making, and their impact on policy theorists. For example, the work on group theory and pluralism in Section 2 had an obvious
impact on the development of typologies (Section 4) and the subsystem literature (Section 5). The readings give the student a basic foundation in the

theories that have influenced much research and thinking in the policy sciences.

Sections 2 through 5 begin with an Introduction by the editor, and end with a Discussion, also written by the editor. Some students have found it helpful to read both of them before they read the selections, and then reread the Discussion after they have finished that section. The Introduction and Discussion place each selection in its larger theoretical context and expose you to related research.

As you read this book, keep in mind that you are being exposed to a single, brief example of each concept. To learn more about each theory, consult the references that accompany each selection and each Introduction and Discussion.

This book will get you started on your quest to understand policy theory. However, this book alone cannot make you a theorist or even a viable theoretical critic; for that you will need patience, a library card, and a strong desire to think theoretically.

REFERENCES

ANDERSON, CHARLES (1988). "Political Judgment and Theory in Policy Analysis." In *Handbook of Political Theory and Policy Science*, pp.184–98. Edited by Edward Portis and Michael Levy. New York: Greenwood Press.

BAUER, RAYMOND, AND KENNETH GERGEN, eds. (1968). *The Study of Policy Formation.* New York: The Free Press.

BERNSTEIN, RICHARD (1976). *The Restructuring of Social and Political Theory.* New York: Harcourt Brace Jovanovich.

_____ (1983). *Beyond Objectivism.* Philadelphia: University of Pennsylvania Press.

BLAIR, JOHN, AND STEVEN MASER (1977). "Axiomatic versus Empirical Models in Policy Studies." *Policy Studies Journal* 5 (Spring): 282-89.

BLUHM, WILLIAM, ed. (1982). *The Paradigm Problem in Political Science.* Durham, NC: Carolina Academic Press.

BOBROW, DAVIS, AND JOHN DRYZEK (1987). *Policy Analysis by Design.* Pittsburgh: University of Pittsburgh Press.

BREWER, GARRY, AND PETER deLEON (1983). *The Foundations of Policy Analysis.* Homewood, IL: The Dorsey Press.

BRUNNER, RONALD (1992). "Science and Responsibility." *Policy Sciences* 25 (no. 3): 295-331.

COCHRAN, CLARKE, LAWRENCE MAYER, T. R. CARR, AND JOSEPH CAYER (1986). *American Public Policy: An Introduction.* 2d ed. New York: St. Martin's Press.

DELEON, PETER (1988). *Advice and Consent: The Development of the Policy Sciences*. New York: Russel Sage Foundation.

DEUTSCH, KARL (1972). "The Contribution of Experiments within the Framework of Political Theory." In *Experimentation and Simulation in Political Science*, pp. 19–36. Edited by J. A. Laponce and Paul Smoker. Toronto: University of Toronto Press.

DORON, GIDEON (1992). Policy Sciences: "The State of the Discipline." *Policy Studies Review* 11 (Autumn/Winter): 303–09.

DOUGLAS, MARY (1989). "A Model of Models: Distinguished Lecture," *American Anthropologist* 91 (4): 855–65.

DRESANG, DENNIS (1983). "Forward" to *The Logic of Policy Inquiry*, by David Paris and James Reynolds. New York: Longman.

DROR, YEHEZKEL (1968). *Public Policy Making Reexamined*. Scranton, PA: Chandler Publishing Co.

_____(1971). *Design for Policy Sciences*. New York: American Elsevier.

DUBIN, ROBERT (1969). *Theory Building*. New York: The Free Press.

DUBNICK, MEL, AND BARBARA BARDES (1983). *Thinking About Public Policy*. New York: John Wiley and Sons.

DUNN, WILLIAM (1981). *Public Policy Analysis*. Englewood Cliffs, NJ: Prentice-Hall.

_____ (1988). "Methods of the Second Type: Coping with the Wilderness of Conventional Policy Analysis." *Policy Studies Review* 7 (Summer): 720–37.

DYE, THOMAS (1972). *Understanding Public Policy*. Englewood Cliffs, NJ: Prentice-Hall.

EULAU, HEINZ (1977). "The Workshop: The Place of Policy Analysis in Political Science: Five Perspectives." *American Journal of Political Science* 21 (May): 415–33.

FORCESE, DENNIS, AND STEPHEN RICHER (1973). *Social Science Research Methods*. Englewood Cliffs, NJ: Prentice-Hall.

FRANKFORT-NACHMIAS, CHAVA, AND DAVID NACHMIAS (1992). *Research Methods in the Social Sciences*. 4th ed. New York: St. Martin's Press.

FROHOCK, FRED (1967). *The Nature of Political Inquiry*. Homewood, IL: Dorsey Press.

_____ (1979). *Public Policy: Scope and Logic*. Englewood Cliffs, NJ: Prentice-Hall.

GOODIN, ROBERT (1976). *The Politics of Rational Man*. John Wiley and Sons.

_____ (1982). *Political Theory and Public Policy*. Chicago: University of Chicago Press.

GRAHAM, GEORGE (1988). "'The Policy Orientation' and the Theoretical Development of Political Science." In *Handbook of Political Theory and Pol-*

icy Science, pp.150–61. Edited by Edward Portis and Michael Levy. New York: Greenwood Press.

GREENBERGER, MARTIN, MATTHEW CRENSON, AND BRIAN CRISSEY (1976). *Models in the Policy Process*. New York: Russel Sage Foundation.

HAM, CHRISTOPHER, AND MICHAEL HILL (1984). *The Policy Process in the Modern Capitalist State*. Brighton, Sussex, GB: Wheatsheaf Books.

HAYES, MICHAEL (1992). *Incrementalism and Public Policy*. New York: Longman.

HECLO, HUGH (1972). "Review Article: Policy Analysis." *British Journal of Political Science* 2 (Jan.): 83–108.

HOGWOOD, BRIAN, AND LEWIS GUNN (1984). *Policy Analysis for the Real World*. London: Oxford University Press.

HOOVER, KENNETH (1992). *Elements of Social Scientific Thinking*. 5th ed. New York: St. Martin's Press.

HOUSE, PETER (1982). *The Art of Public Policy Analysis*. Beverly Hills: Sage Publications.

HOUSE, PETER, AND ROGER SHULL (1988). *Rush To Policy*. New Brunswick: Transaction Books.

JENKINS, W. I. (1978). *Policy Analysis*. London: Martin Robertson.

JENKINS-SMITH, HANK (1990). *Democratic Politics and Policy Analysis*. Pacific Grove, Cal.: Brooks/Cole Publishing.

JENNINGS, BRUCE (1983). "Interpretive Social Science and Policy Analysis." In *Ethics, The Social Sciences, and Policy Analysis*, pp. 3–35. Edited by Daniel Callahan and Bruce Jennings. New York: Plenum Press.

KIMPTON, LAWRENCE (1956). "The Social Sciences Today." In *The State of the Social Sciences*, pp. 348-52. Edited by Leonard White. Chicago: University of Chicago Press.

KING, GARY, ROBERT KEHANE, AND SIDNEY VERBA (1994). *Designing Social Inquiry: Scientific Inference in Qualitative Research*. Princeton, NJ: Princeton University Press.

LANE, RUTH (1990). "Concrete Theory: An Emerging Political Method." *American Political Science Review* 84 (Sept.): 927–40.

LASSWELL, HAROLD (1951). "The Policy Orientation." In *The Policy Sciences*, pp. 3–15. Edited by Daniel Lerner and Harold Lasswell. Stanford, CA: Stanford University Press.

_____ (1971). *A Pre-View of Policy Sciences*. New York: American Elsevier.

LAVE, CHARLES, AND JAMES MARCH (1975). *An Introduction to Models in the Social Sciences*. New York: Harper and Row.

LEVY, MICHAEL (1988). "Political Theory and the Emergence of a Policy Science." In *Handbook of Political Theory and Policy Science*, pp. 1–10. Edited by Edward Portis and Michael Levy. New York: Greenwood Press.

LINDER, STEPHEN, AND B. GUY PETERS (1988). "The Analysis of Design or the Design of Analysis?" *Policy Studies Review* 7 (Summer): 738–50.

LIPPITT, GORDON (1973). *Visualizing Change: Model Building and the Change Process*. La Jolla, CA: University Associates.

MACRAE, DUNCAN JR. (1985). *Policy Indicators*. Chapel Hill: The University of North Carolina Press.

MALECHA, GARY (1989). "From Political Science to Policy Science." Paper prepared for delivery at the 1989 Annual Meeting of the Western Political Science Association, Salt Lake City, Utah, March 29–April 2.

MARSHALL, CATHERINE, AND GRETCHEN ROSSMAN (1989). *Designing Qualitative Research*. New York: Sage Publications.

MAY, PETER (1986). "Politics and Policy Analysis." *Political Science Quarterly* 101 (Spring): 109–25.

MAZMANIAN, DANIEL, AND PAUL SABATIER (1980). "A Multivariate Model of Public Policy-Making." *American Journal of Political Science* 24 (Aug.): 439–68.

MERRIAM, CHARLES (1921). "The Present State of the Study of Politics." *American Political Science Review* XV (May): 173–85.

MILLER, JAMES G. (1956). "Toward a General Theory for the Behavioral Sciences." In *The State of the Social Sciences*, pp. 29–65. Edited by Leonard White. Chicago: University of Chicago Press.

MITCHELL, JERRY (1988). "The Limits of Positivism: Case Studies of Values in Science." *Policy Studies Journal* 17 (Fall): 215–20.

MUZZIO, DOUGLAS, AND GERALD DE MAIO (1988). "Formal Theory and the Prospects of a Policy Science." In *Handbook of Political Theory and Policy Science*, pp.127–45. Edited by Edward Portis and Michael Levy. New York: Greenwood Press.

NOBLE, JAMES B. (1982). "Social Structure and Paradigm Synthesis: Theoretical Commensurability and the Problem of Mannheim's Paradox." In *The Paradigm Problem in Political Science*, pp. 25–64. Edited by William T. Bluhm. Durham, NC: Carolina Academic Press.

PALUMBO, DENNIS (1981). "The State of Policy Studies Research and the Policy of the *New Policy Studies Review*." *Policy Studies Review* 1 (1): 5–10.

PUTT, ALLEN, AND J. FRED SPRINGER (1989). *Policy Research*. Englewood Cliffs, NJ: Prentice-Hall.

QUADE, E. S. (1989). *Analysis for Public Decisions*. 3d ed. Revised by Grace Carter. New York: North Holland.

RANNEY, AUSTIN (1968). "The Study of Policy Content: A Framework for Choice." In *Political Science and Public Policy*, pp. 3–21. Edited by Austin Ranney. Chicago: Markham.

RIPLEY, RANDALL (1985). *Policy Analysis in Political Science*. Chicago: Nelson-Hall.

ROBERTSON, DAVID, AND DENNIS JUDD (1989). *The Development of American Public Policy*. Glenview, IL: Scott-Foresman.

ROGERS, JAMES (1988). *The Impact of Policy Analysis*. Pittsburgh: The University of Pittsburgh Press.

ROTH, PAUL (1987). *Meaning and Method in the Social Sciences*. Ithaca: Cornell University Press.

RUDNER, RICHARD (1966). *Philosophy of Social Science*. Englewood Cliffs, NJ: Prentice-Hall.

SABATIER, PAUL (1989). "Political Science and Public Policy: An Assessment." Paper presented to the annual meeting of the American Political Science Association, Aug. 30–Sept. 2, 1989, Atlanta, GA.

SHARKANSKY, IRA, ed. (1970). *Policy Analysis in Political Science*. Chicago: Markham.

SHILS, EDWARD, AND HENRY FINCH, eds. (1949). *Max Weber on the Methodology of the Social Sciences*. Glencoe, IL: The Free Press.

SIMON, HERBERT, AND ALLEN NEWELL (1956). "Models: Their Uses and Limitations." In *The State of the Social Sciences*, pp. 66–83. Edited by Leonard White. Chicago: University of Chicago Press.

SINGLETON, ROYCE, BRUCE STRAITS, AND MARGARET MILLER STRAITS (1993). *Approaches to Social Research*. 2d ed. New York: Oxford University Press.

SMELSER, NEIL (1968). *Essays in Sociological Explanation*. Englewood Cliffs, NJ: Prentice-Hall.

STOKEY, EDITH, AND RICHARD ZECKHAUSER (1978). *A Primer for Policy Analysis*. New York: W. W. Norton, 1978.

STONE, DEBORAH (1988). *Policy Paradox and Political Reason*. Glenview, IL: Scott, Foresman.

TORGERSON, DOUGLAS (1992). "Priest and Jester in Policy Sciences: Developing the Focus of Inquiry." *Policy Sciences* 25 (no. 3): 225–35.

VAN MAANEN, JOHN, ed. (1983). *Qualitative Methodology*. Beverly Hills: Sage Publications.

WEIMER, DAVID, AND AIDAN VINING (1992). *Policy Analysis: Concepts and Practice*. Englewood Cliffs, NJ: Prentice Hall.

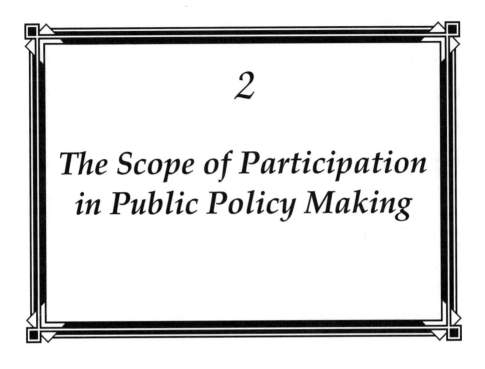

2

The Scope of Participation in Public Policy Making

INTRODUCTION

There is no clear demarcation between contemporary political theory and public policy theory. To some extent, the latter is a subset of the former, although policy theory has established a unique purpose and direction for itself. The readings in this section are usually perceived as political theory, but they also form the foundation for much of the policy theory that is presented in subsequent sections. For example, Section 5 on subsystems owes a great deal to the conceptual work on pluralism and elitism. And the typologies developed in Section 4 correlate with some elements of elitist and pluralist theory.

The debate over "who rules" is an old one. The title of this section, "The Scope of Participation," refers to the breadth and depth of influence, power, and authority that essentially determine policy. Do we really have government by, for, and of the people? Or are we ruled by a small oligarchy of self-appointed elites? Do we exercise control over government through interest groups that speak on our behalf? These are fundamental questions about the character of our political system.

Modern analysis of "special interests" has its genesis in Arthur Bentley's 1908 book, *The Process of Government*, although much of his discussion would sound familiar to the authors of the *Federalist Papers*, who knew that competing interests would try to influence the fledgling democracy for their own benefit. Bentley surmised that "All phenomena of government are phenomena of groups pressing one another, forming one another, and pushing out new groups and group representatives (the organs or agencies of government) to mediate the adjustments" (1908, 269).

Not long after Bentley's work was published, Charles Beard wrote a book that was considered heretical at the time; in *An Economic Interpretation of the Constitution* (1913), he argued that a small, unique clique of closely connected individuals developed the Constitution as a way of protecting their own private interests. These two landmark studies helped initiate a long tradition of scholarly work on elites, interest groups, and democratic government in America. These authors were among the first to examine the scope of participation in American policy making, but the literature on group politics, and especially elites, has a long tradition in Europe. Indeed, we could argue that everything from Plato's *Republic* to Hobbes' *Leviathan* are concerned with the same questions of governance. And Bentley gives Karl Marx credit for being the original group theorist. But Bentley and Beard wrote about the unique character of U. S. democracy, setting in motion a grand effort to develop a theory that explains who governs America.

The readings selected for this section provide just a taste of this voluminous work on group politics, elites, and democracy. The selection from Truman's highly regarded work, *The Governmental Process*, was written over forty years ago, but it serves well as an analysis of interest group politics even today. He notes that many interest groups are increasingly politicized, meaning "they make their claims through or upon the institutions of government" (1951, 505). Indeed, the number of interest groups, registered lobbyists, and political action committees (PACs) has soared in the last two decades—a phenomenon Jeffrey Berry calls the "advocacy explosion" (1989, 16). This process of making "claims" is the focus of much contemporary political science research.

Truman provided a foundation for later research that is characterized loosely as pluralist theory. The doyen of this school of thought is Robert Dahl. His book, *Pluralist Democracy in the United States*, offers a succinct statement of the basic tenets of pluralist theory, listed as follows:

> Because one center of power is set against another, power itself will be tamed, civilized, controlled, and limited to decent human purposes, while coercion, the most evil form of power, will be reduced to a minimum.
>
> Because even minorities are provided with opportunities to veto solutions they strongly object to, the consent of all will be won in the long run.
>
> Because constant negotiations among different centers of power are necessary in order to make decisions, citizens and leaders will perfect the precious art of dealing peacefully with their conflicts, and not merely to the benefit of one partisan but to the mutual benefit of all the parties to a conflict (Dahl 1967, 24).

Dahl's many books on pluralism spawned a great debate over its merits. The selection by William Kelso is from a book "intended as a defense of a pluralistic form of democracy" (1978, xi). Kelso describes three different variations of the pluralist concept, including a variation he developed called *public pluralism*. He champions this form of pluralism in his book and offers it in response to the criticism leveled against pluralism. In contrast, the selection from David Garson's book, *Group Theories of Politics* (1978), reviews the critics of group theory and pluralism, and concludes that group theory has fallen from favor.

Some of the most vociferous criticism of pluralism has come from scholars who argue that public policy is controlled by a small, self-appointed oligarchy of elites: "The core of the elitist doctrine is that there may exist in any society a minority of the population which makes the major decisions in the society. . . . the dominant minority cannot be controlled by the majority, whatever democratic mechanisms are used" (Parry 1969, 30–31). The chapter from Robert Putnam's book, *The Comparative Study of Elites*, provides an overview of the classical elite theorists and identifies the principal conceptual elements of elite theory.

There has been a long and frustrating conflict between pluralist and elite theorists:

> Recent years have witnessed ongoing debates between pluralists and "elitists" concerning elites' role in contemporary democracies. Pluralists have argued that power is significantly decentralized, with opportunities reasonably available to organized groups seeking to influence policies of interest to them. "Elitists" have argued by contrast that most effectively organized interests represent the upper or ruling class, and that opportunities for others to influence public policy are generally open only to the degree they harmonize with upper class interests. This debate has continued interminably (deZerega 1991, 341).

For many years the *American Political Science Review* published numerous articles by the warring theorists. The article by Jack Walker (1966a) is one of the better-known salvos in this exchange, and criticizes the pluralist perspective, which he cryptically labeled the *elitist theory of democracy*. This phrase, borrowed from sociologist Semour Lipset, was purposefully designed to obscure any difference between pluralist and elitist theory; Walker viewed both as a normative threat to "real" democratic theory. He later explained that this essay was "intended as a critique of the prescriptive implications of a set of ideas concerning democratic political systems. . . "(1966b, 391). The "set of ideas" that so intensely perturbed Walker concerned the role of the masses in a democratic political system. He argues that pluralist theory mistakenly minimized the importance of "the common citizen."

Walker's piece did not, of course, end the debate, which continues to this day.

Throughout the readings in this section there are many references to the theoretical utility of these concepts. Critics of a theory often argue it is not really a theory at all, and that in essence it fails the tests identified in the the first chapter of this book. The reader should carefully scrutinize these claims; relying upon the criteria for a good theory, decide for yourself if these concepts clarify, or obfuscate, reality.

In contemporary politics there is much discussion of beltway bandits, special interests at Gucci Gulch, unresponsive government, fat cats, and out-of-touch politicians. Some of this is just political hype, but clearly there is widespread concern over the scope of participation in the policy-making process. Perhaps the debate over group, pluralist, and elite theories is more relevant today than ever.

REFERENCES

BEARD, CHARLES (1913). *An Economic Interpretation of the Constitution of the United States.* New York: Macmillan.

BENTLEY, ARTHUR (1908). *The Process of Government: A Study of Social Pressures.* Evanston, IL: The Principia Press of Illinois (new edition published in 1935).

BERRY, JEFFREY (1989). *The Interest Group Society.* 2d ed. New York: Harper/Collins.

DAHL, ROBERT (1967). *Pluralist Democracy in the United States.* Chicago: Rand McNally.

DEZEREGA, GUS (1991). "Elites and Democratic Theory: Insights from the Self-Organizing Model." *The Review of Politics* 53 (Spring): 340–72.

GARSON, G. DAVID (1978). *Group Theories of Politics.* Beverly Hills: Sage Publications.

KELSO, WILLIAM (1978). *American Democratic Theory.* Westport, CT: Greenwood Press.

PARRY, GERAINT (1969). *Political Elites.* New York: Frederick Praeger.

PUTNAM, ROBERT (1976). *The Comparative Study of Political Elites.* Englewood Cliffs, NJ: Prentice-Hall.

TRUMAN, DAVID (1951). *The Governmental Process.* New York: Alfred Knopf.

WALKER, JACK (1966a). "A Critique of the Elitist Theory of Democracy." *American Political Science Review* 60 (June): 285–95.

_____ (1966b). "A Reply to 'Further Reflections on the Elitist Theory of Democracy'." *American Political Science Review* 60 (June): 391–92.

INTEREST GROUPS AND THE NATURE OF THE STATE
David B. Truman*

Men, wherever they are observed, are creatures participating in those established patterns of interaction that we call groups. Excepting perhaps the
most casual and transitory, these continuing interactions, like all such interpersonal relationships, involve power. This power is exhibited in two
closely interdependent ways. In the first place, the group exerts power over
its members; an individual's group affiliations largely determine his attitudes, values, and the frames of reference in terms of which he interprets
his experiences. For a measure of conformity to the norms of the group is
the price of acceptance within it. Such power is exerted not only by an individual's present group relationships; it also may derive from past affiliations such as the childhood family as well as from groups to which the individual aspires to belong and whose characteristic shared attitudes he also
holds. In the second place, the group, if it is or becomes an interest group,
which any group in a society may be, exerts power over other groups in the
society when it successfully imposes claims upon them.

Many interest groups, probably an increasing proportion in the United
States, are politicized. That is, either from the outset or from time to time in
the course of their development they make their claims through or upon the
institutions of government. Both the forms and functions of government in
turn are a reflection of the activities and claims of such groups. The consti-
tution-writing proclivities of Americans clearly reveal the influence of demands from such sources, and the statutory creation of new functions reflects their continuing operation. Many of these forms and functions have
received such widespread acceptance from the start or in the course of time
that they appear to be independent of the overt activities of organized interest groups. The judiciary is such a form. The building of city streets and the
control of vehicular traffic are examples of such a function. However, if the
judiciary or a segment of it operates in a fashion sharply contrary to the expectations of an appreciable portion of the community or if its role is
strongly attacked, the group basis of its structure and powers is likely to become apparent. Similarly, if street construction greatly increases tax rates or
if the control of traffic unnecessarily inconveniences either pedestrians or
motorists, the exposure of these functions to the demands of competing interests will not be obscure. Interests that are widely held in the society may
be reflected in government without their being organized in groups. They
are what we have called potential groups. If the claims implied by the inter-

* David Truman, *The Governmental Process: Political Interests and Public Opinion.* New York:
Knopf, 1951, 1971 (pp. 505–515). Used by permission

ests of these potential groups are quickly and adequately represented, inter-action among those people who share the underlying interests or attitudes is unnecessary. But the interest base of accepted governmental forms and functions and their potential involvement in overt group activities are ever present even when not patently operative.

The institutions of government are centers of interest-based power; their connections with interest groups may be latent or overt and their ac-tivities range in political character from the routinized and widely accepted to the unstable and highly controversial. In order to make claims, political interest groups will seek access to the key points of decision within these in-stitutions. Such points are scattered throughout the structure, including not only the formally established branches of government but also the political parties in their various forms and the relationships between governmental units and other interest groups.

The extent to which a group achieves effective access to the institu-tions of government is the resultant of a complex of interdependent factors. For the sake of simplicity these may be classified in three somewhat over-lapping categories: (1) factors relating to a group's strategic position in the society; (2) factors associated with the internal characteristics of the group; and (3) factors peculiar to the governmental institutions themselves. In the first category are: the group's status or prestige in the society, affecting the ease with which it commands deference from those outside its bounds; the standing it and its activities have when measured against the widely held but largely unorganized interests or "rules of the game;" the extent to which government officials are formally or informally "members" of the group; and the usefulness of the group as a source of technical and political knowledge. The second category includes: the degree and appropriateness of the group's organization; the degree of cohesion it can achieve in a given situation, especially in the light of competing group demands upon its membership; the skills of the leadership; and the group's resources in num-bers and money. In the third category, are: the operating structure of the government institutions, since such established features involve relatively fixed advantages and handicaps; and the effects of the group life of particu-lar units or branches of the government.

The product of effective access, of the claims of organized and unorga-nized interests that achieve access with varying degrees of effectiveness, is a governmental decision. Note that these interests that achieve effective ac-cess and guide decisions need not be "selfish," are not necessarily solidly unified, and may not be represented by organized groups. Governmental decisions are the resultant of effective access by various interests, of which organized groups may be only a segment. These decisions may be more or less stable depending on the strength of supporting interests and on the severity of disturbances in the society which affect that strength.

A characteristic feature of the governmental system in the United States is that it contains a multiplicity of points of access. The federal system establishes decentralized and more or less independent centers of power, vantage points from which to secure privileged access to the national government. Both a sign and a cause of the strength of the constituent units in the federal scheme is the peculiar character of our party system, which has strengthened parochial relationships, especially those of national legislators. National parties, and to a lesser degree those in the States, tend to be poorly cohesive leagues of locally based organizations rather than unified and inclusive structures. Staggered terms for executive officials and various types of legislators accentuate differences in the effective electorates that participate in choosing these officers. Each of these different, often opposite, localized patterns (constituencies) is a channel of independent access to the larger party aggregation and to the formal government. Thus, especially at the national level, the party is an electing-device and only in limited measure an integrated means of policy determination. Within the Congress, furthermore, controls are diffused among committee chairmen and other leaders in both chambers. The variety of these points of access is further supported by relationships stemming from the constitutional doctrine of the separation of powers, from related checks and balances, and at the State and local level from the common practice of choosing an array of executive officials by popular election. At the Federal level the formal simplicity of the executive branch has been complicated by a Supreme Court decision that has placed a number of administrative agencies beyond the removal power of the president. The position of these units, however, differs only in degree from that of many that are constitutionally within the executive branch. In consequence of alternative lines of access available through the legislature and the executive and of divided channels for the control of administrative policy, many nominally executive agencies are at various times virtually independent of the chief executive.

Although some of these lines of access may operate in series, they are not arranged in a stable and integrated hierarchy. Depending upon the whole political context in a given period and upon the relative strength of contending interests, one or another of the centers of power in the formal government or in the parties may become the apex of a hierarchy of controls. Only the highly routinized governmental activities show any stability in this respect, and these may as easily be subordinated to elements in the legislature as to the chief executive. Within limits, therefore, organized interest groups, gravitating toward responsive points of decision, may play one segment of the structure against another as circumstances and strategic considerations permit. The total pattern of government over a period of time thus presents a protean complex of crisscrossing relationships that change in strength and direction with alterations in the power and standing of interests, organized and unorganized.

There are two elements in this conception of the political process in the United States that are of crucial significance and that require special emphasis. These are, first, the notion of multiple or overlapping membership and, second, the function of unorganized interests, or potential interest groups.

The idea of overlapping membership stems from the conception of a group as a standardized pattern of interactions rather than as a collection of human units. Although the former may appear to be a rather misty abstraction, it is actually far closer to complex reality than the latter notion. The view of a group as an aggregation of individuals abstracts from the observable fact that in any society, and especially a complex one, no single group affiliation accounts for all of the attitudes or interests of any individual except a fanatic or a compulsive neurotic. No tolerably normal person is totally absorbed in any group in which he participates. The diversity of an individual's activities and his attendant interests involve him in a variety of actual and potential groups. Moreover, the fact that the genetic experiences of no two individuals are identical and the consequent fact that the spectra of their attitudes are in varying degrees dissimilar means that the members of a single group will perceive the group's claims in terms of a diversity of frames of reference. Such heterogeneity may be of little significance until such time as these multiple memberships conflict. Then the cohesion and influence of the affected group depend upon the incorporation or accommodation of the conflicting loyalties of any significant segment of the group, an accommodation that may result in altering the original claims. Thus the leaders of a Parent-Teacher Association must take some account of the fact that their proposals must be acceptable to members who also belong to the local taxpayers' league, to the local chamber of commerce, and to the Catholic Church.

The notion of overlapping membership bears directly upon the problems allegedly created by the appearance of a multiplicity of interest groups. Yet the fact of such overlapping is frequently overlooked or neglected in discussions of the political role of groups. James Madison, whose brilliant analysis in the tenth essay in *The Federalist* we have frequently quoted, relied primarily upon diversity of groups and difficulty of communication to protect the new government from the tyranny of a factious majority. He barely touched on the notion of multiple membership when he observed, almost parenthetically: "Besides other impediments, it may be remarked that, where there is a consciousness of unjust or dishonorable purposes, communication is always checked by distrust in proportion to the number whose concurrence is necessary." John C. Calhoun's idea of the concurrent majority, developed in his posthumously published work, *A Disquisition on Gov-*

ernment (1851), assumed the unified, monolithic character of the groups
whose liberties he was so anxious to protect. When his present-day followers unearth his doctrines, moreover, they usually make the same assumption, although implicitly.[1] Others, seeking a satisfactory means of accounting
for the continued existence of the political system, sometimes assume that it
is the nonparticipant citizens, aroused to unwonted activity, who act as a
kind of counterbalance to the solid masses that constitute organized interest
groups.[2] Although this phenomenon may occur in times of crisis, reliance
upon it reckons insufficiently with the established observation that citizens
who are nonparticipant in one aspect of the governmental process, such as
voting, rarely show much concern for any phase of political activity. Multiple membership is more important as a restraint upon the activities of organized groups than the rarely aroused protests of chronic nonparticipants.

Organized interest groups are never solid and monolithic, though the
consequences of their overlapping memberships may be handled with sufficient skill to give the organizations a maximum of cohesion. It is the competing claims of other groups *within* a given interest group that threaten its cohesion and force it to reconcile its claims with those of other groups active
on the political scene. The claims within the American Medical Association
of specialists and teaching doctors who support group practice, compulsory
health insurance and preventive medicine offer an illustration. The presence
within the American Legion of public-housing enthusiasts and labor unionists as well as private homebuilders and labor opponents provides another
example. Potential conflicts within the Farm Bureau between farmers who
must buy supplementary feed and those who produce excess feed grains for
the market, between soybean growers and dairymen, even between traditional Republicans and loyal Democrats, create serious political problems for
the interest group. Instances of the way in which such cleavages impose restraints upon an organized group's activities are infinitely numerous, almost
as numerous as cases of multiple membership. Given the problems of cohesion and internal group politics that result from overlapping membership,
the emergence of a multiplicity of interest groups in itself contains no dangers for the political system, especially since such overlapping affects not
only private but also governmental "members" of the organized group.

But multiple membership in organized groups is not sufficiently extensive to obviate the possibility of irreconcilable conflict. There is little
overlapping in the memberships of the National Association of Manufacturers and the United Steelworkers of America, or of the American Farm
Bureau Federation and the United Automobile Workers. Overlapping membership among relatively cohesive organized interest groups provides an

---

[1]Cf. John Fischer: "Unwritten Rules of American Politics," *Harper's Magazine* (November,
1948), pp. 27-36.
[2]Cf. Hering: *The Politics of Democracy*, p. 32.

insufficient basis upon which to account for the relative stability of an operating political system. That system is a fact. An adequate conception of the group process must reckon with it. To paraphrase the famous words of John Marshall, we must never forget that it is a going polity we are explaining.

We cannot account for an established American political system without the second crucial element in our conception of the political process, the concept of the unorganized interest, or potential interest group. Despite the tremendous number of interest groups existing in the United States, not all interests are organized. If we recall the definition of an interest as a shared attitude, it becomes obvious that continuing interaction resulting in claims upon other groups does not take place on the basis of all such attitudes. One of the commonest interest group forms, the association, emerges out of severe or prolonged disturbances in the expected relationships of individuals in similar institutionalized groups. An association continues to function as long as it succeeds in ordering these disturbed relationships, as a labor union orders the relationships between management and workers. Not all such expected relationships are simultaneously or in a given short period sufficiently disturbed to produce organization. Therefore only a portion of the interests or attitudes involved in such expectations are represented by organized groups. Similarly, many organized groups—families, businesses, or churches, for example—do not operate continuously as interest groups or as political interest groups.

Any mutual interest, however, any shared attitude, is a potential group. A disturbance in established relationships and expectations anywhere in the society may produce new patterns of interaction aimed at restricting or eliminating the disturbance. Sometimes it may be this possibility of organization that alone gives the potential group a minimum of influence in the political process. It is in this sense that Bentley speaks of a difference in degree between the politics of despotism and that of other "forms" of government. He notes that there is "a process of representation in despotisms which is inevitable in all democracies, and which may be distinguished by quantities and by elaboration of technique, but not in any deeper 'qualititative' way." He speaks of the despot as "representative of his own class, and to a smaller, but none the less real, extent of the ruled class as well."[3] Obstacles to the development of organized groups from potential ones may be presented by inertia or by the activities of opposed groups, but the possibility that severe disturbances will be created if these submerged, potential interests should organize necessitates some recognition of the existence of these interests and gives them at least a minimum of influence.

More important for present purposes than the potential groups representing separate minority elements are those interests or expectations that

---

[3]Bentley: *The Process of Government*, pp. 314-5. Copyright 1908 and used with the permission of Arthur F. Bentley.

are so widely held in the society and are so reflected in the behavior of almost all citizens that they are, so to speak, taken for granted. Such "majority" interests are significant not only because they may become the basis for organized interest groups but also because the "membership" of such potential groups overlaps extensively the memberships of the various organized interest groups.[4] The resolution of conflicts between the claims of such unorganized interests and those of organized interest groups must grant recognition to the former not only because affected individuals may feel strongly attached to them but even more certainly because these interests are widely shared and are a part of many established patterns of behavior the disturbance of which would be difficult and painful. They are likely to be highly valued.

These widely held but unorganized interests are what we have previously called the "rules of the game." Others have described these attitudes in such terms as "systems of belief," as a "general ideological consensus," and as "a broad body of attitudes and understandings regarding the nature and limits of authority."[5] Each of these interests (attitudes) may be wide or narrow, general or detailed. For the mass of the population they may be loose and ambiguous, though more precise and articulated at the leadership level. In any case the "rules of the game" are interests the serious disturbance of which will result in organized interaction and the assertion of fairly explicit claims for conformity. In the American system the "rules" would include the value generally attached to the dignity of the individual human being, loosely expressed in terms of "fair dealing" or more explicitly verbalized in formulations such as the Bill of Rights. They would embrace "the democratic mold," that is, the approval of forms for broad mass participation in the designation of leaders and in the selection of policies in all social groups and institutions. They would also comprehend certain semi-egalitarian notions of material welfare. This is an illustrative, not an exhaustive, list of such interests.

The widely held, unorganized interests are reflected in the major institutions of the society, including the political. The political structure of the United States, as we have seen, has adopted characteristic legislative, executive, and judicial forms through the efforts of organized interest groups. Once these forms have been accepted and have been largely routinized, the supporting organized interest groups cease to operate as such and revert to the potential stage. As embodied in these institutional forms and in accepted verbal formulations, such as those of legal and constitutional theory,

---

[4]See the suggestive discussion of this general subject in Robert Bierstedt: "The Sociology of Majorities," *American Sociological Review,* Vol. 13, no. 6 (December, 1948), pp. 700-10.

[5]Kluckhohn: *Mirror for Man,* pp. 248 and *passim*; Sebastian de Grazia: *The Political Community: A Study of Anomie* (Chicago: University of Chicago Press, 1948), pp. ix, 80, and *passim*; Almond: *The American People and Foreign Policy,* p. 158; Charles E. Merriam: *Systematic Politics* (Chicago: University of Chicago Press, 1945), p. 213.

the interests of these potential groups are established expectations concerning not only *what* the governmental institutions shall do, but more particularly *how* they shall operate. To the extent that these established processes remain noncontroversial, they may appear to have no foundation in interests. Nevertheless, the widespread expectations will receive tacit or explicit deference from most organized interest groups in consequence of the overlapping of their memberships with these potential groups.[6] Violation of the "rules of the game" normally will weaken a group's cohesion, reduce its status in the community, and expose it to the claims of other groups. The latter may be competing organized groups that more adequately incorporate the "rules," or they may be groups organized on the basis of these broad interests and in response to the violations.

The pervasive and generally accepted character of these unorganized interests, or "rules," is such that they are acquired by most individuals in their early experiences in the family, in the public schools (probably less effectively in the private and parochial schools), and in similar institutionalized groups that are also expected to conform in some measure to the "democratic mold." The "rules" are likely to be reinforced by later events. Persons who aspire to, or occupy, public office of whatever sort are particularly likely to identify with these expected behaviors as part of their desired or existing roles. With varying degrees of effectiveness the group life of government agencies—legislative, executive, and judicial—reinforces the claims of these unorganized interests, which overlap those of the official group itself and those of "outside" political interest groups. Marked and prolonged deviation from these expected behaviors by public officials, who are expected to represent what Bentley calls the "'absent' or quiescent group interests," will normally produce restrictive action by other governmental functionaries, by existing organized interest groups, by ones newly organized in consequence of the deviations, or by all three.

It is thus multiple memberships in potential groups based on widely held and accepted interests that serve as a balance wheel in a going political system like that of the United States. To some people this observation may appear to be a truism and to others a somewhat mystical notion. It is neither. In the first place, neglect of this function of multiple memberships in most discussions of organized interest groups indicates that the observation is not altogether commonplace. Secondly, the statement has no mystical quality; the effective operation of these widely held interests is to be inferred directly from verbal and other behavior in the political sphere. Without the notion of multiple memberships in potential groups it is literally impossible to account for the existence of a viable polity such as that in the United States or to develop a coherent conception of the political process. The strength of these widely held but largely unorganized interests explains

[6]Cf. Bentley: *The Process of Government*, p. 397, and MacIver: *The Web of Government*, p. 79

the vigor with which propagandists for organized groups attempt to change other attitudes by invoking such interests.[7] Their importance is further evidenced in the recognized function of the means of mass communication, notably the press, in reinforcing widely accepted norms of "public morality."[8]

The role of the widespread unorganized interests and potential groups does not imply that such interests are always and everywhere dominant. Nor does it mean that the slightest action in violation of any of them inevitably and instantly produces a restrictive response from another source. These interests are not unambiguous, as the long history of litigation concerning freedom of speech will demonstrate. Subjectively they are not all equally fundamental. Thus since the "rules" are interests competing with those of various organized groups, they are in any given set of circumstances more or less subject to attenuation through such psychological mechanisms as rationalization. Moreover, the means of communication, whether by word of mouth or through the mass media, may not adequately make known particular deviations from the behavior indicated by these broad interests.

In a relatively vigorous political system, however, these unorganized interests are dominant with sufficient frequency in the behavior of enough important segments of the society so that, despite ambiguity and other restrictions, both the activity and the methods of organized interest groups are kept within broad limits. This interpretation is not far from Lasswell's view of the state as a relational system defined by a certain frequency of subjective events.[9] According to his definition, "the state . . . is a time-space manifold of similar subjective events. . . .That subjective event which is the unique mark of the state is the recognition that one belongs to a community with a system of paramount claims and expectations.[10] All citizens of the state as thus conceived need not experience this "event" continuously or with equal intensity. Nor need the attitudes of all citizens be favorable toward these "claims and expectations." But the existence of the state, of the polity, depends on widespread, frequent recognition of and conformity to the claims of these unorganized interests and on activity condemning marked deviations from them. "All this," says Lasswell, "is frequently expressed as the 'sense of justice'. . . ."[11]

Thus it is only as the effects of overlapping memberships and the functions of unorganized interests and potential groups are included in the

---

[7]Cf. Lazarsfeld *et al.*: *The People's Choice*, preface to 2d edition, pp. xxi-xxii.

[8]Cf. Paul F. Lazarsfeld and Robert K. Merton: "Mass Communication, Popular Taste and Organized Social Act," in Lyman Bryson (ed.): *The Communication of Ideas* (New York: Harper and Brothers, 1948), pp. 102 ff.

[9]Lasswell: *Psychopathology and Politics*, pp. 240-61.

[10]Ibid., p. 245.

[11]Ibid., p. 246.

equation that it is accurate to speak of governmental activity as the product or resultant of interest group activity.

THREE TYPES OF PLURALISM
William Kelso*

In recent years the debate over pluralistic democracy has elicited intense comment from detractors as well as defenders of the doctrine. While supporters of a group theory of democracy contend that the interplay of interests enhances individual freedom and promotes rational decision making, critics claim that it retards comprehensive planning and works to the disadvantage of marginal interests in society. The purpose of this chapter is to argue that the debate has often been somewhat beside the point since the antagonists have failed to realize that there are distinct varieties of pluralism. The pattern of policy making that Robert Dahl and David Truman have described as pluralism has little in common with that form of politics Theodore Lowi has called "interest group liberalism" or Grant McConnell has termed "a group theory of politics." Because of their failure to recognize the existence of different kinds of interest-group democracy, many commentators have not always realized that their criticisms may apply only to specific forms of the doctrine. As we shall soon see, it is analytically possible to identify three distinct varieties: laissez-faire, corporate, and public pluralism. These alternative types make not only very different empirical assumptions about the openness of the present political system, but also very different normative assumptions about the most desirable pattern of group interaction.

Laissez-faire Pluralism

The form of pluralism I have labeled laissez-faire finds its clearest expression in the works of Robert Dahl, David Truman, Wallace Sayre, Herbert Kaufman, Edward Banfield, Charles Lindblom, and William Kornhauser.[1] Despite some variations in their respective views, these authors

*William Kelso, *American Democratic Theory: Pluralism and its Critics*. Westport, CN: Greenwood Press, 1978 (pp. 12-29). Used by permission

[1]In the course of his academic career Robert Dahl has espoused a variety of positions. In *Who Governs?* and *Pluralistic Democracy in the United States* he proposed what we have called a laissez-faire system of pluralism. In contrast, in *A Preface to Democratic Theory* he seems to advocate a polyarchal view of democracy, while more recently in *After the Revolution* he has argued that the most appropriate form of democracy depends on the level of government. See also Wallace Sayre and Herbert Kaufman, *Governing New York City*; David Truman, *The Governmental Process*; Edward C. Banfield, *Political Influence*; Charles Lindblom, *The Intelligence of Democracy*; David Braybrooke and Charles Lindblom, *A Strategy of Decision Making*; Charles Lindblom, "The Science of Muddling Through," pp. 79-88; William Kornhauser, *The Politics of Mass Society*.

conceive of democracy as essentially a twofold process involving competition among political elites and bargaining among interest groups. They insist that whenever members of the public are concerned about a particular issue, they can bring about political change either directly through the process of group bargaining or indirectly through the mechanism of elections. Laissez-faire pluralists reject the argument that the political system is dominated by a single ruling elite and instead insist that it is responsive to a variety of interests with divergent policy preferences. Like their laissez-faire counterparts in economics, they view the political arena as a competitive marketplace in which any entrepreneur can gain entry to merchandise his views. Politics is seen as an open, fluid process in which responsibility for formulating decisions is shared by a diverse array of groups and public officials who constantly bargain and negotiate with one another.

According to Dahl, whose case study of New Haven politics constitutes the classic example of the laissez-faire model, this openness represents the major distinguishing characteristic of the American political system.

> When one looks at American political institutions in their entirety and compares them with institutions in other democracies, what stands out as a salient feature is the extraordinary variety of opportunities these institutions provide for an organized minority to block, modify, or delay a policy which the minority opposes. Consequently, it is a rarity for any coalition to carry out its policies without having to bargain, negotiate, and compromise with its opponents.[2]

In New Haven, the process of bargaining and negotiation has made it possible for such diverse groups as wealthy businessmen, oldtime patricians, and working-class ethnics to wield considerable control over those policies which happen to concern them.[3] Since these groups have a variety of resources at their disposal as well as a number of points at which to influence policy, they cannot be denied access to the bargaining table for any prolonged period of time. Given the decentralized nature of the decision-making process, no single party can succeed in permanently excluding interests that hold opposing views. If a group feels intensely about an issue and is skillful in using its resources, it can win a favorable hearing of its demands even though it may not wield any preponderant strength in terms of wealth, social standing, or the like.[4]

Secondly, laissez-faire pluralists contend that the political system is self-regulating and self-correcting. If particular groups do start to accumulate excessive amounts of power, countervailing forces are likely to become active, which will check or limit their actions. Dahl argues that the phenom-

---

[2]Dahl, *Pluralistic Democracy*, p. 326.
[3]Dahl, *Who Governs?*, pp. 89-168.
[4]See chap. 6 for a more detailed treatment of the explanations laissez-faire pluralists give for the openness of the political system.

enon of unused resources, or what he terms "political slack," constitutes the chief brake on the decision-making process.[5] Since all groups possess some sort of resources, whether they be numbers, skill, or wealth, and since on most occasions groups do not expend all of their available assets to influence the deliberations of the political system, they have a certain amount of political slack on which they can draw when they perceive a threat to their interests. If a group starts to abuse its power or to deny access to other interests, opposing groups can tap previously unused resources in order to counterbalance these developments.

While Dahl speaks of political slack, Truman regards the phenomenon of "potential groups" as the chief restraint on monopoly power. Truman points out that individuals who are concerned with a particular issue do not necessarily need to use their resources overtly in order to wield influence. Established interests that recognize that their actions may elicit hostile reactions from other parties often seek to moderate their demands in order to minimize political opposition to their programs.

> The power of unorganized interests lies in the possibility that, if these wide, weak interests are too flagrantly ignored, they may be stimulated to organize for aggressive counteraction. In a society permitting wide freedom of association, access to power is not confined to the organized groups in the population.[6]

In a slightly different vein, Sayre and Kaufman argue that the self-regulating nature of the political system derives from the existence of multiple decision-making points.[7] In their case study of politics in New York City, they show how the decentralized nature of the city's government structure prevents any one group from monopolizing the political arena. Because there are so many points at which groups can voice their opinions, interests that lose out at one center of decision making can often seek redress of their grievances at another location.

Thirdly, because laissez-faire pluralists see the political system as both open and self-regulating, they believe that the power of the state to guide and regulate the political process is problematic at best. In a fluid political system in which decisions are reached through continual negotiation and compromise, the power of all parties, including that of political elites, is necessarily limited. Truman views government officials as playing primarily a mediative role, reconciling conflicting group demands when particular interests are unable to resolve their differences by themselves.[8] In contrast, Banfield recognizes that political officials can institute change if they want to, but he argues that they often feel the cost is too high. Banfield's case

[5]Dahl, *Who Governs?*, p. 310.
[6]Truman, *Governmental Process*, p. 114.
[7]Sayre and Kaufman, *Governing New York City*, p. 710.
[8]Truman, *Governmental Process*, pp. 45-63, 352-437.

study of Chicago graphically illustrates the constraints political leaders face under a highly pluralistic system of decision making: "In a system in which the political head must continually 'pay' to overcome formal decentralization and to acquire the authority he needs, the stock of influence in his possession cannot all be 'spent' as he might wish."[9] Thus instead of supervising the policy-making arena and orchestrating support for particular issues, leaders like Mayor Daley often choose to play a passive role. "When there is disagreement . . . the rational strategy for the political head usually is to do nothing."[10]

However, if government officials are especially skillful at what Dahl calls "pyramiding resources,"[11] they may be able to initiate significant change. In a laissez-faire system, elites like Mayor Lee of New Haven may be able to have a significant impact on their community by employing previously unused resources. But even when government officials are prominent actors in the political arena and not just mediators or passive bystanders, their power is based more on their personal skills as negotiators than on the institutional authority of their office. Mayor Lee succeeded in initiating an extensive urban redevelopment program in New Haven, but he was able to do so because "he was a negotiator rather than a hierarchical executive."[12]

> He rarely commanded. He negotiated, cajoled, exhorted, beguiled, charmed, pressed, appealed, reasoned, promised, insisted, demanded, even threatened, but he most needed support and acquiescence from other leaders who simply could not be commanded. Because the mayor could not command, he had to bargain.[13]

While the above authors have developed a model that is primarily an empirical theory of politics, their work is not without normative significance. The defenders of laissez-faire pluralism can easily be seen as the inheritors of eighteenth- and nineteenth-century liberalism's interest in the rights and liberties of the individual. Like James Madison before them, they recognize that in a large and diverse society men are prone to infringe on the liberties of those who espouse conflicting values. But as an article of faith, most laissez-faire pluralists insist that the presence of multiple centers of power will be sufficient to deter any party from abusing the rights of others. Instead of attacking what Madison called the cause of faction—the very diversity of human goals—they seek to control its consequences by dividing power among numerous groups. As Dahl argues, when "one center of power is set against another, power itself will be tamed, civilized, controlled

[9]Banfield, *Political Influence*, p. 241.
[10]Ibid., p. 252.
[11]Dahl, *Who Governs?*, p. 308.
[12]Ibid., p. 209.
[13]Ibid., p. 204.

and limited to decent human purposes, while coercion, the most evil form of power, will be reduced to a minimum."[14]

By dispersing power among many parties laissez-faire pluralists believe they will not only inhibit the misuse of government power but also retard the development of coercive mass movements. As William Kornhauser has shown in an important defense of pluralistic democracy, when individuals have no ties to secondary associations, they often lack standards for evaluating the appeals of various mass movements.[15] In such a state of anomie or normlessness, they are more likely to be receptive to movements with authoritarian characteristics. However, if people have an opportunity to participate in a rich and diverse group life, they acquire alternative sources of information and standards for assessing various points of view. A plurality of groups that can shield the individual from the machinations of the government can also protect him from the pressures of an intolerant majority.

Although many laissez-faire pluralists endorse the responsiveness of the political system because it enhances liberal values, they often raise troublesome questions about the rationality of pluralism as a form of decision making. Truman recognizes that the dispersal of political power among many groups protects individual freedom, but he nonetheless suggests that widespread participation might lead to what he calls "morbific" politics, a state in which the political system cannot act quickly enough to deal with pressing problems.[16] Even though Truman is supportive of a pluralistic system of politics, he suggests that it might have offsetting costs. But other laissez-faire pluralists—like Dahl, Banfield, and Kornhauser—overlook or ignore questions dealing with the policy consequences of a pluralistic system of decision making. The fact that it tames the use of power, whether by the government or by the mass public, seems to them reason enough to normatively defend the existence of multiple decision makers.

However, in what constitutes a major revision of laissez-faire pluralism, Charles Lindblom has criticized his fellow pluralists for failing to see that a system of multiple decision makers bargaining and competing with one another fosters the formulation of informed and creative policy decisions.[17] Lindblom argues that a laissez-faire form of pluralism not only enhances individual freedom but also results in better policy making. First of all, a competitive, pluralistic style of politics simplifies the burdens a political system has to bear in deciding among alternative policy choices. The interaction among a variety of parties—or what he prefers to call "partisan mutual adjustment"—is often a convenient device for identifying problems

---

[14]Dahl, *Pluralistic Democracy*, p. 24.

[15]Kornhauser, *Politics of Mass Society*, pp. 65-75.

[16]Truman, *Governmental Process*, pp. 516-24.

[17]Lindblom has developed this thesis in a variety of places but the best statements are found in *The Intelligence of Democracy* and "The Science of Muddling Through."

and acquiring reliable information on issues. Lindblom insists that the ability of any one individual to anticipate and plan for the contingencies associated with a set of programs is limited. While centralized planners may desire to analyze all possible ramifications surrounding a problem, the burden of weighing the evidence bearing on complex issues may prompt them to screen out important bits of information. The attempt to engage in long-range, comprehensive planning is thus likely to be frustrated by the complexity of events. However, a competitive, pluralistic form of decision making avoids these difficulties, since it "imposes on no one the heroic demands for information, intellectual competence, time, energy, and money that are required for an overview of interrelationships among decisions."[18] When decisions are made through the give-and-take of partisan mutual adjustment, numerous groups have responsibility for defending and analyzing a limited set of values.

Moreover, as Lindblom notes, in partisan mutual adjustment there are "powerful motives for groups to mobilize information and analysis on the relations among possible decisions."[19] When decisions are made in a competitive fashion, each party has a vested interest in finding information that will advance the policies it prefers while discrediting the programs it opposes. Thus any attempt by a group to suppress information harmful to a particular course of action is likely to be uncovered by opposing interests. While no one participant is motivated to undertake a comprehensive view of a problem, the bargaining and competition among numerous interests will develop more information bearing on the issue than will more centralized and unified forms of decision making. As in the operation of Adam Smith's marketplace, the "invisible hand" of group competition helps to transform limited, parochial views into much broader, public benefits.

Besides stimulating the production of more information, partisan mutual adjustment can also help soften the consequences of political disagreement. The give-and-take of the bargaining process at times results in various parties' reformulating or modifying their values and therefore helps to narrow, rather than widen, policy differences among groups. Through the process of bargaining and negotiation, individuals often come to a more precise definition of what goals they hope to achieve, since the rank ordering they would attach to particular values may not become clear to them until they are faced with making concrete choices. What at first may appear to be a serious point of disagreement may disappear when a plurality of interests must negotiate over the shape of a particular policy.[20]

While Lindblom often stresses aspects that other laissez-faire pluralists have ignored, taken together their work nonetheless adds up to a uni-

[18]Lindblom, *Intelligence of Democracy*, p. 171.
[19]Ibid., p. 174.
[20]Ibid., pp. 206-25.

fied theory of pluralism. The terms vary from "political slack" to "multiple decision making points," from "the noncumulative distribution of resources" to "potential groups," but they suggest a common theme: whether we look at the operations of local politics or the federal government, we see an open and self-regulating political system. The competitive nature of the political marketplace inhibits the rise of monopolistic power, while the openness of the polity in turn promotes the advancement of both individual freedom and rational policy making. This division of power among many groups curtails the ability of the government or a majority to infringe on individual liberties while enhancing the capability of the political system to identify and respond to pressing social issues. When groups share responsibility for deciding issues, they have not only ample incentives for generating data on important issues confronting the polity but also sufficient reason for containing the worst consequences of partisan disagreement.

Corporate Pluralism

Although the laissez-faire model is the dominant view of pluralism in the academic literature today, analytically it is possible to identify another form, which I have chosen to call corporate pluralism. Its clearest description—albeit a hostile one—is found in Lowi's notion of interest group liberalism and McConnell's group theory of politics.[21] Empirically most laissez-faire pluralists have derived their model of interest-group interaction from the realm of urban politics, but Lowi and McConnell have examined the behavior of federal agencies and their clientele groups and argue that the notion of an open, competitive political arena does not apply. While laissez-faire pluralists envision a self-correcting system in which the invisible hand of political bargaining inevitably restrains the concentration of power, Lowi and McConnell see the fragmentation of the polity into a series of small, autonomous fiefdoms, all of which are independent of one another. Under a corporate form of pluralism, no single party has the ability to monopolize all decisions, but certain groups have been able to acquire controlling power within individual policy areas. Regardless of the political slack in the system or the existence of potential groups, various parties have been able to isolate their detractors and enjoy the luxury of making decisions without negotiating or bargaining with their competitors. Any self-correcting pressures that may once have been present in the political system have been overwhelmed by the organized power of selective interest groups.

The reasons for the breakdown of the laissez-faire model are varied, but critics like Lowi and McConnell usually point to three factors: (1) the capture of government power by interest groups, (2) the efforts of interest

---

[21]Theodore J. Lowi, *The End of Liberalism*; Theodore J. Lowi, "The Public Philosophy: Interest Group Liberalism"; Grant McConnell, *Private Power and American Democracy*.

groups and agencies to narrow the size of the policy making arena, and (3) the tacit agreement among certain interests to refrain from competing with one another. By any criterion, the willingness of government officials to relinquish their power to interest groups has been the most distinctive characteristic of corporate pluralism. While laissez-faire pluralists have tended to view government officials as either neutral mediators of the group process or merely another party competing with private groups for political power, McConnell and others have recognized that public officials often become captured by constituents who use the authority of the state to enhance their own well-being. The process leads to a blurring of the distinction that laissez-faire pluralists have implicitly, if not explicitly, made between private interests and public authority. Private groups come to exercise the regulatory and rule-making powers that were once the exclusive responsibility of public officials, while public officials, having parcelled out their authority, become mere legitimizing agents, sanctioning the decisions agreed upon by private interests.* McConnell points to the War Industries Board of World War I as a classic example involving this kind of surrender of government authority. The board was responsible for drawing up wartime mobilization plans for private industry, but instead of requiring business to implement government-decreed objectives, it allowed private industry to assume responsibility for setting prices and establishing production quotas.[22] A similar willingness to relinquish power to private groups underlay the National Recovery Administration of the New Deal, which sought to combat the economic disruption of the 1930s by encouraging business to draw up codes of fair competition regulating sales and production. As with the War Industries Board, the guiding assumption was that policy should be made through the cooperation and mutual agreement of business and government rather than through the competition of the economic and political arenas.[23]

---

*While it is important to distinguish corporate pluralism from its laissez-faire counterpart, at the same time we must be careful not to confuse it with the doctrine of corporativism. Some of the examples of corporate pluralism, such as the NRA of the New Deal, have often been mistakenly called instances of corporativism. On a superficial level there is some degree of similarity, for both corporate pluralism as practiced in the United States and corporativism as practiced in fascist Italy involve a fusion of public and private authority. But aside from that similarity there are immense differences between the two approaches to government. In a corporativistic political system the government either sets up allegedly private groups or acquires control of private groups in order to advance its own specific objectives. In corporate pluralism, however, the situation is much more complex. Instead of the government attempting to assume exclusive control over the actions of private groups, it relinquishes much of its power to private groups seeking to advance their own special interests. Even when there is a common problem that government and private interest groups wish to resolve, public officials often turn their authority over to various interests to tackle the issue. Corporate pluralism involves the private capture of public agencies and the establishment of semipublic monopolies, while corporativism involves public domination of private groups. See W. Y. Elliot, *The Pragmatic Revolt in Politics*, for a theoretical discussion of the doctrine of corporativism.

[22]McConnell, *Private Power and American Democracy*, p. 64.

[23]Hugh Johnson, *The Blue Eagle*.

Besides capturing government authority, interest groups have also managed to exercise semi-monopoly power by narrowing down and isolating the decision-making process. Established groups realize that the smaller the decision-making arena is, the easier it becomes for a few parties to shut out opposing interests and undermine the competitive nature of the political marketplace. As the decision-making sphere contracts, the advantages enjoyed by the most powerful interest become magnified, while the resources available to the least influential group become increasingly vulnerable.[24] Interest groups have often invoked the rhetoric of grassroots democracy in order to achieve this kind of narrowing of the decision-making arena. Farm groups have utilized such tactics to establish ten separate self-governing systems within the Department of Agriculture, ranging from the soil conservation districts to the various price support districts. As Lowi has shown, each program is run as an independent fiefdom, with little or no interaction among them.[25] But even more importantly, on issues like price supports, commodity growers are able to exercise veto power over any policy recommendations public officials may wish to make. Rather than merely sharing power with government personnel, they have acquired full legal authority to approve or reject any changes that affect their interests.

Other groups, such as professional educators, have achieved similar objectives by calling for the depoliticization of certain policy areas. As Marilyn Gittell argues, once issues are removed from politics, it becomes much more difficult for groups with influence in the larger political realm to wield any appreciable degree of power in isolated decision-making arenas. Gittell's study of the New York school system describes how professional educators sought to limit the influence of local politicians and community groups by taking "politics out of education" and how this attempt served merely to remove educational policy from the-influence of groups, like minorities, who relied on alliances with political officials to achieve their goals. By making school policy independent of the city commission, the educational bureaucracy succeeded in undercutting those opposing groups which might have been able to challenge its decisions in a larger political setting.[26]

If interest groups have not been able to capture public authority or narrow down the policy-making arena, they have often sought to build monopolistic empires through tacit agreements and collusion. As a case in point, McConnell notes that in the 1940s when Congress considered measures for controlling the Missouri River, the Army Corps of Engineers and its clientele groups of construction firms and navigation companies called for the construction of extensive flood levies, while the Bureau of Land

[24]McConnell, *Private Power and American Democracy*, pp. 91-110.
[25]Lowi, *End of Liberalism*, pp. 102-15.
[26]Marilyn Gittell, *Participants and Participation*.

Reclamation and its agricultural supporters were more interested in promoting the development of dams and irrigation canals. Rather than pointing out the deficiencies in each other's programs, the two agencies agreed to refrain from criticizing one another and recommended the implementation of both proposals. In place of partisan mutual adjustment, the two agencies agreed to restrain their competitive impulses in return for mutual noninterference in each other's domains.[27]

Whether we look at the country's past efforts to mobilize for war or to recover from a depression, or at its present efforts to manage agriculture, formulate educational policy, or regulate our rivers, there emerges a pattern of interest-group activity differing significantly from the laissez-faire picture of politics. As is true of the economic marketplace, a competitive political market is neither self-maintaining nor self-correcting. By either persuading political officials to surrender their decision-making power to various interests, or by narrowing down the size of the decision-making arena, or by implicitly or explicitly agreeing not to compete with one another, a variety of groups have been able to exert semi-monopolistic dominance over certain policy areas. Through deft use of the above tactics, many organized interests have succeeded in restraining the countervailing forces which laissez-faire pluralists have posited as the main deterrent to excessive monopoly power.

While McConnell and Lowi are extremely critical of what we have called corporate pluralism, the doctrine is not without its defenders. It is possible to piece together a normative defense of the corporate model from a variety of sources, including the writings of individuals like Herbert Hoover and Raymond Moley or the pronouncements of various interest groups.[28] Despite the rather unsystematic nature of these sources, certain themes reappear constantly. For instance, unlike laissez-faire pluralists, who see numerous benefits accruing to society from competition among interest groups, corporate pluralists attach value to making decisions in a cooperative, rather than a competitive, fashion. Both Hoover, an enthusiastic supporter of the War Industries Board, and Moley, a strong advocate of the National Recovery Administration, maintained that the nation's social problems could be solved through cooperative action between government and business. Neither Hoover nor Moley believed there were any significant differences in the goals that government and business sought to achieve and they therefore did not see any need to pit organizations against one another. Unlike laissez-faire pluralists, who have argued that competition is necessary to tame the misuse of power, corporate pluralists have contended that in turning power over to private groups, government officials need not worry that public authority will be used for parochial or illicit

---

[27]McConnell, *Private Power and American Democracy*, p. 224.
[28]U.S. Department of Commerce, *Annual Report of the Secretary of Commerce*, 1922; Raymond Moley, *The First New Deal*.

ends. As Hoover once argued, "there is a wide difference between the whole social conception of capital combinations against public interest and cooperative action between individuals which may be profoundly in the public interest."[29] Unfortunately, however, corporate pluralists have not always been clear as to how one distinguishes between beneficial and harmful monopolies.[30] While the overriding importance of winning a war or ending a depression has perhaps resulted in a certain degree of convergence among most interests in society, it has nonetheless left a host of other problems unresolved. Especially on more mundane issues like agriculture or education, the most desirable course of action to follow often resists easy definition.

Corporate pluralists have also contended that competition is an inherently wasteful and disorderly process of decision making. In a laissez-faire system, where there is competition among a variety of groups and agencies, government programs often overlap one another. Instead of a unified, coherent attack on a particular issue, there is likely to be considerable duplication of effort in the formulation of various programs. In addition, as the number of parties involved in a particular policy increases, problems of coordination arise and energy has to be expended to resolve divergences of opinion. However, as Hoover and many others have often argued, when decisions are made in self-contained centers, the problems of duplication and coordination are greatly diminished. By establishing independent centers of decision making, public authorities and the private groups they rely on for guidance can develop uniform standards for regulating each separate policy area.

Finally, many of the defenders of a corporate form of pluralism have insisted that the establishment of semi-monopolistic decision-making centers is necessary to guarantee the professional handling of important social issues. For example, the Interior Department has often justified the surrender of government oil policy to the Petroleum Council, a semiprivate group, on purely technical grounds. The problem of developing and processing natural resources is so complex that the agency has sought to tap the expertise of those companies directly involved in the production of the country's basic energy resources. Many professional groups have sought to restrict the decision-making arena for very similar reasons, arguing that the complexity of issues like education or welfare requires the establishment of independent, nonpartisan commissions to supervise these programs. In the corporate view, not all semipublic monopolies are undesirable: when issues are technical or complex in nature, professionals or technicians should have the decisive voice in setting policy.

---

[29]U.S. Department of Commerce, *Annual Report of the Secretary*, p. 29.
[30]See McConnell, *Private Power and American Democracy*, pp. 66-69, for a further discussion of Hoover's outlook on cooperation.

Public Pluralism

Finally, it is analytically possible to identify a third form, which I call public pluralism. This doctrine differs from its predecessors in that it is essentially a prescriptive model of decision making. Whereas both laissez-faire and corporate pluralists attempt to describe the give-and-take of American politics as well as to normatively justify the variety of politics they have empirically identified, I wish to advance public pluralism as a reform-oriented model of decision making for regulating the interplay of interests in society.

Public pluralism recognizes, as does corporate pluralism, that the competitive nature of the political marketplace may break down, but it does not share corporate pluralism's approbation of this phenomenon. In any society as diverse and heterogeneous as the United States, there are bound to be disagreements over both the methods and the goals that the political system seeks to realize. The hope of corporate pluralists to formulate public policy in a cooperative, rather than a competitive, fashion is thus likely to prove illusory. But even more importantly, by insisting that decisions be made in a cooperative fashion, corporate pluralism may inadvertently create a political system that ignores important segments of the population and represses dissenting views.[31] Likewise, its stress on efficiency and technical expertise raises this problem: efficient for what purposes or ends? If a variety of groups must constantly bargain with one another and settle their differences through negotiation, it is true that the process may involve a great deal of time and may even result in a duplication of effort; but a process that may be uneconomical in saving time may be very economical in insuring that many different interests have an opportunity to make their voices heard. Finally, a corporate form of decision making that emphasizes technical expertise may overlook the fact that a large number of policies are not technical at all. Even if issues like education involve questions of a highly specialized nature, we must recognize that most problems have a normative, as well as a technical, aspect to them. While the most successful reading method may be a technical decision that professional educators should determine, the larger purposes schools should serve or the amount of resources they should have at their disposal are political or normative questions that no one group should have the exclusive power to decide. Allocating resources among different segments of society is a political, and not a technical, process.

The doctrine of public pluralism thus represents a reaction to the establishment of cooperative, semi-independent centers of decision making. Like its laissez-faire counterpart, the public variety of pluralism believes that it is imperative to divide power among numerous groups and to pit

---

[31]See Arthur M. Schlesinger, Jr., *The Age of Roosevelt*, Vol II: *The Coming of the New Deal*, pp. 165-75, for a description of how NRA worked to the benefit of large corporations.

one interest against another. But in embracing laissez-faire's normative faith in the beneficial results of partisan mutual adjustment, it does not necessarily accept laissez-faire's contention that the present political system represents an empirical fulfillment of the competitive model. On the contrary, the doctrine of public pluralism identifies three defects in the laissez-faire picture of American politics.

First, it recognizes, as laissez-faire pluralists often do not, that many constituencies, especially marginal groups like the poor or amorphous groups like consumers, lack either the resources or the incentives to defend their interests effectively against opposing elements in society. While Truman often seems to suggest that potential groups will become activated when their wishes are thwarted, the less than successful record of many marginal elements seems to suggest otherwise. Secondly, as we have already seen, public pluralism realizes that various interests often avoid competition with one another either by capturing government authority or by insulating part of the political process from outside pressure. Lindblom's argument that partisan mutual adjustment may enhance the ability of the political system to recognize pressing social issues is based on the assumption that agencies and their clientele groups actually bargain and compete with one another. Unfortunately, as Lowi and McConnell have shown, many groups have been able to shut out their rivals and formulate policy monopolistically in specific areas. Thirdly, as Truman himself points out, a laissez-faire system faces the additional problem of not being able to respond quickly enough to pressing social issues. While Lindblom makes a convincing case that the clash of competing groups will simplify the decision-making process, he fails to show that this same system can resolve problems with any degree of dispatch. A pattern of policy making that is rational in Lindblom's sense of exposing all facets of a problem may be ineffective in the sense that it cannot act expeditiously to resolve issues. Naturally, as more parties participate in the decision-making arena, it becomes increasingly more time consuming to forge acceptable agreements among all concerned interests.

Public pluralism seeks to deal with the above problems through a system of regulated interest-group activity. The operating assumption of the doctrine is that many of the values espoused by laissez-faire pluralism can in effect be achieved if the president and the executive branch adopt a dual policy of organizing marginal elements from the bottom up and regulating the give-and-take among interests from the top down. Even if many groups are not organized or engage in collusion or restraint of trade, judicious government action may mitigate, if not eliminate altogether, the worst defects of an unregulated form of pluralistic government.

Public pluralism thus differs from Lindblom's version in that it rejects a pure or free-market, bargaining style of decision making. Instead it relies heavily on central direction and management to insure that the competitive nature of the political arena remains intact.[32] On those occasions when the political marketplace is no longer self-correcting, it insists that public officials facilitate the process of group competition by playing what must first appear as three mutually antagonistic roles. First, the government can act as an advocate, defending and even organizing interests like the poor or consumers who presently lack political clout. In stimulating previously dormant elements to become more active, government bureaus can assist various potential groups to contest the actions of agencies or groups that are pursuing objectives detrimental to their interests. Such a course of action will necessarily lead to a blurring of the distinction between public and private power, but instead of fostering the development of semi-monopolies, as occurs under a corporate form of pluralism, it will serve to enhance the competitive nature of the political process. Rather than relinquishing their authority to semi-monopolies, public officials will assist potential groups to become mobilized so that the rise of concentrated power can be averted.

Secondly, in order to prevent newly activated groups from being denied access to the bargaining table, the executive branch must also assume the role of political custodian, structuring and arranging the formulation of policy decisions so that interest groups are forced to compete with one another. Just as the government has acquired responsibility in the economic arena for breaking up monopolies, so it must seek to restrain any concentration of power that threatens the openness of the political marketplace. When it appears that the competitive nature of the political system is threatened, the president or central government bureaus, such as the Office of Management and Budget, must intervene to hinder the development of semiclosed centers of decision making.

Finally, in order to focus the bargaining process among different groups, the executive branch must assume responsibility for one additional role, that of political manager. Besides fostering competition among different interests, elected public officials such as the president must at the same time act as arbitrators, mediating disputes and choosing among the proposals of contending groups. Under public pluralism, the numerous interests in society will have to compete against one another not only for specific advantages, as they would under a laissez-faire system, but also for the attention and approval of political elites and their staff agencies. In contrast to a laissez-faire system of politics, in which the power of public officials like Mayor Lee is dependent primarily on their personal negotiating skills, a public form of pluralism seeks to augment the institutional, and not merely the personal, power of elected officials so that they have the capacity to direct the outcome of the group process. If elites acquire these additional re-

---

[32]See Alexander George's excellent article on foreign affairs, "The Case for Multiple Advocacy," pp. 751-86, for another treatment of possible government roles. His analysis of foreign policy has greatly influenced my conception of public pluralism.

sponsibilities, they will be in a position to significantly alter the environment in which groups and their allies interact by vetoing logrolling arrangements that attempt to shut out other interests in society. Similarly, if government officials acquire the power to manage negotiations among interest groups, they may be able to insure that the political system does not become mired down in endless bargaining. Under a decentralized system in which groups must negotiate with many different parties, gradual and even time-consuming incremental changes in policy can give way to fruitless periods of interminable bargaining; but under a centrally coordinated style of decision making, political officials and their staff agencies will be in a position to mediate disputes and force the settlement of issues.

Admittedly, initiating such political changes is bound to be a difficult task, but we must realize that the fragmentation of the political marketplace and the freezing out of weaker competition were often accomplished not in the face of government opposition but with the tacit, if not open, consent of many government agencies and officials. In contrast, if various agencies choose to play advocate, custodial, and managerial roles, the breakdown of the bargaining process can possibly be contained. The visible hand of government regulation may be able to achieve what laissez-faire's self-corrective, invisible hand of bargaining promised but failed to deliver.

THE GOLDEN ERA OF INTEREST GROUP THEORY— ITS RISE AND PASSAGE
G. David Garson*

The pluralist paradigm has come under attack on these grounds: that it erred in its benign assessment of the group process and its cavalier dispensing with the public-interest concept; that groups were, in point of fact, much less important than pluralist imagery suggested; and that pluralist theory was not truly theory at all, and, therefore, was not a basis for a scientific approach to the study of political events. The wave of criticism on these grounds in the early 1960s, combined with the academic radicalization of the late 1960s, dealt the pluralist position blows from which it never recovered. Though lingering on as a description of fragmented politics contrasting with elite theory, pluralism's decline prefigured an onslaught of proposed new paradigms (e.g., communications theory, game theory, public-choice theory, rational-decision-making theory, phenomenology, and so forth) that were to splinter the discipline further without taking on half the influence of group theory.

The charge that normal group process was anything but benign was a position taken in a solid chain of political science literature stretching back

*G. David Garson, *Group Theories of Politics*. Beverly Hills: Sage Publications, 1978 (pp. 104-118). Used by Permission]

into the nineteenth century. Typical was Philip Foss's *Politics and Grass* (1960), showing a "monopolitical" pattern in which entrenched economic interests lacked any significant competition in their attempt, largely successful, to dominate government policy in areas of concern to them. In a much more influential work, Robert Engler described the politics of the oil industry as a form of "private government," making the concept of the rule of law a mere myth and giving rise to the need for regulation in the public interest (Engler, 1961). The public-interest concept was then, moreover, a matter of high interest and popular support, pluralism notwithstanding, as evidenced by the work of the President's Commission on National Goals (1960). Of course, this commission was spawned by the Eisenhower administration and, therefore, tended not to be taken seriously by the pluralists, who were overwhelmingly liberal in persuasion. But this, in itself, was significant. Liberalism was in crisis on this point, Henry Kariel argued in his modern classic, *The Decline of American Pluralism* (1961). In this work Kariel contrasted the traditional liberal vision of centralization, hierarchical accountability, and even nationalization with the pluralist vision of postwar liberals. This vision brought liberalism into crisis as private interests took on ever more public functions without being subjected to correspondingly meaningful public accountability. The decline of representative government was a function of the loss of power to the private power of corporations and unions. To bless this trend with the legitimacy of postwar liberal attitudes, such as those of pluralism, was to abdicate the essential responsibilities of democratic government.

A second line of criticism of pluralism was equally influential in its decline, but, ironically, was itself in more than a little tension with the public interest criticisms just outlined. This was the argument that interest groups were scarcely as important as pluralist theorists (much less those concerned with reasserting the public interest vis-a-vis selfish interests and pressures) had portrayed them. Donald Matthew's widely discussed work, *U.S. Senators and Their World* (1960), for example, emphasized the discretion of political decision makers. "You know, that's an amazing thing," Matthews quoted a senator. "I hardly ever see a lobbyist. I don't know—maybe they think I'm a poor target, but I seldom see them. During this entire natural gas battle (in which he was a prominent figure) I was not approached by either side" (Matthews, 1960:177).

Similarly, John Wahlke and his associates found that state legislators saw themselves as being above the group process. Political culture, not direct group pressures, was the critical factor (Wahlke, Buchanan, Eulau and Ferguson, 1960). And in a study of bureaucrats, Joseph LaPalombara found that, not only did they continually explain their actions in terms of a national interest concept, but they also played a far more active role in the group process than one might expect on the basis of group theory. "The bureaucrat also tends to develop certain skills," he noted, "that permit him to manipulate the interest groups and to play them off against each other for his own purposes. It is for this reason that administrators often welcome group clienteles and, where such do not exist, will seek to create them" (La-Palombara, 1960: 48). LaPalombara went on to condemn group theory as "simplistic" in its attempt to account for political behavior in terms of interest-group conflict.

It might well be argued that these criticisms, while applicable against certain aspects of group theory, were misrepresentations if applied to pluralism. Dahl, for example, *did* discuss the active role of bureaucrats and politicians in the group process and *did* emphasize the importance of political culture as an intervening variable of critical importance. Thus, when the group approach fell under heavy attack in 1960, pluralist theory might be viewed as being something apart. Certainly Truman, Bentley, and group theory of a decade earlier took the brunt of criticism. But if pluralism was to be disassociated from group theory, what was left? What remained after the discrediting of group theory was pluralism not as a theory of political behavior, but merely pluralism in the sense of fragmentation of power, the importance of numerous power-related variables (not just groups, but culture, socialization, psychology, and virtually any other variable), and the decision-making method of studying politics.

In a 1960 symposium on "Bentley Revisited," the *American Political Science Review* published the strongest and most comprehensive attacks on group theory up to that time. The core argument of these articles was that group theory was not a true theory in the scientific sense, and that the great expectations of refounding political science on it were misguided.

"The failure of group theory to serve as an adequate guide to research," Stanley Rothman wrote, "is the result both of the logical inconsistencies of its propositions and its inability to explain what it purports to explain" (Rothman, 1960: 15). Building on Odegard's earlier criticism of the vagueness of group theory (Odegard, 1958), Rothman emphasized the core imprecision of group theory. Herring, Latham, and Truman, he noted, were referring to groups not just as interest groups, but as categoric groups (e.g., Jews, alcoholics) and, even, potential (unorganized) groups. As far as organized, group membership went, evidence by Wright and Hyman (1958) suggested, contrary to Truman, that Americans were not notably joiners, and groups seemed to affect their attitudes little.

More important, the notion of potential groups tended to render group theory tautological. Political attitudes are explained on the basis of group affiliations, but the pattern of group forces in a society is explained by the underlying pattern of potential groups, which in turn are based on categorical attributes, notably, shared attitudes. "In fact the whole concept of potential groups acts as a sort of *deus ex machina* which can be brought in for any purpose," Rothman observed. "Why are British trade unions socialist? Strong socialist potential group. Why did the Germans prefer a strong authoritarian regime? Strong authoritarian potential group. It can explain everything, but fundamentally it explains nothing" (Rothman, 1960: 23). Consequently, in *The Governmental Process's* empirical sections, Truman rarely used a specifically *group* explanation for behavior. Rather, though groups are repeatedly referred to, Truman's work is built around a variety of types of political explanation: group theory, economic causation (e.g., Truman, 1951:53, 67), individual-level analysis, to name a few.

This should bring us back to the question, "What *is* a group explanation of political behavior?" In simple and direct form, as expressed in Arthur F. Bentley's *The Process of Government* (1908), the group theory states that "all interests and all potential interests are a part of the governing process, since each interest is represented in proportion to its pressure" (Hale, 1960: 960). This "physics of group forces," by treating government decisions as a function of interest pressures, assumes an essentially neutral or "umpire" state. The government can never be charged with acting outside the "public interest"; one only may wish that groups other than those prevailing would exert more pressure.

Like most strong social theories on which prediction may be based, Bentleyan physics is a simple model of reality. It is also a profoundly conservative one, expelling not only the notion of the public interest, but also the very possibility that government might engage in long-range acts of foresight that transcend the pressures of the moment. Most social scientists would probably prefer a theory of government that gave greater discretion to decision makers, partly because one may judge this normatively to be beneficial to society, and partly because the acknowledgment of discretion makes better empirical theory. Government officials, as noted earlier, in fact do not act in terms of the physics of group forces. Bentley himself acknowledged this, as Hale has noted (Hale, 1960: 960), in his frequent assertions (Bentley, 1908: 301, 358-359, 449-458) that American government was out of balance with group forces and, hence, in need of reform. Given Bentley's theory in simple form, group theory made impossible such imbalance. To call for "rebalancing" was to call for government decisions on a nongroup basis. With this, Bentley implicitly sabotaged the shorings of the group basis of politics.

Recognizing the simplistic implications of pure Bentley, David Truman, although giving great honor to Bentley, rather clearly avoided a physics-of-group-forces model. Another critic, R. E. Dowling, asked in this context, "What, then, is his (Truman's) avowed debt to Bentley? It is, I suggest, little more than a realization that interest groups are 'very important' in the political process and that a lot of attention should be given to them" (Dowling, 1960:951). But in avoiding Bentley's sometime simplicity, Truman presented no clear alternative. To say that the group process was an integral part of the political process was something deserving emphasis, but it fell far short of constituting theory in a predictive sense. One could not predict government outcomes as the resultant vector of opposing group forces, empirically measured. By introducing a more comprehensive view, emphasizing potential groups, economic factors, and various other variables, Truman's work better described the political process than did Bentley's. But, as Dowling argued pointedly, this was "a bit of very naive methodology." Truman "does not see that the *merit* of a 'group interpretation' of politics (meaning by that a Bentleyan methodology) would, if it were worked out, be precisely that it does 'leave something out'" (Dowling, 1960: 953).

The Passage of an Idea

Group theory and pluralism were not"rebutted" by the arguments just discussed. In a peculiar way, it did not matter if it was true that these ideas, which purported to represent a revolutionary new paradigm for a reconstructed political science, did not add up to scientific theory in the predictive sense. Or, that interest groups and lobbying might not be as important as initially portrayed. Or, even, that group theory was imbued with conservative implications at a time when practitioners in the discipline continued to see the urgent need for a reassertion of the "public interest" over transitory, selfish interests of the day.

What brought group and pluralist theory to a peak by the late 1950s and early 1960s was more a matter of mood and imagery than of science and evidence. Group and pluralist theorists were working neither inductively from comprehensively selected case observations, nor deductively from general principles of political behavior. Rather, their work sought to present a description of American politics sharply at variance with the pessimistic image put forward by elite theorists. At the same time, they were attempting to present a vocabulary of political analysis that contrasted with class-analytic terms without degenerating into traditional, uninspired institutionalism. Group and pluralist theories served a powerful purpose, as Leiserson noted: to provide an orienting framework to which a host of new studies and theories could be attached. The common theme was that American stability might be attributed to a rich, complex, and pluralistic pattern of interaction of groups, individuals, and strata in the context of a culturally legitimated, fragmented polity.

American political science, however, is as fragmented and pluralistic as that which it seeks to explain. Even at the height of its influence, the group approach was not dominant. Most studies of groups did not use a group- or pluralist-theory vocabulary to any significant degree (e.g., Block, 1960; MacKinnon, 1960; Lenczowski, 1960; Harbrecht, 1960). Those that did frequently arrived at conclusions inconsistent with the group approach (e.g., Foss, 1960; Engler, 1961; Wilson, 1961). More importantly, alternative (e.g., developmentalism—Deutsch, 1961) and contradictory (e.g., symbolic action—Edelman, 1960) paradigms were continually proposed, each attracting their own coteries of adherents and promoting new frameworks for discourse without explicitly confronting and rejecting earlier paradigms.

The fascinating process whereby ideas evolve in political science has little to do with "scientific revolutions" and the rational confrontation of paradigms popularized by Kuhn's work. Group theory after World War II did not spring fully grown from the womb of science, nor did it hatch from a Bentleyan egg unearthed by David Truman. The language and imagery of the group approach, rather, is rooted deeply in American political thought and may be traced back to Calhoun and Madison. The specific, Trumanesque revival of group theory emerged, moreover, from the wartime mood of consensus and the ideological defense of democracy against fascism, communism, and other elite conceptions of the state.

While serving an ideological function, the emphasis in the group approach upon the pragmatic and empirical also seemed to justify its identification with a more empirical, behavioral, and even scientific approach to the study of politics. This was compatible with the anti-ideological mood in social science following World War II, and with the "end of ideology" proclaimed by Bell, Lipset, and others.

The Governmental Process   Truman's classic postwar reformulation of the group approach, was a work of tone, not paradigmatic science. When Truman raised a framework to contrast with the group approach, he chose to deal with institutionalism. The institutionalist "paradigm," however, had long since passed from the scene (see Garson, 1974). It was, in short, a straw man. More serious, alternative paradigms, such as Marxism and elite theory, were largely ignored. There was no confrontation of paradigm with paradigm, evidence with evidence. Indeed, most specific group studies, then and later, continually came to conclusions enconsistent with Truman's work (e.g., showing the dangers of group process unregulated by a strong public interest in some areas, the importance of a public interest concept to decision makers, and the relative lack of impact of interest groups on political outcomes in other areas).

All of this might lead one to judge that, if the rational (scientific paradigm) explanation of the passage of ideas in political science is mistaken, perhaps a social explanation would fare better. That is, perhaps group theory would be interpreted better as an idea whose time had been prepared by sociopolitical events. Certainly this was *not* true in terms of the enduring importance of the public interest concept in scholarship on the group process. On the other hand, the revival of group theory *was* timely. As mentioned, it fit in with the postwar mood of consensus, anti-ideological pragmatism, and moderation. Associations with fascism and communism had delegitimized elite theories, and group theory filled a relative void at a time when the discipline was again hearing strong calls to emulate scientific frameworks.

If the shift of political science ideas seemed faddish, each author seeking the psychological satisfaction of being the first to set forth the basic outlines for analysis, it is also true that there were many who endeavored to build upon the works of Truman and Dahl. Not infrequently, the laborers in this particular vineyard, like Eckstein, eventually came to conclusions emphasizing the limits of the group approach. But there was continuity of research, from Truman's restatement of the theory, to Dahl's formulation of the pluralist variant, to the drive to put group research on a comparative basis (Ehrmann, Almond), to Dahl's influential *Who Governs?* in 1961. If the diversity of the discipline allowed for the continual assertion of new frameworks (systems analysis, the economic theory of democracy, developmentalism), those identified with the group approach were not advocates of a faddish succession of frameworks.

The very development of group theory, however, contributed to its eventual decline. It is striking that the articulation of group theory, including pluralism, led to a "revolution of rising expectations." Truman's work, conceived as a descriptive exploration of the relation of group process to politics, was later cited as a classic exposition of paradigmatic theory. That Truman later disavowed such would-be accolades for his work is less important than that it, like Dahl's pluralism, came to represent a "theory" that could be counterposed to others, notably to elite theory. Once this expectation was established, it was then possible to attack group theory for failing to meet the expected standard: it could not be used as a basis for predictive scientific theory because group process was both less important and less benign than portrayed by Truman, Dahl, and other group theorists. The "golden rule" of social science was at work: as Truman had interpreted institutionalism as a straw man and foil for the group approach, now the theoretical expectations placed upon the group approach distorted its nature to serve similar purposes of other scholars.

As David Apter has noted, pluralism drew directly on the inheritance of institutionalism and it was itself interpretable as a form of elite theory (Apter, 1977: 374-375). The jurists and later institutionalists were concerned with questions such as the role of groups in the state; and all critics of group theory, such as Bachrach, accepted the pluralist description of American politics. The pluralists were concerned both to emphasize the jurists' central theme of the responsibility of the governor to the good of the governed, and to emphasize elite theory's central theme of the inevitability of hierarchy and the determining role of leadership in politics. Most critics of pluralism (e.g., Bachrach, Kariel, Pateman) dissented on grounds of normative theory, not empirical theory. But even here an artificial dichotomy was set up by the critics, portraying the group approach as merely a rosy rationale for the status quo, defining away the need for democratic reform. In fact, the concerns of the pluralists for the reform of democracy, such as community size and structure as prerequisites for the ideal democratic polity (Dahl and

Tufte, 1973; Dahl, 1967) and workplace democracy (Dahl, 1970), were not so different from the concerns of the critics. These communalities became observable in retrospect only, however. At the time, there seemed to be a world of difference.

REFERENCES

ALMOND, G. A. (1946) "Politics, Science, and Ethics," *American Political Science Review*, Vol. 40, No. 2 (April): 283-293.

APTER, D. (1977) *Introduction to Political Analysis.* Cambridge, Mass.: Winthrop Publishers.

BACHRACH, P. (1967) *The Theory of Democratic Elitism*: A Critique. Boston: Little, Brown.

BELL, D. (1960) *The End of Ideology.* Glencoe, Ill.: Free Press.

BENTLEY, A. (1908) *The Process of Government: A Study of Social Pressures.* Bloomington, Ind.: Principia Press.

BLOCK, W. J. (1960) *The Separation of the Farm Bureau and the Extension Service.* Urbana: Univ. of Illinois Press.

DAHL, R. A. (1961a) *Who Governs?: Democracy and Power in an American City.* New Haven: Yale Univ. Press.

——— (1967) "The City in the Future of Democracy," *American Political Science Review*, Vol. 61, No. 4 (December): 953-970.

——— (1970) *After the Revolution?: Authority in a Good Society.* New Haven: Yale Univ. Press.

DAHL, R. A. AND E. R. TUFTE (1973) *Size and Democracy.* Stanford: Stanford Univ. Press.

DEUTSCH, K. (1961) "Social Mobilization and Political Development," *American Political Science Review*, Vol. 55, No. 3 (September): 493-514.

DOWLING, R. E. (1960) "Pressure Group Theory: Its Methodological Range," *American Political Science Review*, Vol. 54 No. 4 (December): 944-954.

EDELMAN, M. (1960) "Symbols and Political Quiescence," *American Political Science Review*, Vol. 54, No. 3 (September): 695-704.

EHRMANN, H. W. (1957) *Organized Business in France.* Princeton: Princeton Univ. Press.

ENGLER, R. (1961) *The Politics of Oil.* New York: Macmillan.

FOSS, P. O. (1960) *Politics and Grass.* Seattle: Univ. of Washington Press.

GARSON, G. D. (1974) "On the Origins of Interest-Group Theory: A Critique of a Process," *American Political Science Review*, Vol. 68, No. 4 (December): 1505-1519.

HALE, M. Q. (1960) "The Cosmology of Arthur F. Bentley," *American Political Science Review*, Vol. 54 No. 4 (December): 955-961.

KARIEL, H. S. (1961) *The Decline of American Pluralism.* Stanford: Stanford Univ. Press.

KUHN, T. (1970) *The Structure of Scientific Revolutions, Second Edition.* Chicago: Univ. of Chicago Press.

LAPALOMBARA, J. (1960) "The Utility and Limitations of Interest Group Theory in Non-American Field Situations," *Journal of Politics,* Vol. 22, No. 1 (February): 29-49.

LEISERSON, A. (1951) Review of Truman (1951) in *American Political Science Review,* Vol. 45, No. 4 (December): 1192-1193.

LIPSET, S. M. (1960) *Political Man.* Garden City, N.Y.: Doubleday.

MATTHEWS, D. (1960) *U.S. Senators and Their World.* Vintage.

ODEGARD, P. H. (1958) "A Group Basis of Politics: A New Name for an Old Myth," *Western Political Quarterly,* Vol. 11, No. 3 (September): 689-702.

PATEMAN, C. (1970) *Participation and Democratic Theory.* Cambridge, England: Cambridge Univ. Press.

President's Commission on National Goals (1960) *Goals for Americans.* Englewood Cliffs, N.J.: Prentice-Hall.

ROTHMAN, S. (1960) "Systematic Political Theory: Observations of the Group Approach," *American Political Science Review,* Vol. 54, No. 1 (February): 15-33.

TRUMAN, D. B. (1951) *The Governmental Process.* New York: Knopf.

WAHLKE, J. C., W. BUCHANAN, H. EULAU, AND L. C. FERGUSON (1960) "American State Legislators' Role Orientations Toward Pressure Groups," *Journal of Politics,* Vol. 22, No. 2 (May): 203-227.

WILSON, H. H. (1961) *Pressure Group, The Campaign for Commercial Television in England.* New Brunswick, N.J.: Rutgers Univ. Press.

WRIGHT, C. R. AND H. H. HYMAN (1958) "Voluntary Association Membership of American Adults," *American Sociological Review,* Vol. 23, No. 3 (June): 284-294.

INTRODUCTION: THE COMPARATIVE STUDY OF POLITICAL ELITES
Robert D. Putnam*

"Who rules?" has a fair claim to be the central question of empirical political science, just as its normative counterpart, "Who should rule?" is perhaps the central question of political philosophy. Like any truly fundamental question about social relations, "Who rules?" has generated a long history of speculative answers and a rich store of "common knowledge."

*Robert D. Putnam, *The Comparative Study of Political Elites.* Englewood Cliffs, NJ: Prentice-Hall, 1976 (pp. 2-19). Used by permission

Sage commentators, from Plato and Aristotle to our nightly television newscasters, tell us much about power and leadership, but their profundities, when carefully examined, often turn out to be incomplete and ambiguous. Recently, however, systematic research has begun to produce a modest store of knowledge about political elites that is both reliable and reasonably coherent.

That rulers are fewer in number than ruled might seem an exceptionable first step toward answering our fundamental query. For many centuries, in fact, it was an unquestioned axiom of political thought that power in society is distributed unequally. In eighteenth-century Europe, however, a contrary view began to gain credence among philosophers and men of affairs: that all citizens—or at least all men—might share power equally. The age of the democratic revolutions had dawned. During the nineteenth century radical critics of bourgeois society decried the persistence of oligarchy but insisted that in the long run a society without rulers was desirable and possible—perhaps even inevitable.

At the close of the nineteenth century, however, this democratic optimism began to be questioned by more pessimistic students of society, who argued that behind the diverse facades of government, power was always confined to a ruling few. As Gaetano Mosca phrased the argument:

> In all societies . . . two classes of people appear—a class that rules and a class that is ruled. The first class, always the less numerous, performs all political functions, monopolizes power and enjoys the advantages that power brings, whereas the second, the more numerous class, is directed and controlled by the first.[1]

From the outset the dispute between the elitists and their opponents has been bedeviled by confusions among what *is*, what *could be*, and what *ought to be*. The radical democrats argued that power should be shared equally and, by implication, that it could be. The elitists replied not merely that in fact power was monopolized by the few, but that as a practical matter things neither could nor should be otherwise. Thus, ideologically the elitists seemed merely conservative defenders of the established order.[2] Nevertheless, their writings contained some insights that deserve attention even from their adversaries.

Most prominent among these turn-of-the-century elitists, in addition to Mosca, were Vilfredo Pareto and Robert Michels. The general principles shared by all three are:

1. *Political power, like other social goods, is distributed unequally.* Pareto was the most elegant in his formulation of this initial point.

---

[1]Mosca, 1939, p. 50.

[2]For useful summaries of the classical elite theories, see Bottomore, 1964, pp. 1-41, and G. Parry, 1969, pp. 15-50.

Let us suppose that in every branch of human activity an index or grade can be assigned to each individual as an indication of his capacity, in much the same way that marks are awarded for the various subjects in a school examination. . . . To the man who has earned millions—no matter what means he has employed therein, fair or foul—we will . . . give 10. To the earner of thousands we will give 6, assigning 1 to the man who just manages to keep body and soul together, and zero to him who ends up in the workhouse. . . . The clever swindler who can pull the wool over people's eyes without falling foul of the law will be rated at 8, 9, or 10 according to the number of dupes he catches in his net and the amount of money he squeezes out of them. The wretched pilferer who snaffles the cutlery in a restaurant and bumps redhanded into the nearest policeman will be rated at 1. . . . Let us therefore make a class for those people who have the highest indices in their branch of activity, and give to this class the name of elite. It will help in our investigations into the social equilibrium if we distinguish two further classes within this main class of the elite: the governing elite and the non-governing elite. The first elite class includes those who directly or indirectly play a significant part in government and political life; the second comprises the rest of the elite personnel, those who have no significant role in government and politics.[3]

Already Pareto has introduced a number of complications; we might wonder, for example, about the relations between governing and nongoverning elites. But the fundamental idea is simple and persuasive: people can be ranked by their share of any good—wealth, skill, or political power.

2. *Essentially, people fall into only two groups: those who have "significant" political power and those who have none.* This second point is not logically implied by the first; Pareto's scheme, for example, could encompass intermediate positions on the scales of wealth, skill, and (presumably) power. But the classical elitists generally argued that for most purposes the distribution of power can be conceived in dichotomous terms.

3. *The elite is internally homogeneous, unified, and self-conscious.* This proposition, too, adds a new twist. The elite is not a collection of isolated individuals—a mere statistical artifact. Instead, like the members of some exclusive club, individuals in the elite know each other well, have similar backgrounds, and (though they may have occasional differences of opinion) share similar values, loyalties, and interests. James Meisel has summed up this proposition in his mnemonic "three C's"—group consciousness, coherence, and conspiracy (in the sense of common intentions).[4]

4. *The elite is largely self-perpetuating and is drawn from a very exclusive segment of society.* The classical theorists gave much attention to the long-term rise and fall of elites, but in the short run, they argued, successful leaders select their own successors from among the privileged few. The powerful are the scions and the representatives of the wealthy and the prestigious.

5. Finally and for all these reasons, *the elite is essentially autonomous,* answerable to no one else for its decisions. All important political questions are settled according to the interests or whims of this group.

[3]Pareto, 1966, p. 248.
[4]Meisel, 1962, p. 4.

This, then, is the portrait of society painted by the classical elite theorists: a socially isolated, self-seeking leadership caste that cleverly dominates the abject masses. Theorists have differed on the question of *why* societies were always so organized. Some, like Michels, stressed that the division of labor necessary in any organization implies that some people acquire the skills and perquisites of leadership, while others become accustomed to being led. Others, like Pareto, argued that oligarchy flows from the unequal distribution of innate personal qualities. And some more recent theorists, like Suzanne Keller, have proclaimed elite rule a functional requisite that must be satisfied if society is not to disintegrate. But all agreed that oligarchy is, as Michels put it, an "iron law."[5]

Does a small, cohesive, unresponsive group actually run everything? This deceptively simple question has no single answer, for it is not a single question. The empirical complexities of elite analysis have often been compounded by a tendency to disguise issues of fact as issues of definition. For example, many social scientists have defined "elite" in terms of Meisel's three C's and have referred to the set of propositions outlined above as "the" elite theory of politics.

As Humpty Dumpty explained to Alice, words can mean anything we want. But we must beware of building dubious empirical assumptions into definitions, for, as Alice discovered, if the assumptions are false, the definitions will be very confusing. One well-known study, for example, defined the political elite as "the leadership [of a body politic] and the social formations from which leaders typically come, and to which accountability is maintained, during a given generation."[6] But whether leaders do in fact remain accountable to the groups from which they come is a matter for investigation, not stipulation. The leader who becomes "a traitor to his class" should not be ruled out simply by definition.

There is little consensus among social scientists about the definition of elite, but I propose to define the term broadly, leaving questions of size, composition, and autonomy for later empirical investigation. Let us begin with the first postulate of classical elite theory: some people have more political power than others; they are the political elite. This proposition is hardly profound, but definitions should open questions, not close them.

If we are to define our subject in terms of the distribution of power, we must consider the controversial concept of power itself.[7] Two distinct conceptions of power appear in both social science and common parlance: (1) power as the ability to influence other individuals and (2) power as the ability to influence collective decision making. We often say that one person has

---

[5]Michels, 1959, pp. 32-36, 377; Keller, 1963, pp. 88-106. Keller does not endorse all the elements of classical elite theory.

[6]Lasswell, Lerner, and Rothwell, 1952, p. 13.

[7]For useful introductions to the literature on power, influence, and related concepts, see Dahl, 1968, and Kadushin, 1968.

power over another, meaning that the first can make the second act in ways the second would not otherwise choose. On the other hand, when we speak of the political power of farmers, for example, we are really referring, not to their ability to change the behavior of other individuals, but to their ability to affect the government's agricultural policies. Of course, power over people is often a means to achieve power over outcomes. But in the practical analysis of politics it is often useful to keep these concepts separate.

For studying political elites, it is most useful to think in terms of power over outcomes. The president of General Motors, the general secretary of the Soviet Communist party, the prime minister of Tanzania, or the chairman of the Swedish Labor Federation is a member of the political elite, not by virtue of his ability to issue binding orders to subordinates, but rather because of his influence on national policy. Hence, by *power* here I shall mean the *probability of influencing the policies and activities of the state*, or (in the language of systems theory) *the probability of influencing the authoritative allocation of values*.

Several important kinds of power relations are excluded by this definition. First of all, power over persons that does not affect government policy is omitted. The power of a Chilean general over his men, or of an English mill owner over his workers, or of a wife over her husband will be neglected unless it becomes a factor affecting affairs of state. Secondly, the ability to affect the well-being of others without using the mediating agency of government is also excluded from view. The decision of Henry Ford II to locate a new plant, or of a British union leader to call a strike, or of the pope to proscribe the pill—each has important consequences for many ordinary citizens, but these are not exercises of political power as I define that term.[8] On the other hand, power of these diverse sorts is often convertible into power over public policy and thus may become indirectly relevant to our study of political elites.

Several other distinctions are important here. First, we must carefully specify the *scope* of power—that is, the range of activities over which it extends. Military leaders may have much influence on defense policy, but little on agricultural matters. The chairman of a congressional committee may be quite powerful within a limited domain, whereas the director of the president's Office of Management and Budget probably has less intense influence over a broader range of issues. For some purposes it may be convenient to consider an actor's "average" power across the whole panoply of government activities, but caution is required, because in specific cases this average may be quite misleading.

Even among the very powerful, few people directly decide public pol-

---

[8]The relative importance of government and politics (as opposed to, say, religion or the marketplace) in affecting the lives of ordinary men and women doubtless varies across time and space, but I shall not here discuss this broader question of the social significance of political power.

icy. Hence, we must distinguish direct, indirect, and spurious influence. Figure 2-1 sorts out these possibilities. Actor A has *direct influence* when he participates himself in the final decision. Actor A has *indirect influence* when he influences actor B, who in turn decides policy. For example, the head of a central bank has indirect influence when he persuades the government to modify its fiscal policy. Actor A has *both* direct and indirect influence when he participates himself in the policy-making process and also influences other participants. This case is illustrated when the president successfully urges Congress to pass legislation originally drafted by the White House. Finally, in the case of *spurious influence*, actor B himself directly influences policy and at the same time determines the stand taken by actor A, who has no independent influence on the outcome. Here the policy seems to coincide with actor A's preferences, but his apparent influence is spurious. This possibility is exemplified when a foreign minister merely announces a decision actually taken by the chief executive; the influence of the foreign minister is spurious. Our definition of power (and hence of elite) must allow for both direct and indirect influence, but it must exclude spurious influence.

Many years ago Carl J. Friedrich called attention to a troublesome aspect of power relations. Frequently, even a very powerful decision maker will take into account the possible reactions of other actors. In 1971 the British decision to enter the Common Market was made by the Conservative cabinet; probably they could have carried either a positive or a negative

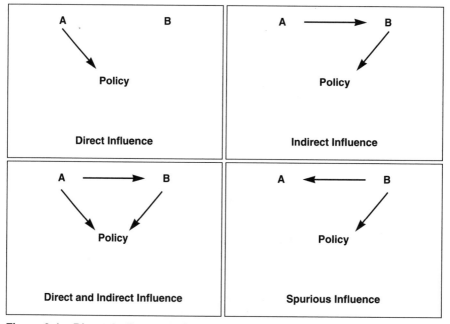

Figure 2-1   Direct, Indirect and Spurious Influence

decision. Yet in reaching their final decision they doubtless considered the probable reactions of many other actors—their rank and file in Parliament, the Labour opposition, leading bankers, industrialists, and trade unionists, prominent journalists and commentators, and even the electorate. Friedrich termed this phenomenon "the rule of anticipated reactions."[9]

This rule plays havoc with any simple analysis of power, because the very real power of those whose reactions are anticipated need not be manifested by any action on their part. Power of this sort—let us call it *implicit power*—is elusive, but it can be detected. For example, if the ultimate decision maker fails to anticipate the reactions of some powerful actor, that actor may reveal his power by direct action. Indeed, holders of implicit power from time to time have to revalidate their claim to power by acting against some objectionable decision. The power of the U.S. Senate over Supreme Court nominations is normally only implicit, for the president usually tries to anticipate senatorial reactions. In 1970 and 1971, however, the senators' power was made explicit, when they rejected two of President Nixon's nominees.

Most important actors in a political system soon learn whose reactions they must anticipate; slow learners quickly become unimportant. Hence, we can often gain valuable clues to the distribution of implicit power by discovering the rules of thumb used by decision makers. Of course, information of this sort must be matched against other evidence, too, for reputation does not always reflect reality.

Implicit power must not be confused with *potential power*. Occasionally, an actor who seems to have the ability to influence policy forbears from exerting that influence. Many scholars, for example, believe that Dwight D. Eisenhower did not fully use the powers inherent in the U.S. presidency. His power, we might say, was in part only potential. Potential power sometimes generates implicit power, as others try to anticipate the reactions of the potentially powerful actor. But for our purposes, consistently unused potential power is much less significant than actual power. We are interested in those who actually influence policy, not in those who could, but never do.

That some people have more power than others is, strictly speaking, axiomatic; I shall treat this proposition as largely self-evident, though I shall offer some collateral evidence shortly. Certainly no national political system displays a distribution of power at all approaching equality. Whether in some sense this, *must be* so is irrelevant here; in the case of all political systems we know, it *is* so. And its empirical universality makes this a particularly useful axiom on which to base political analysis. To describe directly the distribution of power in any national political system would require an exhaustive and very difficult investigation. But just as physicists infer the

---

[9]Friedrich, 1937, pp. 16-18.

shape of subatomic or extragalactic objects that they cannot directly observe, so too we can estimate the contours of the distribution of political power by relying on indirect evidence about the nature of political participation.

In all societies yet studied there is a high correlation among the following variables: interest in politics, political knowledge and sophistication, political skill and resources (particularly education), political participation, political position, and—here the evidence is less direct—political power. Citizens who are unusually interested in politics tend to be more knowledgeable about public affairs; those who have more political resources, such as education, wealth, and social prestige, are both more interested and more knowledgeable; and those who are interested, knowledgeable, and blessed with resources are more likely to participate actively. Furthermore, positions of political prominence are held disproportionately by people of exceptional political motivation and sophistication who have unusually abundant access to socioeconomic and political resources. Few generalizations in political science are so firmly grounded in rigorous research as these.[10]

None of this is very surprising. Nor can there be much doubt that political power itself—the ability to influence public policy—is also highly (though not perfectly) correlated with these variables. Those at the top of these several scales have the desire, the resources, the skill, and the occasion to exert influence. There is no reason to doubt that by and large they use these opportunities nor that their fellow citizens who lack desire, resources, skill, and occasion are normally much less likely to affect the course of public affairs.

We can thus conceive political systems as stratified, much as sociologists speak of social stratification. Individuals toward the bottom of the political stratification system lack nearly all the prerequisites for exercising political power, whereas those toward the top have these characteristics in abundance. The empirical correlations that underlie this notion of political stratification are so strong and so universal that it offers a uniquely valuable key to the study of politics, more susceptible to cross-national comparison than, for example, elections or legislatures or political parties.[11]

To suggest the general outlines of political stratification systems, Figure 2-2 presents data from several nations on the proportion of their citizens

[10]For illustrative evidence, see Milbrath, 1965; Verba, Nie, and Kim, 1971; Verba and Nie, 1972, pp. 25-94, 127-129. Verba and his colleagues show that political participation is multidimensional; that is, some people engage in "harder" activities, like writing to officials, but fail to perform "easier" acts, like voting. Nevertheless, for the dominant modes of participation they confirm the propositions reported in the text.

[11]See Michels, 1959, pp. 52-53, and Key, 1961, pp. 182-202. Because the intercorrelations among the components of political stratification, though high, are not perfect, some people may rank high on one dimension, such as motivation or education, and low on others, such as participation or power. These discrepancies are themselves of considerable interest, because, as we shall discuss in Chapter 7, they may be a source of potential instability in a political system. For a discussion of status, inconsistency, the analogous phenomenon in social stratification, see Lenski, 1966, pp. 85-88, 288-289.

United States	0.0007%	Top 1,000 national decision makers
	0.4%	Elected local or national officials
	8%	Government employees
	8%	Members of a political club or organization
	19%	Attend political meetings or rallies
	35%	At least "somewhat" interested in politics
	72%	Vote in national elections
Yugloslavia	0.0008%	Top 1,000 national decision makers
	4%	Members of municipal self-government councils
	9%	Members of League of Communists
	20%	Members of workers' council
	45%	Attend voters' meetings
	70%	At least "somewhat" interested in politics
	82%	Vote in national elections
India	0.0003%	Top 1,000 national decision makers
	1%	Members of *panchayati* (village council)
	2%	Government employees
	6%	Members of a political club or organization
	14%	Attend political meetings or rallies
	42%	At least "somewhat" interested in politics
	59%	Vote in national elections
Japan	0.001%	Top 1,000 national decision makers
	0.1%	Elected local or national officials
	4%	Government employees
	4%	Members of a political club or organization
	50%	Attend political meetings or rallies
	45%	At least "somewhat" interested in politics
	72%	Vote in national elections
USSR	0.0005%	Top 1,000 national decision makers
	0.004%	Delegates in central Party Congress
	1%	Deputies of local Soviet (legislature)
	10%	Members of Communist party
	14%	Volunteer activists in local government
	99%	Vote in national elections

Figure 2-2   Several Pyramids of Participation (*Source*: Verba, Nie, and Kim, 1971; Verba et al., 1973; Barton, Denitch, and Kadushin, 1973 p. 113; Russett et al., 1964, p. 70; Barghoorn, 1972, p. 245; Mickiewicz, 1973, pp. 163, 173; LaPalombara, 1974, p. 484; and various national statistical yearbooks.)

involved in politics in varying degrees. Our interest here is less in the subtle and complex cross-national differences than in one striking cross-national uniformity: only a tiny proportion of the citizens in any of these countries has more than an infinitesimal chance of directly influencing national policy. We can use this indirect evidence to construct a general model of political stratification, distinguishing for convenience six broad strata, as illustrated in Figure 2-3.

At the top of the pyramid are those individuals directly involved in national policy making, the *proximate decision makers*. Incumbents in key official posts normally comprise most of this stratum, though as we shall discuss in a moment, it need not be limited to them.

Just below come the *influentials*—individuals with substantial indirect or implicit influence, those to whom the decision makers look for advice, whose interests and opinions they take into account, or from whom they fear sanctions. This stratum may include such figures as high-level bureaucrats, large landowners, industrialists, and financiers, interest-group leaders, and official and unofficial consultants. Of particular interest here are national opinion makers, "those who actively try to influence the opinions either of the national decision makers, the public as a whole or large parts of it, or the other opinion makers."[12] On many major issues the opinion makers set the terms within which policy is debated and decisions are framed. The history of American involvement in Indochina illustrates that over the long run opinion makers may be even more influential than official decision makers, although this case also shows that in the short run decision makers may have considerable autonomy.

The third stratum consists of the much larger number of citizens who

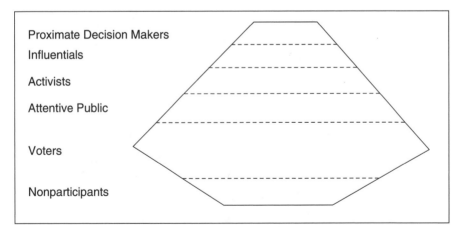

Proximate Decision Makers

Influentials

Activists

Attentive Public

Voters

Nonparticipants

Figure 2-3   A Schematic Model of Political Stratification

[12]Barton, 1969, pp. 1-2.

take some active part in politics and government, perhaps as party members, middle-level bureaucrats, or local editors, perhaps in some more private way, such as by writing to national legislators. This stratum we can term the *activists*. Below them are those for whom politics is a spectator sport. These men and women—the *attentive public*—are distinguished from most citizens by the unusual amount of attention they pay to public affairs. They recognize many of the leading players in the political game, perhaps even without consulting a scorecard, and they may discuss plays and strategy, but they rarely move onto the field themselves.

Next in the political stratification systems of representative democracies come the masses of ordinary citizens whose only impact on national politics comes in the polling booth. Voters have one important collective political resource—numbers—but as individuals they have, for all practical purposes, no political influence. Finally, at the bottom stand those men and women who are, in political terms, objects, not actors. Sometimes by choice, sometimes as a result of deliberate exclusion by the authorities, these *nonparticipants* are politically powerless. (Because in most modern political systems nonvoters constitute a minority of the adult population, Figure 2-3 shows this stratum as smaller than the one above it.)

To say that all political systems are stratified is not to say that all stratification systems are identical, either across countries or across time. The shape of the pyramid of participation—and by implication, the shape of the pyramid of power—is a matter of empirical investigation. Indeed, Harold Lasswell pointed out years ago that "nothing inherent in the geometry of power restricts power to the pyramid. . . . The significant point is that elite patterns are to be discovered by research and not settled by arbitrary definition."[13]

Empirically, distributions of power (pyramidal or not) differ in *height*, *profile*, and *stability*. In some countries differences in power between the top strata and lower layers—the height of the pyramid—may be very great, whereas in other times and places activists, the attentive public, and even voters may have relatively more influence. Profile refers to the varying proportions of the population that fall in particular strata. In most countries, for example, the pyramids of participation and power are more spike-shaped—fewer people have much power—for foreign policy than for domestic issues. Finally, although the contours of some political stratification systems seem to be quite stable, elsewhere patterns of participation and power vary greatly across time. For example, differences in the size (and hence in the composition) of the electoral stratum between primary and general elections help explain the ill-fated presidential nominations of Barry Goldwater and George McGovern.[14] The possibility of historical change is

[13]Lasswell, Lerner, and Rothwell, 1952, p. 13.
[14]Ranney, 1972.

nicely illustrated by the finding that since the end of the nineteenth century "the shape of the American political universe" has been drastically altered by declining rates of citizen participation.[15]

Unless interpreted carefully, the image of a pyramid may be misleading in several important respects. In the first place, we must make no a priori assumption about the cohesion, consciousness, or autonomy of particular strata. In some countries the top echelon may be a closed, cohesive cabal, unconstrained by circumstance or opposition, while elsewhere it may be open and competitive.

Nor should we assume that the political stratification system is organized hierarchically like an army. Members of higher strata cannot necessarily issue orders to members of lower strata, for power as defined here involves influence over policy, not over people. To be sure, people at the top may use their influence over policy to acquire power over other individuals. For example, the head of the secret police may assume special powers of search and imprisonment. Logically, however, it is equally possible for a decision maker to be divested of power over persons, without in any way limiting his power over policy. The development of the rule of law in Western constitutional history to some extent exemplifies this possibility.

In fact, a stratification model of politics highlights the importance of linkages between strata. Friedrich's rule of anticipated reactions points to the possibility of reciprocal influence. By definition, final decisions are taken by proximate decision makers, but they in turn may be subject to indirect or implicit influence from lower strata. On the other hand, the various strata may be mutually isolated, creating a so-called "elite-mass gap."

In many organizations some subordinates have more influence over policy than do their nominal superiors. The ability to control the flow of information, to preformulate decisions for formal ratification, to modify policy while seeming to implement it—all give rise to what Pahl and Winkler term "power from below."[16] This phenomenon appears a contradiction in terms only if one falsely assumes that distributions of power perfectly mirror organization charts.

Just as sociologists debate the number of social classes, political scientists do not agree on how to slice the pyramid of power. The classical elite theorists usually spoke as if there were only two classes, the powerful and the powerless. Others have instead proposed a three-class theory, including an intermediate stratum of leaders who transmit information and opinion between the top elite and the citizenry, help to implement the elite's decisions, and provide new recruits for the upper stratum.[17]

[15]Burnham, 1965, 1974.

[16]Pahl and Winkler, 1974, pp. 109-120.

[17]Mosca, 1939, pp. 404-410. See also Giddens, 1972, pp. 360-362, and Deutsch, 1966, pp. 154-155.

It is sometimes convenient to refer to specific layers in the political stratification system. For example, Figure 2-3 distinguished six different strata. But in the absence of detailed information about the profile of a particular system, indicating natural points of demarcation, this terminology is merely rhetorical shorthand.

This ambiguity is not a major problem, so long as we keep clearly in mind that the underlying variable of participation and power is a matter of more-or-less, not all-or-nothing. For some purposes, we may confine our attention, say, to the top ten decision makers in a country, while for other purposes, we will want to define the elite more broadly to include several thousand individuals who occasionally influence national policy. However, we must not generalize our findings from the narrower to the broader group, or vice versa, without supporting evidence. Similarly, we must beware of comparing incomparable slices of different stratification systems, particularly because the heights and profiles of the systems may be quite different. But these complexities are best addressed in the context of particular research rather than in terms of general theory.

In addition to the horizontal divisions we have been considering, there may be vertical divisions—that is, distinctive groups within the same political stratum. In most modern societies there is considerable division of labor within the elite. Suzanne Keller suggests the term "strategic elites" for these functionally differentiated groups at the top of the pyramid of power.[18]

For our present purposes the most significant of these strategic elites is comprised of the full-time professional politicians—legislators, cabinet ministers, party officials, and their immediate advisors. Most research on political elites has dealt with only this category. However, other politically significant strategic elites include the following: senior civil servants; managers of important economic enterprises, public and private; leaders of mass organizations, such as labor unions, farm groups, and civic associations; high military officials; leading professionals, such as lawyers, doctors, and economists; prominent intellectuals, journalists, and religious leaders.

An elite defined in terms of influence over public policy need not be confined to "establishment" figures. As G. Lowell Field and John Higley point out, this conception "subsumes persons who are often labeled 'counter elite' because these persons quite clearly have the power, although perhaps only through negation, to affect political outcomes individually, regularly, and seriously."[19]

The relative importance of strategic elites varies from country to country and from time to time. For example, businessmen are reputed to play a more significant political role in America and Japan than they do in Western

[18]Keller, 1963.
[19]Field and Higley, 1973, p. 8.

Europe, whereas intellectuals have traditionally been more influential in European politics.

Elite specialization in particular policy areas may produce another set of vertical distinctions. Policy subelites focus on such areas as military affairs, agricultural policy, education, social welfare, or economic planning. As I have already noted, influence in one policy area does not necessarily bring with it influence in others. Sometimes it is crucial to distinguish among separate policy subelites, but for other purposes we shall find it appropriate to group together all individuals and groups having influence in national politics, regardless of their areas of maximum impact.

I have suggested that political systems consist of various strata, some more powerful than others, and that the most powerful stratum includes a number of functionally differentiated groupings. For empirical investigation, however, it is not enough to know that the powerful exist in any political system; we must be able to find them. Broadly speaking, social scientists have used three strategies for identifying elites: positional analysis, reputational analysis, and decisional analysis.[20]

Like most of us most of the time, political scientists using *positional analysis* assume that the formal institutions of government provide a useful map of power relations, and thus that incumbents of high positions in those institutions are likely to be politically powerful. In part this assumption is grounded in the fact that people derive power itself from institutional roles. As C. Wright Mills argued:

> If we took the one hundred most powerful men in America, the one hundred wealthiest, and the one hundred most celebrated away from the institutional positions they now occupy, away from their resources of men and women and money, away from the media of mass communication that are now focused upon them—then they would be powerless and poor and uncelebrated. . . . To be celebrated, to be wealthy, to have power requires access to major institutions, for the institutional positions men occupy determine in large part their chances to have and to hold these valued experiences.[21]

In a slightly different way, membership in some political organizations, such as European parliaments and Communist central committees, is a significant indicator of elite stature, less because these institutions confer power themselves than because membership is mostly confined to persons who derive power from other sources.

Because formal institutions usually keep good records, positional analysis is the easiest and most common technique for finding the powerful. Most empirical studies are based on the analysis of members of parliaments, cabinets, central committees, boards of directors, and other formal institutions. But cogent critics of positional analysis have denied that power

---

[20]On the problem of finding the powerful, see Frey, 1970, and Hough, 1975.
[21]Mills, 1956, pp. 10-11.

is perfectly correlated with institutional position. One recent study of power within business organizations concluded soberingly that "Positional definitions distort organizational reality because organizations are more complex than authority hierarchies. Power is more than role structure. Men with power in organizations exist in various subdivisions, at various levels, and in staff positions outside the normal hierarchy."[22] History is replete with *eminences grises*, men and women of power whispering instructions from the shadows behind the throne.

Moreover, positional analysis assumes that we know which institutions are politically significant and which are shams, and it risks equating institutions that are formally similar, but functionally different. For example, members of the U.S. Congress, the British Parliament, and the Supreme Soviet surely do not hold comparable positions in their respective elites, although formally all are national legislators. We may be misled by positional analysis in two ways: (1) we may include among our elite, figureheads who simply rubber-stamp decisions reached elsewhere, and (2) we may fail to include informal opinion makers who influence the proximate decision makers. Positional analysis tends to overemphasize spurious influence and to underemphasize indirect influence.

Reputational analysis relies, not on formal organization charts, but on informal reputations for power. Some researchers set out to discover who has power by querying informants who are presumed to have observed political machinations from close up. For example, one student of the American elite asked officials in several national organizations (such as the Chamber of Commerce and the National Federation of Business and Professional Women's Clubs) for "the names of persons known to [them] who might be considered top policy makers at the national level." These nominees were then polled "to get their own choices of those whom they consider[ed] to be their peers."[23]

This technique is founded on the assumption that participants in a system will know who is powerful and who is not. It does allow the analyst to discover powerful figures whose influence is only indirect or implicit. However, reputational analysis also has grave weaknesses, for a researcher using this method must decide whom to ask and what to ask. Errors in choosing informants may irreparably bias the results. If the informants have no access to inside information, or if their knowledge is limited to a particular sphere of public affairs, they may innocently purvey a distorted picture of power relations. Moreover, informants are often even more confused than social scientists about what power is and who has it. More cautious reputational analysts ask their informants only about influence relations they have personally witnessed, but the reconstruction of overall patterns

[22]Pahl and Winkler, 1974, p. 121.
[23]Hunter, 1959, pp. 16, 195.

of power from a myriad of such individual reports remains a terrifically complex task.

This last variant of the reputation approach is closely related to the third main technique for identifying the powerful—*decisional analysis*. This method—sometimes also called event analysis—is based on the assumption that if political power is defined in terms of influence over government activities, we can detect it by studying how specific decisions are reached and, in particular, by noting who successfully initiates or vetoes proposals. In the best-known application of decisional analysis, Robert A. Dahl studied decisions in New Haven, Connecticut, on three topics: urban redevelopment, public education, and nominations for public office.[24]

This technique comes closer than either of the other two to capturing the realities of power as I have defined it. Critics, however, have discovered several significant flaws. First, as a practical matter, only a few important decisions can be studied in detail, and the analyst must infer the broader structure of power from his small sample of cases. Yet patterns of power may vary systematically from issue to issue.[25] Bias in the selection of the decisions to be studied may be nearly as damaging for this approach as bias in the selection of informants is for the reputational method.

A second weakness of decisional analysis is that it is best suited for studying matters that have already become recognized public issues. Yet controlling what gets on the agenda for decision is itself clearly an exercise of political power. If the powerful are able to keep certain controversies off the public agenda, their power is harder to detect by the decisional method.[26]

Because none of these methods for finding the powerful is without defects, some sophisticated analysts have merged several different approaches. For example, in a pair of pioneering studies of Yugoslav and American elites, Allen Barton and his collaborators combined positional and reputational analysis in the so-called "snowball" technique. In each country, incumbents of key formal positions constituted the initial elite, as defined operationally. Respondents from these positions were then asked for the names of others to whom they looked for advice or who they thought to be generally influential. People receiving at least five such nominations were themselves added to the elite sample, and they in turn were asked for further nominations.[27]

The vigorous debate among social scientists over methods for identifying the political elite has often proceeded at too abstract a level. Too little attention has been paid to whether, when, and how our conclusions might

[24]Dahl, 1961, pp. 104-162.
[25]Lowi, 1964*b*
[26]Bachrach and Baratz, 1962.
[27]Barton, Denitch, and Kadushin, 1973; Bellisfield, 1973.

be affected by our methods. Some have argued that reputational analysis overestimates the power and cohesiveness of elites, while decisional analysis underestimates these factors. But there is no systematic evidence that this is so. More to the point here, Barton and his colleagues found that in both small, one-party Yugoslavia and large, multiparty America power-as-reputation overlapped almost completely with power-as-position. Virtually everyone whose name appeared on the reputational lists was already in the positional sample. Moreover, the overlap between position and reputation was greatest in the governmental and (in Yugoslavia) party sectors, precisely the sectors of greatest centrality in terms of both reputation and political interaction.[28] Where it matters most, it seems, the differences among the three techniques matter least. Why should this be so?

In complex systems, formal and informal relations of power and coordination are likely to converge at the top. Organization theory suggests that even in small groups inefficiency increases sharply when formal and informal structures are discrepant.[29] The conduct of national affairs in the United States or the Soviet Union would be extremely difficult if institutionally designated leaders did not normally also possess effective power to make and enforce decisions. If petitions from Detroit or Dnepropetrovsk to the president or the party secretary had to be referred to an obscure, but all-powerful chestnut vendor in Lafayette Park or Red Square, organizational imperatives would soon require that the chestnut vendor's informal power be institutionalized. To be sure, institutional analysis must not be blindly legalistic; both the president of the Supreme Soviet and the queen of England are constitutionally prominent and politically impotent. Prudent students of power must be self-skeptical.

Scholars need to investigate the circumstances under which differing research techniques are most likely to be misleading. For instance, decisional, reputational, and positional power are probably more likely to converge in stable political systems than during periods of rapid change. Another example: it is no accident that the hottest methodological debate has centered on studies of local communities, for the divergence between formal and informal structures is likely to be greater in smaller, simpler social systems. We must keep these methodological problems in mind but for the national elites methodological difficulties in finding the powerful should not be exaggerated.

Students of politics and society sometimes assume that definitions and theories are logically prior to empirical investigation. This image of the scientific enterprise is correct insofar as it highlights how concepts guide research. But the relationship between concepts and data is dialectical. Answers to one set of questions invariably raise further questions and suggest

---

[28]Barton, Denitch, and Kadushin, 1973, pp. 24, 166-167; Bellisfield, 1973.
[29]Kadushin and Abrams, 1973, p. 189.

conceptual and even definitional innovations. Hence, the concepts and definitions discussed in this chapter must remain tentative, open to correction as our grasp of the realities of power and politics evolves.

A CRITIQUE OF THE ELITIST THEORY OF DEMOCRACY
Jack L. Walker*

During the last thirty years, there have been numerous attempts to revise or reconstitute the "classical" theory of democracy: the familiar doctrine of popular rule, patterned after the New England town meeting, which asserts that public policy should result from extensive, informed discussion and debate.[1] By extending general participation in decision-making the classical theorists hoped to increase the citizen's awareness of his moral and social responsibilities, reduce the danger of tyranny, and improve the quality of government. Public officials, acting as agents of the public at large, would then carry out the broad policies decided upon by majority vote in popular assemblies.

Although it is seldom made clear just which of the classical democratic theorists is being referred to, contemporary criticism has focused primarily on the descriptive elements of the theory, on its basic conceptions of citizenship, representation and decision-making.[2] The concept of an active, informed, democratic citizenry, the most distinctive feature of the traditional theory, is the principal object of attack. On empirical grounds it is argued that very few such people can be found in Western societies. Public policy is not the expression of the common good as conceived of by the citizenry after widespread discussion and compromise. This description of policy making is held to be dangerously naive because it overlooks the role of demagogic leadership, mass psychology, group coercion, and the influence

*Jack L. Walker, "A Critique of the Elitist Theory of Democracy." *American Political Science Review* 60 (1966): 285-95. Used by permission

[1]For discussions of the meaning of the classical theory of democracy see: George Sabine, "The Two Democratic Traditions," *The Philosophical Review*, 61 (1952), 451-474; and his *A History of Political Theory* (New York, 1958), especially chs. 31 and 32. Also see J. Roland Pennock, *Liberal Democracy: Its Merits and Prospects* (New York, 1950); and Sheldon Wolin, *Politics and Vision* (Boston, 1960), especially chs. 9 and 10.

[2]Criticism of the descriptive accuracy of the classical theory has been widespread in recent years. The best statement of the basic objections usually made is Joseph Schumpeter, *Capitalism, Socialism and Democracy* (New York, 1942), Part IV. See also Bernard Berelson *et al.*, *Voting* Chicago, 1954), chapter 14; articles by Louis Hartz and Samuel Beer in W. N. Chambers and R. H. Salisbery (eds.), *Democracy in the Mid-2oth Century* (St. Louis, 1960); Seymour Martin Lipset, *Political Man* (New York, 1960); Robert Dahl, *A Preface to Democratic Theory* (Chicago, 1956), and *Who Governs?* (New Haven, 1961), especially pp. 223-325; V. O. Key, *Public Opinion and American Democracy* (New York, 1961), especially Part VI; Lester W. Milbrath, *Political Participation* (Chicago, 1965), especially Chapter VI; and for a general summary of the position: Henry Mayo, *An Introduction to Democratic Theory*. (New York, 1960).

of those who control concentrated economic power. In short, classical democratic theory is held to be unrealistic; first because it employs conceptions of the nature of man and the operation of society which are utopian, and second because it does not provide adequate, operational definitions of its key concepts.

Since contemporary scholars have found the classical theory of democracy inadequate, a "revisionist" movement has developed, much as it has among contemporary Marxists, seeking to reconstitute the theory and bring it into closer correspondence with the latest findings of empirical research. One major restatement, called the "elitist theory of democracy" by Seymour Martin Lipset,[3] is now employed in many contemporary books and articles on American politics and political behavior and is fast becoming part of the conventional wisdom of political science.

The adequacy of the elitist theory of democracy, both as a set of political norms and as a guide to empirical research, is open to serious question. It has two major shortcomings: first, in their quest for realism, the revisionists have fundamentally changed the normative significance of democracy, rendering it a more conservative doctrine in the process; second, the general acceptance of the elitist theory by contemporary political scientists has led them to neglect almost completely some profoundly important developments in American society.

Normative Implications of the Elitist Theory

At the heart of the elitist theory is a clear presumption of the average citizen's inadequacies. As a consequence, democratic systems must rely on the wisdom, loyalty and skill of their political leaders, not on the population at large. The political system is divided into two groups: the *elite*, or the "political entrepreneurs,"[4] who possess ideological commitments and manipulative skills; and the *citizens at large*, the masses, or the "apolitical clay"[5] of the system, a much larger class of passive, inert followers who have little knowledge of public affairs and even less interest. The factor that distinguishes democratic and authoritarian systems, according to this view, is the provision for limited, peaceful competition among members of the elite for the formal positions of leadership within the system. As Joseph Schumpeter summarized the theory; "the democratic method is that institutional arrangement for arriving at political decisions in which individuals acquire the power to decide by means of a competitive struggle for the people's vote."[6]

---

[3]Introduction by Lipset to the Collier Books paperback edition of Robert Michel's, *Political Parties* (New York, 1962), p. 33.
[4]The phrase is Dahl's in *Who Governs?*, p. 227.
[5]*Ibid.*, p. 225.
[6]Schumpeter, *op. cit.*, p. 269.

Democracy is thus conceived primarily in procedural terms; it is seen as a method of making decisions which insures efficiency in administration and policy making and yet requires some measure of responsiveness to popular opinion on the part of the ruling elites. The average citizen still has some measure of effective political power under this system, even though he does not initiate policy, because of his right to vote (if he chooses) in regularly scheduled elections. The political leaders, in an effort to gain support at the polls, will shape public policy to fit the citizens' desires. By anticipating public reaction the elite grants the citizenry a form of indirect access to public policy making, without the creation of any kind of formal institutions and even in the absence of any direct communication. "A few citizens who are non-voters, and who for some reason have no influential contact with voters have no indirect influence. Most citizens, however, possess a moderate degree of indirect influence, for elected officials keep the real or imagined preferences of constituents constantly in mind in deciding what policies to adopt or reject."[7] An ambiguity is created here because obviously leaders sometimes create opinions as well as respond to them, but since the leaders are constantly being challenged by rivals seeking to gain the allegiance of the masses it is assumed that the individual citizen will receive information from several conflicting sources, making it extremely difficult for any one group to "engineer consent" by manipulating public opinion. As Lipset puts it: "Representation is neither simply a means of political adjustment to social pressures nor an instrument of manipulation. It involves both functions, since the purpose of representation is to locate the combinations of relationships between parties and social bases which make possible the operation of efficient government."[8]

There has been extensive research and speculation about the prerequisites for a democratic system of this kind. There is general agreement that a well developed social pluralism and an extensive system of voluntary groups or associations is needed, along with a prevailing sense of psychological security, widespread education and limited disparities of wealth. There must be no arbitrary barriers to political participation, and "enough people must participate in the governmental process so that political leaders compete for the support of a large and more or less representative cross section of the population."[9]

Elitist theory departs markedly from the classical tradition at this point. Traditionally it was assumed that the most important prerequisite for a stable democracy was general agreement among the politically active (those who vote) on certain fundamental policies and basic values, and widespread acceptance of democratic procedures and restraints on political

---

[7]Dahl, *Who Governs?*, p. 164.
[8]Lipset, Introduction to Michels, *op. cit.*, p. 34.
[9]Robert Dahl and Charles Lindblom, *Politics, Economics and Welfare* (New York, 1953), p. 309.

activity. Political leaders would not violate the basic consensus, or "democratic mold," if they wished to be successful in gaining their objectives, because once these fundamental restraints were broken the otherwise passive public would become aroused and would organize against the offending leaders. Elitist theorists argue instead that agreement on democratic values among the "intervening structure of elites," the very elements which had been seen earlier as potential threats to democracy, is the main bulwark against a breakdown in constitutionalism. Writing in 1959 David Truman discards his notion of "potential groups," a variation of the traditional doctrine of consensus, and calls instead for a "consensus of elites," a determination on the part of the leaders of political parties, labor unions, trade associations and other voluntary associations to defend the fundamental procedures of democracy in order to protect their own positions and the basic structure of society itself from the threat of an irresponsible demagogue.[10] V.O. Key, in his *Public Opinion and the American Democracy*, concludes that "the critical element for the health of a democratic order consists in the beliefs, standards, and competence of those who constitute the influentials, the opinion-leaders, the political activists in the order."[11] Similarly, Robert Dahl concludes in his study of New Haven that the skillful, active political leaders in the system are the true democratic "legitimists."[12] Since democratic procedures regulate their conflicts and protect their privileged positions in the system the leaders can be counted on to defend the democratic creed even if a majority of the voters might prefer some other set of procedures.[13]

[10]David Truman, "The American System in Crisis," *Political Science Quarterly*, (December, 1959), pp. 481-497. See also a perceptive critique of Truman's change of attitude in Peter Bachrach, "Elite Consensus and Democracy," *The Journal of Politics*, 24 (1962), 439-452.

[11]Key, op. cit., p. 558. See also Key's "Public Opinion and the Decay of Democracy," *The Virginia Quarterly Review*, 37 (1961), 481-494.

[12]Dahl's position on this issue seems to have undergone a transformation somewhat similar to Truman's. Compare Dahl and Lindbloom, *op. cit.*, Chapter 11 with Dahl, *Who Governs?*, Books IV, V, VI.

[13]Dahl, *Who Governs?*, pp. 311-325. It is important to note that these conclusions about the crucial function of an elite consensus in democracy were based on little empirical evidence. Truman, Key and Dahl seem to rely most heavily on Samuel Stouffer, *Communism, Conformity, and Civil Liberties* (New York, 1955), a study based on national opinion surveys which was concerned with only one issue (McCarthyism) and did not investigate the relationship between the expressed opinions of its subjects and their behavior under stress; and James Prothro and Charles Grigg, "Fundamental Principles of Democracy: Bases of Agreement and Disagreement," *Journal of Politics*, 22 (1960), 276-294, a study of attitudes in two small cities. More recently, however, Herbert McClosky has produced a more convincing data in his "Consensus and Ideology in American Politics," this REVIEW, 58 (1964), 361-382. On page 377 McClosky concludes that widespread agreement on procedural norms is not a prerequisite to the success of a democratic system: "Consensus may strengthen democratic viability, but its absence in an otherwise stable society need not be fatal, or even particularly damaging." McClosky's conclusions are called into question by data presented by Samuel Eldersveld, *Political Parties: A Behavioral Analysis* (Chicago, 1964), pp. 183-219; and Edmond Constantini, "Intra-party Attitude Conflict: Democratic Party Leadership in California," *Western Political Quarterly*, 16 (1963), 956-972.

It has also been suggested by several elitist theorists that democracies have good reason to fear increased political participation. They argue that a successful (that is, stable) democratic system depends on widespread apathy and general political incompetence.[14] The ideal of democratic participation is thus transformed into a "noble lie" designed chiefly to insure a sense of responsibility among political leaders. As Lester Milbrath puts it:

> . . . it is important to continue moral admonishment for citizens to become active in politics, not because we want or expect great masses of them to become active, but rather because the admonishment helps keep the system open and sustains a belief in the right of all to participate, which is an important norm governing the behavior of political elites.[15]

If the uninformed masses participate in large numbers, democratic self-restraint will break down and peaceful competition among the elites, the central element in the elitist theory, will become impossible.

The principal aim of the critics whose views we are examining has been to make the theory of democracy more realistic, to bring it into closer correspondence with empirical reality. They are convinced that the classical theory does not account for "much of the real machinery"[16] by which the system operates, and they have expressed concern about the possible spread among Americans of either unwarranted anxiety or cynical disillusionment over the condition of democracy. But it is difficult to transform a utopian theory into a realistic account of political behavior without changing the theory's normative foundations. By revising the theory to bring it into closer correspondence with reality, the elitist theorists have transformed democracy from a radical into a conservative political doctrine, stripping away its distinctive emphasis on popular political activity so that it no longer serves as a set of ideals toward which society ought to be striving.[17]

---

[14]See Bernard Berelson, *et al., op. cit.*, Chapter 14; Lipset, *op. cit.*, pp. 14-16; W. H. Morris-Jones, "In Defense of Apathy," *Political Studies*, II (1954), 25-37.

[15]Milbrath, *op. cit.*, p. 152.

[16]Louis Hartz, "Democracy: Image and Reality," in Chambers and Salisbury (eds.), *op. cit.*, p. 26.

[17]Several articles have recently appeared which attack the elitist theory on normative grounds. The best and most insightful is Lane Davis, "The Cost of Realism: Contemporary Restatements of Democracy," *Western Political Quarterly*, 17 (1964), 37-46. Also see: Graeme Duncan and Steven Lukes, "The New Democracy," *Political Studies*, 11 (1963), 156-177; Steven W. Rousseas and James Farganis, "American Politics and the End of Ideology," *British Journal of Sociology*, 14 (1963) 347-360; and Christian Bay, "Politics and Pseudopolitics," this REVIEW, 59 (1965), 39-51. The subject is also treated in: Henry Kariel, *The Decline of American Pluralism* (Stanford, 1961), Chapters 9 and 11; T. B. Bottomore, *Elites and Society* (London, 1964), 108-110; Robert Presthus, *Men at the Top* (New York, 1964), 3-47; and Robert Agger, Daniel Goldrich and Bert Swanson, *The Rulers and the Ruled* (New York) (1964), 93-99, 524-532. For an insightful critique of the work of Dahl and Mills, conceived of as opposing ideological positions see: William E. Connolly, *Responsible Political Ideology: Implications of the Sociology of Knowledge for Political Inquiry*, (unpublished doctoral dissertation, University of Michigan, 1965), pp. 18-39. This section of this article depends heavily on Lane Davis' analysis.

The most distinctive feature, and the principal orienting value, of classical democratic theory was its emphasis on individual participation in the development of public policy. By taking part in the affairs of his society the citizen would gain in knowledge and understanding, develop a deeper sense of social responsibility, and broaden his perspective beyond the narrow confines of his private life. Although the classical theorists accepted the basic framework of Lockean democracy, with its emphasis on limited government, they were *not* primarily concerned with the *policies* which might be produced in a democracy; above all else they were concerned with *human development*, the opportunities which existed in political activity to realize the untapped potentials of men and to create the foundations of a genuine human community. In the words of John Stuart Mill:

> . . . the most important point of excellence which any form of government can possess is to promote the virtue and intelligence of the people themselves. The first question in respect to any political institutions is how far they tend to foster in the members of the community the various desirable qualities, . . . moral, intellectual, and active.[18]

In the elitist version of the theory, however, emphasis has shifted to the needs and functions of the system as a whole; there is no longer a direct concern with human development. The central question is not how to design a political system which stimulates greater individual participation and enhances the moral development of its citizens, but how "to combine a substantial degree of popular participation with a system of power capable of governing *effectively* and *coherently*?"[19]

The elitist theory allows the citizen only a passive role as an object of political activity; he exerts influence on policy making only by rendering judgements after the fact in national elections. The safety of contemporary democracy lies in the high-minded sense of responsibility of its leaders, the only elements of society who are actively striving to discover and implement the common good. The citizens are left to "judge a world they never made, and thus to become a genteel counter-part of the mobs which sporadically unseated aristocratic governments in eighteenth- and nineteenth-century Europe."[20]

The contemporary version of democratic theory has, it seems, lost much of the vital force, the radical thrust of the classical theory. The elitist theorists, in trying to develop a theory which takes account of the way the political system actually operates, have changed the principal orienting values of democracy. The heart of the classical theory was its justification of broad participation in the public affairs of the community; the aim was the

---

[18]John Stuart Mill, *Considerations on Representative Government* (New York, 1862), pp. 39-40.

[19]Samuel Beer, "New Structures of Democracy: Britain and America," in Chambers and Salisbury (eds.), *op. cit.*, p. 46.

[20]Davis, *Op. Cit.*, p. 45.

production of citizens who were capable enough and responsible enough to play this role. The classical theory was not meant to describe any existing system of government; it was an outline, a set of prescriptions for the ideal polity which men should strive to create. The elitist theorists, in their quest for realism, have changed this distinctive prescriptive element in democratic theory; they have substituted stability and efficiency as the prime goals of democracy. If these revisions are accepted, the danger arises that in striving to develop more reliable explanations of political behavior, political scientists will also become sophisticated apologists for the existing political order. Robert Lane, in concluding his study of the political ideologies of fifteen "common men" in an Eastern city, observes that they lack a utopian vision, a well-defined sense of social justice that would allow them to stand in judgement on their society and its institutions.[21] To some degree, the "men of Eastport" share this disability with much of the American academic elite.

The Elitist Theory as a Guide for Research

The shortcomings of the elitist theory are not confined to its normative implications. Serious questions also arise concerning its descriptive accuracy and its utility as a guide to empirical research. The most unsatisfactory element in the theory is its concept of the passive, apolitical, common man who pays allegiance to his governors and to the sideshow of politics while remaining primarily concerned with his private life, evenings of television with his family, or the demands of his job. Occasionally, when the average citizen finds his primary goals threatened by the actions or inactions of government, he may strive vigorously to influence the course of public policy, but *"Homo Civicus"* as Dahl calls him, "is not, by nature, a political animal."[22]

It was the acceptance of this concept that led the elitist theorists to reject the traditional notion of consensus. It became implausible to argue that the citizenry is watchful and jealous of the great democratic values while at the same time suggesting that they are uninvolved, uninformed and apathetic. Widespread apathy also is said to contribute to democratic stability by insuring that the disagreements that arise during campaigns and elections will not involve large numbers of people or plunge the society into violent disorders or civil war.

No one can deny that there is widespread political apathy among many sectors of the American public. But it is important to ask why this is so and not simply to explain how this phenomenon contributes to the

---

[21]Robert Lane, *Political Ideology* (New York, 1962), p. 475. See also Donald Stokes' comments on the same topic in "Popular Evaluations of Government: An Empirical Assessment," in Harlan Cleveland and Harold Lasswell (eds.), *Ethics and Bigness* (Published by the Conference on Science, Philosophy and Religion in their relation to the Democratic Way of Life, 1962), p. 72.
[22]Dahl, *Who Governs?*, pp. 225.

smooth functioning of the system. Of course, the citizens' passivity might stem from their satisfaction with the operation of the political system, and thus they would naturally become aroused only if they perceived a threat to the system. Dahl, for one, argues that the political system operates largely through "inertia," tradition or habitual responses. It remains stable because only a few "key" issues are the objects of controversy at any one time, the rest of public policy having been settled and established in past controversies which are now all but forgotten. Similarly, Nelson Polsby argues that it is fallacious to assume that the quiescent citizens in a community, especially those in the lower income groups, have grievances unless they actually express them. To do so is to arbitrarily assign "upper- and middle-class values to all actors in the community."[23]

But it is hard to believe, in these days of protest demonstrations, of Black Muslims and the Deacons of Defense and Justice, that the mood of cynical apathy toward politics which affects so many American Negroes is an indication of their satisfaction with the political system, and with the weak, essentially meaningless alternatives it usually presents to them. To assume that apathy is a sign of satisfaction in this case is to overlook the tragic history of the Negroes in America and the system of violent repression long used to deny them any entrance into the regular channels of democratic decision-making.

Students of race relations have concluded that hostile attitudes toward a racial group do not necessarily lead to hostile actions, and amicable feelings do not ensure amicable actions. Instead, "it is the social demands of the situation, particularly when supported by accepted authority figures, which are the effective determinants of individual action..."[24] This insight might apply to other areas besides race relations. It suggests that a society's political culture, the general perceptions about the nature of authority and the prevailing expectations of significant reference groups, might be a major influence on the political behavior of the average citizen regardless of his own feelings of satisfaction or hostility. There have been sizable shifts in rates of political participation throughout American history which suggests that these rates are not rigidly determined. A recent analysis indicates that rates of voter participation are now *lower* than they were in the Nineteenth Century even though the population is now much better educated and the facilities for communication much better developed.[25] Other studies indicate

---

[23]Nelson Polsby, *Community Power and Political Theory* (New Haven, 1963), p. 117.

[24]Herbert Blumer, "Recent Research [on race relations in the] United States of America," *International Social Science Bulletin* (UNESCO), 10 (1958), p. 432. Similar arguments concerning the relationship of beliefs and action can be found in J. D. Lohman and D. C. Reitzes, "Deliberately Organized Groups and Racial Behavior," *American Sociological Review*, 19 (1954), 342-344; and in Earl Raab (ed.), *American Race Relations Today* (Garden City, 1962).

[25]Walter Dean Burnham, "The Changing Shape of the American Political Universe," this Review, 59 (1965), 7-28.

that there are marked differences in the political milieu of towns and cities which lead citizens of one area to exhibit much more cynicism and distrust of the political system than others.[26] Although the studies showed no corresponding changes in feelings of political competence, cynical attitudes might inhibit many forms of participation and thus induce apathy.

Political apathy obviously has many sources. It may stem from feelings of personal inadequacy, from a fear of endangering important personal relationships, or from a lack of interest in the issues; but it may also have its roots in the society's institutional structure, in the weakness or absence of group stimulation or support, in the positive opposition of elements within the political system to wider participation; in the absence, in other words, of appropriate spurs to action, or the presence of tangible deterrents.[27] Before the causes of apathy can be established with confidence much more attention must be directed to the role of the mass media. How are the perceptions of individual citizens affected by the version of reality they receive, either directly or indirectly, from television, the national wire services, and the public schools[28]—and how do these perceptions affect their motivations? Political scientists have also largely neglected to study the use of both legitimate and illegitimate sanctions and private intimidation to gain political ends. How do the activities of the police,[29] social workers, or elements of organized crime affect the desires and the opportunities available for individual political participation?

Certainly the apparent calm of American politics is not matched by our general social life, which is marked by high crime rates, numerous fads and crazes, and much inter-group tension.[30] One recent study showed that during the civil rights protests in Atlanta, Georgia, and Cambridge, Maryland, crime rates in the Negro communities dropped substantially.[31] A finding of this kind suggests that there is some connection between these two realms of social conflict and that both may serve as outlets for individual

[26]Robert Agger, Marshall Goldstein and Stanley Pearl, "Political Cynicism: Measurement and Meaning," *The Journal of Politics* 23 (1961), 477-506; and Edgar Litt, "Political Cynicism and Political Futility," *The Journal of Politics*, 25 (1963) 312-323.

[27]For a brief survey of findings on this subject, see Milbrath, op. cit.; and for a clear, brief summary, see: Morris Rosenburg, "Some Determinants of Political Apathy," *Public Opinion Quarterly.* 18 (1954-55), 349-366. Also see David Apter (ed.), *Ideology and Discontent* (New York, 1964), especially chapters by Converse and Wolfinger, *et al.*

[28]A major study of the influence of secondary schools on political attitudes is underway at the University of Michigan under the direction of M. Kent Jennings.

[29]An extensive investigation of the role of the police and the courts in city politics is being conducted at Harvard University by James Q. Wilson.

[30]It is very difficult to compare crime rates or other indications of social disorganization in the United States with those in other countries. For a discussion of some of the difficulties see: UNESCO 1963 *Report on the World Social Situation* (New York, 1963).

[31]Fredric Solomon, Walter L. Walker, Garrett O'Connor and Jacob Fishman, "Civil Rights Activity and Reduction of Crime Among Negros," *Archives of General Psychiatry*, 12 (March, 1965), 227-236.

distress and frustration. High crime (or suicide) rates and low rates of voting may very well be related; the former may represent "leakage" from the political system[32]

Once we admit that the society is not based on widespread consensus, we must look at our loosely organized, decentralized political parties in a different light. It may be that the parties have developed in this way precisely because no broad consensus exists. In a fragmented society which contains numerous geographic, religious, and racial conflicts, the successful politician has been the man adept at negotiation and bargaining, the man best able to play these numerous animosities off against each other, and thereby build *ad hoc* coalitions of support for specific programs. Success at this delicate business of coalition building depends on achieving some basis for communication among the leaders of otherwise antagonistic groups and finding a formula for compromise. To create these circumstances sharp conflicts must be avoided; highly controversial, potentially explosive issues shunned. Controversy is shifted to other issues or the public authorities simply refuse to deal with the question, claiming that they have no legitimate jurisdiction in the case or burying it quietly in some committee room or bureaucratic pigeonhole.[33]

In other words, one of the chief characteristics of our political system has been its success in suppressing and controlling internal conflict. But the avoidance of conflict, the suppression of strife, is *not* necessarily the creation of satisfaction or consensus. The citizens may remain quiescent, the political system might retain its stability, but significant differences of opinion remain, numerous conflicts are unresolved and many desires go unfulfilled. The frustrations resulting from such deprivations can create conflict in other, non-political realms. Fads, religious revivals, or wild, anomic riots such as those which occurred in the Negro ghettos of several large American cities during the summers of 1964 and 1965, phenomena not directly related to the achievement of any clearly conceived political goals, may be touched off by unresolved tensions left untended by the society's political leaders.

The American political system is highly complex, with conflicting jurisdictions and numerous checks and balances. A large commitment in time

[32]For an excellent study of the Black Muslims which portrays the movement as a non-political outlet for the frustration and bitterness felt by many American Negroes see the study by an African scholar: E. V. Essien-Udom, *Black Nationalism: A Search for an Identity in America* (Chicago, 1962).

[33]Herbert Agar makes a similar analysis and argues for the retention of the system in *The Price of Union*, (Boston, 1950). On page 689 he states:

> The lesson which Americans learned [from the Civil War] was useful: in a large federal nation, when a problem is passionately felt, and is discussed in terms of morals, each party may divide within itself, against itself. And if the parties divide, the nation may divide; for the parties, with their enjoyable pursuit of power, are a unifying influence. Wise men, therefore, may seek to dodge such problems as long as possible. And the easiest way to dodge them is for both parties to take both sides.

and energy must be made, even by a well-educated citizen, to keep informed of the issues and personalities in all levels of government. Most citizens are not able or willing to pay this kind of cost to gain the information necessary for effective political participation. This may be especially true in a political system in which weak or unclear alternatives are usually presented to the electorate. For most citizens the world of politics is remote, bewildering, and meaningless, having no direct relation to daily concerns about jobs or family life. Many citizens have desires or frustrations with which public agencies might be expected to deal, but they usually remain unaware of possible solutions to their problems in the public sphere. This group within our political system are citizens only from the legal point of view. If a high degree of social solidarity and sense of community are necessary for true democratic participation, then these marginal men are not really citizens of the state. The polity has not been extended to include them.[34]

For the elitist theorist widespread apathy is merely a fact of political life, something to be anticipated, a prerequisite for democratic stability. But for the classical democrat political apathy is an object of intense concern because the overriding moral purpose of the classical theory is to expand the boundaries of the political community and build the foundations for human understanding through participation by the citizens in the affairs of their government.

Leaders and Followers

While most elitist theorists are agreed in conceiving of the average citizen as politically passive and uncreative, there seems to be a difference of opinion (or at least of emphasis) over the likelihood of some irrational, antidemocratic outbursts from the society's common men. Dahl does not dwell on this possibility. He seemingly conceives of *homo civicus*, the average citizen, as a man who consciously chooses to avoid politics and to devote himself to the pleasures and problems of his job and family:

> Typically, as a source of direct gratifications political activity will appear to *homo civicus* as less attractive than a host of other activities; and, as a strategy to achieve his gratifications indirectly political action will seem considerably less efficient than working at his job, earning more money, taking out insurance, joining a club, planning a vacation, moving to another neighborhood or city, or coping with an uncertain future in manifold other ways.[35]

Lipset, on the other hand, seems much more concerned with the danger that the common man might suddenly enter the political system, smash-

---

[34]For a study of several important factors affecting the degree of participation in American politics see: E. E. Schattschneider, *The Semi-Sovereign People* (New York, 1960), especially chs. 5 and 6.

[35]Dahl, *Who Governs?*, p. 224.

ing democratic institutions in the process, as part of an irrational, authoritarian political force. He sees "profoundly anti-democratic tendencies in lower class groups,"[36] and he has been frequently concerned in his work with Hitler, McCarthy and other demagogic leaders who have led anti-democratic mass movements.

Although there are obviously some important differences of opinion and emphasis concerning the political capacities of average citizens and the relative security of democratic institutions, the elitist theorists agree on the crucial importance of leadership in insuring both the safety and viability of representative government. This set of basic assumptions serves as a foundation for their explanation of change and innovation in American politics, a process in which they feel creative leadership plays the central role.

Running throughout the work of these writers is a vision of the "professional" politician as hero, much as he is pictured in Max Weber's essay, "Politics as a Vocation." Dahl's Mayor Lee, Edward Banfield's Mayor Daley, Richard Neustadt's ideal occupant of the White House all possess great skill and drive, and are engaged in the delicate art of persuasion and coalition building. They are actively moving the society forward toward their own goals, according to their own special vision. All of them possess the pre-eminent qualities of Weber's ideal-type politician: "passion, a feeling of responsibility, and a sense of proportion."[37] As in Schumpeter's analysis of capitalism, the primary source of change and innovation in the political system is the "political entrepreneur"; only such a leader can break through the inherent conservatism of organizations and shake the masses from their habitual passivity.

It is obvious that political leaders (especially chief executives) have played a very important role in American politics, but it is also clear that the American system's large degree of internal bargaining, the lack of many strong hierarchical controls and its numerous checks and balances, both constitutional and political, place powerful constraints on the behavior of political executives. American presidents, governors and mayors usually find themselves caught in a web of cross pressures which prevent them from making bold departures in policy or firmly attaching themselves to either side of a controversy. The agenda of controversy, the list of questions which are recognized by the active participants in politics as legitimate subjects of attention and concern, is very hard to change.

Just as it can be argued that the common citizens have a form of indirect influence, so it can also be argued that the top leaders of other institutions in the society, such as the business community, possess indirect influence as well. As Banfield suggests in his study of Chicago, the top business

[36]Lipset, *op. cit.*, p. 121.

[37]Hans Gerth and C. Wright Mills (eds.), *From Max Weber: Essays in Sociology* (New York, 1946), p. 115.

leaders have great potential power: "if the twenty or thirty wealthiest men in Chicago acted as one and put all their wealth into the fight, they could easily destroy or capture the machine."[38] The skillful politician, following Carl Friedrich's "rule of anticipated reactions,"[39] is unlikely to make proposals which would unite the business community against him. The aspiring politician learns early in his career, by absorbing the folklore which circulates among the politically active, which issues can and cannot be exploited successfully. It is this constellation of influences and anticipated reactions, "the peculiar mobilization of bias" in the community, fortified by a general consensus of elites, that determines the agenda of controversy.[40] The American political system, above all others, seems to be especially designed to frustrate the creative leader.

But as rigid and inflexible as it is, the political system does produce new policies; new programs and schemes are approved; even basic procedural changes are made from time to time. Of course, each major shift in public policy has a great many causes. The elitist theory of democracy looks for the principal source of innovation in the competition among rival leaders and the clever maneuvering of political entrepreneurs, which is, in its view, the most distinctive aspect of a democratic system. Because so many political scientists have worn the theoretical blinders of the elitist theory, however, we have overlooked the importance of broadly based social movements, arising from the public at large, as powerful agents of innovation and change.

The primary concerns of the elitist theorists have been the maintenance of democratic stability, the preservation of democratic procedures, and the creation of machinery which would produce efficient administration and coherent public policies. With these goals in mind, social movements (if they have been studied at all) have usually been pictured as threats to democracy, as manifestations of "political extremism." Lipset asserts that such movements typically appeal to the "disgruntled and the psychologically homeless, to the personal failures, the socially isolated, the economically insecure, the uneducated, unsophisticated, and authoritarian persons at every level of the society."[41] Movements of this kind throw the political system out of gear and disrupt the mechanisms designed to maintain due process; if the elites were overwhelmed by such forces, democracy would be destroyed. This narrow, antagonistic view of social movements stems from the elitist theorists' suspicion of the political capacities of the

---

[38]Edward Banfield, *Political Influence* (New York, 1961), p. 290

[39]Carl Friedrich, *Constitutional Government and Politics* (New York, 1939), pp. 17-18.

[40]This point is made persuasively by Peter Bachrach and Morton Baratz, "The Two Faces of Power," this REVIEW, 56 (1962), 947-952. Also see their "Decisions and Nondecisions: An Analytical Framework," this REVIEW, 57 (1963), 632-642; and Thomas J. Anton, "Power, Pluralism and Local Politics," *Administrative Quarterly*, 7 (1963), 425-457.

[41]Lipset, *op. cit.*, p. 178

common citizens,[42] their fear of instability and their failure to recognize the elements of rigidity and constraint existing in the political system. But if one holds that view and at the same time recognizes the tendency of the prevailing political system to frustrate strong leaders, it becomes difficult to explain how significant innovations in public policy, such as the social security system, the Wagner Act, the Subversive Activities Control Act of 1950, or the Civil Rights Bill of 1964, ever came about.

During the last century American society has spawned numerous social movements, some of which have made extensive demands on the political system, while others have been highly esoteric, mystical, and apolitical. These movements arise because some form of social dislocation or widespread sense of frustration exists within the society. But dissatisfaction alone is not a sufficient cause; it must be coupled with the necessary resources and the existence of potential leadership which can motivate a group to take action designed to change the offending circumstances.[43] Often such movements erupt along the margins of the political system, and they sometimes serve the purpose of encouraging political and social mobilization, of widening the boundaries of the polity.[44] Through movements such as the Negroes' drive for civil rights, or the Midwestern farmers' crusade for fair prices in the 1890's, the Ku Klux Klan, or the "radical right" movements of the 1960's, *"pre-political* people who have not yet found, or

[42]Ruth Searles and J. Allen Williams, in a study of Negro students who took part in the sit-in demonstrations, found no evidence that they were authoritarian or posed threats to democracy. "Far from being alienated, the students appear to be committed to the society and its middle class leaders": "Negro College Students' Participation in Sit-ins," *Social Forces*, 40 (1962), p. 219. For other studies of this particular social movement see: Robert Coles, "Social Struggle and Weariness," *Psychiatry*, 27 (1964), 305-315; and three articles by Fredric Solomon and Jacob Fishman; "Perspectives on Student Sit-in Movement," *American Journal of Ortho-psychiatry*, 33 (1963), 872-882; "Action and Identity Formation in First Student Sit-in Demonstration." *Journal of Social Issues*, 20 (1964), 36-45; and "Psycho-social Meaning of Nonviolence in Student Civil Rights Activities," *Psychiatry*, 27 (1964) 91-99. Also see the October, 1964 issue of *The Journal of Social Issues*, entitled "Youth and Social Action," edited by Fredric Solomon and Jacob Fishman; and Jack L. Walker, "Protest and Negotiation: A Case Study of Negro Leaders in Atlanta, Georgia," *Midwest Journal of Political Science*, 7 (1963), 99-124.

[43]Sociologists usually study social movements under the rubric of collective behavior. For general treatments see: Herbert Blumer, "Collective Behavior" in J. B. Gittler (ed.), *Review of Sociology* (New York, 1957); Rudolph Heberle, *Social Movements*, (New York, 1951); Lewis Killian, "Social Movements" in Robert Faris (ed.), *Handbook of Modern Sociology* (Chicago, 1964); Charles King, *Social Movements in the United States* (New York, 1956); Karl Lang and Gladys Lang, *Collective Dynamics* (New York, 1961); Neil Smelser, *Theory of Collective Behavior* (New York, 1963); Ralph Turner and Lewis Killian, *Collective Behavior* (Englewood Cliffs, N.J., 1957). For a brief historical sketch of some American social movements see: Thomas Greer, *American Social Reform Movements: Their Pattern Since 1865* (Englewood Cliffs, N.J., 1946).

[44]For a book which investigates social movements which have served this function among Italian peasants see: E. J. Hobsbawn, *Primitive Rebels* (Manchester, 1959). See also: Vittorio Lanternari, *The Religions of the Oppressed* (New York, 1963) for a study of the relationship of Messianic Cults and revolutionary movements on five continents; and George Rude, *The Crowd in History* (New York, 1964) for a study of popular uprisings in England and France from 1730-1848.

only begun to find, a specific language in which to express their aspirations about the world"[45] are given new orientation, confidence, knowledge, sources of information and leadership.

Social movements also serve, in Rudolf Heberle's words, as the "creators and carriers of public opinion."[46] By confronting the political authorities, or by locking themselves in peaceful—or violent [47] — conflict with some other element of the society, social movements provoke trials of strength between contending forces or ideas. Those trials of economic, political or moral strength take place in the court of public opinion and sometimes place enormous strain on democratic institutions and even the social fabric itself. But through such trials, as tumultuous as they may sometimes be, the agenda of controversy, the list of acceptable, "key" issues may be changed. In an effort to conciliate and mediate, the political leaders fashion new legislation, create unique regulatory bodies and strive to establish channels of communication and accommodation among the combatants.

Of course, members of the political elite may respond to the movement by resisting it, driving it underground or destroying it; they may try to co-opt the movement's leaders by granting them privileges or by accepting parts of its program or even by making the leaders part of its program, or part of the established elite; they may surrender to the movement, losing control of their offices in the political system in the process. The nature of the political leader's response is probably a prime determinant of the tactics the movement will adopt, the kind of leadership that arises within it, and the ideological appeals it develops. Other factors might determine the response of the leadership, such as the existence of competing social movements with conflicting demands, the resources available to the political leaders to satisfy the demands of the movement, the social status of the participants in the movement, the presence of competing sets of leaders claiming to represent the same movement, and many other elements peculiar to each particular situation. In this process social movements may be highly disruptive and some institutions may be completely destroyed; the story does not always have a happy ending. But one major consequence (function, if you will) of social movements is to break society's log jams, to pre-

---

[45]Hobsbawn, *op. cit.*, p. 2.

[46]Heberle, op. cit., pp. 417-418.

[47]American political scientists have not been sufficiently concerned with the role of violence in the governmental process. Among all the articles published in *The American Political Science Review* between 1906 and 1963, there was only one whose title contained the word "violence," only one with the word "coercive" (it concerned India), and none with the word "force." During the same period there were forty-nine articles on governmental reorganizations and twenty-four on civil service reform. See Kenneth Janda (ed.), *Cumulative Index to The American Political Science Review* (Evanston, 1964). Efforts to retrieve this situation have begun in: Harry Eckstein (ed.), *Internal War* (New York, 1964).

vent ossification in the political system, to prompt and justify major innovations in social policy and economic organization.[48]

This relationship of challenge and response between the established political system and social movements has gone without much systematic study by political scientists. Sociologists have been concerned with social movements, but they have directed most of their attention to the causes of the movements, their "natural history," and the relationship between leaders and followers within them.[49] Historians have produced many case studies of social movements but little in the way of systematic explanation.[50] This would seem to be a fruitful area for investigation by political scientists. But this research is not likely to appear unless we revise our concept of the masses as politically inert, apathetic and bound by habitual responses. We must also shift our emphasis from theories which conceive of the "social structure in terms of a functionally integrated system held in equilibrium by certain patterned and recurrent processes," to theories which place greater emphasis on the role of coercion and constraint in the political system and which concentrate on the influences within society which produce "the forces that maintain it in an unending process of change."[51] The greatest contribution of Marx to the understanding of society was his realization that internal conflict is a major source of change and innovation. One need not accept his metaphysical assumptions to appreciate this important insight.

Conclusion

In a society undergoing massive social change, fresh theoretical perspectives are essential. Political theorists are charged with the responsibility of constantly reformulating the dogmas of the past so that democratic theory remains relevant to the stormy realities of Twentieth Century American society with its sprawling urban centers, its innumerable social conflicts, and its enormous bureaucratic hierarchies.

In restating the classical theory, however, contemporary political scientists have stripped democracy of much of its radical *élan* and have diluted

---

[48]Lewis Coser has discussed the role of conflict in provoking social change in his *The Functions of Social Conflict* (Glencoe: 1956); and in his "Social Conflict and the Theory of Social Change" *British Journal of Sociology*, 9 (1957) 197-207. See also Irving Louis Horowitz, "Consensus, Conflict and Cooperation: A Sociological Inventory," *Social Forces*, 41 (1962), 177-188.

[49]For an insightful and stimulating example, see Joseph Gusfield, *Symbolic Crusade* (Urbana, 1963), which makes an excellent analysis of the causes of the Temperance movement and changes in its leadership but makes only brief mention of the movement's impact on the government and the responses of political leaders to its efforts.

[50]John Higham is somewhat of an exception of this generalization. See his *Strangers in the Land: Patterns of American Nativism 1860-1925* (New York, 1963). Also see his: "Another Look at Nativism," *Catholic Historical Review*, 44 (1958), 147-158; and his "The Cult of the 'American Consensus': Homogenizing Our History." *Commentary* (February, 1959) p. 159.

[51]Ralf Dahrendorf, *Class and Class Conflict in Industrial Society* (Stanford, 1959), p. 159.

its utopian vision, thus rendering it inadequate as a guide to the future. The elitist theorists generally accept the prevailing distribution of status in the society (with exceptions usually made for the American Negro), and find it "not only compatible with political freedom but even . . . a condition of it."[52] They place great emphasis on the limitations of the average citizen and are suspicious of schemes which might encourage greater participation in public affairs. Accordingly, they put their trust in the wisdom and energy of an active, responsible elite.

Besides these normative shortcomings the elitist theory has served as an inadequate guide to empirical research, providing an unconvincing explanation of widespread political apathy in American society and leading political scientists to ignore manifestations of discontent not directly related to the political system. Few studies have been conducted of the use of force, or informal, illegitimate coercion in the American political system, and little attention has been directed to the great social movements which have marked American society in the last one hundred years.

If political science is to be relevant to society's pressing needs and urgent problems, professional students of politics must broaden their perspectives and become aware of new problems which are in need of scientific investigation. They must examine the norms that guide their efforts and guard against the danger of uncritically accepting the values of the going system in the name of scientific objectivity. Political scientists must strive for heightened awareness and self-knowledge; they must avoid rigid presumptions which diminish their vision, destroy their capacities for criticism, and blind them to some of the most significant social and political developments of our time.

DISCUSSION
Daniel McCool

Traditional democratic theory is predicated on the belief that power flows from the people to political leaders. Accordingly, an informed populace can affect—indeed determine—government decisions through a variety of participatory actions. Pluralist theory modified this simple notion of government-by-the-people, and elite theory stood it on its head.

Truman's goal was not to dismiss democratic theory, but to provide a realistic portrayal of how power was wielded in the democratic process. The key components of group theory—the multiplicity of access points, independent centers of power, and overlapping membership—convey a sense that a tiny oligarchy could never control policy, because power is dispersed among innumerable semiautonomous collective entities. Going even fur-

---

[52]Sabine, "The Two Democratic Traditions," *op. cit.*, p. 459.

ther, his ideas about the "rules of the game," and potential groups,[1] assume that everyone has the option of participating if their interests are "disturbed," and those that do participate must do so within a framework of broadly supported democratic norms. Truman gave voice to the silent majority long before Richard Nixon came on the scene.

Truman also began what later became *subsystem theory* (see Section 5). In summarizing the interplay of groups in the policy-making process, he wrote: "The total pattern of government over a period of time thus presents a protean complex of crisscrossing relationships that change in strength and direction with alterations in the power and standing of interests, organized and unorganized" (1951, 508). Compare this to the discussion of "issue networks" and "advocacy coalitions" in Section 5.[2]

Robert Dahl, like Truman, strove to create a theory that emphasized realism rather than ideology or philosophy. His concept of pluralism placed a greater emphasis on the role of governmental structure, which provided the framework for a system of government based on dispersed, limited sovereignty among government and non-government entities. In essence, Dahl's pluralism was the ultimate articulation of a system of checks and balances; no single interest or institution could dominate governing, and if any interest tried to do so, a vast panoply of competing interests would rise to meet the challenge. This system was characterized by multiple veto points, as well as multiple access points.

Dahl's first comprehensive work on the pluralist concept *Who Governs?* (1961), examined the political structure of New Haven, Connecticut. It was written in part as a response to the charge from elite theorists, such as C. Wright Mills, that government was controlled by a tiny elite. Contrary to that notion, Dahl argued that ". . . the relationship between leaders and citizens in a pluralistic democracy is frequently reciprocal: leaders influence the decisions of constituents, but the decisions of leaders are also determined in part by what they think are, will be, or have been the preferences of their constituents" (1961, 89–90). *Who Governs?* concluded that "New Haven, like most pluralistic democracies. . . has a built-in, self-operating limitation on the influence of all participants, including the [political] professionals" (1961, 305).

---

[1]As Walker notes, Truman later revised his notion of potential groups when he became convinced that the common man often refuses to organize, even when his direct interests are at stake; he had overestimated the willingness of the masses to initiate their own defensive organizations (Truman 1959).

[2]Another interesting comparison is with Bentley, who hinted at the outlines of a theory of subsystem politics: "In the United States we certainly find executive, legislative, and judicial agencies. They are set up with walls built between them, each taking up its work at a certain stage, using certain methods, and continuing its work to a certain further stage, and each entering into formal relations with the others only at specified points. Actually the interactions occur at many presumably forbidden points because the same groups of pressures are working through all of them and seeking always to find their smoothest courses, wherever they may flow" (Bentley 1908, 325).

Six years later Dahl wrote *Pluralist Democracy in the United States,* which was an attempt to refine the concept of pluralism in light of much criticism from both elite theorists and proponents of traditional democratic theory such as Jack Walker. Dahl's basic premise was that pluralist processes of government, which he labeled *polyarchy,* were a necessary and even healthy adaptation to the increased scope of governing that accompanied the evolution from small city-states to the nation-state. Thus polyarchy applied the democratic creed to the greatest extent practicable in a large, diverse country.

Over the years Dahl continued to develop his idea of polyarchy. In a subsequent book he defined it as

> a kind of regime for governing nation-states in which power and authority over public matters are distributed among a plurality of organizations and associations that are relatively autonomous in relation to one another and in many cases in relation to the government of the state as well. These relatively autonomous units include not only organizations that are, legally and sometimes constitutionally, components of the government of the state but also organizations that legally are. . ."private:" that is legally, and to an important extent realistically, they are independent, or mainly independent, of the state. (1986, 242)

In recent years Dahl has argued that our government has evolved even further, from polyarchy I, to polyarchy II, because of the expanded influence of public policy specialists. Dahl fears these specialists could subvert the basic democratic aspects of pluralism through "a kind of quasi guardianship of the policy elites" (1989, 335). Dahl's choice of words does not mean he has acceded to elite theory. On the contrary, he claims that policy specialists are much too diverse in purpose and background to ever constitute a ruling elite class. Nevertheless, he fears the power of these specialists, who are often referred to in the popular press these days as "policy wonks." Dahl warns:

> I am inclined to think that the long-run prospects for democracy are more seriously endangered by inequalities in resources, strategic positions, and bargaining strength that are derived not from wealth or economic position [as the elite theorists argued] but from special knowledge. Perhaps it is not altogether surprising that the danger I see springs from a source that provided Plato with his hopes for guardianship: intellectuals. (1989, 333)

This fear of government by policy analysts has been an important theme in the public policy literature for the last decade. Often labeled *technocracy,* the assumption is that governing is so complex and technical that only those with highly specialized technical expertise can affect policy (see Fischer 1990). This gives rise to fears of a "new elitism." On the other hand, Hank Jenkins-Smith argues convincingly that policy analysts are often ignored and are seldom in a position to dominate policy making (Jenkins-Smith 1990).

The selection from G. David Garson's book *Group Theories of Politics* provides a succinct summary of the critiques of pluralism and group theory and concludes in essence that these concepts have been fully discredited. This is a conclusion many do not share, including William Kelso, who ends his book with a normative plea: "The pluralistic interplay of groups may not be self-sustaining, but if it is properly regulated, it may be far superior to the alternatives from which we have to choose" (1978, 270). Despite the disagreement over its merits, pluralism still plays a dominant role in much political science. Christopher Ham and Michael Hill write that "The importance of pluralist theory is demonstrated by the fact that, implicitly if not always explicitly, its assumptions and arguments now pervade much Anglo-American writing and research. . . " (1984, 27). Jenkins concludes that the influence of pluralism "has been considerable and pervasive" (1978, 109). For example, in Section 5 we will read about the transformation of rigid, closed iron triangles into open, flexible issue networks; to many students of interest group politics, this is evidence of pluralism at work, making government more responsive to a wider variety of interests. In the social sciences theories are like old soldiers—they never die, they just fade from view. But unlike old soldiers, they have a way of reincarnating in revised form. Such is the story of pluralism.[3]

Nevertheless, telling criticisms of the pluralist interpretation exist. Perhaps the most common objection concerns the obvious inequalities among interest groups (see Schattschneider 1960; Connolly 1969). The outcome of competition among interests in conflict is often determined by relative financial resources; this dramatically limits the ability of some elements of society to effectively participate. Groups representing the poor and the disenfranchised may be heard, but still have little substantive impact on policy, because they are out-classed by well-financed, entrenched professional lobbies. Kelso tacitly acknowledges this in his discussion of what he calls corporate pluralism. Manley argues that the failure of pluralist theory to consider the relationship between political equality and economic inequality invalidates the theory and distorts the reality of modern politics (1983). The gross inequalities among interest groups has been documented in literally dozens of studies (Dunleavy 1992, 13–44). A common finding is that particular policy arenas are dominated by one or two powerful interests, which work to exclude others—a theme we will cover in Section 4 "Policy Typologies" and Section 5 "Policy Subsystems. "

Another problem with pluralism concerns the relatively small number of people who are actively involved in interest groups. Smaller still is the number of people who are interest group leaders, who determine the policy preferences of the group. Probably no more than one percent of the Ameri-

[3]The same can be said for institutionalism, the alleged "straw man" of the group theorists. It is now back in vogue as the "new institutionalism," with a healthy dose of pluralist thinking injected into it. See Moe (1990); March and Olsen (1984).

can populace fits that description. What is the difference between a group leader and an elite? Is this simply a problem of semantics? Elite theory emphasizes the cohesiveness of that coterie of people, whereas pluralism does not. But group leaders certainly have a common stake in the system. Pluralism assumes group leaders are in power. Thus they have the most to lose from dramatic challenges to the system; at some point this commitment to preserve their own power must surely weld them together with some degree of cohesiveness. In short the interest groups that speak on our behalf may be controlled by elites that have a strong collective incentive to keep it that way.

Arguments concerning group inequality and the elite nature of group leaders are essentially empirical critiques of pluralism. In other words pluralist theory may lack validity, or at least will omit critically important factors. But pluralist theory has also been criticized as a normative failure. Critics have argued that it represents an apology, in the guise of science, for an unfair system that purports to be democratic but in reality is dominated by a few powerful special interests. Trudi Miller writes that pluralist theory "induces political professionals—on the grounds of science—to accept what, from the traditional liberal [meaning democratic] perspective, is corruption" (1989, 511). This is quite similar to Jack Walker's critique of elitism, attacking it because it fails to provide a better "guide to the future" (1966, 295). In essence, Walker argued that pluralism was no better than elitism—normatively speaking—because both theories failed to stress the significance of social movements and other forms of popular political input. Similarly Gus deZerega claims both pluralism and elitism lack a sound theoretical base, and this creates normative problems: "Elitists have a theoretical framework, albeit a bad one, but pluralists tend to have very little framework at all. This theoretical lack makes pluralist arguments sometimes appear simply as defenses of the status quo" (1991, 371).

Both pluralist and elite theory have provoked a host of detractors, but elite theory has the advantage of a long tradition of thought. As Putnam points out in *The Comparative Study of Political Elites,* the European trilogy of Robert Michels, Vilfredo Pareto, and Gastano Mosca provided a sophisticated conceptualization of the simple idea that, when people get together, a few tend to lead and the rest tend to follow. At its most basic formulation elite theory is difficult to refute. Indeed it is almost tautological if we adopt the definition offered by Putnam: "Some people have more political power than others; they are the political elite" (1976, 5). The real question, of course, is to what extent they have more power, and why. Elite theorists, both classical and modern, have grappled with this. There are two relevant dimensions.

First, all elite theorists conceive of a stratification, but it is nearly always more complicated than a simple dichotomy between the few and the many. Putnam's schematic of political stratification includes six layers; the conceptual difficulty lies in determining the relationship *between* these strat-ifications, especially the point at which a nonelite layer adjoins the elite layer. Can people from one strata enter a higher strata? Under what condi-tions does this elevation take place?

Putnam cites Meisel's "three Cs" (consciousness, coherence, and con-spiracy), but another C could be added to the list: *co-optation,* meaning re-cruits must assume the values of the elite class as a prerequisite of entry. An important element in classical elitism is the issue of recruitment; that is, how one becomes an elite: "The strength of the elite is in many respects in-dicated by its ability to lay down the terms for admission to the circle of the politically influential, terms which may include conformity to standards of wealth, social background, educational attainment and commitment to the elite's interests and ideology" (Parry 1969, 31–32). If recruits are not co-opted, then the other three C's are impossible to attain, and the elite "class" loses it unity. How can we prove that co-optation has occurred? Do those in power really share a consensus on values? Do Jesse Helms and Ted Kennedy conform to the same standards of "wealth, social background, and educational attainment"?

A second issue concerns the extent to which elites actually control pol-icy making. There is considerable empirical evidence to indicate that a small percentage of the population wields a great deal of influence in politi-cal matters (see Dye 1986). However, this may simply indicate that a few people possess disproportionate influence, which is qualitatively different from ruling the country. For example, if three percent of the population wields forty percent of the power, but the other 97 percent wields sixty per-cent (an untestable proposition), then who rules?

These questions do not refute elite theory; they merely point out how difficult it is to validate it. Like pluralism, elite theory attempts to explain the most basic relationships between society and government. It is often the case that the theories that attempt to explain the most (that is, the most powerful theories) are also the most difficult to validate.

Perhaps the most intriguing idea developed by elite theorists is what Thomas Dye and Harmon Ziegler call the *irony of democracy* (1987). They cite evidence that the masses do not understand, and are not committed to, democratic norms; only those in power realize the necessity of adhering to principles such as rule by law, due process, tolerance of the opposition, and guaranteed rights of the minority. The irony is that, if the masses began to participate in government, they would soon destroy its democratic charac-ter. This again points to the importance of cooptation; if a member of a lower strata moves into a higher one, the system must impose democratic values upon them. This notion was particularly troublesome to Walker (1966, 287).

Throughout the debate between elite and pluralist theorists, there was an implicit assumption that the two theories were mutually exclusive. But in recent years scholars have begun investigating ways to combine pluralist and elitist thought. For example, Dunleavy (1981), studying housing policy in Great Britain, found that a small elite controlled policy, but it lacked the cohesiveness and consciousness predicted by elite theory. He proposed a "new pluralist theory," not unlike polyarchy II, to explain political power in postindustrial society. Garson's analysis also concluded with a synthesis: "American politics are neither the marketplace of group theory nor the conspiracy of simple elite theories. If America is elitist, it is elitist in a pluralistic way, or, if pluralist, then pluralist in a way that benefits an elite. . . " (1978, 207).

The long debate between pluralist and elite theorists offers some lessons regarding scientific method. The work of these theorists led to a great deal of further research, an exchange of ideas, and multiple efforts to critique, refine, and adapt various theoretical perspectives. This kind of exchange and development is an integral part of the scientific method, but there are dangers along the way. Theory exists only in the mind as a set of ideas; the written record can only serve as an approximation of that set of ideas. This is especially true of social science theory, which often lacks the mathematical precision of theory in the physical sciences. Thus there is always a high potential for miscommunication, misinterpretation, and abuse. Many theorists claim their work has been misinterpreted by critics, and in some cases these are legitimate complaints. But the alleged misinterpretation may be a result of poorly developed theory rather than a willful, malicious misrepresentation. In the debate over pluralism there have been many charges of misinterpretation. Dahl complained:

> . . . the concept [of pluralism] took on a life of its own. "Pluralist theory" came to designate a strange melange of ideas. In fact, a good deal of the "theory" consisted of interpretations by hostile critics who sometimes constructed a compound of straw men and inferences from the work of assorted writers who by no means held the same views. Frequently the result was a "theory" that probably no competent political theorist—pluralist or not—would find plausible (1986, 235).[4]

The reader should be aware that not all characterizations of theory are faithful reproductions; there is sometimes a tendency to critique caricatures rather than the real thing. This makes the debunking process easier, but ill serves the scientific process of cumulative theory building.

All of the theorists discussed in this section recognized the importance of institutions. Earl Latham, an early group theorist, conceived of government as a kind of neutral referee. Dahl and the pluralists abandoned this notion and considered government institutions as just another part of the

---

[4]Dahl, in his rejoinder that accompanied Walker's article in the *American Political Science Review*, complained that Walker did this in characterizing a vast and diverse set of authors as proponents of a single theory called the elitist theory of democracy (Dahl 1966, 297–98).

group milieu, each with its own set of preferences and biases. Implicit in these concepts is the realization that the power of institutions comes from controlling process, both formal and informal. Indeed Anderson defines institutions in terms of process: "An institution is a set of regularized patterns of human behavior. . . which we often call rules or structures. . . " (1990, 31). Whoever controls the structure of decision making, be it group leaders, elites, or The People, has a power advantage. This led policy scholars to develop process models that attempt to explain the steps, the stages, the reasoning, and the linkages of the policy-making process. These models are the subject of the next section.

REFERENCES

ANDERSON, JAMES (1990). *Public Policy Making.* Boston: Houghton Mifflin.

BENTLEY, ARTHUR (1908). *The Process of Government: A Study of Social Pressures.* Evanston, IL: The Principia Press of Illinois (new edition published in 1935).

CONNOLLY, WILLIAM, ed. (1969). *The Bias of Pluralism.* New York: Atherton Press.

DAHL, ROBERT (1961). *Who Governs?* New Haven: Yale University Press.

_____ (1966). "Further Reflections on the 'Elitist Theory of Democracy'." *American Political Science Review* 60 (June): 285–305.

_____ (1967). *Pluralist Democracy in the United States.* Chicago: Rand McNally.

_____ (1986). *Democracy, Liberty, and Equality.* Oslo: Norwegian University Press.

_____ (1989). *Democracy and Its Critics.* New Haven: Yale University Press.

deZEREGA, GUS (1991). "Elites and Democratic Theory: Insights from the Self-Organizing Model." *The Review of Politics* 53 (Spring): 340–72.

DUNLEAVY, PATRICK (1981). *The Politics of Mass Housing in Britain, 1945–1975.* Oxford: Clarendon Press.

_____ (1992). *Democracy, Bureaucracy, and Public Choice.* Englewood Cliffs, NJ: Prentice-Hall.

DYE, THOMAS (1986). *Who's Running America? The Conservative Years.* Englewood, NJ: Prentice-Hall.

DYE, THOMAS, AND HARMON ZEIGLER (1987). *The Irony of Democracy,* 7th. ed. Monterey, CA: Brooks/Cole.

FISCHER, FRANK (1990). *Technocracy and the Politics of Expertise.* Newbury Park, CA: Sage Publications.

GARSON, G. DAVID (1978). *Group Theories of Politics.* Beverly Hills: Sage Publications.

JENKINS, W. I. (1978). *Policy Analysis: A Political and Organizational Perspective*. London: Martin Robertson.

JENKINS-SMITH, HANK (1990). *Democratic Politics and Policy Analysis*. Pacific Grove, CA: Brooks/Cole.

MANLEY, JOHN (1983). "Neo-Pluralism: A Class Analysis of Pluralism I and Pluralism II." *American Political Science Review* 77 (June): 268–83.

MARCH, JAMES, AND JOHAN OLSEN (1984). "The New Institutionalism: Organizational Factors in Political Life." *American Political Science Review* 78 (Sept.): 734–49.

MILLER, TRUDI (1989). "The Operation of Democratic Institutions." *Public Administration Review* (Nov.): 511–21.

MOE, TERRY (1990). "Political Institutions: The Neglected Side of the Story." *Journal Of Law, Economics and Organization* 6 (Special issue): 213–53.

PARRY, GERAINT (1969). *Political Elites*. New York: Praeger.

SCHATTSCHNEIDER, E. E. (1960). *The Semi-Sovereign People*. New York: Holt, Rinehart, and Winston.

TRUMAN, DAVID (1959). "The American System in Crisis." *Political Science Quarterly* 74 (Dec.): 481–97.

WALKER, JACK (1966). "A Critique of the Elitist Theory of Democracy." *American Political Science Review* 60 (June): 285–95.

3

The Process of Public Policy Making

INTRODUCTION

Much of the research on public policy has focused on its output, that is, the end result of the policy-making process. But policy scholars have always been cognizant of the relationship between process and product. One way to improve our understanding of public policy is to improve our understanding of the processes that create policy.

There is no definitive, discrete category of research called "policy process studies." There is, however, a large and diverse scholarship that examines the enormous variety of policy processes. Some studies focus on decision-making behavior; others emphasize linear or spatial relationships; and still others focus on structures such as institutions, regulations, and laws.

In a sense, process studies grew out of the institutional approach that dominated political science until about midcentury. Institutional studies described how policy was made: the actors, rules, procedures, and government entities that comprise the policy-making process. Quite often these researchers concentrated on the "bias" of the institution, or in other words, how certain design features of the institution tended to predetermine the outcome of policy decisions. Their concept of an institution was fairly narrow: It was a formal structure of government, such as congress, the courts, or the presidency. Early process studies also examined institutions, but focused on activities and behaviors rather than structural entities.

More recently our concept of what constitutes an "institution" has expanded dramatically. A "new institutionalism" has been identified that includes "rules of behavior, norms, roles, physical arrangements, buildings, and archives. . . " [March and Olsen 1984, 741. Also see: Powell and DiMaggio, 1991; Ferris and Tang, 1993]. This expanded definition has clearly moved beyond formal structures and erased the line between the study of institutions and the study of process. Our concept of process has also expanded, and today the study of policy process encompasses a vast array of political phenomena. The selections presented in this section are only a sampling of that disparate literature, but they represent some of the more important themes in recent scholarship on the policy process.

The first selection is by David Easton (1965*a*), whose name is synonymous with systems theory. Much of the thinking regarding the systems approach grew out of the technical specialty of systems analysis developed by the military. Although this approach has lost some of its popularity in recent years, it has had a long-term impact on our concepts of how the policy-making process works, and "has occupied the time and energy of a number of political scientists" (Hines 1982, 59). The book excerpted here is the second in a trilogy, which presented Easton's ideas on how to build a "general political theory" (1957, 383). He defined a political system as consisting of all "interactions through which values are authoritatively allocated for a society" (1965*b*, 21), and depicted it as "a vast and perpetual conversion process. It takes in demands and support as they are shaped in the environment and produces something out of them called *outputs*" (1965*b*, 29). Easton's work was important because it focused on the relationships *between* various elements in the system, including the relationship between the political system and its external environment.

A dramatically different conceptualization of the policy-making process is presented in the second selection. Relying upon the work of Downs (1957), Arrow (1951), and others, James Buchanan and Gordon Tullock began analyzing the political system by applying precepts of market economics. In an influential book *The Calculus of Consent* (1962)[1] they helped develop a theoretical framework that is known as "public choice" theory,[2] which is defined as "the application of economic theory to non-market decision processes" (Paldam 1993, 178). William Riker, a well-known proponent

---

[1]The full title is: *The Calculus of Consent: Logical Foundations of Constitutional Democracy*. However, in the text they explain that a more accurate title would be "An Economic (but Non-Marxian) Theory of Political Constitutions" (p. 161). The "calculus" is, of course, the individual's determination of what constitutes "more" and "less." In addition to this book two other seminal works on public choice should be cited: Anthony Downs' *An Economic Theory of Democracy* (1959), and William Riker's *Theory of Political Coalitions* (1962).

[2]Public choice theory is also known as *collective choice* (the term used by Buchanan and Tullock), and *rational choice* theory.

of public choice theory, describes it as a "combination of economics and political science for the practical study of public issues" (Riker 1988, 252).

Buchanan and Tullock explicitly rejected Easton's notion of an organic system with some kind of "life" of its own. Rather, they argued that analysis should focus on the individual and the political choices he or she makes. To them, there is no such thing as "the public interest," but only the interests of individuals; they criticized systemic concepts of government for their "grail-like search for some 'public interest' apart from, and independent of, the separate interests of the individual. . . " (Buchanan and Tullock 1962, 12). But when they spoke of "individuals," they did not necessarily mean a single person, but rather any autonomous entity that participates in the political marketplace as a "buyer" or "seller" or both. Buchanan and Tullock acknowledged a debt to group theory, and noted: "Throughout our analysis the word 'group' could be substituted for the 'individual' without significantly affecting the result. In this way a group calculus may be developed" (p. 9).

Public choice theory assumes that every individual is "an egoistic, rational, utility maximizer" (Mueller 1979, 1). In other words, "all behavior is self-interested" (Mitchell 1983*a*, 349). This idea is coupled with the assumption that individuals make "rational" decisions in the political system the same way they make decisions in the marketplace: ". . . individuals will, on the average, choose 'more' rather than 'less' when confronted with the opportunity for choice in a political process, with 'more' and 'less' being defined in terms of measurable economic position" (Buchanan and Tullock 1962, 29).

Riker puts the two basic assumptions of public choice in the following terms:

1. Actors are able to order their alternative goals, values, tastes, and strategies. This means that the relation of preferences and indifference among the alternatives is transitive . . . [they can be ranked in linear fashion].
2. Actors choose from available alternatives so as to maximize their satisfaction (Riker 1990, 172).

Thus individuals make political decisions by calculating the decision's relative costs and benefits to them, and then selecting the policy option that maximizes their benefits with the least cost (see McLean 1987). This concept of *individual utility maximization* differs dramatically from what Buchanan and Tullock termed the *power maximizer* approach developed by Dahl and the pluralists. It also conjures up a starkly negative image of government bureaucrats as budget maximizers and politicians as vote maximizers (Niskanen, 1971).

Much early public choice theory was based on the *demand* model, which focused on government as a provider to consumers—a notion not inimical to pluralist assumptions. More recent public choice theorists charge that government is inherently incapable of fulfilling this function because of an innate tendency to accede to too many demands and thus overspend. In the selection reprinted here one of those critics, William Mitchell, explains a *supply* model of public choice that assumes government politicians and bureaucrats act as monopolists (1983*b*). Like all contemporary public choice theorists, he believes government is a poor medium by which to make rational decisions; As Riker states, the "main function of the [governing] institution is to stay out of the way" (Riker 1988, 251). Public choice theorists assume that markets, based on private property rights, are the best way to determine the value of goods and services in an exchange. This assumption is much in evidence in Mitchell's piece.

Although much of public choice theory is an attempt to empirically analyze political phenomena, it is infused with a potent normative dimension. Public choice has a strong libertarian bent and is closely associated with orthodox conservative ideology (Dunleavy 1992, 4). Like the pluralist and democratic theorists in Section 2, public choice theorists have a vision of the government ideal. It is the reader's task to discern empirical theory from wishful thinking.

One of the reasons public choice theorists are antigovernment is because they view it as incapable of making "rational" decisions. Rather, they claim, government just stumbles onward, responding to the demand of the moment. According to the public choice perspective this prevents government from being rational and efficient. But to another set of theorists, who have developed a theory of "disjointed incrementalism," such an approach to policy making is preferable to the so-called rational-comprehensive decision-making model.[3]

The basic notion of disjointed incrementalism can be seen in the title of a well known article by Charles Lindblom, "The Science of Muddling Through" (1959). This article is included in this book because it spawned an entire literature on the subject, including many critiques, revisions, and reformulations, and is "one of the most widely cited ideas in the policy sciences" (Weiss and Woodhouse 1992, 255). At its most basic, incrementalism is simply "political change by small steps" (Lindblom 1979, 517).

Incrementalist theory posits that the *rational–comprehensive model* (Lindbolm's term) is an unrealistic notion of what actually occurs in policy making (in other words, it lacks validity). Lindblom set out to develop a re-

---

[3]Charles Lindblom offers a synopsis of the rational-comprehensive model in his 1979 article (p. 525):

a. Identify and organize in some coherent relation the goal and side values pertinent to the policy choice to be made.
b. Identify all important policy alternatives that might realize the values.
c. Analyze all important possible consequences of each of the considered alternative policies.
d. Choose that policy the consequences of which best match the values of Step a.

alistic model of the "successive limited comparisons" (1959, 81) actually used by policy makers. In contrast to the rational–comprehensive model, incrementalists argue that policy makers proceed in a slow, cautious manner, somewhat akin to tiptoeing into a darkened room full of toe-stubbing obstacles. Lacking adequate information, they experiment with change in modest increments, adjusting their actions as they proceed. This concept has been applied to general policy making as well as public administration and public budgeting. Incrementalism offers some practical advantages over the rational–comprehensive model: "It is much less demanding than the rational method, requiring neither comprehensive information nor agreement among policy makers on objectives. Consequently, incrementalism permits action where the rational ideal is paralyzed. . . " (Hayes 1992, 16).

All of the theories in this section present a linear concept of the process of policy making: One act leads to another in a causal chain of decisions, outcomes, and responses. One way to analyze this chain is to break it down into its constituent links and then describe each link and how it differs from the others. Numerous policy scholars have used this approach by devising a model of the various stages of the policy-making process. There are innumerable variations to this "stages model," but all share the idea that we can improve our understanding of the policy-making process by categorizing and describing its component parts.

The basic idea of the stages concept grew out of attempts to analyze discrete decisions. Harold Lasswell (1956), ever the innovator, produced an early version of a stages model for decision making that is quite similar to subsequent models developed for general policy making. He identified the following seven "functional" stages:

1. Collection of information regarding the problem
2. Formulation of various solutions to the problem
3. Prescription of a preferred alternative
4. *Invocation*, or provisional enforcement of the new policy
5. Actual implementation of the policy
6. Appraisal and monitoring of the impact of the policy
7. Termination, renewal, or revision of the policy.

The stages model is quite popular and often used as an organizing scheme for policy textbooks, which typically devote a chapter to each stage in the policy-making process. The selection by Randall Ripley included in this book is a typical but particularly adroit application of a stages framework. He notes carefully both the advantages and disadvantages of using such a scheme.

Even though all of the models presented in this section deal with the process of making policy, they differ in significant ways. Before you start reading, think about the goal of each theory; that is, what are they attempting to understand? Policy making is an extraordinarily complex process, so there is much to describe, categorize, model, and ultimately, explain. The four concepts that follow examine the policy-making process in a unique way; each attempts to explain a particular aspect of the process.

REFERENCES

ARROW, KENNETH (1951). *Social Choice and Individual Values.* New York: John Wiley.

BUCHANAN, JAMES, and GORDON TULLOCK (1962). *The Calculus of Consent.* Ann Arbor: The University of Michigan Press.

DOWNS, ANTHONY (1957). *An Economic Theory of Democracy.* New York: Harper and Row.

DUNLEAVY, PATRICK (1992). *Democracy, Bureaucracy, and Public Choice.* Englewood Cliffs, NJ: Prentice Hall.

EASTON, DAVID (1953). *The Political System.* University of Chicago Press.

_____(1957). "An Approach to the Analysis of Political Systems." *World Politics* (April): 383–400.

_____ (1965a). *A Framework for Political Analysis.* New York: Prentice-Hall.

_____ (1965b). *A Systems Analysis of Political Life.* University of Chicago Press.

FERRIS, JAMES, and SHUI-YAN TANG (1993). "The New Institutionalism and Public Administration: An Overview." *Journal of Public Administration Research and Theory* 3 (Jan.): 4–10, and accompanying articles.

HAYES, MICHAEL (1992). *Incrementalism and Public Policy.* New York: Longman.

HINES, SAMUEL JR. (1982). "Is Synthesis Philosophically Possible? The Paradigm Problem in the Philosophy of Social Science." In *The Paradigm Problem in Political Science*, pp. 25–64. Edited by William Bluhm. Durham: Carolina Academic Press.

LASSWELL, HAROLD (1956). *The Decision Process: Seven Categories of Functional Analysis.* College Park: University of Maryland.

LINDBLOM, CHARLES (1959). "The Science of Muddling Through." *Public Administration Review* 19 (Spring): 79–88.

_____ (1979). "Still Muddling, Not Yet Through." *Public Administration Review* 39 (Nov./Dec.): 517–26.

MARCH, JAMES, and JOHAN OLSEN (1984). "The New Institutionalism: Organizational Factors in Political Life." *American Political Science Review* 78 (Sept.): 734–49.

McLEAN, IAIN (1987). *Public Choice: An Introduction*. Oxford, United Kingdom: Basil Blackwell.

MITCHELL, WILLIAM (1983*a*). "Efficiency, Responsibility, and Democratic Politics." In *Liberal Democracy*, pp. 343–73. Edited by J. Roland Pennock and John Chapman. New York: New York University Press.

_____. (1983*b*). "Fiscal Behavior of the Modern Democratic State: Public Choice Perspectives and Contributions." In *Political Economy: Recent Views*. pp. 69–114. Edited by Larry Wade. Boston: Kluwer-Nijhoff Publishing.

NISKANEN, WILLIAM (1971). *Bureaucracy and Representative Government*. Chicago: Aldine-Atherton.

PALDAM, MARTIN (1993). "Public Choice: More of a Branch or More of a Sect?" *Public Choice* 77 (1993): 177–84.

POWELL, WALTER, and PAUL DiMAGGIO (1991). *The New Institutionalism in Organizational Analysis*. University of Chicago Press.

RIKER, WILLIAM (1962). *The Theory of Political Coalitions*. New Haven: Yale University Press.

_____ (1988). "The Place of Political Science in Public Choice." *Public Choice* 57 (2): 247–57.

WEISS, ANDREW, and EDWARD WOODHOUSE (1992). "Reframing Incrementalism: A Constructive Response to the Critics." *Policy Sciences* 25 (no. 3): 255–73.

THE POLITICAL SYSTEM UNDER STRESS
David Easton*

How are we to detect the way in which disturbances affect the functioning of a system? Political research has tended to ignore this matter or to assume that there is no special problem in linking up events in the environment with the structures and processes within a political system. What may normally be taken for granted, we shall find rewarding to consider problematic. Indeed, we shall discover that the very method that we find useful for tracing the impact of disturbances upon a political system will also provide us with vital and theoretically manageable indicators of stress. In this chap-

*David Easton, *A Framework for Political Analysis*. Chicago, IL: The University of Chicago Press, 1965 (pp. 103-117). Used by permission

ter I shall examine concepts that will help us to reveal and analyze the precise way in which events and conditions in the environment are transmitted to the political system as potential sources of stress.

The Communication of Disturbances To The Political System

Environmental Disturbances Due to Change   I shall begin in a relatively simple way. We are trying to understand how any political system manages to persist. We assume that it is subject to influences of many kinds coming to it from the environment or from things that happen within a political system. These have already been designated as disturbances. It is one thing to recognize generally that a system may be subject to such influences; it is quite another to devise categories of analysis that will enable us to handle the complexities involved in their transmission to the political system.

Because of the magnitude of the task, for the moment I shall neglect the disturbances occurring within a system and consider only those arising in the environment, especially the intrasocietal part. It is legitimate to do this because theoretically the problems of handling internal and external disturbances have a similar status and will therefore require no special analytic tools.

I shall set out by assuming, for illustrative purposes, that the environmental systems are themselves undergoing considerable change. How are we to link these changes to their consequences for a political system?

For example, it has become commonplace to emphasize the major problems confronting the erstwhile traditional societies resulting from their slow exposure to industrialized civilizations over earlier centuries and the suddenly increased rate and intensity of contacts today. It has led through a complex interlocking of influences to the emergence of new national units in unprecedented numbers; the relocation of populations in overcrowded, tense urban centers; the growth of an elite educated in the ideals of Western civilization; the slow downward percolation of these ideas to the broad indigenous populations; and the implanting of new scales of values associated with the disappearance of a subsistence economy and the spread of cash crops. A money economy, mobility of persons, and new ideals and goals for the individual and for the collectivities have all encouraged the importation and adoption of new technical skills. These have been found critical both to man the developing industrial complex, which may be slow in coming, and to mobilize the members of society in the pursuit of newly discovered ambitions and possibilities. Change has meant a not-so-slow awakening to the potency of organized behavior through trade unions, political parties, and tribal- or ethnic-based groups. It is compelling as well the adoption of rationally oriented bureaucratic structures for the achievement of both economic and political goals.

All of the societal changes mentioned have been or can be shown to have decisive effects on the way in which a political system operates. In many cases, with respect to the developing nations, especially in Africa, they have led to such stress on indigenous political systems that these systems have been unable to cope with the disturbances. The old tribal systems, already somewhat atrophied through varying colonial policies, are simply disappearing, if slowly. There can be little doubt that they will be fully absorbed, in most cases, into secular systems territorially based and bureaucratically organized.

If we sought to link these changes in the environment of a system—in its economy, culture, and social structure—to the destiny of the political system involved, we could continue to list the various elements in the environment that were undergoing change. We could link them on an *ad hoc* basis to the results they seemed to have for the structures and processes of the relevant political systems. Depending upon our interests, we could write volumes to show how change and development, whether in new or old nations, have led to the emergence of parties, legislatures, new patterns of political recruitment, new kinds of political motivations, special forms of interest groups, different kinds of political participation and involvement from what we are familiar with in the West, and novel methods of political leadership and control. But, in the end, we would still be faced with the need to bring some over-all order out of the welter of descriptive material and partial theories or so-called theories of interest groups, parties, personalities, or structural political change in developing areas that might have been evolved. At least, we would require an order that derives from more than the fact that the investigations deal with what all observers would agree are important transformations of political life attributable to changing environmental conditions.

We might seek to bring some theoretical order to the data by postulating functional requirements, substitutability of structures, and the comparison of varying structures for the fulfillment of constant functions. However scientifically valid such an approach may be, it has finally and conclusively been demonstrated to be at best theoretically trivial.[1] At worst, it involves the research worker in a gigantic numbers game to which there is no end: each investigator is encouraged to establish his own favored number of invariant functions and there is no satisfactory way of selecting among the alternatives.[2]

To the extent that there is any validity to the approach, it derives from the fact that it clarifies what lies at the base of all scientific research. Any in-

---

[1]K. Davis, "The Myth of Functional Analysis."
[2]I too have tried my hand at this "numbers game," as in my article "Political Anthropology" previously cited.

quiry postulates some kinds of functions, even though the exact term may not and need not be used. For this reason, the explicit identification of function does not indicate the presence of any special theory. It reflects only a scientific posture, which, of course, is to be encouraged. It also indicates a specific point of departure for theory construction. To stop there and simply compare alternative structures is to leave us waiting in suspense for the "dropping of the next shoe," namely, some kind of theory.

Even to begin to develop theoretical inquiry, it is necessary to go far beyond the relating of varying structures to functions. The order that functional analysis, at least as it has been vaguely outlined in political science, seeks to bring to comparative research, still leaves the basic problems of theory construction entirely untouched and could even do harm if unwittingly it were allowed to stand as an easy substitute for theorizing. It does not offer, at the minimum, a way of ordering data based upon a coherent and consistent body of concepts other than so-called functional terms that are and must be common to all scientific inquiry. Aside from these more general considerations, the so-called functional approach would still leave us struggling for a way of systematically working out the relationships between environmental changes and responses within political systems.

Stability as a Special Case of Change   Even if we drop the assumption that change is taking place in the environment and turn to systems whose environments have been relatively stable (an exception in the modern world but frequent in the past and undoubtedly possible episodically in the future), we continue to face the problem of how to deal economically and systematically with influences on a system that come from the environment. Whether a system is imbedded in a constantly changing environment or in a stable one, the elements of the environment continue to exert an effect upon the operations of the system. The analysis of the effect of the stable environment on a system poses the same theoretical problems as in the case of rapidly changing ones, even though the rate of change may have important additional consequences.

Although social science has recently and suddenly become enamored of problems of change and a tidal wave of theories of change threatens to engulf us, it has at least opened our eyes to the fact that any general theory, if it is even minimally adequate, must be able to handle change as easily as it does stability.[3] But the truth is that in the elaboration of the initial fundamental categories of an analysis, there is no need for special concepts to study change. Indeed to introduce them would be a sign of weakness and a disjunction in the theory, not one of strength and integration.

---

[3]I am here using the concept "change in the usual loose sense of social science. The fact is that stability is not related to change or its antithesis. For the difference between static as against changing conditions on the one hand and stability on the other, see my previously cited article "Limits of the Equilibrium Model in Social Research."

Stability is only a special example of change, not a generically different one. There is never a social situation in which the patterns of interaction are absolutely unchanging. If stability is to have any sensible meaning, it must represent a condition in which the rate of change is slow enough to create no special problems due to change. But some change there always is. Hence, the study of stable systems involves a special case of change, one where the rate is slow. Similarly, so-called change draws attention to another special case in which the rate is high enough to create special consequences of which it is necessary to take note, both analytically and empirically.

Any general theory or conceptual framework, however, should be able to take both special cases simultaneously in its stride. The vital objective at the outset is not to create a special set of categories to examine special cases but, rather, to develop a set that will be useful for identifying the major variables involved in the functioning of the system, regardless for the moment of the rate of change. Whether a system is changing imperceptibly and is, therefore, said to be stable or whether it is changing rapidly and is, therefore, characterized as unstable or in transition does not alter the nature of the fundamental variables that need to be examined. It may add to them, but it cannot detract from them. The categories presented below are designed to be of this generic character.

Environmental Disturbances Under Conditions of Stability Even under conditions of stability, where the rate of change is low, interaction between the environment and a system continues to occur. Hence, even if a special theory of change were required, it could not eliminate the similarity between change and nonchange with respect to the continuing presence of exchanges between a political system and its environment.

To illustrate, let us assume that we were interested in tracing out the consequences of social stratification upon the political structure. At one point, where a change had taken place in the social structure, we might discover that the realignment of social classes had modified the distribution of power in society in such a way that a new political elite had displaced the old one. The French and Russian Revolutions both led to consequences such as these. But once these effects on the political system had been produced, this did not lead to the elimination of the effects of the new class structure on the society, even if the new class relationship remained absolutely static. Once a change is introduced and stabilized, it may continue to exert its influence on other aspects of society. It is not like a bolt of lightning that does its damage and disappears to leave a single deposit of effects. Rather, it constitutes a continuing pressure on the political system.

The new status and class structure of the society would exert its continuing pressure on the political structure in many ways. It might affect the kind of persons recruited to political positions, the variety of issues raised for discussion, and the kind of decisions actually adopted and implemented. The absence of change implies not that politics escapes the influence of its parameters, but the stabilization of these influences. In other words, the exchanges between an environment and the political system imbedded in it continue, but without important modification.

It is vital to realize this fact. Even under the unreal state of absolutely static conditions in the environment of a political system, transactions between the two would still take place. If it were otherwise, we could never understand how a system could experience stress even if its conditions of existence did not change. If the conditions themselves have always been stressful, a system could be destroyed, not as a result of new kinds of stress occurring, but as a consequence of the failure of the members of the system at some point to handle the old and stable kinds as adequately as their predecessors.

The Linkage Variables Between System and Environment

Two things are clear from the preceding discussion. First, there is an enormous variety of influences coming from the environment of a political system capable of disturbing the way in which the system performs its tasks. Second, these influences are there whether the environment is relatively stable or fluctuating wildly. Environmental change which draws so much attention today, and appropriately so, does not create entirely new theoretical problems in the construction of a general structure of analysis. It simply aggravates an analytic problem that is already present, namely: How are we to systematize our understanding of the way in which the disturbances or influences from the environment are transferred to a political system? Do we have to treat each change or disturbance as a particular or general type, as the case may be, and simply work out its specific effects in each instance? If so, because of the obviously enormous variety of influences at work, the problems for systematic analysis are virtually insurmountable. But if we can discover a way of generalizing our method for handling the impact of the environment on a system, there would be some hope for reducing the enormous variety of influences into a relatively few and, therefore, relatively manageable number of indicators or variables. This is precisely what I shall seek to do.

Transactions Across System Boundaries   Since we have been conceiving of a political system as analytically separable from all other social systems, and frequently empirically differentiated as well through an independent political structure, it is useful to treat the disturbances or influences occurring from behavior in the environmental systems as *exchanges* or *transactions* that cross the boundaries of the political system. None of the broad social systems into which I have classified the environment stands completely independent of the other; complex interpenetration occurs. That is, each is coupled to the other in some way, however slight it may be. Exchanges can be used when we wish to refer to the mutuality of the relationship, that is, where each has a reciprocal influence on the other. Transaction may be used when we wish to emphasize the movement of an effect in one direction, simply across the boundary from one system to another.[4]

However scientifically important it may be to point this out, by itself the statement is so obvious as to have little interest. What can and will carry recognition of this coupling beyond a mere truism is the invention of a way to trace out the complex exchanges so that we can readily reduce the immense variety of interactions to theoretically and empirically manageable proportions.

In order to accomplish this, I propose to reduce the major and significant environmental influences to a few indicators. Through the examination of these we should be able to appraise and follow through the potential impact of environmental events on the system. With this objective in mind, I shall designate the effects that are transmitted across the boundary of a system toward some other system as the *outputs* of the first system and, hence, as the *inputs* of the second system, the one that they influence. A transaction between systems will therefore be viewed as a linkage between them in the form of an input-output relationship.

If we now apply this general conceptualization of the points of linkage between systems to a political system and its environmental systems, it offers us a rudimentary model of the type illustrated in Figure 3-1. This is, of course, a gargantuan oversimplification both of reality and of my developing conceptual scheme itself. But the task of analysis is at least to begin by stripping away all incidental relationships in order to lay bare the essential framework. These are the very minimal commitments if we inquire into political life as a system of behavior. In a succeeding volume the objective will be to add complicating relationships of various sorts so that the model will offer a somewhat closer approximation to the relationships in phenomenal systems. Here the analysis will remain macroscopic in intent. We shall be observing political systems from a considerable distance, as through a telescope rather than a microscope. This is in the nature of the case, given the present state of theoretical analysis in political research. Although we have

---

[4]Exchange is sometimes used to suggest some kind of mutually beneficial relationship such as a settlement or contractual tie in which each of the parties feels there is something to be gained. I presume that Talcott Parsons typically uses the concept in this or in a closely related sense. See his use of the term in *The Social System* (New York: Free Press of Glencoe, Inc., 1951), especially at pp. 122 ff and in a volume with N. J. Smelser, *Economy and Society* (New York: Free Press of Glencoe, Inc., 1956), pp. 105 and 184. Here, however, I shall confine the terms to a neutral meaning, one that denotes only that events in two or more systems have reciprocal effects on the systems involved and that these effects are not unrelated to each other. Interaction might well have been used to describe the relationship except that it has been customary to restrict this concept to the actions and reactions among social roles rather than among systems.

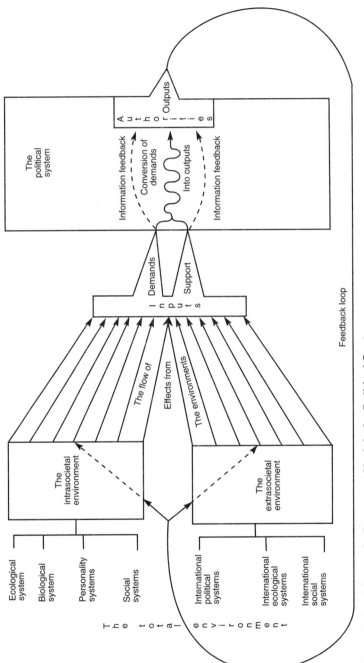

Figure 3-1   A Dynamic Response Model of a Political System.

much empirical detail, we have tended to lose sight of the need to see the outlines of the over-all picture.

A Flow Model of the Political System   Broadly, this diagramatic representation of the functioning of a political system suggests that what is happening in the environment affects the political system through the kinds of influences that flow into the system. Through its structures and processes the system then acts on these intakes in such a way that they are converted into outputs. These are the authoritative decisions and their implementation. The outputs return to the systems in the environment, or, in many cases, they may turn directly and without intermediaries back upon the system itself. In Figure 3-1 the arrows from the environments portray the vast variety of transactions between them and the political system. Here, though, the arrows have only single heads, and they are shown in such a way that they are fed into the system in summary form as demands and support. The exchange or reciprocity of the relationship between the system and its environments, previously depicted as double-headed arrows, is now indicated by arrows that show the direction of flow of the outputs toward the environmental systems. This clearly demonstrates that the inputs of the environment are really just the outputs of the political system. The broken lines in the environmental systems reflect the dynamics of the relationship. They indicate that there is a continuous flow of influences or outputs from the political system into and through the environments. By modifying the environments, political outputs thereby influence the next round of effects that move from the environment back to the political system. In this way we can identify a continuous feedback loop. The meaning of the other lines and designations on the diagram will become apparent as our discussion proceeds.

As detailed as the diagram is, much is omitted, as we would expect. First, many other environmental systems could be added even to take into account the few that were identified in an earlier chapter. Second, the interrelationships among environmental systems themselves are completely omitted since they would have so cluttered the diagram as to leave it virtually indecipherable. Finally, the structures and processes through which a political system converts its inputs into outputs are represented only by the serpentine line within the system. It does suggest, however, that the various inputs from the external system are worked upon and converted into outputs that return to one or another of the external systems as inputs for them.

Figure 3-2 goes even further in stripping the rich and complex political processes down to their bare bones. It depicts in their simplest guise the dynamic relationships among the processes of a political system. It serves to dramatize an image to which we shall return; it reveals that, after all, in its elemental form a political system is just a means whereby certain kinds of

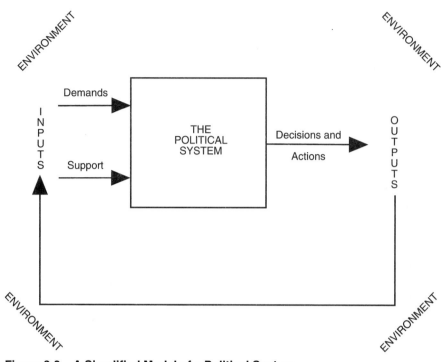

Figure 3-2   A Simplified Model of a Political System.

inputs are converted into outputs. At least, this is a highly useful starting
point from which to begin plugging in the complexities of political life.

The Input Variables

Demands and Support as Input Indicators   The value of inputs as a
concept is that through its use we shall find it possible to capture the effect
of the enormous variety of events and conditions in the environment as
they pertain to the persistence of a political system. Without the inputs it
would be difficult to delineate in any precise operational way how behavior
in the various sectors of society affects what happens in the political sector.
Inputs will serve as summary variables that concentrate and reflect everything in the environment which is relevant to political stress. Because it is
possible to use inputs in this manner, the concept can serve as a powerful
analytic tool.

Whether or not we use inputs as summary variables will depend upon
how we define them. We might conceive of them in their broadest sense.
Then we would interpret them as including any event external to the system—confining ourselves momentarily to environmental inputs—that alters, modifies, or affects the system in any way. If inputs are used in such a

broad sense, we could never exhaust the list of those that leave an impact on the political system.

Let us take only a minute number of illustrations. The effect of the economy on creating and sustaining powerful economic classes, urbanization, interest group segmentation, fluctuations in the business cycle, and the like would constitute inputs, broadly interpreted, that shape the character of the political structure, the distribution of power therein, and the goals of political controversy. The general culture helps to mold the constraints within which political discussion and competition take place (if it is permitted at all), lends color to the style of political life, and signalizes the kinds of issues that will be considered important by the members of the system. Motivational patterns found in modal personality types or in elite personalities within a society will contribute to the availability of personnel to fill the political roles, to the incentives for political participation, and to the types that achieve leadership status and to their perception of policy. We could enlarge this list indefinitely. For each sector of the environment introduced we would need a separate partial theory to explain the effect which its inputs might have. The only unifying element in it all would be that we were seeking to trace out and interrelate the inputs (that is, the general and specific effects) of each of these parameters on a common object—the political system.

However, we can simplify enormously the task of analyzing the impact of the environment on the political systems if we adopt more narrowly defined inputs and use them as indicators that will sum up most of the important effects that cross the boundary between these systems. This conceptualization would relieve us of the need to deal with and trace out the effect on a system of every different type of environmental event separately.

As the analytic tool for this purpose, it is helpful to view the major parameters as focusing their effects on two major inputs: demands and support. Through them a vast range of changes in the environment may be channeled, reflected, and summarized. For this reason they can be used as the key indicators of the way in which environmental events and conditions modify and affect the operations of the political system. On Figure 3–1, the multiple transactions are collapsed into two major inputs, and these alone are conceived as flowing into and affecting the political system.

It will matter little whether we consider these inputs as internal or external to the political system. They stand on the border, bridging and linking the political system with all other intra- and extrasocietal systems. Depending upon the requirements of our analysis, they may be equally conceived to lie within the system or outside it, as long as we recognize that they remain in the neighborhood of the boundary.

"Withinputs" as Intrasystem Indicators At times I have been writing as though all the influences or disturbances that had to be considered in understanding how a system manages to persist occurred in the environment of a system. As we know from what has already been said, many of these influences may occur within a system itself. Insofar as things happening within a system shape its destinies as a system of interactions, it will be possible to take them into account as they are reflected through the inputs of the members of a system. It does not seem reasonable to speak of these events as inputs since they already occur within the system rather than outside. For the sake of logical consistency we might call them "withinputs." All that would be meant by this neologism is that we have decided to treat, in a unified way, the effects that events and conditions both within and without a system may have upon its persistence. Hence, unless the context requires otherwise, in writing of inputs I shall include "withinputs" in the same category.

We need to take the trouble to make the distinction because recognition of the two categories sensitizes us to the value of looking within the system as well as the environment to find the major influences that may lead to stress. Just as a human body may fail because of an infection received from the outside or from the attrition, through old age, of some organ such as the heart, a political system may suffer stress from disturbances in the environment or from failures that can be attributed directly to processes or structural arrangements within the system itself. For example, members of the American political system have from time to time felt that the whole regime has been threatened by the difficulties that the separation of powers has aggravated with regard to the passage of legislation. This is traditionally brought out in discussions of a responsible two-party system for the United States. To signalize the fact that the disturbance has occurred within the system and that the stressing input has been shaped by internal events, the concept "withinputs" can be used.

Illustrations of the Summary Function of Inputs   It will be helpful to have some brief indication of what demands and support comprise and how they could be used, although a full analysis of their role as summary variables through which stress is transmitted will have to await a later work. To take a specific example, let us assume that we are interested in a developing nation which is undergoing a transition from a tribal form of organization based upon village headmen, lineage elders, and a lineage-determined paramount chief with minimal power, toward a national political leadership based upon secular party organization, a legislature, an efficiency-oriented bureaucracy, and a dominant leadership. Presumably the modifications of the old tribal system have been brought about in part through contact with Western ideals of democracy and administration, buttressed by the needs of a changing economy and social structure.

In accordance with current procedures of political research, we might specify the aspect of political change that seems to be important. Normally we would use as the criteria of relevance those changes in the direction of or away from Western democratic institutions. We might then seek to account for the direction, rate, and outcome of these changes by considering all of the external changes that can then be shown to be relevant to the political changes which we have already selected as important according to these criteria.

From the perspectives of our analysis the environmental changes are considered to be disturbances on the existing tribal system because of the stress they impose upon it, leading ultimately to its transformation. In response to the stress the system either becomes extinct and is absorbed by some other society, or it responds and adapts by adopting modernized political structures in the shape of parties, legislatures, rationalized bureaucracy, and a generalized leadership (rather than a lineage, tribal, or ethnically based leadership).

The critical questions for us do not relate to the way in which environmental disturbances modify the particular form of the internal structures or processes of the system. Such changes may take place without any discernible effect upon the capacity of some kind of system to persist, or they may not be fundamentally related to this capacity. That is to say, whether the adopted modernized structure happens to be modeled after the British parliamentary system or the American presidential type may or may not have relevance to the capacity of some kind of system to persist. What is important is that the traditional political forms have given way to at least a semblance of the bureaucratized types. For us the critical questions are: To what extent did the disturbances constitute stress on the pre-existing system? Precisely how did this stress manifest and communicate itself? How did the system cope with this stress, if at all?

A useful way of answering such questions lies in exploring the impact that contacts with the West, both ideological and economical, have upon the inputs. Briefly, exposure to the kind of life possible under Western forms of social organization, together with the emergence of the material means through transition from a subsistence to a cash and wage economy, has unleashed a vast increase in the volume of demands which members of the system now seek to satisfy through political action. This in itself imposes such a severe burden on the old tribal forms of political organization that they could not possibly cope with them.

Further, the changes in the environment serve to broaden the types of demands for which satisfaction is now sought through the political system. Such new demands, at their most inclusive level, are typically capsulated into programs for national freedom and political unity among divergent groups, linked usually to policies advocating a rapid rate of economic development. The kinds of commitments required from the members of the system for the fulfillment of these types of demands are dramatically different from those required under the prior traditional systems. The novelty of the demands themselves create severe crises in the developing nations.

Changes in volume and variety of demands represent a major and fundamentally neglected type of stress that environmental changes may be interpreted as bringing to bear upon a political system. In this way a vast host of different kinds of changes such as these may be drawn together and observed through a single kind of variable, that is, as they influence the volume and variety of demands.

But something more is also at stake in these emerging national units. It is to be found in the need for a new leadership to weld together a group that can offer sufficient support for a new political unit, a new set of structures for getting things done politically, and new political authorities to provide leadership and administrative skills. These are the basic components of a political system which might be labeled the political community, regime, and authorities.[5] The search for rapid economic and social development, combined with political stability, imposes on such systems the need to generate a leadership which can promote and sustain support for these components. To do so they may have to negotiate coalitions among the dominant ethnic, lineage, and new economic groups in the society. They may look for support among young adults, among the politically dispossessed tribes, or among the urban workers deprived of the past security of lineage ties. They may turn to the use of coercion.

However the new leadership may seek to renew the input of support for some system, stress owing to the decline of support for the pre-existing system can be laid at the door of environmental changes of the kinds already mentioned. Where the fact of change indicates that the old systems thereby failed, we can interpret the situation to mean that the members were able to assure the persistence of some kind of system by transforming themselves into and lending support to a modernizing or transitional type of system. Regardless of how the system coped with the stress, the point is that environmental disturbances can be summarized and unified through their influence on the level of support for a system. By thus utilizing support as the connecting link between the environment and a system, we obtain a clue about how this variable serves as the focal point of many different kinds of environmental changes important for an understanding of stress on a system.

A great deal more needs to be said about the way in which the inputs of demands and support sum up and reflect the changes taking place in the environment of a political system, communicate these changes as disturbances to the system, and in turn are acted upon by the system as a way of coping with potential stress. Final validation of the fact that most of the important aspects of environmental events and conditions are refracted through these two indicators will have to wait for the elaboration of each

[5]For a brief discussion of these terms see Easton, "An Approach to the Analysis of Political Systems," and "Political Anthropology." The concepts will be elaborated in detail in another volume.

input and the system response. My purpose is to sketch out and offer only a preliminary view of the role that these inputs do play. Through the adoption of this kind of conceptualization we are able to invent a means for tracing out the way in which stress may be communicated to a system.

FISCAL BEHAVIOR OF THE MODERN DEMOCRATIC STATE: PUBLIC CHOICE PERSPECTIVES AND CONTRIBUTIONS
William C. Mitchell*

> The fundamental business of our representatives is taxing and spending.
> —E.S. Phelps "Rational Taxation" *Social Research* 44 (Winter, 1977): 657

My concerns center on political processes and, more particularly, American governmental decisions pertaining to the raising and spending of public monies. Fiscal choices are at the heart of politics. As Aaron Wildavsky has often noted, budgets are key political documents for they register the allocative and distributive choices that have been made or are being proposed. In this chapter I attempt to describe, integrate, and assess certain contributions of modern pubic choice to these questions of fiscal policy. The work of Bartlett, Borcherding, Breton, Browning, Buchanan and Tullock, Niskanen, and Tollison, to mention some of the more prominent, loom large. My survey is highly selective, but it is hoped not unreasonable or unfair. Nontechnical contributions as well as work with a certain libertarian thrust are emphasized. Highly specialized empirical investigations are occasionally cited but not extensively discussed. Although important in a science of public choice, they are here deemed of lesser import to general students of public choice and finance. While cognizant of the value of surveys of the literature, I seek here a synthesis or a consistent point of view. The synthesis draws unequally upon two divergent perspectives: demand and supply models. In the former, citizen-consumers reign supreme; in the latter, politicians, bureaucrats, and governments play roles not unlike those ascribed to monopolistic businesses by, say, J. K. Galbraith. With important qualifications, I view the consumer as powerful in the economy and the citizen as relatively powerless in the polity.

Elements of Public Choice

The political institutions of a society provide the framework within which the preferences and resource commitments of its citizens are transformed into collective actions that are expected to yield utility. Just as the

*William Mitchell, "Fiscal Behavior of the Modern Democratic State: Public Choice Perspectives and Contributions," in *Political Economy: Recent Views*, edited by Larry Wade. Boston: Kluwer-Nijhoff, 1983 (pp. 69-72, 86-99). Used by permission.

distribution of income and wealth, the availability of markets, et cetera, determine price-quantity-quality outputs in the market, so wealth, votes, and the presence of certain democratic institutions determine the distribution of political power and the responsiveness of policies in achieving the preferences of voters.

Modern public-choice views representative government not as a separate, sentient entity capable of acting in the public interest; rather government is treated as a political activity carried on by rational, self-interested individuals. Public policies are the product of many individuals with different values, preferences, beliefs, and knowledge. Some are office holders and employees of the state, but most are simply citizens with extraordinarily limited roles in collective decision processes. The vast majority of citizens do not get an opportunity to vote directly on most issues, even at local levels of government. Because of the large number of issues, their complexity, and the high cost of adequate information (among other reasons), actual decision-making is delegated to representatives. The important decisions for the ordinary citizen are made by representatives selected in an at—large voting process where the principle of majority rule usually is in force (even if plurality rules formally apply, as in congressional elections).

The individual citizen-voter uses political institutions to shop, as it were, for publicly supplied services in a manner somewhat analogous to shopping behavior in the market. In both systems the citizen seeks to obtain the best or optimal bargain obtainable. Public choice maintains that political institutions and activities can be understood by use of economic analysis quite comparable to that traditionally applied to market institutions and activity.

The politician or elective public official, including aspirants, plays a role analogous to that of an entrepreneur in the economy. Like businessmen, politicians seek to maximize their own utility, an aim accomplished by maximizing either votes or their probability of being returned to office.

Elected officials realize that any given policy stance will please some voters, displease others, and escape the attention of many. The same action can change their power or influence with colleagues, bureaucrats, and organized interests. Reconciling these differences requires bargains, compromises, logrolling, and, in general, strategic choices. Successful politicians are those who can adopt policies which keep them in office, maintain or improve influence with other politicians, and enlist the aid of bureaucrats. Presumably, much of this interaction restrains irresponsible behavior. The extent to which this occurs is a subject of some difference among public-choice theorists. A few, including Anthony Downs and Mancur Olson, have an apparent faith in the efficacy of politics, while others, notably James M. Buchanan and Gordon Tullock, are skeptical about the efficacy of the *unseen hand* of political bargaining. The latter contend that political institutions are highly imperfect reflectors of preferences, that information costs are immense, that the probability of successful action is remote, that cost-benefit calculations are more difficult than in the market, and, that efficiency goes unrewarded. Institutional arrangements, then, serve to increase irresponsible behavior and inefficient policies. Most likely, political processes encourage everyone to distort, dissemble, and exaggerate their demands. The ever-present prospect of receiving substantial gains, at little or no cost to oneself, is a major motivating force in the polity, since costs and benefits are rarely internalized as they must be in most market activity.

It is within this general setting that the fiscal choices of a society are made or enacted. The obvious questions confronting analysts include: (1) the supply of government output or, more precisely, the size of the public budget; (2) composition of the output or expenditures; (3) choice of revenue sources, instruments, and rates; and (4) variations of these magnitudes through time. While public-choice analysts approach these questions within the well-defined paradigm of economics, the theories that have evolved over the past thirty years are by no means fully consistent. In fact, I shall contend that two major schools of thought vie in supplying answers to these questions.

Unlike economic theory, which began with production or supply-oriented models, public choice began with demand-inspired models. But, whereas economics took a century to discover demand and appropriate means for integrating supply and demand analyses, public choice began to emphasize the other side of the market only a decade after the demand-oriented work of Black and of Downs.[1] Indeed, libertarian economists from Virginia Polytechnic Institute have viewed theories of imperfect competition and monopoly as more appropriate and useful in the study of politics than the markets for which they were originally designed.

Government as a Monopolistic Supplier: Supply Models

Dating the emergence of supply-based models is a difficult and possibly fruitless task because supply considerations have rarely been excluded from even the most demand-oriented theories. However, Downs moved far beyond the early analyses with a theory of the politician's behavior and later, but less successfully, of the bureaucrat and bureau. Shifts from demand to supply models may, perhaps, best be explained as responses to both theoretical difficulties and the unrelenting force of real-world developments. Casual observation of real-world politics suggests, among other things, that politicians and governments are not the passive creatures implied by the demand theorists of public choice and by interest-group theorists in political science. Politicians, bureaucrats, and governments have an

[1]Duncan Black. *The Theory of Committees and Elections* (Cambridge: Cambridge University Press, 1958); Anthony Downs, *An Economic Theory of Democracy* (New York: Harper, 1957).

enormous capacity to control and powerful incentives to decide their own fates. In order to survive, politicians and bureaucrats need not always keep their "ears to the ground" and "thumbs to the wind." Officials have considerable control over constituent demands and as governments they act not only as monopolistic suppliers but as the single most authoritative and powerful social institution.

Supply Models: A Thumbnail History

The dramatic growth of bureaucratic activity during the past twenty years has had a profound effect on theory building. The theories of collective choice advanced by Arrow, Black, and even Downs had no role for bureaucracy. Tullock and Niskanen were to have a significant part in writing the role of the missing actor.[2] One suspects, too, that ideological commitments or values had some role to play in sensitizing these two theorists to imperfect political competition as well as the unique power of government to control life. Such sensitivities doubtlessly encouraged scholars of libertarian economic proclivities to note and emphasize the allocative and technical inefficiencies and distributive inequities of politics. Demand models simply do not prepare one to recognize, let alone emphasize, these difficulties. Downs insisted that political competition made politicians responsive and responsible. Common sense has led many to question the fact and some the theory and logic.

In any event, explicit supply considerations began entering the literature about 1965 with the publication of Tullock's *The Politics of Bureaucracy* and, two years later, his *Toward a Mathematics of Politics*.[3] James M. Buchanan had contributed still earlier to these developments with a classic paper on "Social Choice, Democracy, and Free Markets" (1954),[4] and in the series of papers published in the mid 1960s under the title of *Public Finance in Democratic Process*.[5] Although the same author advanced some supply considerations in *The Demand and Supply of Public Goods* (1968), the title of the volume is misleading, since most of it is really about demand.[6] Niskanen's much cited *Bureaucracy and Representative Government* (1971), Randall Bartlett's impressive but little-noted *Economic Foundations of Political Power*

---

[2]Gordon Tullock, *The Politics of Bureaucracy* (Washington. D. C.: Public Affairs Press. 1965); William A. Niskanen. Jr., *Bureaucracy and Representative Government* (Chicago: Aldine-Atherton, 1971).

[3]Gordon Tullock, *Toward a Mathematics of Politics* (Ann Arbor: University of Michigan Press, 1965).

[4]James M. Buchanan, "Social Choice, Democracy, and Free Markets," *Journal of Political Economy*, 62 (April 1954): 114-23.

[5] _____ *Public Finance in Democratic Process*.(Chapel Hill: University of North Carolina Press, 1967).

[6] _____ *The Demand and Supply of Public Goods* (Chicago: Rand McNally, 1968).

(1973),[7] and Albert Breton's *The Economic Theory of Representative Government* (1974)[8] afforded a more complete theory of democracy than demand theory was or is able to attain. Others, notably, Stigler (1971), Tollison and Mc-Cormick (1981), Wittman (1973), Sirkin (1975), Peltzman (1976), Aranson and Ordeshook (1977), Rose-Ackerman (1978), Auster and Silver (1979), Mueller (1979), Wagner (1980), and Mackay and Weaver (1978; 1981), were all to make significant contributions to the realism of public-choice theories of government and politics.[9] Their analyses, some highly technical, were clearly inspired by theories of imperfect market competition and monopoly. Although these many contributions cannot be detailed in these few pages, some of the basic ideas can be summarized as they relate to the problem of fiscal behavior in and by the modern state.

One result of this recent interest in supply-side public choice is a richer, more complete, and realistic approach to politics than that afforded by demand analysis. The latter, as we have seen, was and remains fixated on the voluntary exchanges between citizen/voters and elective officials. The newer supply-side approach does not so much eschew the demand model as expand it to include bureaucracy and add to the complexity of relationships among citizens (beneficiaries, taxpayers, regulated), politicians, and bureaucrats. Certain of these relationships are considered to be not only important but crucial. These include a new emphasis upon regulation, authority, compliance, taxation; in other words, the political science tradition of treating the state as the embodiment of power and authority is revived by public choice. The state is now seen as a monopolist and possible exploiter rather than a neutral, responsive supplier of public goods. Figure 3–3 offers a schematic means for contrasting demand and supply models. The heavier lines indicate some of the new emphases in public-choice studies.

[7]Randall Bartlett, *Economic Foundations of Political Power* (New York: The Free Press, 1973).

[8]Albert Breton, The Economic Theory of Representative Government (Chicago: Aldine, 1974).

[9]Stigler, "The Theory of Economic Regulation"; Robert D. Tollison and Robert E. McCormick, *Politicians, Legislation, and the Economy* (Boston: Martinus Nijhoff, 1981); Donald Wittman, "Parties as Utility Maximizers,'" *American Political Science Review*, 67 (June 1973):490-98; Gerald Sirkin, "The Anatomy of Public Choice Failure," in R. D. Leiter and G. Sirkin, eds., *Economics of Public Choice* (New York: Cyrco Press, 1975); Sam Peltzman, "Toward a More General Theory of Regulation," *Journal of Law and Economics*, 19 (August 1976):2 11-40; Peter H. Aranson and Peter C. Ordeshook, "A Prolegomenon to a Theory of the Failure of Representative Democracy," in R. Auster and B. Sears, eds., *American Revolution: Papers and Proceedings* (Tucson: University of Arizona, 1977); Susan Rose-Ackerman, *Corruption: A Study in Political Economy* (New York: Academic Press, 1978); R. D. Auster and Morris Silver, *The State as a Firm* (Boston: Martinus Nijhoff, 1979); Dennis C. Mueller, *Public Choice* (Cambridge: Cambridge University Press, 1979); Richard E. Wagner, "Boom and Bust: The Political Economy of Economic Disorder," *Journal of Libertarian Studies*, 4 (Winter 1980): 1-37; Robert J. Mackay and Carolyn L. Weaver, "Monopoly Bureaus and Fiscal Outcomes: Deductive Models and Implications for Reform," in Gordon Tullock and Richard E. Wagner, eds., *Policy Analysis and Deductive Reasoning* (Lexington, Mass.: Lexington Books, 1978), pp. 141-66; Robert J. Mackay and Carolyn L. Weaver, "Agenda Control by Budget Maximizers in a Multi-Bureau Setting,'' *Public Choice*, 37 (I98I):447-72.

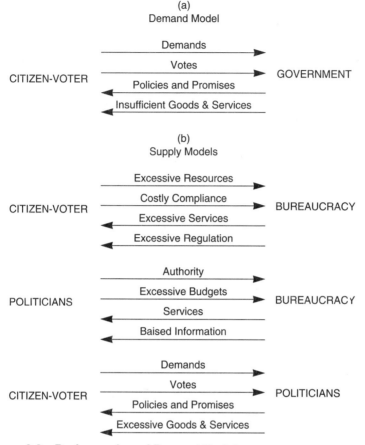

Figure 3-3   Basic supply and Demand Models

Private monopoly has been made an explicit benchmark for the analysis of government and in particular, bureaucracy. Various types of well-known monopolistic practices including all-or-nothing offers, tax share discrimination, and commodity bundling, are examined for their collective counterparts.[10] In addition, the power of government to set agendas and determine the rules of the game have become a major focus of research.[11] Government, then, is viewed as a monopolist, but a somewhat benevolent one following peculiar economic rules but highly rational political goals and strategies.

[10]Mackay and Weaver, "Agenda Control by Budget Maximizers."

[11]Charles R. Plott, "Axiomatic Social Choice Theory," *American Journal of Political Science*, 20 (August 1976):511-96.

The Nature of Public Supply and Excessive Provision

The fundamental insight of the supply-siders is simple: monopolistic governments and their members pursue self-interests and no theory of democracy can possibly be maintained that does not take these interests into account. Richard Wagner put it well when he wrote, "It is contrary to reason and to history to expect that a monopoly position will fail to be exploited for the benefit of those in a position to do so.[12] Early theorists of supply tended to take the discovery too narrowly and assumed that governments had a singular and readily discerned interest that could be readily applied in devising positive theory. This simplistic understanding was soon rectified with the recognition that a government could have different objectives and that they might conflict. Accordingly, theorists began to consider the divergent objectives of different members or agents of government. As previously noted, both Tullock and Niskanen explored the situation and behavior of bureaucrats as distinct from those of elective officials, not to mention divergencies from the voters.[13] The various fiscal roles of legislators, executives, governmental employees, and such unique officials as city managers who are neither elected politicians nor civil servants were delineated and explored. Still other theorists, notably, Peltzman, Stigler, Posner, Hirshleifer, Lindsay, and Owen and Braeutigam were to concentrate on regulatory problems within a public-choice setting.[14] Choices to regulate, including the pricing of governmentally supplied utilities, are now discussed as political rather than purely economic decisions. Not unexpectedly, a small literature on political wage determination in bureaucracy has also emerged.[15]

In addition to viewing government as an interested but peculiar monopolist, supply-side theorists have insisted that governments do not respond to the same economic stimuli as private persons and organizations, that is, the stimuli of prices and price changes. In other words, governments do not necessarily buy less when prices rise or more when prices fall. In

[12]Wagner, "Boom and Bust" p. 2.

[13]Tullock, *The Politics of Bureaucracy*; Niskanen, *Bureaucracy and Representative Government*; Niskanen, "Bureaucrats and Politicians," *Journal of Law and Economics*, 18 (December 1975):617-43.

[14]Sam Peltzman, "Pricing in Public and Private Enterprises: Electric Utilities in the U.S.," *Journal of Law and Economics*, 14 (April 1971): 109-47; Peltzman, "Toward a More General Theory of Economic Regulation"; Richard A. Posner, "Theories of Economic Regulation," *Bell Journal of Economics and Management Science*, 5 (Autumn 1974): 335- 58; Jack Hirschleifer, "Comment" on Sam Peltzman, "Toward a More General Theory of Regulation," *Journal of Law and Economics*, 19 (August 1976):241-44; Cotton M. Lindsay, "A Theory of Government Enterprise," *Journal of Political Economy*, 84(1976): 1061-77; Bruce M. Owen and Ronald Braeutigam, *The Regulation Game* (Cambridge: Ballinger, 1978).

[15]Melvin W. Reder, "The Theory of Employment and Wages in the Public Sector," in Daniel Hamermesh, ed., *Labor in the Public and Non-Profit Sectors* (Princeton: Princeton University Press, 1975); ch. 3, George J. Borjas, *Wage Policy in the Federal Bureaucracy* (Washington, D.C.: American Enterprise Institute, 1980).

fact, under Keynesian precepts, government is advised to act in ways contrary to rational market behavior. Under any regime, governments do not observe the fundamental rule of allocation, that is, do not equalize costs and benefits at the margin. Governments are concerned with the *distribution* of benefits and costs because distributions shape the voting choices and electoral outcomes. Zero- and under-pricing of services is, of course, ubiquitous precisely because of these considerations.

Besides ignoring the marginal equivalence mandate, governments ignore the basic constraint on the financial choices of individuals, namely, income. While an individual's income determines possible expenditure, a government's expenditures determine the amount of its necessary income. To make things worse, under Keynesian rules a government can engage in deficit finance less as a matter of necessity than as a theoretical and ethical imperative.

This brief discussion of the peculiar economics of government cannot be completed without reference to a principle that is everywhere ignored by governments: "Nobody spends somebody else's money as carefully as he spends his own."[16] Voters, politicians, and bureaucrats are engaged in spending the money of others. And, since everyone is spending money on others as well as spending the money of others on themselves, a double inefficiency is incurred: spenders have little incentive either to economize or to provide the goods most valued by the beneficiary.

Traditional public finance and economics generally have maintained that marginal analysis *should* be applied to an analysis of the proper or correct role of government in the economy. Thus, it has been held that the expenditures of government should be carried to the point where the value of the last unit of all governmentally produced goods and services is equal, and the value of the last unit produced for the government sector is equal to the value of the last unit produced for the private sector.[17] Others have claimed that the government should spend until the value of the sums lost by taxation is equal to the value of the last unit bought by the government.[18]

Public choice, whether demand or supply oriented, has insisted that familiarity with actual political processes and historical patterns of expenditures suggests that the marginal calculus is rarely followed; indeed, it cannot be honored. The nature of the political product and the incentives of participants both work against the adoption of conventional economic advice. Furthermore, governments that might desire to apply the marginal calculus would encounter the prescriptive limitations of macroeconomic

---

[16]Milton and Rose Friedman, *Free to Choose* (New York: Harcourt, Brace, Jovanovich, 1980), p. 31.

[17]Hugh Dalton, *Principles of Public Finance* (1922; reprint ed., New York: Augustus M. Kelly, Publishers, 1967).

[18]Richard A. and Peggy B. Musgrave, *Public Finance in Theory and Practice*, 3rd ed. (New York: McGraw-Hill, 1980).

analysis itself. At best, macrotheory has progressed to the point where it can tell us what not to do and sometimes can inform us when it is necessary to reverse the direction of policy. It still, however, cannot tell the policy maker when he should act to prevent a change in economic conditions; what responses to a given act of government will be; or which course, among many possible, is the most desirable at a given time. The confidence generated when the Keynesian system of autonomous and dependent variables was first developed has long since been lost. A long overdue reappraisal is now taking place within macroeconomics. Complementary discoveries within public choice, not the least of which is the realization that the choice between alternative macro-policies is determined not by theoretical considerations but by the effects of those policies upon the careers of politicians and by the welfare of major economic interests, are of major importance.[19] Public choice has also been in the forefront in maintaining that there are no purely scientific criteria that can determine the proper level of government expenditures: at best, we might obtain some second-order efficiencies.

Rent Seeking and Redistribution

More recent treatments of income redistribution appear to offer improvements over the demand models previously cited. While not eschewing the insights of demand-based redistributive efforts by government, these newer theories include more participants, more complex institutions, and varied incentives in their models. The redistributive battle is now considered a major activity of the political process, and not simply a sideshow to the main act of public-good provision. Redistribution is not a direct, class-based conflict of one-way flows of wealth and income. Instead, as Stigler, Tullock, and many empirical investigators have observed, redistribution assumes many forms, directions, and patterns of incidence.

One of the first insights of supply-side public choice suggests that governments have no all-embracing scheme of redistribution in which each instrument of policy is finely tuned to the desired incidence. Much of redistribution is an unintended collective result of other intended individual activities and outcomes. Some redistribution stems from macropolicies, that is, expenditure and revenue decisions that are designed to counter the business cycle and not the redistributive desires of citizens. Still other policies are enacted to control markets but reduce market risks and thereby influence distributive outcomes. In fact, the recent literature on *rent seeking* appears to spring from such considerations. Rent seeking is now a deliberate strategy of nearly everyone. As an inclusive game for improving market shares, large investments in political activity now make considerable sense.

---

[19]Richard E. Wagner, "Economic Manipulation for Political Profit: Macro-Economic Consequences and Constitutional Implication," *Kyklos*, 30 (1977):395-40.

In a world such as ours, political participation becomes mandatory in the same sense that participation in a commons dilemma is obligatory. Individuals and interest groups attempt to improve their lot not simply by adjusting to each economic contingency; instead, they attempt to alter the rules to their own advantage. Demand models seem not to have made room for this strategy. In any event, the effort to seek rents depends on the relationship between costs and gains.

What appears to have happened over the past century is nothing less than a dramatic shift in the cost-benefit schedules of political action. The returns from political action have increased for many at a far greater rate than the mounting costs. Almost any economic policy can be challenged in the political arena and with a reasonable expectation of success.

Citizens attempt to obtain income and wealth at the expense of others, an observation made by both demand and supply analysts. This complex process has produced a number of interesting and even perverse consequences. While definitive estimates of redistribution are elusive, it is clear that 1) income and wealth are redistributed both vertically and horizontally; 2) almost every citizen is both beneficiary and donor; 3) significant transfers take place among members of the same income bracket; 4) lower-income groups have made significant gains during the past forty years; 5) total transfers, which are increasing, have not altered the basic distribution by very much; and, finally, 6) inequality prevails.

Supply-side analysts are apt to emphasize that rent seeking is very costly since the opportunity costs are enormous. They are also apt to stress the additional fact that rent seeking probably serves to make the better-off still better off and some of the poor poorer in a relative sense. And, worse, rent seeking is an essentially unproductive activity. If our economic fate depends less on productive market work than on wheeling and dealing in government halls, everyone will suffer.

Of course, everyone does not. The analytical problem is to determine which groups will gain the most and least, since all do not share equally. Unhappily, many of the answers are contradictory. Demand models tended to emphasize the downward flow of benefits from the rich to the poor. The more sophisticated models, whether demand or supply oriented, point to some limitations on the power and incentives of the poor to exploit the rich. These same models suggest that the middle class may be exploiting both rich and poor. Certainly, one can point to countless policies at all levels of government that were designed to aid middle income groups or to policies that were originated for the purpose of aiding the less well-off, but soon included the middle class as beneficiaries. The latter possibility may well be the political payment necessary to enact any redistribution to the low income strata. Such possibilities alert one to the fact that the substantial amounts allocated to the poor cannot be the products of the political power of the poor alone. Coalition efforts with other classes, altruistic impulses among higher income groups, and an historically increasing national income all have some role in explaining the success of the poor.

Different income and occupational groups tend to obtain their gains in quite different forms. Neither demand nor supply models have adequately considered this important policy choice. As noted elsewhere in this chapter, the rich tend to gain much of their rents through tax reductions, whereas the poor obtain their gains via welfare programs involving both cash income and benefits in kind. The middle class seems to derive its improvements from a combination of tax reduction and subsidies. Occupational groups seem to prefer or obtain market privileges such as tariffs, quotas, licenses, zoning laws, building codes, tax moratoriums, and preferential contracts.

But each form is also accompanied by the *quid pro quo* demanded by the politicians who enacted the laws and the bureaucrats who administer them. The regulated have found a means of increasing their incomes, but at a cost; the cost of regulation includes red tape, delay, petty decisions, and unreasonable requirements. The poor face humiliation, means tests, and often overbearing bureaucrats. Only the wealthy seem not to confront such personal relationships with government. Their checks come in the mail and their taxes are managed by lawyers and accountants.

Supply models have enriched our understanding of political redistribution beyond the somewhat confusing view of demand models which presumed that redistribution occurs from the rich to the poor and that producer groups are more powerful than consumer groups. Supply models correct the former error and integrate the Downsian view of producer power within a more complex rent-seeking model. Empirical evidence appears to support this newer view of redistribution.

Entrepreneurs, Policy Innovation, and Supplies

Collective goods do not emerge from the logic of rational, self-interested private action; if they are to be produced by collective action, political entrepreneurs must be willing to campaign on the behalf of the good. We owe this fundamental insight to Frohlich, Oppenheimer, and Young.[20] The earlier insight concerning the nature of public goods and free-riding was, of course, that of Olson.[21] The important point for us is the recognition not only of the activist role of the politician but the unique character of policy innovation in the public realm. Political and market entrepreneurs may have some attributes in common, but none is significant. Their situations, roles, and incentives differ in profound ways.

[20]Norman Frohlich, Joe A. Oppenheimer, and Oran R. Young, *Political Leadership and Collective Goods* (Princeton: Princeton University Press, 1971).

[21]Mancur Olson, Jr., *The Logic of Collective Action* (Cambridge: Harvard University Press, 1965).

Market entrepreneurs innovate by inventing new products and services, offering better conditions or contracts, devising new sales techniques, et cetera. All this is accompanied by some personal risk or uncertainty. No such risk is imposed on the politician. The politician can promise new policies and fail in their delivery yet remain in office. Still, the political entrepreneur must win an election before the policy can be considered and enacted, whereas market competitors need not convince majorities to permit them to produce and retail an innovation. Paradoxically, once a policy is enacted it usually becomes exceedingly difficult to dislodge; a coalition of beneficiaries, resource suppliers, and bureaucrats will see to that end. The market knows no such powerful array behind the status quo. In short, innovation in politics is difficult because, as Friedman has written, "It is hard to start small, and once started, almost impossible to fail. That is why governmental intervention is at once so rigid and so unstable."[22] Perhaps Friedman's contention can be refined and extended: diffused losses and concentrated gains account for the initial success in securing the adoption of inefficient policies, whereas the diffused gains and concentrated losses that will result from reform account for the frequent failure of efforts to repeal policies.

But innovation does occur. What sort of innovation? And why? How can innovation take place in a political system with properties of the sort just outlined?

The kind of innovation that politicians offer is conditioned by their desire to remain in office or to achieve a still higher office. Such innovations are not apt, as W. Allen Wallis has observed, to be truly innovative; instead, the politician offers not a new product or service, but free access to one with which they are already familiar and whose price they cannot or wish not to pay.[23] In short, the politician is an innovator in redistributive schemes. Public provision of education in the nineteenth century is a fine example; publicly provided medical services is a singularly depressing example of a current effort at redistributive innovation. The first task of the politician is to discover a service in widespread demand which is increasingly burdensome for private persons to finance. Once such a large potential voting group has been located, the politician must devise a scheme that will transfer costs from the intended beneficiaries to third parties. And, ideally the regime's scheme must be such that the beneficiary knows he is a substantial beneficiary while the taxed are left unaware of their increased burden. Private market entrepreneurs are denied these opportunities; they must convince those who will benefit to pay and those who will pay that the benefits are worth the price.

This peculiar form of political innovation has serious consequences, many of them perverse. For example, the genuinely poor are less apt to ben-

[22]Milton Friedmtigler, "Director's Law of Public Income Redistribution"; Tullock, "The Charity of the Uncharitable."

[23]W. Allen Wallis, *The Overgoverned Society* (New York; Macmillan, 1976).

efit under such regimes, a distributive outcome that is not usually intended nor predicted by those who would aid the poor. The reason is simple: the genuinely poor lack most of the critical political resources that might compel the attention of politicians. The poor are neither numerous enough nor inclined to pursue political action, including the simple act of voting. Accordingly, the politician interested in redistributive innovations will turn to the better-off who wish to become still better off. The vast middle class is one such group according to Stigler and Tullock; the wealthy are another.[24] Sooner or later these groups manage to be included among the eligible for monies and services usually meant for the less well-off. A not unusual example: the removal of family income as a disqualification for low-cost student loans. Families earning over $40,000 per year and having offspring at Harvard and Stanford eventually came to qualify for these loans. Another program, unique to Oregon, began as a home and farm loan service (at half market interest rates) for veterans who had actually served during wars and were in need of assistance. The program then began making substantial sums available to nearly everyone who served whether during wars or peacetime and regardless of income. Public choice could have predicted both outcomes. This leads us into a more explicit consideration of the strategic elements of political entrepreneurship.

Although supply-side models have emphasized questions of the overall size and composition of budgets, there is a related literature stressing the strategic aspects of spending. I refer not to Downs' spending rule or Riker's minimal-size principle but to a variety of ad hoc generalizations concerning governmental spending as well as taxing proclivities.[25] Some have been rigorously generated as theorems, but many remain as informed but somewhat casual observations made in the context of general fiscal discussions. A few have been tested as ad hoc hypotheses.[26] Regardless, most, if not all, are probably consistent with one or another basic model of public choice.[27]

In spending money, governments want to purchase support, notably votes and campaign monies. The benefits that accrue from these expenditures will best ensure support if 1) the benefits are highly visible to the intended beneficiaries; 2) they are sufficiently large to make a difference to the beneficiaries; 3) they are received in the immediate present or short-run future and just before elections; 4) their flow is more or less continuous; and 5) they are given especially to those beneficiaries in a position to switch

[24]Stigler, "Director's Law of Public Income Redistribution"; Tullock, "The Charity of the Uncharitable."

[25]D. G. Hartle, *A Theory of the Expenditure Budgetary Process* (Toronto: University of Toronto Press, 1976).

[26]Edward R. Tufte, *Political Control of the Economy* (Princeton: Princeton University Press, 1978).

[27]William D. Nordhaus, "The Political Business Cycle," *Review of Economic Studies*, 42 (April 1975): 169-90; Bruno S. Frey, *Modern Political Economy* (New York: John Wiley & Sons, 1978).

their votes. The loyalties of confirmed ideological opponents and supporters are less apt to be swayed by governmental spending.

Spending on highly visible goods for the visibly well-off must be at least partially concealed in order to avoid charges of favoritism. Accordingly, such spending must be accomplished in intricate if not devious ways so as not to anger others. This can be accomplished by the substitution of tax privileges, use of market controls (restricted entry), guaranteed loans, complex programs that conceal incidence, and culturally approved justifications including defense needs, stockpiling of strategic resources, and market failure.

If the spending is on the less well-off, legislators are well advised to confer goods and services rather than income; such an arrangement will satisfy many taxpayers and business suppliers. A large bureaucratic delivery system will be politically advantageous because it increases the number of persons beholdened to the program. Programs must also be encumbered by vast and complicated controls so as to satisfy taxpayers and create work for lawyers and bureaucrats. Again, justifications should reflect invariant but unfulfilled needs of the recipients.

Legislators, bureaucrats, and advocates of additional spending, whether for public goods or transfers, are also advised to adopt certain tactical measures that will increase the probability of enactment of the proposal/s.[28] For example, bureaucrats are advised to request less than the preferred amount/s in order to appear responsible and economy-minded. Additional funds can be subsequently gained through supplemental appropriations which have the further virtues of being quick, quiet, and unpublicized. Another popular tactic is to claim that the program is designed to meet a temporary condition. While bureaucrats prefer highly specified and not readily altered distributive formulas, they may have to concede more discretionary control to the legislators as a quid pro quo.

Recent constitutional spending-limitation proposals as well as tax limitation and budget balancing requirements would, if adopted, create a new and challenging set of circumstances for governments. While public choice supply-siders are hardly in agreement, they do argue that each proposal has its separate virtues—virtues dependent upon the definition of or sources of fiscal irresponsibility. In any event, these same theorists have yet to adequately explore the probable responses of government to enactments of their proposals. Increased skepticism about the possibilities of constraining self-interested and powerful political agents is a distinct likelihood.[29]

Interestingly, theorists who oppose these particular basic fiscal constraints are among those who have alerted us to governmental counterat-

[28]Aaron Wildvasky, *How to Limit Government Spending* (Berkeley: University of California Press, 1979).
[29]Rudolph G. Penner, "The Nonsense Amendment," *New York Times*, 28 March 1982, p. 1.

tacks. For example, Bennett and DiLorenzo and Penner have argued that the balanced budget requirement would simply induce governments to increase use of public corporations[30] Promises of future spending programs, for example, could be offered in place of current income. Fiscally strapped governments might monetize the debt in order to lower interest payments. Conscription for military service might be substituted for a voluntary military in order to reduce the outlay for wages. Finally, since most balanced budget proposals contain an emergency clause, emergencies could become a way of life or simply pro forma responses on the part of government.

Others have maintained that a spending limitation will not succeed because governments can resort to all sorts of "off-budget" programs and "backdoor spending."[31] Guaranteed loans are an egregious example. Increased use of regulation will be employed to force the private sector to do that which in the public sector is prohibited.[32] Spending limitations on state governments have been easily circumvented by some legislatures. The state of Tennessee devised a formula to govern growth, but the formula itself was written by the legislature and is interpreted by the legislature. Spending has not been limited in any significant sense. Friedman, while a supporter of Jarvis-Gann, has noted that that particular tax limitation (property taxes) does nothing about halting the use of inflation as a tax by government.[33] And, worse, such tax limitation laws do nothing to correct the constitutional defect which prohibits the public from ever voting on the *total* budget of government. Our system is one which determines totals by treating each expenditure separately. Friedman also contends that balanced budget requirements at the state and local levels have not and cannot limit the growth of both expenditures and taxation. Similarly, he claims that tax limitations are but stopgaps and that they do not prevent all further growth. Many of the worst forms of government intervention do not involve much spending: often cited examples include tariffs, price controls, and regulation of industry. The regulators spend little, but in meeting regulations the regulated incur considerable costs.[34]

Although public choice has had something to say about the likely responses of government to these fiscal restraints it has had less to offer on the political feasibility of the proposals, that is, the probabilities that any of them might become law. One might have thought otherwise, since public

---

[30]Penner, "The Nonsense Amendment"; James T. Bennett and Thomas J. DiLorenzo, "Underground Government: Subverting Constraints on Public Sector Expansion," *Journal of Social, Political and Economic Studies*, 6 (Fall, 198 l):219-33.

[31]James T. Bennett and Thomas J. DiLorenzo, "How the Government Evades Taxes," *Policy Review*, 19 (Winter 1982):71-89.

[32]Wagner, "Boom and Bust."

[33]Milton Friedman, "The Limitations of Tax Limitation," *Policy Review*, 5(Summer 1978):7-14.

[34]Murray L. Weidenbaum, *Business, Government, and the Public* (Englewood Cliffs, N.J.: Prentice-Hall, 1977).

choice is defined by some as the study of constitutions, decision-rules, and outcomes. Balanced budget requirements are typical at the state and local levels. Tax limitations are less so in one sense but not in another; the equal treatment provision of the Constitution provides a basis for all sorts of legal requirements that define tax law. Nevertheless, spending limitations are not apt to be popular among politicians and bureaucrats.

The scanty evidence which exists suggests that the property tax revolts of recent years have not slowed spending at the local level. In 1981, the *Wall Street Journal* cited a Census Bureau study showing property tax receipts falling by nearly $2 billion in the nation's 75 largest metropolitan areas while spending was increasing for schools, libraries, police and fire protection, and even parks. Supporters of tax limitations may find this disturbing, but it is all highly predictable: governments simply substitute other sources of revenue for the lost property tax. Increases in state and federal aid, boosts in other local taxes, and user fees more than made up for the drop in property tax income. In fact, overall direct local spending and taxes each rose by more than ten percent in 1979. And, in spite of all the misleading claims by the Reagan administration, federal expenditures and tax revenues continued to increase under that so-called conservative government.

Working Bureaucrats and Nonworking Bureaucracy

The role of voters in demand models has been explored and found to be exceedingly limited; they have voices but few choices. In turn, we examined the active role of politicians in supply models and showed how the nature of the political process makes it possible for the elected official to be much more influential than voters, even in the aggregate. We have now to consider the calculus and actions of the bureaucrats who actually provide services wanted and unwanted by citizens, authorized by the politicians, and financed by taxpayers. Theories of bureaucratic behavior and outcomes have proliferated during the decade since Niskanen's *Bureaucracy and Representative Government*. Niskanen's original model has been amended in important ways, but none so critical as to negate its basic approach.[35] We set forth the model without aid of mathematics or even elementary graphics and take but brief note of some of the suggested changes.

Like many brilliant innovations, Niskanen's theory is actually based on quite simple assumptions and reasoning. He argues that the bureaucrat and bureau are, like politicians and voters, self-interested and rational in their work. This orientation leads them to request and usually obtain budgets from their legislative sponsors that are excessive, that is, exceed the social optimum as defined by the equality of marginal costs and marginal benefits that would be achieved in a competitive market. Bureaucrats are able to overspend because, in part, their superior informational capacities

[35]Niskanen, "Bureaucrats and Politicians."

enable them to identify a budget size that will equate total costs and total benefits and thus meet the electoral needs of the politician who wants to cover costs of whatever is provided. But the quantity preferred by bureaucrats is excessive because the additional costs, that is, costs beyond the social optimum, eliminate, in effect, the *consumer surplus* afforded at the optimum level of production.

The model provides a useful basis for understanding how bureaucrats can specify the positions and slopes of the relevant cost- and benefit-curves and "get away with it.'" Costs that are difficult to identify can be easily underestimated while vague and distantly received benefits, especially from public goods, can be significantly overestimated. Thompson[36] has questioned the assumption that legislators can be readily fooled by bureaucrats, while Breton and Wintrobe[37] have maintained that politicians can buy the relevant information. Accordingly, these critics argue that bureaucratic budgets are less outsized than envisaged in the Niskanen model; indeed, they may approximate the politically optimal levels. Others, including McKenzie and Tullock have set forth models that have bureaucrats more concerned with maximizing "waste" (their own salaries, perks, et cetera), than budget size and services.[38] The main outlines of the models are identical, but the levels of production are different in each, depending on the maximand/s set forth. McKenzie and Tullock think that most bureau budgets (quantity of service) are smaller than those predicted by Niskanen, yet larger than the quantity of services offered by a private firm operating under competition or even by a private monopoly. Ironically, then, the public monopoly, while self-interested and more powerful than a private monopoly, desires to offer the consumers more than would a private monopolist and, of course, at zero prices. Overproduction is, necessarily, a wasteful activity; too much of a good thing is generated! The resources could be better employed elsewhere.

Politicians and bureaucrats have different tasks and objectives in the Niskanen model. In this instance, the politicians rather than bureaucrats are thought to better represent the preferences of the voters. The reason: politicians must face voters who are taxpayers as well as beneficiaries, while bureaucrats face voters only indirectly and, in any case, as pure beneficiaries. Politicians are apt, therefore, to prefer lower levels of spending than are bureaucrats, but both sets of preferences are nonoptimal in the Paretian sense.[39]

---

[36]Earl A. Thompson, review of *Bureaucracy and Representative Government* by William A. Niskanen, *Journal of Economic Literature*, 11 (September-December 1973):950-53.

[37]Albert Breton and R. Wintrobe, "The Equilibrium Size of a Budget Maximizing Bureau," *Journal of Political Economy*, 83 (February 1975): 195-207.

[38]Richard D. McKenzie and Gordon Tullock, *Modern Political Economy* (New York: McGraw-Hill, 1978).

[39]Hans van den Doel, *Democracy and Welfare Economics* (Cambridge: Cambridge University Press, 1979).

The importance of bureaucracy in a democracy is difficult to exaggerate. Whether one is a poet or an economist, the fact of extensive bureaucracy cannot be denied, for it is felt in the impersonality of its treatment of citizens, the arbitrariness of its decisions, the boredom of its internal life, and the wastefulness of its allocations. Recent public choice has made this latter consequence a permanent element of modern political economy.

THE SCIENCE OF MUDDLING THROUGH
Charles E. Lindblom*

Suppose an administrator is given responsibility for formulating policy with respect to inflation. He might start by trying to list all related values in order of importance, e.g., full employment, reasonable business profit, protection of small savings, prevention of a stock market crash. Then all possible policy outcomes could be rated as more or less efficient in attaining a maximum of these values. This would of course require a prodigious inquiry into values held by members of society and an equally prodigious set of calculations on how much of each value is equal to how much of each other value. He could then proceed to outline all possible policy alternatives. In a third step, he would undertake systematic comparison of his multitude of alternatives to determine which attains the greatest amount of values.

In comparing policies, he would take advantage of any theory available that generalized about classes of policies. In considering inflation, for example, he would compare all policies in the light of the theory of prices. Since no alternatives are beyond his investigation, he would consider strict central control and the abolition of all prices and markets on the one hand and elimination of all public controls with reliance completely on the free market on the other, both in the light of whatever theoretical generalizations he could find on such hypothetical economies.

Finally, he would try to make the choice that would in fact maximize his values.

An alternative line of attack would be to set as his principal objective, either explicitly or without conscious thought, the relatively simple goal of keeping prices level. This objective might be compromised or complicated by only a few other goals, such as full employment. He would in fact disregard most other social values as beyond his present interest, and he would for the moment not even attempt to rank the few values that he regarded as immediately relevant. Were he pressed, he would quickly admit that he was

*Charles E. Lindblom, "The Science of Muddling Through." *Public Administration Review* 19 (Spring, 1950): 79-88. Used by permission

ignoring many related values and many possible important consequences of his policies.

As a second step, he would outline those relatively few policy alternatives that occurred to him. He would then compare them. In comparing his limited number of alternatives, most of them familiar from past controversies, he would not ordinarily find a body of theory precise enough to carry him through a comparison of their respective consequences. Instead he would rely heavily on the record of past experience with small policy steps to predict the consequences of similar steps extended into the future.

Moreover, he would find that the policy alternatives combined objectives or values in different ways. For example, one policy might offer price level stability at the cost of some risk of unemployment; another might offer less price stability but also less risk of unemployment. Hence, the next step in his approach—the final selection—would combine into one the choice among values and the choice among instruments for reaching values. It would not, as in the first method of policy-making, approximate a more mechanical process of choosing the means that best satisfied goals that were previously clarified and ranked. Because practitioners of the second approach expect to achieve their goals only partially, they would expect to repeat endlessly the sequence just described, as conditions and aspirations changed and as accuracy of prediction improved.

By Root or by Branch

For complex problems, the first of these two approaches is of course impossible. Although such an approach can he described, it cannot be practiced except for relatively simple problems and even then only in a somewhat modified form. It assumes intellectual capacities and sources of information that men simply do not possess, and it is even more absurd as an approach to policy when the time and money that can be allocated to a policy problem are limited, as is always the case. Of particular importance to public administrators is the fact that public agencies are in effect usually instructed not to practice the first method. That is to say, their prescribed functions and constraints—the politically or legally possible—restrict their attention to relatively few values and relatively few alternative policies among the countless alternatives that might be imagined. It is the second method that is practiced.

Curiously, however, the literatures of decision-making, policy formulation, planning, and public administration formalize the first approach rather than the second, leaving public administrators who handle complex decisions in the position of practicing what few preach. For emphasis I run some risk of overstatement. True enough, the literature is well aware of limits on man's capacities and of the inevitability that policies will be approached in some such style as the second. But attempts to formalize rational policy formulation—to lay out explicitly the necessary steps in the process—usually describe the first approach and not the second.[1]

The common tendency to describe policy formulation even for complex problems as though it followed the first approach has been strengthened by the attention given to, and successes enjoyed by, operations research, statistical decision theory, and systems analysis. The hallmarks of these procedures, typical of the first approach, are clarity of objective, explicitness of evaluation, a high degree of comprehensiveness of overview, and, wherever possible, quantification of values for mathematical analysis. But these advanced procedures remain largely the appropriate techniques of relatively small-scale problem-solving where the total number of variables to be considered is small and value problems restricted. Charles Hitch, head of the Economics Division of RAND Corporation, one of the leading centers for application of these techniques, has written:

> I would make the empirical generalization from my experience at RAND and elsewhere that operations research is the art of sub-optimizing, i.e., of solving some lower level problems, and that difficulties increase and our special competence diminishes by an order of magnitude with every level of decision making we attempt to ascend. The sort of simple explicit model which operations researchers are so proficient in using can certainly reflect most of the significant factors influencing traffic control on the George Washington Bridge, but the proportion of the relevant reality which we can represent by any such model or models in studying, say, a major foreign-policy decision, appears to be almost trivial.[2]

Accordingly, I propose in this paper to clarify and formalize the second method, much neglected in the literature. This might be described as the method of *successive limited comparisons*. I will contrast it with the first approach, which might be called the rational-comprehensive method.[3] More impressionistically and briefly—and therefore generally used in this article—they could be characterized as the branch method and root method, the former continually building out from the current situation, step-by-step and by small degrees; the latter starting from fundamentals anew each time,

---

[1] James G. March and Herbert A. Simon similarly characterize the literature. They also take some important steps, as have Simon's recent articles, to describe a less heroic model of policy-making, See *Organizations* (John Wiley and Sons, 1958), p. 137.

[2] "Operations Research and National Planning—A Dissent," *Operations Research* 718 (October, 1957), Hitch's dissent is from particular points made in the article to which his paper is a reply: his claim that operations research is for low-level problems is widely accepted.

For examples of the kind of problems to which operations research is applied, see C. W. Churchman, R. L. Ackoff and E. L. Arnoff, *Introduction to Operations Research* (John Wiley and Sons, 1957); and J. F. McCloskey and J. M. Coppinger (eds.), *Operations Research for Management*, Vol, II (The Johns Hopkins Press, 1956),

[3] I am assuming that administrators often make policy and advise in the making of policy and am treating decision-making and policy-making as synonymous for purposes of this paper.

building on the past only as experience is embodied in a theory, and always prepared to start completely from the ground up.

Let us put the characteristics of the two methods side by side in simplest terms. (See Table 3-1.)

Assuming that the root method is familiar and understandable, we proceed directly to clarification of its alternative by contrast. In explaining the second, we shall be describing how most administrators do in fact approach complex questions, for the root method, the "best" way as a blueprint or model, is in fact not workable for complex policy questions, and administrators are forced to use the method of successive limited comparisons.

Intertwining Evaluation and Empirical Analysis (lb)

The quickest way to understand how values are handled in the method of successive limited comparisons is to see how the root method often breaks down in *its* handling of values or objectives. The idea that values should be clarified, and in advance of the examination of alternative policies, is appealing. But what happens when we attempt it for complex social problems? The first difficulty is that on many critical values or objectives, citizens disagree, congressmen disagree, and public administrators

Table 3-1

Rational-Comprehensive (Root)	Successive Limited Comparisons (Branch)
Clarification of values or objectives distinct from and usually prerequisite to empirical analysis of alternative policies.	Selection of value goals and empirical analysis of the needed action are not distinct from one another but are closely intertwined.
Policy-formulation is therefore approached through means-end analysis: First the ends are isolated, then the means to achieve them are sought.	Since means and ends are not distinct, means-end analysis is often inappropriate or limited.
The rest of a "good" policy is that it can be shown to be the most appropriate means to desired ends.	The rest of a "good" policy is typically that various analysts find themselves directly agreeing on a policy (without their agreeing that it is the most appropriate means to an agreed objective.)
Analysis is comprehensive; every important relevant factor is taken into account.	Analysis is drastically limited: Important possible outcomes are neglected. Important alternative potential policies are neglected. Important affected values are neglected.
Theory is often heavily relied upon.	A succession of comparisons greatly reduces or eliminates reliance on theory.

disagree. Even where a fairly specific objective is prescribed for the administrator, there remains considerable room for disagreement on subobjectives. Consider, for example, the conflict with respect to locating public housing, described in Meyerson and Banfield's study of the Chicago Housing Authority[4]—disagreement which occurred despite the clear objective of providing a certain number of public housing units in the city. Similarly conflicting are objectives in highway location, traffic control, minimum wage administration, development of tourist facilities in national parks, or insect control.

Administrators cannot escape these conflicts by ascertaining the majority's preference, for preferences have not been registered on most issues; indeed, there often *are* no preferences in the absence of public discussion sufficient to bring an issue to the attention of the electorate. Furthermore, there is a question of whether intensity of feeling should be considered as well as the number of persons preferring each alternative. By the impossibility of doing otherwise, administrators often are reduced to deciding policy without clarifying objectives first.

Even when an administrator resolves to follow his own values as a criterion for decisions, he often will not know how to rank them when they conflict with one another, as they usually do. Suppose, for example, that an administrator must relocate tenants living in tenements scheduled for destruction. One objective is to empty the buildings fairly promptly, another is to find suitable accommodation for persons displaced, another is to avoid friction with residents in other areas in which a large influx would be unwelcome, another is to deal with all concerned through persuasion if possible, and so on.

How does one state even to himself the relative importance of these partially conflicting values? A simple ranking of them is not enough; one needs ideally to know how much of one value is worth sacrificing for some of another value. The answer is that typically the administrator chooses— and must choose—directly among policies in which these values are combined in different ways. He cannot first clarify his values and then choose among policies.

A more subtle third point underlies both the first two. Social objectives do not always have the same relative values. One objective may be highly prized in one circumstance, another in another circumstance. If, for example, an administrator values highly both the dispatch with which his agency can carry through its projects *and* good public relations, it matters little which of the two possibly conflicting values he favors in some abstract or general sense. Policy questions arise in forms which put to administra-

[4]Martin Meyerson and Edward C. Banfield, *Politics, Planning and the Public Interest* (The Free Press, 1955).

tors such a question as: Given the degree to which we are or are not already achieving the values of dispatch and the values of good public relations, is it worth sacrificing a little speed for a happier clientele, or is it better to risk offending the clientele so that we can get on with our work? The answer to such a question varies with circumstances.

The value problem is, as the example shows, always a problem of adjustments at a margin. But there is no practicable way to state marginal objectives or values except in terms of particular policies. That one value is preferred to another in one decision situation does not mean that it will be preferred in another decision situation in which it can be had only at great sacrifice of another value. Attempts to rank or order values in general and abstract terms so that they do not shift from decision to decision end up by ignoring the relevant marginal preferences. The significance of this third point thus goes very far. Even if all administrators had at hand an agreed set of values, objectives, and constraints, and an agreed ranking of these values, objectives, and constraints, their marginal values in actual choice situations would be impossible to formulate.

Unable consequently to formulate the relevant values first and then choose among policies to achieve them, administrators must choose directly among alternative policies that offer different marginal combinations of values. Somewhat paradoxically, the only practicable way to disclose one's relevant marginal values even to oneself is to describe the policy one chooses to achieve them. Except roughly and vaguely, I know of no way to describe—or even to understand—what my relative evaluations are for, say, freedom and security, speed and accuracy in governmental decisions, or low taxes and better schools than to describe my preferences among specific policy choices that might be made between the alternatives in each of the pairs.

In summary, two aspects of the process by which values are actually handled can be distinguished. The first is clear: evaluation and empirical analysis are intertwined: that is, one chooses among values and among policies at one and the same time. Put a little more elaborately, one simultaneously chooses a policy to attain certain objectives and chooses the objectives themselves. The second aspect is related but distinct: the administrator focuses his attention on marginal or incremental values. Whether he is aware of it or not, he does not find general formulations of objectives very helpful and in fact makes specific marginal or incremental comparisons. Two policies, X and Y, confront him. Both promise the same degree of attainment of objectives a, b, c, d, and e. But X promises him somewhat more of f than does Y, while Y promises him somewhat more of g than does X. In choosing between them, he is in fact offered the alternative of a marginal or incremental amount of f at the expense of a marginal or incremental amount of g. The only values that are relevant to his choice are these increments by which the two policies differ; and, when he finally chooses between the two marginal values, he does so by making a choice between policies.[5]

As to whether the attempt to clarify objectives in advance of policy selection is more or less rational than the close intertwining of marginal evaluation and empirical analysis, the principal difference established is that for complex problems the first is impossible and irrelevant, and the second is both possible and relevant. The second is possible because the administrator need not try to analyze any values except the values by which alternative policies differ and need not be concerned with them except as they differ marginally. His need for information on values or objectives is drastically reduced as compared with the root method; and his capacity for grasping, comprehending, and relating values to one another is not strained beyond the breaking point.

Relations Between Means and Ends (2b)

Decision-making is ordinarily formalized as a means-ends relationship: means are conceived to be evaluated and chosen in the light of ends finally selected independently of and prior to the choice of means. This is the means-ends relationship of the root method. But it follows from all that has just been said that such a means-ends relationship is possible only to the extent that values are agreed upon, are reconcilable, and are stable at the margin. Typically, therefore, such a means-ends relationship is absent from the branch method, where means and ends are simultaneously chosen.

Yet any departure from the means-ends relationship of the root method will strike some readers as inconceivable. For it will appear to them that only in such a relationship is it possible to determine whether one policy choice is better or worse than another. How can an administrator know whether he has made a wise or foolish decision if he is without prior values or objectives by which to judge his decisions? The answer to this question calls up the third distinctive difference between root and branch methods: how to decide the best policy.

The Test of "Good" Policy (3b)

In the root method, a decision is "correct," "good," or "rational" if it can be shown to attain some specified objective, where the objective can be specified without simply describing the decision itself. Where objectives are defined only through the marginal or incremental approach to values described above, it is still sometimes possible to test whether a policy does in fact attain the desired objectives; but a precise statement of the objectives

---

[5]The line of argument is, of course, an extension of the theory of market choice, especially the theory of consumer choice, to public policy choices.

takes the form of a description of the policy chosen or some alternative to it. To show that a policy is mistaken one cannot offer an abstract argument that important objectives are not achieved; one must instead argue that another policy is more to be preferred.

So far, the departure from customary ways of looking at problem-solving is not troublesome, for many administrators will be quick to agree that the most effective discussion of the correctness of policy does take the form of comparison with other policies that might have been chosen. But what of the situation in which administrators cannot agree on values or objectives, either abstractly or in marginal terms? What then is the test of "good" policy? For the root method, there is no test. Agreement on objectives failing, there is no standard of "correctness." For the method of successive limited comparisons, the test is agreement on policy itself, which remains possible even when agreement on values is not.

It has been suggested that continuing agreement in Congress on the desirability of extending old age insurance stems from liberal desires to strengthen the welfare programs of the federal government and from conservative desires to reduce union demands for private pension plans. If so, this is an excellent demonstration of the ease with which individuals of different ideologies often can agree on concrete policy. Labor mediators report a similar phenomenon: the contestants cannot agree on criteria for settling their disputes but can agree on specific proposals. Similarly, when one administrator's objective turns out to be another's means, they often can agree on policy.

Agreement on policy thus becomes the only practicable test of the policy's correctness. And for one administrator to seek to win the other over to agreement on ends as well would accomplish nothing and create quite unnecessary controversy.

If agreement directly on policy as a test for "best" policy seems a poor substitute for testing the policy against its objectives, it ought to be remembered that objectives themselves have no ultimate validity other than they are agreed upon. Hence agreement is the test of "best" policy in both methods. But where the root method requires agreement on what elements in the decision constitute objectives and on which of these objectives should be sought, the branch method falls back on agreement wherever it can be found.

In an important sense, therefore, it is not irrational for an administrator to defend a policy as good without being able to specify what it is good for.

Noncomprehensive Analysis (4b)

Ideally, rational-comprehensive analysis leaves out nothing important. But it is impossible to take everything important into consideration unless "important" is so narrowly defined that analysis is in fact quite limited.

Limits on human intellectual capacities and on available information set definite limits to man's capacity to be comprehensive. In actual fact, therefore, no one can practice the rational comprehensive method for really complex problems, and every administrator faced with a sufficiently complex problem must find ways drastically to simplify.

An administrator assisting in the formulation of agricultural economic policy cannot in the first place be competent on all possible policies. He cannot even comprehend one policy entirely. In planning a soil bank program, he cannot successfully anticipate the impact of higher or lower farm income on, say, urbanization—the possible consequent loosening of family ties, possible consequent eventual need for revisions in social security and further implications for tax problems arising out of new federal responsibilities for social security and municipal responsibilities for urban services. Nor, to follow another line of repercussions, can he work through the soil bank program's effects on prices for agricultural products in foreign markets and consequent implications for foreign relations, including those arising out of economic rivalry between the United States and the U.S.S.R.

In the method of successive, limited comparisons, simplification is systematically achieved in two principal ways. First, it is achieved through limitation of policy comparisons to those policies that differ in relatively small degree from policies presently in effect. Such a limitation immediately reduces the number of alternatives to be investigated and also drastically simplifies the character of the investigation of each. For it is not necessary to undertake fundamental inquiry into an alternative and its consequences; it is necessary only to study those respects in which the proposed alternative and its consequences differ from the status quo. The empirical comparison of marginal differences among alternative policies that differ only marginally is, of course, a counterpart to the incremental or marginal comparison of values discussed above.[6]

Relevance as Well as Realism

It is a matter of common observation that in Western democracies public administrators and policy analysts in general do largely limit their analyses to incremental or marginal differences in policies that are chosen to differ only incrementally. They do not do so, however, solely because they desperately need some way to simplify their problems; they also do so in order to be relevant. Democracies change their policies almost entirely through incremental adjustments. Policy does not move in leaps and bounds.

---

[6]A more precise definition of incremental policies and a discussion of whether a change that appears "small" to one observer might be seen differently by another is to be found in my "Policy Analysis," 48 *American Economic Review* 298 (June, 1958).

The incremental character of political change in the United States has often been remarked. The two major political parties agree on fundamentals; they offer alternative policies to the voters only on relatively small points of difference. Both parties favor full employment, but they define it somewhat differently; both favor the development of water power resources, but in slightly different ways; and both favor unemployment compensation, but not the same level of benefits. Similarly, shifts of policy within a party take place largely through a series of relatively small changes, as can be seen in their only gradual acceptance of the idea of governmental responsibility for support of the unemployed, a change in party positions beginning in the early 1930s and culminating in a sense in the Employment Act of 1946.

Party behavior is in turn rooted in public attitudes, and political theorists cannot conceive of democracy's surviving in the United States in the absence of fundamental agreement on potentially disruptive issues, with consequent limitation of policy debates to relatively small differences in policy.

Since the policies ignored by the administrator are politically impossible and so irrelevant, the simplification of analysis achieved by concentrating on policies that differ only incrementally is not a capricious kind of simplification. In addition, it can be argued that, given the limits on knowledge within which policy-makers are confined, simplifying by limiting the focus to small variations from present policy makes the most of available knowledge. Because policies being considered are like present and past policies, the administrator can obtain information and claim some insight. Nonincremental policy proposals are therefore typically not only politically irrelevant but also unpredictable in their consequences.

The second method of simplification of analysis is the practice of ignoring important possible consequences of possible policies, as well as the values attached to the neglected consequences. If this appears to disclose a shocking shortcoming of successive limited comparisons, it can be replied that, even if the exclusions are random, policies may nevertheless be more intelligently formulated than through futile attempts to achieve a comprehensiveness beyond human capacity. Actually, however, the exclusions, seeming arbitrary or random from one point of view, need be neither.

Achieving a Degree of Comprehensiveness

Suppose that each value neglected by one policy-making agency were a major concern of at least one other agency. In that case, a helpful division of labor would be achieved, and no agency need find its task beyond its capacities. The shortcomings of such a system would be that one agency might destroy a value either before another agency could be activated to safeguard it or in spite of another agency's efforts. But the possibility that important values may be lost is present in any form of organization, even where agencies attempt to comprehend in planning more than is humanly possible.

The virtue of such a hypothetical division of labor is that every important interest or value has its watchdog. And these watchdogs can protect the interests in their jurisdiction in two quite different ways: first, by redressing damages done by other agencies; and, second, by anticipating and heading off injury before it occurs.

In a society like that of the United States in which individuals are free to combine to pursue almost any possible common interest they might have and in which government agencies are sensitive to the pressures of these groups, the system described is approximated. Almost every interest has its watchdog. Without claiming that every interest has a sufficiently powerful watchdog, it can be argued that our system often can assure a more comprehensive regard for the values of the whole society than any attempt at intellectual comprehensiveness.

In the United States, for example, no part of government attempts a comprehensive overview of policy on income distribution. A policy nevertheless evolves, and one responding to a wide variety of interests. A process of mutual adjustment among farm groups, labor unions, municipalities and school boards, tax authorities, and government agencies with responsibilities in the fields of housing, health, highways, national parks, fire, and police accomplishes a distribution of income in which particular income problems neglected at one point in the decision processes become central at another point.

Mutual adjustment is more pervasive than the explicit forms it takes in negotiation between groups; it persists through the mutual impacts of groups upon each other even where they are not in communication. For all the imperfections and latent dangers in this ubiquitous process of mutual adjustment, it will often accomplish an adaptation of policies to a wider range of interests than could be done by one group centrally.

Note, too, how the incremental pattern of policy-making fits with the multiple pressure pattern. For when decisions are only incremental—closely related to known policies, it is easier for one group to anticipate the kind of moves another might make and easier too for it to make correction for injury already accomplished.[7]

Even partisanship and narrowness, to use pejorative terms, will sometimes be assets to rational decision-making, for they can doubly insure that what one agency neglects, another will not; they specialize personnel to distinct points of view. The claim is valid that effective rational coordination of the federal administration, if possible to achieve at all, would require an

---

[7]The link between the practice of the method of successive limited comparisons and mutual adjustment of interests in a highly fragmented decision-making process adds a new facet to pluralist theories of government and administration.

agreed set of values[8]—if "rational" is defined as the practice of the root method of decision-making. But a high degree of administrative coordination occurs as each agency adjusts its policies to the concerns of the other agencies in the process of fragmented decision-making I have just described.

For all the apparent shortcomings of the incremental approach to policy alternatives with its arbitrary exclusion coupled with fragmentation, when compared to the root method, the branch method often looks far superior. In the root method, the inevitable exclusion of factors is accidental, unsystematic, and not defensible by any argument so far developed, while in the branch method the exclusions are deliberate, systematic, and defensible. Ideally, of course, the root method does not exclude; in practice it must.

Nor does the branch method necessarily neglect long-run considerations and objectives. It is clear that important values must be omitted in considering policy, and sometimes the only way long-run objectives can be given adequate attention is through the neglect of short-run considerations. But the values omitted can be either long-run or short-run.

Succession of Comparisons (5b)

The final distinctive element in the branch method is that the comparisons, together with the policy choice, proceed in a chronological series. Policy is not made once and for all; it is made and re-made endlessly. Policy-making is a process of successive approximation to some desired objectives in which what is desired itself continues to change under reconsideration.

Making policy is at best a very rough process. Neither social scientists, nor politicians, nor public administrators yet know enough about the social world to avoid repeated error in predicting the consequences of policy moves. A wise policy-maker consequently expects that his policies will achieve only part of what he hopes and at the same time will produce unanticipated consequences he would have preferred to avoid. If he proceeds through a *succession* of incremental changes, he avoids serious lasting mistakes in several ways.

In the first place, past sequences of policy steps have given him knowledge about the probable consequences of further similar steps. Second, he need not attempt big jumps toward his goals that would require predictions beyond his or anyone else's knowledge, because he never expects his policy to be a final resolution of a problem. His decision is only one step, one that if successful can quickly be followed by another. Third, he is in effect able to test his previous predictions as he moves on to each further step. Lastly, he often can remedy a past error fairly quickly—more

[8]Herbert Simon, Donald W. Smithburg, and Victor A. Thompson, *Public Administration* (Alfred A. Knopf, 1950), p. 434.

quickly than if policy proceeded through more distinct steps widely spaced in time.

Compare this comparative analysis of incremental changes with the aspiration to employ theory in the root method. Man cannot think without classifying, without subsuming one experience under a more general category of experiences. The attempt to push categorization as far as possible and to find general propositions which can be applied to specific situations is what l refer to with the word "theory." Where root analysis often leans heavily on theory in this sense, the branch method does not.

The assumption of root analysts is that theory is the most systematic and economical way to bring relevant knowledge to bear on a specific problem. Granting the assumption, an unhappy fact is that we do not have adequate theory to apply to problems in any policy area, although theory is more adequate in some areas—monetary policy, for example—than in others. Comparative analysis, as in the branch method, is sometimes a systematic alternative to theory.

Suppose an administrator must choose among a small group of policies that differ only incrementally from each other and from present policy. He might aspire to "understand" each of the alternatives—for example, to know all the consequences of each aspect of each policy. If so, he would indeed require theory. In fact, however, he would usually decide that, *for policy-making purposes*, he need know, as explained above, only the consequences of each of those aspects of the policies in which they differed from one another. For this much more modest aspiration, he requires no theory (although it might be helpful, if available), for he can proceed to isolate probable differences by examining the differences in consequences associated with past differences in policies, a feasible program because he can take his observations from a long sequence of incremental changes.

For example, without a more comprehensive social theory about juvenile delinquency than scholars have yet produced, one cannot possibly understand the ways in which a variety of public policies—say on education, housing, recreation, employment, race relations, and policing—might encourage or discourage delinquency. And one needs such an understanding if he undertakes the comprehensive overview of the problem prescribed in the models of the root method. If, however, one merely wants to mobilize knowledge sufficient to assist in a choice among a small group of similar policies—alternative policies on juvenile court procedures, for example—he can do so by comparative analysis of the results of similar past policy moves.

Theorists and Practitioners

This difference explains—in some cases at least—why the administrator often feels that the outside expert or academic problem-solver is sometimes not helpful and why they in turn often urge more theory on him. And it explains why an administrator often feels more confident when "flying by the seat of his pants" than when following the advice of theorists. Theorists often ask the administrator to go the long way round to the solution of his problems, in effect ask him to follow the best canons of the scientific method, when the administrator knows that the best available theory will work less well than the more modest incremental comparisons. Theorists do not realize that the administrator is often in fact practicing a systematic method. It would be foolish to push this explanation too far, for sometimes practical decision-makers are pursuing neither a theoretical approach nor successive comparisons, nor any other systematic method.

It may be worth emphasizing that theory is sometimes of extremely limited helpfulness in policy-making for at least two rather different reasons. It is greedy for facts; it can be constructed only through a great collection of observations. And it is typically insufficiently precise for application to a policy process that moves through small changes. In contrast, the comparative method both economizes on the need for facts and directs the analyst's attention to just those facts that are relevant to the fine choices faced by the decision-maker.

With respect to precision of theory, economic theory serves as an example. It predicts that an economy without money or prices would in certain specified ways misallocate resources, but this finding pertains to an alternative far removed from the kind of policies on which administrators need help. On the other hand, it is not precise enough to predict the consequences of policies restricting business mergers, and this is the kind of issue on which the administrators need help. Only in relatively restricted areas does economic theory achieve sufficient precision to go far in resolving policy questions; its helpfulness in policy-making is always so limited that it requires supplementation through comparative analysis.

Successive Comparison as a System

Successive limited comparisons is, then, indeed a method or system; it is not a failure of method for which administrators ought to apologize. Nonetheless, its imperfections, which have not been explored in this paper, are many. For example, the method is without a built-in safeguard for all relevant values, and it also may lead the decision maker to overlook excellent policies for no other reason than that they are not suggested by the chain of successive policy steps leading up to the present. Hence, it ought to be said that under this method, as well as under some of the most sophisticated variants of the root method—operations research, for example—policies will continue to be as foolish as they are wise.

Why then bother to describe the method in all the above detail? Because it is in fact a common method of policy formulation, and is, for complex problems, the principal reliance of administrators as well as of other policy analysts.[9] And because it will be superior to any other decision-making method available for complex problems in many circumstances, certainly superior to a futile attempt at superhuman comprehensiveness. The reaction of the public administrator to the exposition of method doubtless will be less a discovery of a new method than a better acquaintance with an old. But by becoming more conscious of their practice of this method, administrators might practice it with more skill and know when to extend or constrict its use. (That they sometimes practice it effectively and sometimes not may explain the extremes of opinion on "muddling through," which is both praised as a highly sophisticated form of problem-solving and denounced as no method at all. For I suspect that in so far as there is a system in what is known as "muddling through," this method is it.)

One of the noteworthy incidental consequences of clarification of the method is the light it throws on the suspicion an administrator sometimes entertains that a consultant or adviser is not speaking relevantly and responsibly when in fact by all ordinary objective evidence he is. The trouble lies in the fact that most of us approach policy problems within a framework given by our view of a chain of successive policy choices made up to the present. One's thinking about appropriate policies with respect, say, to urban traffic control is greatly influenced by one's knowledge of the incremental steps taken up to the present. An administrator enjoys an intimate knowledge of his past sequences that "outsiders" do not share, and his thinking and that of the "outsider" will consequently be different in ways that may puzzle both. Both may appear to be talking intelligently, yet each may find the other unsatisfactory. The relevance of the policy chain of succession is even more clear when an American tries to discuss, say, antitrust policy with a Swiss, for the chains of policy in the two countries are strikingly different and the two individuals consequently have organized their knowledge in quite different ways.

If this phenomenon is a barrier to communication, an understanding of it promises an enrichment of intellectual interaction in policy formulation. Once the source of difference is understood, it will sometimes be stim-

---

[9]Elsewhere I have explored this same method of policy formulation as practiced by academic analysts of policy ("Policy Analysis." 48 *American Economic Review* 298 [June, 1958]). Although it has been here presented as a method for public administrators, it is no less necessary to analysts more removed from immediate policy questions, despite their tendencies to describe their own analytical efforts as though they were the rational-comprehensive method with an especially heavy use of theory. Similarly, this same method is inevitably resorted to in personal problem-solving, where means and ends are sometimes impossible to separate, where aspirations or objectives undergo constant development, and where drastic simplification of the complexity of the real world is urgent if problems are to be solved in the time that can be given to them. To an economist accustomed to dealing with the marginal or incremental concept in market processes, the central idea in the method is that both evaluation and empirical analysis are incremental. Accordingly I have referred to the method elsewhere as "the incremental method."

ulating for an administrator to seek out a policy analyst whose recent experience is with a policy chain different from his own.

This raises again a question only briefly discussed above on the merits of likemindedness among government administrators. While much of organization theory argues the virtues of common values and agreed organizational objectives, for complex problems in which the root method is inapplicable, agencies will want among their own personnel two types of diversification: administrators whose thinking is organized by reference to policy chains other than those familiar to most members of the organization and, even more commonly, administrators whose professional or personal values or interests create diversity of view (perhaps coming from different specialties, social classes, geographical areas) so that, even within a single agency, decision-making can be fragmented and parts of the agency can serve as watchdogs for other parts.

STAGES OF THE POLICY PROCESS
Randall B. Ripley*

Numerous treatments of the policy process lay out stages of that process, with various nominal labels attached, in order to help organize discussion and analysis. Such stage-oriented discussions do not form the direct basis for hypothesizing causal relationships, although such hypotheses may emerge. Rather, they are rough chronological and logical guides for observers who want to see important activities in some ordered pattern or sequence. Such organizational helpers are useful and, in fact, essential for anyone trying to plow through the complexities of policy making and policy analysis. At best, such maps—even with their rough spots and simplifications—lend some clarity to the observer/reader/student as he or she grapples with a complicated and sometimes murky set of interactions and processes.

I see no point to repeating a lot of different authors' versions of policy stages. There are many versions. Most of them have some similarities. Many analysts agree pretty well on the central activities requiring attention. Instead, I will offer my guide to the stages of the policy process.

Major Stages

Figure 3–4 lays out the basic flow of policy stages, major functional activities that occur in those stages, and the products that can be expected at each stage if a product is forthcoming. Naturally, a policy process may be aborted at any stage. Beginning a process does not guarantee that products

*Randall Ripley, *Policy Analysis in Political Science.* Chicago: Nelson-Hall, 1985 (pp. 48-55). Used by permission.

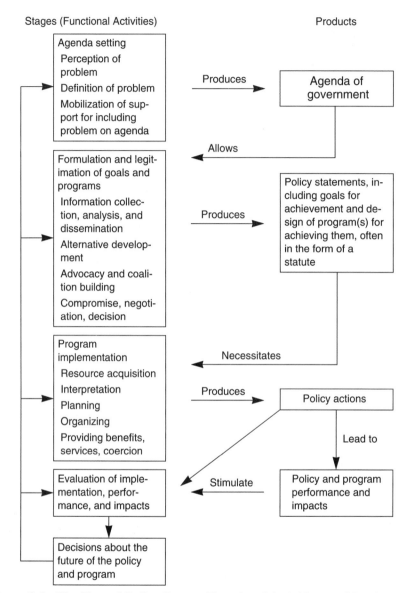

Stages (Functional Activities)   Products

Agenda setting
Perception of problem
Definition of problem   —Produces→   Agenda of government
Mobilization of support for including problem on agenda

                           ←Allows—

Formulation and legitimation of goals and programs
Information collection, analysis, and dissemination   —Produces→   Policy statements, including goals for achievement and design of program(s) for achieving them, often in the form of a statute
Alternative development
Advocacy and coalition building
Compromise, negotiation, decision

                           ←Necessitates—

Program implementation
Resource acquisition
Interpretation   —Produces→   Policy actions
Planning
Organizing
Providing benefits, services, coercion   Lead to

Evaluation of implementation, performance, and impacts   ←Stimulate—   Policy and program performance and impacts

Decisions about the future of the policy and program

Figure 3-4   The Flow of Policy Stages, Functional Activities, and Products

will emerge or that a stage will be "completed" and so lead to the next stage. Figure 3–4 presents the general flow of stages, activities, and products that can be expected in a policy that is generated and transformed into a viable and ongoing program. "Stages" are the names attached to major clusters of activities that result in identifiable products if they reach conclu-

sion. "Functional activities" are the major subroutines of actions and interactions engaged in by policy actors. "Products" are the output, or end result, of any general stage.

Agenda setting   Somehow the organs of government must decide
what they will pay attention to. The stage at which this decision is made in
any given policy area is here called agenda setting. Thousands of issues are
constantly vying for inclusion on the governmental agenda. Only some of
them make it at any given time. The form in which they come on the
agenda can vary over time and influence subsequent concrete decisions.
The functional activities in the agenda-setting stage include the necessity
for some individuals and/or groups to perceive a problem to exist, to decide the government should be involved in the problem, to define the problem, and to mobilize support for including the problem on the governmental agenda.

Competition enters these activities in several ways. First, different
people compete to attract the attention of governmental actors for inclusion
of any specific problem on the agenda. There is not a fixed number of
agenda item "slots" available at any one time. On the other hand, the capacity for the government to include items on its action agenda at any point in
time is not unlimited. Second, even within the groups and among individuals concerned with a general issue area there will be competition over the
specific definition of the problem and, subsequently, competition over
which groups and views to mobilize and how to do it.

Formulation and Legitimation of Goals and Programs   Not all
agenda items receive specific treatment in the form of decisions about policies and programs. Not all of them even get translated into a form that allows specific formulation and legitimation activities to take place. But if an
item on the agenda is treated in any concrete way, the next step is for it to
become the subject of formulation and legitimation.

Formulation and legitimation are complex activities that involve four
major sets of functional activities, each complex in its own right. Part of formulating alternatives and then choosing one alternative for possible ratification is collecting, analyzing, and disseminating information for purposes
of assessing alternatives and projecting likely outcomes and for purposes of
persuasion.

Alternative development is one of the successor subroutines to the one
dealing with information. Another is advocacy, in which different persons
and groups advocate different points of views and alternatives and seek to
build supporting coalitions in support of their views and their preferred alternative. Finally, usually as a result of compromise and negotiation, a decision is reached. If the compromise and negotiation process breaks down, no
decision is reached.

The generic products of the formulation and legitimation stage are policy statements (declarations of intent, including some form of goal statement) and the design of programs for making the intent concrete and pursuing achievement of the goals. Both the goals and the program designs may be vague and sketchy. Grandiose goal statements that lack clarity are usually the result of the compromise process. Too much specificity and clarity might prevent compromise of forces that don't really agree on fundamental concrete goals and aspirations. If the goals are raised to a more general and murky level, they can attract the support of persons and groups that might otherwise disagree.

Reasons for lack of specificity and clarity in program design are more numerous. Partly it is a matter of not proliferating details that might also proliferate disagreements, and partly it is a matter of time on the part of Congress, since program designs usually appear first in a statute. Congress must address hundreds, even thousands, of agenda items in any given two-year period. The members cannot fool with any one too long. Throughout the course of history, Congress has gotten into the habit of delegating administrative power to the president and/or to the agencies and secretaries concerned to flesh out rudimentary program designs. From the early 1930s to 1983, Congress could hedge its bets by inserting some form of legislative veto in a statute, which in effect made the president or agency check with Congress before proceeding with some specific actions. The Supreme Court ruled this invention unconstitutional in mid-1983. This ruling may force Congress to fill in a few more details some of the time, but it is doubtful if it will have more effect than that. The pressures producing extensive delegation by Congress will not change.

Program Implementation   The next stage (assuming that a policy has been stated and a program created) is program implementation. In order to implement a program, resources need to be acquired. The law needs to be interpreted, usually in written regulations and then in elaborations of those regulations. A variety of planning activities typically take place. Various organizing routines are part of implementation. Finally, the payoff—routines of providing benefits, services, and/or coercion (whatever the tangible manifestation of the program) are developed. All of these activities, although they sound more dull than advocacy and negotiation, are political. Conflict and disagreement can erupt. Various techniques of conflict resolution are necessarily brought into play. Policy actions are the products of the various routines and activities that comprise the program implementation stage.

Evaluation of Implementation, Performance, and Impacts   After policy actions lead to various kinds of results (what I call performance and impact), evaluation of both the actions (implementation) and the results (performance and impacts) takes place. The word *evaluation* often conjures up an image of "objective" social scientists applying rigorous analytic techniques and letting the chips fall where they may. Some of that may transpire. But, as used in this book, evaluation is a much broader concept and refers to the assessment of what has happened or, in many cases, what is thought to have happened. The "what" can refer to implementation, to short-run results (performance), or to long-run results (impacts). That assessment takes place constantly and is done by all kinds of people—officials of all descriptions, interest groups, legislators, researchers inside the government, and researchers outside the government. Some evaluation is completely based on political instincts and judgments. A good deal is based on a mix of a little information (often anecdotal) and political judgments. Some (a small portion) is based on systematic analysis of fairly extensive information (data).

Policy analysts coming from political science or any other discipline have a role to play in evaluation of implementation, performance, and impacts. But they should realize that their form of evaluation is only one form and that probably it is less politically relevant than almost any other form of evaluation that takes place. Not too much should be expected in terms of attention to or subsequent actions based on evaluation. On the other hand, evaluation should not be written off entirely. It has a place.

Decisions about the Future of the Policy and Program The evaluative processes and conclusions, in all of their diversity, lead to one or more of many decisions about the future (or nonfuture) of the policy and program being evaluated. The necessity for such decisions means that the cycle can be entered again at any of its major stages. Conceivably, a problem will be taken off the agenda either because it has been "solved" or because it is viewed as no longer relevant. Or the nature of its most salient features as an agenda item may be changed. Thus, decisions about the future might reset the cycle to the agenda setting stage.

Those decisions may lead back to policy formulation and legitimation. The necessity or legitimacy of keeping an item on the agenda may not be questioned, but legislative (statutory) revisions may be viewed as necessary or desirable, at least by some actors. Thus, the cycle is reentered somewhere in the activity cluster comprising formulation and legitimation. In some cases, decisions about the future may not require new legislation or amendments to existing legislation, but they may require some adjustments in program implementation.

Principal Limits on and Utility of a Stage Conception of the Policy Process

Remember when looking at the policy process as a succession of stages that any such conception is artificial. It may also not be true to what happens. It has a logical appeal, and it is presented chronologically, but chronological reality as it emerges in any case may vary significantly from what the stage-based model says "should" happen in a specific order. The process can be stopped at any point, and, in most cases, the policy process is truncated at some fairly early stage. Only some fairly modest subsets of all possible policies go through the entire process. And the process can be reentered or reactivated at any point and at any time.

In short, reality is messy. Models, particularly a nice listing of stages with an implied tidy chronology, are not messy. In a collision between tidiness and untidiness the analyst must not be so struck by the values of order as to force reality into a model in which it might not fit.

These are only caveats, however. The utility of organizing data and thoughts about complicated reality in this way is great. It allows the analyst to look for patterns and, more important, to explain the causes of different patterns.

DISCUSSION
Daniel McCool

All of the concepts introduced in this section, while disparate, attempt to explain how the process of governing works (or does not work). The macrolevel model of the entire political system presented by Easton is the most ambitious. As Easton points out, he is trying to "bring some over-all order" (1965, 105) to a process that is by its very nature extremely chaotic.

There are some advantages to such an all-encompassing view of reality: "The main merit of systems theory is that it provides a way of conceptualizing what are often complex political phenomena. In emphasizing processes as opposed to institutions or structures, Easton's approach represents an advance over more traditional analyses" (Ham and Hill 1984, 13–15). Stewart also sees merit in the systems approach: "The great advantage of systems theory for the understanding of policy is that it invites us to consider how crucial information is in the business of politics" (1992, 245). By moving beyond formal institutional processes, systems theory can account for the informal processes that connect the political system to external influences. Sylvia, Meier, and Gunn attribute the popularity of systems theory to its ability to examine this interaction between a political program and its environment (1985, 1).

But the strength of systems theory is also its weakness; it has achieved generality by sacrificing specificity. Note the following comments:

> Easton's systems analysis gives a verbal accounting system, which is of little help in specific policy analysis. (Heclo 1972, 105)
> [systems analysis] has fallen from favor in part because nobody can really describe it." (Bobrow and Dryzek 1987, 10)

Perhaps the greatest omission in the model is the conspicuous blank space labeled "the political system." Easton tells us this is where the "conversion of demands into outputs" occurs. This conversion process is really the heart of what goes on in politics, but the systems model tells us little about causal relationships that shape this conversion. Easton admits that the conversion process is the central element of the system: "a system is a means whereby the inputs of demands and support are converted into outputs. This is the allocative aspect of the system behavior. It creates the basic political problem. . . ." (1979, 478). But he has spent very little time explaining this aspect of the model. His original formulation of the model, which appeared in *World Politics* in 1957, made no mention of the black box of the "political system" except to say this is where the "withinputs" originate. His subsequent book *A Systems Analysis of Political Life* devotes all of two pages to the conversion of demands into outputs (1979, 478–79). Instead he simply views policy makers as mere "gatekeepers" (1979, 86–96) who regulate the flow of demands through the system. Obviously politics is more than this housekeeping role suggests. Despite these limitations Easton's systems model has provoked a great deal of discussion and prompted numerous attempts to apply—and improve—the theory.[1]

In contrast to systems theory public choice attempts to explain the conversion of demands into outputs with exacting specificity. Analyses focus on the individual decision maker as a person who acts only in self-interest. Public choice is an elaborate, formalized theory of governing that relies upon economic models to give it "a more elegant technical apparatus" (Riker 1988, 256). To its adherents public choice is "a most impressive intellectual achievement" (McLean 1987, 183). Even its detractors recognize its importance: "In just three decades rational [i.e., public] choice theory has emerged as one of the most active, influential, and ambitious subfields in the discipline of political science" (Petracca 1991, 289).

Public choice theory has been most helpful in pointing out the inadequacies of government: the wastefulness of logrolling; the tendency of legislators and bureaucrats to engage in porkbarrel spending; the exploitive use of public resources for private gain; the urge to spend more and more money. Applications of public choice theory to particular policy issues have produced insightful new ways of examining old issues and have led to innovative policy prescriptions (see, e.g., Anderson 1983; Butler 1985; Baden and Leal 1990). But much of the literature on public choice—both pro and con—is infused with ideological bias, and this has made it more difficult to evaluate its utility as a theory of the policy-making process.

The critics of public choice are legion (see, e.g., Ball 1976; Lyons and Lowery 1989; Petracca 1991; Dunleavy 1992). In a comment that accompa-

---

[1]For an interesting application of a modified systems model to administrative law, see Warren 1982, 22–27. For a more general application of systems theory to public administration, see Sharkansky 1978. A recent application of systems theory is found in Stewart (1992).

nied the article by William Mitchell excerpted here, Margaret Levi succinctly listed many of the common criticisms:

> Who is unaware of the fact that the behavioral assumption of public choice is flawed, that the model tends to oversimplify reality, that many of the questions public choice can authoritatively answer are trivial, and that many, too many, of the most intelligent proponents of public choice suffer from a libertarian, conservative, or an out-and-out right-wing bias? (1983, 114)[2]

Of course, many of the critics of public choice have a left-wing bias.

The ideologically charged debate over public choice is voluminous and complex. However, with some simplification we can discern three common criticisms of public choice theory. First, critics attack the assumption that individuals make all decisions based only on a consideration of what it will gain for them. This permits no consideration of altruism, concern for the public interest, or a value system predicated on duty to others. While we presumably choose more rather than less in a marketplace, individuals often make political choices based on a much broader array of values. By insisting that all behavior is simply a matter of calculated self-interest, public choice theory trivializes the human spirit. Indeed, there is empirical evidence that citizens make decisions that go beyond simple calculations of self-interest. Muller and Opp (1986) demonstrated that individuals participate in rebellious political activity—which can be fraught with personal risk—even though they could have let others do the dangerous work for them (be "free riders"); their commitment to cause was greater than their desire to benefit themselves exclusively. Brodsky and Thompson studied referendum voting and concluded that voters justified their votes "in terms which suggest altruistic (selfless) rather than self-interested motivations" (1993, 297).

The debate over self-interest versus public interest has been especially vociferous regarding the behavior of public bureaucrats. Following Niskanen (1971), public choice theorists argue that bureaucrats are only interested in maximizing their budgets and personal remuneration. Others, primarily in the field of public administration, claim that most bureaucrats have a well-developed sense of public service (Goodsell 1982, Kelman 1987) and a commitment to constitutional and professional norms that override selfish desires (Rohr 1989). Furthermore, there is empirical evidence that bureaucrats are not primarily motivated by direct economic benefits to themselves (see Heffron 1989, 266–87).

In recent years many public choice theorists have begun to recognize that the self-interest axiom is inadequate (see Cook and Levi 1990). For example, William Mitchell recently noted that, in regard to altruism, "stan-

---

[2]Martin Paldam admits that "several of the founding fathers of public choice are surely very right wing" but argues this is good because "some extremism gives a movement zest" (1993, 182).

dard public choice admits but does little with such motives" (1993, 141). Others remain convinced that all behavior is based soley on self-interest (Mueller 1986). Mansbridge argues that this single-minded devotion to the self-interest axiom has forced public choice into a corner: "Within the group that insists on self-interest, some, who recognize that a great deal of observed behavior cannot be accounted for by self-interest, are nevertheless so wedded to the concept that they are prepared to salvage it by sacrificing the [public choice] modeler's other stock-in-trade—rationality" (1990, 254). The debate over self-interest raises some interesting questions regarding the validity of public choice theory.

A second assumption of public choice theory is that markets are inherently more rational than governments in determining value (Mitchell 1983, 346, 367). This may be true for items that have a clearly discernable economic value—for example, consumer goods—but is problematic when decisions involve values that are very difficult to quantify in economic terms. For example, the most honorable way to solve a problem, and the most economically efficient way to solve that problem, may be different; which approach is more "rational"? Markets have no sense of fair play, no commitment to justice, culture, or history. As a result, markets evaluate goods and services, not according to their contribution to society, but according to their economic value. To take one simple example, consider the following comparison:

> A basketball player makes $5 million a year.
> A highly paid CEO of a large corporation is paid an annual bonus of $1 million even though his company lost millions of dollars.
> A teacher in a private school is paid $18,000 a year.

We must ask, In what sense are these incomes a "rational" allocation of resources?

Furthermore, there is a well-known set of market failures that prevent markets from achieving optimum rationality. There are plenty of examples of government foolishness, but there are also innumerable examples of market decisions that produced outcomes clearly contrary to the public interest. The real question is whether the inherent disadvantages of government decision making are more onerous than the inherent disadvantages of the market, and which alternative—governments or markets—is more susceptible to reforms that can reduce these disadvantages? The question is further complicated if we want to maintain democratic input; do we want to emphasize popular input, or efficiency?

The third criticism of public choice is the assumption that government is unresponsive and beyond democratic control. In Mitchell's article he clearly states his belief that the citizen is virtually powerless to affect public policy—a notion that is congruent with elite theory. Public choice theorists are particularly adamant about the bureaucracy being beyond the control of the people and their elected officials. In another article Mitchell writes that politicians have "little influence on the bureaucrats and the programs they administer" (1983, 356). Yet many scholars claim just the opposite; bureaucrats are constantly bombarded with demands from elected officials, interest groups, and individuals (Lowi, 1979). This argument is especially relevant to the discussion of iron triangles and policy subsystems in Section 5. The real question is whether it is easier to become a player in the marketplace, or the government. Public choice theorists have developed devastating critiques of how some private interest groups have exploited government for their own private gain at public expense—the so-called rent-seeking discussed by Mitchell. These are certainly valid claims, but participation in the marketplace can also be quite exclusive. Market proponents claim that anyone with a *willingness* to buy and sell can participate in an open market, but such participation also requires the *ability* to pay. In short it takes money to convince government to distribute largess to private interests, but it also takes money to buy what you want in the open market. Thus the elements of society that are disadvantaged in political competition are also disadvantaged in market competition.[3]

This brief review of some main points—and criticisms—of public choice theory demonstrates how difficult it can be to assess the contribution of theory to our understanding of political reality. This challenge becomes even more difficult when it is affected by powerful normative and ideological forces.

Many conceptualizations of policy making assume that individuals are capable of making informed choices by ranking alternatives and then selecting the best one. Public choice assumes this type of "rational" decision is, or at least should be, the norm. But Lindblom, in "Muddling Through," offers what he views as a much more realistic interpretation of how the policy-making process really works. Lindblom later refined his concept in his book *A Strategy of Decision*, which was written with David Braybrooke (1963). In that book they argue that, not only is incrementalism an accurate depiction of the way decisions are really made, but that it is preferable in many ways to alternative forms of decision making: "Disjointedness has its advantages—the virtues of its defects—chief among them the advantage of preserving a rich variety of impressions and insights that are liable to be 'coordinated' out of sight by hasty and inappropriate demands for a common plan of attack" (1963, 106). In the ensuing years there has been a lengthy debate over both the theoretical and normative dimensions of incrementalism.

---

[3]Public choice theorists counter that government could provide vouchers for the disadvantaged, but such vouchers would be subject to all the same political pressures as existing subsidies; who would decide the eligibility requirements and amounts of these vouchers?

In terms of its theoretical utility, there is widespread agreement that incrementalism offers an accurate description of how the policy process actually works much of the time (Ham and Hill 1984, 83). A critic of the incrementalist approach admitted it was an "undeniable success, in purely descriptive terms" (Goodin 1982, 19). Another author gives Lindblom's work even more credit: "[it] constitutes a uniquely valuable source of such knowledge and theory. It is applicable to virtually all public administrators, it is enduring, it is concise and disciplined, it is insightful, and it is realistic" (Balzer 1979, 539). Thus it would appear that incrementalism possesses great theoretical validity. But a closer look reveals problems; a good theory must be much more than mere description; it must permit us to determine causal relationships and thus explain otherwise inexplicable phenomena. And while incrementalism is descriptively accurate, many have questioned whether it is good theory:

> . . . the problem here is less the lack of any scale by which to measure size than it is the demands on theory. . . to help us distinguish incremental from non-incremental adjustments. . . . Aside from being unable to tell us much about the actual size of an increment, weak theory [i.e., incrementalism] cannot tell us how to construct an experiment for testing itself, especially with respect to the influences that need to be controlled (Dryzek and Ripley 1988, 708).

Other critics argue that incrementalism omits critically important elements of the policy-making process:

> Incremental approaches focus on just one kind of decision-making process. . . ignoring the problem orientation of decision makers and the contexts in which they operate. . . . Context does not matter to the incrementalist. Goals are dismissed by assuming that decisions taken are right because, lacking sufficient support, they would not have been made in the first place. The assumption is grievously faulty. (Brewer and DeLeon 1983, 24)

Indeed, incrementalism may not be theory at all; Goodin describes it as an atheoretical decision-making routine (1982, 20). And Braybrooke and Lindblom claim that incrementalism is utilized in the absence of a "large formal theoretical system" (1963, 118). The title of their book, *A Strategy of Decision*, suggests that perhaps incrementalism is a description of a certain way to make decisions, not a theory.

A second critique of incrementalism concerns its normative implications. Many proponents of incrementalism have argued that it "is not only inevitable in practice but also desirable on principle" (Goodin 1982, 19). There have been two responses to this claim. First, critics argue that incrementalism is undesirable because it favors the status quo, makes real reform nearly impossible, and has an ideological bias. These critics claim that incrementalism "is the planning model for ideological conservatism" (Frohock 1979, 52) and "an ideological reinforcement of the pro-inertia and anti-innovation forces. . . . " (Dror 1964, 155. Also see Weiss and Woodhouse 1992). Lindblom has responded to these critics:

> Incrementalism in politics is not, in principle, slow moving. It is not necessarily, therefore, a tactic of conservatism. A fast-moving sequence of small changes can more speedily accomplish a drastic alteration of the status quo than can an only infrequent major policy change. (Lindblom 1979, 520)

To a great extent the conflict over whether incrementalism is inherently conservative is a symptom of the theoretical problems described earlier; if the "theory" does not provide sufficient specification, that is, what constitutes an increment, then it is impossible to assess the validity—and the bias—of the theory. I ask the reader to review the incrementalist strategy as described in the "muddling through" article, and then compare it with the previous quote by Lindblom; does the strategy sound like it is capable of "fast-moving sequences" and "drastic alterations" in policy? Apparently an increment is like pornography; it cannot be defined but you know it when you see it.

A second normative response to incrementalism is that it fails as a guide to moral decision making and thus fails as a preferred strategy regardless of its empirical validity. Paris and Reynolds argue that "incrementalism cannot distinguish positive, fair meliorative change from mere change, i. e. the result of the incremental process; it is blind to its actual normative impact" (1983, 131). They conclude that proponents of incrementalism "provide no reason to believe that incremental systems will consistently or even typically yield morally acceptable results" (1983, 134. Also see Hayes 1992, 24, 197). Etzioni characterizes incrementalist decision making as "drifting—action without direction" (1967, 388. For an opposing opinion see Weiss and Woodhouse 1992).

Incrementalism's greatest contribution may be its utility as a critique of the rational–comprehensive approach; to a great extent the characteristics of the strategy read like a list of reasons why the rational approach does not work. But even here, incrementalism has been criticized. Starling notes that Lindblom's description of the rational approach was overdrawn in order to contrast it with incrementalism; Lindblom's characterization "has something of a straw man in it. None of the model's advocates would press maximization to this absurd length" (1988, 297). This is the same "caricature" issue we discussed in the precious section.

The debate over incrementalism has generated a number of attempts to offer alternative models. Yehezkel Dror (1968) developed a "normative–optimum" model that combines elements of both rational and incremental decision making . Similarly Amatai Etzioni created a combination model called *mixed-scanning* (1967). And Paul Schulman has introduced a theory of how large-scale, nonincremental decisions are made (1980).

It is clear that Lindblom's original "muddling through" piece, published in 1959, has had a heuristic effect. Despite its limitations this seminal idea has had a widespread impact on theories of public policy making.

The stages model of policy making is nearly as pervasive as incrementalism, although it has generated less debate. It is most effective when it is used to explain the *differences* between the stages; if this is not accomplished, research utilizing the stages model becomes merely a chronology of events.

Many textbooks are arranged according to some variation of this model. (See, for example, Brewer and DeLeon 1983; Hogwood and Gunn 1984; Jones 1984; Anderson 1990). There is a clear set of advantages—and disadvantages—to using the stages approach for analyzing the policy-making process.

James Anderson succinctly identifies the advantages of the stages approach:

> It is a fairly accurate description of how the process works.
> It can be easily modified; stages can be added, deleted, or altered.
> It emphasizes the relationships between actors as they proceed through the stages.
> It can be utilized across many different cultures (1990, 35–37).

The stages approach permits a simple, straightforward, linear view of the policy-making process. But as Ripley points out in the piece excerpted here, reality is rarely so tidy. Hogwood and Gunn offer a similar caveat regarding the stages model: ". . . it is a framework for organizing our understanding of what happens—and does not happen. The policy process applied to any given issue in practice may be truncated (e.g. the option selected my be to do nothing). The dividing lines between the various activities are artificial and policy-makers are unlikely to perform them consciously or in the implied 'logical' order" (1984, 4). In short the model sacrifices validity for economy.

Another problem is that the stages model tells us little or nothing about causal relationships; does one stage "cause" a successive stage? Sabatier points out that this approach "contains no coherent assumptions about what forces are driving the process from stage to stage and very few falsifiable hypotheses. . . . there is little theoretical coherence across stages" (1989, 5–6). Jenkins notes that "the utility of such an approach, particularly as a vehicle for hypothesis generation, becomes problematic" (1978, 18).

By now it should be clear to the reader that no perfect theories are going to emerge from this set of readings. Each has its own unique set of insights and liabilities. I have pointed out numerous shortcomings, but this does not mean that these theories are without value; quite the contrary, they are included because policy scholars have found them useful. I suggest that we follow the advice of James Anderson: ". . . it is wise not to be bound too dogmatically or rigidly to a single model or approach" (1990, 34).

At this point you should be developing a sense of how the various theories and concepts relate to each other. Is incrementalism an artifact of pluralist democracy? Is it possible that some of these theories work well in some of the stages of the policy-making process, but not others? What does systems theory have in common with advocacy coalitions (Section 5)? How does group theory fit into Lowi's typology (Section 4): And what can public choice theory tell us about distributive policy (Section 4), and iron triangles? (Section 5)?

REFERENCES

ANDERSON, JAMES (1990). *Public Policy Making*. Boston: Houghton Mifflin Co.

ANDERSON, TERRY (1983). *Water Crisis: Ending the Policy Drought*. Baltimore: Johns Hopkins University Press.

BADEN, JOHN, AND DONALD LEAL (1990). *The Yellowstone Primer*. San Francisco: Pacific Research Institute for Public Policy.

BALL, TERRENCE (1976). "From Paradigms to Research Programs: Toward a Post-Kuhnian Political Science." *American Journal of Political Science* 20 (Feb.): 151–75.

BALZER, ANTHONY (1979). "Reflections on Muddling Through." *Public Administration Review* 39 (Nov./Dec.): 537–44.

BOBROW, DAVIS, AND JOHN DRYZEK (1987). *Policy Analysis by Design*. Pittsburgh: University of Pittsburgh Press.

BRAYBROOKE, DAVID, AND CHARLES LINDBLOM (1963). *A Strategy of Decision*. London: The Free Press of Glencoe.

BREWER, GARRY, AND PETER DELEON (1983). *The Foundations of Policy Analysis*. Homewood, IL: Dorsey Press.

BRODSKY, DAVID, AND EDWARD THOMPSON (1993). "Ethos, Public Choice, and Referendum Voting." *Social Science Quarterly* 74 (June): 286–99.

BUTLER, STUART (1985). *Privatizing Public Spending*. New York: Universe Books.

COOK, KAREN, AND MARGARET LEVI, eds. (1990). *The Limits of Rationality*. University of Chicago Press.

DROR, YEHEZKEL (1964). "Muddling Through—'Science' or Inertia?" *Public Administration Review* 24 (Sept.): 153–57.

_____ (1968). *Public Policy Making Reexamined*. New York: Chandler.

DRYZEK, JOHN, AND BRIAN RIPLEY (1988). "The Ambitions of Policy Design." *Policy Studies Review* 7 (Summer): 705–19.

DUNLEAVY, PATRICK (1992). *Democracy, Bureaucracy, and Public Choice*. Englewood Cliffs, NJ: Prentice-Hall.

EASTON, DAVID (1957). "An Approach to the Analysis of Political Systems." *World Politics* IX (April): 383–400.

_____ (1965). *A Framework for Political Analysis*. Chicago: The University of Chicago Press.

ETZIONI, AMITAI (1967). "Mixed-Scanning: A 'Third' Approach to Decision-Making." *Public Administration Review* 27 (Dec.): 385–92.

FROHOCK, FRED (1979). *Public Policy: Scope and Logic*. Englewood Cliffs, NJ: Prentice-Hall.

GOODIN, ROBERT (1976). *The Politics of Rational Man*. New York: John Wiley and Sons.

GOODSELL, CHARLES. (1982). *The Case for Bureaucracy*, 2nd. ed. Chatham, NJ: Chatham House.

HAM, CHRISTOPHER, AND MICHAEL HILL (1984). *The Policy Process in the Modern Capitalist State*. Brighton, Sussex: Wheatsheaf Books/Harvester Press.

HAYES, MICHAEL (1992). *Incrementalism and Public Policy*. New York: Longman.

HECLO, HUGH (1972). "Review Article: Policy Analysis." *British Journal of Political Science* 2 (Jan.): 83–108.

HEFFRON, FLORENCE (1989). *Organization Theory and Public Organizations*. Englewood Cliffs, NJ: Prentice-Hall.

HOGWOOD, BRIAN, AND LEWIS GUNN (1984). *Policy Analysis for the Real World*. Oxford, England: Oxford University Press.

JENKINS, W. I. (1978). *Policy Analysis*. London: Martin Robertson.

JONES, CHARLES (1984). *An Introduction to the Study of Public Policy*, 3rd. ed. Monterey, CA: Brooks/Cole.

KELMAN, STEVEN (1987). "'Public Choice' and Public Spirit." *The Public Interest* 87 (Spring): 81.

LEVI, MARGARET (1983). "Comment." in *Political Economy*, pp. 114–19. Edited by Larry Wade. Boston: Kluwer-Nijhoff Publishing.

LINDBLOM, CHARLES (1979). "Still Muddling, Not Yet Through." *Public Administration Review* 39 (Nov./Dec.): 517–26.

LOWI, THEODORE (1979). *The End of Liberalism*, 2nd. ed. New York: W. W. Norton.

LYONS, W. E., AND DAVID LOWERY (1989). "Governmental Fragmentation Versus Consolidation: Five Public Choice Myths about How to Create Informed, and Happy Citizens." *Public Administration Review* (Nov./Dec.): 533–43.

MANSBRIDGE, JANE (1990). "Expanding the Range of Formal Modeling." In *Beyond Self-Interest*, pp. 254–63. Edited by Jane Mansbridge. Chicago: University of Chicago Press.

MCLEAN, IAIN (1987). *Public Choice: An Introduction*. Oxford, United Kingdom: Basil Blackwell.

MITCHELL, WILLIAM (1983). "Efficiency, Responsibility, and Democratic Politics." In *Liberal Democracy*, pp. 343–73. Edited by J. Roland Pennock and John Chapman. New York: New York University Press.

MUELLER, DENNIS (1986). "Rational Egoism vs. Adaptive Egoism." *Public Choice* 51 (1): 3–23.

MULLER, EDWARD, AND KARL-DIETER Opp (1986). "Rational Choice and Rebellious Collective Action." *American Political Science Review* 80 (June): 471–87.

NISKANEN, WILLIAM (1971). *Bureaucracy and Representative Government*. Chicago: Aldine-Atherton.

PALDAM, MARTIN (1993). "Public Choice: More of a Branch or More of a Sect." *Public Choice* 77 (Sept.): 177–84.

PARIS, DAVID, AND JAMES REYNOLDS (1983). *The Logic of Policy Inquiry*. New York: Longman.

PETRACCA, MARK (1991). "The Rational Choice Approach to Politics: A Challenge to Democratic Theory." *The Review of Politics* 53 (Spring): 298–319.

RIKER, WILLIAM (1988). "The Place of Political Science in Public Choice." *Public Choice* 57 (2): 247–57.

ROHR, JOHN (1989). *Ethics for Bureaucrats*, 2nd. ed. New York: Marcel Dekker.

SABATIER, PAUL (1989). "Political Science and Public Policy: An Assessment." Presented at the Policy Studies Organization special conference on "Advances in Policy Studies," American Political Science Association annual meeting, Washington, D.C.

SCHULMAN, PAUL (1980). *Large-Scale Policy Making*. New York: Elsevier.

SHARKANSKY, IRA (1978). *Public Administration: Policy-Making in Government Agencies*, 4th ed. Chicago: Rand McNally.

STARLING, GROVER (1988). *Strategies for Policy Making*. Chicago, IL: Dorsey Press.

STEWART, JENNY (1992). "Corporatism, Pluralism, and Political Learning: A Systems Approach." *Journal of Public Policy* 12 (July–Sept.): 243–55.

SYLVIA, RONALD, KENNETH MEIER, AND ELIZABETH GUNN (1985). *Program Planning and Evaluation for the Public Manager*. Prospect Heights, IL: Waveland Press.

WARREN, KENNETH (1982). *Administrative Law In the American Political System*. St. Paul: West Publishing.

WEISS, ANDREW, AND EDWARD WOODHOUSE (1992). "Reframing Incrementalism: A Constructive Response to the Critics." *Policy Sciences* 25 (no. 3): 255–73.

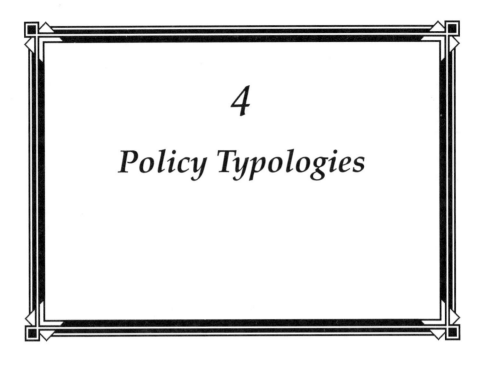

4

Policy Typologies

INTRODUCTION

The first step in the scientific process is classification: identifying common-alities in phenomena and grouping them accordingly. In science this process is called *taxonomy*, and it is a necessary precursor to advanced analysis: ". . .there is a direct line of logical continuity from qualitative classification to the most rigorous forms of measurement, by way of intermediate devices of systematic ratings, ranking scales, multidimensional classifications, ty-pologies, and simple quantitative indices. . ." (Lazarsfeld and Barton 1951, 155). In the social sciences typologies are quite common because they serve a distinct purpose:

> A typology goes beyond sheer description by simplifying the ordering of the elements of a population, and the known relevant traits of that population, into distinct groupings; in this capacity a typological classification creates order out of the potential chaos of discrete, discontinuous, or heterogeneous observations. . . . it also permits the observer to seek and predict relationships between phenomena. . . (Tiryakian 1968, 178).

A policy typology is like other taxonomies; it is an effort to classify policies according to their attributes. But classification in political science did not start with the policy typologies; nearly all research entails an effort to group according to common attributes: elites versus masses; the formula-tion stage versus the implementation stage; legislative versus judicial; incremental versus nonincremental; inputs versus outputs; good versus bad, and so forth. The validity of such classifications depends upon the extent to which we can discern the differences between the groups and then classify them accordingly. The best typologies are those that clearly identify a coherent set of characteristics that enable us to classify the objects of our study into Group A, Group B, and so forth. Thus a good policy typology is both *inclusive*, meaning all policies can be placed into one of the categories, and *mutually exclusive*, meaning that each policy falls clearly into one and only one category (Froman 1968, 46).

Initial attempts to classify policies into identifiable types followed fairly obvious lines of distinction. The most obvious policy typology is substantive: farm policy, energy policy, or foreign policy, for example. Other obvious modes of classification are time period (postwar policy); ideology (conservative policy); or institutional (legislative policy). And of course, nearly everyone has a penchant for dividing policy into normative categories: good versus bad; progressive versus regressive, and so on.

There are literally dozens of attempts to classify policies into two or more groups, and many of these studies are identified in the article in this section by Peter Steinberger. But Theodore Lowi's 1964 article in *World Politics*—the first selection you will read—was fundamentally different from other policy typologies. Until Lowi, policy was viewed as a product—an outcome—of government. In other words politics determined policies. But Lowi reversed this relationship; his typology is based on the assumption that the perceived attributes of the policy determine the attributes of the political process that makes that policy.

The first selection by Lowi establishes his basic typology, based on the assumption that policies determine politics. This piece was originally a book review by Lowi and has been edited to include only the basic description of his policy types and the rationale for the categorization. The second selection is also by Lowi, and is an attempt to refine and improve the typology and respond to various critics.

The third selection, by Greenberg, Miller, Mohr and Vladeck, is a critique of policy typologies in general, with a special emphasis on Lowi's scheme. In a sense this is a measure of just how influential Lowi's typology is: An entire article in the *American Political Science Review* is devoted to describing its limits! They critique policy typologies from the perspective of positivist science.

The following article by Steinberger is also a critique of typologies, but from a perspective that contrasts dramatically with Greenberg et. al. Steinberger writes from a perspective called *phenomenology*.[1] The contrast be-

---

[1]Phenomenology has a long and complicated lineage going back to the eighteenth century. In modern usage this concept refers to an interpretive view of reality. Unlike positive science it does not objectify reality. Rather it interprets the meaning of each phenomenon as a distinct and unique event as seen through the eyes of the actor or observer. There are no presuppositions or metaphysical assumptions: You observe, then intuit reality (Schutz 1967).

tween the two is quite revealing. The reader will recall from the introductory chapter that there is an ongoing debate in the social sciences as to whether research can truly be objective and value free. On one side of this debate are the proponents of positivist science, such as Greenberg et al., and on the other side are scholars such as Steinberger and other proponents of *meaning construction*. Their different reactions to policy typologies permit us to learn how policy theory is viewed from each of these perspectives.

The final selection, by Spitzer, is an attempt to improve the Lowi typology by making some important modifications. There have been numerous attempts to modify the basic Lowi typology, and a number of them will be reviewed in the discussion that follows the readings. Spitzer's article is included here because it is quite creative, and it raises some very important questions about policy theory in general. In that sense it is representative of this literature.

The readings in this section are different from previous sections in that they represent a more coherent and integrated set of ideas; all of them are attempts to create, modify, and critique policy typologies, often using Lowi as a focal point. One can clearly see the "building block" aspect of the scientific process; ideas are proposed, subjected to peer review, and modified, rejected, or accepted accordingly. This review process produces a new understanding of the phenomena, which in turn is subjected to another round of critical scrutiny. After reading these articles you may wonder: Will this seemingly endless debate go on forever? The answer is, hopefully so. Hendrick and Nachmias are correct in saying that "a research project that does not generate other research questions which, in turn, generate more research questions is hardly worth pursuing" (1992, 312). If it ends we stop theory building, we stop learning, we stop improving our understanding of public policy.

REFERENCES

FROMAN, LEWIS (1968). "The Categorization of Policy Contents." In *Political Science and Political Theory*." Edited by Austin Ranney. Chicago, IL: Markham Publishing.

HENDRICK, REBECCA, AND DAVID NACHMIAS (1992). "The Policy Sciences: The Challenge of Complexity." *Policy Science Review* 11 (Autumn/Winter): 310–28.

LAZARSFELD, PAUL, AND ALLEN BARTON (1951). "Qualitative Measurement in the Social Sciences: Classification, Typologies, and Indices." In *The Policy Sciences*. Edited by Daniel Lerner and Harold D. Lasswell. Stanford, CA: Stanford University Press.

SCHUTZ, ALFRED (1967). *The Phenomenology of the Social World.* Translated by George Walsh and Frederick Lehnert, Evanston, IL: Northwestern University Press.

TIRYAKIAN, EDWARD (1968). "Typologies." In *International Encyclopedia of the Social Sciences,* pp. 177–86. Edited by David Sills. New York: Macmillan and the Free Press.

AMERICAN BUSINESS, PUBLIC POLICY, CASE-STUDIES, AND POLITICAL THEORY
Theodore J. Lowi*

It seems to me that the reason for lack of interesting and non-obvious generalization from cases and other specific empirical studies is clearly that the broad-gauged theories of politics are not related, perhaps are not relatable, to observable cases. In general, American political science seems to be subject to a continuing fission of theory and research, in which the empiricist is not sufficiently mindful of his role as system-builder and the system-builder is not sufficiently mindful (if at all) of the role that theory is supposed to play. What is needed is a basis for cumulating, comparing, and contrasting diverse findings. Such a framework or interpretative scheme would bring the diverse cases and findings into a more consistent relation to each other and would begin to suggest generalizations sufficiently close to the data to be relevant and sufficiently abstract to be subject to more broadly theoretical treatment.

An attempt at such a framework follows.

The scheme is based upon the following argument: (1) The types of relationships to be found among people are determined by their expectations—by what they hope to achieve or get from relating to others. (2) In politics, expectations are determined by governmental outputs or policies. (3) Therefore, a political relationship is determined by the type of policy at stake, so that for every type of policy there is likely to be a distinctive type of political relationship. If power is defined as a share in the making of policy, or authoritative allocations, then the political relationship in question is a power relationship or, over time, a power structure. As Dahl would say, one must ask, "Power for *what?*" One must control for the *scope* of power and look for elites, power structures, and the like within each of the predefined scopes or "issue areas."[1] My analysis moves in this direction, but far-

---

*Theodore J. Lowi, "American Business, Public Policy, Case Studies, and Political Theory." *World Politics* 16 (1964): 687–91, 713. Used by permission.

[1]Dahl, *Who Governs?*, and Polsby, *Community Power*, esp. chap. 6.

ther. Issues as such are too ephemeral; it is on the basis of established expectations and a history of earlier government decisions *of the same type* that single issues are fought out. The study of single issues provides a good test of hypotheses about structure, but the hypotheses must be arrived at in some other, independent way.

Obviously, the major analytic problem is that of identifying types of outputs or policies. The approach I have taken is to define policies in terms of their impact or expected impact on the society. When policies are defined this way, there are only a limited number of types; when all is said and done, there are only a limited number of functions that governments can perform. This approach cashiers the "politics of agriculture" and the "politics of education" or, even more narrowly but typically, "the politics of the ARA bill" or "the politics of the 1956 Aid to Education bill," in which the composition and strategy of the participants are fairly well-known before the study is begun. But it maintains the pluralist's resistance to the assumption that there is only one power structure for every political system. My approach replaces the descriptive, subject-matter categories of the pluralists with functional categories. There is no need to argue that the classification scheme exhausts all the possibilities even among domestic policies; it is sufficient if most policies and the agencies that implement them can be categorized with little, if any, damage to the nuances.

There are three major categories of public policies in the scheme: distribution, regulation, and redistribution. These types are historically as well as functionally distinct, distribution being almost the exclusive type of national domestic policy from 1789 until virtually 1890. Agitation for regulatory and redistributive policies began at about the same time, but regulation had become an established fact before any headway at all was made in redistribution.[2]

These categories are not mere contrivances for purposes of simplification. They are meant to correspond to real phenomena—so much so that the major hypotheses of the scheme follow directly from the categories and their definitions. Thus, *these areas of policy or government activity constitute real arenas of power*. Each arena tends to develop its own characteristic political structure, political process, elites, and group relations. What remains is to identify these arenas, to formulate hypotheses about the attributes of each, and to test the scheme by how many empirical relationships it can anticipate and explain.

---

[2]Foreign policy, for which no appropriate "-tion" word has been found, is obviously a fourth category. It is not dealt with here for two reasons. First, it overly extends the analysis. Second, and of greater importance, it is in many ways not part of the same universe, because in foreign policy-making America is only a subsystem. Winston Churchill, among other foreigners, has consistently participated in our foreign policy decisions. Of course, those aspects of foreign and military policy that have direct domestic implications are included in my scheme.

Areas of Policy Defined

In the long run, all governmental policies may be considered redistributive, because in the long run some people pay in taxes more than they receive in services. Or, all may be thought regulatory because, in the long run, a governmental decision on the use of resources can only displace a private decision about the same resource or at least reduce private alternatives about the resource. But politics works in the short run, and in the short run certain kinds of government decisions can be made without regard to limited resources. Policies of this kind are called "distributive," a term first coined for nineteenth-century land policies, but easily extended to include most contemporary public land and resource policies; rivers and harbors ("pork barrel") programs; defense procurement and R & D; labor, business, and agricultural "clientele" services; and the traditional tariff. Distributive policies are characterized by the ease with which they can be disaggregated and dispensed unit by small unit, each unit more or less in isolation from other units and from any general rule. "Patronage" in the fullest meaning of the word can be taken as a synonym for "distributive." These are policies that are virtually not policies at all but are highly individualized decisions that only by accumulation can be called a policy. They are policies in which the indulged and the deprived, the loser and the recipient, need never come into direct confrontation. Indeed, in many instances of distributive policy, the deprived cannot as a class be identified, because the most influential among them can be accommodated by further disaggregation of the stakes (see Table 4-1).

Regulatory policies are also specific and individual in their impact, but they are not capable of the almost infinite amount of disaggregation typical of distributive policies. Although the laws are stated in general terms ("Arrange the transportation system artistically." "Thou shalt not show favoritism in pricing."), the impact of regulatory decisions is clearly one of directly raising costs and/or reducing or expanding the alternatives of private individuals ("Get off the grass!" "Produce kosher if you advertise kosher!"). Regulatory policies are distinguishable from distributive in that in the short run the regulatory decision involves a direct choice as to who will be indulged and who deprived. Not all applicants for a single television channel or an overseas air route can be propitiated. Enforcement of an unfair labor practice on the part of management weakens management in its dealings with labor. So, while implementation is firm-by-firm and case-by-case, policies cannot be disaggregated to the level of the individual or the single firm (as in distribution), because individual decisions must be made by application of a general rule and therefore become interrelated within the broader standards of law. Decisions cumulate among all individuals affected by the law in roughly the same way. Since the most stable lines

Table 4-1 Arenas and Political Relationships: A Diagrammatic Summary

Arena	Primary Political Unit	Relation Among Units	Power Structure	Stability of Structure	Primary Decisional Locus	Implementation
Distribution	Individual, firm corporation	Log-rolling, mutual noninterference, uncommon interests	Non-conflictual elite with support groups	Stable	Congressional committee and/or agency**	Agency centralized to primary functional unit ("bureau")
Regulation*	Group	"The coalition," shared subject-matter interest, bargaining	Pluralistic, multi-centered, "theory of balance"	Unstale	Congress, in classic role	Agency decentralized from center by "delegation," mixed control
Redistribution	Association	The "peak association," class, ideology	Conflictual elite, i.e., elite and counterlite	Stable	Executive and peak associations	Agency centralized toward top (above "bureau"), elaborate standards

*Given the muliplicity of organized interests in the regulatory areana, there are obviously many cases of successful log-rolling coalitions that resemble the coalitions prevailing in distributive politics. In this respect, the difference between the regulatory and the distributive arenas is thus one of degree. The *predominant* form of coalition in regulatory politics is deemed to be that of common or tangential interest. Although the difference is only one of degree, it is significant because this prevailing type of coalition makes the regulatory arena so much more unstable, unpredictable, and non-elitist ("balance of power"). When we turn to the redistributive arena, however, we find differences of principle in every sense of the word.

**Distributive politics tends to stabilize around an institutional unit. In most cases, it is the Congressional committee (or subcommittee). But in others, particularly in the Department of Agriculture, the focus is the agency or the agency and the committee. In the cities, this is the arena where machine domination continues, if machines were in control in the first place.

of perceived common impact are the basic sectors of the economy, regulatory decisions are cumulative largely along sectoral lines; regulatory policies are usually disaggregable only down to the sector level.[3]

Redistributive policies are like regulatory policies in the sense that relations among broad categories of private individuals are involved and, hence, individual decisions must be interrelated. But on all other counts there are great differences in the nature of impact. The categories of impact are much broader, approaching social classes. They are, crudely speaking, haves and have-nots, bigness and smallness, bourgeoisie and proletariat. The aim involved is not use of property but property itself, not equal treatment but equal possession, not behavior but being. The fact that our income tax is in reality only mildly redistributive does not alter the fact of the aims and the stakes involved in income tax policies. The same goes for our various "welfare state" programs, which are redistributive only for those who entered retirement or unemployment rolls without having contributed at all. The nature of a redistributive issue is not determined by the outcome of a battle over how redistributive a policy is going to be. Expectations about what it *can* be, what it threatens to be, are determinative.

FOUR SYSTEMS OF POLICY, POLITICS, AND CHOICE
Theodore J. Lowi*

The politics vocabulary is not rich in distinctions among governmental functions and policies. Even the great Cushman seems to have been satisfied with a distinction between regulation and nonregulation, based upon an even simpler dichotomy between coercion and noncoercion.[1] Perhaps this poverty of language is due to the widespread liberal attitude that since government itself is not a problem, the best approach is simply to point out and describe the unit or activity of concern. Part of the problem also lies in the fact that prevailing fashions in political science have put heaviest stress on the politics rather than the government side of the field. In many dimensions of politics there are well-developed vocabularies, indicating indeed where the major theoretical interests have been. Students of politics do oc-

---

[3]A "sector" refers to any set of common or substitutable commodities or services or any other form of established economic interaction. Sectors therefore vary in size because of natural economic forces and because of the different ways they are identified by economists or businessmen. They vary in size also because they are sometimes defined a *priori* by the observer's assessment of what constitutes a common product and at other times are defined *a posteriori* by the trade associations that represent the identification of a sector by economic actors themselves.

*Theodore Lowi, "Four Systems of Policy, Politics, and Choice." *Public Administration Review* 33 (July–Aug., 1972): 298–310. Used by permission.

[1]Robert Cushman, President's Committee on Administrative Management, *Report with Special Studies* (Washington, D.C.: U.S. Government Printing Office, 1937); and Cushman, *The Independent Regulatory Commissions* (London: Oxford University Press), p.3.

casionally turn to policy and government, but the tendency has been to do so only because the interesting conflicts are around issues, and many issues involve basic policies. But the issue of policy was not the part of these issues that came in for serious analysis.

Regulation is obviously only one of several ways governments seek to control society and individual conduct. There are rather specific purposes that are best pursued through regulatory techniques, and the reading of any account of regulatory administration suggests that there is a distinct set of moral and political-process consequences associated with this kind of governmental commitment. But this implies that there might be other governmental commitments to serve other ends involving other moralities and other processes. If this is the case, then no one type is meaningful except in comparison to other types.

There is more to the urge for classification than the desire for complexity. Finding different manifestations or types of a given phenomenon is the beginning of orderly control and prediction. Taxonomy before ontogeny *or* phylogeny. Moreover, to find the *basis* for classification reveals the hidden meanings and significance of the phenomenon, suggesting what the important hypotheses ought to be concerned with.

This is precisely what a policy taxonomy might do for the study of politics. To break through the weak and designative vocabulary of public law is perhaps to bring public policy—government—into a proper analyzable, relationship with those dimensions of political science that are already well developed. In hard and practical terms, a good taxonomy of policies might ennoble this under-developed part of the field by converting these important phenomena into "variables," which make them more esthetic to the scientist in political science.

One such attempt to formulate a politically relevant policy taxonomy has been made, and, although still in the process of development, it is possible to report upon it here, in fact, using this as part of the process of developing the scheme. The purpose here will be to bring broad theoretical policy considerations concretely to bear upon some real political situations to see if each enriches the other. It should soon be amply clear why one can say little new about the politics of regulation without introducing the general policy context within which regulation is only one small, albeit important, part.

Since reference can readily be made to the earlier publications, only scant attention will be paid here to the rationale and the details of the scheme.[2] The perspective of the entire approach is the very opposite of the typical perspective in political science, for it begins with the assumption

[2]Theodore Lowi, "American Business and Public Policy, Case Studies and Political Theory," *World Politics* (July 1964); and Lowi, "Decision Making vs. Policy Making: Toward an Antidote for Technocracy," *Public Administration Review* (May/June 1970).

that *policies determine politics*. But the assumption is without value unless the taxonomy of policies captures features of real government that are politically significant; and the most significant political fact about government is that government coerces. Different ways of coercing provide a set of parameters, a context, within which politics takes place.

Figure 4-1 is an attempt to identify and derive logically the types of coercion available to governments.[3] According to the vertical dimension, coercion can be remote or immediate; in a governmental context it can be remote if sanctions are absent, or if they are indirect—as for example a pro-

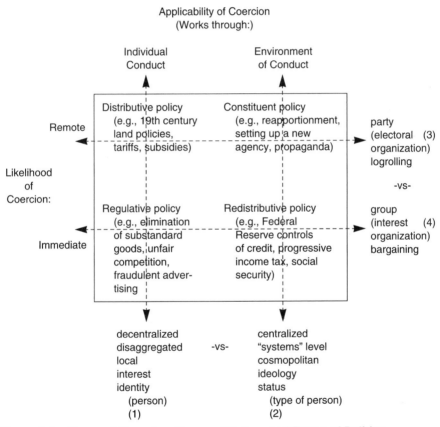

Figure 4-1 Types of Coercion, Types of Policy, and Types of Politics

[3]To visualize the analysis best, the reader should substitute "statute" for "policy." This gives up a great deal of information about policies in the real world, but clarity is gained by having a clear and common unit to classify. Moreover, even from this partial and formalized operational definition of policy, there is a great deal of predictive and ethical value in the classification scheme.

gram based on a service or subsidy where the coercive element is displaced onto the general revenue system.

While the vertical dimension is usually easy to locate in the statute, the horizontal dimension offers a few more difficulties. Nonetheless it is clear that some policies do not come into operation until there is a question about someone's behavior. For example, there is a general rule covering all fraudulent advertising, but it is applicable only to the conduct of individual advertisers. In strong contrast, some policies do not need to wait for a particular behavior, but rather do not touch behavior directly at all. Instead they work through the environment of conduct. For example, a minor change in the Federal Reserve discount rate can have a major impact on my propensity to invest, yet no official need know of my existence.

Beyond the examples provided in each cell, there does not seem to be need for providing elaborate definitions here. The essential aspect of each type is provided or strongly implied in the cross-tabulation of each of the properties along the margins. This is the beauty of finding a basis of distinction to work with.

There are various ways to work from the scheme toward its normative and empirical implications. Some of the process variables are indicated around the margins of the paradigm. Cross-tabulations among these common-sense relationships produces many complex hypotheses that are systematically related to each other and to a common and known analytic posture. For example, it is not hard to document historically that the overwhelming proportion of policies produced by the federal government during the 19th century were distributive; it is also not hard to place alongside that the other well-documented fact, that the period produced a strong partisan politics, then became dominated by localized, logrolling, nonideological parties. The paradigm puts the two sets of facts into an intimate interrelation. The two separate sets of facts can be pulled together systematically in detail and yet in relation to other sets of facts by mixing marginal characteristics (1) and (3) in a context established for them on Figure 4-1. Oblique turns in politics can be anticipated systematically by moving to another cell and mixing the marginal characteristics accordingly, as for example combining items (1) and (4) for an initial look at what tends to develop around regulatory policies. And so on.

Of all the ways of testing the hypotheses drawn from this scheme, perhaps the most effective, as well as the most useful one to begin with, is that of looking through the eyes of the top-most officials at the political system and how and to what extent the system shifts obliquely as their view of it shifts from one policy prism to another. The way to do this is with actual accounts; one of the virtues of the policy scheme is that it converts ordinary case studies from chronicles and teaching instruments into data. Yet the cases themselves require some preparation for this somewhat novel usage;

and this can be provided by a brief and superficial review of variations in the lives of a few Presidents, as these were seen, or could have been seen, by them.

From Cleveland to FDR:
What Makes Presidential Politics?

The "Republican Era" of 1869–1901 is generally thought of as a period of congressional dominance and presidential passivity. To Woodrow Wilson, the period was not merely congressional government; congressional government meant committee government. And in his overview of that era, Leonard White observed that the presidency was at "low ebb" and that despite hard-fought battles between the two branches, the theory and practice of government was congressional supremacy. This went virtually unchallenged, according to White, Binkley, and others, from Grant through McKinley.[4] To students of that period it was for good reason that Woodrow Wilson could write *Congressional Government* and Bryce could ask Why Great Men Are Not Chosen President. The only thing Presidents were strong about was their faith in the separation of powers, which meant steadfast passivity in the policy-making process.[5]

Even Grover Cleveland, despite his standing as one of the stronger Presidents, was unquestionably passive in his relations with Congress. According to Woodrow Wilson, Cleveland "thought it not part of his proper function to press his preference in any other way than by recommendation in a message and upon acceptance of Congress. . . ."[6] It was simply an established fact about Presidents and had been true of all Presidents during and before the Republican Era, virtually from Jefferson to Buchanan, when, except for brief moments, Congress dominated.

This kind of dominance, especially by the committees, has been experienced whenever distributive policies have prevailed, and it so happened that such was the case for most of the 19th century, when the federal government turned out little but land disposal programs, shipping subsidies, tariffs, internal improvements. and the like.

The federal level of politics was stable, and could have been governed by congressional committee and party logrolling precisely because policies

---

[4]Leonard White, *The Republican Era* (New York: The Free Press, 1958); and W. Binkley, *President and Congress* (New York: Vintage Ed 1962), pp. 215 ff.

[5]See especially Binkley, *op. cit.*, pp. 217–218.

[6]Quoted in *ibid.*, p. 217. The essence of Wilson's treatment will be found in *Congressional Government* (New York: Meridian Edition, n.d.), pp. 58–81.

dealing with slavery, public health, property. and so on were left to the states—which were duly radicalized.[7]

Out of this stable situation, politically speaking, grew the practice, then the theory, of presidential obligation that prevailed until the Wilson Administration. Yet there were exceptional moments, and these underscore the influence that policy has upon politics. For, whenever politics took an exceptional turn, there seems to have been an exceptional policy issue at the bottom of it. Interesting cases, actually anticipating the New Deal, can be found in the Cleveland and the Harrison Administrations.[8]

President Cleveland seems to have allowed himself a single important exception to the accepted presidential posture of his day. On the one issue of repeal of the Silver Purchase Act he exerted strong leadership, legislative leadership in particular. In his efforts to secure the repeal "he gave one of his few instances of leadership," even though he had to compromise with "his theory of separated powers to do it." He was "humiliated by the necessity of purchasing the support of a Democratic member of the finance committee of the upper house. . .," but he did it all the same, as part of a pattern of leadership not to be seen on a regular basis again for many years to come. Thus, when later an important tariff was being framed, "he played no effective part."[9]

Actually Harrison, though a much weaker man, headed a more vigorous Administration. Central leadership was of course not characteristic of it. Harrison more than shared Cleveland's views; to him, the President should be guided by his party in Congress. Nevertheless, his Administration is associated with many important political changes, all in the direction of greater vigor, greater political centrality and responsibility. It was during his Administration that Congress began the most far-reaching reforms in its history. In brief, the House gave itself a new constitution by adopting at long last an organized and codified set of rules. These were "Reed's Rules," named after their author, Speaker Thomas B. Reed, and they were concerned in particular with controlling individual congressmen, reducing dilatory tactics, and confining deliberation to relevant and efficient channels. All of this in turn amounted to an assertion of central leadership and of the parliamentary Congress over the tightly entrenched committees and individual, power-seeking congressmen.

After Harrison, Presidents would, at least more frequently, see a real

---

[7]This goes a long way toward explaining the Huntington paradox, the spectacle of a highly dynamic economy developing in the context of a stable, "underdeveloping" policy. See Samuel P. Huntington, "Political Modernization: America vs. Europe," *World Politics* (April 1966), pp. 378–414.

[8]Earlier instances, such as the Fugitive Slave Act of 1850, are dealt with in another article.

[9]Binkley, *op. cit.*, pp. 225, 217, 227.

Congress and deal directly with legislative problems. Presidents would thereafter also see more and more nationally organized interest groups, for the late 19th century witnessed the most phenomenal growth of such organizations oriented to political influence and capable of sustaining pressure. It began somewhat earlier at the state level with commodity associations, but it spread to labor and business, the most effective eventually being the trade associations, almost all of whose foundings date during or after the mid-1890's. The number and strength of these interest groups provided political alternatives to the parties in policy formulation, and by 1900 parties in Congress went into a decline in their capacity to discipline members, a decline from which they have never fully recovered.

All of this is associated in turn with the rise of new kinds of public policy, new at least at the national level. These are regulatory and redistributive policies. As earlier observed, state governments had from the beginning of the Republic regularly enacted regulatory laws—for example, in the fields of property, quarantine and public health, crime, construction, banking, marriage and the family, trade, occupations, etc. On rarer occasions states also attempted to redistribute wealth. Surely state politics had a radical reputation because of the policies they were obliged to make. These kinds of policies kept state politics perpetually on the edge of organized turmoil. When this type of policy entered national government in large enough numbers, the politics would surely follow soon thereafter. And the policies would change the politics regardless of the character of the men or the party that inhabited the presidency or organized the Congress.

The Roosevelt Era

All of these tendencies came to a head in the 1930's, because Roosevelt was responsible for expanding national government on all fronts through all kinds of policies. The politics of the New Deal cannot be understood except by identifying and appreciating the multiple patterns of policy and of politics. Multiple patterns can be found before, but in the 1930's and thereafter, passage of large numbers of all four types of policies was so regular and frequent that these patterns began to institutionalize themselves into clear and distinct systems of politics.

Lack of full appreciation of these multiple patterns of policy and politics had led to many and conflicting interpretations of Roosevelt. For example, Leuchtenberg could argue that the New Deal was a "broker state," yet that this clashed with the fact that he was agent, both willingly and unwillingly, of forces of reform that business found unacceptable."[10] On top of

---

[10]Leuchtenberg, *Franklin D. Roosevelt and the New Deal, 1932–1940* (1963), pp. 87–94, esp. 90.

this, many have argued that he was the savior of capitalism while others argued he was the chief enemy. He was to some a social democrat, to others a corporativist, to others simply a savvy and scheming politician.

These conflicting characterizations and interpretations become more interesting when all of them are taken as accurate and correct. Each simply applies to a special set of conditions; and each loses value when over-generalized to the whole man rather than to aspects of his behavior. Each interpretation comes out of one set of policy issues; the observer must have had that set in mind as he tried to describe, vainly, the entire man and the whole New Deal.

For example, Binkley, like most students of the period, stressed Roosevelt's unqualified and unprecedented leadership during the 100 days, and goes on to explain it as an emergency phenomenon. Yet, almost immediately, he saw that Roosevelt faced a "crucial test" over the economy bill (a constituent policy providing for severe reduction in the salaries of government personnel and the compensation of veterans). Only the most strenuous party discipline kept dissident Democrats line.[11] Thus, here the pattern was not president power but national party power, which tends, if at all, to re-emerge whenever constituent issues emerge. This could have been predicted, with some degree of confidence, by knowing only the formal provisions of the bill.

Roosevelt was indeed a strong President, but his strength was conditioned and shaped by its environment, and the most determinative part of that environment was the policy environment. Roosevelt responded to more pressures than any national leader ever had. And in translating those pressures into public policies he also transformed those pressures into special and meaningful political forces that were shaped by the type of policy the demand became. It is in this sense that the Roosevelt Revolution is the key to American politics even into the 1970's. Granted, it was a bit of a revolution in terms of the scale of its expansion, and in terms of the extent to which it turned round the Constitution. But the precise meaning of the revolution will be found in the multiplicity rather than the scale of policy actions. This multiplicity of policies differentiated politics.

Thus, the impression of Roosevelt the strong, Roosevelt the opinion leader, the social democrat, is gained primarily from the unprecedentedly large number of redistributive programs he formulated and sent up to Congress. On these, during and after the 100 days, he overwhelmed the opposition with the support of the masses and the force of rhetoric heavily laden with class fear and antagonism. Congress operated like a meek Parliament before a mighty Crown. During the first two months alone these programs included: suspension of the convertibility of dollars into gold, suspension of gold export, the Emergency Banking Act loosening Federal Reserve autho-

---

[11]Binkley, *op. cit.*, pp. 296–298.

rization on loans to member banks, broad authority to issue unsecured greenbacks up to $3 billion under the Thomas Amendment to the AAA, temporary deposit insurance, and authority to purchase up to $2 billion in gold or foreign exchange—the first step toward devaluation. These were all presidential in that they were created there, were approved quickly by a co-operative Congress, and amounted to large and explicit grants of power back to the President.

But on other matters Roosevelt looked more like the classic politician, playing the role of broker, the cajoler, the man in the center more by place-ment than power. Indeed, his broker role included an unprecedented will-ingness to alienate a large share of national sovereignty in order to get enough consensus for formulation and passage of legislation. And this is why Roosevelt looks, through the prism of regulatory issues, like a 1930's European corporate syndicalist. Only a brief look at such programs as AAA (parity provisions), the Securities Act, the Glass Steagall Banking Bill, and NIRA will reveal the distinctly different political process around the Presi-dent—and this was going on exactly at the same time the President was also the social democratic leader. In these regulatory matters he was willing to share power and to co-opt business support because neither his presi-dency nor anyone else's has had sufficient independent power to pass im-portant regulatory programs without paying a big price to build a coalition for the purpose. Access to public opinion and use of lofty rhetoric are re-sources that simply do not spend well in the regulatory area.

Thus, to this vastly popular and unilaterally powerful President (as he could easily have seen himself through the prism of redistributive policies), it must have been something of a comedown to look out at the world through the prism of securities and banking and labor regulatory legisla-tion. Every account of these policies in 1933 and 1934 stresses the pro-nouncedly congressional factor. Despite the fact that the Securities Act of 1933 and the Securities and Exchange Act of 1934 were drafted by Landis, Cohen, and Corcoran in the White House (or Cambridge), both acts were gone over carefully and were very creatively rewritten in Congress.[12] House treatment of the Public Utility Holding Company Act of 1935 was "one of the most comprehensive and complete. . .ever given. . .any bill."[13] House and Senate versions were different from one another, and both were differ-ent from the White House. The final draft, worked out in conference com-mittee, was quite different from all of these. And to any observer, President, or casual reader of the accounts, this looks like congressional, not presiden-tial, power.

[12]Landis' own account has been republished in Lowi, *Legislative Politics USA* (Boston: Little, Brown, 1965), pp. 143 ff.; see also Chamberlain, *The President, Congress and Legislation* (New York: Columbia University Press, 1946), pp. 58 ff.

[13]*Ibid.*, p. 72.

Or, take the Wagner Act, well after the opening blast of the New Deal. It was of congressional origin and was dominated by congressional forces. President Roosevelt held out for a few changes in particularly objectionable parts, but he was dragged along more as an unhappy supplicant than as a leader of nation, government, and party.[14]

But Roosevelt does not constitute a sufficient case. The real question here is whether this differentiated pattern, set during the 1930's, became institutionalized into separate and predictable systems of policy and politics. Rather than concentrate only on the 1930's, it would be better to span the entire period since those formative days. Strong *and* weak Presidents have been in the office since then, and the test will be whether, regardless of that, they face the same kinds of politics when the policy conditions are the same. If this is true, it would mean that strong Presidents may increase the amount of political action or the level of intensity, but they are less likely to alter the pattern of politics except insofar as they pursue one type of policy overwhelmingly more than the three others.

The Record Since Roosevelt:
Stabilized Variation

The "Summary of Case Studies" (Table 4-2) presents a pattern of stabilized variation. Once we began regularly to get a goodly number of policies of all four types, we also began to witness four quite different types of politics. Were it not for the possibility of overstating the argument, one could say that each is a distinct subsystem.

The summary is comprised of 17 published case studies. Many are book-length, all are very detailed, and each was written by a reputable scholar. Our task was essentially to "interview" each author by addressing certain questions to his case study. The questions are presented in shorthand across the top of the summary. For example, it was important to learn what each author had to say about the typical participant in his story (column 1)—if indeed the author was struck by anything worth reporting on that subject. As is clear, almost all authors did stress some characteristic of the participants that could be coded, as indicated by the adjectives running down column (1). To take one case, Bailey and Samuel were impressed by

---

[14]Leuchtenberg, *op. cit.*, pp. 150 ff; and compare James MaG. Burns, *The Lion and the Fox* (New York: Harcourt, 1956): "Quite unwittingly the President acted as midwife in the rebirth of labor action" (p. 215. "Neither Roosevelt nor Miss Perkins had much to do with this provision (Sec. 7A, NRA). Framed mainly by congressmen and labor leaders, it was simply part of a bargain under which labor joined the NRA's great 'concert of interest'" (pp. 215–216). ". . .Roosevelt failed to see the potentialities of an enlarged labor movement. . ." (p. 216). The Wagner Act: "was the most radical legislation passed during the new Deal. . . yet . . .he threw his weight behind the measure only at the last moment, when it was due to pass anyway" (p. 219). These are not the portrait of a lion *or* a fox, but only of a man running hard to keep up with history.

the quality of "every man for himself," in the formulation of the Rivers and Harbors Act of 1950.[15] For another that has been covered in enormous detail, the politics of the traditional tariff has by all observers been considered highly individualized.[16]

Each author, through his case, was also asked if he had anything special to report on how the actors seemed to relate to each other (column 2). Did they mainly engage in mutual back scratching? Or, does the author report that he found careful strategy over long periods along broad, ideological lines? Or was there careful plotting and coalition building but along sector or other more special lines of cleavage? Idealogical ties and long and stable lines of cleavage were reported by McConnell in his accounts of Farm Security and Farmers Home Administrations, as did Munger and Fenno in the fight over aid to education. In contrast, all of the authors of the middle six grouping of cases reported unstable cleavages (coalitions) based on sector and trade lines. It was this type of case, of which there were so many in the 1940's and 50's, that provided the empirical basis for the formalizing of the pluralist interpretation of American politics.[17]

The President is most likely to perceive for himself the patterns reported on columns (5) through (8) of the summary. Here the authors were asked what they had to report about the relative importance of lobbying, congressional committees, the floor, and the White House, respectively, to the final outcome of the program. No author undertakes to write a policymaking case study unless he intends to have something significant to say about the relative importance of these "loci of power."

The first thing one is struck by in the returns from these 17 cases is their sheer variation. Yet, if we could really generalize about national politics, would there not be a great deal of similarity in these adjectives?

The second thing one is struck by is the pattern of variation. Other readers might use different adjectives, but that is not likely to change the pattern much, since the adjectives used here were either used in the original or were careful translations of longer accounts. Even if something is lost by converting a paragraph or section into a single, summary word, the repetition and regular variation of these words across 17 important cases cannot be taken lightly.[18]

[15]Bailey and Samuel, cited on the bibliography accompanying the summary.

[16]Schattschneider, and also Bauer, *et al.*, cited in the bibliography.

[17]See David B. Truman, *The Governmental Process* (New York: Knopf, 1951), especially his notes on sources in chapters XI-XV, dealing with policy formulation; see also Earl Latham, *The Group Theory of Politics* (Ithaca: Cornell University Press, 1952), whose opening theoretical chapter generalized on a pattern developed in the rest of his book, a case study of the federal attempt to regulate basing points practices in the cement industry and elsewhere. This case is very frequently cited in Truman.

[18]Eighteen additional cases have been given the same treatment, but they are not yet ready for the same presentation. The pattern is about the same, although a few surprise exceptions bear checking out or explaining.

Table 4-2 Variations in the Policy Process
Summary of Case Studies I: Actors and Their Roles

Case	Attribute			
	(1) *Primary* *Units*	*(2)* *Relationships* *Among*	*(3)* *Stability* *Among*	*(4)* *Bu.-Prof.* *Factor*
Distributive				
Rivers—Harbors '50	single	logrolling	highest	some
Airports Aid '58-'59	single	logrolling	very high	low
ARA	single	logrolling	highest	low
Tariff, '50's	single	logrolling	highest	low
Regulative				
FDA, '38	tr. assn.	bargaining	high	high
Rent Control '50	tr. assn.	bargaining	low	low
Robinson-Patman	tr. assn.	bargaining	low	low
AAA '38	tr. assn.	bargaining	low	low
Taft-Hartley	tr. assn.	bargaining	moderate*	low
Landrum-Griffin	tr. assn.	bargaining	low	low
Redistributive				
Farm Security Administration	(Bu. only)	ideal.	high	highest
Farmers Home Administration	(Bu. only)	ideol.	very high	highest
Social Security '35	Peaks	ideol.	very high	highest
Federal Aid to Education	Peaks	ideol.	very high	high**
Employment Act '46	Peaks	ideol.	very high	high**
Excess Profits	***	ideol.	very high	high**
Internal Revenue '54 (exemption and rates)	Peaks	ideol.	high	highest

* Pro's high, anti's low.

** Professional very high; agency personnel involvement as lobbyists or draftsmen not high.

*** No mention is made of any groups or associations. The "business community" is termed "unanimous" and "concerted" but not managed.

What the Roosevelt watchers report as exceptions to the general rule of Roosevelt mastery, therefore, turn out on closer examination to be not exceptions at all, but the rule under certain conditions that can be known in advance and understood in theoretically and jurisprudentially interesting terms. In all four of the distributive cases—the top group on the summary—the authors report that the President was either out of the picture altogether or was in it as a very weak and striving supplicant. Often the only way the President has been able to get into this act has been to try to con-

Table 4-2, Continued

Case	Attribute			
	(5) *Lobby* *Role*	*(6)* *Committee* *Role*	*(7)* *Floor* *Role*	*(8)* *Executive* *Role*
Rivers-Harbors '50	very high	determinative	consensual	supplicative
Airports Aid	high	determinative	consensual	supplicative
ARA	high	creative	consensual	supplicative
Tariff, 50's	low	creative	contentious	supplicative
FDA '38	low	creative	very creative	supplicative
Rent Control '50	low	creative	creative	supplicative
Robinson-Patman	very high	creative	creative	passive
AAA '38	very high	creative	not asc.	coordinative
Taft-Hartley	very high	creative	creative	passive (stalemated)
Landrum-Griffin	high	conduit	very creative	coordinative & supplicative
Farm Security Administration	very high	none	none	legislative
Farmers Home Administration	high	lobbyist	not ascertained	legislative
Social Security Act	moderate	conduit	consensual	legislative
Aid to Education '59*	high	lobbyist	contentious	inactive*
Employment Act of '46	moderate	very low	very creative	legislative
Excess Profits '50	moderate	lobbyist	contentious	supplicative
Internal Revenue '54	moderate	low-creative**	contentious	legislative

Legend

Lobby role: *Very high* if prominent and creative in legislature, executive, and grass roots; *high* if prominent and creative at any point; *moderate* if only prominent; and *low* if no evidence of anything.

Committee role: *conduit, lobbyist, creative, determinative*, in that rough order of importance.

Floor role: *consensual, contentious* (if a lot of debate but little alteration of the bill), *creative* (if evidence of alteration).

Executive role: *passive, coordinative, supplicative, legislative* in that order.

*Failed of passage. As a general rule, if executive activity is low on a redistributive activity, the bill is probably doomed. This is not true of the other two types.

**Joint Committee on Internal Revenue Taxation very creative—especially its staff; but it is not a legislative committee. The Ways and Means Committee and Finance Committee were much less creative, much more ratifiers of accords reached between JCIRT and Treasury lawyers.

vert the legislation into something else besides pork barrel—as Roosevelt succeeded in doing once and no more on TVA, and as Kennedy succeeded once in doing with his emergency public works proposal, which he tied to fiscal planning and general redistribution. But usually the committees succeed in severing these redistributive features from distributive bills.

A variety of words describe Presidents in the six cases of regulatory legislation, but one thing runs dramatically through all of them: Whether the President is strongly involved (as in AAA legislation on parity), or is stalemated due to squabbles within his own branch and party (as was true in the case of Taft-Hartley), Congress dominates the regulatory process. And this is the parliamentary Congress—the floor, not the committees. Sometimes the President has presented full-blown draft legislation, and sometimes the relevant committee will draft the original version. But in either event, according to the authors of the six regulatory cases, there is likely to be a lot of rewriting on the floor, through the amending process, and through conference.

Table 4-3 is a statistical confirmation of the results in the summary. It is a count of the actual amending actions involved in the 13 post-1948 bills on the summary, plus all bills in the 87th Congress, First Session, that received roll call vote in both houses. We used eight types of amending activity, and we ranked them according to degree of difficulty: (1) number of amendments offered (2) per cent passed; (3) number of important amendments offered; (4) per cent of those that passed, (5) number of amendments offered over objections of the sponsor; (6) per cent of those that passed; (7) number of important amendments offered over objections of sponsor; (8) per cent of these that passed. The average amending activity using each of the eight types, were tallied, and the results of three of these are presented in the table. We then attached weights from 1 to 8 to these categories to reflect roughly the degree of difficulty a member would have in getting each type of amendment adopted, and the "weighted mean" for each chamber is presented in the last column.

First, we can see that floor activity jumps up dramatically from distributive to redistributive bills. Since other evidence (see the summary) indicates presidential dominance over redistributive legislation, this finding suggests that on redistributive bills we get something like an acting out of the intent of the framers: direct communication between Executive and Legislative Branches. But the evidence in Table 4-3 is really classic for regulative bills. The goose egg for significant creativity in distributive legislation tends to dramatize the fact that on 67 per cent of all regulative bills at least two significant amendments were added during floor debate in the House despite the objections of the sponsor, who is usually the committee chairman. Indeed, that is a lot of rewriting, a lot of creativity, especially in the era of the "rise of the presidency" when Congress' reputation for creativity has declined.

Table 4-3   Evidence of Floor Creativity: Amendments
Three examples of straight amendment counts:

	(1) Average Number of Amendments Offered Per Bill	(2) Per Cent of These Passed	(3) Per Cent of Significant Amendments Passed Over Sponsor	Weighted Means, a Summary of all Levels of Amending Action:	
				House	Senate
Distributive Bills (N=22)	5.8	41.8%	0	.05	.16
Redistributive Bills (N=25)	9.1	62.4%	24%	.15	.45
Regulative Bills (N=15)	12.8	48.9%	67%	.46	.50

The "weighted mean" adds considerable confirmation.[19] Obviously the overall level of floor action was much higher in the Senate, where smaller size and permissive rules prevail. But within the Senate the amounts of floor action, i.e., the evidence of floor creativity, varied from policy type to policy type, in a predictable way.

In House and Senate the dramatic jump upward was from distributive to regulative. This is much more significant in the House because of the many rules that discourage access to the floor under any circumstances. But even in the Senate, the reputation for floor creativity would hardly exist if we went back to the period when federal legislation was all distributive.

Finally, in the Senate, as in the House, there is a significant jump from distributive to redistributive, in evidence of floor creativity. This finding will bear further examination. Since history and the cases have revealed the special role of the executive on redistributive matters, and since we now see also the considerable creativity of Congress as well, we might be led to reformulate our notions of policy and institutions, and how they relate to each other. It is quite conceivable that political scientists can develop criteria for policy choice in terms of predicted and desired impacts on the political system, just as economists, biologists, and the like attempt to predict and guide policies according to their societal impacts.

Implications for Prediction and Choice

Neither these data nor data of any other sort would support a drastically diminished interpretation of presidential power. His freedom to commit us to war, his command of secret information and diplomacy, his power to use executive agreements are all too impressive. But these impressive powers have overshadowed real variations even in that area defined, quite erroneously, as "foreign policy."[20] One need only note the amount of revi-

[19]Each category of amending activity was dichotomized, so that the action on each bill and for each type of amendment could be scored 0 or 1—then multiplied by the difficulty weights, as described above. For example, if two or more significant amendments were added to a bill despite the objections of the sponsor, that was scored 1 and multiplied by 8. (If fewer than two such amendments passed, it was then scored 0 and did not increase the score.) These scores were then cumulated for all bills in each policy category, and the average shown on the table was the result of dividing by each of the N's.

[20]Some of these variations can be captured in the fourth category, constituent or system maintenance policy. These are not dealt with in this essay because of many considerations too complicating for this first effort at reanalyzing cases. However, I have dealt with some of these patterns elsewhere, and have argued at length that the so-called foreign policy area actually breaks down into the four types captured in the paradigm. The break comes when one asks about the kinds of disciplines governments place upon their own populations in order to carry out foreign influence. For example, setting up a Marshall Plan is not the same kind of policy as actions revising our relations with Red China. Foreign policy is no more of a single piece than agriculture policy or any other conventional, subject-matter designation. And, as shown with the different types of agriculture policy, the politics of each type of foreign policy will vary accordingly. See my chapter in James Rosenau (ed.). *The Domestic Sources of Foreign Policy* (New York: The Free Press, 1967).

sion of factual and normative interpretation about presidential power since the Vietnam failures to realize the variability that was probably masked in the political science of national power during the 1950's and 60's.

All of this is to say that presidential power, and all other political phenomena, must be put in proportion and perspective. Whether we are concerned about the issue of presidential power or the issue of adopting a regulatory approach to a social problem, and whether we are concerned with the objective business of prediction or the normative business of choosing a particular outcome, perspective must reside in at least two considerations: (1) prediction or choice must begin by recognizing the possibility of more than one pattern, and by pattern we must mean whole models rather than incremental differences in specific behavior patterns; and (2) if predictions can be made at this massive, institutional level, then they can, and inevitably will, become a major criterion for policy choice—i.e., really good theory is unavoidably, normative.

(1) If this essay has shown anything, it is that almost any generalization about national politics is inapplicable to as many as two-thirds of the cases of policy formulation. If we reverse the generalization by adding a "not," the new generalization would also tend to be inapplicable to about two-thirds of the known cases. The policy framework provides a basis for stating the conditions under which a given proposition is applicable, rather than merely helping improve the batting average from .333 to .335, or something of the sort. The policy framework locates the smaller universe where the batting average might be .677 or higher, and additionally it puts each of the generalizations into a theoretically orderly relation to all others. In turn, this produces new insights but, more important, it builds the propositions toward whole models rather than merely stringing out specific x-y statements.

One example alluded to earlier, where whole models of government and politics are seen to be involved, has to do with the conventional wisdom that American politics is all subsumed under a "presidential system," with exceptions. The cases and statistics here suggest first that several models have been masked over by the notion of a single system with multiple centers of power. One of the worst consequences of this assumption is its central construct, the "rise of presidential power, the decline of legislative power." *Sub rosa* it is then recognized that presidential power is not unilateral, nor is it even remotely equivalent to executive power; but those ambiguities are left theoretically unsettled. When one allows for multiple models rather than multiple power centers in a single model, many tendencies that must be left as ambiguities or anomalies can be brought explicitly to the center and handled rather easily. At least two such models involve a very strong Congress, and in one or perhaps both of these, presidential and congressional power are consonant, not zero-sum.

This bears further pursuit. Evidence of floor creativity is stronger for strong Presidents, such as Kennedy and Johnson, than for weak Presidents, such as Eisenhower, or Truman during his first three years in office. And floor creativity, as Table 4-3 shows is high for redistributive bills, when the presidential role is most pronounced, for strong as well as for weak Presidents. What this really means is that the levels of political responsibility in the two branches tend to be consonant, and that they exist together in counterpoise to the administrative or bureaucratic levels of both branches. When the President is weak it is his bureaucracies and the congressional committees—the levels of low political responsibility—that tend to dominate the process; when the President is strong it is because he controls the bureaucratic levels.

(2) If the policy scheme developed in this essay, or some superior one to come along, can predict when a President will be strong and weak, as well as when other gross institutional patterns will prevail, then it is no step at all to a policy science for political scientists. This kind of wisdom provides criteria for choosing among policies, criteria that do not require the imposition of private goals upon legislators or the people. To illustrate, if two policies have about an equal chance of failure or success in the achievement of some social purpose the legislature has agreed upon, then that one should be preferred that has the most desirable impact on the political system. It should be the expertise of the political scientist to specify these kinds of consequences, and a policy framework would be necessary to do this. This is science, yet it reaches to the very foundations of democratic politics and the public interest. Let us pursue both, the second first.[21]

For a public interest to be involved at all, at least one of two properties must be present: The policy should be large enough in scope to affect a large number of people in a consistent way. This could be true of constituent policies, where a basic structural change in the system tends to create class even where it does not directly define one, for example in electoral reforms.

Or, the policy must, regardless of its scope, express a clear rule of law. A rule of law identifies the citizen in each person, the public part of each of us. The making of a real law (as contrasted with a policy-without-law) is an act of setting a public morality upon some action or status hitherto considered private.[22]

Distributive policy, in this context, clearly comes closest to being a complete privatization of the public. Much of it is intended to be *sub rosa*, and usually succeeds, given the capacity of these policies for continual fis-

---

[21]A more elaborate argument, with many more illustrations, will be found in my companion paper, "Population Policies and the Political System," mimeo., 1971.

[22]Cf. Hannah Arendt, *The Human Condition*, Chapter II and pp. 193–199, especially her treatment of the Greek concept of law making as akin to architecture in that laws define a space entirely restricted to citizens.

sion according to the number of individuals making claims. To take but one contrasting example, regulatory politics that embody even vague rules of law cannot be full privatized. The directly coercive element introduces public concerns of increasingly general applicability.[23] The overriding point is that these policy considerations, within the arena's framework, provide a systematic and plausible basis for defining good and bad legislation—without holding one moral code absolutely above another.

We can also judge public policy as good or bad in still another sense, a sense that leads toward fundamental questions about the relationship between public policy and democracy. If we want an open and public politics, we are limited to certain kinds of policies—regardless of whether the manifest goals of these policies are fulfilled. Again we would try to avoid distributive policies, because nothing open and democratic can come of them. But more nuance can be added. There can be moments in history, or changes of fashion, where the presidency is thought to be too powerful—perhaps we live in such a period today. In such a situation, Keynesian fiscal policies should be resisted, and regulatory policies should be preferred, for the latter tend to bring things to Congress and tend to invigorate interest group action. If anxiety about unlimited presidential power in international affairs continues to grow, regulatory provisions could even be tied to treaties or executive agreements. To trace this out is to illustrate rather dramatically the possibilities of looking at politics through policies: The best way, in other words, to open up the presidency and to expose the relations he is developing with another country is to put into policy terms some reciprocal commitments that require internal controls in both countries. For example, a provision requiring exchange of stock between two or more corporations, or their countries, in order to deal with air or water pollution would destabilize the politics of both countries, at least enough to gain entree into what is going on. Requirements for inspection of financial institutions dealing in our foreign aid would do about the same thing.

Finally, if we wished to introduce strong national parties into our system, we might try to pursue more goals through constituent policies—like effective public propaganda in the birth control field, or dealing with monopolies by changing the rules protecting their limited liability rather than by adding regulations affecting their conduct.

---

[23]Obviously a distinction is being made here when a continuum is involved. There are degrees of vagueness, degrees to which a rule of law is present. However, any rule, no matter how vague, begins to transform distributive into regulatory patterns. For example, adding a vague and very mild anti-discrimination provision to an education subsidy statute can turn established distributive patterns literally inside out. On the other hand, it should be added that very broad delegations of regulatory authority to an agency can lead in the long run to a decline into an all too stable and private politics. Thus, the rule of law criterion is a good one that is often not provided in quantity sufficient to produce the predicted results. Cf. my *The End of Liberalism*, (New York: Norton, 1969), esp. chapters V and X.

The point is that if we can discover empirically the policy conditions underlying our political patterns, we have a basis for better public policies as well as better political science. Should we regulate? If there is the slightest contribution to political theory or policy science in this article, it would be in having established a basis for actually answering that question.

Sources for Table 4-2

Rivers and Harbors Act of 1950. Stephen K. Bailey and Howard Samuel, *Congress at Work* (New York: Holt, 1952).

Airports Aid, 1958–59. Randall P. Ripley. "Congress Champions Aid to Airports." in F.N. Cleaveland, *Congress and Urban Problems* (Washington, D.C.: The Brookings Institution, 1968).

Area Redevelopment Act, John Bibby and Roger Davidson, *On Capitol Hill* (New York: Holt, Rinehart and Winston, 1967).

Tariff. Raymond Bauer, *et al.*, *American Business and Public Policy* (New York: Atherton, 1963).

Food, Drug and Cosmetic Act. David Cavers, "The Food, Drug and Cosmetic Act of 1938: Its Legislative History and Its Substantive Provisions." *Law and Contemporary Problems* (Winter 1939).

Rent Control, 1950. Bailey and Samuel, *op. cit.*

Robinson-Patman. Joseph C. Palamountain, *The Politics of Distribution* (Cambridge: Harvard University Press, 1955).

Agricultural Adjustment Act. Charles Hardin, *The Politics of Agriculture* (New York: The Free Press, 1952); and Gilbert Fite, *George Peek and the Fight for Farm Parity* (Norman: University of Oklahoma Press, 1954).

Taft-Hartley. Bailey and Samuel. *op. cit.*

Landrum-Griffin. Alan McAdams, *Power Politics in Labor Legislation* (New York: Columbia University Press, 1964).

Farm Security and Farmers Home Administrations. Grant McConnell, *The Decline of Agrarian Democracy* (Berkeley: University of California Press, 1953).

Social Security. Paul H. Douglas, *Social Security in the U.S..* (New York: Whittlesey House, 1936); and Edwin E. Witte, *The Development of the Social Security Act* (Madison: University of Wisconsin Press, 1962).

Aid to Education. Frank Munger and Richard Fenno, *National Politics in Federal Aid to Education* (Syracuse: Syracuse University Press, 1962).

Employment Act of 1946. Stephen K. Bailey, *Congress Makes a Law* (New York: Columbia University Press, 1950).

Excess Profits. Bailey and Samuel, *op. cit.*

Internal Revenue. Stanley S. Surrey, "The Congress and the Tax Lobbyist: How Special Tax Provisions Get Enacted," *Harvard Law Review* (1957). pp. 1145 ff.

DEVELOPING PUBLIC POLICY THEORY: PERSPECTIVES FROM EMPIRICAL RESEARCH
*George Greenberg, Jeffrey Miller, Lawrence Mohr, and Bruce Vladeck**

The emerging discipline of public policy studies is characterized by a growing disjunction between theory and research. While there are many provocative and potentially important theories, systematic empirical research to test them has largely been lacking.[1] Most importantly, there seems to have been little progress in the critical intermediate stage of refining and then operationalizing the important variables.

In the course of our own research—an attempt to employ aggregated case-study data in order to test quantitatively a number of important public policy hypotheses[2]—we experienced enormous difficulty at this intermediate stage. We attempted to translate leading hypotheses into operational variables suitable for employment in quantitative analysis. The difficulty we experienced did not lie in the question of whether the hypotheses were supported or not, but in whether they were testable or not. Although the theories seemed perfectly applicable to the few cases used by their authors to illustrate them originally, the propositions did not fit so neatly when applied to a number of examples not expressly chosen for explanation and illustration. As we attempted to deal with problems of operationalization in connection with a variety of theories and dozens of cases, we noted that many of the problems recurred. While the theories were plausible, they seemed to fall into certain traps that appear to be endemic to the systematic

---

*George Greenberg, Jeffrey Miller, Lawrence Mohr, and Bruce Vladeck, "Developing Public Policy Theory: Perspectives from Empirical Research." *American Political Science Review* 71 (Dec., 1977): 1532–1543. Used by permission.

[1] By "systematic empirical research" we mean the use of quantitative data gathered from a number of instances of policy making in order to test specific hypotheses. Examples of recent work in this direction are provided by Robert K. Yin and Douglas Yates, *Street-Level Governments*, R-1527-NSF (Santa Monica: Rand, 1974); William A. Lucas, *The Case Survey Method*, R-1515-RC (Santa Monica: Rand, 1974); and Robert K. Yin and Karen A. Heald, "Using the Case Survey Method to Analyze Policy Studies," *Administrative Science Quarterly*, 20 (September 1975), 371-81.

[2] For a description of that project, see our "Case Study Aggregation and Policy Theory," *Proceedings*, 1973 Annual Meeting of the American Political Science Association, New Orleans, La., September 4-8, 1973.

study of public policy. This led us to adopt the purpose of the present paper—to comment on these peculiarities of public policy theory and describe these pitfalls, as an avenue toward both building better theory and illuminating some of the significant characteristics of public policy itself.

The plausible and provocative theories of public policy formation offered by Lowi, Banfield, Froman, Gamson, Dahl, and others, appear in general to be no more or less adequate than those in any area of political science. *But the kinds of phenomena that the theories seek to explain* are radically different from most of the other phenomena we study. It is this difference in the objects of analysis that is the source of the difficulty.

In brief, public policy as a focus of systematic comparative analysis is *more complex* than such phenomena as electoral votes, legislative roll calls, incidents of political violence, and elite ideologies. It is more complex on at least four counts, which we will elaborate and illustrate in the discussion to follow. These are:

1. The policy process takes place over time, sometimes over a long period of time. This leads to difficulty in explaining "the process" as a simple unit. Even if one attempts to explain specific outcomes, the explanatory forces invoked almost invariably involve characteristics of this long and shifting process. Two sorts of difficulty arise: As the process proceeds over time, it can involve a large number of decision points, e.g., the decision of a subcommittee chairman, a Senate roll call, a presidential compromise, and the decision of an appellate court. The contents of each of these outputs might be called "public policy" and might be predictable by public policy theory. But we do not want theories to be oriented toward or tested upon inconclusive or tentative decisions. Nor do we want them constructed so as to predict the characteristics of the rubber-stamping process. We want somehow to focus only on "significant" outputs.

The idea of a predictive theory of public policy demands that the values of the predictors be determined at some beginning point. Such values, however, are likely to change with the unfolding of the process itself, their final status being achieved only at its termination. Many presumably predictive theories are thereby weakened substantially, and become, in final analysis, post hoc explanations.

2. Any given policy proposal, or "output," or "outcome"[3] is in itself complex; it may have several important aspects. This multiplicity can make the whole policy extremely difficult to place in any single category, as is de-

---

[3]Our use of the terms "output" and "outcome" follows Ranney's definition of those terms. See his "The Study of Policy Content," in *Political Science and Public Policy*, ed. Austin Ranney (Chicago: Markheim, 1968), pp. 8-9.

manded, for example, by the categorization schemes that currently abound in public policy theory.

3. As a focus of analysis, policy making is complicated by the presence of a large number of participants. When a characteristic of the participants becomes a variable of interest, as it often does, variation among participants with regard to that characteristic causes difficulty. The difficulty takes two forms:

Subjective The state of the world as perceived by participants yields many important policy-analytic variables. But perceptions vary considerably, of course, depending upon the participant consulted or described.

Objective Still more variables are generated in existing theory by "objectively" determined participant characteristics—as determined, that is, by the researcher, interviewer, casewriter, or other outside observer. Ambiguity is introduced when the heterogeneous group of all participants, or heterogeneous subcollections of participants, must be assigned a single score on such a characteristic (e.g., level of involvement, or point of access to decision makers).

4. Lastly, public policy as a research focus is complex because the process cannot be described by simple additive models. On the contrary, the forces interact; the impact of one depends in large measure upon the value of another.

In sum, "public policy" is almost never a single, discrete, unitary phenomenon. Indeed, the appeal of public policy studies as a focus of intellectual endeavor lies precisely in its richness; the complexity of the unit of analysis simply and appropriately reflects the fact that an action of government is rarely meaningful if conceived of as a discrete, disembodied event, and that the impacts of a single government action on society are not understood properly if taken in isolation from one another.

In this essay, then, we seek to specify in some detail the kinds of difficulties these characteristics create, illustrating them by exploring the problems arising from attempts to apply specific theoretical propositions to concrete events taken from the case-study literature. We hope that our conclusions will not only provide some assistance to developers of public policy theory who are concerned to avoid problems of conceptualization and operational definition, but will also highlight certain important characteristics of public policy itself that have heretofore been inadequately understood or explained.

An Initial Illustration

Many of the problems arising from the complexity of using "policy" as a unit of analysis can be illustrated by the work of Theodore Lowi. No single theoretical construct has been more important to the development of public policy studies than Lowi's categorization scheme,[4] yet the way in which he defines his fundamental terms is seriously weakened by the problems inherent in the unit of analysis, which make his hypotheses almost impossible to operationalize meaningfully in order to test them empirically. Since these problems of operationalization bear upon several of the challenges inherent in developing public policy theory, and since Lowi's idea is so well known and so well received, we refer to his work by way of general introduction, to be recalled briefly at several points in the more schematic discussion to follow.

The heart of Lowi's argument is that "policies determine politics." He developed, in a series of articles, a typology containing "regulatory," "distributive," "redistributive," and (subsequently) "constituency" policies and argued that policy processes will differ significantly depending on the policy type involved. As a result of those differences in process, he suggests, relationships among important concepts or variables that may be quite strong when policies of one kind are involved may be much weaker or even totally absent when other types of policies are concerned. Instead of attempting to find relationships that hold across the entire range of public policy, he argues that one should focus one's investigation within one of the four policy classifications.

Lowi generates a number of important hypotheses from his typology. For example, he predicts that congressional committees will be able to retain control of the process of coalition building on distributive amendments and that, therefore, few amendments will be offered to committee bills on the floor.[5] He also predicts that peak associations can be expected to be more cohesive when confronted with redistributive issues that unite their memberships than when they are faced with regulatory issues that divide them.[6]

The explicitness of the predictions Lowi derives from his policy classification is not matched, however, by a similar explicitness in explaining

---

[4]We refer, of course, to the ideas presented in the series of three articles: "American Business, Public Policy, Case-Studies and Political Theory," *World Politics,* 16 (July 1964), 677-715; "Decision Making vs. Policy Making: Toward an Antidote for Technocracy," *Public Administration Review,* 30 (May-June 1970), 314-25; "Four Systems of Policy, Politics, and Choice," *Public Administration Review,* 32 (July-August 1972), 298-310.

[5]This is why Lowi found the '60s tariff to be so different. In earlier times, tariff policy was distributive, but "The true nature of tariff in the 1960s emerges as regulatory policy. . . . Issues that could not be thrashed out through the 'group process' also could not be thrashed out in committee but had to pass on to Congress and the floor," Lowi, "American Business," p. 701. Lowi presented data on amendments to bills in Congress from the floor in "Decision Making vs. Policy Making," pp. 321-22.

[6]"If there is ever any cohesion within the peak associations, it occurs on redistributive issues, and their rhetoric suggests that they occupy themselves most of the time with these" (Lowi, "American Business," p. 707).

how one can determine the correct policy type for a given policy. Since the correct determination of policy type is obviously central to the predictive ability of Lowi's theory, this limitation has crucial importance. Lowi contends that distributive decisions are made without reference to their implications for other decisions; that regulatory decisions imply a direct choice "as to who will be indulged and who will be deprived"; and that redistributive decisions involve the greatest interconnection, since they imply choices among broad classes of individuals.[7] But the "decisions" of which Lowi is speaking are not simple and discrete; they are *policy* decisions. Many can be expected to contain at least some characteristics of each of Lowi's types, and there is little guidance for determining how a policy is to be classified in any but the simplest cases.

The problem of classifying a policy correctly thus becomes a central stumbling block to the empirical testing of Lowi's hypotheses. For instance, policies often have distributive programmatic characteristics but redistributive or regulatory financing mechanisms, as the case of the Chicago Transit Authority aptly illustrates. The CTA approached the state of Illinois for subsidization—a handout, precisely in the distributive tradition of the pork barrel and the pre-1960s tariff. The matter might easily have been processed and settled as a distributive issue, but the method for financing the subsidy became controversial. The proposal was eventually defeated, largely because of the dispute on regulatory or redistributive concerns—the question of whose particular pockets the money was to come from.[8] More generally, for *any* policy lacking explicit income transfers, there is some financing method either built in or implied that may or may not fall into the same category (in Lowi's typology) as the policy's other characteristics.

James Q. Wilson discusses this difficulty at some length. He maintains that a single policy may have aspects of each policy type, and he offers several examples. "A bill barring discrimination in public accommodations," for instance:

> ...could be seen as a measure regulating the use of hotels and restaurants or as one redistributing a benefit (access to hotels and restaurants) from one social stratum to another. . . . Urban renewal programs regulate the use of land, redistribute the housing supply, and distribute benefits to certain contractors and labor unions. Monetary and fiscal policy has both regulatory and redistributionist implications depending on whether one thinks of it as simply controlling the interest rate or as benefiting creditors at the expense of debtors (or vice versa).[9]

---

[7]Ibid., pp. 690-91.

[8]Edward C. Banfield, "The Chicago Transit Authority," in *Political Influence* (New York: Free Press, 1961), pp. 91-125.

[9]James Q. Wilson, *Political Organizations* (New York: Basic Books, 1973), p. 329.

Lowi never specifically addresses the problem of how to classify a policy correctly when it has attributes of more than one of his policy types, but one can infer from the general tone of his articles that he does not expect classification to present a major problem. His basic argument in this respect appears to be that expectations based on past experience with similar issues objectively structure policy choices for the entire policy process. Thus he might well respond to Wilson by contending that one particular aspect of any of the policies Wilson cites can be expected to dominate the expectations of the actors in the process, so that there will be no problem in making the classification. Hotel and restaurant accommodations policy, for example, would undoubtedly evoke regulatory expectations from virtually all those connected with the policy process, based on their past experience and the past debate on similar issues.

That answer, however, is adequate only when expectations are virtually unanimous. Yet the policy process is as likely to be characterized by multiple perceptions as policies are likely to be characterized by multiple attributes. Whenever there are any significant disagreements among perceptions of a policy, the problem in classification according to Lowi's typology has simply shifted from one of determining "which aspect" to one of determining "whose perceptions." In the CTA example, it would be quite difficult to decide whose views should predominate—those concerned with mode of financing or those concerned with the costs and benefits of the transit service. Moreover, as Wilson notes, the problem becomes even more difficult in the cases of new or innovative policy, where there is little relevant past experience to structure the perceptions of any of the participants.[10]

Variations in perception of a policy are especially likely to occur when participants in the process actively seek to redefine the issue. Lowi himself suggests that "one of the important strategies in any controversial issue is to attempt to define it in redistributive terms in order to broaden the base of opposition or support."[11] In classifying a policy in which this strategy has been employed, Lowi's method will work only if the strategy has been almost a complete success (almost all perceptions have been redefined) or almost a complete failure (almost no perceptions have been redefined). If the strategy succeeds in altering some perceptions but not all, one has no guidance for deciding which perceptions will provide the basis for classification.

Take the controversy over Medicare.[12] Initially, since the proposal called for an additional tax on workers to provide benefits for the elderly,

---

[10]Ibid., p. 339.

[11]Lowi, "American Business," p. 707, footnote 28.

[12]Theodore R. Marmor, "The Congress: Medicare Politics and Policy," in *American Political Institutions and Public Policy*, ed. Allan P. Sindler (Boston: Little, Brown, 1969), pp. 3-68.

one would probably classify the policy as redistributive. The AMA, however, attempted to redefine the issue as one of government regulation of physicians and the practice of medicine. The AMA's argument undoubtedly influenced the perceptions of at least some individuals on the issue, but it certainly did not succeed in restructuring the perceptions of all. There is simply no objective way to determine which set of perceptions should be dominant in classifying a policy issue when there is substantial disagreement among the participants themselves about what is at stake.

The problems in operationalizing Lowi's hypotheses illustrate the special difficulties of theory construction and testing in the field of public policy studies. His provocative ideas cannot be meaningfully operationalized without considerable effort by the researcher to add greater specificity and precision, a process in which the researcher must often, without adequate guidance, make important assumptions about what the theory is really trying to say. As it stands, Lowi's theory is not testable because the basic concepts are not operationalizable; in order to operationalize them, researchers must make a number of guesses and assumptions that create a situation where they can no longer be sure just whose theory they are testing.

The discussion of Lowi's paradigm illustrates the obstacles one encounters in attempting to apply policy theory across many cases, each of which is a full-scale instance of the operation of a policy-making system. We will now consider somewhat more explicitly the forms of complexity enumerated earlier, after which we will conclude with a brief listing of implications.

Problems of Temporality

Multiple Outputs Several important hypotheses become mired in ambiguity for want of a time-stopping criterion. A whole host of variables is difficult to operationalize without being arbitrary until some decision is reached as to when, over a protracted period of development and struggle, "policy is made." For example, many of the most important hypotheses attempt to predict, as a dependent variable, the success or effectiveness of employing various resources or strategies in influencing outputs. Both Gamson and Dahl have discussed this problem at length, and both suggest measuring success by comparing the output of the process with the intentions of the relevant actors.[13] The output, however, keeps changing! There are simple cases, to be sure, such as those studied in Gamson's research on fluoridation, but there are complex cases as well. In fluoridation, points of beginning and ending were generally clear; someone at some time initiated the controversy with a proposal to fluoridate the water and policy was

---

[13]William A. Gamson, *Power and Discontent* (Homewood, Ill.: Dorsey, 1968), p. 71; Robert A. Dahl, *Modern Political Analysis* (Englewood Cliffs, N.J.: Prentice-Hall, 1963), pp. 39-54.

"made" when a community voted. More frequently, though, policy making consists of an ongoing process in which beginning and ending states are unclear, and in which both outputs and intentions are continually modified.

Policy struggles are usually preceded by a background period during which intentions and opinions are being formed. Later, outputs are issued, modified, and remodified as administrators respond to continuing pressures or as losers initiate appeals to higher authorities. At times, reviews by higher authorities create real opportunities to change results; at other times the decision is merely rubber-stamped. At what points are researchers to slice into the ongoing policy process to measure the relevant intentions and outputs? How many and what sorts of appeals are to be considered before a decision process is regarded as complete? These questions are important because the measurement of such variables as the number of participants, the duration of conflict, the resources employed, etc., will be significantly altered depending on the time period over which they are measured.

An illustration can help clarify some of these difficulties. In the case study of "The Glavis-Ballinger Dispute,"[14] the controversy progressed through several stages. At stake was the validity of the Cunningham claim to large tracts of public land in Alaska. At first there was an administrative determination that the claim was valid. Then Glavis, an official in the Bureau of Land Management, began a routine investigation into the validity of the claim, ultimately recommending that the land not be turned over to Cunningham. Secretary of the Interior Ballinger overruled Glavis. Glavis then appealed to President Taft, who supported Ballinger. But Forest Service Director Gifford Pinchot then helped Glavis publicize the issue and take his case to the Congress, and ultimately a law was passed which prohibited the sale of public lands in the future, but which still did not resolve the Cunningham dispute. Several years later a federal court found against Cunningham.

It may seem obvious that the court decision decided the case, but is this the most important point to examine? And what if the court had found *for* Cunningham? The determinative decision might then be considered to have been either that of Ballinger, or Taft, or Congress, or the court, with all of the subsequent decisions essentially ratifying the first. Similarly, one might argue that the case began at any of several different points: congressional authorization of the sale of land; Cunningham's violation of the law in amassing his claim; Glavis's investigation; or the rejection of Glavis's recommendations. Depending upon the points chosen, a number of important variables, such as the degree of conflict in the dispute and the number of participants, would vary.

---

[14][Winifred McCulloch,] "The Glavis-Ballinger Dispute," in *Public Administration and Policy Development*, ed. Harold Stein (New York: Harcourt, 1952), pp. 77-87.

Treatment of this particular quandary not only affects decisions about the analysis of an individual case, such as the Glavis–Ballinger dispute, but might also artificially predetermine certain results of a quantitative analysis. Defining the duration of policy conflicts in such a way as to be as inclusive as possible, for instance, might well yield the finding that most important administrative decisions are determined in the courts, while in fact one suspects that there are many appeals in which there is no real hope of overruling an administrative determination—appeals that are taken largely pro forma in order to symbolically satisfy aggrieved interest groups. Another artificial result of inclusiveness would, no doubt, be the finding that congressional committees hardly ever have the final say about anything—although in fact they make an enormous amount of policy—simply because their decisions are routinely passed upon by the full chamber, conference committees, and the president. On the other hand, defining the time parameters of the process too narrowly—by attempting, say, to single out each discrete decision—would force the systematic analyst to consider thousands of decisions, jamming any data set with useless, unimportant, and misleading information.

It is thus essential, both when policy hypotheses are proposed and when they are tested, to have in mind some reasonable criteria for demarcating the process temporally. The reader and writer must agree somehow on the outputs that are theoretically crucial, otherwise doubt and confusion must inevitably arise regarding the consistency of theory and data.

Postdictive Theory   Another complication of temporality arises from the annoying tendency of variables not to stand still as the process unfolds. The duration, scope, or complexity of a given policy struggle are rarely strictly determined at the outset; not only are outcomes often unpredictable, but so too is the process. Thus predictive hypotheses that fail to account for this contingency often become extremely difficult to apply to concrete cases and are often best tested—and thus rendered most meaningful—by being converted into postdictive hypotheses. But that change may seriously dilute their significance.

An example is provided by the concept of "requisite actions" suggested by Banfield in *Political Influence*. Banfield introduces the concept as a way of explaining why some policy proposals are adopted and others are not. He employs the following definitions:

> Performance of a specified set of actions by specified actors, or by a specified number of, or proportion of, the actors who constitute a specified group, constitutes *adoption*, i.e., adoption is defined as the performance by these actors of these actions, which will be called *requisite* actions. . . . An actor who can perform a requisite action has *authority* over the action. He may perform it or not

as he likes, or, in the language to be used here, he may *give* or *withhold* it from the system of activity being concerted toward adoption of the proposal.[15]

In any situation, certain actors will be controlled while others are autonomous—that is, free to withhold the performance of requisite actions. In highly centralized systems, there are few autonomous actors; in highly decentralized systems there are many. Adoption of proposals in a highly decentralized system is uncertain, according to Banfield, because it cannot be predicted whether or not autonomous actors will perform the requisite actions.

Banfield goes on to derive a number of interesting and nontrivial hypotheses from his argument. For example, he argues that, "as the number of autonomous actors in a situation increases, the probability of adoptions decreases,'"[16] and that "corruption will tend to increase as the distribution of authority widens."[17] Banfield believes that these derived propositions can be tested: "If when tested— and some of them cannot be tested by any data in this volume—these derived hypotheses prove false, doubt will be cast upon the factual premises from which they were deduced."[18] But in order to test Banfield's model, it is necessary to identify and count the number of requisite actions that must be concerted in order for a policy to be adopted. And while Banfield asserts that it is uncertain that any given requisite action will be performed, it must be possible, in order for his theory to have predictive value, to at least specify what the requisite actions are before the policy struggle begins.

The number of requisite actions may, however, change dramatically during the course of a policy struggle, as controversy heats up; and it may become clear that some actions were in fact requisite actions only after the policy struggle is over. Take the case, *Defending "The Hill" Against the Metal Houses*, as an example.[19] A developer wished to erect a questionable type of housing in a lower-middle-class neighborhood. Given the legal requirements of the jurisdiction, certain zoning and building clearances would undoubtedly have to be obtained. Are there other requisite actions? How long and harsh will the decision be in the making? Can we predict the probability of adoption from our initial count of the requisite actions?

If we are to count the neighborhood residents as "an autonomous actor," the struggle could be protracted, but the residents of such neighborhoods typically do not organize to make their wishes known. Thus, predictively, the number of requisite actions would seem to be, say, two or three.

[15]Banfield, p. 309.

[16]Ibid., p. 318.

[17]Ibid., p. 322.

[18]Ibid., p. 308.

[19]William K. Muir, Jr., *Defending "The Hill" Against the Metal Houses*, ICP Case #26 (University, Ala.: University of Alabama Press, 1955).

As the particular case turned out, however, the residents of the neighborhood did organize, and as a result—though not even then a clearly predictable result—a substantial number of aldermen, the mayor, the city's corporation counsel, the state board of health, and the opposition candidate for mayor all eventually became autonomous actors as well. The developer was defeated, but only after a long and emotional struggle.

The specific dynamics of the policy process, in this case at least, thus determined not only whether or not significant actors would give or withhold requisite actions, but how many requisite actions there would have to be. This is not to say that Banfield's theory is not correct as a post hoc generalization about the extent to which two interesting attributes of the policy process covary; but the implied causality in the original hypothesis becomes impossible to test empirically.

It is now clear that Lowi's central hypothesis, that characteristics of the process can be predicted from characteristics of an input (policy type) is fettered by this same difficulty. The policy type and perceptions of it by relevant actors often are determined well after the process has begun. Of course, one might predict new characteristics of the process continuously as a policy changes or is perceived to change from distributive to regulatory, regulatory back to distributive, and so forth, but this complicates the job of comparative analysis to the point of impracticability.

The Problem of Multiplicity of Policy Aspects

A public policy is only rarely the result of a simple binary decision, or even a chain of such decisions. Even the simplest government policy is likely to spring from a complex chain of causes and relationships and to have a set of subtly interrelated consequences for the general social network. Unless there is adequate awareness of this complexity, and adequate precautions are taken to cope with it, even those theories of public policy which seem most sensible are likely to evaporate on close inspection into a cloud of ambiguity. We have already discussed at some length the problems of complexity arising from the temporal nature of policy making. The point of this and succeeding sections is that policy research would be complex even if the process were instantaneous.

Lewis Froman, for instance, hypothesizes that homogeneous communities will adopt "areal" policies, while heterogeneous communities will adopt "segmental" policies. He defines areal policies as those which affect the total population of a city simultaneously by a single action, and segmental policies as continuing policies which affect different people at different times in separate sections of the city.[20] In his segmental category, Fro-

---

[20]Lewis A. Froman, Jr., "An Analysis of Public Policy in Cities," *Journal of Politics*, 29 (February 1967), 94-108.

man thus seems to take cognizance of the fact that the same policy can have different impacts in different places over time. Yet that awareness is of no help to a researcher trying to fit a policy such as, for example, "promoting industrial development," into Froman's categories. Industry may locate in a carefully zoned, narrowly circumscribed area, but (1) its pollution may affect surrounding neighborhoods; (2) it may provide jobs to residents of a much larger area; and (3) its property taxes may pay for services uniformly consumed throughout the whole jurisdiction. There is *no* a priori way for the researcher to determine which of its impacts are to be considered in deciding whether the policy is "areal" or "segmental."

The same problem is illustrated by Alan Altshuler's description of an intercity freeway dispute: should the freeway be built along a southerly route through a black neighborhood or along a railroad line to the north?[21] The route through the black neighborhood was "scientifically chosen" for the shortest and best traffic patterns. The benefits from that route certainly appeared to be areal. The highway would be used by virtually everyone, and even those who didn't use it would benefit from the generally improved transportation and commerce in the area. More importantly, state and federal assistance was available for that route, lowering the tax burden for everyone in choosing it. On the other hand, the costs of the decision were quite clearly segmental. Many families were displaced from the area immediately surrounding the construction, with little or no counseling or provision for replacement housing. The displaced residents moved primarily into nearby buildings, seriously increasing already severe congestion and suffering the noise and pollution consequences of their continued proximity to the freeway. From the point of view of the winners, then, the freeway location decision was areal; from the point of view of the losers, it was segmental. From the point of view of a researcher trying to assign the policy to one of Froman's types in order to test his hypotheses, the decision was not easily classifiable.

The difficulty we encountered above in treating Lowi's stimulating hypothesis in its illustrative application to the subsidy for the Chicago Transit Authority also fits into this category. The policy proposal took on at least two separate and salient aspects, service and financing, which made difficult its classification into one and only one category of Lowi's policy typology.

The Problem of Multiple Participants

Even if the policy-making process were both instantaneous and unitary, it would still be complex as a focus of analysis because of the multi-

---

[21]Alan Altshuler, *Locating the Intercity Freeway*, ICP Case #88 (New York: Bobs-Merrill, 1965).

plicity of participants involved and the towering importance of participant characteristics, both subjective and objective, as elements of policy theory.

Subjective   The perceptions of relevant actors are important determinative variables in many theories about public policy, but policy theories rarely specify whose perceptions are to be taken into account. An illustration of the necessity of specifying from whose point of view a concept is to be defined is provided by hypotheses in which the status quo is an important concept. Gamson, for example, argues that it takes fewer resources to defend the status duo successfully than to bring about change.[22] While the status quo seems to be an objective characteristic of a state of the policy process, it may often be defined only in terms of participants' perceptions, which may in fact differ substantially from one another. Take the following example: in the case study, Shooting Down the Nuclear Plane,[23] all agreed that the specific purpose of an existing $75 million appropriation was to carry out a small development program. From the Air Force's perspective, however, that appropriation was only a first step and constituted a commitment to the actual construction of a nuclear plane. To the Air Force, it was that commitment which defined the status quo. Failure to expand the program and build the plane would be a negation of the commitment and thus a serious departure from the status quo. From the perspective of the members of the congressional appropriations committees, on the other hand, the small development program represented only a limited venture; from their point of view, confining the future program to reactor development, for example, would represent no change whatever in the status quo. In a situation of this sort, how is one to evaluate Gamson's hypothesis? Each protagonist, the Air Force and the Congress, thought that it alone was defending the status quo and that the other was opposing it; there is no objective criterion on which the outside observer can base a decision as to whose perception was correct. It might well be considered sound to decree in this case that the most relevant perception of the status quo is that of the Congress. Its perception anchors the concept of "change" in Gamson's hypothesis; *Congress* must be changed. The generalization to be recognized, however, is that such a determination must be made on a priori theoretical grounds for each variable and each hypothesis subject to this kind of ambiguity in research.

Again, the example helps to pinpoint a problem noted in our earlier discussion of Lowi's typology. Lowi argues explicitly that the perceptions of actors determine the category into which a given policy must be classified, but he does not treat theoretically the question of whose perceptions must be dominant in the event that there are differences.

---

[22]Gamson, p. 63.

[23]W. Henry Lambright, *Shooting Down the Nuclear Plane*, ICP Case #104 (New York: Bobbs-Merrill, 1967).

Objective   In many hypotheses, the independent variable seeks to describe a subjective characteristic of participants—that is, a state of the world as seen through a particular lens. When theorists fail to specify adequately whose subjectivity is to be measured, the problem described in the previous section arises. Other hypotheses, however, seek to link *objective* characteristics of participants—their resources, explicit attitudes, or demographic characteristics—to aspects of process or output. But those hypotheses are of little help in determining *which* participants the characteristics describe. It is useful to keep subjective and objective characteristics of participants distinct. Hypotheses regarding the former often are deceptively simple, because they refer explicitly to impersonal conditions (e.g., the status quo, the divisibility of the benefits), which in reality are subjective perceptions of conditions; where as the latter tend to refer quite obviously to people (e.g., resources used, strategy used). Both, of course, are troublesome for the same basic reasons—the multiplicity and heterogeneity of participants.

In *Democracy in the United States*, Dahl suggests that, "how severe a conflict is depends on how much is at stake."[24] Empirically, we might estimate how much is at stake ourselves as outside observers, or we might depend on the relevant actors' own views of what is to be lost or gained. Even if we elect the former, "objective" course, however, so that perceptions of actors are not relevant, we are still left with the unanswered question: What is at stake *for whom*? Variation is possible here, just as it is for factors such as social class or resources employed. The following concrete instance illustrates how answering that question may be critical to an empirical test of Dahl's hypothesis.

The issue in the case of *The Florida Milk Commission Changes Minimum Prices* was a proposal for the complete deregulation of milk prices, replacing a system of controls at all levels from the dairymen to the consumer.[25] Three different groups were primarily affected. Consumers could be expected to benefit in the short run from increased competition within the milk industry. The "big three" dairies would be hurt in the short run, since they would have to lower prices and curtail profits. Most seriously affected of all, however, would be the independent distributors, who would not be able to compete with the "big three" and might eventually be forced out of business altogether, if past history in the market area were any guide. In the long run, the "big three" would then benefit from the reinstitution of an oligopolistic market in which they each had a larger market share. Conversely, consumers could expect the long-run outcome to be neutral at best, and possibly negative.

---

[24]Robert A. Dahl, *Democracy in the United States*, 2nd ed. (Chicago: Rand-McNally, 1972), p. 303.

[25]Harmon Zeigler, *The Florida Milk Commission Changes Minimum Prices*, ICP Case #77 (University, Ala.: University of Alabama Press, 1963).

Dahl's hypothesis could thus be applied to this case in at least three different ways. If one looked primarily at the consumers, one would predict very little conflict; for them, the stakes were quite small. For the "big three," the stakes were large but not overwhelming. For the independents, the issue was virtually one of life or death, since they could not compete in either buying power or production efficiency if prices were deregulated. The choice of which group to focus on is thus crucial. If one takes the party with the most at stake, one would expect the conflict in this case to be quite severe; if the party with the least at stake were used, very little conflict would be expected. To take an average would similarly be to predict a relatively low or at most a moderate level of conflict. More to the point—unless one attaches a way of surmounting the problem to the original formulation of the hypothesis—the theory cannot be tested. It remains, in an important sense, incomplete.

The Problem of Interaction

Interaction among independent variables in determining an outcome is of course common in social theory and in research findings. By "interaction" we mean that the existence or strength of an effect is contingent upon some other condition or the value of some additional variable; for example, the effect of financial resources upon success in a policy struggle may depend upon the arena of decision—legislative, executive, or judicial. The phenomenon is quite obviously not peculiar to public policy. We suggest, however, as the complexity emphasized repeatedly in the foregoing discussion would indicate, that interaction is endemic to public policy—it is perhaps its most salient characteristic—yet, it is rarely recognized in theoretical offerings.

Many important theories about public policy are probably incorrect as generalizations encompassing everything that falls within *anyone's* image of policy making, while essentially accurate for that subset of examples which theorists implicitly take as their *own* definition of the universe of applicable instances. The failure to demarcate that universe is potentially a failure to recognize important statistical interaction. We will offer a specific illustration in a moment, but we note in passing that the general definition of "policy" itself may be a contingent condition upon which the applicability of a theory is meant to depend. There exists in the literature a rather astounding number and variety of suggested boundaries (or lack thereof) about the concept, "policy": all government action,[26] a program of goals, values, and

---

[26]Lowi criticizes Dror for defining policy as simply any output of any decision maker in his book *Public Policy Making Reexamined* (San Francisco: Chandler, 1968). Dror never formally defines policy but his discussion indicates Lowi is correct. See Lowi, "Decision Making vs. Policy Making," p. 317. Thomas R. Dye defines public policy as "Whatever governments choose to do or not to do," *Understanding Public Policy* (Englewood Cliffs, N.J.: Prentice-Hall, 1972), p. 1.

practices,[27] the impacts of government activity;[28] general rules to subsume future behavioral instances;[29] the consequences of action and inaction;[30] important government decisions;[31] and "a particular object or set of objects which are intended to be affected . . . [together with] a desired course of events . . . a selected line of action . . . a declaration of intent . . . and an implementation of intent. . . ."[32] It is perhaps too much to ask at this stage that we all agree on our usage of the term "policy," but in the absence of such agreement, it is well to recognize that hypotheses might receive more or less support if tested on all government decisions and actions or on some one of the many alternative subsets referred to as "policy" in current theoretical writings.

To illustrate the problem of unspecified interaction more specifically, we will consider hypotheses about group size as a political resource. Pluralists in general postulate that group size is an important potential resource. Murray Edelman, on the other hand, argues that large groups are more likely to be bought off with symbolic reassurances than small, well-organized groups.[33] E. E. Schattschneider argued still a third position: that group size may be of relatively minor significance because the relevant group may be able to involve wider publics or disinterested government officials in a dispute.[34] It is easy to think of examples to illustrate the persuasiveness of each of these conflicting hypotheses, and, indeed, each author provides several. None, however, attempts to place his propositions in the context of more general theory by specifying the conditions under which they are valid. One is thus left with three opposing theories, all of which may very well be valid for a broad class of decisions, but with no clue as to when they are valid and when they are not, and why.

---

[27]Harold D. Lasswell and Abraham Kaplan define policy as "a projected program of goal values and practices," *Power and Society* (New Haven: Yale University Press, 1970), p. 71. See also Carl J. Friedrich, *Man and His Government* (New York: McGraw-Hill, 1963), p. 70.

[28]For example, Easton writes: "Arriving at a decision is the formal phase of establishing a policy; it is not the whole policy in relation to a particular problem. A legislature can devise to punish monopolists; that is the intention. But an administrator can destroy or reformulate the decision by failing either to discover offenders or prosecute them vigorously. The failure is as much a part of the policy with regard to monopoly as the formal law. When we act to implement a decision therefore we enter the second or effective phase of a policy." *The Political System*, 2nd ed. (New York: Knopf, 1971), p. 130.

[29]This is our own preferred definition of policy. See our "Case Study Aggregation and Policy Theory," p. 11.

[30]Dye includes the consequences of inaction as well as action, whether intended or not, in his definition of policy. Dye, p. 2.

[31]Lowi suggests the need to look at only important substantive government decisions, "Decision Making vs. Policy Making," p. 317.

[32]Ranney, p. 7.

[33]Murray Edelman, *The Symbolic Uses of Politics* (Urbana: University of Illinois Press, 1974).

[34]E. E. Schattschneider, *The Semi-Sovereign People* (New York: Holt, 1960), pp. 3-77, passim.

By way of contrast, it might be useful to offer the work of one theorist who appears to have adequately stated the conditions under which his hypotheses can be expected to be supported. In his *The Logic of Collective Action*, Mancur Olson takes exception to the pluralist position concerning group size as a resource, contending that large groups may be ineffective in pursuing their interests in comparison with smaller groups.[35] Although his hypothesis is derived from more general economic theory, Olson also relies heavily on the kind of illustrative material used by Edelman and Schattschneider. Yet Olson carefully delimits the scope of his theory by specifying the circumstances under which the behavior he predicts is most likely to occur. Large groups, for example, will be able to organize effectively when they are seeking collective goods if their members benefit disproportionately, or if they are able to coerce their memberships or provide members with side payments of selective goods. Because Olson makes such contingent conditions explicit, his hypothesis is testable without requiring further refinement—without the researcher having to guess at the theorist's intentions.[36]

Implications

We have argued from our own research experience that the systematic study of public policy is seriously complicated by the nature of the beast. "Policy" is complex—because of temporality, because of multiplicity of aspects and participants, and because of interaction. Yet complexity need not prohibit systematic empirical research. So long as it is accounted for and confronted directly, so long as hypotheses are sufficiently precise, theoretical models may adequately represent reality. We suggest that most of the lessons to be learned have to do, not so much with the conduct of data analysis, as with the formulation of hypotheses and the elaboration of theory.[37] Specifically, we suggest the following:

[35]Mancur Olson, *The Logic of Collective Action* (Cambridge, Mass.: Harvard University Press, 1965).

[36]This does not mean that Olson's theory is necessarily correct. There may be additional contingent conditions which he failed to state that would further refine or modify his theory. John Chamberlin, for example, has recently suggested some additional contingent conditions under which large groups are likely to provide large amounts of a collective good in contradiction to Olson's predictions. All we want to imply is that the concepts in Olson's theory are reasonably well specified and the theoretical relationships among concepts are stated with reasonable precision, allowing others successfully to re-examine and test them. See John Chamberlin, "Provision of Collective Goods as a Function of Group Size," *American Political Science Review*, 68 (June 1974), 707-16.

[37]For illustrations of how this process can both permit the elaboration of theory and provide operationalized hypotheses for empirical testing, see Jeffrey A. Miller, "Welfare Criteria and Policy Outcomes: An Empirical Assessment" (Ph.D. dissertation, University of Michigan, 1975).

Temporality: Multiple Outputs   Optimally, we should all agree on how to identify key developmental points in the policy process, such as the beginning point and the point at which it might be said that policy was indeed "made." Such agreement is undoubtedly premature. In its absence, however, systematic comparative analysis still requires that key stages be identified. In this one instance, it is the data analyst who perhaps has more to contribute than the theorist. We can learn by experience which identification criteria are reliably operationalizable and which among them seem to yield fair tests of hypotheses. In our own work, we have found it both practical and productive to identify a "point of last significant controversy" and, somewhat less importantly, a "point of first significant controversy." The terms are almost self-explanatory, although an elaboration of their meaning and use is available elsewhere.[38] We commend these criteria to others for consideration and trial and urge the formulation and trial of alternatives as well. Most importantly, we emphasize that objective comparisons cannot be made unless a criterion is consistently applied to each case in order to determine which of its many decision points establishes "policy."

Temporality: Postdictive Theory   One must simply be sensitive to the problem and avoid creating predictive hypotheses that fall into the postdictive trap. Specifically, one must not attempt to predict characteristics of the policy *process* either (a) by variables (such as number of requisite actions or resources committed to the struggle) whose value or score for a given case is not known until too late in the process itself, or (b) by variables (such as "policy type") that are offered predictively by theorists as inputs but that in actuality are characteristics of outputs. For a policy hypothesis to be predictive, the causal variable must obviously be observable and measurable at a point in time before the effect and should not be subject to significant change beyond that point of evaluation.

Multiplicity of Policy Aspects   The general implication of this problem is that we must either avoid variables that may differ significantly in value depending upon the aspect of a given policy to which they are applied, or that we must provide a means of selecting the aspect that is most relevant for the operationalization of a given variable. Two guidelines on this issue stand out in our experience to date. One is that any typology of whole policies runs a substantial risk of ambiguity at the stage of operationalization; typologies can be extremely valuable, but they should optimally be offered along with well-considered ground rules for classification. The other guideline is that a major (but not exclusive) source of ambiguity lies in the possible divergence of the benefits from the costs or the substan-

---

[38]See our "Case Study Aggregation and Policy Theory," p. 14.

tive from the financial aspects of a public policy. In creating hypotheses, it may be profitable for the theorist to consider whether the variables are subject to differential rating depending upon whether benefits or costs form the basis of evaluation.

Multiple Participants: Subjective   The question of whether it is most important to consider a given possible state of the world as it in some sense actually or objectively exists or as it is perceived by participants in the policy process is generally given inadequate attention. If there are good theoretical or methodological grounds for choosing the latter, it is essential to consider whether different participants might perceive the status of affairs differently. If so, it is necessary to translate those grounds into guidelines on whose perceptions are to govern the scoring of that particular dimension for research purposes.

Multiple Participants: Objective   This problem is potentially the most troublesome of all, since characteristics and behaviors of participants emerge so commonly in policy theory as important variables. The theoretical considerations that necessitate testing a hypothesis comparatively—by assigning a value to each policy struggle to represent some objective characteristic or behavior of "participants"—should make possible some decision as to how those characteristics should be operationalized. Theory might provide criteria for selecting *one* participant or homogeneous group as the basis for assigning a value to the variable, or, perhaps, criteria for aggregating the value across one or more groups of heterogeneous participants. We have had substantial success in dividing the participants in each struggle into two opposing camps and, for most participant-oriented variables, giving an aggregate score on the variable to each camp. However, this attempt at a universal method is much less satisfactory for some variables than for others, and for some cases of policy making than for others. Sometimes it does not work at all. Other schemes might be devised, but such tinkering by the data analyst is in general less desirable than explicit criteria generated within the theoretical proposition to be tested; for example: "In predicting the severity of conflict by 'how much is at stake,' the true predictor is the average of the perceived stakes across all major participants."

Interaction   It is clear that not all hypotheses can be valid for all types of policy making in all kinds of circumstances. To the extent that a theory fails to specify major conditions defining its applicability, it is inadequate theory. If the conditions of validity are specified, not only is the analyst's job made easier and a fair test of the proposition likely to ensue, but also direct benefits result for the development of the content of policy theory itself. Theory should be parsimonious, to be sure, but not oversimplified.

Conclusion

Because of the complexities of public policy as an object of study, we may never be able to obtain hard knowledge of the policy process of the type available in the advanced physical sciences. Yet improving our understanding of policy phenomena is clearly possible, if only through advancing the conceptual sophistication of theoretical formulations.[39] Our own experience has convinced us that such advances will be more rapid and certain as theory encounters systematic empirical data. As the brief comments in this paper illustrate, the collision between theory and data, while perhaps frustrating at first, can have important benefits for both researchers and theorists. Those lacunae in theory, painfully identified by difficulties in operationalization, become foci for efforts at additional theorizing that, however much they may do violence to the intentions of the original theorist, can add considerably to the richness and utility of hypotheses. The necessity of separating benefit aspects from cost aspects in theories of policy type, or the notion of "last significant controversy" in a policy process, are small, but not trivial examples. If present theoretical levels in public policy are to progress, obstacles of the kind identified here should not be viewed as roadblocks. They cannot be wished away, nor can they be evaded. But by grappling with them directly, it is possible to add to the precision and sophistication of theory while proceeding with the essential conduct of supporting empirical research.

TYPOLOGIES OF PUBLIC POLICY: MEANING CONSTRUCTION AND THE POLICY PROCESS*
*Peter J. Steinberger***

The burgeoning field of public policy analysis seems finally to have acquired a fairly well-articulated research agenda. While many ambiguities and disputes inevitably remain, most scholars can agree on the need to in-

[39]For an illuminating discussion of the role of "hard" research in developing social theory of various types, see the following two papers by Anatol Rapoport: "Various Meanings of 'Theory'," *American Political Science Review*, 52 (December 1958), 972-88, and "Explanatory Power and Explanatory Appeal" (Paper prepared for the Conference on Explanatory Theory in Political Science, Department of Government, University of Texas at Austin, Feb. 19-23, 1968). Rapoport argues that because of the limitations of social science, improved conceptualization is often a more important criterion in judging good theory than predictive power. In this regard, the value of the application of hard methods in social science would not necessarily lie so much in improved prediction as in better conceptualization and the reformulation of thinking about problems.

*I am grateful to Maureen Farnan Steinberger, Sheldon Edner and Noel Reynolds for the valuable comments and suggestions.

**Peter J. Steinberger, "Typologies of Public Policy: Meaning Construction and their Policy Process." *Social Science Quarterly* 61 (Sept., 1980): 185-197. Used by permission.

vestigate (among other things) the environmental correlates of public policy, the various processes of implementation and the complex nature of policy impact (for a convenient summary, see Hofferbert, 1974). In pursuing these kinds of tasks, moreover, scholars have produced a good deal of important research, frequently building upon—and improving upon—one another's work. Indeed, the development of research on the environmental and systemic correlates of policy is almost a model of how a cumulative and rigorous social science should proceed (see, for example, the literature described by Godwin and Sheperd, 1976.

Although most of this work is certainly of great interest, we might also suggest that the most intriguing aspect of the field has been the effort to *classify* public policies, or, more specifically, the attempt to categorize policies in such a way that the relationship between substance and process can be more clearly understood. Especially relevant is the "typological" tradition of policy analysis. Dating back to Lowi's (1964) now classic review article, the typological tradition has produced a variety of conceptions that have proven to be immensely appealing and influential. Nearly all summarizations of the policy field make reference to the typological literature, and usually do so in a favorable light, emphasizing the conceptual and theoretical insights it provides. And, indeed, there appears to be good reason for this. There can be no doubt, for example, that Lowi's typology of distributive, redistributive and regulatory policies seems to zero in on some useful and very fundamental distinctions. There is a certain plausibility in the formulation, and a fortuitous clarifying of common sense understandings, that has led numerous scholars to accept its accuracy and relevance virtually on the face of it. Even more importantly, Lowi's typology does indeed suggest a powerful and useful *theory* of the policy process. By arguing that different kinds of policies have different kinds of politics associated with them, Lowi provides an attractive explanatory scheme, one in which linkages between substance and process would appear to be concrete, testable and entirely credible.

Much the same can be said for several of the other typologies that have been influential in the field. Particularly notable, of course, is the "public goods/non-public goods" distinction from economics which has been enthusiastically adopted by contemporary policy analysts (see Olson, 1965). But one must also mention several other important classificatory schemes, especially Froman's (1967) "areal/segmental" distinction, Eulau and Eyestone's (1968) taxonomy of "adaptive" and "control" policies, and Edelman's (1974) emphasis on the "symbolic" dimension of politics. Each of these typologies seems to focus on a particularly salient aspect of public policy and to provide a basis for sound theorizing. It makes sense that redistributive policies will engender more conflict; or that public goods will produce the kinds of problems described by Olson; or that homogeneous cities are more likely to pursue areal policies than heterogeneous cities. As Lowi indicates, it is only through such efforts to conceptualize—to typify— that policy analysts can overcome the limitations inherent in the case-study method.

Unfortunately, this most promising of approaches has also proven to be most frustrating. What originally looked like a useful set of theories has, in fact, turned out to have serious practical limitations. There have been at least two reasons for this.

First, the various typologies may each be understood as an attempt to identify what is most fundamental, most distinctive, in public policy. Thus, in an important sense they have developed as rivals. One typology is offered, at least tacitly, as an improvement over another and, yet, there seems to be little to choose between them. The result is that policy analysis has retained at least some of its noncumulative character. An analyst interested in this approach must select one of the typologies, but the criteria for selection are by no means clear. Moreover, any particular study will be truly comparable only with other studies using the same typology. Thus, the effort to establish a general conceptual scheme has not been successful.

The second and more important difficulty has to do with the classification of actual cases. In brief, it has proved nearly impossible to confidently identify a particular policy as being of this type or that (Lineberry and Sharkansky, 1971). Most actual policies tend, upon analysis, to overlap categories. For example, in examining the "areal-segmental" distinction, Froman (1967) classifies urban renewal policy as segmental (i.e., affecting only a section of the city) and annexation policy as areal (affecting the entire city). Yet there are numerous reasons for finding this a dubious, indeed misleading, classification. It can hardly be denied that annexation has a certain segmental quality; the area annexed, as well as adjacent areas, will likely be affected in special ways. Similarly, while urban renewal certainly is segmental in one sense, there can also be no doubt that it is likely to have a profound impact on the entire urban area. Thus, an objective classification appears to be impossible (Greenberg et al., 1977; Dornan, 1977). This problem has proved to be a general one. Few policies can be easily pigeonholed in terms of any of the typologies. Lowi himself notes, for example, that virtually every policy has a redistributive aspect of some kind.

The upshot of this has been well outlined by Hofferbert (1964): "To date, little empirical work has been fruitfully conducted with any of these typologies. . . The evidence is as yet incomplete regarding the typologies discussed here. It is disturbing, however, at least with respect to the Lowi scheme, that the bait has not been taken by other researchers. Lowi's insightful review is often noted in critical essays, but there is no instance in the literature I have read where his classification scheme has been examined with specific data and tested propositions" (Cf. Greenberg et al., 1977; Wilson, 1973).

This is disturbing indeed. The seemingly fruitful and enlightening conceptualizations outlined above have thus far been barren, and for very good reasons as we have seen. We appear to have a set of theories that are clearly insightful and perceptive but which seem to be, in practical terms, useless.

The purpose of this article is to offer, if only provisionally, a way out of this situation. Specifically, it suggests an approach to policy analysis which would fully utilize the insights of typological theory while recognizing, and indeed taking advantage of, the very limitations described above. As will be shown, such an effort must involve a significant reorientation of the typologies, and a considerable change in perspective. But, hopefully, the result will be an approach to policy analysis that vindicates our interest in, and demonstrates the usefulness of, the typological tradition.

A Phenomenological Approach to Policy Analysis

Appropriately enough, our starting point is the complex and ambiguous nature of public policy. As indicated above, this frustrating complexity has made it difficult to classify policies with confidence. Such a consistent lack of success must, at some point, raise the possibility that the enterprise is not merely difficult but, in a fundamental way, impossible.

Indeed, the premise of this paper is that we should regard ambiguity not as a defect in understanding but, rather, as a salient and ineluctable characteristic of public policy. The elusiveness of policy should not be considered a nuisance, an obstacle in the way of sound analysis. Rather, it should be regarded as a fundamental, defining element. By and large, policies are not self-explanatory. Once we accept this, the way may be open for a methodological approach to typological analysis that is both feasible and fruitful.

The central hypothesis is that most particular policies can be, and are, coherently understood and defined in a wide variety of ways. Indeed, policy-related controversies rarely involve simple questions of pro and con, or good versus bad. Rather, they generally involve two (or more) entirely different and competing understandings or definitions of the very same policy, of its purpose, its substance and its potential impact. That is, for one group a particular proposal or initiative may be fundamentally a matter of (say) regulatory policy, while for another it may be a question of distribution or redistribution. The implications are that each policy is likely to have different *meanings* for different participants; that the exact meaning of a policy, then, is by no means self-evident but, rather, is ambiguous and manipulable; and that the policy process is—at least in part—a struggle to get one or another meaning established as the accepted one.

Indeed, we must go a bit further than this and suggest—again provisionally—that a particular policy has virtually *no* relevant meaning *until* one is attached to it by some kind of participant. Normally, of course, policy is initially formulated by a participant who has an explicit meaning in mind. But this meaning is by no means final or definitive. The import and significance of any particular policy is, in the most general sense, indeterminate and open to interpretation and dispute.

As indicated above, Lowi himself appears to recognize something like this when he admits, for example, that in the long run virtually all government policies have redistributive impacts, and regulatory ones as well. But he seems to think that this is the case only in a trivial sense, and that most policies are clearly more of one type than another. The present argument, on the other hand, suggests that we regard ambiguity as fundamental and unavoidable. Few policies are obviously or "objectively" distributive rather than redistributive or regulatory; few are clearly more "adaptive" than "control," or "segmental" rather than "areal." In general, we should at least consider the possibility that the meaning of a particular policy must therefore be constituted by the various participants in the policy process.

The idea of reality and meaning as a social construct is an old one in epistemology, traceable, without doubt, to Kant and to his philosophical heirs. However, it has also had a profound impact on the social sciences. Berger and Luckmann's classic work on the social construction of reality is merely a recent example of an important, if controversial, social science tradition that dates back to Dilthey, Weber, Mead and especially Schutz. According to this general view, the social world—and its institutions, roles, ideas, etc.—is essentially a series of socially constructed meanings. In the words of Berger and Luckmann (1966):

> Men *together* produce a human environment, with the totality of its socio-cultural and psychological formations . . . (S)ocial order is a human product, or more precisely, an ongoing human production. It is produced by man in the course of his ongoing externalization. . . Social order exists *only* as a product of human activity.

Clearly this perspective is intended to apply to all of social reality, including (we must presume) the realm of policy meanings. It is precisely here, then, that the typological tradition can be especially useful. The interpretive approach to social science relies heavily on the concept of "type." Indeed, Berger and Luckmann, following the lead of both Weber and Schutz, indicate that socially constructed meanings generally appear as "typifications." That is, meanings tend to take on a variety of basic, more-or-less agreed-upon, typical forms. Such typifications, taken together, describe not merely social meanings but also social reality, since that reality can be nothing more than structures of meaning. Thus, the central function of the social scientist is to discover and analyze these forms. In this sense, and most importantly, we can suggest that the achievement and insight of the typological tradition is not in its analysis of "objective" policy characteristics. Rather, the best of the typologies are plausible and useful in that they describe (or, rather, can be used to describe) *typifications* that are generally and commonly employed by participants in the political process to define public policies. In other words, they are insightful in elucidating and in specifying socially constructed meanings.

Thus, when we talk about distributive, redistributive and regulatory policies, for example, we are not talking about objectively different kinds of policy. Rather, we are conceptualizing some of the ways in which participants tend to define policies. The participants inevitably engage in typification, in meaning construction, and the typological tradition is useful in specifying, categorizing and conceptualizing those various typifications. It is thus that we can explain the appeal of the typological approach and can begin to show its research potential.

Most emphatically, the argument is *not* that policies have no concrete, objective characteristics. Obviously, any policy proposal specifies courses of action, allocations of resources, methods of implementation, etc. These characteristics are salient, real and, indeed, crucial. They work to shape and constrain and mold the policy's meaning (though they do so in ways we can only hypothesize about). But they are not identical with that meaning. By the *meaning* of a policy (and, hence, of its objective characteristics) we refer essentially to the understandings that participants have regarding the policy's purpose, its potential impact and its relationship to other policies. Even when these things are somehow "spelled out" in the policy, there can—indeed must—be interpretation and reinterpretation. Thus, the meaning of a policy can only be something which has been attached to it by the various participants in the policy process (Edner, 1976).

Meaning Construction and the Policy Process

Interestingly, Lowi (1964:707) has suggested something rather like the approach here outlined. In his own words:

> . . . it is not the actual outcomes but the expectations as to what the outcomes can be that shape the issues and determine their politics. One of the most important strategies in any controversial issue is to attempt to define it in redistributive terms in order to broaden the base of opposition or support.

But unfortunately, and revealingly, Lowi relegates this comment to a footnote and does not pursue it. Nor do the other writers in the typological tradition. Thus, the perspective described above has been largely overlooked in favor of what has proven to be a less promising approach. This is particularly surprising in light of the influential literature on the *strategy* of the policy process, most notably the work of Schattschneider. Indeed, the method suggested in the present paper is largely useful in bringing together, and thereby broadening, the insights of Schattschneider (among others) and those of the typological writers. Schattschneider (1960) has taught us much about the way in which participants attempt to manipulate the scope of conflict in order to further their policy preferences. His formulation provides a good perspective on the policy process, and has been valuable as a research tool. But in at least a couple of ways, the approach here suggested can extend and improve upon Schattschneider's theory.

First, by emphasizing the social construction of reality, the present perspective helps to clarify the nature of the processes involved. For what we are concerned with is not just questions of good and bad, nor simple efforts to control the scope of conflict. Rather, we are interested in broad questions of social meaning. This emphasis tends to locate the policy process more squarely within the social world generally, helps to specify the mechanisms by which contexts are manipulated, and suggests a particular research agenda, viz., the empirical examination of typifications. Further, the present approach does away with certain pejorative connotations by demonstrating the very necessity of meaning construction. Efforts to define and redefine policies are not, as Schattschneider would have it, simply matters of strategy or distortion; they are in fact unavoidable if policies are to be at all relevant and meaningful. This, of course, implies also that various participants will define a single policy in various ways not simply out of tactical or prudential considerations but, rather, because of contrasting perspectives or worldviews. In this sense, the sociology of knowledge is obviously relevant; different groups are likely to see things differently. Conflict can therefore be a result of genuine definitional disagreements about the meaning of a policy.

Moreover, the typological tradition broadens Schattschneider's insight by demonstrating the wide variety of possible policy meanings. The typologies show that conflict or disagreement is not limited to the issue of scope, of public versus private, but may also include an entire range of other questions dealing with political impact, economic impact, motive, relationships to basic values, etc. The possibilities are numerous. And as indicated below, this greater complexity can, in turn, significantly broaden our theoretical and research opportunities.

Even a casual reexamination of the case study literature in public policy would turn up a good deal of support for the perspective outlined in this essay. The literature on the War on Poverty presents an interesting example. A reading of the numerous relevant case studies suggests that this set of policies was initially defined as "adaptive," in the sense outlined by Eulau and Eyestone. That is, proponents of the War on Poverty understood it as an attempt by government to adapt its practices to meet the special political needs of the poor (see, for example, Kramer, 1969). Thus, the establishment of community action agencies would considerably change the decision-making process so as to include representatives of the poor and give them real power over the allocation of resources. But the same literature indicates that certain key opponents thought the War on Poverty had a rather different meaning (see especially Piven and Cloward, 1971). They defined it as, perhaps, a series of "control" policies. According to this view, the government wasn't actually adapting itself in any real sense. Rather, the purpose was to control the environment, to co-opt the poor and take the sting out of social protest. No real change in the distribution of power resources was involved.

Of course, space limitations forbid even a cursory examination of the case study literature along these lines. But among the many other cases that could be reinterpreted in this way are Bailey's (1950) analysis of the Full Employment Bill of 1946, Banfield's (1961) description of a transit subsidy dispute in Chicago, Altshuler's (1965) study of an inter-city freeway controversy, Art's (1968) research on the TFX decision, Halperin's (1972) history of the ABM decision, Pressman and Wildavsky's (1973) discussion of an EDA job program in Oakland, and Greenstone and Peterson's (1973) research on citizen participation and the War on Poverty. In each case, a dispute over policy meaning appeared to be crucial in shaping the nature of political controversy and in influencing the nature of ultimate policy settlements.

Before considering more specifically the research consequences of this perspective, one additional question presents itself immediately. This concerns the *evaluation* of meaning and definition. Even assuming the variability of meanings that can be attached to a single policy, one may still wonder if some meanings are more correct, or more appropriate, than others. If so, then surely one of the primary tasks of the policy analyst would be to determine the truest meaning of a particular policy.

There are a number of feasibility problems here, especially relating to the vagaries of the implementation process. But, more importantly, we may wonder if such an evaluation effort, even if possible, would be at all appropriate. To evaluate a particular meaning as more or less "correct" would surely be to violate one of the basic premises of the approach here suggested. The emphasis on social construction implies that, for practical purposes, there is no objective "right" and "wrong", at least in an a priori sense. The objective elements of a policy (e.g., specific conferrals of power, allocations of resources, proscriptions, etc.) do, in all likelihood, tend to shape the kinds of meanings attached to it. But those meanings, rather than being judged according to some objective standard of truth, in fact create the truth of the policy. They give it its definition. Hence, for the researcher to impose his own standards on the definitional process would be for him to become, in effect, a part of the political process itself, just another participant with biases and predispositions of his own.

However, we may still be able to identify a useful and legitimate "political" role for the policy analyst, one that he can adopt without compromising his scholarly status. Insofar as policies can be defined in numerous ways, we have said that their potential socially relevant impacts are also numerous. Any policy is likely to have distributive, redistributive and regulatory consequences, as well as various other kinds. However, the political process is likely to focus on only a limited number of such consequences. Actors are apt to seize upon one or two dimensions and to frame their definitions accordingly. In this way, many potential implications of a policy are almost certain to be ignored.

Thus, the policy analyst can perform a useful function in trying to unearth and specify possible consequences. And it is here, again, that the typological tradition can be of help. By identifying a number of socially generated dimensions along which policy meanings can be formulated, the various typologies point to the kinds of impacts which, when made manifest, are likely to be considered socially relevant. They can serve, then, as a guide or a checklist for the politically oriented researcher. And he can play a valuable public role by pointing out potential consequences which the political process has, for whatever reason, failed to uncover.

Research Consequences

While this kind of evaluative procedure might have a good deal of merit, the primary value of the typological tradition would seem to involve analysis of the policy process itself. More specifically, it promises to provide the basis for a sound theoretical approach to the relationship between substance and process. This, of course, was Lowi's central concern in initiating typological analysis. He hypothesized that different types of policy would have different kinds of politics associated with them. Once again, little progress has been made in actually examining this thesis. But the transformation that has been suggested here can, in my view, significantly facilitate research in this regard.

In order to fully utilize the typological tradition, some coherence, some semblance of order, must be made out of the various existing schemes. The major typologies have generally been formulated in isolation from one another and, moreover, have never been adequately integrated. However, once we accept each of the major typologies as presenting a useful and enlightening perspective on public policy, then a unified approach is both possible and desirable. It would seem, most importantly, that none of the typologies are antipathetical to any of the others. Thus, we may suggest that each typology simply reflects one of the several ways in which policies can be conceptualized. Taken together, they indicate the various salient dimensions of public policy. This is illustrated in Table 4-4.

There is, of course, no pretense that the list outlined here is definitive or final. But the implications of the table are numerous. For example, it suggests that participants in the policy process do not merely select certain meanings; they also select, or emphasize, thereby certain *dimensions* of meaning. Thus, it is entirely conceivable that two sides of any particular

Table 4-4 Typologies of Public Policy

Dimensions of Public Policy	Categories of Public Policy		
Substantive impact:	Distributive	Redistributive	Regulatory
Political impact:	Adaptive	Control	
Scope of impact:	Areal	Segmental	
Exhaustibility:	Public Goods	Private goods	
Tangibility:	Symbolic	Tangible	

controversy will choose not only different meanings but also different dimensions. Further, the table suggests that the potential socially-relevant impacts of a policy are—in theoretical terms—much more numerous than previously expected. Rather than three possibilities, as Lowi has suggested, the table indicates a much more complex conceptual scheme. Indeed, if combinations of multiple meanings are considered (e.g., "distributive–areal" or "control–symbolic"), the range of possibilities is obviously enormous.

At least three different sets of substantive issues may be addressed in terms of this table, issues which, taken together, would seem to comprise a stimulating research agenda. One such group of issues concerns the *definitional process* itself. This would especially refer to the way in which particular policy meanings are developed and disseminated. Among the more specific questions that could be raised here are the following:

Do certain policies (that is, policies having certain objective characteristics) tend to be defined in characteristic ways? For example, it seems likely that tax policies will usually be defined in terms of "substantive impact" (see, for example, Friedman, 1962). But this may not be generally true. In some circumstances, tax policies might be defined as primarily "control," or "symbolic," or even "segmental" policies. Moreover, there is the further question of (what might be called) historical paradigms. It may well be that certain policies are defined one way in a particular era and rather differently in another. The recent history of environmental politics in America, for example, might be understandable in these terms.

Do certain actors and groups tend to see all policies in terms of one or two specific dimensions? Rather than the policy itself being the decisive factor, here we raise the possibility that the participants' particular perspectives are crucial. For example, it seems plausible that business groups, labor organizations, environmental groups, professional associations, etc., will each have a distinctive and particular set of concepts with which to make sense out of the political world. These concepts might be usefully analyzed in terms of the typological tradition. Thus, it could be hypothesized that business groups see everything in terms of "substantive impact," environmental groups in terms of "exhaustibility," and so on.

How are definitions actually formulated and disseminated? There is a good deal of research on interest group behavior, but little of it focuses on the question of meaning selection. It is important to understand the ways in which meanings are thought up, ratified and propagated by organized political forces. This, indeed, might well get to the crux of the entire group process.

A second set of substantive questions concerns the *decision-making process*. Here the focus would be on "politics" as Lowi understands it, that is, on the process by which policy initiatives are approved or rejected. Again, several specific questions arise: Are there characteristic juxtapositions of meaning? That is, does the adoption of one particular meaning by Group A tend to lead Group B to adopt a logically alternative meaning? If so, one might then be able to formulate a taxonomy of oppositions and, ultimately, of decision-making processes in general.

Does the nature of political conflict, for example, its intensity, correlate with the juxtaposition of definitions? It may well be that certain kinds of meaning disputes are particularly conducive to rancor. In this regard, we would ask if it makes a difference whether opposed meanings are intra- or interdimensional. Controversies involving interdimensional juxtaposition might be more diffuse, less focused, hence less rancorous. Indeed, conflict may actually be most intense if opposing groups *agree* on definition but disagree on evaluation. For example, opponents on certain welfare proposals might well agree that the proposals are essentially "redistributive" but disagree violently as to whether or not redistribution is a good thing. In such a case, the controversy would perhaps be especially pointed, the issues clear, and the interest obvious.

Are meanings likely to multiply during the course of the decision process or are they likely to become fewer? This is roughly the same as asking if things are likely to grow more complex or more simple. Since both phenomena undoubtedly do occur at various times, we would also want to know under what circumstances these changes take place.

A third and final set of substantive questions concerns the process of *implementation*. In this regard, one could ask, among other things: To what extent are implementors conscious of, and interested in, policy meanings? The discretion of many administrative institutions may well include leeway in terms of which particular policy meaning to adopt. This, in turn, may have a profound effect on the way a particular policy is implemented. From a research point of view, the problem is a particularly complex one, but it may be crucial in formulating a comprehensive theory of the policy process.

A related question would be the following: to what extent do implementors ignore the meanings generated by the "political" process and redefine policies to suit themselves? Again, this is a complex problem, but it seems to put the issue of administrative discretion in a particularly interesting light.

Does meaning ambiguity, i.e., the lack of clear-cut definitions, make implementation especially difficult? An example of this might again be the community action provision of the War on Poverty in which such crucial but vague phrases as "maximum feasible participation" made it nearly impossible for planners to decide how to proceed.

This has been an exploratory and provisional discussion. Indeed, the purpose has been merely to suggest an alternative approach to policy analysis in the hopes of generating some dialogue. Clearly, the essential question is whether or not the research agenda outlined above can amount to a feasible and valuable approach to the study of public policy.

In their intelligent and provocative article on policy analysis, Greenberg et al. (1977) offer some stimulating suggestions relating to the policy field in general and include a discussion of the typological tradition. But though they point to the usual criticisms of typological analysis, they too fail to free themselves from the limitations inherent in the older approach. Thus, for example, they show that "there is *no* a priori way for the researcher to determine which . . . impacts are to be considered in deciding whether a policy is 'areal' or 'segmental' (p. 1538); but they offer nothing very tangible in the way of an alternative strategy. Similarly, they demonstrate several problems inherent in the inevitable existence of a multiplicity of "perceptions" (or meanings), but all they can tell us is that we must somehow decide whose perceptions are most important (p. 1543).

The present discussion can be usefully considered supplemental to the analysis provided by Greenberg et al. It is, in effect, an attempt to meet their challenge by placing certain conceptual insights from the existing literature on a firmer theoretical foundation. Thus, the tentative list of hypotheses outlined above can provide a starting point for policy analysts interested in pursuing more fully the insights of the typological tradition.

REFERENCES

ALTSHULER, ALAN. 1965. *Locating the Intercity Freeway.* (New York: Bobbs Merrill).

ART, ROBERT. 1968. *The TFX Decision: McNamara and the Military.* (Boston: Little, Brown).

BAILEY, STEPHEN K. 1950. *Congress Makes a Law.* (New York: Columbia University Press).

BANFIELD, EDWARD. 1961. *Political Influence.* (New York: Free Press).

BERGER, PETER AND THOMAS LUCKMANN. 1966. *The Social Construction of Reality* (Garden City: Doubleday).

DORNAN, PAUL. 1977. "Whither Urban Policy Analysis: A Review Essay," *Polity,* 9 (Summer): 503-27.

EDELMAN, MURRAY. 1974. *The Symbolic Uses of Politics.* (Urbana: University of Illinois Press).

EDNER, SHELDON. 1976. "Intergovernmental Policy Development: The Importance of Problem Definition," pp. 149-68 in Charles O. Jones and Robert D. Thomas, eds., *Public Policy Making in a Federal System* (Beverly Hills, Calif.: Sage Publications).

EULAU, HEINZ AND ROBERT EYESTONE. 1968. "Policy Maps of City Councils and Policy Outcomes," *American Political Science Review,* 62 (March): 124-43.

FRIEDMAN, MILTON. 1962. *Capitalism and Freedom.* (Chicago: University of Chicago Press).

FROMAN, LEWIS. 1967. "An Analysis of Public Policy in Cities," *Journal of Politics,* 29 (February): 94-108.

GODWIN, R. KENNETH AND W. BRUCE SHEPARD. 1976. "Political Processes and Public Expenditures: A Re-Examination Based on Theories of Representative Government," *American Political Science Review,* 70 (December): 1127-35.

GREENBERG, GEORGE et al. 1977. "Developing Public Policy Theory: Perspectives from Empirical Research," *American Political Science Review,* 71 (December): 1532-44.

GREENSTONE, J. DAVID AND PAUL PETERSEN. 1973. *Race and Authority in Urban Politics.* (New York: Russell Sage).

HALPERIN, MORTON. 1972. "The Decision to Deploy the ABM," *World Politics,* 25 (October): 62-95.

HOFFERBERT, RICHARD. 1974. *The Study of Public Policy.* (New York: Bobbs Merrill).

KRAMER, RALPH. 1969. *Participation of the Poor.* (Englewood Cliffs, N.J.: Prentice-Hall).

LINEBERRY, ROBERT AND IRA SHARKANSKY. 1971. *Urban Politics and Public Policy.* (New York: Harper & Row).

LOWI, THEODORE. 1964. "American Business, Public Policy, Case Studies, and Political Theory," *World Politics,* 16 (July): 677-715.

OLSON, MANCUR. 1965. *The Logic of Collective Action.* (Cambridge, Mass.: Harvard University Press).

PIVEN, FRANCES FOX AND RICHARD CLOWARD. 1971. *Regulating the Poor.* (New York: Vintage).

PRESSMAN, JEFFREY AND AARON WILDAVSKY. 1973. *Implementation.* (Berkeley: University of California Press).

SCHATTSCHNEIDER, E. E. 1960. *The Semi-Sovereign People.* (New York: Holt, Rinehart & Winston).

WILSON, JAMES Q. 1973. *Political Organizations.* (New York: Basic Books).

PROMOTING POLICY THEORY: REVISING THE ARENAS OF POWER
*Robert J. Spitzer**

Lowi's arenas of power has been one of the most durable and widely used schemes applied to the study of public policy. This article seeks to clarify some persistent ambiguities concerning the scheme, and to propose some specific revisions for one of the four categories. These revisions conform to general suggestions for making the four policy categories more sensitive to the degree to which actual policies possess the traits of more than one policy type. When the concepts giving rise to the four categories are thought of as continua rather than discrete entitles, the scheme resolves for itself what many have perceived as its key weakness.

The process of theory-building, whether in the realm of policy studies or elsewhere, often incorporates an ad hoc admixture of deductive and inductive explorations. Indeed, approaching a problem from both broad theoretic outlines and specific cases and facts can provide an incisive avenue to learning.

The focus of this article is a policy scheme that was conceived on a broad scale—Lowi's arenas of power (1964, 1967, 1970, 1971, 1972, 1972a). This scheme has been subject to both wide use, and extensive critical attention (Beer, 1973; Grant, 1972; Greenberg et al., 1977; Hartmann, 1973; Hayes, 1978; Hill and Plumlee, 1984; Hudson III, 1972; Kjellberg, 1977; Kornblith, 1968; Mann, 1975; Meier, 1979; Penbera, Jr., 1973; Peters, Doughtie and Mc-Culloch, 1977; Price, 1972; Rakoff and Schaefer, 1970; Ripley and Franklin, 1976; Roos, 1969; Salisbury and Heinz, 1970; Schneider, 1979; Shiry, 1977; Shull, 1983, 1984; Smith, 1969, 1975; Spitzer, 1979, 1983, 1983a; Steinberger, 1980; Tatalovich and Daynes, 1984; Vogler, 1974; Wilson, 1973; Wootton, 1985; Zimmerman, 1973). Though the scheme has attracted much attention, misunderstanding persists regarding its conception and nature; in particular, attention is often focused on only three of its four policy categories (distributive, regulatory and redistributive) excluding the fourth category, con-

*Robert Spitzer, "Promoting Policy Theory: Revising the Arenas of Power." *Policy Studies Journal* 15 (June, 1987): 675–689. Used by permission.

stituent; moreover, inadequate attention is focused on the underlying logic behind the categories. Therefore, some attention to these elements is warranted.

The Arenas of Power

Lowi's approach to the study of policy began as a critique and synthesis of the prevailing approaches to the study of power and policy making, focusing in particular on the role of groups and elites.[1] From this critique emerged an important and unusual argument—that different types of policies engender their own unique politics or sets of political relationships. Since policy itself is viewed as state-inspired coercion, it is then divided into two realms: how coercion is applied (applicability of coercion) and the consequences of that coercion (likelihood of coercion). Each of these two components is dichotomized to produce a four-cell matrix.

When the applicability of coercion applies to the individual, the policy and its political consequences are likely to be decentralized and disaggregated; when the applicability of coercion applies to the environment, the policy and political consequences will be more systemic and centralized. When the likelihood of coercion is remote, we are likely to find consensual political patterns, whereas coercion of an immediate nature engenders a more conflictual process.

The pairing of these characteristics produces the familiar four categories. Each category has its own unique policy characteristics, which in turn engenders its own consequent political characteristics.[2] Distributive policies are those which can be dispensed and disaggregated on a unit-by-unit basis, in a non–zero-sum way. Classic examples include pork barrel, patronage and subsidy policies, like public works projects. Distributive politics, in turn, are characterized by accommodation, logrolling, and the prevalence of subgovernments following a pattern of mutual noninterference.

Regulatory policies, though individualized and specific in impact, cannot be disaggregated into a series of unrelated items. Classic regulatory policies involve laws that explicitly manipulate conduct through the use of sanctions, penalties and prohibitions. Consequent political characteristics are pluralistic, with interest groups heavily involved. Examples include

---

[1] Though the scheme's conception was broadly deductive in this sense, it also grew from his very detailed study of New York City politics (Lowi, 1964a, 1971).

[2] Care must be taken to avoid the fallacy of inverting the independent and dependent variables; this is, some are tempted to use political characteristics to categorize policies, rather than relying on policy characteristics themselves (the independent variable) as the basis for categorization. This and subsequent discussion of the categories is drawn from Spitzer, 1983, Ch. 2.

laws restricting substandard goods, unfair competition, and antitrust legislation.

Redistributive policies incorporate those that are broad in scope, affecting classes of people—black versus white, poor versus rich, etc. Redistributive policies are long-range, insofar as they deal with the long-term allocation or reallocation of resources among these broad classes. The attendant political configuration most nearly resembles the elitist view of politics, characterized by the struggle between haves and have-nots. Opposing political forces tend to polarize into two sides, though the political struggles here are less fractious and intense than for regulatory policies. Examples include social security, monetary policy and the income tax.

Constituent policies have received less attention than the other three areas, partly because this category was added later, and because it is less well understood than the others (probably for the former reason). These policies are, in essence, the "rules of the game." They focus on the overhead function of government, and therefore the nature of governmental authority. Constituent policies usually attract relatively little public attention, as only the top political stratum tends to be concerned with these political issues. This often leads to accommodative, if not collusive political arrangements. Examples include election laws, reapportionment, and administrative/departmental reorganization.

As mentioned, the arenas of power scheme has been the subject of both wide use and criticism. Though the criticisms raise important questions, these have been dealt with elsewhere.[3]

Revising the Arenas

Many who have worked with or studied the arenas scheme have observed that the degree of categorical "fit" for various policies is more precise for some than for others. For example, crime control legislation, which usually includes specific prohibitions backed by firm sanctions, is classic regulatory policy. But what about efforts to regulate that are less explicit in language, and/or that rely on sanctions such as fines alone, or license withdrawal, or that even offer positive incentives to encourage or discourage behavior? Similarly, some policies are classically redistributive. such as the income tax. But what about policies that are similarly broad in scope, but that seem to be closer to distributive policies, such as aid to education? Such questions arise about all four categories, and are often raised as evidence of the inadequacy of the scheme. I argue, however, that these questions do not undercut the scheme, but rather illustrate the viability of the categories when they are treated in a slightly different way.

---

[3]Criticisms of the schemes are discussed in Spitzer, 1983:26-29.

Based on the notion that some policy cases represent a more "pure" categorical fit, whereas other cases are more "mixed," I proposed several years ago the revision depicted in Figure 4-2 (Spitzer, 1983:29-31).

Each box in the figure is cut in half, with the resulting inner diamond indicating the location of policies with mixed characteristics. The outer triangles represent the location of policies with more nearly pure cases. In the case of distributive policies, for example, the pure cases on the outside include examples such as parks, land-grant and most public works policies. The mixed cases are policies that are mixed either by virtue of the nature of the policy itself, such as urban mass transit, or by virtue of amendments and/or additions included in the policy. In the case of regulation, pure cases articulate relatively unambiguous rules of conduct backed by sanctions, whereas mixed cases prescribe conduct through less directly coercive means, such as the use of incentives. A pure redistributive policy is one that

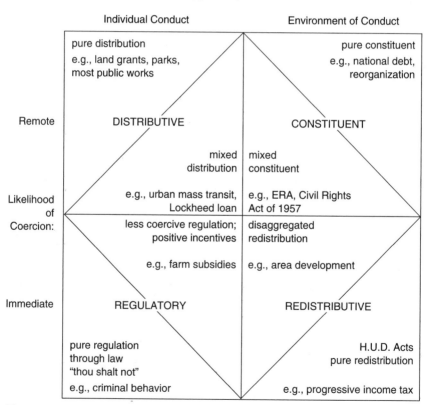

Figure 4-2   Revised Arenas of Power Scheme

involves a direct transfer between classes (a relatively uncommon phenom-enon in American politics), whereas mixed cases reveal some degree of pol-icy disaggregation (in a distributive sense), as with area redevelopment pol-icy, or the Housing and Urban Development acts of 1965 and 1968. A pure constituent case would include one that deals with purely administra-tive/overhead matters, such as election law or agency reorganization. A mixed case also involves governmental-administrative matters, but in the context of a policy that also deals at least partly with substantive govern-mental concerns, like civil rights. The actual determination of how policies are categorized is predicated on a series of classification rules that appear elsewhere (Spitzer, 1983:32-33, 1983a:556-574).

This distinction between pure and mixed cases was tested empirically elsewhere, relying on both cases studies and aggregate analysis, and was found to be valid (Spitzer, 1983, Chs. 3, 4, and 6). In general, the political patterns of policies followed those predicted by the category characteristic, according to the degree to which a case was pure or mixed. For example, Lowi posits that regulatory policies will have highly pluralistic, and there-fore conflictual political patterns. When a case involved pure regulation, conflict was indeed high. When it was a mixed case, however, conflict was less. An important political characteristic of redistributive policy was that the president had great influence over its attendant political process and therefore over the ultimate political outcome. Yet when a redistributive pol-icy possessed mixed attributes, the president's influence was also less. And so on. These past findings are mentioned here briefly to point out that em-pirical verification of this revision does exist. We turn now to another re-finement, dealing only with a single category.

Regulatory Policy

In a recent policy studies article, Tatalovich and Daynes (1984) focus on a single of Lowi's policy areas, regulatory policy. Their interest in this area arises from their prior work on abortion policy (Tatalovich and Daynes, 1981), which they conclude falls under the regulatory rubric. Yet they observe that abortion policy differs from most of the regulatory poli-cies identified by Lowi and others, which are primarily economic in nature. To resolve this apparent divergence, they researched other literature on reg-ulatory policy. They then made the distinction, drawing on past work, be-tween economic regulation (so-called "old" regulation) and social ("new") regulation (Tatalovich and Daynes, 1984:208; Lilley and Miller, 1977; Weaver, 1978; Wilson, 1980). Thus, they divide regulation into two forms, economic and social, with abortion falling into the latter category. Tat-alovich and Daynes (1984:208) define social regulation as "involving the use of authority to modify or replace social values, institutional practices, and norms of interpersonal behavior with new modes of conduct based upon legal proscriptions." They find that the politics of social regulatory policy differ from those of economic regulation by virtue of a greater involvement of the courts, ideology, and single-issue groups (Tatalovich and Daynes, 1984:209). Their study of abortion confirms this, as does a similar study of another social regulatory policy, gun control (Spitzer, 1987).

The key point to make about the two types of regulatory policy is that, though different, they are equally regulatory. In the context of Figure 4-2, each can have pure or mixed cases. As Figure 4-3 proposes, economic regulation is located closer to distributive policy, by virtue of its concern with the regulation of prices and conditions of market entry (Kelman, 1978; Wilson, 1980; Salamon, 1981). This focus on concrete economic terms and consequences in the policy (so-called "old" regulation) should logically yield a political configuration that resembles the policy-politics relationship of the

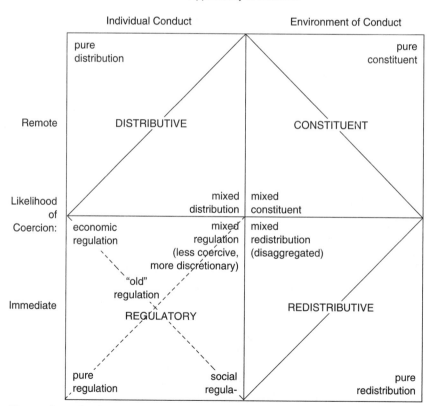

Figure 4-3   Revised Arenas Scheme With Attention to Regulatory Policy

distributive area (as distributive policy deals mostly in the realm of the concrete). A brief example will help to illustrate such a policy.

In their analysis of regulatory policy, Ripley and Franklin (1976:116–117) discuss a relatively minor, but instructive regulatory case involving cranberry growers. Shortly before Thanksgiving in 1959, the Food and Drug Administration (FDA) reported to the Secretary of Health, Education and Welfare (HEW) that some of the cranberries then available had been contaminated with a harmful weed killer. The Secretary went public with the news, advising consumers not to purchase tainted cranberries—though there was no way for consumers to distinguish tainted from untainted berries. The announcement sent panic throughout the industry, as 70 percent of its sales occurred during this period. Hurried negotiations between HEW and the FDA, on the one hand, and the cranberry growers and their congressional supporters, on the other, produced a labeling program to identify safe berries for consumers. Unfortunately, the cranberry growers had already suffered significant losses, so they sought compensation from the government for $15-$20 million in losses (they ultimately received $10 million). According to Ripley and Franklin (1976:117), "[a] distributive subgovernment in effect intervened in the aftermath of a regulatory decision. . . ." Admittedly, the "regulatory decision" was not the issuance of a conventional rule or prohibition. Yet, the statement was the product of the FDA, and it represented the policy of that agency. It was also an effort to curtail certain market activity. Lacking from the statement was the issuance of an explicit penalty. One might argue, however, that the agency was simply relying on a less coercive form of manipulation of conduct (impelled, perhaps, by time constraints and/or political considerations).

Given the argument that regulation can be pure (explicit prohibitions backed by sanctions) or mixed (less coercion, more discretion), as summarized in Figure 4-3, the cranberry case illustrates an example in the administrative realm of "mixed regulation" where the policy characteristics and consequent political patterns resemble those of distributive policies and politics. It also involves "economic regulation." Thus, the location of the cranberry case within the regulatory box in Figure 4-3 would be at the top center, nearest the distributive box.[4]

Moving counter-clockwise in the regulatory box, economic regulation embodies regulation of prices, conditions of market entry and the like ("old" regulation is located closely to this); pure regulation embodies stan-

---

[4]One might speculate that the likelihood of "agency capture" is enhanced the closer a regulatory policy is located to the distributive box; and similarly, that "capture" is less of a political problem when dealing with pure/social regulation, given the higher visibility and broader scope of the latter, as compared to the narrower scope and possible subgovernment involvement in the case of the former.

dard thou-shalt-not provisions, like criminal penalties; and social regulation, defined above as using authority to alter social values, institutional practices and behavioral norms, brings us closest to policy and political characteristics of classic redistribution. In terms of policy characteristics, we find that social regulation shares the broad scope of impact, winners-versus-losers, symbolically zero-sum traits of redistributive policy. Located near to this is what several have referred to as "new" regulation (Kelman, 1978:16–18; Salamon, 1981:150–151), involving non-market behavior including businesses. Cited examples include environmental issues, consumer protection and workplace safety laws (and agencies such as the Environmental Protection Agency, the Occupational Health and Safety Administration, and the Equal Employment Opportunity Commission). This "new" regulation is not purely social, but it does represent a departure from purely narrow economic/market concerns.

The political traits of social regulation are also similar to those of redistribution. Social regulation engenders bi-factional opposing coalitions. Such issues often involve the president as a key symbolic actor (e.g. abortion, gun control, obscenity, school prayer; this also tends to be true of "new" regulation—see Salamon, 1981:150–152) to a greater extent than economic regulation. Moreover, the political reverberations of social regulation arouse passions on a wider scale, as compared to economic regulation (consistent with social regulation's closer proximity to redistribution).

Despite these similarities, however, it is important to remember that social regulatory policies are still regulatory, as defined by the characteristics of the policy. According to the underlying argument of the arenas scheme, the particular political characteristics of social regulation resemble those of redistribution because the policy characteristics of social regulation differ from other forms of regulation, leaning in the redistributive direction. This brief sketch of the proposed sub-components of regulatory policy leads us to a final, more general consideration for the arenas scheme.

Splitting Hairs or Meaningful Distinctions?

The reader having gone this far might query whether these added distinctions represent overly narrow, or even trivial refinements. Naturally, this may be the case. I argue not, however, as all of this leads to a larger conclusion about the arenas of power—namely, that the dichotomization of coercion (immediate versus remote, individual versus environment) yielding four categories is, in a sense, both misleading and simplistic. To say this is not to criticize, however, but merely to recognize that complex concepts must often be simplified to make them manageable and useful.

Still, after more than 20 years of study and application, perhaps we are now at a point where we can recognize the obvious about the concepts underlying the scheme—that immediate versus remote, and individual versus environment as applied to coercion are not dichotomous at all, but rather are continua, as indicated by the arrows connecting coercion traits in Figure 4-3. The four key types upon which so much attention has focused imply semantically, as well as substantively, that policies falling under each are discrete and unique, and that it does not make sense to discuss degrees of distributiveness or degrees of regulation. The main point of this essay, however, is that the oft-neglected underlying logic of the scheme indicates that, in fact, it is perfectly logical and consistent to think in terms of degrees, instead of simple discrete categories. The refinements proposed in Figures 4-2 and 4-3 are aimed specifically at this goal, though they focus principally on only one category of policy. If we think of Lowi's scheme not as a matrix, but as a two-dimensional map, where location of a policy is determined by the appropriate intersection of horizontal and vertical axes based on policy characteristics, then the scheme takes on greater richness and intricacy that is still entirely consistent with the concepts first outlined in 1964. In addition, the fundamental logic underlying the scheme—that policies engender politics—is sustained and, if anything, strengthened. The operational problems of implementing the two-dimensional map approach are, of course, considerable. For example, precise measurement of the relative likelihood of coercion across various policies remains, as of now, an important but unaddressed task. Still, a shift in thinking about the arenas scheme along the lines suggested here might prove to be very rewarding. One hopes that others will be sufficiently intrigued to continue this inquiry, perhaps through an inductive exploration of the other policy areas.

REFERENCES

BEER, SAMUEL. 1973. "The Modernization of American Federalism." *Publius* 3:49-96.

GRANT, JAMES. 1972. "The Administration of Politics." Ph.D. dissertation, University of Chicago.

GREENBERG, GEORGE, et al. 1977. "Developing Public Policy Theory." *American Political Science Review* 71:1532-1543.

HARTMANN, JUDITH. 1973. "Bureaucracy, Democracy and the Administrative Official." Ph.D. dissertation, University of Chicago.

HAYES, MICHAEL T. 1978. "The Semi-Sovereign Pressure Groups." *Journal of Politics* 40:134-161.

HILL, KIM QUAILE, AND JOHN PATRICK PLUMLEE. 1984. "Policy Arenas and Budgetary Politics." *Western Political Quarterly* 37:84-99.

HUDSON III, ROBERT B. 1972. "Public Policy Formation in France." Ph.D. dissertation, University of North Carolina.

KELMAN, STEVEN. 1978. "Regulation That Works." *The New Republic* (November 25):16-20.

KJELLBERG, FRANCESCO. 1977. "Do Policies (Really) Determine Politics? and Eventually How?" *Policy Studies Journal* (Special Issue):554-570.

KORNBLITH, NANCY. 1968. "The Congressional Committee: Variance in Role and Function." M.A. thesis, University of Chicago.

LILLEY, W., AND MILLER, J. C. 1977. "The New 'Social' Regulation." *The Public Interest* 47:49-161.

LOWI, THEODORE J. 1964. "American Business, Public Policy, Case Studies, and Political Theory." *World Politics* 16:677-715.

LOWI, THEODORE J. 1964a. *At the Pleasure of the Mayor* (New York: Free Press).

LOWI, THEODORE J. 1967. "Making Democracy Safe for the World." in James Rosenau, ed., *Domestic Sources of Foreign Policy* (New York: Free Press).

LOWI, THEODORE J. 1970. "Decision Making vs. Policy Making." *Public Administration Review* 30:314-325.

LOWI, THEODORE J. 1971. "The Development of the Arenas of Power." in Oliver Walter, ed., *Political Scientists at Work* (Delmont, CA: Duxbury Press).

LOWI, THEODORE J. 1972. "Four Systems of Policy, Politics, and Choice." *Public Administration Review* 32:298-310.

LOWI, THEODORE J. 1972a. "Population Policies and the American Political System." Pp. 283-300 in *Governance and Population, Commission Research Reports*, Vol. 4. (Washington, DC: Government Printing Office).

MANN, DEAN E. 1975. "Political Incentives in U.S. Water Policy: Relationships Between Distributive and Regulatory Politics." Pp. 94-123 in Matthew Holden and Dennis L. Dresang, eds., *What Government Does* (Beverly Hills, CA: Sage Publications).

MEIER, KENNETH J. 1979. *Politics and the Bureaucracy* (North Scituate, MA: Duxbury Press).

PENBERA, JR., JOSEPH. 1973. "A Test of the Lowi Arenas of Power Policy Approach." Ph.D. dissertation, American University.

PETERS, B. GUY, JOHN C. DOUGHTIE, AND M. KATHLEEN McCULLOCH. 1977. "Types of Democratic Systems and Types of Public Policies." *Comparative Politics* 9:327-355.

PRICE, DAVID. 1972. *Who Makes the Laws* (Cambridge, MA: Schenkman).

RAKOFF, STUART, AND GUENTHER SCHAEFER. 1970. "Politics, Policy and Political Science: Theoretical Alternatives." *Politics and Society* 1:51-77.

RIPLEY, RANDALL, AND GRACE FRANKLIN. 1976. *Congress, the Bureaucracy, and Public Policy* (Homewood, IL: Dorsey Press).

ROOS, L. JOHN. 1969. "Committee-Floor Relations in the U.S. Congress." M.A. thesis, University of Chicago.

SALAMON, LESTER M. 1981. "Federal Regulation: A New Arena for Presidential Power." in Hugh Heclo and Lester M. Salamon, eds., *The Illusion of Presidential Government* (Boulder, CO: Westview Press.

SALISBURY, ROBERT, AND JOHN HEINZ. 1970. "A Theory of Policy Analysis and Some Preliminary Applications. In Ira Sharkansky, ed., *Policy Analysis in Political Science* (Chicago: Markham).

SCHNEIDER, JERROLD. 1979. *Ideological Coalitions in Congress* (Westport, CT: Greenwood Press).

SHIRY, JOHN D. 1977. "Political Patterns in Selected Areas in Ontario." Ph.D. dissertation, Queen's University, Kingston, Ontario, Canada.

SHULL, STEVEN A. 1983. "Changes in Presidential Policy Initiatives." *Western Political Quarterly* 36:491-498.

SHULL, STEVEN A. 1984. *Domestic Policy Formation* (Westport, CT: Greenwood Press).

SMITH, T. ALEXANDER. 1969. "Toward a Comparative Theory of the Policy-Process." *Comparative Politics* 1:498-515.

SMITH, T. ALEXANDER. 1975. *The Comparative Policy Process* (Santa Barbara, CA: Clio Books).

SPITZER, ROBERT J. 1979. *The Presidency and Public Policy: A Preliminary Inquiry* (University, AL: University of Alabama Press).

SPITZER, ROBERT J. 1983. *The Presidency and Public Policy* (University, AL: University of Alabama Press).

SPITZER, ROBERT J. 1983a. *Presidential Policy Determinism Presidential Studies Quarterly* (Fall) :556-574.

SPITZER, ROBERT J. 1987. "Gun Control and the Mythology of the Second Amendment." in Raymond Tatalovich and Byron Daynes, eds., *Social Regulatory Policy* (Boulder, CO: Westview Press).

STEINBERGER, PETER J. 1980. "Typologies of Public Policy: Meaning Construction and the Policy Process." *Social Science Quarterly* 61:185-197.

TATALOVICH, RAYMOND, AND BYRON DAYNES. 1981. *The Politics of Abortion* (New York: Praeger).

TATALOVICH, RAYMOND, AND BYRON DAYNES. 1984. "Moral Controversies and the Policymaking Process." *Policy Studies Journal* 3:207-322.

TATALOVICH, RAYMOND, AND BYRON DAYNES, eds. 1987. *Social Regulatory Policy* (Boulder, CO: Westview Press).

VOGLER, DAVID. 1974. *The Politics of Congress* (Boston: Allyn and Bacon).

WEAVER, P.H. 1977. "Regulation, Social Policy and Class Conflict." *The Public Interest* 50:45-63.

WILSON, JAMES Q. 1973. *Political Organizations* (New York: Basic Books).

WILSON, JAMES Q., ed. 1980. *The Politics of Regulation* (New York: Basic Books).

WOOTTON, GRAHAM. 1985. *Interest Groups: Policy and Politics in America* (Englewood Cliffs, NJ: Prentice-Hall).

ZIMMERMAN, WILLIAM. 1973. "Issue Area and Foreign-Policy Process." *American Political Science Review* 67:1204-1212.

DISCUSSION
Daniel McCool

In the thirty years since the publication of Lowi's *World Politics* article, a lot of ink has been spilled attempting to make the world safe for policy typologies. Many writers, including Steinberger and Greenberg et al., express both appreciation and doubt; Jenkins says the response "has been at best schizophrenic" (1978, 102). It is, of course, difficult to dismiss policy typologies outright; they have been successfully applied by numerous scholars and have clearly increased our understanding of the policy-making process. But they remain underdeveloped in regard to their theoretical utility.

Policy typologies are popular among scholars because they provide insights that might otherwise go undetected. However, there is still plenty of room for improvement, and many scholars have attempted to modify the Lowi typology, or they have offered their own. A brief review of these will provide a larger perspective from which to evaluate the concepts covered in this section.

You recall that *economy* is one of the criteria for good theory. Aynsley Kellow criticized the modifications to Lowi offered by Spitzer and argued that the additions sacrificed economy and made the typology too complex. To Kellow, "the simpler and more powerful the theory the better" (1988, 713). He calls the tendency toward increasingly complex and detailed theory "the bane of social science" (1988, 714). Kellow also questioned the validity of the typology and presented one of his own. He discarded Lowi's "constituent policy" and instead offers two types of regulatory policy: "public interest regulation" and "private interest regulation" (1988, 718). The axes for his four-cell matrix are *public/private costs* and *public/private benefits*.

Kellow's critique sparked a lively exchange between him and Spitzer and Lowi. Lowi responded by noting that his 1964 piece is remembered "not for what it accomplished but for what it started" (1988, 725). He then offered an explanation of what he was trying to accomplish with his original typology: "it had a double purpose: The first purpose was to classify policies. The second purpose was to identify the (behavioral) political dynamic associated with each category of policy—on the assumption that every category of policy has its own political dynamic" (1988, 726).

Spitzer takes issue with Kellow's claim that simplicity is the ultimate virtue in policy theory. On the contrary, he argues that "little in social science is susceptible to broad-based, generalizable, meaningful, law-like propositions" (1989, 530). Thus what Kellow calls the "bane of social science" is "the stuff of social science" to Spitzer because "the exploration of particularities is inextricably bound up with theory-building. . . " (1989, 530). Spitzer concludes that the "philosophy of science and the nature of theoretical inquiry demand continued interaction between prevailing frameworks and new knowledge, including both the general and the particular" (1989, 533).[3] In a sense, then, the debate between Kellow and Spitzer is over the relative importance of the criteria for good theory; is economical theory preferable to more powerful theory? Should testability be sacrificed for greater generalization?

Many efforts to improve and/or apply the Lowi typology combined it with other approaches. Fred Frohock (1979) developed a rather ingenious combination of the Lowi typology, a stages approach, and systems theory. He also subdivided regulatory policy and distributive policy into two categories each. His work was clearly an attempt to increase both the inclusivity and mutual exclusivity of the typology by adding greater specification to the model. It is precisely the kind of approach that Kellow opposes, but it clearly helps solve some of the problems associated with the application of typologies.

Steven Shull applied the Lowi model to various policy stages and concluded that the policy types correspond with different stages of policy making due to the different roles of the president and Congress at different stages of the policy-making process: "The relative influence of Congress and the President. . . is expected to differ widely across stages in the policy process and according to the policy content and the political environment" (1983, 5). Grover Starling's textbook also applied the Lowi typology to a

---

[3]It would appear that Tiryakian agrees with Spitzer but not Kellow. He notes that simplicity has its costs: "...categorizing a given population into a few types or subtypes may reduce validity if the variance within single categories or types is thereby unduly increased. Parsimony, therefore, is not always a virtue" (1968, 178).

stages approach (1988). And Salisbury (1968) expanded Lowi's typology to include a "self-regulatory" category, and combined it with a modified systems approach.

One of the best known and most widely cited modifications of the Lowi typology was developed by Ripley and Franklin (1987). They attempted to make the typology more inclusive by adding policy types that cover policies that clearly do not fit into Lowi's categories. They made a distinction between domestic policy types, and foreign and defense policy types. In the former category are *distributive, competitive regulatory, protective regulatory*,[4] and *redistributive*. In foreign and defense policy are *structural, strategic*, and *crisis policy*.[5] In separate books Ripley and Franklin applied this modified typology to the formulation/legitimation stage (1987) and the implementation stage (1986).

Other applications of Lowi's typology are even more novel. Heckathorn and Maser (1990) offered a "transaction space analysis" based on public choice theory to modify the typology, and find that Lowi's scheme works quite well under some conditions but not others. Miller attempted to overcome the exclusivity problems of the Lowi typology by combining it with the social action theory developed by the famous German sociologist Max Weber (1990). He argues that these "newly synthesized criteria enable more analytically precise categories, resolving much of the disagreement about where in Lowi's framework a policy belongs" (1990, 887).

Certainly Lowi's typology is not the only one on the market. A number of other authors have also developed typologies, some of which were briefly reviewed by Steinberger. A widely cited alternative to Lowi is Wilson's matrix built upon two axes: *concentrated/diffused benefits* and *concentrated/diffused costs* (1973, 1992, 426–37). This results in four policy types: If a policy is perceived to have diffused costs and benefits, it is made by way of "majoritarian politics;" if it is perceived to have diffused costs but concentrated benefits, it is called "client politics;" if the policy is perceived to concentrate costs but diffuse benefits, it is "entrepreneurial politics;" and if the perception of a policy is that it concentrates both costs and benefits, it is characterized as "interest-group politics."

---

[4]Competitive regulatory policies are "aimed at limiting the provision of specific goods and services to only one or a few designated deliverers who are chosen from a larger number of competing potential deliverers" (1984, 26). Protective regulatory policies "are designed to protect the public by setting the conditions under which various private activities can be undertaken" (1984, 27). In the 1991 edition of this book the authors eliminated the "protective regulatory" policy type because it was obsolete.

[5]Structural policy is distributive policy applied to defense-related matters such as procurement and funding for military bases. Strategic policy affects our nation's relationship with other nations (1984, 28–29).

Wilson, like Lowi, based his typology on the *perception* of policy impacts. This permits us to anticipate—and possibly to predict—what the political contest over that policy will look like. But as Steinberger and others have pointed out, there is an inherent risk in assuming that we can verify an identifiable perception of an issue. Deborah Stone makes this point quite succinctly:

> . . . issues are portrayed in terms of who and how many people benefit precisely in order to mobilize support for and against proposals. Programs do not themselves have inherent distributions of costs and benefits. Rather, political actors strategically represent programs as contests between different types of costs and benefits. (1988, 180)

A quite different approach to the problem of perceptions has been taken by Schneider and Ingram. They have taken the concept of social construction—discussed by Steinberger—and developed a distinct and innovative typology of how we perceive "target populations," meaning "the cultural characterizations or popular images of the persons or groups whose behavior and well-being are affected by public policy" (1993, 334). Their work explains why earlier typologies often failed to predict the outcome of certain types of policy making.

Other attempts to categorize policy have been made by Hayes (1978) and Hansen (1984). Each of them developed a complex six-part typology that captures a wide array of policies. Both of these authors utilize economic concepts in their policy types. Like other scholars, they strove for a typology that can place every policy in one of the categories. Hayes writes of his scheme: "Insofar as the categories. . . are exhaustive and mutually exclusive, the resulting six policy processes should be quite distinct and comprehensive" (1978, 145).

As you can see, there is a tremendous variety of policy typologies; and there is a league of critics almost as diverse as the typologies themselves. Two of the best known are Steinberger and Greenberg et al., but it is worth briefly identifying the concerns of some others. Wilson called Lowi's formulation "bold and imaginative" but also "ambiguous and incomplete" (Wilson 1973, 328). Howlett argues that the typological tradition has lead policy studies astray because it focuses on the *substance* of policies rather than policy *instruments*, meaning the techniques of action and the tools chosen by policy makers (1991, 4).

Other critics point out what they see as inherent limitations in typologies. May writes that "typologies are of little value in predicting the political feasibility of particular policies. . . these criticisms suggest the policy typology literature has little relevance for the task of predicting 'probabilities of success' of particular policy proposals" (1986, 116). Heclo argues that the problem is with validity, not just predictability: "[a typology] usually pays for its analytic credentials at the price of realism. The main reason for this unrealism is that typologies of components are essentially static; attention is devoted to categories rather than to relationships" (1972, 105). And Jenkins raises questions regarding both validity and causality: "To link process and content, in the way Lowi advocates. . . demands a theory of motivation and a model of behavior. This undoubtedly leads to severe problems of analysis, from which escape may only be possible through drastic simplification" (1978, 104).

All of these critiques raise valid points regarding the limitations of typologies. But the student of public policy should not jump to the conclusion that such typologies are theoretically useless. It is quite the contrary; they improve our understanding of policy and the impacts they have on the political process. They also form a valuable foundation upon which we can construct other theories that offer a greater level of specification, which ultimately leads to insights regarding causation and prediction. Like all of the theories covered in this book, if we expect typologies to solve all of our theoretical shortcomings—and they are legion—we are bound to be disappointed.

And finally it is appropriate to end with a statement concerning the importance of typologies. It may appear that the attempts to improve typologies merely create increasingly detailed microtheory—that we are arguing over trivialities. Indeed, there is some truth to Kellow's charge that we continue to build more elaborate typologies in order to reduce the number of unexplained cases. But it is also true that the debate over typologies involves basic questions about how the governing system works. For example, a prominent element in these typologies concerns the relationship between various forms of government *coercion* and government *largess*. These are not insignificant details, but rather they are broad questions that must be addressed if policy theory is ever to move beyond its current parameters (the reader need only return to Section 1 for a litany of those). Lowi has written that, in regard to his typology, "The purpose of this classifying activity is to produce theory that can manage the empirical patterns in policy making and yet keep them attached to the basic functions of the state" (1970, 321). Thus the research reviewed in this discussion is more than just an attempt to refine categories; it is an effort to describe some of the most fundamental features of our form of government.

REFERENCES

FROHOCK, FRED (1979). *Public Policy: Scope and Logic*. Englewood Cliffs, NJ: Prentice-Hall.

HANSEN, SUSAN. "On the Making of Unpopular Decisions: A Typology and Some Evidence." *Policy Studies Journal* 13 (Sept.): 23–42.

HAYES, MICHAEL (1978). "The Semi-Sovereign Pressure Groups: A Critique of Current Theory and an Alternative Typology." *Journal of Politics* 40 (Feb.): 134–61.

HECKATHORN, DOUGLAS, AND STEVEN MASER (1990). "The Contractual Architecture of Public Policy: A Critical Reconstruction of Lowi's Typology." *Journal of Politics* 52 (Nov.): 1101–123.

HECLO, HUGH (1972). "Review Article: Policy Analysis." *British Journal of Political Science* 2 (Jan.): 83–108.

HOWLETT, MICHAEL (1991). "Policy Instruments, Policy Styles, and Policy Implementation: National Approaches to Theories of Instrument Choice." *Policy Studies Journal* 19 (Spring): 1–21.

JENKINS, W. I. *Policy Analysis* (1978). London, England: Martin Robertson.

KELLOW, AYNSLEY (1988). "Promoting Elegance in Policy Theory: Simplifying Lowi's Arenas of Power." *Policy Studies Journal* 16 (Summer): 713–24.

LOWI, THEODORE (1970). "Decision Making vs. Policy Making: Toward and Antidote for Technocracy." *Public Administration Review* (May/June): 314–25.

_____ (1988). "Comment," *Policy Studies Journal* 16 (Summer): 725–28.

MILLER, HUGH (1990). "Weber's Action Theory and Lowi's Policy Types in Formulation, Enactment, and Implementation." *Policy Studies Journal* 18 (Summer): 887–905.

RIPLEY, RANDALL, AND GRACE FRANKLIN (1987). *Congress, the Bureaucracy, and Public Policy*, 4th ed. Chicago: Dorsey Press.

_____ (1986). *Bureaucracy and Policy Implementation*, 2nd ed. Chicago: Dorsey Press.

SALISBURY, ROBERT (1968). "The Analysis of Public Policy: A Search for Theories and Roles." In *Political Science and Public Policy*, pp. 151–75. Edited by Austin Ranney. Chicago: Markham.

SHULL, STEVEN (1983). *Domestic Policy Formation: Presidential Congressional Partnership?* Westport, CT: Greenwood Press.

SPITZER, ROBERT (1989). "From Complexity to Simplicity: More on Policy Theory and the Arenas of Power." *Policy Studies Journal* 17 (Spring): 529–36.

STARLING, GROVER (1988). *Strategies for Policy Making*. Chicago: Dorsey Press.

STONE, DEBORAH (1988). *Policy Paradox and Political Reason*. Glenview, IL: Scott, Foresman and Co.

TIRYAKIAN, EDWARD. "Typologies." In the *International Encyclopedia of the Social Sciences*, pp. 177–86. Edited by David Sills. New York: The Macmillan Company and the Free Press.

WILSON, JAMES Q. (1973). *Political Organizations*. New York: Basic Books.

_____(1992) *American Government: Institutions and Policies*, 5th ed. Lexington, MA: D. C. Heath.

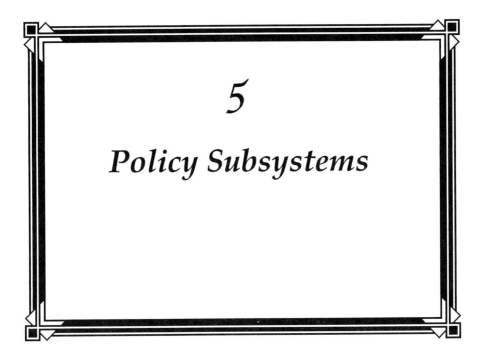

5

Policy Subsystems

INTRODUCTION

If you had to summarily characterize—with just one word—changes in the federal government over the past thirty years, that word would be *fragmentation*. The old power centers have been balkanized; political parties have lost much of their clout; interest groups have become enormously diverse and numerous; legislative power is divided into innumerable committees and subcommittees and the days of strong committee chairs are gone; the number and diversity of administrative agencies has increased dramatically; the president's power is compromised by a host of new realities; and "The People" can attend hearings, comment on proposals, sit on advisory boards, go to "scoping meetings," and, with the help of computers, send millions of letters.

   This does not mean that the resulting fragments of governing power are wholly disconnected. Quite the contrary, those wielding power—no matter how sectoral—learned long ago that they could increase their leverage by forming informal alliances with other players in the policy-making process. In a truly seminal book published in 1939, Ernest Griffith described a set of informal relationships that are still the focus of intense scholarly interest:

> Looking at our government from another angle, one can see it to be composed of a number of dispersive and virtually uncoordinated units, each whirling in

its own orbit. . . . the relationship among these men—legislators, administrators, lobbyists, scholars—who are interested in a common problem is a much more real relationship than the relationships between congressmen generally or between administrators generally. In other words, he who would understand the prevailing pattern of our present governmental behavior, instead of studying the formal institutions. . . may possibly obtain a better picture of the way things really happen if he would study these 'whirlpools' of special social interest and problems. (Griffith 1939, 182–83)

Griffith's basic notion was that by studying informal alliances rather than formal institutions we can obtain a better understanding of how policy is made. Subsequent scholars and journalists have also worked under this assumption, and they have come up with other terms—*iron triangles*, or *subgovernments* , for example—to describe similar arrangements.[1] Allowing for some variation, these terms refer to the symbiotic alliances of convenience between committees in Congress, administrative agencies, and interest groups, all concerned with the same substantive policy area. A whole set of behaviors became associated with these alliances:

They dispense distributive policy as a payoff to the participants.

They operate autonomously with little public visibility.

Conflict is minimal and often mitigated through logrolling and extending benefits to potential opponents.

Participants in the triangle are cohesive and have common policy goals (McCool 1990).[2]

Policies that have been characterized in the literature as being dominated by iron triangles at some point in time include agricultural policy, water development policy, defense procurement, veteran's affairs, public works, and maritime policy. In each issue area the assumption is that coordination and cooperation among the participants in the triangle can yield votes for the congressmen, larger budgets for the agencies, and government largess for the interest groups. Thus they all have a vested interest in the continued operation of their triangle.

---

[1]Other terms for these informal alliances are *policy whirlpools, cozy little triangles, triple alliances, power triads, subsystems, issue networks, policy networks*, and *advocacy coalitions*. You will encounter most of these in this section and discern differences between some of them.

[2]The four books most often cited as the source of the concept of iron triangles do not even use the term (Cater, 1964; Freeman, 1965; McConnell, 1966; Lowi, 1979). The history of the iron triangle concept offers an object lesson in how theory can be abused by both scholars and practitioners. The scholars abused it by creating a caricature of the original concept; it was misapplied to regulatory and redistributive policies, and its attributes were viewed as absolutes. Not surprisingly these scholars could not find many "real" iron triangles. The iron triangle concept also proved to be a valuable political weapon. Opponents of specific programs often saddle them with the sinister-sounding iron triangle label (it was a favorite with President Reagan), implying that the programs are wasteful porkbarrel doled out by secretive collusions (Wamsley 1985, 76; McCool 1989, 264–65).

The iron triangle concept became quite popular, but its applicability was limited to distributive policy made under a fairly specific set of conditions. Johnson points out that the "subgovernment analysis provides little insight into the relationships between agencies and committees beyond the distributive policy area" (1992, 9). In the last twenty years scholars have developed a number of different concepts that attempt to explain the behavior of all informal alliances, not just those involved in distributive policy. Although a number of labels are in use, most scholars simply refer to these studies as the subsystem literature. This body of research has played an important role in policy theory. Berry notes that "Few approaches for analyzing the American political system have endured as long or as well as that of the policy subgovernment" (1989, 239). Johnson calls the subgovernment concept "the dominant way in which political scientists model the making of public policy in the United States" (1992, 7. Also see Hansen 1987, 183).

The readings in this section begin with a selection from *The Political Process*, by J. Leiper Freeman, first published in 1955 (a revised edition came out ten years later). He defined a subsystem as the "pattern of interactions of participants, or actors, involved in making decisions in a special area of public policy" (1955, 5). He begins his book by noting that the relationship between "key personnel of executive bureaus," "leading members of congressional committees," and "other actors, especially from interest groups," "form crucial subsystems of the larger political system for making decisions in their special areas" (1955, 1). Citing both Ernest Griffith and David Truman, he contrasts these "plural patterns of power" to the perception held by some that the federal government is some sort of "well-ordered monolith" (1955, 2). Although he used the Bureau of Indian Affairs as his subject, his analysis was stated in sufficiently abstract and generalizable terms so that it can be applied to numerous substantive policy areas. The excerpt reprinted here is the final chapter, which summarizes his generalizations about subsystems.

In addition to Freeman's book, other studies of specific policies described the kinds of relationships that fit the subsystem model, although that term was not used in most of them. Typically these studies were polemics or critiques that attempted to expose how private interests receive special treatment and generous subsidies when they join forces with allies in Congress and the bureaucracy. Classics of this genre include Maass (1951), Foss (1960), Cater (1964), McConnell (1966), Theodore Lowi (1969, 2d. ed. 1979) and Ferejohn (1974). Cater's book was especially helpful because he explicitly developed and defined the concept of a subgovernment:

> In one important policy after another, substantial efforts to exercise power are waged by alliances cutting across the two branches of government and including key operatives from outside. In effect, they constitute subgovernments of Washington comprising the expert, the interested, and the engaged. . . . the subgovernment's tendency is to strive to become self-sustaining in control of

power in its own sphere. Each seeks to aggregate the power necessary to its purposes. Each resists being overridden. (1964, 17)

Cater's concept of a subgovernment was an apt description of much policy making in the early 1960s, but the ensuing decades have brought profound changes to national politics. As a result the subgovernment concept has lost some of its validity because this new mode of policy making cannot not be explained solely by a concept developed for an earlier era. Hugh Heclo was the first to develop an alternative to the traditional model; his piece on *issue networks* is the second reading in this section. The reader should be careful to note that Heclo does not claim that the old subgovernments have been supplanted by issue networks. Indeed he says "it would be foolish" to do so (1978, 105). Instead he argues that the issue networks "overlay" the subgovernments (1978, 105. Also see Michaels 1992). An important question then, is what is the relationship between the old iron triangles and the new overlay of issue networks?

Heclo's chapter offers an interesting smorgasbord of ideas concerning coalition politics at the federal level. It is a thought-piece, not an attempt to construct a highly specified theory. There was still a need to identify a more specific set of relationships and attributes that would enable scholars to clearly identify and analyze subsystems. The third selection, by Keith Hamm (1983), offers a specific list of subsystem characteristics, and explains how subsystem participants interact. Pay special attention to his idea that a set of continua can be utilized to explain the differences between different types of informal alliances. How does an iron triangle differ from an issue network?

The final selection, by Paul Sabatier (1988), also uses the subsystem concept, but adds considerable sophistication by tying it to two related concepts: "advocacy coalitions," and "policy learning." Sabatier's work is an attempt to improve both the power and validity of subsytem theory by specifying clearly and in detail how coalitions compete in the policy-making process. Both Heclo and Sabatier are quoted widely as the sources of the new concept of informal alliances in government. One can see a definite progression of ideas, from policy whirlpools to advocacy coalitions. At the same time there are notable continuities throughout the subsystem literature. The astute reader will pick out these continuities; it is important to learn, not just how policy making—and our theories about it—have changed, but also how some elements identified by Griffith fifty-five years ago are still very much a part of our governing process.

REFERENCES

BERRY, JEFFREY (1989). "Subgovernments, Issue Networks, and Political Conflict." In *Remaking American Politics*, pp. 239–60. Edited by Richard Harris and Sidney Miklas. Boulder, CO: Westview Press.

CATER, DOUGLASS (1964). *Power in Washington*. New York: Random House.

FEREJOHN, JOHN (1974). *Pork Barrel Politics: Rivers and Harbors Legislation, 1947–1968*. Stanford, CA: Stanford University Press.

FOSS, PHILIP (1960). *Politics and Grass*. Seattle: University of Washington Press.

FREEMAN, J. LEIPER (1955, rev. ed. 1965). *The Political Process*, rev. ed. New York: Random House.

GRIFFITH, ERNEST (1939). *The Impasse of Democracy*. New York: Harrison-Hilton Books.

HANSEN, JOHN MARK (1987). "Choosing Sides: The Creation of an Agricultural Policy Network in Congress, 1919–1932." *Studies in American Political Development* 2 (annual): 183–235.

JOHNSON, CATHY (1992). *The Dynamics of Conflict Between Bureaucrats and Legislators*. Amonk, NY: M. E. Sharpe.

LOWI, THEODORE (1969; 2d. ed. 1979). *The End of Liberalism*. New York: W. W. Norton.

MAASS, ARTHUR (1951). *Muddy Waters*. Cambridge, MA: Harvard University Press.

MCCONNELL, GRANT (1966). *Private Power and American Democracy*. New York: Random House.

MCCOOL, DANIEL (1989). "Subgovernments and the Impact of Policy Fragmentation and Accommodation." *Policy Studies Review* 8 (Winter): 264–87.

_____ (1990). "Subgovernments as Determinants of Political Viability." *Political Science Quarterly* 105 (Summer): 269–93.

MICHAELS, SARAH (1992). "Issue Networks and Activism." *Policy Studies Review* 11 (Autumn/Winter): 241–58.

WAMSLEY, GARY (1985). "Policy Subsystems as a Unit of Analysis in Implementation Studies: A Struggle for Theoretical Synthesis." In *Policy Implementation in Federal and Unitary Systems*, pp. 71–96. Edited by Kenneth Hanf and Theo Toonen. Boston: Martinus Nijhoff.

THE SUBSYSTEM IN PERSPECTIVE
J. Leiper Freeman*

A Summary Justification of the Study's Focus

In focusing upon the relations among executive bureau participants, congressional committee personnel, and leaders of interest groups in subsystems of public policy-making in American government, this study has attempted to demonstrate a useful way of examining the political process. It has argued for the utility of this kind of analytical approach partially upon the basis that the study of national policy-making at the more general, institutional level of Congress, the Administration, and the political parties does not always furnish the most meaningful understanding of the decisive factors. The case has been argued that the social diversity, the multiplicity of types of special groups of people promoting and defending particular values in American life, results in selective concentration of public interest and attention in politics. Concomitantly, the legislative and executive branches of the federal government cloak plural patterns of power and decision-making which mirror the functional specialization and diversity of interests in the society to a great extent. Furthermore, the legal framework in which this overall governmental system is cast contributes a permissive code not only making for a maximum of interplay between the legislative and executive branches in policy-making, but also allowing considerable decentralization of authority within each branch.

Consequently, we find that the overall, institutional system which forms the general setting for the executive bureau-legislative committee subsystem tends to have definite limitations as a decisive policy-making mechanism. While the Administration, Congress, and the major parties in their general structures and relationships tend to reflect gross distribution of public sentiment and public power, the resolution of issues tends to be accomplished through specialized lesser units. These subunitsóbureaus, committees, and interest groups—enjoy considerable autonomy in the special policy areas with which they are concerned. Furthermore, these are the units which provide the immediate setting of the subsystem here under analysis. The leading members of these subunits are the major, constant participants in a process through which special issues are discussed and policy solutions are formed. In their interactions which form the subsystem, the behavior of the participants is most immediately affected by the nature and interests of the subunits which they lead.

*J. Leiper Freeman, *The Political Process: Executive Bureau-Legislative Committee Relations.* New York: Random House, 1955, revised edition 1965. Used by permission.

The patterns of interaction in the subsystem are, of course, not by any means completely beyond the pale of influence of the leaders of the Administration, of Congress, or of the political parties. The nature and also the limitations of top-level influence, however, were seen to be such that, except under rather unusual and optimum conditions, the subsystem is likely to be sufficiently decisive so as to warrant an orderly and detailed examination of the relations within it.

Some Propositions About the Subsystem

The major types of strategy and means of influence of the participants in the subsystem will be summarized here as a conclusion to the study.

Summary Propositions Regarding the Bureau Leaders in the Subsystem Crucial to the bureau leader's objective of obtaining favorable responses from committee members to his policy proposals is his *strategic sensitivity* or his ability to recognize and to anticipate the expectations of committee members and to relate this to his own actions. Of course, a critical part of this strategic sensitivity lies in recognizing the interests of powerful committee members and making the necessary accommodations.

In attempting to influence committee members, the bureau leader has numerous direct and indirect means at his disposal. *One alternative is the exploitation of high-level power and prestige symbols by using the support of dominant figures in the Administration.* This strategy is most likely to be employed where there are strong and mutually reinforcing bonds of an interest or ideological nature (or both) between the bureau leader and the higher echelon figures. The strategy is most likely to have an effect upon the committee members when the general public acclaim and support for the Administration is so overwhelming as to offset possible negative reactions which committee members might develop against the bureau leader's use of such pressures. Furthermore, even though this strategy may maximize the influence of the bureaucrat in the subsystem, it is also likely to enlarge the area of controversy in which he and his organization become involved.

Increasingly, attempts of bureau leaders to influence committee members are being routinized through provision in the departmental organizational structure for specialists in legislative liaison. This organized legislative liaison is most important as a communications device on day-to-day matters and for dealing with the extensive number of routine requests from legislators. Its cumulative effect, however, is an important conditioner of the official's relations with committee members and key individuals in the legislative liaison setup may be important adjuncts to the bureau leader's efforts.

Personal friendship or other personal sentiments between a bureau leader and key committee members can also be crucial elements in his ability to gain favorable responses from the committees. The oversimplified use of personality factors to explain a bureau leader's success or failure along this line nevertheless probably should be avoided. It is sometimes too simple and easy just to attribute the consequences to the compatibility or incompatibility of certain personalities. *The chances are that personal relationships of a favorable type may be as frequently disrupted by the diverse roles which bureaucrat and legislative committeemen have to play as the other way around.* Furthermore, while length of tenure of office may give a bureaucrat time to develop favorable personal relationships in a committee, there is no assurance that the obverse may not also occur in which once-favorable personal relationships deteriorate over the years under the conflicting demands of bureaucratic and legislative roles and conflicting interests.

Still further, *what holds true for a bureau leader's personal relations with committee members can hold true also in his relations with group leaders who may support or oppose his proposals before the committees.* In his relations with group leaders, however, the bureau leader may maintain the support of some by institutionalizing his friendship with them by appointing them to official posts in the bureau. On the other hand, such action is likely to be regarded as favoritism by group leaders not thus honored, thereby increasing their efforts against the bureau leader's objectives.

Although committee hearings are manifestly means for the rational communication of factual information, often the exploitation of the non-rational aspects of committee hearings is more important to the type and degree of response which the bureau leader elicits than are the facts which he presents. This means, on the one hand, that his influence with the committee may depend not so much upon what he says as upon the impression the committee members form of him as a communicator and as a bureaucrat. On the other hand it also means that the skill with which a bureau leader is able to exploit the supposed public impact of his testimony in the minds of the committee members will be closely related to his ability to influence them.

In the use of publicity and propaganda, the bureau leader may capitalize upon two conditions to influence the course of decision in the subsystem. First, the interested publics of the subsystem are usually sufficiently restricted in size so that extensive propaganda campaigns are not ordinarily necessary to reach the critical audience. Second, because the inside or trade media are likely to reach the most interested publics, the bureau leader by virtue of his status may not only enjoy ready access to most of the nonofficial trade channels but also has the advantage of controlling the official media emanating from the bureau. Nevertheless, undue exploitation of either type may generate adverse reactions in the long run by violating the committee members' conceptions of the proper publicity role for bureaucrats.

A bureau leader generally finds it necessary to have at least the support of most of the bureau's employees and most of its clientele in order to assert his policy views successfully before committee members. Such support is likely to be one of the minimum conditions for committee acceptance of his policy proposals. This is not as easily accomplished as one might think at first glance, since employee and clientele groups are not cohesive units in most instances. Furthermore, besides a tendency to resist too much pressure from the bureau leadership, these groups usually show considerable propensity for internal schisms in which the bureau leaders often alienate one faction in the attempt to win the affections of another. If bureau leaders can mobilize the support of employees and clientele in the home territories of committee members, the consequences in the short run may be quite helpful in getting committee acceptance of proposed policies, especially if committee members are consulted in the process. Over the long run, however, such action runs the risk of involving the bureau leadership in the political affairs of committee members' constituents, which may very likely produce results adverse to the objectives of the bureaucrats. Local reaction may develop against the use of this strategy by bureau officials, and local interests may consolidate against them.

In mobilizing support among non-internal groups, bureau leaders are more likely to find initial sympathy among those segments of the public which are interested in the clientele, though not a part of it, which are less local and more cosmopolitan in their orientations, and which are more prone to be concerned with the bureau's policies on ideological grounds rather than material interests. The ability of such groups to influence committee members, however, is often not as great as that of the locally-based groups who frequently have the advantage in working through those constituents of committee members who are not clients of the bureau.

By admitting members of certain groups to the policy-making councils of the bureau, either through consultation or by official appointment, bureau leaders can often maximize the support of such groups in behalf of the bureau before the committees. Conversely, leaders and members of groups not thus coopted may tend to be the most vociferous opponents of the bureau leaders and may serve as strong counterforces to the acceptance of their proposals by committee members.

Summary Propositions Regarding Committee Participants in the Subsystem By exploiting the broad sanctions which are available to them, committee participants can wield great influence in the subsystem, both in determining the content of legislation and in shaping its administration. The three major types of committee sanctions are approval or disapproval of substantive legislation, approval or disapproval of appropriations, and investigation of subsystem affairs.

The substantive committee leaders tend to constitute the most constant congressional influentials in subsystem policy-making. They are frequently able to exercise a major degree of censorship over the final legislative product; especially, is this true of the veteran members of the committee in-group. They are likely to be the most powerful and most concerned members of Congress in a given policy area. Their interests become major factors in the process.

Substantive committees frequently attract a predominance of members with particular social backgrounds and characteristics. The major enduring social characteristics in such cases help in understanding the members' behavior in policy-making over the long run insofar as that behavior tends to reflect value patterns of the subcultures in which the members have achieved political success. *The predominance of one major set of subcultural values among the members of a committee will tend to lend a consistent pattern to their policy-making activities which transcends such factors as partisan differences.*

Also, length of service of committee members produces a degree of stability in committee membership patterns, lending a cohesiveness which is reflected in the members' behavior. The longer average tenure of senators may be relevant to a greater constancy in the reactions of Senate committee members to bureau leaders' proposals in comparison to the reactions of House committee members.

Though legislative committee members are perhaps the most constant influentials on the legislative side of the subsystem and though they may ultimately give the bureau leaders much of what they desire in the way of authorized policies, the members of the appropriations committees possess what is probably the strongest single sanction and may effectively negate authorized policies and force administrative changes by refusing the necessary resources. Here the decisive part tends to be played by leaders of the subcommittees on appropriations who are the real specialists in the financial affairs of particular bureaus. Especially is this true of the chairman of a given House appropriations subcommittee. His function is frequently that of basic arbiter over the allocation of financial resources for a bureau, a power which he may use to accomplish ends well beyond the overt objectives of the appropriations process. As a general rule, the strongest pressures for cutting a bureau's funds emanate from members of the House appropriations subcommittee, who are by custom the first and closest legislative scrutinizers of the budget proposals. Senate appropriations subcommittee members tend to concern themselves with questions of whether to restore cuts made in the House.

Investigating committee participants in the subsystem vary in their influence to a considerable degree in accordance with their ability to break through settled channels of opinion formation and conventional stereotypes about issues among public groups. They tend to increase in impact as they enlarge the public interested in the subsystem. Over the long run, however, members of investigating committees which have exploited the potentialities for sensational-ism to the utmost and have consistently widened the targets of their opera-tions are likely to reach a point of diminishing effect. This may be due to the accumulation of opposition which is likely to crystallize eventually in an ef-fort to halt the investigation or may result from eventual public weariness with the committee's repetitive theme. Furthermore, where the investiga-tion is used as an adjunct to the political hopes of the committee leader, the leaders of one or both of the major parties may intervene in the subsystem in an effort to protect the balance of power in the party system.

Due to demands upon committee members' time, knowledge, and attention, their dependency upon others for information, judgment, and executive action con-tributes to the influential roles played by committee staff. High-ranking, long-time committee staff members tend to control the communications channels of committees, draft committee reports, and as committee agents may inject their views into the subsystem in ways and to degrees that their formal roles might not imply.

The committee member's role, in which he is expected to choose wisely among policy alternatives as well as to represent his local constituency, tends to create blocks against his receptivity to the views of bureau leaders, despite their often-al-leged superior technical knowledge. Frequently, the committee member feels a strong urge to protect his status as the lawmaker in the face of bureaucratic challenge. Consequently, the committee member often prefers information and suggestions about policy from sources other than bureau leaders and their allies. Furthermore, he may often play something less than a neutral role in the deliberations within the subsystem by giving encouragement to non-bureau spokesmen. Certainly, even if the committee member does not feel especially sensitive about his status relative to that of bureaucrats, on occasions in which the committee member's interests lie counter to the bu-reau leader's, he may find it convenient to pretend that the bureaucrat is at-tempting to pre-empt the legislative function and to lay claim to a superior-ity of knowledge that is based on theory rather than on practicality.

The influence and effectiveness of groups in a subsystem may well fol-low long-range cyclical patterns. Over a period of more than a decade, dur-ing which the bureau leadership and the supporting leadership of the Ad-ministration were both unchanged, the pattern of group alignments for and against the policies of the bureau leaders remained fairly constant. But this was in one subsystem during an exceptionally long continuity in the policy orientation of the bureau. On the basis of a wider observation of the pat-terns of group-leader intervention in the subsystem, the broadest pattern appeared likely to be that tendencies toward extremes in policy were modi-fied by a process in which the "outs" used the committee members as sounding boards to work against the bureau leaders and their associated group leaders.

ISSUE NETWORKS AND THE EXECUTIVE ESTABLISHMENT
Hugh Heclo*

The connection between politics and administration arouses remarkably little interest in the United States. The presidency is considered more glamorous, Congress more intriguing, elections more exciting, and interest groups more troublesome. General levels of public interest can be gauged by the burst of indifference that usually greets the announcement of a new President's cabinet or rumors of a political appointee's resignation. Unless there is some White House "tie-in" or scandal (preferably both), news stories about presidential appointments are usually treated by the media as routine filler material.

This lack of interest in political administration is rarely found in other democratic countries, and it has not always prevailed in the United States. In most nations the ups and downs of political executives are taken as vital signs of the health of a government, indeed of its survival. In the United States, the nineteenth-century turmoil over one type of connection between politics and administration—party spoils—frequently overwhelmed any notion of presidential leadership. Anyone reading the history of those troubled decades is likely to be struck by the way in which political administration in Washington registered many of the deeper strains in American society at large. It is a curious switch that appointments to the bureaucracy should loom so large in the history of the nineteenth century, when the federal government did little, and be so completely discounted in the twentieth century, when government tries to do so much.

Political administration in Washington continues to register strains in American politics and society, although in ways more subtle than the nineteenth-century spoils scramble between Federalists and Democrats, Pro- and Anti-tariff forces, Nationalists and States Righters, and so on. Unlike many other countries, the United States has never created a high level, government-wide civil service. Neither has it been favored with a political structure that automatically produces a stock of experienced political manpower for top executive positions in government.[1] How then does political administration in Washington work? More to the point, how might the expanding role of government be changing the connection between administration and politics?

Received opinion on this subject suggests that we already know the answers. Control is said to be vested in an informal but enduring series of

*Hugh Heclo, "Issue Networks and the Executive Establishment," in *The New American Political System*, pp. 87-107, 115-124. Edited by Anthony King. Washington, D. C.: American Enterprise Institute, 1978. Used by permission.
[1]Hugh Heclo, *A Government of Strangers: Executive Politics in Washington* (Washington, D.C.: Brookings Institution, 1977).

"iron triangles" linking executive bureaus, congressional committees, and interest group clienteles with a stake in particular programs. A President or presidential appointee may occasionally try to muscle in, but few people doubt the capacity of these subgovernments to thwart outsiders in the long run.

Based largely on early studies of agricultural, water, and public works policies, the iron triangle concept is not so much wrong as it is disastrously incomplete.[2] And the conventional view is especially inappropriate for understanding changes in politics and administration during recent years. Preoccupied with trying to find the few truly powerful actors, observers tend to overlook the power and influence that arise out of the configurations through which leading policy makers move and do business with each other. Looking for the closed triangles of control, we tend to miss the fairly open networks of people that increasingly impinge upon government.

To do justice to the subject would require a major study of the Washington community and the combined inspiration of a Leonard White and a James Young. Tolerating a fair bit of injustice, one can sketch a few of the factors that seem to be at work. The first is growth in the sheer mass of government activity and associated expectations. The second is the peculiar, loose-jointed play of influence that is accompanying this growth. Related to these two is the third: the layering and specialization that have overtaken the government work force, not least the political leadership of the bureaucracy.

All of this vastly complicates the job of presidential appointees both in controlling their own actions and in managing the bureaucracy. But there is much more at stake than the troubles faced by people in government. There is the deeper problem of connecting what politicians, officials, and their fellow travelers are doing in Washington with what the public at large can understand and accept. It is on this point that political administration registers some of the larger strains of American politics and society, much as it did in the nineteenth century. For what it shows is a dissolving of organized politics and a politicizing of organizational life throughout the nation.

Government Growth in an Age of Improvement

Few people doubt that we live in a time of big government. During his few years in office, President Kennedy struggled to avoid becoming the first President with a $100 billion budget. Just seventeen years later, President Carter easily slipped into history as the first $500 billion President. Even in

---

[2]Perhaps the most widely cited interpretations are J. Leiper Freeman, *The Political Process* (New York: Random House, 1965); and Douglass Cater, *Power in Washington* (New York: Vintage, 1964).

(1949 = 100)

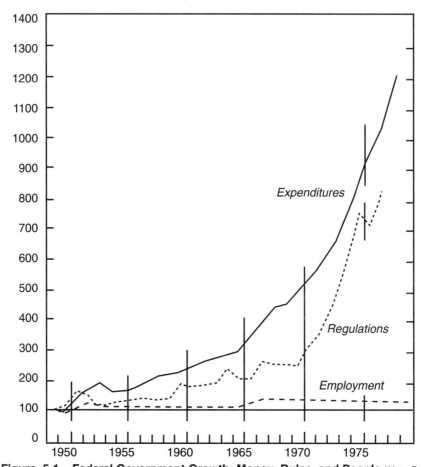

Figure 5-1   **Federal Government Growth: Money, Rules, and People** (*Note:* Federal spending on income and product account. Figures are on an accrual basis and include trust account transactions with the public as well as grants-in-aid to state and local governments. Employment covers total end-of-year civilian employees in full-time, permanent, temporary, part-time, and intermittent employment in the executive branch, including the Postal Service. Regulations are indicated by numbers of pages in *The Federal Register.* *Source:* The Tax Foundation, *Facts and Figures on Government Finance, 1977,* table 20, p. 33; U.S. Office of Management and Budget, *Special Analyses, Budget of the U.S. Government, 1979,* p. 210. Figures are taken from an unpublished table compiled by the Executive Agencies Division, Office of the Federal Register, Washington, D.C. I wish to express my gratitude to this division for their cooperation in supplying information.)

constant prices, the 1979 federal budget was about double that of 1960.[3] The late 1950s and the entire 1960s witnessed a wave of federal initiatives in health, civil rights, education, housing, manpower, income maintenance, transportation, and urban affairs. To these, later years have added newer types of welfare concerns: consumer protection, the environment, cancer prevention, and energy, to name only a few. Whatever today's conventional skepticism about the success of these programs, posterity will probably regard the last twenty-odd years as an extraordinarily ambitious, reform-minded period. The dominant feeling behind our age of improvement was best expressed by Adlai Stevenson in 1955 when he sensed a new willingness "to feel strongly, to be impatient, to want mightily to see that things are done better."[4]

However, we need to be clear concerning what it is that has gotten big in government. Our modern age of improvement has occurred with astonishingly little increase in the overall size of the federal executive establishment. Figure 5-1 traces changes in the raw materials of government: money, rules, and people from 1949 to 1977. The year 1955 represented a return to more normal times after the Korean conflict and may be taken as a reasonable baseline. Since that year national spending has risen sixfold in current dollars and has more than doubled in constant terms. Federal regulations (as indicated by pages in the *Federal Register*) have also sextupled. In the cases of both money and regulations, it was during the second Eisenhower administration that a new and expensive activism in public policy began to sweep through the national government. The landslide congressional victory by liberal Democrats in 1958, the challenge of Sputnik, the new stirrings of the civil rights movementóthese and other factors created a wave of government spending and regulation that has continued to roll ever since. The force of this growth was felt at least as much in the Nixon-Ford years as in the earlier decade of New Frontier/Great Society programs under Democratic Presidents.

Yet federal employment grew hardly at all in comparison with spending and regulations (up by less than one-fifth since 1955). Despite widespread complaints about the size of government, the federal bureaucracy is entitled to join foreign aid as one of that small band of cases where close to zero-growth has been the norm for the last twenty-five years.

The paradox of expanding government and stable bureaucracy has two explanations. In purely budgetary terms, much of the increase in federal outlays has been due to higher costs of existing policies. It does not nec-

---

[3]Office of Management and Budget, *The United States Budget in Brief, 1979* (Washington, D.C., 1978), p. 21.
[4]Adlai E. Stevenson, quoted in James L. Sundquist, *Politics and Policy* (Washington, D.C.: Brookings Institution, 1968), p. 385.

essarily require more bureaucrats to write larger checks. Such cost increases have been especially important in the area of income maintenance programs. Federal payments to individuals (social security, medical care, veterans' pensions, unemployment insurance, and public assistance) increased from $22 billion in 1960 to $167 billion in 1977, accounting for well over half of the total increase in federal domestic spending during these years.[5] Much of this increase came not from adding new programs but from higher bills for existing programs, particularly social security. Thus at the end of 1977, when federal outlays were at $402 billion, President Carter proposed a $500 billion budget for fiscal year 1979. Of the $98 billion increase, about 90 percent was due to the higher cost of existing policies and only 10 percent to new spending recommended by the President.[6] About one-quarter of the total cost increase was due simply to income security programs.

This sort of momentum in government obviously presents serious challenges to politicians in general and to politically appointed executives in particular. These are the people who tend to feel they have a mandate to "change things, shake up the bureaucracy" and who even in the best of circumstances have only a few years in which to do so. But there is a second and at least equally important explanation for the stability of the national bureaucracy in an era of increased policy interventionism. This factor creates even more profound problems for government leadership.

In the main, Washington has not attempted to apply its policies by administering programs directly to the general population. It has therefore been able to avoid bureaucratic giantism. This is true in many programs classified as payments to individuals (for example, Medicare and Medicaid funds pass through large numbers of administrative middlemen), and it is especially true in several of the policy areas that have grown the fastest since the mid-fifties. One such area is investment and subsidies for the physical environment. Grants for mass transit, waste treatment plants, highways, and the like have tripled in real terms since 1960. Another area rich in indirect administration falls under the heading of social investment and services; spending for education, health care, employment training, urban development, and social services has risen more than tenfold since 1960.[7] Rather than building and staffing its own administrative facilities for these programs, the federal government has preferred to act through intermediary organizations—state governments, city halls, third party payers,

[5]Office of Management and Budget, *The Budget in Brief, 1979,* p. 21.

[6]Office of Management and Budget, *Special Analyses, Budget of the United States Government, 1979* (Washington, D.C., 1978), table A-4, p. 12.

[7]Charles L. Schultze, "Federal Spending: Past, Present, and Future," in Henry Owen and Charles L. Schultze, *Setting National Priorities: The Next Ten Years* (Washington, D.C.: Brookings Institution, 1976), p. 335.

consultants, contractors, and many others. Administratively, the result is that what was true during the Eisenhower administration remains true today: despite huge increases in government programs, about the only time an ordinary citizen sees a federal bureaucrat is when his mail is delivered, his taxes are audited, or a trip to the local social security office becomes necessary (unless of course an FBI agent knocks on his door).

New policies associated with our modern age of improvement have tended to promote the idea of government by remote control. Political administration in Washington is heavily conditioned by an accumulation of methods for paying the bills and regulating the conduct of intermediary organizations. This pattern is consistent with a long tradition of fragmented and decentralized administration. Moreover, it offers important political and bureaucratic advantages. Spreading cash grants among various third party payers is an important way of building support for policies, translating otherwise indivisible collective goods into terms suitable for distributive politics. Rather than having to convince everyone of the value of a clean environment, government administrators can preside over a scramble for federal funds to subsidize construction of local sewage treatment plants. Likewise, in spending for health, manpower, transportation, and so on, the federal government has sidestepped the tremendously difficult task of creating a broad national consensus for its own administered activities. It has done so by counting on third parties to crave the funds which the national government makes available to serve its purposes. Recently Charles Schultze has argued that Washington should make greater use of market incentives to meet public ends.[8] Yet as far as fiscal relations in the political marketplace are concerned, a strong case could be made that in fact the federal government has done little else.

In terms of using intermediaries to administer the new melioristic policies, the mushrooming of federal regulations has much in common with federal spending. Rather than having to work at building and policing its own delivery mechanisms, the Washington bureaucracy can use regulations and then rest content with telling other public and private bureaucracies what should be done. This has the added advantage of allowing federal policy makers to distribute not only funds but also much of the blame when things go wrong.

One might suppose that the executive establishment in Washington has put itself in an extremely comfortable position, retailing the promise of improved policies and wholesaling the administrative headaches connected with delivery. Unfortunately, life has not been so kind. People increasingly expect Washington to solve problems but not to get in anyone's way in the

---

[8] Charles L. Schultze, *The Public Use of Private Interest* (Washington, D.C.: Brookings Institution, 1977).

process. The result is that policy goals are piled on top of each other without generating any commitment to the administrative wherewithal to achieve them. Even in the depths of anti-Washington sentiment, the overwhelming majority of Americans agreed that the federal government should control inflation, prevent depressions, assure international peace, regulate private business, and also ensure that the poor are taken care of, the hungry fed, and every person assured a minimum standard of living. A comparably large majority also felt that the federal government was too "big and bureaucratic.[9] As it turns out, therefore, the executive establishment in Washington tends to get the worst of both worlds—blamed for poor delivery by its public customers and besieged with bills from its middlemen.

Fraying at the Center

The strategy of responding to aspirations for improvement while maintaining a no-growth national administrative machine and relying on middlemen has succeeded in doing one thing. It has saved Washington policy makers from having to cope with what would otherwise have been an immense, nationwide bureaucracy. Yet far from simplifying operations, this "success" has vastly complicated the connection between administration and politics in Washington. Lacking their own electoral mandates, political administrators have always been in an ambivalent position in American government. Every ambitious new program, every clever innovation in indirect administration has merely deepened this ambivalence.

What is occurring at the national level is a peculiar "push-pull effect" on the relation between democratic politics and the executive establishment. On the one hand, government growth has pushed more and more policy concerns out of the federal government's own structure and into masses of intermediary, issue-conscious groups. On the other hand, the requirements for managing such a complex system are pulling government leadership further and further away from the nontechnical, nonspecialist understanding of the ordinary citizen and politician. It is worth looking more closely at how it is possible to be both politicizing organizational life and depoliticizing democratic leadership.

All Join In   During 1977-1978, Harvard University hired a Washington lobbyist and joined a loose group called Friends of DNA in an effort to influence federal regulation of research into the creation of new forms of

[9]U.S. Congress, Senate, Subcommittee on Intergovernmental Relations of the Committee on Government Operations, *Confidence and Concern: Citizens View American Government*, committee print, 93d Cong., 1st sess., 1973, part 2, pp. 111, 117, 118-19, 238.

life. The same year, the former militant chairman of the Black Panther party, Bobby Seale, founded a new Washington organization to lobby for community-controlled poverty programs. And the president of the national machinists' union convened a National Energy Coalition composed of environmentalists, neighborhood organizers, and consumer advocates. Perhaps not coincidentally, forty-seven congressmen announced their retirement, citing as the major reason a lack of enjoyment in the job.

Trivial in their own right, these incidents suggest something deeper than the feeling (probably true) that exercising power is not as much fun as it used to be in the clubby days of Washington politics. As more and more puzzling, unfamiliar policy issues have been thrust on government, more and more fluid groups have been unexpectedly mobilized. As proliferating groups have claimed a stake and clamored for a place in the policy process, they have helped to diffuse the focus of political and administrative leadership.

What has happened at the subnational level of government is a striking illustration of this process. Much of the bureaucratic expansion that might otherwise have occurred nationally has taken place in state and local governments. Between 1955 and 1977 state and local public employment grew by more than two and one-half times, to 12 million people, while federal employment hovered at around 2.5 million.[10] The increased interdependence of subnational and national bureaucracies has led to the growth of what Samuel H. Beer has termed the intergovernmental lobby.[11] Those in Washington whose memories go back a generation or more can recall a time when it was something of an occasion for a governor to undertake a mission to Washington. As Senator Moynihan (who was a junior aide to Governor Averell Harriman in the 1940s) put it, "You'd spend time planning how many shirts to take. Going to Washington was a very big deal."[12] Today, not only do governors or mayors as groups have their own specialized staffs permanently stationed in Washington, but large state governments, major units within state governments, and individual cities frequently have their own Washington offices or hired representatives. In addition to umbrella organizations such as the National Governors' Conference, the Conference of State Governments, the U.S. Conference of Mayors, the National League of Cities, the National Conference of State Legislatures, and the National Association of Counties, one finds the intergovernmental lobby peopled with representatives from groups such as the New York State Association of Counties, cities such as Detroit and Boston, major counties, various state water districts, boards of regents, and so on and on and on.

---

[10]Office of Management and Budget, *Special Analyses, 1979 Budget*, p. 33.
[11]Samuel H. Beer, "Political Overload and Federalism" *Polity*, vol. 10 (March 1977).
[12]Unpublished talk at the Brookings Institution, June 8, 1977.

Similarly, an even larger number of private and semi-private organizations have grown up as important extensions of the new federal policies. One of the enduring legacies of every reform movement in the United States—whether it was the Progressives' good government movement, Hoover's attempts at engineering voluntarism, or FDR's New Deal—has been to create new groups with a stake in the reformed processes and programs.[13] So too our own age of improvement his encouraged a blossoming of policy participants and kibitzers. In this instance (and this differentiates it somewhat from earlier periods) virtually everyone has accepted the idea that the national government in Washington is the decisive arena and will continue to be so indefinitely.

Some groups are nurtured by the government's own need for administrative help. For example, new neighborhood associations have been asked to take a major part in Washington's urban and housing programs. Or when the Consumer Product Safety Commission sets new standards for extension cords, the National Electrical Manufacturers' Association plays a major part in drawing up the new designs. Some groups are almost spontaneously called into being by what they can gain or lose from new federal policies or—perhaps just as often—the unforeseen consequences of these policies. For example, in the early 1970s Washington launched vigorous new efforts to promote grain exports. This generated not only new borrowing by farmers to expand production but also a new, militant farmers' organization (American Agriculture) when prices later fell from their export-led highs.

A key factor in the proliferation of groups is the almost inevitable tendency of successfully enacted policies unwittingly to propagate hybrid interests. The area of health care is rich in examples. Far from solidifying the established medical interests, federal funding and regulation of health care since the mid-1960s have had diverse impacts and therefore have tended to fragment what was once a fairly monolithic system of medical representation. Public policy has not only uncovered but also helped to create diverging interests among hospital associations, insurance companies, medical schools, hospital equipment manufacturers, local health planning groups, preventive medicine advocates, nonteaching research centers, and many others.[14] This does not necessarily mean that every group is in conflict with all of the others all of the time. The point is that even when government is not pursuing a deliberate strategy of divide and conquer, its activist policies greatly increase the incentives for groups to form around the differential ef-

[13]See for example Ellis Hawley, "Herbert Hoover and the Associative State," *Journal of American History*, June 1974; and Grant McConnell, *Private Power and American Democracy* (New York: Alfred Knopf, 1966), pp. 50, 69.

[14] A similar tendency for public involvement to divide private interests occurred with earlier health initiatives in other countries. See Arnold Heidenheimer, Hugh Heclo, and Carolyn Adams, *Comparative Public Policy* (New York: St. Martin's Press, 1976).

fects of these policies, each refusing to allow any other group to speak in its name.

While nothing should necessarily be assumed about their political power, trade and professional associations offer a revealing pattern of growth. The number of such groups has grown sharply during three periods: during the First World War, the first half of the 1930s, and the Second World War. Since 1945 the total number has been continuously increasing, and in recent years more and more of these groups have found it useful to make their headquarters in Washington. During the 1970s the number of trade and professional associations headquartered in Washington surpassed that in New York for the first time, climbing to 1,800 organizations with 40,000 employees in 1977. Well over half of the nation's largest associations (those with annual budgets of over $1 million) are now located in the Washington metropolitan area.[15] This takes no account of the large number of consumer and other public interest groups that have sprouted all over the nation's capital since the early 1960s.[16]

Of course Americans' love affair with interest groups is hardly a new phenomenon. From abolitionists to abortionists there has never been a lack of issue-conscious organizations; in the 1830s, Tocqueville described how the tariff question generated an early version of local consumer groups and a national lobbying association.[17] Yet if the current situation is a mere outgrowth of old tendencies, it is so in the same sense that a 16-lane spaghetti interchange is the mere elaboration of a country crossroads. With more public policies, more groups are being mobilized and there are more complex relationships among them. Since very few policies ever seem to drop off the public agenda as more are added, congestion among those interested in various issues grows, the chances for accidental collisions increase, and the interaction tends to take on a distinctive group-life of its own in the Washington community. One scene in a recent Jacques Tati film pictures a Paris traffic circle so dense with traffic that no one can get in or out; instead, drivers spend their time socializing with each other as they drive in endless circles. Group politics in Washington may be becoming such a merry-go-round.

How these changes influence the substance of public policy processes depends on what it is that the burgeoning numbers of participants want.

[15]Craig Colgate, Jr., ed., *National Trade and Professional Associations* (Washington, D.C.: Columbia Books, 1978).

[16]For example, a statement issued by Ralph Nader on April 24, 1978, criticizing the Carter energy program included endorsements by the Natural Resources Defense Council Inc., Friends of the Earth Inc., the Environmental Policy Center, the Environmental Action Foundation, Environmentalists for Full Employment, the Wilderness Society, Consumer Action Now, the Sierra Club, the Environmental Defense Fund Inc., the National Parks and Conservation Association, and the National Consumers League.

[17]Alexis de Tocqueville, *Democracy in America* (New York: Harper and Row, 1966), p. 176.

Obviously their wants vary greatly, but to a large extent they are probably accurately reflected in the areas of greatest policy growth since the late 1950s—programs seeking social betterment in terms of civil rights, income, housing, environment, consumer protection, and so on—what I will simply refer to as "welfare policies." The hallmark of these policies seems to reflect attitudes in the general public.[18] What is wanted is not more equal outcomes or unfair preferences. No, if there is a theme in the clamor of group politics and public policy, it is the idea of compensation. Compensation for what? For past racial wrongs, for current overcharging of consumers, for future environmental damage. The idea of compensatory policy—that the federal government should put things right—fits equally well for the groups representing the disadvantaged (special treatment is required for truly equal opportunity to prevail) and for those representing the advantaged (any market-imposed loss can be defined as a special hardship). The same holds for newer public interest groups (government action is required to redress the impact of selfish private interests). If middle-class parents have not saved enough for college costs they should be compensated with tuition tax credits. If public buildings are inaccessible to the physically handicapped, government regulations should change that. If farmers overinvest during good times, they should be granted redress from the consequences of their actions. The old American saying "there oughtta be a law" had a negative connotation of preventing someone from getting away with something. Today the more prevalent feeling is "there oughtta be a policy," and the connotation of getting in on society's compensations is decidedly positive.

In sum, new initiatives in federal funding and regulation have infused old and new organizations with a public policy dimension, especially when such groups are used as administrative middlemen and facilitators. Moreover, the growing body of compensatory interventions by government has helped create a climate of acceptance for ever more groups to insist that things be set right on their behalf. What matters is not so much that organizations are moving to Washington as that Washington's policy problems are coming to occupy so many different facets of organizational life in the United States.

Policy as an Intramural Activity   A second tendency cuts in a direction opposite to the widening group participation in public policy. Expanding welfare policies and Washington's reliance on indirect administration have encouraged the development of specialized subcultures composed of highly knowledgeable policy-watchers. Some of these people have ad-

---

[18]Seymour Martin Lipset and William Schneider, "The Bakke Case: How Would It Be Decided at the Bar of Public Opinion?" *Public Opinion* (March/April 1978), pp. 41-42.

vanced professional degrees, some do not. What they all have in common is the detailed understanding of specialized issues that comes from sustained attention to a given policy debate.

Certain of these changes are evident in the government's own work force. Employees in the field and in Washington who perform the routine chores associated with direct administration have become less prominent. More important have become those officials with the necessary technical and supervisory skills to oversee what other people are doing. Thus the surge in federal domestic activities in the 1960s and 1970s may not have increased the overall size of the bureaucracy very much, but it did markedly expand the upper and upper-middle levels of officialdom. Compared with an 18 percent rise in total civilian employment, mid-level executive positions in the federal government (that is, supergrade and public law 313 equivalents) have increased approximately 90 percent since 1960. Some of these changes are due to a slow inflation of job titles and paper credentials that can be found in private as well as public organizations. But case studies in the 1960s suggested that most of this escalation occurring in the Washington bureaucracy could be traced to the new and expanded public programs of that decade.[19] The general effect of these policy changes has been to require more technical skills and higher supervisory levels, overlaying routine technicians with specialist engineers, insurance claims examiners with claims administrators, and so on. Approximately two-fifths of mid-level executives in the bureaucracy (grades 16—18 or the equivalent) are what might loosely be termed scientists, though frequently they are in fact science managers who oversee the work of other people inside and outside of the government.

Increasing complexity and specialization are affecting leaders in all modern organizations, even profit-oriented enterprises with stable sets of clear goals. For decision makers in government—where the policy goals have been neither stable nor clear in the last twenty years—the pressures for more expert staff assistance have become immense. This is as true for legislators as it is for public executives. President Nixon estimated that he personally saw no more than 200,000 of the 42 million pieces of paper in his own presidential materials. Recent studies of Congress estimate that the average member of the House of Representatives has, out of an eleven-hour workday, only eleven minutes to devote personally to reading and only twelve minutes in his or her own office to spend personally on writing legislation and speeches.[20] Congress, like the executive branch, has responded to the pressures by creating more specialists and top-side staff. Since 1957

[19]McKinsey and Company, Inc., "Strengthening Control of Grade Escalation" (Office of Management and Budget Archives: processed, June 1966).

[20] *Washington Post*, August 28, 1977, p. 1.

the total number of personal and committee staff on the Hill has climbed from 4,300 to 11,000 and over 20,000 more persons service the legislature from institutional staff positions (the General Accounting Office, Congressional Budget Office, and so on).[21] At the core of this blossoming congressional bureaucracy are bright, often remarkably young, technocrats who are almost indistinguishable from the analysts and subject matter specialists in the executive branch.

There are many straws in the wind to indicate the growing skill base of policy professionals in Washington. Executive search firms (so-called headhunters) have found a booming market in recent years, with many new firms being founded and prestigious New York organizations opening up Washington offices. One indicator of this movement, the amount of "professional opportunity" advertising in the press, now puts Washington on a par with Los Angeles and New York as an executive hunting ground for the private sector. The reason is clear. As government activities and regulations have grown, the value of policy specialists who understand the complex Washington environment has appreciated in the eyes of all of the private organizations with a stake in government activity. Another indicator is the mushrooming of new Washington law firms. Typically these firms are headed by former government officials and practice in substantive areas of law and policy that did not exist twenty years ago.

Again it is tempting to borrow a term from Professor Beer and to refer to these groups of policy specialists as constituting a "professional-bureaucratic complex." Certainly there are many core groups with scientific or professional training which have carved out spheres of bureaucratic influence over health, highways, education, and so on. Likewise the familiar nexus of less professional, economic interests can still be found linking various parts of the Washington community. But the general arrangement that is emerging is somewhat different from the conventional image of iron triangles tying together executive bureaus, interest groups, and congressional committees in all-powerful alliances.

Unfortunately, our standard political conceptions of power and control arc not very well suited to the loose-jointed play of influence that is emerging in political administration. We tend to look for one group exerting dominance over another, for subgovernments that are strongly insulated from other outside forces in the environment, for policies that get "produced" by a few "makers." Seeing former government officials opening law firms or joining a new trade association, we naturally think of ways in which they are trying to conquer and control particular pieces of government machinery.

Obviously questions of power are still important. But for a host of pol-

---

[21] Harrison W. Fox, Jr. and Susan Webb Hammond, *Congressional Staffs* (New York: Free Press, 1977).

icy initiatives undertaken in the last twenty years it is all but impossible to identify clearly who the dominant actors are. Who is controlling those actions that go to make up our national policy on abortions, or on income redistribution, or consumer protection, or energy? Looking for the few who are powerful, we tend to overlook the many whose webs of influence provoke and guide the exercise of power. These webs, or what I will call "issue networks," are particularly relevant to the highly intricate and confusing welfare policies that have been undertaken in recent years.

The notion of iron triangles and subgovernments presumes small circles of participants who have succeeded in becoming largely autonomous. Issue networks, on the other hand, comprise a large number of participants with quite variable degrees of mutual commitment or of dependence on others in their environment; in fact it is almost impossible to say where a network leaves off and its environment begins. Iron triangles and subgovernments suggest a stable set of participants coalesced to control fairly narrow public programs which are in the direct economic interest of each party to the alliance. Issue networks are almost the reverse image in each respect. Participants move in and out of the networks constantly. Rather than groups united in dominance over a program, no one, as far as one can tell, is in control of the policies and issues. Any direct material interest is often secondary to intellectual or emotional commitment. Network members reinforce each other's sense of issues as their interests, rather than (as standard political or economic models would have it) interests defining positions on issues.

Issue networks operate at many levels, from the vocal minority who turn up at local planning commission hearings to the renowned professor who is quietly telephoned by the White House to give a quick "reading" on some participant or policy. The price of buying into one or another issue network is watching, reading, talking about, and trying to act on particular policy problems. Powerful interest groups can be found represented in networks but so too can individuals in or out of government who have a reputation for being knowledgeable. Particular professions may be prominent, but the true experts in the networks are those who are issue-skilled (that is, well informed about the ins and outs of a particular policy debate) regardless of formal professional training. More than mere technical experts, network people are policy activists who know each other through the issues. Those who emerge to positions of wider leadership are policy politicians—experts in using experts, victuallers of knowledge in a world hungry for right decisions.

In the old days—when the primary problem of government was assumed to be doing what was right, rather than knowing what was right—policy knowledge could be contained in the slim adages of public administration. Public executives, it was thought, needed to know how to execute. They needed power commensurate with their responsibility. Nowadays, of course, political administrators do not execute but are involved in making highly important decisions on society's behalf, and they must mobilize policy intermediaries to deliver the goods. Knowing what is right becomes crucial, and since no one knows that for sure, going through the process of dealing with those who are judged knowledgeable (or at least continuously concerned) becomes even more crucial. Instead of power commensurate with responsibility, issue networks seek influence commensurate with their understanding of the various, complex social choices being made. Of course some participants would like nothing better than complete power over the issues in question. Others seem to want little more than the security that comes with being well informed. As the executive of one new group moving to Washington put it, "We didn't come here to change the world; we came to minimize our surprises."[22]

Whatever the participants' motivation, it is the issue network that ties together what would otherwise be the contradictory tendencies of, on the one hand, more widespread organizational participation in public policy and, on the other, more narrow technocratic specialization in complex modern policies. Such networks need to be distinguished from three other more familiar terms used in connection with political administration. An issue network is a shared-knowledge group having to do with some aspect (or, as defined by the network, some problem) of public policy. It is therefore more well-defined than, first, a shared-attention group or "public"; those in the networks are likely to have a common base of information and understanding of how one knows about policy and identifies its problems. But knowledge does not necessarily produce agreement. Issue networks may or may not, therefore, be mobilized into, second, a shared-action group (creating a coalition) or, third, a shared-belief group (becoming a conventional interest organization). Increasingly, it is through networks of people who regard each other as knowledgeable, or at least as needing to be answered, that public policy issues tend to be refined, evidence debated, and alternative options worked out—though rarely in any controlled, well-organized way.

What does an issue network look like? It is difficult to say precisely, for at any given time only one part of a network may be active and through time the various connections may intensify or fade among the policy intermediaries and the executive and congressional bureaucracies. For example, there is no single health policy network but various sets of people knowledgeable and concerned about cost-control mechanisms, insurance techniques, nutritional programs, prepaid plans, and so on. At one time, those expert in designing a nationwide insurance system may seem to be operating in relative isolation, until it becomes clear that previous efforts to control costs have already created precedents that have to be accommodated in

---

[22] Steven V. Roberts, "Trade Associations Flocking to Capital as U.S. Role Rises," *New York Times,* March 4, 1978, p. 44

any new system, or that the issue of federal funding for abortions has laid land mines in the path of any workable plan.

The debate on energy policy is rich in examples of the kaleidoscopic interaction of changing issue networks. The Carter administration's initial proposal was worked out among experts who were closely tied in to conservation-minded networks. Soon it became clear that those concerned with macroeconomic policies had been largely bypassed in the planning, and last-minute amendments were made in the proposal presented to Congress, a fact that was not lost on the networks of leading economists and economic correspondents. Once congressional consideration began, it quickly became evident that attempts to define the energy debate in terms of a classic confrontation between big oil companies and consumer interests were doomed. More and more policy watchers joined the debate, bringing to it their own concerns and analyses: tax reformers, nuclear power specialists, civil rights groups interested in more jobs; the list soon grew beyond the wildest dreams of the original energy policy planners. The problem, it became clear, was that no one could quickly turn the many networks of knowledgeable people into a shared-action coalition, much less into a single, shared-attitude group believing it faced the moral equivalent of war. Or, if it was a war, it was a Vietnam-type quagmire.

It would be foolish to suggest that the clouds of issue networks that have accompanied expanding national policies are set to replace the more familiar politics of subgovernments in Washington. What they are doing is to overlay the once stable political reference points with new forces that complicate calculations, decrease predictability, and impose considerable strains on those charged with government leadership. The overlay of networks and issue politics not only confronts but also seeps down into the formerly well-established politics of particular policies and programs. Social security, which for a generation had been quietly managed by a small circle of insiders, becomes controversial and politicized. The Army Corps of Engineers, once the picturebook example of control by subgovernments, is dragged into the brawl on environmental politics. The once quiet "traffic safety establishment" finds its own safety permanently endangered by the consumer movement. Confrontation between networks and iron triangles in the Social and Rehabilitation Service, the disintegration of the mighty politics of the Public Health Service and its corps—the list could be extended into a chronicle of American national government during the last generation.[23] The point is that a somewhat new and difficult dynamic is

---

[23] For a full account of particular cases, see for example Martha Derthick, *Policy-Making for Social Security* (Washington, D.C.: Brookings Institution, forthcoming); Daniel Mazmanian and Jeanne Nienaber, *Environmentalism, Participation and the Corps of Engineers: A Study of Organizational Change* (Washington, D.C.: Brookings Institution, 1978). For the case of traffic safety, see Jack L. Walker, "Setting the Agenda in the U.S. Senate," *British Journal of Political Science*, vol. 7 (1977), pp. 432-45.

being played out in the world of politics and administration. It is not what has been feared for so long: that technocrats and other people in white coats will expropriate the policy process. If there is to be any expropriation, it is likely to be by the policy activists, those who care deeply about a set of issues and are determined to shape the fabric of public policy accordingly.

The Technopols

The many new policy commitments of the last twenty years have brought about a play of influence that is many-stranded and loose. Iron triangles or other clear shapes may embrace some of the participants, but the larger picture in any policy area is likely to be one involving many other policy specialists. More than ever, policy making is becoming an intramural activity among expert issue-watchers, their networks, and their networks of networks. In this situation any neat distinction between the governmental structure and its environment tends to break down.

Political administrators, like the bureaucracies they superintend, are caught up in the trend toward issue specialization at the same time that responsibility is increasingly being dispersed among large numbers of policy intermediaries. The specialization in question may have little to do with purely professional training. Neither is it a matter of finding interest group spokesmen placed in appointive positions. Instead of party politicians, today's political executives tend to be policy politicians, able to move among the various networks, recognized as knowledgeable about the substance of issues concerning these networks, but not irretrievably identified with highly controversial positions. Their reputations among those "in the know" make them available for presidential appointments. Their mushiness on the most sensitive issues makes them acceptable. Neither a craft professional nor a gifted amateur, the modern recruit for political leadership in the bureaucracy is a journeyman of issues.

Approximately 200 top presidential appointees are charged with supervising the bureaucracy. These political executives include thirteen departmental secretaries, some half a dozen nondepartmental officials who are also in the cabinet, several dozen deputy secretaries or undersecretaries, and many more commission chairmen, agency administrators, and office directors. Below these men and women are another 500 politically appointed assistant secretaries, commissioners, deputies, and a host of other officials. If all of these positions and those who hold them are unknown to the public at large, there is nevertheless no mistaking the importance of the work that they do. It is here, in the layers of public managers, that political promise confronts administrative reality, or what passes for reality in Washington.

At first glance, generalization seems impossible. The political executive system in Washington has everything. Highly trained experts in medicine, economics, and the natural sciences can be found in positions where there is something like guild control over the criteria for a political appointment. But one can also find the most obvious patronage payoffs; obscure commissions, along with cultural and inter-American affairs, are some of the favorite dumping grounds. There are highly issue-oriented appointments, such as the sixty or so "consumer advocates" that the Ralph Nader groups claimed were in the early Carter administration. And there are also particular skill groups represented in appointments devoid of policy content (for example, about two-thirds of the top government public relations positions were filled during 1977 with people from private media organizations). In recent years, the claims of women and minorities for executive positions have added a further kind of positional patronage, where it is the number of positions rather than any agreed policy agenda that is important. After one year, about 11 percent of President Carter's appointees were women, mainly from established law firms, or what is sometimes referred to as the Ladies' Auxiliary of the Old Boys' Network.

How to make sense of this welter of political executives? Certainly there is a subtlety in the arrangements by which top people become top people and deal with each other. For the fact is that the issue networks share information not only about policy problems but also about people. Rarely are high political executives people who have an overriding identification with a particular interest group or credentials as leading figures in a profession. Rather they are people with recognized reputations in particular areas of public policy. The fluid networks through which they move can best be thought of as proto-bureaucracies. There are subordinate and superordinate positions through which they climb from lesser to greater renown and recognition, but these are not usually within the same organization. It is indeed a world of large-scale bureaucracies but one interlaced with loose, personal associations in which reputations are established by word of mouth. The reputations in question depend little on what, in Weberian terms, would be bureaucratically rational evaluations of objective performance or on what the political scientist would see as the individual's power rating. Even less do reputations depend on opinions in the electorate at large. What matters are the assessments of people like themselves concerning how well, in the short term, the budding technopol is managing each of his assignments in and at the fringes of government.

The Executive Leadership Problem

Washington has always relied on informal means of producing political leaders in government. This is no less true now than in the days when party spoils ruled presidential appointments. It is the informal mechanisms that have changed. No doubt some of the increasing emphasis on educational credentials, professional specialization, and technical facility merely reflects changes in society at large. But it is also important to recognize that government activity has itself been changing the informal mechanisms that produce political administrators. Accumulating policy commitments have become crucial forces affecting the kind of executive leadership that emerges. E. E. Schattschneider put it better when he observed that "new policies create new politics."[24]

For many years now the list of issues on the public agenda has grown more dense as new policy concerns have been added and few dropped. Administratively, this has proliferated the number of policy intermediaries. Politically, it has mobilized more and more groups of people who feel they have a stake, a determined stake, in this or that issue of public policy. These changes are in turn encouraging further specialization of the government's work force and bureaucratic layering in its political leadership. However, the term "political" needs to be used carefully. Modern officials responsible for making the connection between politics and administration bear little resemblance to the Party politicians who once filled patronage jobs. Rather, today's political executive is likely to be a person knowledgeable about the substance of particular issues and adept at moving among the networks of people who are intensely concerned about them.

What are the implications for American government and politics? The verdict cannot be one-sided, if only because political management of the bureaucracy serves a number of diverse purposes. At least three important advantages can be found in the emerging system.

First, the reliance on issue networks and policy politicians is obviously consistent with some of the larger changes in society. Ordinary voters are apparently less constrained by party identification and more attracted to an issue-based style of politics. Party organizations are said to have fallen into a state of decay and to have become less capable of supplying enough highly qualified executive manpower. If government is committed to intervening in more complex, specialized areas, it is useful to draw upon the experts and policy specialists for the public management of these programs. Moreover, the congruence between an executive leadership and an electorate that are both uninterested in party politics may help stabilize a rapidly changing society. Since no one really knows how to solve the policy puzzles, policy politicians have the important quality of being disposable without any serious political ramifications (unless of course there are major symbolic implications, as in President Nixon's firing of Attorney General Elliot Richardson).

Within government, the operation of issue networks may have a second advantage in that they link Congress and the executive branch in ways

---

[24] E. E. Schattschneider, *Politics, Pressures and the Tariff* (Hamden: Archon, 1963), p. 288 (originally published 1935).

that political parties no longer can. For many years, reformers have sought to revive the idea of party discipline as a means of spanning the distance between the two branches and turning their natural competition to useful purposes. But as the troubled dealings of recent Democratic Presidents with their majorities in Congress have indicated, political parties tend to be a weak bridge.

Meanwhile, the linkages of technocracy between the branches are indeliberately growing. The congressional bureaucracy that has blossomed in Washington during the last generation is in many ways like the political bureaucracy in the executive branch. In general, the new breed of congressional staffer is not a legislative crony or beneficiary of patronage favors. Personal loyalty to the congressman is still paramount, but the new-style legislative bureaucrat is likely to be someone skilled in dealing with certain complex policy issues, possibly with credentials as a policy analyst, but certainly an expert in using other experts and their networks.

None of this means an absence of conflict between President and Congress. Policy technicians in the two branches are still working for different sets of clients with different interests. The point is that the growth of specialized policy networks tends to perform the same useful services that it was once hoped a disciplined national party system would perform. Sharing policy knowledge, the networks provide a minimum common framework for political debate and decision in the two branches. For example, on energy policy, regardless of one's position on gas deregulation or incentives to producers, the policy technocracy has established a common language for discussing the issues, a shared grammar for identifying the major points of contention, a mutually familiar rhetoric of argumentation. Whether in Congress or the executive branch or somewhere outside, the "movers and shakers" in energy policy (as in health insurance, welfare reform, strategic arms limitation, occupational safety, and a host of other policy areas) tend to share an analytic repertoire for coping with the issues. Like experienced party politicians of earlier times, policy politicians in the knowledge networks may not agree; but they understand each other's way of looking at the world and arguing about policy choices.

A third advantage is the increased maneuvering room offered to political executives by the loose-jointed play of influence. If appointees were ambassadors from clearly defined interest groups and professions, or if policy were monopolized in iron triangles, then the chances for executive leadership in the bureaucracy would be small. In fact, however, the proliferation of administrative middlemen and networks of policy watchers offers new strategic resources for public managers. These are mainly opportunities to split and recombine the many sources of support and opposition that exist on policy issues. Of course, there are limits on how far a political executive can go in shopping for a constituency, but the general tendency over time has been to extend those limits. A secretary of labor will obviously pay close attention to what the AFL-CIO has to say, but there are many other voices to hear, not only in the union movement but also minority groups interested in jobs, state and local officials administering the department's programs, consumer groups worried about wage-push inflation, employees faced with unsafe working conditions, and so on. By the same token, former Secretary of Transportation William Coleman found new room for maneuver on the problem of landings by supersonic planes when he opened up the setpiece debate between pro- and anti-Concorde groups to a wider play of influence through public hearings. Clearly the richness of issue politics demands a high degree of skill to contain expectations and manage the natural dissatisfaction that comes from courting some groups rather than others. But at least it is a game that can be affected by skill, rather than one that is predetermined by immutable forces.

These three advantages are substantial. But before we embrace the rule of policy politicians and their networks, it is worth considering the threats they pose for American government. Issue networks may be good at influencing policy, but can they govern? Should they?

The first and foremost problem is the old one of democratic legitimacy. Weaknesses in executive leadership below the level of the President have never really been due to interest groups, party politics, or Congress. The primary problem has always been the lack of any democratically based power. Political executives get their popular mandate to do anything in the bureaucracy secondhand, from either an elected chief executive or Congress. The emerging system of political technocrats makes this democratic weakness much more severe. The more closely political administrators become identified with the various specialized policy networks, the farther they become separated from the ordinary citizen. Political executives can maneuver among the already mobilized issue networks and may occasionally do a little mobilizing of their own. But this is not the same thing as creating a broad base of public understanding and support for national policies. The typical presidential appointee will travel to any number of conferences, make speeches to the membership of one association after another, but almost never will he or she have to see or listen to an ordinary member of the public. The trouble is that only a small minority of citizens, even of those who are seriously attentive to public affairs, are likely to be mobilized in the various networks.[25] Those who are not policy activists depend on the ability of government institutions to act on their behalf.

If the problem were merely an information gap between policy experts and the bulk of the population, then more communication might help.

---

[25]An interesting recent case study showing the complexity of trying to generalize about who is "mobilizable" is James N. Rosenau, *Citizenship Between Elections* (New York: The Free Press, 1974).

Yet instead of garnering support for policy choices, more communication from the issue networks tends to produce an "everything causes cancer" syndrome among ordinary citizens. Policy forensics among the networks yield more experts making more sophisticated claims and counterclaims to the point that the non-specialist becomes inclined to concede everything and believe nothing that he hears. The ongoing debates on energy policy, health crises, or arms limitation are rich in examples of public skepticism about what "they," the abstruse policy experts, are doing and saying. While the highly knowledgeable have been playing a larger role in government, the proportion of the general public concluding that those running the government don't seem to know what they are doing has risen rather steadily.[26] Likewise, the more government has tried to help, the more feelings of public helplessness have grown.

No doubt many factors and events are linked to these changing public attitudes. The point is that the increasing prominence of issue networks is bound to aggravate problems of legitimacy and public disenchantment. Policy activists have little desire to recognize an unpleasant fact: that their influential systems for knowledgeable policy making tend to make democratic politics more difficult. There are at least four reasons.

Complexity Democratic political competition is based on the idea of trying to simplify complexity into a few, broadly intelligible choices. The various issue networks, on the other hand, have a stake in searching out complexity in what might seem simple. Those who deal with particular policy issues over the years recognize that policy objectives are usually vague and results difficult to measure. Actions relevant to one policy goal can frequently be shown to be inconsistent with others. To gain a reputation as a knowledgeable participant, one must juggle all of these complexities and demand that other technocrats in the issue networks do the same.

Consensus A major aim in democratic politics is, after open argument, to arrive at some workable consensus of views. Whether by trading off one issue against another or by combining related issues, the goal is agreement. Policy activists may commend this democratic purpose in theory, but what their issue networks actually provide is a way of processing

---

[26]Since 1964 the Institute for Social Research at the University of Michigan has asked the question, "Do you feel that almost all of the people running the government are smart people, or do you think that quite a few of them don't seem to know what they are doing?" The proportions choosing the latter view have been 28 percent (1964), 38 percent (1968), 45 percent (1970), 42 percent (1972), 47 percent (1974), and 52 percent (1976). For similar findings on public feelings of lack of control over the policy process, see U.S. Congress, Senate, Subcommittee on Intergovernmental Relations of the Committee on Government Operations, *Confidence and Concern: Citizens View American Government,* committee print, 93d Cong., 1st sees., 1973, pt. 1, p. 30. For a more complete discussion of recent trends see the two articles by Arthur H. Miller and Jack Citrin in the *American Political Science Review* (September 1974).

dissension. The aim is good policy—the right outcome on the issue. Since what that means is disputable among knowledgeable people, the desire for agreement must often take second place to one's understanding of the issue. Trade-offs or combinations—say, right-to-life groups with nuclear-arms-control people; environmentalists and consumerists; civil liberties groups and anti-gun controllers represent a kind of impurity for many of the newly proliferating groups. In general there are few imperatives pushing for political consensus among the issue networks and many rewards for those who become practiced in the techniques of informed skepticism about different positions.

Confidence Democratic politics presumes a kind of psychological asymmetry between leaders and followers. Those competing for leadership positions are expected to be sure of themselves and of what is to be done, while those led are expected to have a certain amount of detachment and dubiety in choosing how to give their consent to be governed. Politicians are supposed to take credit for successes, to avoid any appearance of failure, and to fix blame clearly on their opponents; voters weigh these claims and come to tentative judgments, pending the next competition among the leaders.

The emerging policy networks tend to reverse the situation. Activists mobilized around the policy issues are the true believers. To survive, the newer breed of leaders, or policy politicians, must become well versed in the complex, highly disputed substance of the issues. A certain tentativeness comes naturally as ostensible leaders try to spread themselves across the issues. Taking credit shows a lack of understanding of how intricate policies work and may antagonize those who really have been zealously pushing the issue. Spreading blame threatens others in the established networks and may raise expectations that new leadership can guarantee a better policy result. Vagueness about what is to be done allows policy problems to be dealt with as they develop and in accord with the intensity of opinion among policy specialists at that time. None of this is likely to warm the average citizen's confidence in his leaders. The new breed of policy politicians are cool precisely because the issue networks are hot.

Closure Part of the genius of democratic politics is its ability to find a nonviolent decision-rule (by voting) for ending debate in favor of action. All the incentives in the policy technocracy work against such decisive closure. New studies and findings can always be brought to bear. The biggest rewards in these highly intellectual groups go to those who successfully challenge accepted wisdom. The networks thrive by continuously weighing alternative courses of action on particular policies, not by suspending disbelief and accepting that something must be done.

For all of these reasons, what is good for policy making (in the sense of involving well-informed people and rigorous analysts) may be bad for democratic politics. The emerging policy technocracy tends, as Henry Aaron has said of social science research, to "corrode any simple faiths around which political coalitions ordinarily are built."[27] Should we be content with simple faiths? Perhaps not; but the great danger is that the emerging world of issue politics and policy experts will turn John Stuart Mill's argument about the connection between liberty and popular government on its head. More informed argument about policy choices may produce more incomprehensibility. More policy intermediaries may widen participation among activists but deepen suspicions among unorganized nonspecialists. There may be more group involvement and less democratic legitimacy, more knowledge and more Know-Nothingism. Activists are likely to remain unsatisfied with, and nonactivists uncommitted to, what government is doing. Superficially this canceling of forces might seem to assure a conservative tilt away from new, expansionary government policies. However, in terms of undermining a democratic identification of ordinary citizens with their government, the tendencies are profoundly radical.

A second difficulty with the issue networks is the problem that they create for the President as ostensible chief of the executive establishment. The emerging policy technocracy puts presidential appointees outside of the chief executive's reach in a way that narrowly focused iron triangles rarely can. At the end of the day, constituents of these triangles can at least be bought off by giving them some of the material advantages that they crave. But for issue activists it is likely to be a question of policy choices that are right or wrong. In this situation, more analysis and staff expertise—far from helping—may only hinder the President in playing an independent political leadership role. The influence of the policy technicians and their networks permeates everything the White House may want to do. Without their expertise there are no option papers, no detailed data and elaborate assessments to stand up against the onslaught of the issue experts in Congress and outside. Of course a President can replace a political executive, but that is probably merely to substitute one incumbent of the relevant policy network for another.

It is, therefore, no accident that President Carter found himself with a cabinet almost none of whom were either his longstanding political backers or leaders of his party. Few if any of his personal retinue could have passed through the reputational screens of the networks to be named, for example, a secretary of labor or defense. Moreover, anyone known to be close to the President and placed in an operating position in the bureaucracy puts him-

---

[27]Henry J. Aaron, *Politics and the Professors* (Washington, D.C.: Brookings Institution, 1978), p. 159.

self, and through him the President, in an extremely vulnerable position. Of the three cabinet members who were President Carter's own men, one, Andrew Young, was under extreme pressure to resign in the first several months. Another Carter associate, Bert Lance, was successfully forced to resign after six months, and the third, Griffin Bell, was given particularly tough treatment during his confirmation hearings and was being pressured to resign after only a year in office. The emerging system of political administration tends to produce executive arrangements in which the President's power stakes are on the line almost everywhere in terms of policy, whereas almost nowhere is anyone on the line for him personally.

Where does all this leave the President as a politician and as an executive of executives? In an impossible position. The problem of connecting politics and administration currently places any President in a classic no-win predicament. If he attempts to use personal loyalists as agency and department heads, he will be accused of politicizing the bureaucracy and will most likely put his executives in an untenable position for dealing with their organizations and the related networks. If he tries to create a countervailing source of policy expertise at the center, he will be accused of aggrandizing the Imperial Presidency and may hopelessly bureaucratize the White House's operations. If he relies on some benighted idea of collective cabinet government and on departmental executives for leadership in the bureaucracy (as Carter did in his first term), then the President does more than risk abdicating his own leadership responsibilities as the only elected executive in the national government; he is bound to become a creature of the issue networks and the policy specialists. It would be pleasant to think that there is a neat way out of this trilemma, but there is not.

Finally, there are disturbing questions surrounding the accountability of a political technocracy. The real problem is not that policy specialists specialize but that, by the nature of public office, they must generalize. Whatever an influential political executive does is done with all the collective authority of government and in the name of the public at large. It is not difficult to imagine situations in which policies make excellent sense within the cloisters of the expert issue watchers and yet are nonsense or worse seen from the viewpoint of ordinary people, the kinds of people political executives rarely meet. Since political executives themselves never need to pass muster with the electorate, the main source of democratic accountability must lie with the President and Congress. Given the President's problems and Congress's own burgeoning bureaucracy of policy specialists, the prospects for a democratically responsible executive establishment are poor at best.

Perhaps we need not worry. A case could be made that all we are seeing is a temporary commotion stirred up by a generation of reformist policies. In time the policy process may reenter a period of detumescence as the new groups and networks subside into the familiar triangulations of power.

However, a stronger case can be made that the changes will endure. In the first place, sufficient policy-making forces have now converged in Washington that it is unlikely that we will see a return to the familiar cycle of federal quiescence and policy experimentation by state governments. The central government, surrounded by networks of policy specialists, probably now has the capacity for taking continual policy initiatives. In the second place, there seems to be no way of braking, much less reversing, policy expectations generated by the compensatory mentality. To cut back on commitments undertaken in the last generation would itself be a major act of redistribution and could be expected to yield even more turmoil in the policy process. Once it becomes accepted that relative rather than absolute deprivation is what matters, the crusaders can always be counted upon to be in business.

A third reason why our politics and administration may never be the same lies in the very fact that so many policies have already been accumulated. Having to make policy in an environment already crowded with public commitments and programs increases the odds of multiple, indirect impacts of one policy on another, of one perspective set in tension with another, of one group and then another being mobilized. This sort of complexity and unpredictability creates a hostile setting for any return to traditional interest group politics.

Imagine trying to govern in a situation where the short-term political resources you need are stacked around a changing series of discrete issues, and where people overseeing these issues have nothing to prevent their pressing claims beyond any resources that they can offer in return. Imagine too that the more they do so, the more you lose understanding and support from public backers who have the long-term resources that you need. Whipsawed between cynics and true believers, policy would always tend to evolve to levels of insolubility. It is not easy for a society to politicize itself and at the same time depoliticize government leadership. But we in the United States may be managing to do just this.

PATTERNS OF INFLUENCE AMONG COMMITTEES, AGENCIES, AND INTEREST GROUPS
Keith Hamm*

This essay examines research on the patterns of influence among legislative committees, executive agencies, and interest groups. While the essay summarizes and synthesizes literature covering a number of political systems, it draws a substantial number of theoretical and descriptive statements from studies of legislatures whose policy-making powers are relatively strong (i.e., active or vulnerable legislatures [Mezey, 1979]) and whose committee systems are considered moderately important in the legislative process (see Lees and Shaw, 1979).

The literature review is organized around six major topics.[1] The essay first examines research on the conceptual characteristics of subgovernments, emphasizing different classificatory criteria. Second, the essay summarizes research on the effect of a commonality of interests or priorities among the interest groups, legislative committees, and executive agencies.

*Keith Hamm, "Patterns of Influence Among Committees, Agencies, and Interest Groups." *Legislative Studies Quarterly* VIII (Aug., 1983): 379-426. Used by permission.

[1]Several decision rules were employed in writing this paper.

Preference was given to studies which develop theoretical statements or test relationships; descriptive case studies are cited typically only where they can be linked to some theoretical point.

Studies which treat either the committee, interest group, or agency or the individual committee members, lobbyists, or administrators as the unit of analysis are included.

Studies are not included if they only analyzed the relative importance of a particular subsystem in the policy formulation or policy implementation process; in addition, to be included, the study had to contain discussions of the conditions under which the various subsystem participants (e.g., interest groups) are able to affect the behavior of individuals in other parts of the subsystem (e.g., agencies or committees).

Given the emphasis on legislative studies, this essay does not concentrate on research which only examines the linkages between interest groups and administrative agencies. However, an expanded review could analyze the general patterns of interaction (e.g., Peters, 1977; Ehrmann, 1961), the extent of agency "capture" by interest groups (e.g., Bernstein, 1955; Sabatier, 1975; Culhane, 1981), interest group representation on agency committees (e.g., Christensen and Egeberg, 1979; Buksti and Johansen, 1979; Helander, 1979; Kvavik, 1975; Olsen, 1977; Leiserson, 1942), or parentela relationships (e.g., LaPalombara, 1964).

Given that the topic of oversight is being covered in another review piece, most studies in this area have not been included (e.g., Bibby, 1966; Scher, 1960,1963; Cotter and Smith, 1957; Fiorina, 1981; Ogul, 1976; Kaiser, 1977; Johnson, 1980; Jahnige, 1968; Aberbach, 1979; Schubert, 1958; Kerr, 1965; Ethridge, 1981; Harris, 1964), although those which specifically focus on legislative control, interest groups, and agencies are analyzed.

Research which focuses on the entire legislature (e.g., city council) without discussing the committees is typically excluded.

Because of translation and acquisition difficulties, most studies not printed in English are excluded.

I wish to acknowledge the helpful written comments of Morris Fiorina, Malcolm Jewell, and Samuel Patterson as well as suggestions by numerous participants at the Legislative Research Conference in Iowa City, Iowa, October 25-27,1982.

The literature reviewed demonstrates the extent of commonality within and across different legislative bodies. The literature also describes the types of individuals who occupy the strategically placed decision-making positions within the subsystem and their effect on the influence patterns which develop. Finally, it describes the effects of variable committee recruiting processes, the overrepresentation of "interesteds" on committees, and the circulation of personnel among different parts of the subsystem.

A third body of literature describes interaction patterns among members of the triad. Emphasis is on information search patterns, communication networks, methods of communication, and role orientations. The research here deals with whether and how committee members differ from the non- members in their interaction patterns with interest groups and executive agency personnel. Researchers have also studied what techniques of communication are employed, what the shape of the communications network among members of the subsystem is, and what the consequences of this network may be.

The fourth area of research reviewed here examines exchange relationships—mutually beneficial transactions—among interest groups, agencies, and committee members. There are several major research questions here: What are the bases for, and behavioral consequences of, transactions between agencies and committees, and between interest groups and committees and secondarily between agencies and interest groups? To what extent do these exchanges differ in kind or magnitude from those which interest groups or agencies have with nonmembers? How does this exchange process vary by issue, level of support, or type of legislature?

A fifth area of the literature ascertains the unique contributions that committees, agencies, and interest groups make to the policy process. The influence of the participants is evaluated according to the stage in the policy making process, the type of committee, the type of issue, the type of environmental factors, and so on. Necessary conditions for agency or interest group impact are examined as well as the consequences of different strategic decisions.

The final section of this essay reviews the literature on appropriations politics. It summarizes research on agency-committee relationships, the impact of internal and external factors on committee budget decisions, variations in agencies' budget strategies, committee impact on agencies' substantive policy, methods of legislative control, and variations in subcommittees' supervision and control.

Subsystem Characteristics

Scholars have noted that in some political systems particular policy areas are dominated by an executive agency, legislative committees with the appropriate jurisdiction, and relevant interest groups. An early observer of this phenomenon commented that

> the relationship among these men—legislators, administrators, lobbyists, scholars—who are interested in a common problem is a much more real relationship than the relationships between congressmen generally or between administrators generally (Griffith, 1939, pp. 182-183).

To describe these relationships, the researcher's lexicon came to include such terms as "whirlpools," "cozy triangles," "subgovernments," "subsystems," "iron triangles," and so on.

Researchers have traced the development and change in subgovernments (Dodd and Schott, 1979), the extent to which subgovernments predominate in various policy areas (Ripley and Franklin, 1980), and the extent to which legislators accept bureaucratic and clientele-group interaction (Aberbach and Rockman, 1978). Electoral security among congressmen is traced, in part, to the existence of many subgovernments.

> In sum, the decentralization of congressional power has created numerous subgovernments that enable individual members to control policy decisions and influence elements of the bureaucracy which are of particular concern to their districts. Increased electoral security is the natural result (Fiorina, 1977, p. 67).

Research has also produced a plethora of single-policy studies, including studies of river development (Maass, 1950, 1951), Indian affairs (Freeman, 1965), civil aviation (Redford, 1960), agricultural policy (Lowi, 1973), sugar and military affairs (Cater, 1964), manpower programs (Davidson, 1975), and merchant shipping policies (Lawrence, 1966), to name only a few.

While most of these case studies are descriptive and limited to one topic and may be time bound, they provide a glimpse of the variety of interaction and influence patterns. Each functional subsystem falls somewhere on a continuum for several leading characteristics: (1) internal complexity (Davidson, 1975, p. 105); (2) functional autonomy (Davidson, 1975, pp. 105-106); (3) unity within type of participant (Redford, 1969, p. 97); and (4) cooperation or conflict among different participants (Freeman, 1965, pp. 113-114). "Internal complexity" refers to the number and variety of participants in the subsystem. Some are relatively simple, composed of a few key individuals in each sector, as are the sugar or Indian affairs subsystems; others are more complex, loosely defined systems involving numerous agencies and interest groups, as are the civil aviation, manpower, military-industrial, and maritime subgovernments. In some cases, change occurs within a policy area. For example, "the *cozy little triangles* which had come to characterize the development of energy policies had become *sloppy large hexagons*" (Jones, 1979, p. 105). Some argue that the complexity of the various subsystems in Congress has increased as a result of decentralization of power

(Dodd and Schott, 1979, p. 124), and that "several committees could claim responsibility for particular bureaus, agencies, and programs" (p. 125).

"Functional autonomy" refers to the extent to which policies are formulated and implemented within the subsystem, "with scant attention from actors in other subsystems, much less the public at large" (Davidson, 1975, p. 105). As a later section of this essay indicates, researchers have shown that the autonomy of the subsystem can vary as a function of the type of policy (see Ripley and Franklin, 1980). Case study material also highlights this variation; for example, Freeman (1965) indicates that administrators in the Bureau of Indian Affairs tried to obtain departmental or executive support, but Lawrence (1966) shows that the participants in merchant marine policy tried to "resolve problems through negotiation rather than referring them to the president or the Congress as a whole" (p. 331).

Third, most studies describe the unity among the individuals in each sector—agencies, interest groups, and committees. Some subsystems display considerable disunity. As Freeman (1965) shows in his analysis of Indian affairs, various positions are taken by the substantive committees and the appropriations subcommittees or by the clientele groups and the nonclientele groups. On the other hand, Maass's studies (1950, 1951) of river and harbor development suggested much more harmonious relations within each sector.

Finally, the patterns of cooperation or conflict among the interest groups, committees, and agencies vary across different policies within the same legislature. Thus, Maass presents a picture of a significantly cohesive subsystem, while Freeman indicates more disagreement and tension. In addition, analysis of the same policy in different legislatures uncovers dissimilar relationships. For example, Masters, Salisbury, and Elliot (1964) describe different patterns for education policy in different states, ranging from a significantly cooperative system in which no deep-seated controversies emerge to one in which uncertainty and conflict prevail. What factors account for these patterns of conflict or cooperation and subsequent patterns of influence? A major factor is the sharing of common interest among participants.

Commonality of Interests

An initial consideration of the influence patterns among committees, agencies, and interest groups may take into account the extent to which these sectors have similar perspectives or similar interests. To understand any similarities or variations in perspectives, it is necessary to know how committees recruit members, whether committees overrepresent a given interest, and whether the various sectors interchange personnel or have overlapping memberships.

Recruitment   Under what conditions do interest groups influence the recruitment of legislators to committees? On occasion, a particular group is said to have been involved in the appointment process. For example, the business lobby group was "directly influential in the appointments of chairmen and members of the committees considered of probable concern to the business group" (Garceau and Silverman, 1954, p. 673). Or we find that in Italy, a major objective of the interest group is to affect the appointment of the *relatore*, since this person can expedite or delay any bill he investigates (LaPalombara, 1964,p. 222).

One perspective on the interest group—committee recruitment linkage—is provided in Buchanan's (1963) study of the California legislature during a relatively nonpartisan period. In this system of reciprocal influence, a set of interest groups provided campaign funds or endorsements to supporters during elections to office. Then, on the vote for speaker, lobby supporters would typically vote for the candidate recommended. The lobby would recommend supporters for powerful and strategic committee assignments, the supporters would request assignments strategic to the lobby, and the speaker would act upon the suggestions and requests. The speaker would refer relevant bills to committees controlled by supporters, the lobby would testify to provide "reasons" for supporters actions, and the supporters would speak, make motions, act, and vote in support of the lobby (p. 46). However, given the lack of necessary data, it is impossible to test the relationships.

What if interest groups do not necessarily control the appointment process? Do the "interesteds" "gravitate to decision arenas in which their interests are promoted," thus providing "the fertile environment in which clientelism flourishes" (Shepsle, 1978, p. 248)?

This question has been studied by researchers who focus on either the legislator's articulated goals or his/her interests, as defined by constituency or background. In the former, the motivating force is the member's specific goals. Interviewing a new class of House members, Bullock (1976) used Fenno's (1973) typology of committee preference motives—reelection, policy making, and prestige—to determine among other things the relative importance of each goal and the extent to which each goal is associated with a particular committee. Because Congress has legislators with different goals and committees with varying degrees of attractiveness, its committees "are often unrepresentative of the chamber, not to mention the political system at large" (Davidson, 1974, p. 52).

Studies of the committee recruitment process also relate legislators' interests to actual committee assignment requests. Studies analyzing requests by Democratic members of the U.S. House focus on district and personal characteristics or federal spending in specific policy areas in each legislative district.

Rohde and Shepsle (1973) develop a social choice process involving requestors, the Committee on Committees, and leadership. Committees are found to differ in their relative attractiveness to various groups of legislators: for the five committees specifically studied, interesteds are at least twice as likely to apply for a specific committee position as are indifferents (pp. 895-896), and the Committee on Committees serves a management goal, satisfying requestor demands rather than trying to match individuals to committees on the basis of constituency characteristics (p. 900).

In a second study Shepsle (1978) concludes that the committee assignment process can be characterized as "an *interest-advocacy-accommodation syndrome* in which interests are articulated, advanced, and accommodated in a highly institutionalized . . . fashion" (p. 231). Request behavior is based on a member's interests—involving a set of constituency and personal background factors—plus a set of likelihood of assignment variables (pp. 64-68). The findings, while varying somewhat from committee to committee, indicate that "for all of the major legislative committees (plus Interior), 'interest' variables exert a strong independent effect on request likelihood" (p. 232). The effect is greatest where there is an obvious linkage between committee jurisdiction and constituency-clientele interests, and the effect is least for committees which have jurisdictions of general interest to many constituencies (p. 232). Individual Committee on Committee members, because of a series of factors, adopt an advocacy role (pp. 234-235); party leaders, "as they negotiate a new committee structure, give significant weight to the wishes of their followers" (p. 236); and the full Committee on Committees accommodates a substantial proportion of freshman committee requests (p. 237). The major consequence is that "the accommodation of interests at the stage at which members seek committee assignments is the necessary first step in the creation of enduring relationships among legislators, lobbyists and agency personnel in particular policy areas" (p. 247).

In the third study, Ray (1980c) examines whether "the pre-existing geographic distribution of federal spending dictates representatives' committee assignments" (p. 495). The major independent variables are the federal outlays in congressional districts for six spending areas. Findings indicate that most members who request a committee with jurisdiction over one of these spending areas represent districts in which federal spending in that area is higher-than-average; in addition, in multivariate analysis, "those whose constituencies have the highest levels of involvement in a spending area are most likely to request a matching committee assignment" (p. 505).

What effect can party leaders have on controlling the gravitation of interesteds to specific committees? In some legislatures their appointment power varies across different subject-matter committees. Thus, as Loewenberg shows, the fact that interest groups are overrepresented on some committees of domestic policy in the German Bundestag is "due to the influ-

ence of the interests within the parliamentary parties . . . and to the dependence of the party leaders on the subject expertise which often only the 'interested' member can supply" (1967, p. 199). Yet, these interests do not
dominate a particular subject-matter committee since they are not distributed uniformly across all parties. The parliamentary parties are thought to
encourage a heterogeneous membership on the committee, although "success varies with the pressure exerted by the interest groups" (p. 113).

Beth and Havard (1961) and Havard and Beth (1962), in their studies
of committee stacking in the Florida legislature, note that presiding officers
not only overrepresented some committees with members who agreed with
their own political policies but also stacked certain committees whose jurisdiction included a specific economic interest so that the committee represented that interest (1961, p. 69). Thus, "legislators with personal or representative stakes in the interest with which the committee deals make up all
or almost all of the membership" (1962, pp. 141-142).

Interest Overrepresentation   Some studies do not examine the process of appointment but instead focus on distribution of obvious interesteds
on the committees and comment on possible consequences. For example, in
one of the earliest studies, the relationship between a legislator's occupa-
tion and the topic of his/her committee assignment was explored in the
Maryland and Pennsylvania legislatures, although no complete profile was
provided (Winslow, 1931).

In one of the more complete studies, Damgaard (1977) systematically
links sectoral politics to committee composition in the Danish Folketinget, a
unicameral legislature, during the 1972-1973 and 1973-1974 periods. Examining the legislator's occupational position and experiences which may be
related to a committee's jurisdiction, Damgaard finds that

> in both sessions, and without exceptions, committee members are very fre-
> quently associated with the relevant sector of society and have related inter-
> ests outside the legislative arena. . . . On the average it applies to at least one-
> half of the committee members whereas only one-fifth could be expected to
> have such affiliations by chance (1977, p. 301).

However, it is unclear whether the affiliations of the members always pre-
cede the appointment to the committee, an important causal question
(1977, pp. 300-301). A diachronic analysis over two sessions lends further
support to the idea of sectoral specialization. Among members who actually continue on a committee, 58 percent have sectoral affiliation, while
among members leaving the committee, the figure is only 37 percent (1977,
p. 303).

Scholars, whether focusing on an interest group perspective (Brown,
1956, 1957; Ehrman, 1958) or concentrating on the legislative perspective
(Williams, 1954, 1964; Harrison, 1958), have noted that certain interests were

frequently overrepresented on specific committees during the Fourth French Republic due to defense of local interests, electoral considerations, advancement of personal interests, and previous experiences (Harrison, 1958, p. 174; Williams, 1954, p. 240). The overrepresentation effect was actually greater than it appeared since the *bureaux* of the committee and the *rapporteurs* were said to contain an excessive number of members representing the interested groups (Harrison, 1958, pp. 177-178). However, in the Fifth Republic, the discipline maintained by the majority in the committee, coupled with the increased size of the new committees, "made it harder than before for a few pressure-group spokesmen to win a majority by packing a meeting, or by skillful log-rolling" (Williams, 1968, p. 64).

Overrepresentation of a particular interest can be exacerbated by assigning committee members to subcommittees according to the interests of their constituency. Thus, Jones (1961, 1962) points out that Agriculture Committee members are assigned to subcommittees dealing with commodities mainly of concern to their constituencies; these representatives are then permitted to write legislation in the specialized commodity subcommittees (1962, p. 331).

Even in legislatures where the committees are not an important factor, legislators with perceived ties to major interest groups are sometimes accommodated. Thus, in the Japanese Diet, committee members are given assignments in order to perform an errand-running function for interest groups (Kim, 1975, p. 73). However, members serve on a committee for only a few years, since the leadership does not want strong ties to develop among committee members, relevant government personnel, and interest groups (p. 72).

Overlapping Membership and Circulation of Personnel The circulation of personnel among interest groups, agency positions, committee staffs, and personal staffs is often seen as one way to increase access and interaction. Such circulation patterns have been described in studies of committee staff in the U.S. Congress (Fox and Hammond, 1977) and of *rapporteurs* in the French Senate Finance Committee (Lord, 1973, pp. 153- 154). One case study indicates that interest group-committee ties expanded when a former chairperson and a staff member of a committee left congressional service and became staff consultants to lobbying groups (Haider, 1974, pp. 237-238); another case study showed that committee-agency ties expanded when the administrative assistant to the chairperson of a committee became administrator of the agency under its supervision (Vinyard, 1968).

Consequences of Variations in Commonality of Interests Freeman's (1965) study of Indian affairs examines committees whose members overrepresented distinct sociocultural values, values which diverged from those of the agency administering the program. Here the substantive committees dealing with Indian affairs were overrepresented by legislators elected by white majorities in constituencies with Indian minorities. Freeman suggests that one can "better understand the committee's frequent tendencies to work counter to a Bureau that promoted the interests of Indian minorities in the face of objections by local whites" (p. 100).

By contrast, Maass's (1950, 1951) studies of river and harbor development indicate how commonality of interests affected policy decisions. Members of Congress from areas that traditionally had great need for flood protection, drainage, or river navigation requested positions on committees which had jurisdiction over the Corps of Engineers. Thus, the Committee on Public Works and the Corps developed a very close identity of interests (1951, p. 580). These legislators, strategically located, became honorary members of major relevant interest groups (1951, p. 46). Interest group-agency relations were also close (1951, p. 46). These relationships seemed to routinize a series of decision-making rules. The Projects Committee of the Rivers and Harbors Congress would not, as a general rule, endorse a project unless the Corps had given a favorable or noncommittal report (1951, p. 49), and the Committee on Public Works did not usually authorize any project which had not received a favorable survey report from the Corps (1951, p. 30). Moreover, the committees in charge of writing the navigation and flood control legislation blocked even from the president, major initiatives (e.g., establishment of river valley authorities) which the Corps opposed (1950, p. 589).

Does overrepresentation have direct, significant effects on policy outcomes? Several studies hint at the effects, or try to describe them in very general terms without examining any alternative factors. Two studies very thoroughly investigate the overrepresentation phenomena. Oppenheimer (1974), using a comparative case study approach, focuses on the effects of the constituency-interests variable, rules and procedures, interest group competition, and policy type in two major policy areas—oil depletion allowance and water pollution legislation. After reviewing the linkages extensively and acknowledging that constituency ties are an important factor in the success of an interest group, he summarizes the material on overrepresentation.

> When we compile all this evidence, we find that the level of constituency ties is in some way related to the industry's success on each issue. At best, however, it operates in a haphazard fashion. It is certainly not a sufficient explanatory variable for understanding the degree of industry success. But just as clearly it is not an unrelated variable (1974, p.60).

Studying one of the same policies but using a longitudinal design, Bond (1979) indicates the extent of overrepresentation of oil states on congressional tax committees and its relationship to the oil depletion allowance from 1900 to 1974. Two points raised in Bond's article are important. First, in testing for overrepresentation on a committee, other factors must be taken into account and controlled. When Bond controlled other factors (i.e., previous committee assignments for both tax committee equations and delegation size in the Ways and Means equation), he found "no evidence that oil states exhibit a greater preference for representation on the tax committees than non-oil states at any time in the legislative history of the oil depletion allowance" (p. 657). Second, the analysis of changes in the oil depletion allowance must be tested using a longitudinal design covering several years. Bond's longitudinal study revealed that changes in the legislation which increased the oil depletion allowance were not related to periods in which oil states were overrepresented on the tax committees nor to the number of key congressional leaders from oil states (p. 659). He suggests caution "about extending the subgovernment explanation to different types of committees and to different policy arenas" (p. 662).

Information, Communication, and Influence

Several scholars have investigated the interaction patterns of members of the triad. Most studies use only one political system, typically the national level of the United States, to test their hypotheses, and some analyze only one committee or the behavior of members of one committee or subcommittee. Therefore, additional research to test the various hypotheses in different legislative settings is necessary. Research conducted to date may be classified by whether it concentrates on information usage patterns, direct techniques of communication, committee hearings, role orientations, or the influence of communications.

Information Usage Patterns   Research on legislators' information usage patterns has produced numerous published studies (e.g., Porter, 1974, 1975; Robert B. Bradley, 1980; Wissel, O'Connor, and King, 1976; van Schendelen, 1976). As a specific subgroup, committee members have been analyzed to determine what their important information sources are, whether they have different information search patterns than nonmembers, and what role uncertainty plays in the type of source they consult.

To what extent do committee members or staff rely on interest groups and agency personnel for information? Maisel (1981), in his study of U.S. House members and patterns of using personal staff, found that "members rely most heavily on their own staffs in order to learn what they need to know to perform all aspects of their jobs" (pp. 258-259). The legislative assistants, in turn, rely most heavily on committee staff, also an important source for legislators, for committee work (pp. 259, 263). A greater percentage of legislators and their assistants indicate that lobbyists, rather than the administration, are more important as an information source for committee work (pp. 259, 263). Committee staff at the congressional level, and in some state legislatures, also rely heavily on executive agencies (Fox and Hammond, 1977, pp. 121-122; Balutis, 1975, p. 126).

Do committee and noncommittee members rely on different information sources? In interviews with 40 members of Congress, Scott and Hunt (1966) try to ascertain interest group activity in one field in which the legislators specialized and one in which they did not. Specialization was not always equated with membership on the appropriate committee, limiting the utility of the findings for this analysis. However, one useful finding is that members with low seniority on the committee generally attributed greater importance to organized groups than those with high seniority (p. 66).

Zwier (1979) compares the search processes for specialists (i.e., members who sit on the subcommittee initially considering a bill) and nonspecialists in the U.S. House by interviewing 50 members on one specialist bill and one nonspecialist bill. While nonspecialists tended to rely heavily on congressional sources, subcommittee members utilized external sources, such as executive branch personnel and interest groups. Confirmation of a loose subgovernment phenomena is forthcoming: "when legislators did mention the administration as a source of information, most of them referred to the department or agency that had proposed the legislation or would have responsibility for executing it" (p- 38); moreover, most of these contacts were with program people, not with those who specialize in liaison work (p. 38).

To what extent is uncertainty a critical variable motivating committee members to tap external sources of information (Francis, 1971)? Entin (1974), in his survey of House Armed Services Committee members and associated private groups, found that committee decision patterns are routinized, group norms further group communication, and the committee is relatively cohesive (p. 148). Thus, uncertainty is reduced and the need for outside information sources is minimal (p. 148). Most committee members stated that information provided by the private associations was of little consequence, and relatively few members rated the private groups as being part of their information environment (p. 147). Yet groups saw themselves as providing information which is important to the committee members (p. 148). Why the discrepancy? It appears to evolve from differing assumptions about the role of communications in the lobbying process: "groups consider themselves effective because they have been given the opportunity to present a case," while for committee members the "transfer of information serves to legitimate decisions already made" (p. 149).

Direct Techniques of Communication   How do lobbyists convey their messages to committee members? An initial assumption is that to be effective, lobbyists have to interact with legislators regularly and frequently (Zeigler and Baer, 1969, p. 146). Studies indicate that there are cross-national differences in interaction patterns, due in part to the political structure (Presthus, 1974; Von Nordheim and Taylor, 1976) and that there are cross-state differences and substantial intrastate differences in legislators' and lobbyists' perceptions as to the frequency of interaction (Zeigler and Baer, 1969).

What generalizations have been developed in this literature about the effectiveness of various techniques? In interviews, lobbyists in certain states and in Washington indicated direct communication techniques—personal presentation of viewpoints, presenting research results, and testifying at hearings—as being most effective, while indirect contacts via intermediaries are somewhat less effective and the wining and dining least useful (Porter, 1974, p. 718; Zeigler and Baer, 1969, p. 176; Milbrath, 1963, pp. 392-393). What are the conditions, variations, or qualifications associated with the direct personal approach? From interviews with legislators and lobbyists in four state legislatures, Zeigler and Baer (1969) found that in three of the four states, legislators and lobbyists believe that direct, personal communication is most effective the longer they have been engaged in either legislating or lobbying (p. 178). As to the effectiveness of various techniques, lobbyists, more than legislators, perceive personal presentation of requests to be more effective, while they perceive presentation of research results and testimony at hearings to be less effective (p. 175). Committee hearings provide for a substantial amount of interchange between legislators and lobbyists, although there is some variation among state legislatures (p. 162). Finally "communication unrelated to hearings is not important," although "it is probably best to look upon the formal hearing as a climax to a series of communications" (p. 165).

Under what conditions will lobbyists vary their behavior? Bacheller (1977) suggests that a key factor is the type of issue being considered. He hypothesizes that lobbyists dealing with group-defined, noncontroversial issues will concentrate lobbying efforts on the committee, rely on techniques that are most appropriate in committee, and interact primarily with committee staff. Lobbyists dealing with campaign-defined, controversial issues will be more oriented to floor activity, rely on techniques more appropriate for floor action, and will be more likely to approach members of Congress themselves. If lobbyists are dealing with a group-defined controversial issue, their behavior should fall somewhere between that for the other two cases just described (p. 254). Analysis of responses from 118 Washington lobbyists confirms these hypotheses. One interesting finding is that the use of committee specialized techniques, such as submitting statements or testifying before committees, does not vary by type of issue; but nonspecialized techniques, such as contacting congressmen or other interest groups, are utilized more by lobbyists dealing with campaign-related issues. In addition, "mass groups were found to rely more on letters and telegram campaigns, while nonmass groups rely on telephone and direct contact by a few influential constituents" (p.262). Since few of the issues are campaign defined, Bacheller suggests that to study political outcomes, emphasis should be placed on ascertaining how committee decision makers are recruited and how committee decisions are made (p. 262).

Importance of Committee Hearings   One type of direct communication technique which is seen as important, at least in the United States, is testifying at the committee hearing. In fact, Herring ([1929], 1967) suggested that the new lobby concentrates its efforts on the hearing, not on entertaining or on unethical dealings behind the scenes. Rather, "it is at the hearings held by the committees of Congress that the lobbyist today performs his heavy work" (1967, pp. 71-72).

Aside from general statements as to the functions the hearings perform for the various legislative participants (e.g., Zeigler and Peak, 1972, p. 140; Truman, 1971, p. 372; Huitt, 1973, p. 108; Gross, 1953, pp. 284-308), there are analyses as to who testifies in a policy area (Cahn, 1974), case studies which focus on testimony on a particular bill (e.g., Schattschneider, 1935—see the fifth section of this literature review, on policy making), and general studies which use information from the hearing to find clusters of interest group cooperation patterns (Ross, 1970) or to determine attitudes of citizen witnesses (Van der Slik and Stenger, 1977).

From interviews with lobbyists, generalizations about the lobbyists' behavior emerge. Rather than have the lobbyist testify, the typical case has a "working member of the lobby group speak" (Milbrath, 1963, p. 231). In their four-state study of lobbyists, Zeigler and Baer (1969) note that generally the more experienced lobbyists spend more time at committee hearings than novices do (p. 170), but the more influential lobbyists do not rely upon committee hearings as much as do less influential ones (p. 171), and those scoring lower on the persuasibility index are more likely to rely on the hearings(p. 171).

Committee Members' Role Orientations   Legislative role orientations have been emphasized as one way to understand interest group access and influence (e.g., Wahlke, Buchanan, Eulau, and Ferguson, 1960; Davidson, 1969; Bell and Price, 1975). When role orientations have been applied to studying committee-interest group-agency relationships, different roles have been determined from interactions at committee hearings. Huitt (1954) is able to provide a description of the various roles (e.g., representatives of sectional interests) members assumed at a hearing on a controversial program, although no data on the distribution of roles is presented. In testing whether the committee is a fact finding agency or a participant in the political struggle, a major theoretical point is noted.

> The Committee and its witnesses were made up of two loose groups of people who disagreed, not so much in their opinions upon what should be done about a known or ascertainable fact situation, as upon what the underlying facts themselves were. . . .The interest group orientation furnished the pattern of preconceptions through which the facts were screened (p. 367).

DelSesto (1980) ascertained, in systematic empirical fashion, whether members of the Joint Committee on Atomic Energy displayed different role behaviors toward different witnesses testifying at committee hearings. Using hearings from the 1973-1974 period, witnesses were categorized into one of four groups. Committee member roles were dichotomized into those which were cooperative—investigator, instrumentalist, and organizer/administrator—and those which were antagonistic—debunker of facts, procedural antagonist, and debunker of qualifications (pp. 231-232). The major finding is that the members' role behaviors varied tremendously, depending on the witnesses' affiliation. Antagonistic committee roles occurred less than 4 percent of the time toward the Atomic Energy Commission, nuclear power industry, or nuclear community witness groups, while for environmental and concerned citizens, the figure rises to 64 percent (p. 235). As DelSesto notes,

> on the basis of the analysis there is strong evidence that the Committee appeared very closely aligned and cooperative with the subsystem, while appearing antagonistic and unresponsive to outside groups who brought their views before the Committee hoping for support (p. 240).

Communication and Influence Patterns   Research focusing on the frequency of communication has examined the structure of communication patterns, the importance of the receiver's orientation toward the group, and impact of such communication. Thomas (1970) analyzed the perceived frequencies of communication during an 18-month period among members of the U.S. national education policy system. Acknowledging that the existence of communication does not imply that an influence relationship exists, he still suggests that "the greater the frequency of communication between two individuals, the greater the probability that an influence relationship can develop" (p. 56). Using smallest space analysis, the sender and receiver of communication are arrayed along three dimensions—institutional affiliation, level of education toward which the person is oriented, and exclusiveness of contacts with governmental personnel (pp. 63-64). A major finding is that the principal operating agency occupies a central position in the communication network, confirming Freeman's contention that bureaus have a more influential role than do their departments in relationships with Congress (1965, p. 75). As to the role of legislative committees in this particular network,

> as one would expect, the data reveal that there is frequent communication between key congressional figures such as committee and subcommittee chairmen and staff directors and bureaucrats having legislative liaison and program control functions. Congress does not, however, appear to be as effectively integrated with the operating agencies as are interest groups, but along with the agency, Congress does serve as a major point of access for the lobbies (p. 76).

The receptivity of the decision maker to the communicator is taken into account in Wolman's analysis of the national housing subsystem (1971). While access is related to frequency of communication, effective access requires that a group's views be represented within the decision-making elite (p. 67). While two different groups have the same amount of communication with decision makers, the receptivity of the individuals to the particular group's message may vary substantially. For the housing policy system during the 1960s, this differential response translates into the following:

> it is the groups which in general terms supported the Johnson Administration programs which are best represented. Moreover, it is the more conservative groups rather than the more radical groups whose views were most rejected by members of the elite (pp. 68-699).

In the only published study to systematically link influence to communications, Kovenock (1973) utilized a communication audit technique to compile data on six representatives of the U.S. Congress, all members of the same "interest" subcommittee. This design was chosen intentionally to test Freeman's (1965) ideas regarding a policy subsystem (p. 449). Communication was defined as "premises transmitted from one relevant person to another" (pp. 410-411); influence occurs "when person B accepts an X-relevant premise communicated by person A regarding decision X" (pp. 410-411). Both legislator attribution and subsequent behavior tests were used for gauging influence. In terms of integration and autonomy of the policy-making subgovernment, nearly three out of four influential premises came from legislators, staffers, governmental officials, and interest groups with formal roles in the specific policy area, with these government officials and organized interest groups each contributing 15 percent of the influential premises (Table 7, p. 451). When communications by members within the subsystem are compared to communications with those outside, the closed nature of the process is apparent.

> A representative with a formal J role (i.e., a J subcommittee member) was over 50 times as likely to receive an influential J premise from another individual with a J role than from a 'typical' House colleague without such a role. Our Ss received 25 times as many influential J legislative premises from J subcommittee and K committee staff personnel than from all other congressional committee and party staffers combined, eight times as many from governmental officials with formal roles in J matters than from all those without them, and nearly eight times as many from interest groups whose paramount legislative interests were in J policy than from all groups whose major interests lay in non-J policy fields (p. 451).

On the other hand, these individuals within the subsystem accounted for only a few percent of the influential communications in other policy areas (pp. 451-452).

Exchange Relationships

From one perspective, the operation of the subsystem is a series of exchange relationships. Since each sector of the subsystem can influence, to a certain degree, the goal attainment of the others, there is an incentive for exchanges to transpire which are mutually beneficial. Committee members provide interest groups with legislation suitable to their requests and influence the agency in the implementation of programs, particularly where discretion is available. Legislators provide agencies with secure and expanded budgets as well as programs they requested. From interest groups, committee members receive electoral support, policy information, research, and so on. From agencies, legislators receive an expeditious and favorable consideration of requests from their districts, programs which benefit their constituents, and implementation of laws to benefit their constituents. Finally, agencies provide favorable programs to interest groups in exchange for a supportive environment, including influence with the committee (e.g., Dodd and Schott, 1979, p. 103; Gryski, 1987,pp. 164-173; Arnold, 1979; Fiorina, 1977).

Interest Group Exchanges with Committees In describing the exchange relationship between legislators and interest groups, researchers assume that committee members benefit most in the exchange, that they receive a disproportionate share of publicity, campaign workers, money, and so on. To what extent is this assumption accurate?

Ogul (1976), in his study of legislative oversight, analyzes the tactics utilized by the employee groups with members of the U.S. House Post Office and Civil Service Committee. The various postal employee organizations gave committee members recognition in their periodicals, invited them to speak at association meetings, provided campaign support, bought tickets to testimonial dinners, and provided transportation, theater tickets, and so on (pp. 65-73). In addition, the employee groups had a skilled, well-financed lobbying organization, testified before congressional committees, held breakfasts for congressmen, and had their members petition or write to their congressmen (pp. 74-81). What were the effects? To answer this question, knowledge of committee member priorities is useful. Few members sought a seat on this committee, and a substantial number sought a voluntary transfer from it. Members who stayed were concerned with an early rise to positions of power, with constituency interests, with high political salience for reelection campaigns, and with the pace of committee work (pp. 56-70). Given these conditions, Ogul finds that in this case the interest groups were able to affect the committee's agenda and time, its information sources, its staffing, and its behavior generally (pp. 81-85). Although no quantitative measurement is provided, Ogul feels he is able "to demonstrate that these groups have had a substantive impact on committee behavior" (p. 90).

Few studies provide such a complete analysis. Instead, the consequences of providing a single resource, usually money, are examined. Since "giving campaign contributions is easily the most publicized tactic of groups for access and influence in the political process" (Ornstein and Elder, 1978, p. 71) and since, behaviorally, there are some data to suggest that "campaign contributions do stimulate legislators toward interaction" (Zeigler and Baer, 1969, p. 190), the obvious question is whether interest groups provide a disproportionate share of their campaign resources to committee members who have jurisdiction over their legislation. Quantitative research published on this topic exists only for the U.S. Congress.

At the congressional level, no published academic study has documented a total distribution of funds to various committee members nor tried to link campaign contributions directly to committee behavior, although some descriptive information is provided on the extent of the contributions by a few groups. Thus, in discussing campaign contribution patterns for the dairy industry, the American Medical Association, the banking industry, and the maritime union's political action committees, Jacobson (1980) indicates that "they give overwhelmingly to incumbents in both parties who sit on committees that handle matters directly affecting their financial interests, although if the election is in doubt, they may contribute to both candidates" (p. 77). Yet, even for interest groups known to make substantial contributions, indications are that they "were not a major source of funds for any of the committee's members, except for the chairman" (Malbin, 1979, p. 36). An interesting, but untested, observation is that "if campaign contributions from Washington-based organizations were prohibited, the rest of what the Washington 'issue networks' do would remain untouched" (p. 37).

If "lobbying is conceived as a matter of bargaining" (Matthews, 1960, p. 190), then interest groups can be seen as being asked to provide a series of services for the legislator. In one perspective, "the lobbyist becomes, in effect, a service bureau for those congressmen already agreeing with him, rather than an agent of direct persuasion" (Bauer, Pool, and Dexter, 1963, p. 353). That legislators request these services of lobbyists at times is not disputed. Findings from certain state legislatures demonstrate the proportion of lobbyists who are called upon to offer their services (Zeigler and Baer, 1969). Even a moderate proportion of Washington's public interest groups provide information on a frequent basis (Berry, 1977, pp. 280-284). While it appears that committee members use a different information search pattern, no statistical evidence exists as to whether committee members request lobbyists to write speeches, prepare reports, answer correspondence, write legislative bills, and so forth at a different rate than do noncommittee members, and with what consequences.

Agency Exchanges with Committees: Geographic Distribution of Programs Research in this area may be divided into that which concentrates on how agencies distribute resources and projects throughout the various parts of the country and that which examines the response by the agency to discrete requests from legislators for constituent services and information.

Do the relevant authorization and appropriations committee members influence the geographical distribution of benefits emanating from governmental agencies? Descriptive case study information is available (e.g., Murphy, 1971) and general theoretical work on the question of distribution rules exist (Buchanan and Tullock, 1962; Barry, 1965). Recent theoretical work, from a rational choice perspective, accounts for the inefficiency of pork barrel distributive projects by focusing on the biases of democratic institutions, with emphases on the politicization of economic costs, representation by geographical districts, and the financing of projects through generalized taxation (Weingast, Shepsle, and Johnsen, 1981). However, for this review, two theories are most appropriate: a "distributive" theory, explicitly formulated by Rundquist and Ferejohn (1975), and Arnold's theory of influence (1979).

Distributive Theory The greatest amount of empirical research has been given to testing the distributive theory, which does not apply to all policies, just "those which can be subdivided into many parts, each of which can be implemented in different areas of the country and regarding which separate choices can be made by legislative or bureaucratic decision-makers" (Rundquist and Ferejohn, 1975, p. 88). In this theory, it is assumed that members of Congress want to serve the economic interests of their constituencies. This objective is best obtained when legislators are assigned to a committee with jurisdiction over those activities which most affect their constituencies. In those legislatures in which the major decisions are made in the committee, the most important legislators will be found within the committee, and "this means that committee members who wish to withhold their support for an agency's request until it is changed to include consideration for their constituencies will tend to obtain that objective" (Rundquist and Ferejohn, 1975, p. 89). Three hypotheses are presented.

1. Recruitment hypothesis: "Members from constituencies with a pecuniary interest in a particular form of government activity seek membership on a constituency-relevant authorizing committee or appropriations subcommittee."
2. Overrepresentation hypothesis: "When the districts of committee members are compared with those of other congressmen, the committees will be found to overrepresent constituencies with a stake in the matter."
3. Benefit hypothesis: "Relative to those of other congressmen, the constituencies of committee members benefit disproportionately from the distribution of expenditures under their jurisdiction" (p. 88).

In testing the benefit hypothesis, researchers have examined executive-oriented decisions, legislative-oriented decisions, and legislative-and-executive-oriented decisions. While the second set is most germane to this discussion, consideration of the other two provides comparison and contrast.

For a considerable number of programs, the formal authority for making distributional decisions resides with the executive agencies. Bureau and agency leaders, striving for budgetary growth and security, are thought to have strategic sensitivity "in recognizing the interests of powerful committee members and making necessary accommodations" (Freeman, 1965, p. 121). In doing so, the administrators are seen as responding to the influence of the various legislators. In most empirical studies, a legislator is perceived as being influential whenever "bureaucrats' allocational decisions reflect in some way the congressman's preferences regarding allocation" (Arnold, 1979, p. 73).

Research testing the benefit hypothesis has produced mixed findings. For the most studied sector—military-industrial subgovernment—the results have been generally negative. Goss (1972) investigated whether there was a relationship between military committee membership and excess benefits, benefits measured as numbers of military personnel, civilian personnel on military bases, and private defense plant personnel. The general conclusion is that the impact is variable, depending on the specific committee analyzed and type of employment examined. Using prime military contracts as the dependent variable, the benefit and overrepresentation hypotheses were rejected for the U.S. House, although the recruitment hypothesis was verified for the Armed Service Committee (Rundquist and Ferejohn, 1975). No support for the benefit hypothesis is forthcoming when a comparison is made of the ratio of disaggregated prime military contracts to manufacturing capability in the districts represented by members on the military committees and districts of nonmembers. Also, when the relative impact of the district's manufacturing capability and military committee representation are assessed using a regression analysis, the null hypothesis is accepted (Rundquist, 1978). Finally, using an interrupted time-series design, little support is found for the hypothesis that if states obtain representation on the congressional military committees, they will show increased military procurement expenditures; conversely, those states which lose representation on the same committee will exhibit a decreased amount of these expenditures (Rundquist and Griffith, 1976).

More positive results are found from analysis of programs which have more domestic content. Thus, in one of the first published studies of the geographical distribution of government programs, Plott (1968) analyzed how the Urban Renewal Agency allocated projects and spending throughout the United States. Using both state- and district-level data, he found support for the benefit hypothesis. At the district level, for example, "in all cases it was expected that about 37 percent of the expenditures should have occurred during the time of representation. However, about 70 percent of the expenditures took place at the time of representation" (p. 310).

Another study indicates some support for the proposition with modifications. Anagnoson (1980) examines the executive-oriented decision making of the Economic Development Administration, using a basic model consisting of two major factors: the need or eligibility of each area and political representation of that area (p 70). Most of the variance is explained by need variables—number of eligible areas per congressional district, population, and income (p. 83). Anagnoson, however, suggests that "the distributive theory should not be abandoned, for there are significant benefits to some of those overseeing the agency" (p. 83). But the specific process in which influence is exercised is more complicated than it was initially thought to be.

> Thus it is not simply a position overseeing the agency which produces benefits for influential congressmen, but the combination of position, choice on the part of the congressmen that these are the kinds of benefits he wishes to emphasize, and local initiative in producing good quality applications. It does not appear that the agency is favoring politically well-situated congressmen with easier standards of approval, and the decentralized EDA project selection process argues against this (p. 84).

Studies concentrating on programs in which the legislature (i.e., Congress) makes the major distributional decisions usually find an influential role for the committee. For example, Strom (1975) analyzed the distribution of funds relative to demand for the Environmental Protection Agency's waste treatment construction grant program. Using data gathered for the decade 1962 to 1971, Strom found that states represented on the House Public Works Committee received more funds from the grant relative to the demand than did states which did not have membership on the committee (p. 723). In addition, a series of other factors—party, delegation size on committee, and so on—appeared to affect the amount of positive policy benefits. Ferejohn (1974) analyzes the politics surrounding the geographical distribution of the rivers and harbors projects administered by the Corps of Engineers. In this discretionary program, most of the major decisions are made by Congress. His major findings are that

1.   members of the public works committees of both chambers get more new projects than nonmembers do;
2.   members of the public works subcommittees get more new projects than nonmembers do;
3.   appropriations subcommittee members receive better treatment than authorization committee members (by several different measures) in both chambers;
4.   the committee leaders of the public works committees (subcommittees and full committee chairmen and ranking minority members) receive more favorable treatment for their state's budget requests than do nonleaders on the committees in both chambers and for both the authorization and appropriations committees;
5.   within the appropriations subcommittee of both chambers, the budgets of states represented by Democrats fared better than those of states represented by Republicans (p. 234).

Results of a second study supported the benefit hypothesis at the state and district level for both the authorizing and appropriations committees, but it did not support the recruitment or overrepresentation hypotheses (Rundquist and Ferejohn, 1975, pp. 92-97).

A study of multiple programs indicates the variations which may exist within the same policy area. Reid (1980), in an analysis of five different health programs, tried to identify how variations in grant-in-aid programs—formula versus project type—may affect congressional influence, presidential influence, and state aggressiveness. Congressional influence, in this case, is defined as "where members of the authorizing and appropriations committees are able to direct greater shares of the grant-in-aid funds to their district" (p. 46). Findings reveal that formula grants are more tightly governed by programmatic criteria than are project grants (p. 48) and that the clearer the formula language, the less the impact of political factors (p. 48). As to congressional influence,

> no single committee or subcommittee appears to exercise dominant influence over the distribution of health grant funds. Rather, the regression coefficients suggest that individual committees tend to specialize in the exercise of influence (pp. 48-49).

What is the cumulative effect of committee influence on the distribution of total expenditures for an agency? In general, research conducted at this level has not substantiated a benefit hypothesis. Three studies are pertinent. Ritt (1976) examines how committee and subcommittee assignments, seniority, party, and region affect the distribution of total expenditures and expenditures for six departments among congressional districts during 1972. Membership on the exclusive committees does not result in a higher comparative expenditure, except for Republicans on the Ways and Means Committee (p. 479). For Democrats, membership on the Public Works Committee and interest committees enhances the chances of obtaining additional funds (p. 479). When one controls for the nature of constituency, "the benefits appearing to accrue to committee members diminish substantially" (p. 479). Membership on the subcommittee does not increase constituency benefits automatically (p. 481), and seniority on the committee is not predominately related to expenditures even when constituency effects are controlled. Thus, "although it is contrary to what is said about the operation of Congress, it would appear that seniority per se is simply not a significant factor in determining a congressman's ability to get dollars for his district" (p. 486).

What is the effect of committee position on incremental change in expenditures—that is, change from year to year? Ray addresses this question in three separate articles. In one study he tests whether constituencies of powerful representatives receive larger increases than those districts with less powerful congressmen (1980a, p. 12). His analysis covers seven budget areas for eight years of data, his unit of analysis the congressional district rather than the representative. This complex analysis includes variables which control for district characteristics, variables which deal with possibilities for logrolling, and eight variables which tap congressional influence rooted in institutional position. In summarizing the regression analysis, he states that "the most obvious conclusion is that there is little evidence of a consistent pattern of successful promotion rooted in institutional influence" (p. 18). Substantive committee assignment and appropriations subcommittee assignment exhibit no consistent pattern (p. 25). In terms of seniority, "the more seniority Democrats accrue on a committee with jurisdiction over a spending area, the more benefits their districts receive within that subsystem" (p. 26). For the minority party members, no such relationship emerges clearly.

In a second study, Ray (1980b) analyzes whether members of the appropriate legislative committees are able to prevent losses of existing federal activities in their district. The major finding is that "representation in a jurisdiction is no guarantee that a constituency will not suffer losses in federal activity within that jurisdiction" (p. 362). In a third article, he tries to ascertain the causal relationship between congressional position and federal spending, concluding that

> it has been shown that congressmen are more likely to follow their districts' dependencies upon specific segments of federal activities than they are to create dependencies by exercising the influence resulting from their committee assignments. This is why committee positions positively correlate with the geographic distribution of federal spending (1982d, p. 690).

An Alternative Theory of Influence   A different theoretical perspective is developed by Arnold (1979) for he focuses explicitly on bureaucratic behavior. He theorizes that bureaucrats, in an attempt to provide budget security and growth, exchange benefits "in an effort to maintain and expand their supporting coalitions" (p. 207). In making strategic decisions regarding the distribution of benefits, bureaucrats take into account the general-benefit preferences among congressmen (that is, whether there is consensus, indifference, or a polarized distribution of preferences) and allocate accordingly. Extra consideration is given to committee members who have jurisdiction over the agencies' activities, since they determine the agenda for all legislative activity dealing with a program (p. 63), influence bureaucratic behavior through nonstatutory techniques not available to nonmembers (p. 63), and have a legislative veto. In addition, most committee members are potential coalition leaders (p. 66). Yet, bureaucrats' estimates of the probability that committee sanctions may be used "vary from committee to committee or from program to program" (p. 67) depending on the amount of oversight, committee members' willingness to approve budget requests, and the type of congressmen who are attracted to the committees (pp. 67-68).

Previous studies have employed the constituency or district. Noting the limitations with these studies (pp. 83-85), Arnold argues for the program decision as the appropriate unit. Thus, the military installation is the analytic unit for studying military employment (p. 102), while the program application is the unit for water and sewer grant programs (p. 139). Given the specific set of decision rules for the model cities program, Arnold is forced to adopt districts (rather than program decisions) as the analytic units in this case (p. 178).

As for the empirical analysis, Arnold indicates that congressional influence accounts for between 10 and 30 percent of the allocational decisions in these three public programs (p. 214). To what extent do committee members have an effect on this allocation process? Arnold's summary indicates the complex nature of bureaucratic decision making.

> Ordinarily, bureaucrats choose to allocate disproportionate shares of benefits to members of those committees that have jurisdiction over their programs. But these extra shares do not come automatically. They accrue to members who have performed important services, who control resources the bureaucrats desire, or who threaten in some way the achievement of bureaucratic goals. Committees that merely have the potential to threaten bureaucrats' fortunes but fail to develop that potential do not ordinarily obtain extra benefits for their members (p. 207).

Agency–Committee Exchanges: Constituent Services   Additional studies have examined exchange strategies focusing on constituent needs or legislative needs. In this regard, Freeman's proposition that bureau leaders, in their attempts to influence committees, had to go through the legislative liaison specialists in the various departments (1965, p. 122) becomes appropriate. Specific research on these liaison operations has either focused on a single agency or department, such as the Agency for International Development, the Department of State, or NASA (e.g., DeGrazia, 1966; Robinson, 1962; Murphy, 1972) or has concentrated on a comparative analysis of liaison activities in different departments (e.g., Pipe, 1966; Holtzman, 1970).

Studies of individual agencies indicate that legislative requests more often involve service functions than policy functions (Robinson, 1962, p. 159) and that agencies receive a disproportionate number of requests from committee members (e.g., Murphy, 1972, p. 202). To what extent and with what effects do agencies utilize a strategy which emphasizes constituent needs of committee members? Liaison officers in a number of departments "agreed that members of their substantive committees or appropriations subcommittees took precedence in time and attention as well as services and favors over other members of the legislative system" (Holtzman, 1970, p. 183). The element of partisanship was also an important factor in terms of offering services and favors (Holtzman, 1970, p. 184). It has been shown that members of the committees which have jurisdiction over NASA received marginally better treatment than other legislators, save for personnel referrals (Murphy, 1972, pp. 200-201).

Does the handling of constituent services have a noticeable effect on committee member behavior? No comparative quantitative study exists and those studies that have been completed vary in their assessment. Robinson (1962) argues that satisfaction is a necessary but not a sufficient condition for "establishing congressional support for Departmental policies" (p. 185). Murphy (1972) observes that NASA, in providing constituent services to members of Congress "cannot change any Congressman's basic position on issues, but it is likely to make him a bit more disposed to give NASA the benefit of the doubt" (1972, p. 202); however, he presents no data on this point. Replies from liaison personnel in domestic agencies indicate that "more positive results accrued to them and to their departments as a result of their employing a strategy of services and favors" (Holtzman, 1970, p. 188). On the other hand, Robinson (1962) collected data on legislators' satisfaction with the information provided them by the State Department and on their approval of State Department policies. For members of committees with foreign policy responsibilities, but not for nonmembers, he found a statistically significant relationship between satisfaction and approval (p. 186). Finally, what is the overall impact of the liaison activity? In one assessment, the "prevailing influences seem clearly to be factors relating to NASA's program relationship with Congress rather than influences of the legislative liaison office" (Murphy, 1972, p. 213).

Impact on Policy

This section examines the extent to which the committees, agencies, and interest groups affect policy outcomes. The influence of participants is evaluated in light of theoretical perspectives, issues selected, methodologies, and so on.

Interest Group–Committee Relationships   A considerable body of political science literature focuses on interest groups as "the fundamental units of analysis" (Hayes, 1981, p. 7). Research in this vein ranges from a general presentation of group theory (e.g., Truman, 1971) to an analysis of the impact of groups on a particular legislature (Zeller, 1937) to case studies of the impact of specific interest groups (e.g., Odegard, 1928) to studies of group impact on a single bill (e.g., Latham, 1952; Morgan, 1956).

One study meriting attention for this essay is Schattschneider's analysis (1935) of the role played by interest groups on tariff legislation. The pattern of interest group activity was characterized as being more or less sporadic, conflict as occasional, and pressure as enormously unbalanced (p. 109). Among several factors which account for this distribution of interests, two are worth noting. First, Schattschneider distinguishes between "insiders" and "outsiders" (p. 166); committee members would help the insiders by not adequately circulating committee hearings notices, so that only the most knowledgeable lobbyists would be informed and able to obtain necessary, but confidential, information (pp. 164-213). Second, the contestants operated under the norm of reciprocal noninterference, and committee members were inclined to enforce this policy, thus tending to reduce the level of conflict (p. 143).

Schattschneider's discussion of the conduct of the committee hearings indicates how process and interest identification are intertwined. Committee members permitted interest groups to choose what information to submit, did not check to see if material contained the requested information, and did not ask difficult questions of the protected interests (pp. 38-41). Communication between the members of the committee and those testifying was "rather in the style and manner of equals engaged in negotiation" (p. 43). The hearings were expedited, since "agreements may be reached speedily in a friendly proceeding in which every major premise of the petitioners is conceded in advance" (p. 44).

Since committee members had no workable criterion for determining tariff rates, they adopted a decision rule of universalization in which they sought political support for the system by "giving limited protection to all interests strong enough to furnish formidable resistance to it" (p. 85). Yet, the Committee on Ways and Means did not simply acquiesce to the demands of the industries for a specific tariff; instead, they "granted only a small percentage of the tariff increases desired" (p. 80).

An alternative perspective developed by Bauer, Pool, and Dexter (1963, 1972) on interest group impact downplays the role of "pressures." While pressure may occasionally be applied, there is no linear causal relationship analogous to fluid mechanics in which "the pressure is applied here and the results come out there" (1972, p. 455). These researchers see the relationship instead as transactional; that is they view "all the actors in the situation as exerting continuous influence on each other" (1972, p. 457). All the actors are to some extent "in a situation of mutual influence and interdependence" (1972, p. 457). The authors try to merge the empirical-influence model from psychology with the teleological-maximizing model from economics (p. 472). Communications, in this perspective, tend to act "more as triggers than as forces" (1972, p. 467), becoming one factor in a sociopsychological system (1972, p. 470). In this communication process, lobbyists are seen as contacting and assisting those who agree with them (1972, p. 442).

In a study of the relative importance of interest groups and the executive branch and committees on policy making in the U.S. Congress, Price (1972) argues that it is erroneous to concentrate solely on the "causal" impact of external factors since there is sufficient "slack" in the system and substantial variations in behavior (pp. 310-311). Thus, in analyzing the impact of external actors, he suggests a different perspective.

> Patterns of legislative influence were found which approximated the classic 'pressure group' model. But the characteristic relationship to sympathetic interest groups among legislative activists was 'entrepreneurial,' the initiatives taken were best seen not as a response to group demands but as an anticipation or projection of group demands and stimulation of their active concern (p. 322).

This is not to say that the groups have no impact, since interest group orientations are seen as constraining, stimulating, and shaping committee behavior (p. 323).

The lack of interest group impact is also to be seen in a study of the New Zealand Parliament. Using a sample of ten bills considered by the committees, Willie (1972) tries to determine the relationship between evidence presented to the committees by interest groups and the type of amendments subsequently proposed by the committees. For the ten bills studied, 106 groups and individuals, covering different levels of society, presented testimony (p. 112). Noting that all bills considered were amended and that most of the amendments had their origin in the group testimony, he comments that, "this indicates both government sensitivity to the groups and the close attention paid by the groups to the legislation" (p. 111). At the same time, though, groups do not appear to assert a large amount of influence. "In fact, a considerable amount of evidence was given in vain" (p. 111).

Interest Group Importance in Agency–Committee Relationships   A different perspective on the role of interest groups focuses on their role in helping the agency attain its goals. Freeman's (1965) proposition serves to structure this literature: "A bureau leader generally finds it necessary to have at least the support of most of the bureau's employees and most of its clientele in order to assert his policy views successfully before committee members" (p. 124). The importance of clientele groups may be evaluated under two conditions: (1) when there is no clientele group involved and (2) when clientele groups oppose the bureau's position.

Several studies indicate that a mobilized constituency is crucial to the agency's development. Morrow (1968), in his study of foreign aid, comments that "the relative lack of support for a program from a structured constituency tends to encourage legislative limitations on administration discretion and subsequent executive-legislative conflict" (p. 1005).

Green and Rosenthal (1963) provide a complete analysis of the Joint Committee on Atomic Energy's sources of influence, including the importance of nonconstituency ties. The influence of the committee was extensive; it could achieve its program objectives "by persuasion, negotiation, and pressure, not through legislation" (p. 105). The committee in this case had unique statutory power (pp. 79-103), but its institutional bases of power were also extensive. First, the Atomic Energy Commission was in a "no-man's land" between the president and Congress (p. 77). Second, the members of the committee had longer continuity than those on the commission and a relatively stable and skilled staff. Third, because of its highly technical and secret subject area, the committee's position within the Congress increased and therefore the AEC's dependence on the committee increased (p. 78). Finally, "unlike most other government agencies, the AEC had no significant constituency; there were no important segments of American society with a special interest in the atomic-energy program which might serve as sources of strength or influence" (p. 75). This created a situation in which, aside from the Joint Committee on Atomic Energy and the committees dealing with appropriations, the AEC was relatively isolated from Congress (pp. 75-76). Thus, the concessions on legislation were made by the agency, not by the committee (p. 137).

What happens when the clientele group takes a position opposite that of the bureau? There are several case studies of this phenomenon and its consequences. We have already discussed Freeman's study of Indian affairs. An analogous situation occurs in the Federal grazing policy area (Foss, 1960). When administrators of the Federal grazing agency were in general agreement with the clientele group of stockmen, the administrators could serve as major lobbyists for the clientele. However, when the administrators acted contrary to the wishes of the stockmen, the administrators have been unsuccessful with the committees (p. 201). Levantrosser's (1967) analysis of the armed forces reserve also demonstrates that the agency must have the support of the major interest group. In his study of seven cases, he concludes, "whenever one of the two associations representing citizen soldiers has differed with a Department of Defense proposal Congress has sustained association objections in considering that proposal for enactment" (p. 220).

The importance of interest groups may be stated in a slightly different way: "the amount of bargaining and compromising of executive branch proposals in Congress varies inversely with the amount of bargaining and compromising that occurs between interest groups and the executive branch" (Manley, 1970, p. 356). Studying a particular committee, he finds that "the stronger the opposition (by interest groups) to Treasury proposals the more Ways and Means will tend to reject or seriously amend the proposals; the stronger the support the less likely Ways and Means will reject or amend the proposal" (pp. 359-360). Analyzing a series of Treasury proposals, Manley demonstrates some support for the hypothesis, although the similarity of committee response to majority demands does not indicate the exact extent to which the groups and individuals influenced the committee's decision (p. 362). In addition, the committee decision did not always agree with the position of the majority of groups testifying (pp. 365-366). Manley concludes that for executive agencies "on major policy initiatives some group support is probably necessary to gaining congressional approval, especially if there are groups in opposition to the proposals" (p. 374). It does not say, however, that the support must necessarily be a majority of all demands made.

What if agencies and interest groups oppose the legislation? Hamm (1980), in research on decision making in state legislative committees, addresses this question. Using two state legislatures, differentiating the lower house from the senate, and using two different sessions for one legislature, he calculated support and opposition scores for each bill by counting how many of seven significant sectors (e.g., state agencies or labor unions) testified at the committee hearing. In both the bivariate and multivariate analysis, he found that among eight independent variables (e.g., complexity of legislation) the most consistently significant factor is the extent of opposition expressed by the significant actors (p. 47).

Factors Affecting Variations in Relationships   Studies also indicate that agency-committee relationships vary with the type of policy, the stage in the policy process, the type of committee, environmental constraints, and issue characteristics. Recognizing that different types of policies have different characteristics and thus different political relationships, several scholars have developed policy typologies (Huntington, 1961; Lowi, 1964; Froman, 1968; Hayes, 1978; Salisbury, 1968; Edelman, 1960), although some difficulties have been noted with them (Froman, 1968, pp. 45-52). Ripley and Franklin (1980) analyze congressional-bureaucratic relationships using a hybrid of these typologies. The focus is basically on the impact which the subgovernment has in different policy areas, although some analysis is devoted to the outcomes of conflict among members of the subgovernment. In distributive policy and structural defense policy, where subgovernments are thought to hold sway, the ordinary relationship involves cooperation among members of the subgovernment. In each policy area, however, when conflict arises, its resolution is weighted slightly more toward the subcommittee preferences than toward bureaucratic preferences (pp. 92, 119,185).

In regulatory policy, the conflict is thought to originate when members of the subcommittee want a variance from a regulation for favored constituents rather than when they want more stringent enforcement of the regulations (p. 124). However, in some cases "the Senators and representatives involved were more aggressive in asking for regulatory action than were the agencies themselves" (p. 152). In cases of disagreement, a compromise is likely between the initial specific measures, with the congressional position probably prevailing more often, particularly if the full Congress gets involved (p. 124). Generalizations regarding influence are difficult for other policy areas, since there is either minimal subsystem interaction or resolution of the issue at a higher level.

Price (1972), in trying to assess the influence exercised by different participants at different stages in the legislative policy process, conceptualized six separate stages of activity. He assessed the relative responsibility of certain actors—including members of the committees—on 13 major bills handled by three committees, all of which passed the U.S. Senate during the 89th Congress. He concludes that the committee dominates in the modification stage while the executive—mainly agencies and departments—are pre-eminent in information-gathering activities (pp. 293-294). For the other four stages, it is more difficult to assign responsibility. One function (formulation) may be shared, while another (interest aggregation) "generally takes place in different ways and under different conditions in the two arenas" (p. 295).

Fenno's (1973) analysis of committees presents a different conceptualization of the relationship between groups, agencies, and committees. His analytic scheme for comparing committees involves environmental constraints, along with member goals, as the major independent variables in explaining decision-making processes and decisions, with strategic premises or decision rules acting as intervening variables. For the purposes of this essay, a key point is that "each committee operates within a distinctive set of environmental constraints—most particularly the expectations of influential external groups" (p. xv).

Outside groups include clientele groups and members of the parent house, executive branch, or party leadership. Each committee is subject to influence from a specific policy coalition of these "outside groups." For some committees, clientele groups target the relevant agencies and spend little direct communication with the committee. For other committees, the policy coalitions may be described as "clientele-led." Fenno argues that "it is not possible to predict the characteristics of a committee's environment by knowing only its members' goals. Nor is it possible to predict the goals simply by knowing the environment" (p. 44). Thus, even though the two committees with a high percentage of legislators whose major goal is reelection are clientele led, the complexity of the policy coalition varies substantially (p. 44).

Committee decision-making autonomy is also variable: Fenno states that "the greater the relative influence of the members, the more autonomous the committee; the greater the relative influence of outside groups, the less autonomous the committee" (p. 137). Fenno concludes the analysis by suggesting that there are two "ideal types" of committees—"corporate and permeable." Permeable committees tend to be "more responsive but less influential than corporate committees" (p. 279).

Price (1978) elaborated on the impact of "environmental" factors on committee policy making. Rather than focusing on the entire committee, he analyzes factors associated with each issue. Legislators are assumed to be rational-economic persons trying to maximize chances of reelection and to ingratiate themselves with outside actors with whom the committee must deal (p. 549). Committee outputs are a function of individual initiatives (p. 549), and the analysis centers on how variations in environmental forces across a range of policy areas affect the level and content of committee output for one clientele-centered committee—Commerce—in each house from 1969 to 1974.

Summarizing the influence of perceived incentives and constraints, Price concludes that committee members, when deciding where to direct policy-making time and effort, take into account the degree of public salience and amount of conflict (p. 568). Thus, issues which have low conflict but high salience "offer the highest incentives to legislators calculating the likely consequences of initiative and involvement" (p. 569), while low-salience, high-conflict areas present the least incentive (p. 569). His analysis indicates that all policy areas are not equally closed in terms of particularistic groups and agencies, but rather "that the inclination of legislators to take their bearings from broader public policy will be dependent in large part on an issue's perceived public salience" (p. 569). It should be noted that these are perceptual variables, that they may tend to vary over time, between chambers, and so on (p. 570). Finally, the level and direction of the executive's involvement is seen as an intervening variable: committee initiative is more likely if there is executive neglect or if the executive's decisions run counter to the "expressed interests of the groups dominating the congressional landscape" (p. 572), a theme already developed.

Weingast's (1981) analysis of the political foundations of agency-clientele relationships in regulatory policy areas indicates another constellation of factors. The model of regulatory policy equilibrium, using social choice models of voting, produces a policy that remains stable and beneficial to congressional agency clientele as long as the relevant variables of public opinion, balance of power of interests groups, presidential initiative, and precedential legal decisions are stable" (p. 160). However, change in these variables may affect the operation of the subgovernment. These effects are demonstrated in an analysis of regulatory policy movement in three areas: deregulation of the airlines by CAB, broadcast and telephone regulation by FCC, and influence of the environmentalists on nuclear power. This analysis includes a discussion of the impact of judicial constraints, an overlooked topic in the literature (see Fiorina, 1982).

That influence of the participants can change over time is nicely illustrated by Bresnick's (1979) study of the national educational policy system. While the enactment of the Elementary and Secondary Education Act was a major executive policy initiative (Eidenberg and Morey, 1969), the revision of the act produced a different set of influences. In this case, the committees in each house, not the agencies or interest groups, tended to dominate the issues of formula allocation. Why didn't interest groups have greater effect in this institutionalized policy-making process? The issue of competing formulae was so divisive among the national interest groups, given their diverse geographical base, that "they became for the most part immobilized" (1979, p. 202). Moreover, the executive was relatively uninvolved due to recent defeats in educational policy and difficulty in mustering majority support in the Congress (1979, p. 200).

Appropriations Politics

Researchers have tended to treat relationships involving appropriations politics as a distinct subsystem (Dodd and Schott, 1979). And an identifiable body of literature surrounding this topic has developed (e.g., Huzar, 1943, 1950; MacMahon, 1943; Knapp, 1956; Wallace, 1960; Wildavsky, 1964; Sharkansky, 1965a, 1965b; Fenno, 1966; Kingdon, 1966; Knight, 1968; Kirst, 1969; Horn, 1970; Thomas and Handberg, 1974; Meier and Van Lohuizen, 1978a, 1978b; John P. Bradley, 1980).

Agency-Committee Relationships   What agency-committee factors tend to influence the committee budgetary decisions? In Huzar's (1943, 1950) study of the relationships between the military agencies and the appropriations committees, committee members are shown to concentrate on those areas "which fall within the experience, competence, and interest of the legislators" (1943, pp. 665- 666). Huzar emphasizes that when committee members examine the agency witnesses, they place importance on the witnesses' personal relations, impressions, reputation in military circles, accuracy in previous statements, and so on (1943, p. 664). Thus, during the hearings, the extent to which the committees scrutinize agency proposals is a function of the confidence members have in a particular administrator (1943, p. 665).

Kingdon (1966) accounts for variation in subcommittee behavior toward four agencies under its jurisdiction. He emphasizes individual subcommittee members' policy values, particularly as they affect their perception that the agency is cuttable, and the members' recognition that the agency has something to offer their constituents or clientele groups (pp. 69-70). Given the emphasis on cutting the budget, a value is placed on information. Thus, agencies which make effective presentations, particularly by presenting quantifiable activities, may have greater influence. The extent to which an administrator conforms to a particular role enhances the committee members' confidence. The more an administrator is perceived as efficient and effective, as one who keeps the subcommittee informed about developments in the agency, spends the money for the appropriated purposes, and follows the directives of the committee, the greater the confidence the committee will have. Finally, agencies are seen as crafting their strategies "to values which they think the subcommittee considers important" (p. 75). However, Kingdon argues that "strategies can exploit advantages, but they cannot create them" (p. 77).

In the most complete treatment of the topic, Fenno (1966) conceives of the U.S. House Appropriations Committee as a political system, with identifiable, interdependent internal parts, existing in an identifiable external environment (p. xviii), engaged in adaptation, integration, and decision making (p. xviii). He ascertains observable behavior, expectations as to what should happen, and images (attitudes and perceptions) which participants hold (p. xx).

While Fenno uses these concepts to explain the committee's integration and its relationship to the House, for purposes of this review, their application to committee-agency relationships is most relevant. Thus, committee members have numerous goals (e.g., protecting the power of the purse) and view the typical agency with suspicion, "the natural suspicion which a legislative body . . . has for an executive body" (p. 317).

A major problem for Appropriations Committee members is uncertainty as to whether they have the necessary information to make appropriate budget judgments (p. 320). This adaptation problem of informed decision making is reflected in various types of committee behavior (e.g., collecting information via travel to the agency activity sites) (pp. 320-324), although constraints do not permit members to undertake a thorough technical information search. Rather, they develop strategies for sampling information at committee hearings which culminates, via an inductive process, in a general judgment of agency activity (pp. 332-340).

The typical agency has these goal expectations: that the Appropriations Committee accept the agency's base and focus on the incremental increase (p. 267), that it accept the entire agency budget request (p. 269), and that it deal with the budget requests in programmatic terms(pp. 269-271). In terms of maintenance expectations, agencies want predictability or certainty in committee relations, stability in these relations, and fair procedures (pp. 273-274).

A considerable portion of agency behavior is an attempt to adapt to a situation of uncertainty. To maintain a semblance of a stable relationship with the Appropriations Committee, the agency tends to obey reports, prepare for hearings, build confidence in the hearing, and maintain informal contacts (pp. 291-312).

In summary, Fenno suggests that the committee-agency relationships involve conflict, since the agency has program-oriented goals and the committee has economy-oversight goals (p. 348), and uncertainty, since the committee is concerned about relevant information and the agency about what the members will ask (p. 348). Attempts are made to reduce uncertainty and conflict via the methods previously discussed.

Internal and External Influences on Committee Decisions   To what extent do committee-agency relationships or external factors affect committee decisions on the budget and substantive policy? All major published empirical studies on these topics have been at the congressional level. Taking the individual bureaus as the unit of analysis and examining the U.S. House Appropriations Committee decisions for a 16-year period, Fenno

(1966) argues that the extent of increase in the bureaus' appropriations from year to year is mainly a function of "the strength of the demands made in support of the bureau by people outside the committee" (p. 412). On the other hand, when examining the extent to which bureaus obtain their requests, he emphasizes factors "internal to the bureau, to the committee, and to the bureau-committee relationship" (p. 412).

However, the conclusions are not generalizable to the Senate, since those bureaus least successful in obtaining the requested amount from the House Appropriations Committee are most successful in the Senate Finance Committee. This is due, in part, to the fact that the Finance Committee acts as an appeals court; in addition, however, the agencies with relatively low success in the House are "bureaus whose programs command an especially large degree of extra-Committee support" (p. 587).

Additional studies have focused on different bureaus, on different years, or on different combinations of bureaus and time periods (Knight, 1968; Fox, 1971; Thomas and Handberg, 1974). An interesting finding emerges from a study of the budgets of eight agencies from 1947 to 1962: "highly constituency oriented agencies (e.g., Corps, Bureau of Reclamation, and the TVA) were found to receive more generous treatment from both the House and Senate Appropriations Committees" (Thomas and Handberg, 1974, p. 184).

Meier and Van Lohuizen undertake actual measurement of group and bureau lobbying in two articles. While the dependent variable is not the committee decision, the findings are worth noting given the importance of the committee in each house in the appropriations process. In one study (1978a), they investigate the impact of interest group support, using as the unit of analysis the 20 bureaus in the Department of Agriculture, concluding that congressional budgeting behavior was responsive to strong (in the sense that many groups supported the bureau) interest group support for bureaus. On the other hand, the percentage of groups favorably testifying and the intensity of group support do not influence the budget process positively (p. 461), nor does the type of clientele support have much impact (p. 462).

In the second study (1978b), data were gathered from 1974 to 1976 for 107 major operating bureaus of the Federal Government. Using basically the same measurement process as they did in the other study, the authors correlate eight independent variables with bureau growth rate and bureau success rate. In none of the three years studied do they find a group measure positively and significantly correlated with a budget measure (p. 488). In addition, there is no support for the oft-stated relationship between interest group support or intensity and budgetary decisions—growth and success rates—for distributive agencies; in fact, the relationships are mostly negative. Regulatory agencies with strong interest group support have a slower growth rate, and budget success is unrelated to interest group involvement. For constituent agencies, there is a slight benefit from large interest group coalitions but no effect from intense groups. For redistributive policies, the impact is negative, although the few cases reduce confidence in the findings. Finally, when examining specific subcommittees, "even in a narrow substantive policy subfield with only nonregulatory bureaus, the size and intensity of interest group coalitions are unrelated to the growth and success rates of agency appropriations" (p. 492). From these findings, the authors conclude that "agencies with large and/or intense clientele support . . . fare no better in the appropriations process than agencies without such support" (p. 493).

That a subcommittee of the Appropriations Committee, along with the relevant interest groups, can affect an agency's substantive policies and programs can be seen in Knapp's study (1956) of the agricultural conservation policy. In this case, the members of the subcommittee had extensive personal experience and seniority and the Farm Bureau had a strong influence in the subcommittee between 1940 and 1945. However, in post-war years, "most of the major changes came from other sources and were often enacted over the objections of the Farm Bureau" (p. 269). This waning of influence coincided with changes in the leadership of the Farm Bureau and of the House appropriations subcommittee (p. 278). A conclusion is that "interest groups, it would appear, by no means controlled policy-making in the appropriations process, but tended to influence decisions most when an identity of interests existed between members of appropriations subcommittees and interest-group officials" (p. 279).

This lack of identity of interest can result in situations where bureau-committee cooperation prevails in the face of clientele group opposition. For example, John P. Bradley (1980) demonstrates that the Bureau of Health Insurance and the Senate Finance Committee cooperated on changes in Medicare policy, even with the various provider groups exhibiting opposition. In this case, neither of the cooperating participants exercised exclusive influence; instead, mutual interaction prevailed (p. 498).

Variations in Agencies' Budget Strategies   Research has also been conducted into the factors which account for variations in agency budgetary behavior. Sharkansky (1965a), using published records, focuses on the assertiveness of four agencies as they interact with one subcommittee of the House Appropriations Committee. He constructs a causal model to explain differences among agencies' budget strategies, although he performs no actual statistical testing. Stated simply, the revised model indicates that the pattern of influence is from the nature of the program to public support, administration support, and subcommittee support; from the perceptions, values, attitudes, or beliefs of agency administrators to the assertiveness of the agency budget strategy. Reciprocal interaction among the various supporting actors is also hypothesized (pp. 280-281). In addition, the nature of the budget strategy should be considered as a factor influencing the nature of its programs and its support (p. 281). One finding which runs counter to the model is that there is little or no support for the idea "that administrators have considered changing—or have actually changed—their basic strategies in response to the subcommittee's behavior" (p. 280).

Methods of Legislative Control   One technique by which committees can affect agency behavior is the use of nonstatutory controls. These include committee hearings, committee reports, floor debates, and informal meetings. The clearest statements of these have been forthcoming in the studies of the control exercised by the appropriations committees of the U.S. Congress. For example, MacMahon (1943) indicates, in a descriptive sense, how these activities operate, and the effect which they have. Kirst (1969) examines how nonstatutory controls are used in various departmental appropriations bills. For three of the four bills he examines, he finds that an overwhelming majority of the controls over a four year period are nonstatutory (p. 117). Bureaucrats typically comply with nonstatutory language, although Kirst suggests that noncompliance may be traced to either bureaucratic inertia (p. 68, 70) or to "administrators' determination that language will prevent implementation of crucial policy" (p. 67). Interest groups are able to influence language in nonstatutory devices, and they do not have to go through the requirements of legal enactment (p. 134). Finally, agencies and subcommittees cooperate on nonstatutory controls to affect higher level administrators (p. 135).

Horn (1970), in his study of the Senate Finance Committee, analyzes both statutory and nonstatutory controls. After analyzing one year of committee reports, he concludes that

> the directives pertained mainly to the goals and emphasis of the agency activity (program), the distribution of costs among the programs and groups (budget procedure), and the administrative means to implement the activity (management) (pp. 187-188).

While bureaus and departments are often allied in trying to have the subcommittee provide specific nonstatutory language for implementation of a program, at times one may try to have language inserted which may offset the activities of the other (p. 187). Lobbyists often use the report as a way to influence not only executive departments and agencies, but also semiautonomous regulatory bodies (p. 189). Horn indicates that the members of the Committee are doubtful as to the effectiveness of the reports (pp. 191-192).

Variations in Subcommittee Supervision and Control   Sharkansky (1965b), studying one subcommittee and four agencies during the budget years 1949 to 1963, examines how a subcommittee divides its supervisory and control activities among the agencies under its jurisdiction. He suggests that the concept of "oversight" is not unidimensional but has numerous facets. Thus, subcommittee supervision may vary in the attention paid to agency operations, the thoroughness of supervision, the incisiveness of supervision, the frequency of independent investigations, control over expenditures, and control via committee reports. What accounts for the major oversight differences among the agencies? Subcommittee members

> devote more than the average amount of supervisory and control efforts to agencies that spend the most money, whose requests have increased the most rapidly, and whose behavior toward the subcommittee has deviated most frequently from subcommittee desires (p. 628).

Conclusion

The major perspectives for analyzing the patterns of relationships among legislative committees, interest groups, and executive agencies are reviewed in this essay. Although numerous studies have been undertaken in recent years, major research gaps still exist.

One obvious difficulty is having only one or two research studies for a specific topic, covering only one committee or one narrow policy area. At the beginning of this article, I outlined the thesis that the subgovernments fall on a series of continua with regard to internal complexity, functional autonomy, unity, and cooperation or conflict. Most studies focus only on the relationships which occur at a specific point on the continuum, usually conforming to the characteristics of the "iron triangle." These studies are valuable. However, analysis of numerous and more complex subsystems should be undertaken. Then more complex, but more useful, generalizations can be developed.

The problem is exacerbated by the tendency to focus on only one legislature—the U.S. Congress. While this may be useful for initial hypothesis testing, more resources should be devoted to comparative studies on cross-national or cross-state bases. For example, given the important role committees play in the Italian Parliament (See DiPalma, 1976; LaPalombara, 1964), it would appear most appropriate to investigate the relationships among the committees, interest groups, and administrative agencies. In addition, given the variation in the extent to which the committees are the major loci of decision making in state legislatures (Francis and Riddlesperger, 1982), some of the theories and hypotheses developed in a congressional setting could be tested in different contexts.

Several neglected research areas could also be studied. For example, the extent to which private interests of committee members affect their behavior should be explored. Initial research indicates that, at least for the U.S. House of Representatives, "members of standing committees have significantly higher financial holdings in the policy domain of the committee than nonmembers" (Welch and Peters, 1982, p. 554). In fact, "the proportion having substantial financial holdings, which we defined as over $10,000, is from 2 1/2 to 50 times higher for members of relevant committees than for the Congress as a whole" (p.552). Also, there has been an acknowledgement that, in some cases, the triangular metaphor is not accurate. Rather, there is a fourth actor—the courts—which has not been adequately taken into account (Fiorina, 1982,p. 8).

In summary, our knowledge of this area, while expanding, must be more comparative and take into account additional internal and external factors. Then, subsequent reviews may be able to present statements which have a wider applicability and have been tested in different contexts.

REFERENCES

ABERBACH, JOEL D. 1979. "Changes in Congressional Oversight," *American Behavioral Scientist* 22:493-515.

ABERBACH, JOEL D. AND BERT A. ROCKMAN. 1978. "Bureaucrats and Clientele Groups: A View from Capitol Hill," *American Journal of Political Science* 22:818-832.

ANAGNOSON, J. THEODORE. 1980. "Politics in the Distribution of Federal Grants: The Case of the Economic Development Administration," in Barry S. Rundquist, ed., *Political Benefits: Empirical Studies of American Public Programs.* Lexington, MA: Lexington Books, pp. 61-91.

ARNOLD, R. DOUGLAS. 1979. *Congress and the Bureaucracy: A Theory of Influence.* New Haven: Yale University Press.

BACHELLER, JOHN M. 1977. "Lobbyists and the Legislative Process: The Impact of Environmental Constraints," *American Political Science Review* 71:252-263.

BAER, M. A. 1974. "Legislative Lobbying: In Washington and the States," *Georgia Political Science Association Journal* 2:17-27.

BALUTIS, ALAN P. 1975. "Legislative Staffing: A View From the States," in James J. Heaphey and Alan P. Balutis, eds., *Legislative Staffing: A Comparative Perspective.* New York: Sage Publications, pp. 106-137.

BARRY, BRIAN. 1965. *Political Argument.* London: Routledge and Kegan Paul.

BAUER, RAYMOND A., ITHIEL DE SOLA POOL, AND LEWIS A. DEXTER. 1963. *American Business and Public Policy: The Politics of Foreign Trade.* New York: Atherton Press.

_____ . 1972. American Business and Public Policy: *The Politics of Foreign Trade*. 2d ed. Chicago: Aldine-Atherton.

BELL, CHARLES G. AND CHARLES M. PRICE. 1975. *The First Term: A Study of Legislative Socialization*. Beverly Hills, CA: Sage Publications.

BERNSTEIN, MARVER. 1955. *Regulating Business by Independent Commission*. Princeton: Princeton University Press.

BERRY, JEFFREY M. 1977. *Lobbying for the People*. Princeton: Princeton University Press.

BETH, LOREN P. AND WILLIAM C. HAVARD. 1961. "Committee Stacking and Political Power in Florida," *Journal of Politics* 23:157-183.

BIBBY, JOHN F. 1966. "Committee Characteristics and Legislative Oversight of Administration," *Midwest Journal of Political Science* 10:78-98.

BOND, JON R. 1979. "Oiling the Tax Committee in Congress, 1900-1974: Subgovernment Theory, the Overrepresentation Hypothesis, and the Oil Depletion Allowance," *American Journal of Political Science* 23:651-664.

BRADLEY, JOHN P. 1980. "Shaping Administrative Policy With the Aid of Congressional Oversight: The Senate Finance Committee and Medicare," *Western Political Quarterly* 33:492-501.

BRADLEY, ROBERT B. 1980. "Motivations in Legislative Information Use," *Legislative Studies Quarterly* 5:393-406.

BRESNICK, DAVID. 1979. "The Federal Educational Policy System: Enacting and Revising Title I," *Western Political Quarterly* 32:189-202.

BROWN, BERNARD E. 1956. "Pressure Politics in France," *Journal of Politics* 18:702-719.

_____ . 1957. "Alcohol and Politics in France," *American Political Science Review* 51:976-995.

BROWN, MACALISTER. 1961. "The Demise of State Department Public Opinion Polls: A Study in Legislative Oversight," *Midwestern Journal of Political Science* 5:1-17.

BUCHANAN, JAMES M. AND GORDON TULLOCK. 1962. *The Calculus of Consent*, Ann Arbor: University of Michigan Press.

BUCHANAN, WILLIAM. 1963. *Legislative Partisanship: The Deviant Case of California*. Berkeley: University of California Press.

BUKSTI, JACOB A. AND LARS NORBY JOHANSEN. 1979. "Variations in Organizational Participation in Government: The Case of Denmark," *Scandinavian Political Studies* 2:197-220.

BULLOCK, CHARLES S. 1976. "Motivations for U.S. Congressional Committee Preferences: Freshmen of the 92nd Congress," *Legislative Studies Quarterly* 1:201-212.

CAHN, ANNE H. 1974. *Congress, Military Affairs and (a Bit of) Information*. Beverly Hills, CA: Sage Publications.

CATER, DOUGLAS. 1964. *Power in Washington*. New York: Random House.

CHRISTENSEN, TOM AND MORTEN EGEBERG. 1979. "Organized Group-Government Relations in Norway: On the Structured Selection of Participants, Problems, Solutions, and Choice Opportunities," *Scandinavian Political Studies* 2:239-259.

COHEN, BERNARD C. 1957. *The Political Process and Foreign Policy*. Princeton: Princeton University Press.

COHEN, BERNARD C. 1959. *The Influence of Non-Governmental Groups on Foreign Policy Making*. Boston: World Peace Foundation.

COLE, TAYLOR. 1958. "Functional Representation in the German Federal Republic," *Midwest Journal of Political Science* 2:256-277.

COTTER, CORNELIUS P. AND MALCOLM J. SMITH. 1957. "Administrative Accountability: Reporting to Congress," *Western Political Quarterly* 10:405-415.

CRANE, WILDER, JR. 1960. "A Test of the Effectiveness of Interest-Group Pressures on Legislators," *Social Science Quarterly* 41:335-340.

CULHANE, PAUL T. 1981. *Public Lands Politics: Interest Group Influence on the Forest Service and the Bureau of Land Management*. Baltimore: Johns Hopkins University Press, published for Resources for the Future, Inc.

DAMGAARD, ERIK. 1977. *Folketinget under forandring. Aspekter af Folketingets udvikling, virkemade og stilling idet politiske system*. Copenhagen: Samfundsvidenskabeligt Forlag.

DAVIDSON, ROGER H. 1969. *The Role of the Congressman*. New York: Pegasus.

_____ . 1974. "Representation and Congressional Committees," *Annals of the American Academy of Political and Social Science* 411:48-62.

_____ . 1975. "Policy Making in the Manpower Subgovernment" in M.P. Smith et al., eds., *Politics in America*. New York: Random House.

_____ . 1977. "Breaking Up Those Cozy Triangles: An Impossible Dream?" in Susan Welch and John G. Peters, eds., *Legislative Reform and Public Policy*. New York: Praeger, pp. 30-53.

DAWSON, RAYMOND H. 1962. "Congressional Innovation and Intervention in Defense Policy: Legislative Authorization of Weapons Systems," *American Political Science Review* 56:42-57.

DE GRAZIA, EDWARD. 1966. "Congressional Liaison—An Inquiry into Its Meaning for Congress," in Alfred de Grazia, ed., *Congress: The First Branch*. Washington, DC: American Enterprise Institute, pp. 297-335.

DELSESTO, STEVEN L. 1980. "Nuclear Reactor Safety and the Role of the Congressman: A Content Analysis of Congressional Hearings," *Journal of Politics* 42:227-241.

DIPALMA, GIUSEPPE. 1976. "Institutional Rules and Legislative Outcomes in the Italian Parliament," *Legislative Studies Quarterly* 1:147-179.

DODD, LAWRENCE C. AND RICHARD L. SCHOTT. 1979. *Congress and the Administrative State*. New York: John Wiley.

EDELMAN, MURRAY. 1960. "Symbols and Political Quiescence," *American Political Science Review* 54:695-704.

EHRMANN, HENRY W. 1958. "Pressure Groups in France," *The Annals of the American Academy of Political and Social Science* 319:141-148.

————. 1961. "French Bureaucracy and Organized Interests," *Administrative Science Quarterly* 5:534-555.

EIDENBERG, EUGENE AND ROY D. MOREY. 1969. *An Act of Congress: The Legislative Process and the Making of Education Policy*. New York: Norton.

ENTIN, KENNETH. 1973. "Information Exchange in Congress: The Case of the House Armed Services Committee," *Western Political Quarterly* 26:427-439.

————. 1974. "Interest Group Communication with a Congressional Committee," *Policy Studies Journal* 3:147-150.

————. 1977. *Bureaucratic Politics and Congressional Decision Making: A Case Study*. Providence: Brown University Press.

ETHRIDGE, MARCUS E. III. 1981. "Legislative-Administrative Interaction and 'Intrusive Access': An Empirical Analysis," *Journal of Politics* 43:473-492.

EULAU, HEINZ. 1964. "Lobbyists: The Wasted Profession," *Public Opinion Quarterly* 28:27-38.

FENNO, RICHARD F., JR. 1966. *The Power of the Purse: Appropriations Politics in Congress*. Boston: Little, Brown.

————. 1969. "The House of Representatives and Federal Aid to Education," in Robert L. Peabody and Nelson W. Polsby, eds., *New Perspectives on the House of Representatives*. Chicago: Rand McNally.

————. 1973. *Congressmen in Committees*. Boston: Little, Brown.

FEREJOHN, JOHN A. 1974. *Pork Barrel Politics: Rivers and Harbors Legislation, 1947-1968*. Stanford: Stanford University Press.

FIORINA, MORRIS P. 1977. *Congress: Keystone to the Washington Establishment*. New Haven: Yale University Press.

————. 1981. "Congressional Control of the Bureaucracy: A Mismatch of Incentives and Capabilities," in Lawrence C. Dodd and Bruce I. Oppenheimer, eds., *Congress Reconsidered*. 2d ed. Washington, DC: Congressional Quarterly Press, pp. 332-348.

————. 1982. "Assorted Thoughts on the Study of Subgovernments," unpublished comments on Keith E. Hamm, "Patterns of Influence Among Committees, Agencies and Interest Groups." Delivered at the Legislative Research Conference, Iowa City, Iowa.

FOSS, PHILLIP O. 1960. *Politics and Grass: The Administration of Grazing on the Public Domain*. Seattle: University of Washington Press.

FOX, DOUGLAS M. 1971. "Congress and the U.S. Military Service Budgets in the Post-War Period: A Research Note," *Midwest Journal of Political Science* 15:382-393.

FOX, HARRISON W. AND SUSAN W. HAMMOND. 1977. *Congressional Staffs: The Invisible Force in American Lawmaking*. New York: Free Press.

FRANCIS, WAYNE L. 1971. "A Profile of Legislator Perception of Interest Group Behavior Relating to Legislative Issues in the States," *Western Political Quarterly* 24:702-712.

FRANCIS, WAYNE L. AND JAMES W. RIDDLESPERGER. 1982. "U.S. State Legislative Committees: Structure, Procedural Efficiency, and Party Control," *Legislative Studies Quarterly* 7:453-371.

FREEMAN, J. LEIPER. 1958. "The Bureaucracy in Pressure Politics," *The Annals of the American Academy of Political and Social Science* 319:10-19.

_____. 1965. *The Political Process: Executive Bureau-Legislative Committee Relations*. Rev. ed. New York: Random House.

FROMAN, LEWIS A., JR. 1968. "The Categorization of Policy Contents," in Austin Ranney, ed., *Political Science and Public Policy*. Chicago: Markham Publishing, pp. 41-52.

GARCEAU, OLIVER AND CORINNE SILVERMAN. 1954. "A Pressure Group and the Pressured," *American Political Science Review* 49:672-691.

GLADIEUX, LAWRENCE E. AND THOMAS R. WOLANIN. 1976. *Congress and the Colleges: The National Politics of Higher Education*. Lexington, MA: Lexington Books.

GOSS, CAROL F. 1972. "Military Committee Membership and Defense Related Benefits in the House of Representatives," *Western Political Quarterly* 25:215-233.

GREEN, HAROLD P. AND ALAN ROSENTHAL. 1963. *Government of the Atom: The Integration of Powers*. New York: Atherton Press.

GRIFFITH, ERNEST S. 1939. *The Impasse of Democracy*. New York: Harrison-Hilton Books.

GROSS, BERTRAM M. 1953. *The Legislative Struggle: A Study in Social Combat*. New York: McGraw-Hill.

GRYSKI, GERARD S. 1981. *Bureaucratic Policy Making in a Technological Society*. Cambridge, MA: Schenkman.

HAIDER, DONALD H. 1974. *When Governments Come to Washington: Governors, Mayors. and Intergovernmental Lobbying*. New York: The Free Press.

HAMM, KEITH E. 1980. "U.S. State Legislative Committee Decisions: Similar Results in Different Settings," *Legislative Studies Quarterly* 5:31-54.

HARRIS, JOSEPH P. 1964. *Congressional Congress of Administration.* Washington, DC: Brookings Institution.

HARRISON, M. 1958. "The Composition of the Committees of the French National Assembly," *Parliamentary Affairs* 11:172-179.

HAVARD, WILLIAM C. AND LOREN P. BETH. 1962. *The Politics of Mis-Representation: Rural-Urban Conflict in the Florida Legislature.* Baton Rouge: Louisiana State University Press.

HAYES, MICHAEL T. 1978. "The Semi-Sovereign Pressure Groups: A Critique of Current Theory and An Alternative Typology," *Journal of Politics* 40:134-161.

_____ . 1979. "Interest Groups and Congress: Toward a Transactional Theory," *The Congressional System: Notes and Readings.* 2d ed. North Scituate, MA: Duxbury Press, pp. 252-273.

_____ . 1981. *Lobbyists and Legislators: A Theory of Political Markets.* New Brunswick, NJ: Rutgers University Press.

HELANDER, VOITTO. 1979. "Interest Representation in the Finnish Committee System in the Post-War Era," *Scandinavian Political Studies* 2:221-238.

HERRING, E. PENDLETON. [1929],1967. *Group Representation Before Congress.* New York: Russell and Russell.

_____ . 1933. "Special Interests and the Interstate Commerce Commission, I," *American Political Science Review* 27:738-751.

_____ . 1933. "Special Interests and the Interstate Commerce Commission, II," *American Political Science Review* 27:899-917.

HOLTZMAN, ABRAHAM. 1970. *Legislative Liaison: Executive Leadership in Congress.* Chicago: Rand McNally.

HORN, STEPHEN. 1970. *Unused Power: The Work of the Senate Committee on Appropriations.* Washington, DC: Brookings Institution.

HUITT, R.K. 1954. "The Congressional Committee: A Case Study," *American Political Science Review* 48:340-365.

_____ . 1973. "The Internal Distribution of Influence: The Senate," in David B. Truman, ed., *The Congress and America's Future.* Englewood Cliffs, NJ: Prentice-Hall, pp. 91-117.

HUNTINGTON, SAMUEL P. 1961. *The Common Defense.* New York: Columbia University Press.

HUZAR, ELIAS. 1943. "Congress and the Army: Appropriations," *American Political Science Review* 37:661-676.

_____ . 1950. *The Purse and the Sword: Control of the Army by Congress Through Military Appropriations, 1933-1950.* Ithaca, NY: Cornell University Press.

JACOBSON, GARY C. 1980. *Money in Congressional Elections.* New Haven: Yale University Press.

JAHNIGE, THOMAS P. 1968. "Congressional Committee System and the Oversight Process: Congress and NASA," *Western Political Quarterly* 21:227-239.

JOHNSON, LOCH. 1980. "The U.S. Congress and the CIA: Monitoring the Dark Side of Government," *Legislative Studies Quarterly* 5:477-499

JONES, CHARLES O. 1961. "Representation in Congress: The Case of the House Agriculture Committee," *American Political Science Review* 55:358-367.

_____ . 1962. "The Role of Congressional Subcommittees," *Midwest Journal of Political Science* 6:327-344.

_____ . 1979. "American Politics and the Organization of Energy Decision Making," *Annual Review of Energy* 4:99-121.

KAISER, FRED. 1977. "Oversight of Foreign Policy: The U.S. House Committee on Foreign Relations," *Legislative Studies Quarterly* 2:255-279.

KERR, JAMES R. 1965. "Congress and Space: Overview or Oversight?" Public Administration Review 25:185-192.

KIM, YOUNG C. 1975. "The Committee System in the Japanese Diet: Recruitment, Orientation, and Behavior," in G.R. Boynton and Chong Lim Kim, eds., *Legislative Systems in Developing Countries.* Durham, NC: Duke University Press, pp. 69-85.

KINGDON, JOHN W. 1966. "A House Appropriations Subcommittee: Influence on Budgetary Decisions," *Social Science Quarterly* 47:68-78.

KIRST, MICHAEL W. 1969. *Government Without Passing Laws: Congress' Non-Statutory Techniques of Appropriations Control.* Chapel Hill: University of North Carolina Press.

KNAPP, DAVID C. 1956. "Congressional Control of Agricultural Conservation Policy: A Case Study of the Appropriations Process," *Political Science Quarterly* 71:257-281.

KNIGHT, JONATHAN. 1968. "The State Department Budget, 1933-1965: A Research Note," *Midwest Journal of Political Science* 12:587-598.

KOVENOCK, DAVID M. 1973. "Influence in the U.S. House of Representatives: A Statistical Analysis of Communications," *American Politics Quarterly* 1 :407-464.

KVAVIK, ROBERT. 1975. *Interest Groups in Norwegian Politics.* Oslo: Universitetsforlaget.

LANE, EDGAR. 1954. "Interest Groups and Bureaucracy," *The Annals of the American Academy of Political and Social Science* 292:104-110.

LaPalombara, Joseph G. 1960. "The Utility and Limitations of Interest Group Theory in Non-American Field Stations," *Journal of Politics* 22:29-49.

_____. 1964. *Interest Groups in Italian Politics*. Princeton: Princeton University Press.

Latham, Earl. 1952. *The Group Basis of Politics: A Study of Point Basing Legislation*. Ithaca, NY: Cornell University Press.

Lawrence, Samuel A. 1966. *United States Merchant Shipping Policies and Politics*. Washington, DC: Brookings Institution.

Lees, John D. and Malcolm Shaw, eds. 1979. *Committees in Legislatures: A Comparative Perspective*. Durham, NC: Duke University Press.

Leiserson, Avery. 1942. *Administrative Regulation: A Study in Representation of Interests*. Chicago: University of Chicago Press.

Levantrosser, William F. 1967. *Congress and the Citizen-Soldier: Legislative Policy-Making for the Federal Armed Forces Reserve*. Columbus: Ohio State University Press.

Liske, Craig and Barry S. Rundquist. 1974. *The Politics of Weapons Procurement: The Role of Congress*, Denver: University of Colorado Press.

Loewenberg, Gerhard. 1967. *Parliament in the German Political System*. Ithaca, NY: Cornell University Press.

Lord, Guy. 1973. *The French Budgetary Process*. Berkeley: University of California Press.

Lowi, Theodore J. 1964. "American Business, Public Policy, Case Studies and Political Theory," *World Politics* 16:677-715.

_____. 1967. "The Public Philosophy: Interest Group Liberalism," *American Political Science Review* 61:5-24.

_____. 1969. *The End of Liberalism*. New York: Norton.

_____. 1972. "Four Systems of Policy, Politics, and Choice," *Public Administration Review* 32:298-310.

_____ 1973. "How the Farmers Get What They Want," in Theodore J. Lowi and Randall B. Ripley, eds., *Legislative Politics, U.S.A.* 3d ed. Boston: Little, Brown, pp. 184-191.

Maass, Arthur A. 1950. "Congress and Water Resources," *American Political Science Review* 44:576-593.

_____. 1951. *Muddy Waters*. Cambridge: Harvard University Press.

MacMahon, Arthur W. 1943. "Congressional Oversight of Administration: The Power of the Purse," *Political Science Quarterly* 58:161-190,380-414.

Maisel, Louis Sandy. 1981. "Congressional Information Sources," in Joseph Cooper and G. Calvin MacKenzie, eds., *The House at Work*. Austin: University of Texas Press, pp. 247-274.

MALBIN, MICHAEL J. 1979. "Campaign Financing and the 'Special Interests'," *The Public Interest* 56:21-42.

MANLEY, JOHN F. 1968. "Congressional Staff and Public Policy Making: The Joint Committee on Internal Revenue Taxation," *Journal of Politics* 30:1046-1067.

_____. 1970. *The Politics of Finance: The House Ways and Means Committee.* Boston: Little, Brown.

MASTERS, NICOLAS A. 1961. "House Committee Assignments," *American Political Science Review* 55:345-357.

MASTERS, NICOLAS A., ROBERT H. SALISBURY, AND THOMAS H. ELIOT. 1964. *State Politics and the Public Schools: An Exploratory Analysis.* New York: Knopf.

MATTHEWS, DONALD R. 1960. *U.S. Senators and Their World.* Chapel Hill: University of North Carolina Press.

MEIER, KENNETH J. AND J.R. VAN LOHUIZEN. 1978a. "Bureaus, Clients and Congress," *Administration and Society* 9:447-466.

_____. 1978b. "Interest Groups in the Appropriations Process: The 'Wasted Profession' Revisited," *Social Science Quarterly* 59:482-495.

MEZEY, MICHAEL. 1979. *Comparative Legislatures.* Durham, NC: Duke University Press.

MILBRATH, LESTER W. 1963. *The Washington Lobbyists.* Chicago: Rand McNally.

_____. 1967. "Interest Groups and Foreign Policy," in James Rosenau, ed., *Domestic Sources of Foreign Policy.* New York: The Free Press, pp. 231-261.

MITCHELL, DOUGLAS E. 1981. *Shaping Legislative Decisions: Education Policy and the Social Sciences.* Lexington, MA: Lexington Books.

MORAN, MARK J. AND BARRY R. WEINGAST. 1982. "Congress as the Source of Regulatory Decisions: The Case of the Federal Trade Commission," *American Economics Association Papers and Proceedings* 72:109-113.

MORGAN, ROBERT J. 1956. "Pressure Politics and Resources Administration," *Journal of Politics* 18:39-60.

MORROW, WILLIAM L. 1968. "Legislative Control of Administrative Discretion: The Case of Congress and Foreign Aid," *Journal of Politics* 30:985-1011.

MURPHY, THOMAS P. 1971. *Science, Geopolitics, and Federal Spending.* Lexington, MA: Heath, Lexington Books.

_____. 1972. "Congressional Liaison: The NASA Case," *Western Political Quarterly* 25:192-214.

NELSON, GARRISON. 1974. "Assessing the Congressional Committee System: Contributions from a Comparative Perspective," *The Annals of the American Academy of Political and Social Science* 411:120-132.

ODEGARD, PETER H. 1928. *Pressure Politics: The Story of the Anti-Saloon League*. New York: Columbia University Press.

OGUL, MORRIS. 1976. *Congress Oversees the Bureaucracy: Studies in Legislative Supervision*. Pittsburgh: University of Pittsburgh Press.

OLSEN, MARVIN E. 1977. "Influence Linkages Between Interest Organizations and the Government in Sweden," *Journal of Political and Military Sociology* 5:35-51.

OPPENHEIMER, BRUCE IAN. 1974. *Oil and the Congressional Process: The Limits of Symbolic Politics*. Lexington, MA: Heath, Lexington Books.

ORNSTEIN, NORMAN J. AND SHIRLEY ELDER. 1978. *Interest Groups, Lobbying and Policymaking*. Washington, DC: Congressional Quarterly Press.

PETERS, B. GUY. 1977. "Insiders and Outsiders: The Politics of Pressure Group Influence on Bureaucracy," *Administration and Society* 9:191-218.

PIPE, G. RUSSELL. 1966. "Congressional Liaison: The Executive Branch Consolidates Its Relations with Congress," *Public Administration Review* 26:14-24.

PLOTT, CHARLES R. 1968. "Some Organizational Influences on Urban Renewal Decisions," *American Econometric Review* 58:306-321.

POLSBY, NELSON W. 1975. "Legislatures," in Fred I. Greenstein and Nelson W. Polsby, eds., *Government Institutions and Process, Handbook of Political Science*. Vol. 5. Reading, MA: Addison-Wesley, pp. 257-319.

PORTER, H. OWEN. 1974. "Legislative Experts and Outsiders: The Two-Step Flow of Communication," *Journal of Politics* 36:703-730.

_____. 1975. "Legislative Information Needs and Staff Resources in the American States," in James Heaphey and Alan Balutis, eds., *Legislative Staffing: A Comparative Perspective*, New York: Halstead, pp. 39-59.

PRESTHUS, ROBERT. 1971. "Interest Groups and the Canadian Parliament: Activities, Interaction, Legitimacy, and Influence," *Canadian Political Science* 4:444-460.

_____. 1974. "Interest Group Lobbying: Canada and the United States," *The Annals of the American Academy of Political and Social Science* 413:44-57.

PRICE, DAVID E. 1971. "Professionals and 'Entrepreneurs': Staff Orientations and Policy Making on Three Senate Committees," *Journal of Politics* 33:316-336.

_____. 1972. *Who Makes the Laws?* Cambridge, MA: Schenkman.

_____. 1978. "Policy Making in Congressional Committees: The Impact of `Environmental' Factors," *American Political Science Review* 72:548-574.

_____. 1979. *Policymaking in Congressional Committees: The Impact of "Environmental" Factors*. Tucson: University of Arizona Press.

_____ . 1981. "Congressional Committees in the Policy Process," in Lawrence C. Dodd and Bruce I. Oppenheimer, eds., *Congress Reconsidered*. 2d ed. Washington, DC: Congressional Quarterly Press, pp. 156-185.

RAY, BRUCE A. 1980a. "Congressional Promotion of District Interests: Does Power on the Hill Really Make a Difference?" in Barry S. Rundquist, ed., *Political Benefits: Empirical Studies of American Public Programs*. Lexington, MA: Heath, Lexington Books, pp. 1-36.

_____ . 1980b. "Congressional Losers in the U.S. Spending Process," *Legislative Studies Quarterly* 5:359-372.

_____ . 1980c. "Federal Spending and the Selection of Committee Assignments in the U.S. House of Representatives," *American Journal of Political Science* 24:495-510.

_____ . 1982. "Causation in the Relationship Between Congressional Position and Federal Spending," *Polity* 14:676-690.

REDFORD, EMMETTE S. 1960. "Case Analysis of Congressional Activity: Civil Aviation1957-1958," *Journal of Politics* 22:228-258.

_____ . 1969. *Democracy in the Administrative State*. New York: Oxford University Press.

REID, J. NORMAN. 1980. "Politics, Program Administration and the Distribution of Grant-In-Aid: A Theory and a Test," in Barry S. Rundquist, ed., *Political Benefits: Empirical Studies of American Public Programs*. Lexington, MA: Lexington Books, pp. 37-60.

RHODE, WILLIAM E. 1959. *Committee Clearance of Administrative Decisions*. East Lansing: Bureau of Social and Political Research, Michigan State University.

RIGGS, FRED W. 1950. *Pressures on Congress: A Study of the Repeal of Chinese Exclusion*. New York: Columbia University, Kings Crown Press.

RIPLEY, RANDALL B. AND GRACE A. FRANKLIN. 1980. *Congress, Bureaucracy and Public Policy*. Rev. ed. Homewood, IL: Dorsey Press.

RITT, LEONARD. 1976. "Committee Position, Seniority, and the Distribution of Governmental Expenditures," *Public Policy* 24:463-489.

ROBINSON, JAMES A. 1962. *Congress and Foreign Policy-Making: A Study in Legislative Influence and Initiative*. Homewood, IL: Dorsey Press.

ROHDE, DAVID W. AND KENNETH A. SHEPSLE. 1973. "Democratic Committee Assignments in the House of Representatives: Strategic Aspects of a Social Choice Process," *American Political Science Review* 67:889-905.

ROSS, ROBERT L. 1970. "Relations Among National Interest Groups," *Journal of Politics* 32:96-114.

RUNDQUIST, BARRY S. 1978. "On Testing a Military Industrial Complex Theory," *American Political Quarterly* 6:29-54.

_____ . 1980. "On the Theory of the Political Benefits in American Public Programs," in Barry S. Rundquist, ed., *Political Benefits: Empirical Studies of American Public Programs*. Lexington, MA: Lexington Books, pp. 229-254.

RUNDQUIST, BARRY S. AND JOHN A. FEREJOHN. 1975. "Observations on a Distributive Theory of Policy Making," in Craig Liske, William Loehr, and John McCarrant, eds., *Comparative Public Policy*. New York: John Wiley, pp. 87-108.

RUNDQUIST, BARRY S. AND DAVID E. GRIFFITH. 1976. "An Interrupted Time Series Test of the Distributive Theory of Military Policy Making," *Western Political Quarterly* 29:620-626.

SABATIER, PAUL. 1975. "Social Movements and Regulatory Agencies: Toward a More Adequate—Less Pessimistic—Theory of 'Clientele Capture', *Policy Sciences* 6:301-342.

SALISBURY, ROBERT H. 1968. "The Analysis of Public Policy: A Search for Theories and Roles," in Austin Ranney, ed., *Political Science and Public Policy*. Chicago: Markham Publishing, pp. 151-175.

SCHATTSCHNEIDER, E.E. 1935. *Politics, Pressures and the Tariff*. New York: Prentice-Hall.

SCHER, SEYMOUR. 1960. "Congressional Committee Members as Independent Agency Overseers: A Case Study," *American Political Science Review* 54:911-920.

_____ . 1962. "The Politics of Agency Organization," *Western Political Quarterly* 15:328-344.

_____ . 1963. "Conditions for Legislative Control," *Journal of Politics* 25:526-551.

SCHUBERT, GLENDON. 1958. "Legislative Adjudication of Administrative Legislation," *Journal of Public Law* 7:135-161.

SCOTT, ANDREW M. AND MARGARET A. HUNT. 1966. *Congress and Lobbies*. Chapel Hill: University of North Carolina Press.

SHARKANSKY, IRA. 1965a. "Four Agencies and an Appropriations Subcommittee: A Comparative Study of Budgeting Strategies," *Midwest Journal of Political Science* 9:254-281.

_____ . 1965b. "An Appropriations Subcommittee and Its Client Agencies, "*American Political Science Review* 59:622-628.

SHEPSLE, KENNETH A. 1978. *The Giant Jigsaw Puzzle: Democratic Committee Assignments in the Modern House*. Chicago: University of Chicago Press.

STEPHENS, HERBERT W. 1971. "Role of the Legislative Committees in the Appropriations Process: A Study Focused on the Armed Services Committee," *Western Political Quarterly* 24:146-162.

STROM, GERALD S. 1975. "Congressional Policy Making: A Test of a Theory," *Journal of Politics* 37:711-734.

TEUNE, HENRY. 1967. "Legislative Attitudes Toward Interest Groups," *Midwest Journal of Political Science* 11 :489-504.

THOMAS, NORMAN C. 1970. "Bureaucratic Congressional Interaction and the Politics of Education," *Journal of Comparative Administration* 2:52-80.

THOMAS, ROBERT O. AND ROGER B. HANDBERG. 1974. "Congressional Budgeting for Eight Agencies, 1947-1972," *American Journal of Political Science* 78:179-185.

THURBER, JAMES A. 1976. "Legislative-Administrative Relations," *Policy Studies Journal* 5:56-65.

TRICE, ROBERT H. 1977. *Interest Groups and the Foreign Policy Process.* Beverly Hills, CA: Sage Publications.

TRUMAN, DAVID B. 1951. *The Governmental Process.* New York: Knopf.

_____ . 1971. *The Governmental Process.* 2d ed. New York: Knopf.

VAN DER SLIK, JACK R. AND THOMAS C. STENGER. 1977. "Citizen Witnesses before Congressional Committees," *Political Science Quarterly* 92:465-485.

VAN SCHENDELEN, M.P.C.M. 1976. "Information and Decision Making in the Dutch Parliament," *Legislative Studies Quarterly* 1:231-250.

VINYARD, DALE. 1968. "The Congressional Committees on Small Business: Patterns of Legislative Committee-Executive Agency Relations," *Western Political Quarterly* 21:391-399.

_____ . 1973. "The Senate Committee on Aging and the Development of a Policy System," *Michigan Academicians* :281-299.

VON NORDHEIM, M. AND R.W. TAYLOR. 1976. "The Significance of Lobbyist-Legislator Interaction in German State Parliaments," *Legislative Studies Quarterly* 1:511-531.

WALLACE, ROBERT ASH. 1960. *Congressional Control of Federal Spending.* Detroit: Wayne State University Press.

WAHLKE, JOHN C., WILLIAM BUCHANAN, HEINZ EULAU, AND LEROY C. FERGUSON. 1960. "American State Legislators' Role Orientations Toward Pressure Groups," *Journal of Politics* 22:203-227.

WEINGAST, BARRY R. 1980. "Congress, Regulation, and the Decline of Nuclear Power," *Public Policy* 28:231-255.

_____ . 1981. "Regulation, Reregulation, and Deregulation: The Political Foundations of Agency Clientele Relationships," *Law and Contemporary Problems* 44:147-177.

WEINGAST, BARRY R., KENNETH A. SHEPSLE, AND CHRISTOPHER JOHNSEN. 1981. "The Political Economy of Benefits and Costs: A Neoclassical Approach to Distributive Politics," *Journal of Political Economy* 89:642-664.

WELCH, SUSAN AND JOHN G. PETERS. 1982. "Private Interests in the U.S. Congress: A Research Note," *Legislative Studies Quarterly* 7:547-555.

WILDAVSKY, AARON B. 1964. *The Politics of the Budgetary Process*. Boston: Little, Brown.

WILLIAMS, PHILIP M. 1954. *Politics in Post-War France*. Hamden, CT: Archon Books.

_____ . 1964. *Crisis and Compromise: Politics in the Republic*. 3d ed. Hamden, CT: Archon Books.

_____ . 1968. *The French Parliament 1958-1967*. London: Allen and Unwin.

WILLIE, FRANK. 1972. "Pressure Groups and Parliamentary Select Committees," in Les Cleveland, ed., *The Anatomy of Influence: Pressure Groups and Politics*. Wellington, New Zealand: Hicks, Smith, pp. 98-112.

WINSLOW, CLINTON IVAN. 1931. "State Legislative Committees: A Study in Legislative Procedure," *Johns Hopkins University Studies in Historical and Political Science* 49:1-158.

WISSEL, PETER, ROBERT O'CONNOR, AND MICHAEL KING. 1976. "The Hunting of the Legislative Snark: Information Searches and Reforms in U.S. State Legislatures," *Legislative Studies Quarterly* 1:251-267.

WOLMAN, HAROLD. 1971. *Politics of Federal Housing*. New York: Dodd, Mead.

ZEIGLER, L. HARMON. 1961. *The Politics of Small Business*. Washington, DC: The Public Affairs Press.

_____ . 1969. "The Effects of Lobbying: A Comparative Assessment," *Western Political Quarterly* 22:122-140.

ZEIGLER, L. HARMON AND MICHAEL BAER. 1969. *Lobbying*. Belmont, CA: Wadsworth.

ZEIGIER, L. HARMON AND WAYNE G. PEAK. 1972. *Interest Groups in American Politics*. 2d ed. Engelwood Cliffs, NJ: Prentice-Hall.

ZELLER, BELLE. 1937. *Pressure Politics in New York*. New York: Russell and Russell.

ZWIER, ROBERT. 1979. "The Search For Information: Specialists and Nonspecialists in the U.S. House of Representatives," *Legislative Studies Quarterly* 4:31-42.

AN ADVOCACY COALITION FRAMEWORK OF POLICY CHANGE
AND THE ROLE OF POLICY-ORIENTED LEARNING THEREIN
Paul Sabatier*

In the mid-1950s, air pollution was scarcely a subject of public policy in the U.S. Federal efforts were limited to a tiny program of technical assistance, and only a few states had more than paper programs. Governmental entities with active control programs were largely limited to a few cities—New York, Chicago, Pittsburgh, St. Louis, Los Angeles—where the problem was perceived to be one of dirty air arising primarily from coal combustion.

Ten years later, federal expenditures had risen over 20-fold and the number of states with pollution control budgets over $100,000 had increased from 3 to 22 (Davies 1970:105,129). Then in 1970 the Federal Clean Air Amendments were passed, transferring principal responsibility for pollution control from local and state governments to Washington, and instituting a massive regulatory program designed to dramatically improve air quality by the mid-1970s. This coincided with a dramatic change in problem perception: the air was no longer simply dirty, it was now perceived as unhealthy in many areas of the country. And perceptions of the principal sources had shifted from coal-burning residences and factories to include automobile emissions and a variety of other sources.

But the consensus in favor of stringent pollution control soon dissipated, as new issues (e.g. energy) came to the fore and as people became aware of the technical and political difficulties of implementating such ambitious legislation. By the end of the decade, while emissions and air quality levels in many areas had improved, the program was under periodic attack and much of the real authority had been delegated to state and local governments (Ingram 1977, Mazmanian and Sabatier 1983: Chap. 4, Downing, 1984: Chaps. 11–13).

This is merely a capsule summary of an enormously complicated story. But it contains many of the key elements which anyone familiar with policymaking in the U.S. will instantly recognize: the importance of problem perception; shifts in elite and public opinion concerning the salience of various problems; periodic struggles over the proper locus of governmental authority; incomplete attainment of legally-prescribed goals; and an iterative process of policy formulation, problematic implementation, and struggles over reformulation.

How is one to understand the incredibly complex process of policy change over periods of one or several decades? What are the principal

*Paul Sabatier, "An Advocacy Coalition Framework of Policy Change and the Role of Policy-oriented Learning Therein." *Policy Sciences* 21 (1988): 129-168. Used by permission.

causal factors? Political demographers point to the role of changing social and economic conditions, e.g. population migrations, the emergence of new social movements, critical elections, macro-economic changes in inflation and unemployment (Hofferbert 1974, Hibbs and Fassbender 1981, Burnham, 1970). These are undoubtedly important. But, in one of the surprisingly few serious analyses of policy change over several decades, Heclo (1974) concluded that such 'macro' factors could account for only a portion of changes in British and Swedish welfare policy during the first several decades of this century. Equally important, he argued, was the interaction of specialists within a specific policy area, as they gradually learned more about various aspects of the problem over time and experimented with a variety of means to achieve their policy objectives. In essence, Heclo saw policy change as being a product of both (1) large scale social, economic, and political changes and (2) the strategic interaction of people within a policy community involving both competition for power and efforts to develop more knowledgeable means of addressing the policy problem.

In many respects, this paper represents an attempt to translate Heclo's basic insight into a reasonably clear conceptual framework of policy change over time.[1] It continues his focus on the interaction of political elites within a policy community/subsystem attempting to respond to changing socio-economic and political conditions. And it expands his interest into the effects of policy-oriented learning on the broader process of policy change by analyzing the manner in which elites from different advocacy coalitions gradually alter their belief systems over time, partially as a result of formal policy analyses and trial and error learning.

The first part of the paper presents an overview of the conceptual framework. Subsequent sections deal with specific aspects, including external events effecting policy subsystems, the internal structure of subsystems, and the dynamics of policy-oriented learning. The concluding section reviews some of the contributions and limitations of the framework.

An Overview of the Framework

The framework has at least three basic premises: first, that understanding the process of policy change—and the role of policy-oriented learning therein—requires a time perspective of a decade or more. Second, that the

---

[1]Heclo (1974) was an exploratory case study which took as its point of departure political demographers' emphasis on socio-economic conditions and then added several factors to their conception. This framework seeks to systematize many of the factors suggested by Heclo, as well as adding new factors suggested by the literatures on political belief systems, political coalitions, policy implementation, the use of policy analysis, etc. The presentation of such a framework is based on the epistemological assumptions that (1) falsifiability is desirable and (2) that neutral perception is impossible; thus that one should always clarify the theoretical 'lenses' through which one views the world (Popper 1959, Hanson 1969, Fiske and Taylor 1984).

most useful way to think about policy change over such a timespan is through a focus on 'policy subsystems,' i.e. the interaction of actors from different institutions interested in a policy area. Third, that public policies (or programs) can be conceptualized in the same manner as belief systems, i.e. as sets of value priorities and causal assumptions about how to realize them.

The focus on timespans of a decade or more comes directly from findings concerning the importance of the 'enlightenment function' of policy research. Weiss (1977a, b) has argued persuasively that a focus on short-term decision-making will underestimate the influence of policy analysis because such research is used primarily to alter the perceptions and conceptual apparatus of policy-makers over time. A corollary of this view is that it is the cumulative effect of findings from different studies and from ordinary knowledge (Lindblom and Cohen 1979) which has the greatest influence on policy. The literature on policy implementation also points to the need for utilizing time-frames of a decade or more, both in order to complete at least one formulation/implementation/reformulation cycle and to obtain a reasonably accurate portrait of program success and failure (Mazmanian and Sabatier, 1983). Numerous studies have shown that ambitious programs which appeared after a few years to be abject failures received more favorable evaluations when seen in a longer timeframe; conversely, initial successes may evaporate over time (Bernstein 1955, Kirst and Jung 1982, Hogwood and Peters 1982).

The framework's second basic premise is that the most useful aggregate unit of analysis for understanding policy change in modern industrial societies is not any specific governmental institution but rather a policy subsystem, i.e. those actors from a variety of public and private organizations who are actively concerned with a policy problem or issue such as air pollution control, mental health, or surface transportation. Following a number of recent authors, this framework argues that our conception of policy subsystems should be broadened from traditional notions of 'iron triangles'—limited to administrative agencies, legislative committees, and interest groups at a single level of government —to include actors at various levels of government active in policy formulation and implementation, as well as journalists, researchers, and policy analysts who play important roles in the generation, dissemination, and evaluation of policy ideas (Heclo 1978, Dunleavy 1981, Milward and Wamsley 1984, Sharpe 1984).

The third important premise is that public policies/programs incorporate implicit theories about how to achieve their objectives (Pressman and Wildavsky 1973, Majone 1980) and thus can be conceptualized in much the same way as belief systems. They involve value priorities, perceptions of important causal relationships, perceptions of world states (including the magnitude of the problem), perceptions of the efficacy of policy instruments, etc. Assuming that people get involved in politics at least in part to translate their beliefs into public policy, this ability to map beliefs and policies on the same 'canvas' provides a vehicle for assessing the influence of various actors on public policy over time.

Figure 5-2 presents a general overview of the framework. On the left side are two sets of exogenous variables—the one fairly stable, the other more dynamic—which affect the constraints and opportunities of subsystem actors. Air pollution policy, for example, is strongly affected by the nature of air quality as a collective good, by the geographical contours of air

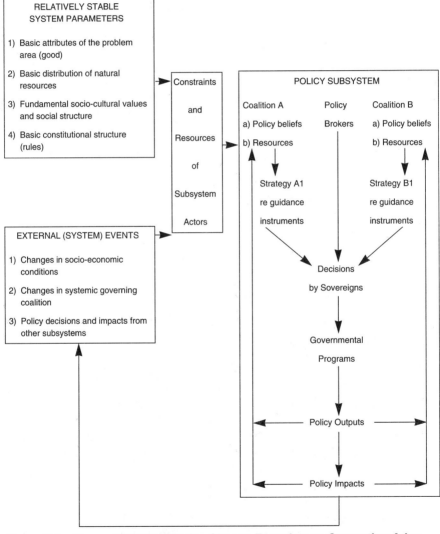

Figure 5-2 General Model of Policy Change Focusing on Competing Advocacy Coalitions within Policy Subsystems.

basins, and by political boundaries which are usually quite stable over time. But there are also more dynamic factors, including changes in socio-economic conditions (e.g. public opinion and oil prices) and in the systemic governing coalition, which provide some of the principal sources of policy change.

Within the subsystem, it is assumed that actors can be aggregated into a number of advocacy coalitions composed of people from various organizations who share a set of normative and causal beliefs and who often act in concert. At any particular point in time, each coalition adopts a strategy(s) envisaging one or more institutional innovations which it feels will further its policy objectives. Conflicting strategies from various coalitions are normally mediated by a third group of actors, here termed 'policy brokers,' whose principal concern is to find some reasonable compromise which will reduce intense conflict. The end result is one or more governmental programs, which in turn produce policy outputs at the operational level (e.g. agency permit decisions). These outputs—mediated by a number of other factors—result in a variety of impacts on targeted problem parameters (e.g. ambient air quality), as well as side effects.

On the basis of perceptions of the adequacy of governmental decisions and/or the resultant impacts, as well as new information arising from search processes and external dynamics, each advocacy coalition may revise its beliefs and/or alter its strategy. The latter may involve the seeking of major institutional revisions at the collective choice level, more minor revisions at the operational level, or even going outside the subsystem by seeking changes in the dominant electoral coalition at the systematic level.[2]

Within the general process of policy change, this framework has a particular interest in policy-oriented learning. Following Heclo (1974:306), policy-oriented learning refers to relatively enduring alterations of thought or behavioral intentions which result from experience and which are concerned with the attainment (or revision) of policy objectives. Policy-oriented learning involves the internal feedback loops depicted in Figure 5-2, perceptions concerning external dynamics, and increased knowledge of the state of problem parameters and the factors affecting them. The integration of

---

[2]The framework generally follows that meta-theoretical approach of Kiser and Ostrom (1982) who argue that individual decision-making should be conceptualized as the product of individual attributes (preferences, information processing capabilities) confronted with an action situation which itself is the result of institutional rules, problem attributes, and socio-cultural values (i.e. roughly analogous to our list of external factors). Kiser and Ostrom also suggest the presence of at least three levels of action situations: the constitutional, the collective choice (e.g. legislation), and the operational (e.g. the disposition of individual cases). A logical extension of this approach is to view policy change as partially the product of attempts by various actors to structure action situations—chiefly via institutional rules regarding the range and authority of participants—so as to produce the desired operational decisions. It is worth nothing, however, that William Dunn (personal communication) insists this advocacy coalition framework is quite compatible with an alternative meta-theory which he terms constructivism' (Dunn, 1982).

this knowledge with the basic values and causal assumptions comprising the core beliefs of advocacy coalitions is the focus of policy learning. The framework assumes that such learning is instrumental, i.e. that members of various coalitions seek to better understand the world in order to further their policy objectives. They will resist information suggesting that their basic beliefs may be invalid and/or unattainable, and they will use formal policy analyses primarily to buttress and elaborate those beliefs (or attack their opponents'). Within this assumption of the prevalence of advocacy analysis, the framework identifies several factors which may nevertheless facilitate learning *across* advocacy coalitions.

Such learning comprises, however, only *one* of the forces affecting policy change over time. In addition to this cognitive activity, there is a real world which changes. This involves, first of all, the realm of system dynamica in Figure 5-2: changes in relevant socioeconomic conditions and system-wide governing coalitions—such as 1973 Arab oil boycott or the 1980 election of Ronald Reagan—can dramatically alter the composition and the resources of various coalitions and, in turn, public policy within the subsystem. Turnover in personnel—sometimes resulting from external conditions, sometimes merely from death or retirement —constitutes a second non-cognitive source of change which can substantially alter the political resources of various advocacy coalitions and thus the policy decisions at the collective choice and operational levels.

The basic argument of this framework is that, while policy-oriented learning is an important aspect of policy change and can often alter secondary aspects of a coalition's belief system, changes in the *core* aspects of a policy are usually the results of perturbations in non-cognitive factors external to the subsystem such as macro-economic conditions or the rise of a new systemic governing coalition. The framework certainly borrows a great deal from Heclo (1974; 1978), but differs from him in its emphasis on ideologically-based coalitions and in its conception of the dynamics of policy-oriented learning. It can also be clearly distinguished from analyses which view formal organizations as the basic actors (e.g. Krasnow et al. 1982), or those which focus on individuals seeking to attain their self-interest through the formation of short-term 'minimum winning coalitions' (Riker 1962).

In order to facilitate continuity of presentation, concepts and hypotheses will generally be illustrated with examples from U.S. air pollution policy. The framework should be applicable to policy change in most industrial polyarchies (Dahl 1971).

External Factors Affecting Policy Change within Subsystems

Policy-making in any political system or policy subsystem is constrained by a variety of social, legal, and resource features of the society of which it is a part (Heclo 1974, Hofferbert 1974, Kiser and Ostrom 1982).

Our concern with the analysis of policy change means that stable external factors must be distinguished from more dynamic ones. And the focus on policy subsystems means that the relationship to other subsystems and to the broader political system must be taken into account. Thus the framework distinguishes between (A) relatively stable (over several decades) parameters and (B) those aspects of the system which are susceptible to significant fluctuations over the course of a few years and thus serve as major stimuli to policy change.

Relatively Stable Parameters The following set of very stable factors may be either within, or external to, the policy subsystem. While the difficulty of changing the following sets of factors discourages actors from making them the object of strategizing behavior, these factors can certainly limit the range of feasible alternatives or otherwise affect the resources and beliefs of subsystem actors.

1. *Basic attributes of the problem area (or 'good')*. Public choice theorists have shown how various characteristics of goods, such as excludability, affect institutional (policy) options. For example, ocean fisheries and large underground aquifers give rise to common pool problems which markets cannot deal with efficiently and which make them candidates for governmental regulation (Ostrom 1986).

    Other aspects of the good or problem/issue area affect the degree of policy-oriented learning likely to take place. For example, a problem's susceptibility to quantitative measurement affects the ability to ascertain performance gaps. The extent of learning is likewise contingent upon the ease of developing good causal models of the factors affecting a problem. One would thus expect more learning on air pollution than on mental health.

2. *Basic distribution of natural resources*. The present (and/or past) distribution of natural resources strongly affects a society's overall wealth and viability of different economic sectors, many aspects of its culture, and the feasibility of options in many policy areas. For example, the U.S. could encourage utilities to switch from oil to coal in the mid-1970s—with its potentially significant effects on sulfur emissions—while the French, lacking abundant coal reserves, turned to nuclear power as an alternative means of generating electricity.

3. *Fundamental cultural values and social structure*. Large-scale nationalization of the means of production is a viable policy option in many European countries, but not the U.S. While such norms are not immutable, change usually requires decades.

    Similarly, political power in most countries tends to be rather highly correlated with income, social class, and large organizations. Significant changes in the influence of various social groups—blacks and Chicanos in the U.S., the coloured in Britain, the rural poor virtually everywhere—normally take several decades. Likewise, the influence on air pollution policy of automobile corporations in the U.S. is unlikely to decline in the near future. The political resources (or lack there of) of many interest groups are slowly-changing 'facts of life' which actors within a subsystem must take into account in formulating their strategies in the short- or moderate-term.

4. *Basic legal structure.* In most political systems, basic legal norms are quite resistant to change. The U.S. Constitution has not been significantly altered since the granting of women's suffrage in 1920. The institutions of the French Fifth Republic have remained virtually unchanged for 25 years; those of the German Federal Republic for 35. Basic legal traditions—such as the role the courts and the fundamental norms of administrative law—also tend to be rather stable over periods of a decade or more.

Constitutional and other fundamental legal norms can also affect the extent of policy-oriented learning. For example, Ashford (1981:16-17) has argued that the concentration of policy-making authority in the British cabinet and higher civil service—coupled with the secrecy which permeates the system—inhibit outsiders from making intelligent evaluations of present policy. In a similar vein, public choice theorists have long argued that decentralized political systems with relatively autonomous local governments facilitate learning by providing arenas for policy experimentation and realistic points of comparison for evaluating different policy instruments (Ostrom, Tiebout and Warren 1961; Ostrom 1982).

Dynamic (System) Events   The following factors external to a policy subsystem can vary substantially over the course of a few years or a decade. By altering the constraints and opportunities confronting subsystem actors, they constitute one of the principal dynamic elements affecting policy change. They also present a continuous challenge to subsystem actors to learn how to anticipate and to respond to them in a manner consistent with their basic beliefs and interests. The process must be frustrating at times, as actors who have worked for years to gain an advantage over their competitors within a subsystem suddenly find their plans knocked awry by (external) events—such as the Arab oil boycott—over which they have little control.

1. *Changes in socio-economic conditions and technology.* These can substantially affect a subsystem, either by undermining the causal assumptions of present policies or by significantly altering the political support of various advocacy coalitions. For example, the dramatic rise in public concern with environmental degradation in the late 1960s played an important role in the passage of the 1970 Clean Air Amendments (Ingram 1978). On the other hand, the Arab oil boycott of 1973-74 contributed to such a depression in the domestic automobile industry that the United Auto Workers—previously a strong supporter of stringent air pollution programs—began echoing industry calls for a relaxation of costly and allegedly energy-inefficient automotive pollution controls (Mazmanian and Sabatier 1983:104).

2. *Changes in systemic governing coalitions.* Air pollution policy was only a trivial issue in the 1980 election of President Reagan and a conservative majority in the Senate—an election dominated by stagflation, the Iranian hostage crisis, and the perceived incompetence of the incumbent President. Nevertheless, Reagan's election led to the appointment of administrators at the Environmental Protection Agency (EPA) who were committed to a drastic reduction

in federal enforcement of environmental legislation (Vig and Kraft 1984). While that position had previously been supported by a minority coalition within the relevant subsystems, it was Reagan's election on *other* issues which brought the minority to power at EPA.

3. *Policy decisions and impacts from other subsystems.* Subsystems are only partially autonomous. In fact, the decisions and impacts from other policy sectors are one of the principal dynamic elements affecting specific subsystems.

   Examples are legion. The search for 'energy independence' in the mid-1970s had significant repercussions on U.S. pollution control policy, as the Nixon and Ford Administrations sought to require utilities to change from (clean burning) natural gas to more abundant coal. Britain's entry into the Common Market (largely on foreign policy and economic grounds) has had repercussions on subsystems from taxation to pollution control because of the need to comply with EEC mandates. And there is evidence that drastic reductions in local tax revenues brought about by Proposition 13 have affected California land use policy by encouraging local governments to become more leery of the service costs of dispersed new housing developments (Inan 1979).

The paper thus far has basically reminded readers of two sets of factors which affect the constraints and resources facing subsystem actors. While the list may strike some readers as rather obvious, the critical role accorded external events by the framework—see Hypothesis 1, for example—means that such factors must he explicated at least briefly if the framework is to be operationalized and rendered falsifiable. We can now turn to an analysis of strategic interaction *within* subsystems.

Policy Subsystems: Internal Structure

The complexity of modern society, the expansion. of governmental functions, and the technical nature of most policy problems create enormous pressures for specialization. It is exceedingly difficult, except perhaps in small communities, to be knowledgeable about more than one or two policy sectors. When others specialize—as they do in any moderately large political system—generalists find it difficult to compete.

Thus it has long been recognized that political elites actively concerned with a specific problem or policy area tend to form relatively autonomous subsystems (Griffith 1961, Fritschler 1975, Dodd and Schott 1979, Hamm 1983). But traditional notions of 'whirlpool' and 'iron triangles' suffer because they are generally limited to interest groups, administrative agencies, and legislative committees at a single level of government. They need to be expanded to include journalists, analysts, researchers, and others who play important roles in the generation, dissemination, and evaluation of policy ideas, as well as actors at other levels of government who play important roles in policy formulation and implementation (Heclo 1978, Wamsley 1983, Kingdon 1984, Sabatier and Pelkey 1987).

Delimiting Subsystem Boundaries   Let us define a policy subsystem as the set of actors who are involved in dealing with a policy problem such as air pollution control, mental health, or energy. While it is often useful to begin with a networking approach to identify the actors involved at any particular point in time (Hjern and Porter 1981), the analyst must also be willing to identify potential (latent) actors who would become active if they had the appropriate information.[3]

The latter approach is important for understanding the role of technical information in policy change over time. For example, Federal air pollution officials in the late 1960s identified a number of latent supporters of stricter pollution control programs and then developed several information and participation programs to encourage their involvement (Sabatier 1975). This explicit effort at using information to expand the range of subsystem actors fundamentally altered air pollution politics in Chicago and several other cities. It would never have been possible, however, had officials (or the analyst studying the case) been content to limit subsystem participants to those previously active. Some means of identifying latent interests is absolutely critical because information can be used to activate those interests and thus alter the balance of power within subsystems.

Origins of Subsystems   The most likely reason for the emergence of new subsystems is that a group of actors become dissatisfied enough with the neglect of a particular problem by existing subsystems to form their own. For example, dissatisfaction with the laissez-faire approach to food safety (e.g. meat inspections) by the agriculture subsystem became so intense in the early 1900s that a new subsystem—centered around what was to become the Food and Drug Administration—gradually separated from the agricultural subsystem over a period of several decades (Nadel 1971:7-17). Whereas this case involved a minority coalition breaking away to form its own subsystem, in other cases a new system is essentially the product of a subset of a dominant coalition becoming large and specialized enough to form its own; an example would be the emergence of housing out of the urban policy subsystem during the 1960s (Farkas 1971).

Subsystem Actors: Advocacy Coalitions and Policy Brokers   Whatever their origins, subsystems normally contain a large and diverse set of ac-

---

[3]The basic argument for including latent interests is found in Balbus (1971). Knoepfel and Weidner (1982) used a list of potential interests as a checklist against the range of present participants in their study of air pollution policy in several European countries. In principle, delimitation of subsystem boundaries should be based upon (1) frequency of interaction (2) and transitivity of influence.

tors. For example, the U.S. air pollution control subsystem includes the following:

1. The Environmental Protection Agency
2. Relevant Congressional committees
3. Portions of peer agencies such as the Department of Energy which are frequently involved in pollution control policy
4. Polluting corporations, their trade associations, unions, and, occasionally, consumer associations
5. The manufacturers of pollution control equipment
6. Environmental and public health groups
7. State and local pollution control agencies
8. Research institutes and consulting firms with a strong interest in air pollution
9. Important journalists who frequently cover the issue
10. On some issues such as acid rain, actors in other countries

Given the enormous number and range of actors involved, it becomes necessary to find ways of aggregating them into smaller and theoretically useful sets of categories.

After considering several alternatives, I have concluded that the most useful means of aggregating actors in order to understand policy change over fairly long periods of time is by 'advocacy coalitions'. These are people from a variety of positions (elected and agency officials, interest group leaders, researchers) who share a particular belief system—i.e. a set of basic values, causal assumptions, and problem perceptions—and who show a nontrivial degree of coordinated activity over time.

I find this superior to the most likely alternative—that viewing formal institutions as the dominant actors—because in most policy subsystems there are at least 20-30 organizations at various levels of government which are active over time. Developing models involving changes in the positions and interaction patterns of that many units over a period of a decade or more would be an *exceedingly* complex task (Sabatier and Pelkey 1987). Moreover, institutional models have difficulty accounting for the importance of specific individuals who move about from organization to organization within the same subsystem (Heclo 1978). Finally, institutional models have difficulty accounting for the huge variation in behavior among individuals within the same institution, e.g. Congress, the federal district courts, the AFL-CIO, or even the same governmental agency (Mazmanian and Nienaber 1979, Liroff 1986). Thus I prefer to utilize advocacy coalitions as a more manageable focus of analysis, while certainly acknowledging that institutions bring critical resources—e.g. the authority to make certain types of authoritative decisions—to the members of a coalition.

In most subsystems, the number of politically-significant advocacy coalitions will be quite small. In quiescent subsystems there may only be a single coalition. In most cases, however, there will be 2-4 important coalitions—the number being limited by all the factors which push actors to coalesce if they are to form effective coalitions (Jenkins-Smith, personal communication; Kingdon 1984). If one's opponents pool their resources under a common position, to remain without allies is to invite defeat; but allies create all sorts of pressures for common positions, which tend to harden over time. This hardening of positions is strengthened by the importance of organizational actors (whose positions are usually slow to change) and by the tendency to perceive one's opponents as being more hostile and powerful than they probably are (Sabatier et al. 1987). This argument suggests, then, that there will be greater fragmentation of beliefs in recently-formed subsystems than in more established ones. Since most subsystems have existed for decades, however, one would expect the number of coalitions in each to be relatively small.

For example, the American air pollution subsystem in the 1970s was apparently divided into two rather distinct advocacy coalitions. One, which might be termed 'the Clean Air Coalition', was dominated by environmental/public health groups, their allies in Congress (e.g. Senator Muskie), most pollution control officials in EPA, a few labor unions, many state and local pollution control officials (particularly in large cities with serious problems), and some researchers. It had a belief system which stressed *i)* the primacy of human health over economic development and efficiency; *ii)* a perception that air pollution was a serious health problem in many urban areas; *iii)* a focus on the inability of markets to deal with 'negative externalities' such as air pollution; *iv)* a causal assumption that state and local governments' preoccupation with competitive advantage in attracting industry made them susceptible to industrial 'blackmail' and thus required a strong federal presence; *v)* a deep distrust of the motives of corporate officials and a consequent assumption of the necessity of forcing the pace of technological innovation; and *vi)* a strong preference for a legal command and control approach rather than heavy reliance on economic incentives.

The competing 'Economic Feasibility Coalition' was dominated by industrial emission sources, energy companies, their allies in Congress (e.g. Congressman Broyhill), several labor unions (particularly after the Arab oil boycott), some state and local pollution control officials, and a few economists. Its belief system *i)* stressed the need to balance human health against economic development and efficiency; *ii)* questioned the alleged seriousness of the health problem except in isolated instances; *iii)* believed that increasing social welfare generally required a deference to market arrangements; *iv)* generally disapproved of a strong federal role (largely on the assumption that their leverage was greater with local officials); *v)* placed great emphasis on legally requiring only what was technologically feasible; and *vi)* expressed support (at least in principle) for the flexibility and cost-effectiveness of economic incentives rather than general legal commands (Downing 1984).

Not everyone active in a policy subsystem will 'belong to' an advocacy coalition or share one of the major belief systems. Some researchers and others may participate simply because they have certain skills to offer, but otherwise be indifferent to the policy disputes (Meltsner 1976). In addition, there will almost certainly be a category of actors—here termed 'policy brokers'—whose dominant concern is with keeping the level of political conflict within acceptable limits and with reaching some 'reasonable' solution to the problem. This is a traditional function of some elected officials (particularly chief executives) and, in some European countries like Britain and France, of high civil servants (Doggan 1975). The courts, 'blue ribbon commissions', and other actors may also play the role of policy broker. The distinction between 'advocate' and 'broker' is, however, a continuum. Many brokers will have some policy bent, while advocates may show some serious concern with system maintenance. The framework merely insists that this is an empirical question which may or may not be correlated with institutional affiliation. While high civil servants may be brokers, they are also often policy advocates—particularly when their agency has a clearly defined mission.[4]

The concept of an 'advocacy coalition' assumes that it is shared beliefs which provide the principal 'glue' of politics. Moreover, as shall be discussed shortly, it is assumed that people's 'core' beliefs are quite resistant to change. This leads to one of the critical hypotheses of the entire framework:

> *Hypothesis 1:* On major controversies within a policy subsystem (i.e. when core beliefs are in dispute), the lineup of allies and opponents will tend to be rather stable over periods of a decade or so.[5]

Thus the framework explicitly rejects the view that actors are primarily motivated by their short-term self-interest and thus that 'coalitions of conve-

---

[4]Floyd Dominy of the U.S. Bureau of Reclamation is an example of an administrator who was clearly a policy advocate (McPhee, 1971).

[5]A weaker hypothesis would suggest that an advocacy coalition will consist of (a) a set of fairly stable members with compatible policy cores and (b) temporary members who float in and out depending upon the particular policy dispute. For example, Ackerman and Hassler (1981) report that the ranks of the Clean Air Coalition were augmented during the mid-1970s by western coal companies, whose supply of low-sulfur coal led them to join environmentalists in seeking stringent emission controls on utilities (which would give them a competitive advantage against high-sulfur midwestern coal). But this alliance was subsequently disrupted when Congressman Henry Waxman, one of the leaders of the Clean Air Coalition, suggested a uniform nationwide tax on utilities as a means of dealing with the acid rain problem which would deal equitably with the concerns of midwestern coal companies and utilities.

nience' of highly varying composition will dominate policy-making over time. This is consistent with the evidence from a number of studies, including (1) the history of U.S. energy policy by Wildavsky and Tenenbaum (1981), (2) Marmor's (1970) analysis of the politics of medicare in the U.S., (3) the work of Jenkins-Smith and St. Clair (1988) on offshore oil development and (4) numerous analyses of the composition of majority coalitions in multiparty European parliaments over the past several decades, which have found that —in contrast to Riker's (1962) 'minimum winning coalition' model—coalition formation has been quite constrained by ideology.[6]

Of course, coalition stability could be the result, not of stable beliefs, but rather of stable economic/organizational interests. This raises very thorny methodological issues, in part because belief systems are normally highly correlated with self-interest and the causation is reciprocal.[7] For example, while Sierra Club leaders and steel company executives typically have quite different views on air pollution control, is this because (a) their organizations have quite different (economic) interests or because (b) people join organizations—and put in the effort to rise to prominence in them—out of affinity with the organization's stated goals? This framework uses belief systems, rather than 'interests,' as its focus because beliefs are more inclusive and more verifiable. Interest models must still identify a set of means and performance indicators necessary for goal attainment; this set of interests/goals, perceived causal relationships, and perceived parameter states constitutes a 'belief system.' While belief system models can thus incorporate self/organizational interests, they also allow actors to establish goals in quite different ways (e.g. as a result of socialization) and are therefore more inclusive. In addition, I personally have great difficulty in specifying *a priori* a clear and falsifiable set of interests for most actors in policy conflicts. Instead, it seems preferable to allow actors to indicate their belief systems (via questionnaires and content analysis of documents) and then empirically examine the extent to which these change over time.

---

[6]The literature on coalition formation in multi-party parliamentary regimes has found both minimum size and ideological constraints to be important factors, with their relative importance varying by country (Browne 1970, de Swann 1973, Taylor and Laver 1973, Dodd 1976, Warwick 1979, Hinckley 1981, Browne and Dreijamis 1982, Franklin and Mackie 1984, Zariski 1984). Unfortunately, the literature on (interest group) coalitions within subsystems over periods of at least a decade appears to be remarkably sparse and unsophisticated, with the study by Wildavsky and Tenenbaum (1981) among the more suggestive. The problem probably resides in methodological difficulties in determining what constitutes a coalition using, for example, legislative/budgetary hearings as a data base.

[7]In the case of air pollution control, the willingness of western coal companies to side with environmentalists against midwestern coal companies would be a case of self-interest (competitive market advantage) over laissez-faire ideology (Ackerman and Hassler, 1981). But the reluctance of manufacturers of pollution control equipment to openly ally themselves with environmentalists in most controversies over the past 20 years would suggest that ideology can likewise restrain the pursuit of self-interest.

Advocacy Coalitions and Public Policy   Coalitions seek to translate their beliefs into public policies (programs). While pressures for compromise generally result in governmental programs incorporating elements advocated by different coalitions, the 1970 Federal Clean Air Amendments incorporated to an unusual degree most elements of the belief system of the Clean Air Coalition.

In any decentralized system, however, different coalitions may be in control of various governmental units. For example, the Economic Efficiency Coalition was apparently more powerful in Sun Belt states during most of the 1970s than at the national level. In fact, one of the basic strategies of any coalition is to manipulate the assignment of program responsibilities so that governmental units which it controls have the most authority (Schattschneider, 1960).

While belief systems will determine the *direction* in which an advocacy coalition (or any other political actor) will seek to move governmental programs, *its ability to do so* will be critically dependent upon its resources. These include such things as money, expertise, number of supporters, and legal authority. With respect to the last, this framework acknowledges one of the central features of institutional models—namely, that rules create authority (power)—but views these rules as the product of competition among advocacy coalitions and views institutional members as providing resources to different coalitions.

The resources of various coalitions change, of course, over time. Some of this is intentional. In fact, most coalitions seek to augment their budgets, recruit new members (especially those with legal authority, expertise, or money) place their members in positions of authority, and employ the variety of other means long identified by interest group theorists (Truman 1951, Berry 1977). But there is also substantial evidence that some coalitions have a more difficult time maintaining an effective presence over time than others. This is particularly true in consumer and environmental protection, where the groups which originally championed regulation have had more difficulty than the regulated industries in finding sufficient organizational resources to monitor and to intervene in the extended process of policy implementation (Bernstein 1955, Nadel 1971, Quirk 1980). Even more severe difficulties confront economically disadvantaged groups in their efforts to muster the resources necessary to remain active over any extended period of time (Goodwin and Moen 1981).

Although the framework focuses on the belief systems of advocacy coalitions—both in themselves and insofar as they are translated into public policy—as the critical vehicle for examining policy change over time, it must not be forgotten that the political resources available to different coalitions will strongly affect their ability to actually translate their beliefs into authoritative policy decisions.

Policy-Oriented Belief Systems   In its conception of the belief systems of individuals and collectivities, the framework has three basic points of departure. The first is Ajzen and Fishbein's (1980) 'theory of reasoned action'—basically an expected utility model in which actors weigh alternative courses of action in terms of their contribution to a set of goals, but in which the preferences of reference groups (such as members of one's coalition) are accorded a more prominent role than in most utilitarian models. Second, rationality is limited rather than perfect. Thus the framework relies heavily upon the work of March and Simon (1958), Nisbett and Ross (1980), Kahneman et al. (1982), and many others in terms of satisficing, cognitive limits on rationality, limited search processes, etc. Third, because subsystems are composed of policy elites rather than the general public, there are strong grounds for assuming that most actors will have *relatively* complex and internally consistent belief systems in the policy area(s) of interest to them (Wilker and Milbrath 1972, Cobb 1973, Axelrod 1976, Putnam 1976:87-93, Buttel and Flinn 1978).

These, however, are only starting points, for they tell us very little about what will happen when experience reveals anomalies—internal inconsistencies, inaccurate predictions, invalid assertions—among beliefs. Assuming some social and psychological pressures for belief consistency and validity, are conflicts resolved in an essentially random process—i.e. with all beliefs accorded the same logical status—or are some more fundamental than others and thus more resistant to change? What, in short, is the *structure* of the belief systems of policy elites?

This is a mine field of conflicting theories and evidence.[8] But the most useful approach seems to be a synthesis of Putnam's (1976:81-89) review of the normative and cognitive orientations of political elites, Axelrod's (1976) work on the complexity of their causal assumptions, an adaptation of Lakatos' (1971) distinction between 'core' and other elements of scientific belief systems, and Converse's (1964) contention that abstract political beliefs are more resistant to change than specific ones (also Peffley and Hurwitz 1985).

Given that the basic strategy of the framework is to use the structure of belief systems to predict changes in beliefs and attempted changes in policy over time, that structure must be stipulated *a priori* if the argument to

---

[8]Among the major strands in this literature are (a) the work of Converse (1964), and many others which view the Left-Right continuum as critical; (b) the 'operational code' studies examining elite assumptions concerning the nature of political conflict (George 1969, Putnam 1973), (c) the work of Axelrod (1976) diagramming the causal assumptions of policy elites, and (d) the work of Conover and Feldman (1984) on schema 'theory.' For a summary of much of this literature, see Putnam (1976: Chap. 4). The distinction between 'secondary aspects' and 'core' is rather similar to Steinbruner's (1974) distinction between 'cybernetic' and 'cognitive' levels of thinking and to Argyris and Schon's (1978) analysis of 'single' and 'double loop' learning.

come in Hypotheses 2 and 3 is to be falsifiable. The unsettled nature of the field makes this a risky undertaking. Nevertheless, on the assumption that clarity—even if wrong—begets clarity and eventually improved under- standing of a phenomenon, the framework proposes the structure of elite belief systems outlined in Table 5-1.[9]

As can be seen, Table 5-1 outlines three structural categories: a Deep Core of fundamental normative and ontological axioms which define a per- son's underlying personal philosophy, a Near (Policy) Core of basic strate- gies and policy positions for achieving Deep Core beliefs in the policy area/subsystem in question, and a set of Secondary Aspects comprising a multitude of instrumental decisions and information searches necessary to implement the Policy Core in the specific policy area. The three structural categories are arranged in order of decreasing resistance to change, i.e. the Deep Core being much more resistant than the Secondary Aspects.

Using U.S. air pollution policy to illustrate the structure of belief sys- tems, the Clean Air Coalition and the Economic Efficiency Coalition have been fundamentally divided over the extent to which the pursuit of individ- ual freedom in a market economy should be constrained in order to protect the health of 'susceptible populations' (e.g., those already suffering from respiratory diseases). Members of the Clean Air Coalition argue that the protection accorded susceptible populations should be virtually absolute, while members of the Economic Efficiency Coalition have been more will- ing to put them at some risk in the interests of individual liberty and in- creased production. This normative difference in the Policy Core of the two coalitions probably reflected a Deep Core difference in the relative priority accorded freedom (or efficiency) versus equality, a conflict underlying many policy disputes (Rokeach 1973; Okun 1975).

Differences on this (and other) issues helped members of the two coalitions to adopt quite different positions on such Policy Core issues as the proper scope of governmental (vs. market) activity, the proper role of the federal government, the advantages of using coercion vs. other policy instruments, the overall seriousness of the air pollution problem in the U.S., etc. These are the sorts of issues which were decided in the 1970 Clean Air Amendments and which, despite numerous attacks, have remained largely unchanged in law since then (Mazmanian and Sabatier 1983: Chap. 4). While there have been since 1970 some issues (most notably, non-degrada- tion and acid rain) which have involved core disputes, most policy-making has focused on secondary aspects such as the determination of which air quality standards are adequate to protect susceptible populations, the feasi- bility of using parking surcharges as a tool for reducing vehicle miles trav-

---

[9]This is a slightly improved version over that previously published in Sabatier (1986), Table 3.

Table 5-1 Structure of Belief Systems of Policy Elites[a]

	Deep (Normative) Core	Near (Policy) Core	Secondary Aspects
Defining characteristics	Fundamental normative and ontological axioms	Fundamental policy positions concerning the basic strategies for achieving normative axioms of deep core.	Instrumental decisions and information searches necessary to implement policy core.
Scope	Part of basic personal philosophy. Applies to all policy areas.	Applies to policy area of interest (and perhaps a few more).	Specific to policy/subsystem of interest.
Susceptibility to change	Very difficult; akin to a religious conversion.	Difficult, but can occur if experience reveals serious anomalies.	Moderately easy; this is the topic of most administrative and even legislative policy-making.

Illustrative components	1) The nature of man
	  i) Inherently evil vs. socially redeemable.
	  ii) Part of nature vs. dominion over nature.
	  iii) Narrow egoists vs. contractarians.
	2) Relative priority of various ultimate values; freedom, security, power, knowledge, health, love, beauty, etc.
	3) Basic criteria of distributive justice: Whose welfare counts? Relative weights of self, primary groups, all people, future generations, non-human beings, etc.
		1) Proper scope of govern-mental vs. market activity.
		2) Proper distribution of authority among various units (e.g. levels) of government
		3) Identification of social groups whose welfare is most critical.
		4) Orientation on substantive policy conflicts, e.g. environmental protection vs. economic development.
		5) Magnitude of perceived threat to those values.
		6) Basic choices concerning policy instruments, e.g. coercion vs. inducements vs. persuasion.
		7) Desirability of participa-tion by various segments of society:
		  i) Public vs. elite participation.
		  ii) Experts vs. elected officials.
		8) Ability of society to solve problems in this policy area:
		  i) Zero-sum competition vs. potential for mutual accommodation.
		  ii) Technological optimism vs. pessimism.
			1) Most decisions concerning administrative rules, budgetary allocations, disposition of cases, statutory interpretation, and even statutory revision.
			2) Information concerning program performance, the seriousness of the problems, etc.

[a] The policy core and secondary aspects also apply to governmental programs.

eled, the determination of which auto emission standards would minimize emissions without wrecking the domestic auto industry, and the technical validity of various techniques for monitoring atmospheric emissions.

It would be absurd to assume that all members of an advocacy coalition have precisely the same belief system. But, based upon Converse's (1964) premise that abstract beliefs are more salient and more resistant to change than more specific ones, most members of a coalition will presumably show substantial agreement on the Policy Core issues outlined in Table 5-1 which need to be addressed by any belief system. In addition, positions on these issues will be slower to change than those concerning the Secondary (implementing) Aspects of a belief system. This leads to the following corollary hypotheses:

> *Hypothesis 2*: Actors within an advocacy coalition will show substantial consensus on issues pertaining to the policy core, although less so on secondary aspects.
>
> *Hypothesis 3*: An actor (or coalition) will give up secondary aspects of his (its) belief system before acknowledging weaknesses in the policy core.

While this leaves open the precise amount of consensus on the policy core which is necessary for an advocacy coalition to be said to 'exist,' the basic thrust of the argument should be quite clear. It is also far from self-evident, as it disagrees with those who proclaim the end of ideology (Bell 1960), perceive the domination of short term 'coalitions of convenience' (Riker 1962), view specific beliefs as more salient than abstract ones (Wilker and Milbrath 1972), or see policy change as a muddled process in which policy technocrats play a major role (Heclo 1978).

Methods for investigating the content of belief systems include elite surveys, panels of knowledgeable observers (Hart 1976), and content analysis of relevant documents (Axelrod 1976). Given the rather technical nature of many Secondary Aspects and the focus on changes in beliefs over a decade or more, content analyses of government documents (e.g. legislative and administrative hearings) and interest group publications probably offer the best prospects for systematic empirical work on changes in elite beliefs.[10]

The entire notion of a belief system organized around a set of core values and policy strategies, plus implementing activities, assumes some psychological predilection for instrumental rationality and cognitive consis-

---

[10]The author and Hank Jenkins-Smith of the University of New Mexico are currently developing a methodology for content analyzing government documents which applies the structure of belief systems in Table 1; it is being applied to (a) OCS drilling and (b) land use at Lake Tahoe (Jenkins-Smith and Sabatier, 1987).

tency on the part of policy elites. It does not, however, take issue with the implications of Simon's recent work suggesting that cognitive structures resemble semi-autonomous filing cabinets into which one places new information (Newell and Simon 1972, Simon 1979). Instead, the framework supposes that policy elites seek to better understand the world within a particular policy area ('filing cabinet') in order to identify means to achieve their fundamental objectives. Such thought produces pressures for evaluative consistency (Tesser, 1978:295).

The framework also presumes some (modest) selection pressures towards those with a capacity for reasoned discourse *within* the 'filing cabinet' directly concerned with the policy subsystem(s) in which they are active. Insofar as policy discussions among insiders are based on reasoned argument, actors holding blatantly inconsistent or unsubstantiated positions will lose credibility. That may not be completely debilitating for their position, but it will force them to expend scarce political resources in its support and eventually be to their competitive disadvantage (Brewer and de Leon, 1983).

Once something has been accepted as a *core* belief, however, powerful egodefense, peer-group, and organizational forces create considerable resistance to change even in the face of countervailing empirical evidence or internal inconsistencies (Festinger 1957, Argyris and Schon 1978, Janis 1983). The literature on cognitive dissonance and selective perception is enormous and far from conclusive (Abelson et al. 1968, Wicklund and Brehm 1976, Greenwald and Ronis 1978, Innis 1978). But, *when* salient beliefs and/or the egos of policy elites are at stake, the evidence of selective perception and partisan analysis is strong enough to warrant a prominent place in any model (Schiff 1962, Smith 1968, Steinbruner 1974, Cameron 1978, Innis 1978, Nelkin 1979, Mazur 1981, Fiske and Taylor 1984, Etheridge 1985).

Policy Change within Subsystems: the View thus Far   Policy change within a subsystem can be understood as the product of two processes: First, the efforts of advocacy coalitions within the subsystem to translate the policy cores and the secondary aspects of their belief systems into governmental programs. While most programs will involve some compromise among coalitions, there will usually be a dominant coalition and one or more minority coalitions (Wamsley, 1983). Each will seek to realize its objectives over time through increasing its political resources and through policy-oriented learning (to be discussed in the next section). The second process is one of external perturbation, i.e. the effects of *systemic* events—changes in socio-economic conditions, outputs from other subsystems, and changes in the system-wide governing coalition—on the resources and constraints of subsystem actors.

The framework argues, however, that the policy core of an advocacy coalition is quite resistant to change over time. This leads to the following hypothesis:

> *Hypothesis 4:* The core (basic attributes) of a governmental program are unlikely to be significantly revised as long as the subsystem advocacy coalition which instituted the program remains in power.

This assumes that a coalition seeks power to translate its core beliefs into policy. It will not abandon those (core) beliefs merely to stay in power, although it may well abandon secondary aspects and even try to incorporate some of the opponents' core as *secondary* aspects of the program.

Likewise, the relative strength of different advocacy coalitions within a subsystem will seldom be sufficiently altered by events *internal* to the subsystem (i.e. by efforts to increase resources or to 'outlearn' opponents) to overthrow a dominant coalition. Hence:

> *Hypothesis 5:* The core (basic attributes) of a governmental action program are unlikely to be changed in the absence of significant perturbations external to the subsystem, i.e. changes in socio-economic conditions, system-wide governing coalitions, or policy outputs from other subsystems.

These hypotheses suggest that, while minority coalitions can seek to improve their relative position through augmenting their resources and 'outlearning' their adversaries, their basic hope of gaining power within the subsystem resides in waiting for some *external* event to significantly increase their political resources.

If Hypothesis 5 is correct, the type of policy-oriented learning discussed in the next section is unlikely by itself to significantly alter the *core* attributes of a governmental action program. But it can still lead to substantial changes in the secondary aspects. And learning by a minority coalition may demonstrate such major deficiencies in the core of a program that the majority acknowledges these deficiencies or, more likely, that a system-wide learning process occurs in which system-wide leaders eventually overturn the dominant coalition. A possible example would be the efforts of economists over the past 20 years to demonstrate the inefficiencies of governmental regulation of airline fares and entry—a campaign which eventually led to the abolition of the Civil Aeronautics Board (Derthick and Quirk 1985, Brown 1987, Nelson 1987). In short, policy-oriented learning is an important process in understanding changes in at least the secondary aspects of governmental action programs and, contrary to Hypothesis 5, may occasionally even lead to a revision of core aspects in the absence of perturbations from beyond the subsystem (see also Foley, 1975).

Policy-Oriented Learning within Subsystems

While only individuals can learn,[11] the distribution of attitudes within, and the official position of, collectivities such as interest groups and advocacy coalitions certainly change over time. In general, this will be a function of (1) individual learning and attitudinal change; (2) the diffusion of new beliefs/attitudes among individuals (Petty and Cacioppo, 1981); (3) turnover in individuals within any collectivity (Pierce and Rochon 1984); (4) group dynamics, such as the polarization of homogeneous groups (Rajecki 1982:129-158, Janis 1983); and (5) rules for aggregating preferences and for promoting (or impeding) communication among members (Kiser and Ostrom, 1982).

Policy-Oriented Learning   This framework is particularly concerned with 'policy-oriented learning,' i.e. with relatively enduring alterations of thought or behavioral intentions which result from experience and which are concerned with the attainment or revision of the percepts of one's belief system. Learning can be about a variety of things:

1. *Improving one's understanding of the state of variables defined as important by one's belief system (or secondarily, by competing belief systems).* For example, participants in the Clean Air Advocacy Coalition have expended a great deal of effort monitoring air quality because that is a critical variable affecting one of their core values, the protection of public health. Conversely, members of the Economic Efficiency Coalition have concentrated on estimating the economic costs of pollution control programs, because that is critical to them. Of course, the interactive process within a policy subsystem forces one to gather information on variables defined as critical by others, but this is primarily done to counter opponents' claims (see Figure 5-3).

2. *Refining one's understanding of logical and causal relationships internal to a belief system.* This typically focuses on the search for improved mechanisms to attain core values. For example, automotive emissions are a function of *(a)* emissions per vehicle mile and *(b)* vehicle miles traveled. Members of the Clean Air Coalition tried hard during the 1970s to find effective means of reducing both. The former included R & D into low-emission propulsion systems and contracts with American and foreign manufacturers. The latter involved a series of studies and experiments with carpooling, parking surcharges, etc.

    While proponents will be loathe to reexamine core beliefs, experience and opponents' activities may eventually force them to acknowledge erroneous assumptions or implicit goal contradictions. For example, EPA's efforts to experiment with a variety of mechanisms to reduce vehicle miles traveled met with numerous local debacles, Congressional rebuffs, and discouraging

---

[11]This is consistent with the meta-theory of Kiser and Ostrom (1982) upon which this framework is based. While one may want to argue that an organization, advocacy coalition, or some other collectivity has 'learned' something, such statements are metaphors and should only be used on the basis of explicit decision rules; for example, see Argyris and Schon (1978:19-20).

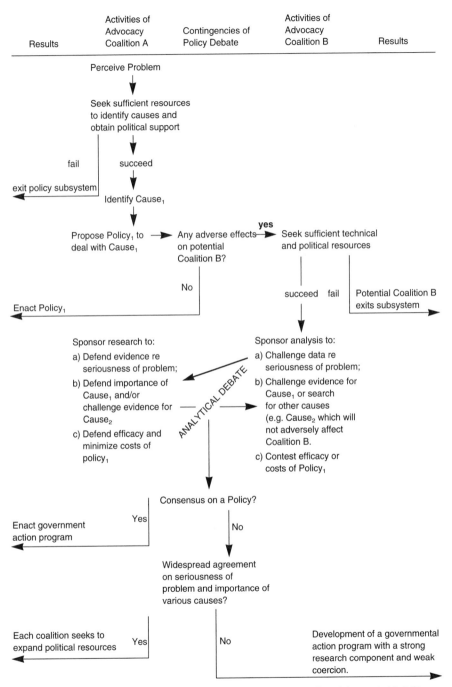

Figure 5-3   Analytical Interactions Between Advocacy Coalitions: Initial Stages

conclusions from contracted research. The agency was eventually forced by Congress in 1977 to give up its efforts to reduce vehicle miles traveled. While its reasons for persisting for so long were multiple, one of the more important was probably its (causal) assumption that such programs were *necessary* to achieve ambient air quality levels in many urban areas. Thus its inability to find effective and politically palatable policy instruments would entail a strategic retreat on its *core* value of protecting human health (Mazmanian and Sabatier, 1983: Chap. 4). [For similar examples in other policy areas, see Cameron (1978) and Robinson (1982).]

3. *Identifying and responding to challenges to one's belief system.* Exogenous events, a loss of political resources, opponents' activities, or a variety of other factors may force proponents to revise their belief systems by incorporating some new elements, e.g. aspects of opponents' beliefs. But every effort will be made to restrict change to the secondary aspects, thus keeping one's core intact.

Since the early 1970s, for example, economists have criticized the inefficiency of the legal command and control approach of the 1970 Clean Air Amendments and argued instead for a variety of economic incentives such as emission fees, transferable pollution rights, etc. (Kneese and Bower 1968, Schultze 1977). The criticism eventually became too important to ignore. Rather than rethink the basic approach of the 1970 Clean Air Act, however, most EPA officials and their Congressional supporters simply incorporated into the 1977 Clean Air Amendments a few variants of economic incentives, e.g. offsets and bubbles, as optional instruments in their overall command and control strategy (Liroff 1986, Cook 1988).

Policy-oriented learning, then, is an ongoing process of search and adaption motivated by the desire to realize core policy beliefs. When confronted with constraints or opportunities, actors attempt to respond in a manner which is consistent with their core. Although exogenous events or opponents' activities may eventually force the reexamination of core beliefs, the pain of doing so means that most learning occurs in the secondary aspects of a belief system and/or governmental program.[12]

The Ambiguity of Experience   Policy-oriented learning normally entails experimenting with a variety of implementing mechanisms over time (Dewey 1938, Brewer 1974, Campbell 1977). Dissatisfaction with the performance of a specific mechanism—in terms of either its policy outputs at the operational level or its resultant inability to ameliorate the problem—will lead program proponents to reexamine their strategy (see Figure 5-2).

---

[12]When change in a governmental action program cannot be restricted to the secondary aspects, one might wish to hypothesize that adherents will seek to modify the core in the following sequence: first, add a portion of the opposing coalition's core; second, delete a portion of the existing core; third, arrange a synthesis of the two cores; and, finally, acquiesce to a replacement of one's core by the challenger's, but try to get portions of it incorporated into the new secondary aspects. It should be noted that the general argument concerning the difficulty of changing core elements is similar to that made by Argyris and Schon (1978) concerning 'double loop' learning.

But learning from experience is very difficult in a world where performance gaps are difficult to measure, well-developed causal theories are often lacking, controlled experimentation is virtually impossible, opponents are doing everything possible to muddle the situation and otherwise to impede one from learning, and even allies' motives are often suspect because of personal and organizational rivalries. Little wonder that advocacy coalitions are constantly arguing about the advisability of different strategies, or that many seek to explore simultaneously many strategies in the hope that a few will fall on fertile soil.

The ambiguity of experience also provides a clue to lag times, to the phenomenon of always preparing to fight the preceding war (Katzenbach 1958, Scharpf 1982). Part of the answer can be found in sunk costs in personnel, capital equipment, and prestige (Kaufman 1971). Part can be attributed to actors' reluctance to revise core beliefs. But part of the explanation lies in the enormous difficulty of assessing the extent of performance gaps and the reasons for them. Without such knowledge, accurate learning from experience is difficult.

Nevertheless it does occur. In a world of scarce resources, those who do not learn are at a competitive disadvantage in realizing their goals. We now turn to a model of that process.

The Advocacy Use of Analysis, Policy-Oriented Learning, and Policy Change   There are at least four points of departure to an understanding of the role of policy analysis/information in policy-oriented learning and eventually in policy change. First, it is primarily perceived threats to people's core values or interests which motivate them to expend scarce resources in policy debates. Second, the crucial role of information and (policy) analysis is to alert people to the extent to which a given situation affects their interests/values. Third, once political actors have developed a position on a policy issue, analysis is used primarily in an 'advocacy' fashion, i.e. to justify and elaborate that position (Sabatier 1978, Wildavsky 1979, Mazur 1981, Jenkins-Smith 1985). And, fourth, actors generally find it necessary to engage in an analytical debate—i.e. to present technical substantiation for their positions—if they are to succeed in translating their beliefs into policy because, in political systems with dispersed power, they can seldom develop a majority position through the raw exercise of power. Instead, they must seek to *convince* other actors of the soundness of their position concerning the nature of the problem and the consequences of one or more policy alternatives.

One scenario is depicted in Figure 5-3. A few people perceive a problem—e.g. air pollution—which affects their core values and search for information concerning the seriousness of the problem and its causes. They identify one or more causes—such as emissions from a local steel mill—

and, based upon certain understandings of the institutional arrangements needed to correct emitters' behavior, they propose one or more policies (or governmental action programs) to accomplish their objectives. Those who feel themselves aggrieved by the proposed policy and have the resources to do something have a number of options. They can:

1. Challenge the validity of the data concerning the seriousness of the problem
2. Challenge the validity of causal assumptions concerning:
   a) Technical aspects, e.g. the links between emissions, ambient air quality, and health effects
   b) Institutional arrangements which will provide the necessary changes in behavior
3. Attempt to mobilize political opposition to the proposal by pointing to costs to themselves and others, i.e. by creating/enlarging their coalition.

The original group normally responds to these challenges, thus initiating a political and analytical debate. The process is usually mediated by policy brokers interested in keeping the conflict within acceptable limits, and the result is often some sort of governmental action program.

In a new policy area, knowledge about the seriousness of the problem and the validity of various causal assumptions is normally sufficiently uncertain—and the political resources of those challenging the *status quo* sufficiently modest —that the initial governmental program involves a significant research component but little coercion.

If such research and policy analysis provides evidence of a reasonably serious problem, identifies one or more probable causes, and convinces people that a proposed set of institutional arrangements will address the problem without politically unacceptable costs, a more substantial governmental action program will result. Implementation will be assigned to one or more agencies and the problem will disappear into a relatively closed subsystem. Participants usually will seek to refine their understanding of the causal factors and the efficacy of various policy instruments over time. In order to keep potential losers from appealing to outsiders for assistance, efforts will be made to provide inclusive negotiated compromises within the parameters of the program core (Derthick 1979, Wamsley 1983). This will normally continue until external (i.e. systemic) conditions change sufficiently to alter the balance of power within the subsystem.

In some cases, however, research can so substantially alter actors' perceptions of the nature of the problem that major changes result. For example, early pollution control efforts in Los Angeles were based on the assumption that household furnaces were the major source of emissions. But when Dr. A. J. Haagen-Smit of Cal Tech in the mid-1950s identified photochemical smog—not particulates—as the major pollutant and automobiles as one of its major sources, local control of the problem no longer made much sense and authority was gradually transferred to state and federal officials (Hagevik 1970, Krier and Ursin 1977). In a somewhat similar fashion, federally-sponsored research into the health effects of various pollutants—combined with a very imaginative program for diffusing that information to interested citizens—led directly to the formation of clean air interest groups in many urban areas during the late 1960s, in the process significantly altering the balance of power in several local and state subsystems (Sabatier, 1975).

But 'knowledge' does not suddenly appear, become universally accepted, and suggest unequivocal changes in governmental action programs. Instead, findings challenging the accepted wisdom concerning the seriousness of a given problem and its principal causes tend to emerge gradually over time, be challenged by those who perceive their interests to be adversely affected, and thus give rise to the sort of analytical debate depicted in Figure 5-3. In the case of Los Angeles air pollution, for example, Haagen-Smit's findings implicating automobiles and oil refineries first emerged about 1950 and were challenged by *(a)* the refineries, which hired the Stanford Research Institute to dispute them, *(b)* the automobile companies, which launched their own research program, and *(c)* local citizens, who were outraged that they—rather than nasty corporate interests—might be implicated. It was not until 6-8 years later, under the aegis of the independent Air Pollution Foundation (a policy broker), that most parties to the dispute accepted Haagen-Smit's argument about the nature and sources of the problem (Krier and Ursin, 1977: Chap. 6). There then ensued an equally long debate about control measures, with initial efforts focusing on relatively inexpensive technological fixes designed to get the pollutants out of the Basin. Only when those were proven to be infeasible did primary attention shift to reducing automotive emissions, and thus to increasing state and federal involvement (Krier and Ursin, 1977: Chaps. 7-10).

Conditions Conducive to Policy-Oriented Learning Across Belief Systems   This brings us to the distinction between 'learning *within* a belief system' versus 'learning *across* belief systems.' The former is relatively unproblematic: Members of an advocacy coalition are always seeking to improve their understanding of variable states and causal relationships which are consistent with their Policy Core. Likewise, they find it easy to convince each other that attacks on their core programs are based on invalid understandings of the world. When two cores conflict, however, the tendency is for each coalition to talk past the other and thus for a 'dialogue of the deaf' to persist until external conditions dramatically alter the power balance within the subsystem. An example is the debate between proponents of 'soft' vs. 'hard' energy paths in the U.S. (Robinson 1982, also Wildavsky and Tenenbaum 1981, Greenberger et al. 1983).

The task, then, is to identify the conditions under which a productive analytical debate between members of *different* advocacy coalitions is likely to occur. The indicator of such a debate is that one or both coalitions are led to alter Policy Core aspects of their belief system—or at least very important Secondary Aspects—as a result of an observed dialogue rather than a change in external conditions.[13]

The first condition deals with the level of informed conflict. On the one hand, both sides must have sufficient technical resources to be able to criticize the other's causal models and data. They must also have the incentive to expend scarce resources to engage in such an analytical debate. We thus come to the first condition:

> *Hypothesis 6*: Policy-oriented learning across belief systems is most likely when there is an intermediate level of informed conflict between the two. This requires: a) each have the technical resources to engage in such a debate; and that b) the conflict be between secondary aspects of one belief system and core elements of the other or, alternatively, between important secondary aspects of the two belief systems.

A frontal attack by two coalitions on each other's core energizes such defensive reactions that more heat than light is generated, while conflict between unimportant aspects of each other's belief systems does not lead to an allocation of the resources necessary to engage in informed technical debate. Thus an intermediate level of conflict is most conducive to policy-oriented learning (Sabatier 1978:409, Argyris and Schon 1978:112).

The second, and probably most important, condition to informed analytical debate between coalitions in which policy core aspects of at least one belief system are at stake involves the presence of a relatively apolitical forum in which experts of the respective coalitions are forced to confront each other:

> *Hypothesis 7*: Policy-oriented learning across belief systems is most likely when there exists a forum which is: a) prestigious enough to force professionals from different coalitions to participate; and b) dominated by professional norms.

The purpose is to force debate among professionals from different belief systems in which their points of view must be aired before peers. Under such conditions, a desire for professional credibility and the norms of scientific debate will lead to a serious analysis of methodological assumptions, to

---

[13]For arguments somewhat similar to that found in this section, see Lindblom and Cohen (1979) and Taylor (1984).

the gradual elimination of the more improbable causal assertions and invalid data, and thus probably to a greater convergence of views over time concerning the nature of the problem and the consequences of various policy alternatives.

Such fora can take a variety of forms. They may be somewhat specialized institutions such as the Air Pollution Foundation in the Los Angeles case, committees of the National Academy of Sciences (Boffey, 1975), or the proposed 'science court' (Mazur, 1981). Some policy subsystems are dominated by a single professional journal or annual conference in which researchers feel obliged to present their views. Perhaps the ideal institutions are the Swedish commissions, which provide for analytical debate among professionals within an institution which has considerable political legitimacy (Anton 1980, Bulmer 1980, Premfors 1983). Thus, one would predict that the debate between proponents of 'soft' and 'hard' energy paths would be more effectively joined in Sweden than in the U.S., where there has apparently been no such prestigious energy forum (Robinson, 1982).

In addition to these two conditions of informed analytical debate across belief systems, there is a third set of factors which increase the likelihood of policy-oriented learning (whether within or between coalitions). These relate to what might be termed the 'analytical tractability' of a problem (Jenkins-Smith, 1985). Of particular importance are the presence of good performance indicators and the ease of developing causal models:

> *Hypothesis 8*: Problems for which accepted quantitative performance indicators exist are more conducive to policy-oriented learning than those in which performance indicators are generally qualitative and quite subjective.
>
> *Hypothesis 9*: Problems involving natural systems are more conducive to policy-oriented learning than those involving purely social systems because in the former many of the critical variables are *not* themselves active strategists and because controlled experimentation is more feasible.

For both of these reasons, then, one would expect more policy-oriented learning in air pollution control than, for example, mental health. On the other hand, even meeting these two conditions does not guarantee continually improved understanding, as there may still be some issues—e.g. the effects of extremely small doses of pathogens on diseases with long latency periods—which are extremely difficult for science to deal with (Weinberg, 1972).

Policy-oriented learning is concerned with the development of a better understanding of the factors affecting a specific policy area over time. There can be no doubt, for example, that we know much more about air pollution—its atmospheric concentrations, causes, and health effects—than we did thirty years ago. We also know a great deal more about the costs and benefits of various control techniques.

That does not mean, however, that policy conflict has ceased. As long as actors with the requisite political resources find the costs of present policies unacceptable, the agreement on some aspects of the problem and on the probable consequences of some policy alternatives will not lead to a *policy consensus*. Instead, the analytical debate among different coalitions will continue to refine actors' understanding of the seriousness of the problem, the importance of various causal relationships, and the consequences of various alternatives. This problem area is sufficiently complex that new aspects—such as acid rain—are continually arising. But because air pollution control receives reasonably high ratings on at least Hypotheses 6, 8, and 9, the base of empirical agreement should gradually expand over time. It is even possible that the aspiration levels of the various coalitions may be converging, as environmentalists become more circumspect about the possibilities of achieving 'clean' air and as emitters become more resigned to internalizing their externalities. Conflict will continue, however, until all major interests find a given mix of policies to be acceptable.

One must remember, however, that policy-oriented learning, both within and between coalitions, has been only one of several factors affecting changes in air pollution policy over the last few decades. External events—such as the Arab oil boycott, the rise of the environmental movement, Presidential politics (Ingram, 1977)—have also played critical roles, as has changeover in key subsystem personnel such as Haagen-Smit, Muskie, and Ruckelshaus.

Conclusions

Political scientists have traditionally perceived policy change as primarily the product of a power struggle among groups with different resources and values/interests operating within a given regime structure and a changing socio-economic environment (Truman 1951, Easton 1965, Wilson 1973). Over the past decade, however, research has indicated that governmental action programs are based upon (often implicit) causal theories of how the world operates, and thus that much of the policy debate can be understood as disputes over the validity of those causal theories and the adequacy of the data bases involving critical state variables (Pressman and Wildavsky 1973, Berman 1978, Majone 1980, Wildavsky and Tenenbaum 1981, Mazmanian and Sabatier 1981, 1983). One of the principal goals of this framework has been to integrate traditional concerns with political resources and values/interests, on the one hand, with the role of knowledge and policy analysis, on the other.

The framework starts from the premises that (1) policy subsystems constitute a useful focal point for this analysis and (2) that such analyses must incorporate time-spans of a decade or more if they are to do justice to the related topics of 'policy-oriented learning' and 'the enlightenment function of policy research.' The framework argues that policy change is best seen as fluctuations in the dominant belief system (i.e. those incorporated into public policy) within a given policy subsystem over time. While policy analysis and learning can strongly affect secondary aspects of such belief systems, changes in the core aspects of subsystem policy are usually the result of alterations in non-cognitive systemic parameters.

The framework makes at least three important contributions to our understanding of the role of policy analysis in policy-oriented learning and the role of such learning in policy change. First, it takes the concept of policy subsystems—heretofore imbedded in a largely descriptive literature of 'iron triangles'—and uses it as the basis for developing a preliminary theory of policy change both by relating it to the larger political system and by viewing advocacy coalitions (rather than formal organizations or free-floating actors) as the key units of internal structure.

Second, the framework attempts to advance our understanding of the nature of elite belief systems by expanding political scientists' traditional focus on normative elements to include perceptions of causal relationships and variable states (Sabatier and Hunter, 1988). It also goes out on a limb by proposing that the belief systems of policy elites have a three-fold structure composed of a Deep Core of fundamental normative and ontological axioms, a Policy Core of basic policy choices and causal assumptions, and a set of Secondary (implementing) Aspects.

The third, and perhaps most important, innovation of this framework is its focus on policy-oriented learning. This is an effort to show how—despite the partisan nature of most analytical debates and the cognitive limits on rationality—actors' desires to realize core values in a world of limited resources provide strong incentives to learn more about the magnitude of salient problems, the factors affecting them, and the consequences of policy alternatives. If the different coalitions have access to a minimum of technical resources and if authoritative and relatively 'depoliticized' communication fora exist which force competing professionals to address each others' findings, the framework suggests that more adequate causal models and a better understanding of policy impacts will gradually emerge over time (particularly on analytically tractable problems).

It should be clear, however, that—as with any conceptual framework—this is only the beginning of a rather extensive research program. At least six tasks can be identified. First, and most obviously, aspects of the framework need to be tested empirically in a variety of settings. This has begun, but much more needs to be done.[14] Second, alternative frameworks

---

[14]In addition to the case studies by Jenkins-Smith, Heintz, and Weyent found in this symposium, the advocacy coalition framework is also being applied to cases involving airline deregulation, offshore oil development, land use at Lake Tahoe, California water policy, urban renewal, telecommunications regulation, ocean policy (Lester and Hamilton, 1987), and public lands management (Davis and Davis, 1988).

of the role of policy analysis in policy change over periods of a decade or more need to be developed and to be tested against this framework. Third, the relative importance of 'interests' versus 'belief systems' needs to be explored. To what extent, for example, do economists' models based upon individual self-interest provide more parsimonious and equally valid explanations of policy change over time? Fourth, this framework has done little more than mention the role of 'policy brokers.' Yet MacIntyre (personal communication) suggests that brokers can learn even while advocacy coalitions continue to talk past each other and that such learning on their part may play pivotal roles in arranging policy compromises. And Gormley (1986) suggests that the institutional locus of key brokers will vary with the technical complexity and political conflict surrounding an issue. Those are both interesting propositions which merit serious empirical analysis. Fifth, the framework has said very little about the generation and diffusion of new ideas concerning, e.g., causal relationships and policy instruments. One would assume that they are often developed by neutral experts in e.g., universities, and then adopted and popularized by advocates from the appropriate coalitions (Nelson, 1987), but more needs to be done on this process. Finally, subsystem dynamics may vary by policy type (Ripley and Franklin 1982, Meier 1987). For example, one might expect regulatory and redistributive subsystems to be characterized by multiple coalitions, while distributive policies may usually have a single (pork-barrel) coalition except during periods when cost-bearers (e.g. taxpayers or environmentalists) are activated.

Clearly the work has just begun. But I hope that this framework—by dealing with an ambitious topic in a clear and provocative fashion—will stimulate good empirical work and thus lead to a significant improvement in our understanding of the role of relatively technical information in policy-oriented learning and, thence, in policy change over periods of a decade or more.

REFERENCES

ABELSON, ROBERT et at. (1968). *Theories of Cognitive Consistency* Chicago: Rand McNally.

ACKERMAN, BRUCE AND HASSLER, WILLIAM (1981). *Clean Coal Dirty Air*. New Haven: Yale Univ. Press.

AJZEN, ICEK AND FISHBEIN, MARTIN (1980). *Understanding Attitudes and Predicting Social Behavior*. Englewood Cliffs: Prentice Hall.

ANTON, THOMAS (1980). *Administered Politics*. Boston: Martinus Nijhoff.

ARGYRIS, CHRIS AND SCHON, DONALD (1978). *Organizational Learning*. N.Y.: Wiley.

ASHFORD, DOUGLAS (1981). *Policy and Politics in Britain.* Philadelphia: Temple Univ. Press.

AXELROD, ROBERT, ed. (1976). *Structure of Decision.* Princeton: Princeton Univ. Press.

BALBUS, ISAAC (1971). 'The Concept of Interest in Pluralist and Marxian Analysis,' *Politics and Society* 1 (Feb.) 151-177.

BELL, DANIEL (1960). *The End of Ideology.* New York: Free Press.

BERMAN, PAUL (1978). 'Macro- and Micro-Implementation,' *Public Policy* 26 (Spring): 165-179.

BERNSTEIN, MARVER (1955). *Regulating Business by Independent Commission.* Princeton: Princeton University Press.

BERRY, JEFFREY (1977). *Lobbying for the People.* Princeton: Princeton University Press.

BEYER, JANICE AND TRICE, HARRISON (1982). 'The Utilization Process: A Conceptual Framework and Synthesis of Empirical Findings', *Administrative Science Quarterly* 27 (December): 591-622.

BOFFEY, PHILIP (1975). *The Brain Bank of America.* N.Y.: McGraw-Hill.

BREWER, GARRY (1973). *Politicians, Bureaucrats, and the Consultant.* N.Y.: Basic Books.

BREWER, GARRY (1974). 'The Policy Sciences Emerge,' *Policy Science* 15 (Sept.): 239-244.

BREWER, GARRY AND DE LEON, PETER (1983). *Foundations of Policy Analysis.* Homewood: Dorsey.

BROWN, ANTHONY (1987). *The Politics of Airline Deregulation.* Knoxville: University of Tennessee Press.

BROWNE, ERIC (1970). *Coalition Theories.* Beverly Hills, CA: Sage.

BROWNE, ERIC AND DREIJAMIS, JOHN, eds. (1982). *Government Coalitions in Western Democracies.* London: Longmans.

BULMER, MARTIN (1980). *Social Research and Royal Commissions.* London: Allen and Unwin.

BURNHAM, WALTER DEAN (1970). *Critical Elections and the Mainsprings of American Politics.* New York: Norton.

BUTTEL, FREDERICK AND FLINN, WILLIAM (1978). 'The Politics of Environmental Concern,' *Environment and Behavior* 10 (March): 17-36.

CAMERON, JAMES (1978). 'Ideology and Policy Termination: Restructuring California's Mental Health System,' in *The Policy Cycle,* ed. Judith May and Aaron Wildavsky (Beverly Hills: Sage), pp. 301-328.

CAMPBELL, DONALD (1977). 'Reforms as Experiments,' *Readings in Evaluation Research,* ed. by Francis Caro (N.Y.: Russell Sage), pp. 172-204.

CAPLAN, NATHAN et al. (1975). *The Use of Social Science Knowledge in Policy Decisions at the National Level.* Ann Arbor: Institute for Social Research.

COBB, ROGER (1973). 'The Belief Systems Perspective.' *Journal of Politics* 35 (Feb.): 121-153.

CONOVER, PAMELA J. AND FELDMAN, STANLEY (1984). 'How People Organize the Political World: A Schematic Model,' *American Journal of Political Science* 28 (February): 95-126.

CONVERSE, PHILLIP (1964). 'The Nature of Belief Systems in Mass Publics,' in *Ideology and Discontent.* ed. David Apter. N.Y.: Free Press, pp. 206-261.

COOK, BRIAN J. (1988). *Bureaucratic Politics and Regulatory Reform: The EPA and Emissions Trading.* Westport, Conn.: Greenwood Press.

DAHL, ROBERT (1971). *Polyarchy.* New Haven: Yale Univ. Press.

DAVIES, J. CLARENCE (1970). *The Politics of Pollution.* N.Y.: Pegasus.

DAVIS, CHARLES AND DAVIS, SANDRA (1988). 'Analyzing Change in Public Lands Policymaking: From Subsystems to Advocacy Coalitions,' *Policy Studies Journal* (forthcoming).

DE HAVEN-SMITH, LANCE AND C. VAN HORN (1984). 'Subgovernment Conflict in Public Policy', *Policy Studies Journal* 12 (June): 627-642.

DE SWANN, ABRAM (1973). *Coalition Theories and Cabinet Formations.* Amsterdam: Elsevier.

DERTHICK, MARTHA (1979). *Policymaking for Social Security.* Washington: Brookings.

DERTHICK, MARTHA AND QUIRK, PAUL (1985). *The Politics of Deregulation.* Washington, D.C.: Brookings.

DEWEY, JOHN (1938). *Logic: The Theory of Inquiry.* N.Y.: Holt, Rinehart and Winston.

DODD, LAWRENCE (1976). *Coalitions in Parliamentary Governments.* Princeton: Princeton University Press.

DODD, LAWRENCE AND SCHOTT, RICHARD (1979). *Congress and the Administrative State.* N.Y: John Wiley.

DOGGAN, MATTEI (1975). *The Mandarins of Western Europe.* New York: Wiley.

DOWNING, PAUL (1984). *Environmental Economics and Policy.* Boston: Little, Brown & Co.

DUNLEAVY, MICHAEL (1981). *The Politics of Mass Housing in Britain, 1945-75.* Oxford: Clarendon Press.

DUNN, WILLIAM (1980). 'The Two-Communities Metaphor and Models of Knowledge Use,' *Knowledge* 1 (June): 515-536.

DUNN, WILLIAM (1982). 'The Theory of Exceptional Clinicians,' Paper presented at the Conference on the Production of Useful Knowledge, University of Pittsburgh, Oct. 28-30, 1982.

EASTON, DAVID (1965). *A Systems Analysis of Political Life.* N.Y.: Wiley.

ELMORE, RICHARD (1979). 'Backward Mapping,' *Political Science Quarterly* 94 (Winter): 601-616.

ETHEREDGE, LLOYD (1981). 'Political Learning,' in *Handbook of Political Psychology*, ed. by S. Long. N.Y.: Plenum.

ETHEREDGE, LLOYD (1985). *Can Governments Learn? American Foreign Policy and Central American Relations.* New York: Pergamon Press.

FARKAS, SUZANNE (1971). *Urban Lobbying.* New York: New York Univ. Press.

FESTINGER, LEON (1957). *A Theory of Cognitive Dissonance.* Evanston: Row, Peterson.

FISKE, SUSAN AND TAYLOR, SHELLEY (1984). *Social Cognition.* Reading, Mass: Addison-Wesley.

FOLEY, HENRY (1975). *Community Mental Health Legislation.* Lexington, Mass.: D.C. Heath.

FRANKLIN, MARK AND MACKIE, THOMAS (1984). 'Reassessing the Importance of Size and Ideology for the Formation of Governing Coalitions in Parliamentary Democracies,' *American Journal of Political Science* 28 (November): 671-692.

FREEDMAN, P. E. AND FREEDMAN, ANNE (1981). 'Political Learning,' in *The Handbook of Political Behavior* ed. Samuel Long. New York: Plenum, pp. 255-304.

FRITSCHLER, A. LEE (1975). *Smoking and Politics*, 2d ed. Englewood Cliffs: Prentice Hall.

GEORGE, ALEXANDER (1969). 'The Operational Code,' *International Studies Quarterly* 13 (June):110-222.

GOODWIN, LEONARD AND MOEN, PHYLLIS (1981). 'The Evolution and Implementation of Federal Welfare Policy,' in *Effective Policy Implementation*, ed. D. Mazmanian and P. Sabatier. (Lexington: Heath), pp. 147-168.

GORMLEY, WILLIAM (1986). 'Regulatory Issue Networks in a Federal System,' *Polity* (Summer):595-620.

GREENBERGER, MARTIN et al. (1983). *Caught Unawares.* Cambridge, Mass.: Ballinger.

GREENWALD, ANTHONY AND RONIS, DAVID (1978). 'Twenty Years of Cognitive Dissonance: Case Study of the Evolution of a Theory,' *Psychological Review* 85 (No. 1): 53-57.

GRIFFITH, ERNEST (1961). *Congress: Its Contemporary Role*, 3d ed., N.Y.: New York Univ. Press.

HAGEVIK, GEORGE (1970). *Decision-Making in Air Pollution Control.* New York: Praeger.

HAMM, KEITH (1983). 'Patterns of Influence among Committees, Agencies and Interest Groups,' *Legislative Studies Quarterly* 8 (August): 379-426.

HANSON, NORWOOD (1969). *Patterns of Discovery*. Cambridge: Cambridge University Press.

HART, JEFFREY (1976). 'Comparative Cognition: Politics of International Control of the Oceans,' in *Structure of Decision*, ed. R. Axelrod. Princeton: Princeton University Press, Chap. 8.

HECLO, HUGH (1974). *Social Policy in Britain and Sweden*. New Haven: Yale Univ. Press.

HECLO, HUGH (1978). 'Issue Networks and the Executive Establishment,' in *The New American Political System*, ed. A. King. Washington: AEI.

HIBBS, DOUGLAS AND FASSBENDER, H., eds. (1981). *Contemporary Political Economy*. Amsterdam: North Holland.

HINCKLEY, BARBARA (1981). *Coalitions and Polities*. New York: Harcourt, Brace, Jovanovich.

HJERN, BENNY AND PORTER, DAVID (1981). 'Implementation Structures,' *Organization Studies* 2:211-227.

HOFFERBERT, RICHARD (1974). *The Study of Public Policy*. Indianapolis: Bobbs-Merrill.

HOGWOOD, BRIAN AND PETERS, B. GUY (1983). *Policy Dynamics*. N.Y.: St. Martins.

INAN, MICHELE (1979). 'Savior of the Cities—Would You Believe, Howard Jarvis?' *California Journal* 10 (April): 138-139.

INGRAM, HELEN (1977). 'Policy Implementation through Bargaining: Federal Grants in Aid,' *Public Story* 25 (Fall):

INGRAM, HELEN (1978). 'The Political Rationality of Innovation: The Clean Air Act Amendments of 1970,' in *Approaches to Controlling Air Pollution*, ed. by Ann Friedlaender. Cambridge: MIT Press, pp. 12-67.

INNIS, J. M. (1978). 'Selective Exposure as a Function of Dogmatism and Incentive,' *Journal of Social Psychology* 106:261-265.

JANIS, IRVING (1983). *Groupthink*, 2nd ed. Boston: Houghton Mifflin.

JENKINS-SMITH, HANK (1985). 'Adversarial Analysis in the Bureaucratic Context,' in *Advocacy Analysis*, ed. Peter Brown. Baltimore: University of Maryland Press.

JENKINS-SMITH, HANK AND SABATIER, PAUL (1987). 'The Use of Content Analysis to Examine Changes in Elite Beliefs and Public Policy over Time,' Paper submitted to the *American Journal of Political Science*.

JENKINS-SMITH, HANK AND ST. CLAIR, GILBERT (1988). 'Analysis of Change in Elite Policy Beliefs within Subsystems.' Paper presented at the Annual Meeting of the Western Political Science Assn., San Francisco.

JORDAN, A. G. AND RICHARDSON, J. J. (1983). 'Policy Communities: The British and European Style,' *Policy Studies Journal* 11 (June): 603-615.

KAHNEMAN. DANIEL, SLAVIC, PAUL AND TVERSKY, AMOS (1982). *Judgment Under Uncertainty*. Cambridge: Cambridge Univ. Press.

KATZENBACH, EDWARD (1958). 'The Horse Cavalry in the Twentieth Century,' *Public Policy* 8:120-149.

KAUFMANN, HERBERT (1971). *The Limits of Organizational Change*. University, Ala.: University of Alabama Press.

KINGDON, JOHN (1984). *Agendas, Alternatives, and Public Policies*. Boston: Little, Brown.

KIRST, MICHAEL AND JUNG, RICHARD (1982). 'The Utility of a Longitudinal Approach in Assessing Implementation: Title l, ESEA,' in *Studying Implementation*, by Walter Williams. Chatham, N.J.: Chatham House, pp. 119-148.

KISER, LARRY AND OSTROM, ELINOR (1982). 'The Three Worlds of Action,' in *Strategies of Political Inquiry*, ed. E. Ostrom. Beverly Hills: Sage, pp. 179-222.

KNEESE, ALLEN AND BOWER, BLAIR (1968). *Water Quality Management*. Baltimore: John Hopkins.

KNOEPFEL, PETER AND WIEDNER, HELMUT (1982). 'A Conceptual Framework for Studying Implementation,' in T*he Implementation of Pollution Control Programs*, ed. by Paul Downing and Kenneth Hanf. Tallahassee: Policy Sciences Program.

KRASNOW, ERWIN, LAWRENCE LONGLEY, AND HERBERT TERRY (1982). *The Politics of Broadcast Regulation*, 3rd. ed. N.Y.: St. Martin's.

KRIER, JAMES AND URSIN, EDMUND (1977). *Pollution and Policy*. Berkeley: University of California Press.

LAKATOS, IMRE (1971). 'History of Science and Its Rational Reconstruction,' *Boston Studies in the Philosophy of Science* 8:42-134.

LESTER, JAMES AND HAMILTON, MICHAEL (1987). 'Intergovernmental Relations and Marine Policy Change,' in *Ocean Resources and U.S. Intergovernmental Relations in the 1980s*, ed. by Maynard Silva. Boulder: Westview Press, pp. 197-220.

LINDBLOM, CHARLES AND COHEN, DAVID (1979). *Usable Knowledge*. New Haven: Yale University Press.

LIROFF, RICHARD (1986). *Reforming Air Pollution Regulation: The Toil and Trouble of EPAs Bubble*. Washington, D.C.: Conservation Foundation.

MAJONE, GIANDOMENICO (1980). 'Policies as Theories,' *Omega* 8:151-162.

MARCH, JAMES AND SIMON, HERBERT (1958). *Organizations*. N.Y.: Wiley.

MARGOLIS, HOWARD (1974). *Technical Advice on Policy Issues*, Sage Professional Paper on Administrative and Policy Studies (Beverly Hills: Sage).

MARMOR, THEODORE (1970). *The Politics of Medicare*. Chicago: Aldine.

MAZMANIAN, DANIEL AND NIENABER, JEANNE (1979). *Can Organizations Change?* Washington, D.C.: Brookings Institution.

MAZMANIAN, DANIEL AND SABATIER, PAUL. eds. (1981). *Effective Policy Implementation*. Lexington, Mass.: D.C. Heath.

MAZMANIAN, DANIEL AND SABATIER, PAUL (1983). *Implementation and Public Policy*. Chicago: Scott Foresman.

MAZUR, ALLAN (1981). *The Dynamics of Technical Controversy*. Washington, D.C.: Communication Press.

McGUIRE, WILLIAM (1968). 'Theory of the Structure of Human Thought,' in *Theories of Cognitive Consistency* ed. R. Abelson et al., Chicago: Rand McNally, pp. 148-162.

McPHEE, JOHN (1971). *Encounters with the Archdruid*. New York: Farrar, Straus, and Giroux.

MEIER, KENNETH (1987). *Politics and the Bureaucracy*, 2d ed. Monterey, CA.: Brooks/Cole.

MELTSNER, ARNOLD (1976). *Policy Analysts in the Bureaucracy*. Berkeley: University of California Press.

MILWARD, H. BRINTON AND WAMSLEY, GARY (1984). 'Policy Subsystems, Networks, and the Tools of Public Management,' *Public Policy Formation and Implementation*, ed. by Robert Eyestone. N.Y.: JAl Press, Chap. l.

NADEL, MARK (1971). *The Politics of Consumer Protection*. Indianapolis: Bobbs-Merrill.

NELKIN, DOROTHY (1979). *Controversy: Politics of Technical Decisions*. Beverly Hills: Sage.

NELSON, ROBERT (1987). 'The Economics Profession and the Making of Public Policy,' *Journal of Economic Literature* 25 (March): 42-84.

NEWELL, ALLEN AND SIMON, HERBERT (1972). *Human Problem Solving*. Englewood Cliffs: Prentice Hall.

NISBETT, RICHARD AND ROSS, LEE (1980). *Human Inference. Strategies and Shortcomings of Social Judgment*. Englewood Cliffs, NJ.: Prentice Hall.

OKUN, ARTHUR (1975). *Equality and Efficiency: The Big Tradeoff* Washington, D.C.: Brookings.

OSTROM, ELINOR (1982). 'Institutional Arrangements and Learning,' Paper delivered at the ZIF, University of Bielefeld, 20 July.

OSTROM, ELINOR (1986). 'Institutional Arrangements for Managing the Commons Dilemma,' in Bonnie McCay and Janis Acheson, eds., *Capturing the Commons*. Tucson: University of Arizona Press.

OSTROM, VINCENT (1982). 'European Public Administration,' Paper presented at the European Institute of Public Administration, Maastricht, The Netherlands.

OSTROM, VINCENT, TIEBOUT, CHARLES, AND WARREN, ROBERT (1961). 'The Organization of Government in Metropolitan Areas,' *American Pol. Sci. Review* 55 (Dec.): 831-842.

PEFFLEY, MARK AND HURWITZ, JON (1985). 'A Hierarchical Model of Attitude Constraint,' *American Journal of Political Science* 29 (November): 871-890.

PETTY, RICHARD AND CACIOPPO, JOHN (1981). *Attitudes and Persuasion.* Dubuque: Wm. C. Brown.

PIERCE, ROY AND ROCHON, THOMAS (1984). 'Attitudinal Change and Elite Conversion: French Socialist Candidates in 1967 and 1978,' *American Journal of Political Science* 28 (May):379-398.

POPPER, KARL (1959). *The Logic of Scientific Discovery.* London: Hutchinson.

PREMFORS, RUNE (1983). 'Governmental Commissions in Sweden,' *American Behavioral Scientist* 26 (May/June): 623-642.

PRESSMAN, JEFFREY AND WILDAVSKY, AARON (1973). *Implementation.* Berkeley: Univ. of California Press.

PRIMACK, JOEL AND VON HIPPEL, FRANK (1974). *Advice and Dissent.* N.Y.: New American.

PUTNAM, ROBERT (1973). *The Beliefs of Politicians.* New Haven: Yale University Press.

PUTNAM, ROBERT (1976). *The Comparative Study of Political Elites.* Englewood Cliffs: Prentice Hall.

QUIRK, PAUL (1981). *Industry Influence in Federal Regulatory Agencies.* Princeton: Princeton Univ. Press.

RAJECKI, D. W. (1982). *Attitudes: Themes and Advances.* Sunderland, Mass.: Sinauer.

REIN, MARTIN AND WHITE, SELDON (1977). 'Policy Research: Belief and Doubt,' *Policy Analysis* 3 (Spring): 239-271.

RICH, ROBERT ed. (1981). *The Knowledge Cycle.* Beverly Hills: Sage.

RIKER, WILLIAM (1962). *The Theory of Political Coalitions.* New Haven: Yale University Press.

RIPLEY, RANDALL AND FRANKLIN, GRACE (1982). *Bureaucracy and Policy Implementation.* Homewood, Ill.: Dorsey Press.

ROBINSON, JOHN B. (1982). 'Apples and Horned Toads: On the Framework-Determined Nature of the Energy Debate.' *Policy Sciences* 15:23-45.

ROKEACH, MILTON (1973). *The Nature of Human Values.* New York: MacMillan.

ROKKAN, STEIN (1970). *Citizens, Elections, and Parties*. Oslo: Universitaetsforlaget.

SABATIER, PAUL (1975). 'Social Movements and Regulatory Agencies' *Political Science* 6 (Sept.):301-342.

SABATIER, PAUL (1978). 'The Acquisition and Utilization of Technical Information by Administrative Agencies.' *Administrative Science Quarterly* 23 (Sept.): 386-411.

SABATIER, PAUL (1986). 'Top-Down and Bottom-Up Models of Policy Implementation: A Critical Analysis and Suggested Synthesis,' *Journal of Public Policy* 6 (January): 21-48.

SABATIER, PAUL AND HUNTER, SUSAN (1988). 'The Incorporation of Causal Perceptions into Models of Elite Belief Systems,' Paper submitted to the *Western Political Quarterly*.

SABATIER, PAUL AND PELKEY, NEIL (1987). 'Incorporating Multiple Actors and Guidance Instruments into Models of Regulatory Policy-Making: An Advocacy Coalition Framework,' *Administration and Society* 19 (Sept.):236—263.

SABATIER, PAUL, SUSAN HUNTER, AND SUSAN MCLAUGHLIN (1987). 'The Devil Shift: Perceptions and Misperceptions of Opponents.' *Western Political Quarterly* 41 (Sept.): 449-476.

SCHARPF, FRITZ (1982). 'The Political Economy of Inflation and Unemployment in Western Europe: An Outline,' Discussion Paper 81-21 (Berlin: International Institute of Management

SCHATTSCHNEIDER, E. E. (1960). *The Semi-Sovereign People*. N.Y: Holt, Rinehart and Winston.

SCHIFF, ASHLEY (1962). *Fire and Water: Scientific Heresy in the Forest Service*. Cambridge: Harvard Univ. Press.

SCHULTZE, CHARLES (1977). *The Public Use of Private Interest*. Washington, D.C.: Brookings.

SHARPE, L. J. (1984). 'National and Subnational Government and Coordination,' in *Guidance Control and Evaluation in the Public Sector*, ed. F. X. Kaufmann, V. Ostrom and G. Majone (Berlin: de Gruyter).

SIMON, HERBERT (1955). 'A Behavioral Model of Rational Choice,' *Quarterly Journal of Economics* 69:99-118.

SIMON, HERBERT (1979). *Models of Thought*. New Haven: Yale Univ. Press.

SMITH, DON (1968). 'Cognitive Consistency and the Perception of Others' Opinions,' *Public Opinion Quarterly* 32:1-15.

STEINBRUNER, JOHN (1974). *The Cybernetic Theory of Decision*. Princeton: Princeton University Press.

TAYLOR, MICHAEL AND LAVER, MICHAEL (1973). 'Government Coalitions in Western Europe,' *European Journal of Political Research* 1 (September): 205-248.

TAYLOR, SERGE (1984). *Making Bureaucracies Think.* Stanford: Stanford University Press.

TESSER, ABRAHAM (1987). 'Self-Generated Attitude Change,' *Advances in Experimental Social-Psychology* 11:289-338.

TRUMAN. DAVID (1951). *The Governmental Process.* New York: Alfred Knopf.

VIG, NORMAN AND KRAFT, MICHAEL, eds. (1984). *Environmental Policy in the 1980s.* Washington, D.C.: Congressional Quarterly Press.

WAMSLEY, GARY (1983). 'Policy Subsystems as a Unit of Analysis in Implementation Studies,' Paper presented at Erasmus University, Rotterdam, June.

WARWICK, PAUL (1979). 'The Durability of Coalition Governments in Parliamentary Democracies,' *Comparative Political Studies* 11 (January): 465-498.

WEBBER, DAVID (1983). 'Obstacles to the Utilization of Systematic Policy Analysis,' *Knowledge* 4 (June): 534-560.

WEINBERG, ALVIN (1972). 'Science and Trans-Science,' *Minerva* 10 (April): 209-222.

WEISS, CAROL (1977a). *Using Social Research in Public Policy Making.* Lexington: D.C. Heath.

WEISS, CAROL (1977b). 'Research for Policy's Sake: The Enlightenment Function of Social Research,' *Policy Analysis* 3 (Fall): 531-545.

WICKLUND, ROBERT AND BREHM, JACK (1976). *Perspectives on Cognitive Dissonance.* Hillsdale, N.J.: Lawrence Erlbaum Assoc.

WILDAVSKY, AARON (1979). *Speaking Truth to Power.* Boston: Little, Brown.

WILDAVSKY. AARON AND TENENHAUM, ELLEN (1981). *The Politics of Mistrust.* Beverly Hills, Sage.

WILKER, HARRY AND MILBRATH, LESTER (1972). 'Political Belief Systems and Political Behaviour,' in *Political Attitudes and Public Opinion*, ed. D. Nimmo and C. Bonjean. N.Y.: David McKay, pp. 41-57.

WILSON, JAMES Q. (1973). *Political Organizations.* New York: Basic Books.

WITTROCK, BJORN (1983). 'Planning, Pluralism, and Policy Intellectuals,' in *Researchers and Policy-Makers in Education*, ed. T. Husen and M. Kogan. Oxford: Pergamon.

ZARISKI, RAPHAEL (1984). 'Coalition Formation in the Italian Regions,' *Comparative Politics* 16 (July): 403-420.

DISCUSSION
Daniel McCool

The family of concepts grouped under the rubric of "subsystem" theory has a long and popular tradition in political science. A content analysis of twenty popular American government textbooks reveals that eighteen of them refer to iron triangles, ten refer to subgovernments, and issue networks are discussed in eight.[1] Most of them provide no citation for the source of the iron triangle concept; a few cite Freeman or Cater, although neither of these authors used the term. In other words one of the most popular concepts in political science is of obscure, if not totally unknown, origins.

There have been relatively few attempts to systematically validate subsystem theory. However, there are many case studies that utilize some variation of subsystems, which suggests it is a useful way to conceptualize some types of policy making (see, e.g., Gormley 1986; Hansen 1987; King and Shannon 1987; McCool 1987; Adams 1988; Davis and Davis 1988; Heintz 1988; Klay and McElveen 1991). Its popularity is due to its intuitive appeal; many political scientists, politicians, and public administrators apparently feel this is "the way things really are." However, much of the "support" for subsystem theory is anecdotal and impressionistic. For example, nearly half of the textbooks I surveyed stated as fact that most policy was now made by way of Heclo's issue networks, even though the concept is virtually untestable and there is little empirical evidence to support it. In short there is a kind of paradox surrounding subsystem theory; many people like to use it, yet we have made only limited progress in developing it into a coherent, highly specified and testable theory. Like most policy theory, its potential has yet to be fully developed.

There are a number of fundamental issues regarding subsystems that are currently being explored in the literature. A review of these issues gives us a better sense of what subsystem theory can—and cannot—explain.

One of the most significant research questions concerns the role of conflict in subsystem theory. The biggest difference between the traditional notion of iron triangles, and more current concepts of networks and coalitions, is their treatment of conflict. According to the iron triangle concept, conflict is minimized by excluding or co-opting opponents. But this is much more difficult today due to the explosion of interest group activity and budgetary pressures. Thus an important question is, what happens when an iron triangle becomes the focus of a pitched battle over policy?

---

[1] All of these textbooks were published since 1985.

For a policy subsystem to function effectively, there must be some way to limit conflict (Wamsley 1985). Indeed it could be argued that the principle reason for their existence is to either accommodate potential adversaries, or overwhelm them with superior political strength; both of these are responses to conflict (McCool 1989). Under certain conditions conflict cannot be effectively controlled by these methods. In such instances subsystems undergo a series of changes, or collapse altogether (Gormley 1986; Levine and Thurber 1986; Hansen 1987; Ripley and Franklin 1987; Baumgartner and Jones 1993).

In some situations increased conflict gives rise to new subsystems that are in competition with existing subsystems. Fritschler documents the rise of an antismoking alliance that challenged the old tobacco subsystem (1989). Smith noted the rise of a *dissident triangle* that opposed continued increases in defense spending (1988, 163). And a number of authors have characterized coalitions by their relative strength in these conflicts. Sabatier writes of a *dominant coalition* and a *minority coalition* (1988, 148. Also see Wamsley 1985, 83), and Thurber makes a distinction between dominant and competitive subsystems (1991, 328).

Another promising line of research investigates how subsystems change across policy types, time, and policy stages. In regard to the latter, Charles Jones traced how the actors in a subsystem change as an issue proceeds through the stages of policy (1982, 358–408). Palumbo investigated the role of subsystems at the agenda-setting stage and concluded that their influence at that stage was "very powerful" (1988, 51).[2] And Heineman (1986) argues that subgovernments should be treated as a given in the implementation stage.

Other researchers have explored the connection between the subsystem concept and distributive policy. The traditional notion of iron triangles assumes that they exist primarily to dole out porkbarrel,[3] and they do this solely out of self-interest. But there is mounting evidence that porkbarreling is of limited utility or appeal to legislators and bureaucrats (Johannes 1984, 202–3; Fleisher 1985; Lineberry 1985; Rich 1989; Savage 1991; Ellwood and Patashnik 1993; Hamman 1993), and many of them are more interested in making what they perceive to be good policy than simply distributing goodies back home (Johnson, 1992; Lindsay 1991; Mayer 1991; Hird 1993. For an opposing point of view, see: Smith 1988; Uslaner 1989; Cohen and Noll 1991; Kelly 1992). If the subgovernment concept is only applicable to distributive policy, then there is a great deal of policy making that cannot be

[2]For an alternative point of view, see Schull (1983, 4). Capturing the agenda may not be an advantage; see Bender and Moe (1986).
[3]Porkbarrel is the allocation of government largess according to political advantage rather than a neutral, objective criteria.

explained by that concept. This has provided much of the impetus to expand the concept to networks that are involved in all types of policy, not just distributive policy.

Much recent research focuses on how subgovernments have evolved in recent years in response to changes in the political system. Johnson (1991) found that the housing policy subgovernment during the Reagan years switched from distributive to redistributive policy output. And other studies have documented the decline of iron triangles in specific policy arenas such as wildlife policy (Klay and McElveen 1991), agriculture (Browne 1986), western water policy (Miller 1985), and social policy (Weaver 1978). Salisbury et. al. argue that the only true iron triangle left is the veteran's subgovernment (1988, 28).

There are many reasons why iron triangles have been forced to change in recent years. In a word they have been *pluralized*: All three "corners" of the triangle now have multiple participants instead of one or two dominant players. In addition external entities such as the media, policy analysts, and individual policy entrepreneurs now play a larger role. Subsystems also involve different levels of government. But perhaps the most significant question, at least from a theoretical perspective, concerns the impact that the president has on subsystems. The traditional assumption was that subsystems operated largely beyond the control of the president because it just was not worth it politically for a president to interfere persistently with programs that had the intense support of a specific clientele (Jordon 1981, 101). Peterson writes that "a popular conception among academics has long been that [subgovernments]. . . are relatively impervious to outside intervention, even from the president" (1990, 114).

Recent research has attempted to clarify the impact presidents have on subsystems. However, there is no consensus in the literature on this question. A number of studies have examined efforts by the Reagan administration to curtail spending for certain domestic programs. LeLoup writes that the top-down budgeting of the Reagan era "was a direct effort to reduce the power of. . . subgovernments which promote higher spending" (1986, 124. Also see Berry 1989, 252) Rubin examined five programs that Reagan tried to cut; four of these were redistributive social programs, and Reagan succeeded in reducing funding for these. But the fifth program—mass transit— was more of a distributive program, and Rubin found that "Congress defied the president's all-out determination to eliminate operating subsidies for mass transit" (1985, 197). Johnson (1991) investigated another social program—funding for housing. Like Rubin, he found that President Reagan succeeded in cutting spending and challenging the housing subgovernment.

Other scholars have researched the general relationship between subsystems and the president. Shull argues that the president has greatly increased his influence: "Domestic policy formation is anticipated to have changed greatly over the years. Once the province of Congress and subgovernments, agenda-setting and initiation have largely come under the purview of the institutionalized Presidency" (1983, 4). Salisbury makes an even broader claim for enhanced presidential influence: "In the executive branch the most significant development affecting established interest triangles has been the centralization of policy initiatives within the Executive Office of the President and particularly the White House staff" (1990, 214). Hammond and Knott (1988) also conclude that the president now has a major impact on subsystems.

Other scholars have come to a different conclusion. Francis Rourke sums up the response that iron triangles had to the Reagan Administration:

> What the Reagan years rather demonstrate is that the celebrated alliances that link executive agencies, congressional committees and outside groups together in tightly knit policy making systems have defenses in depth against White House efforts to turn existing politics around at the behest of a new President. . . . they can always fall back, quickly regroup in Congress and the courts, and reclaim much of the ground they may initially have lost. (1990, 6–7)

Peterson and Walker reached the same conclusion (1986, 175–76). It should be noted that, while it may be difficult for presidents to cut spending favored by subsystems, presidential support can certainly help them in their quest for funding. One of the largest and most powerful subsystems—defense procurement—received an extraordinary boost from the Reagan presidency. Perhaps the degree of presidential influence over subsystems is a function of two factors: the extent to which the president is willing to sacrifice political capital to fight the subsystem, and the extent to which the president's policy goals are in harmony with the subsystem. The point is we should not assume that presidential "interference" with a subsystem will have a detrimental impact on that subsystem. Indeed some of the domestic subsystems that suffered under Reagan and Bush may have a new lease on life under the Clinton administration.

Another important debate in the literature concerns the relationship between subsystem politics and democracy. There has long been an assumption in the literature that specialized policy alliances are antidemocratic. Griffith characterized the policy whirlpools as a form of *dispersive disintegration* (1939, 340), and Robert Dahl claimed that subgovernments were "nothing less than a shocking outrage to the democratic vision" (1986, 242). Jones advocated a series of reforms to make subsystems more responsive to popular input (1982, 406–8).

But others view subsystems in a more benign light. Redford called them "arenas for adjustment of contending interests" (1969, 104) and concluded that even weaker interests could access government by way of subsystems:

> [S]ubsystems provide some access and representation to interests that are not dominant. While the systems tend to maintain the interests represented in the existing equilibriums, they still provide some access to other interests. And those which find the door to one forum shut may turn to another door, for the subsystems provide multiple channels of access. Occasional victories are won by even the normally excluded. (1969, 105)

Heclo argues that contemporary networks are more democratic than the closed iron triangles of the past (1978, 116). Other authors agree: "issue networks show more potential for fulfilling the pluralist prescription for democratic politics than do subgovernments" (Berry 1989, 257). Thurber characterized subsystems as a "form of functional representation" (1991, 326). Subsystems may be imperfect instruments of democracy, but they may provide access to government.

On the other hand multiple competitive subsystems may produce too much access, too much conflict; the result is overspending in some policy areas, and deadlock in others. In an insightful book about how subsystems rise and fall, Baumgartner and Jones note that "the American political system may be more difficult to control in the 1980s and the 1990s than it was in the 1940s and 1950s. . . ." (1993, 215). Perhaps this helps explain why deficits have skyrocketed while at the same time the federal government seems unable to act decisively on many issues.

Of course the ultimate research question is whether subsystem theory is good theory. Have the numerous studies of subsystems improved it to the point where it can fulfill its role as the foundation of policy theory? There is no doubt that significant progress has been made, but still, there is no shortage of critics.

> We lack...a coherent theory of their [policy networks] origins, their causes, and the precise range of their occurrence. Instead of an explicit set of propositions about why these networks come into being in some places and at some times, we have only scattered and generally unsystematic notions about political exchange, and about the absence of effective centralized control, and about deeply held beliefs in decentralization and self-government. (Hansen 1987, 184)

This inadequate theoretical specification leads to methodological problems:

> Unless the reader is given some notion of the reasons for why a particular actor qualifies as a member of a policy subsystem and for why another actor does not, he or she will have no chance of assessing the validity and reliability

of what the analyst has done. That is the acid test of social science, and it is why the unit-of-analysis problem in (not only) policy research is a pre-eminently methodological one. (Hull 1985, 103)

Despite these shortcomings, subsystem theory still offers a unique perspective of how policy is made. It also permits us to apply, and ultimately improve, our understanding of other theories of policy making:

> ...the power triad is a simple concept. But it has the special capacity to link together a variety of theories of the policy process; traditional pluralism, plural elitism, state autonomy, corporatism, social movements and... traditional institutions. One hopes theorizing will move in this direction. (McFarland 1987, 147)

The great advantage to subsystem theory is that, like the alliances it models, it cuts across innumerable dimensions of policy making.

1. It improves our understanding of who participates. Are iron triangles the vehicles of elite preference? Are issue networks the fulfillment of pluralist theory, as Cigler and Loomis suggest (1986, 307)?

2. It improves our understanding of the policy-making process. Does subsystem theory help explain why incrementalism is a common strategy? Does subsystem theory point out the limitations of systems theory? Can it help us understand the differences between policy stages?

3. It improves our understanding of typologies. If we correlate iron triangles with distributive policy, and issue networks with regulatory and redistributive policy, can we increase our understanding of each of those policy types?

And finally subsystem theory tells us something about our governing institutions and how they interact with each other and with nongoverning entities such as interest groups, the media, and policy specialists. In this sense subsystem theory is potentially the most powerful policy theory of all. It would be a mistake, however, to assume—as many writers do—that a subsystem can be found for every issue. For that to be true the concept would have to be so generic as to lose much of its meaning. The research challenge is to explain the differences between various subsystems and identify the conditions under which they operate.

Writing fifty-five years ago, Ernest Griffith ended his book with a question regarding whether society and its government will be able to control policy whirlpools: "Can institutional adjustments and an integrating motivation move quickly enough to stem the existing dispersive disintegration" (1939, 340)? We still do not have an adequate answer to that question. But the enormous body of literature on subsystems has added immeasurably to our understanding of the problem.

REFERENCES

ADAMS, GORDON (1988). "The Iron Triangle: Inside the Defense Policy Process." In *The Domestic Sources of American Foreign Policy*, pp. 70–78. Edited by Charles Kegley and Eugene Wittkopf. New York: St. Martin's Press.

BAUMGARTNER, FRANK, AND BRYAN JONES (1993). *Agendas and Instability in American Politics*. Chicago: University of Chicago Press.

BENDER, JONATHAN, AND TERRY MOE (1986). "Agenda Control, Committee Capture, and the Dynamics of Institutional Politics." *American Political Science Review* 80 (Dec.): 1189–1207.

BERRY, JEFFREY (1989). "Subgovernments, Issue Networks, and Political Conflict." In *Remaking American Politics*, pp. 239–60. Edited by Richard Harris and Sidney Milkis. Boulder, CO: Westview Press.

BROWNE, WILLIAM (1986). "Policy and Interests: Instability and Change in a Classic Subsystem." In *Interest Group Politics*, 2d. ed., pp. 183–201. Edited by Allen Cigler and Burdett Loomis. Washington, D.C.: Congressional Quarterly Press.

CIGLER, ALLAN, AND BURDETT LOOMIS (1986). "Moving On: Interests, Power, and Politics in the 1980s." In *Interest Group Politics*, 2d. ed., pp. 303–16. Edited by Allen Cigler and Burdett Loomis. Washington, D.C.: Congressional Quarterly Press.

COHEN, LINDA, AND ROGER NOLL (1991). *The Technology Porkbarrel*. Washington, D.C.: The Brookings Institution.

DAHL, ROBERT (1986). *Democracy, Liberty, and Equality*. Norwegion University Press.

FLEISHER, RICHARD (1985). "Economic Benefit, Ideology, and Senate Voting on the B-1 Bomber." *American Politics Quarterly* 13 (April): 200–11.

FRITSCHLER, LEE (1989). *Smoking and Politics*, 4th ed. Englewood Cliffs, NJ: Prentice-Hall.

GORMLEY, WILLIAM (1986). "Regulatory Issue Networks in a Federal System." *Polity* 18 (Summer): 595–620.

GRIFFITH, ERNEST (1939). *The Impasse of Democracy*. New York: Harrison-Hilton Books.

HAMMAN, JOHN (1993). "Bureaucratic Accommodation of Congress and the President: Elections and the Distribution of Federal Assistance." *Political Research Quarterly* 46 (Dec.): 863–79.

HAMMOND, THOMAS, AND JACK KNOTT (1988). "Accountability in Agency-Legislative Committee Interaction." Paper presented at the annual meeting of the American Society for Public Administration, Portland, OR.

HANSEN, JOHN MARK (1987). "Choosing Sides: The Creation of an Agricultural Policy Network in Congress, 1919–32." *Studies in American Political Development* 2 (annual): 183–235.

HEINEMAN, ROBERT (1986). "Teaching Program Implementation." *News for Teachers of Political Science* (no. 48): 10–11.

HEINTZ, THEODORE (1988). "Advocacy Coalitions and the OCS Leasing Debate." *Policy Science* 21 (nos. 2–3): 213–38.

HIRD, JOHN (1993). "Congressional Voting on Superfund: Self-Interest or Ideology?" *Public Choice* 77 (2): 333–57.

HULL, CHRISTOPHER (1985). "Comment." Accompanying article by Gary Wamsley. In *Policy Implementation in Federal and Unitary Systems*, pp. 97–103. Edited by Kenneth Hanf and Theo Toonen. Boston: Martinus Nijhoff.

JONES, CHARLES (1982). *The United States Congress*. Chicago, IL: Dorsey Press.

JOHNSON, CATHY MARIE (1992). *The Dynamics of Conflict Between Bureaucrats and Legislators*. Armonk, NY: M. E. Sharpe.

JOHNSON, WILLIAM (1991). "Housing Policy Under the Reagan Presidency: The Demise of an Iron Triangle." *Policy Studies Review* 10 (Winter): 69–87.

JORDON, A. GRANT (1981). "Iron Triangles, Woolly Corporatism and Elastic Nets: Images of the Policy Process." *Journal of Public Policy* 1 (Winter): 95–123.

KELLY, BRIAN (1992). *Adventures in Porkland*. New York: Villard Books.

KING, LAURISTON, AND WAYNE SHANNON (1987). "Political Networks in the Policy Process: The Case of the National Sea Grant College Program." *Polity* 19 (Winter): 213–31.

KLAY, WILLIAM, AND JAMES MCELVEEN (1991). "Planning as a Vehicle for Policy Formulation and Accommodation in an Evolving Subgovernment." *Policy Studies Journal* 19 (nos. 3–4): 527–33.

LELOUP, LANCE (1986). *Budgetary Politics*, 3d. ed. Brunswick, OH: King's Court Communications.

LEVINE, CHARLES, AND JAMES THURBER (1986). "Reagan and the Intergovernmental Lobby: Iron Triangles, Cozy Subsystems, and Political Conflict." In *Interest Group Politics*, 2d. ed., pp. 202–20. Edited by Allen Cigler and Burdett Loomis. Washington, D.C.: Congressional Quarterly Press.

LINDSAY, JAMES (1991). *Congress and Nuclear Weapons*. Baltimore: The Johns Hopkins University Press.

MAYER, KENNETH (1991). *The Political Economy of Defense Contracting*. New Haven: Hale University Press.

McCOOL, DANIEL (1987). *Command of the Waters: Iron Triangles, Federal Water Development, and Indian Water.* Berkeley: University of California Press.

_____ (1989). "Subgovernments and the Impact of Policy Fragmentation and Accommodation." *Policy Studies Review* 8 (Winter): 264–87.

MILLER, TIM (1985). "Recent Trends in Federal Water Resource Management: Are the 'Iron Triangles' in Retreat?" *Policy Studies Review* 5 (Nov.): 395–412.

PALUMBO, DENNIS (1988). *Public Policy in America.* New York: Harcourt Brace Jovanovich.

PETERSON, MARK (1990). *Legislating Together.* Cambridge, MA: Harvard University Press.

PETERSON, MARK, AND JACK WALKER (1986). "The Impact of the Reagan Administration upon the National Interest Group System." In *Interest Group Politics,* 2d. ed., pp. 162–82. Edited by Allan Cigler and Burdett Loomis. Washington, D.C.: Congressional Quarterly Press.

RICH, MICHAEL (1989). "Distributive Politics and the Allocation of Federal Grants." *American Political Science Review* 83 (March): 193–213.

RIPLEY, RANDALL, AND GRACE FRANKLIN (1987). *Congress, The Bureaucracy, and Public Policy,* 4th ed. Homewood, IL: Dorsey Press.

REDFORD, EMMETTE (1969). *Democracy in the Administrative State.* New York: Oxford University Press.

ROURKE, FRANCIS (1990). "Executive Responses to Presidential Politics: The Reagan Presidency." *Congress and the Presidency* (Spring): 1–11.

RUBIN IRENE (1985). *Shrinking the Federal Government.* New York: Longman.

SABATIER, PAUL (1988). "An Advocacy Coalition Framework of Policy Change and the Role of Policy-Oriented Learning Therein." *Policy Science* 5 21 (nos. 2–3): 129–68.

SALISBURY, ROBERT (1990). "The Paradox of Interest Groups in Washington—More Groups, Less Clout." In *The New American Political System, Second Version,* pp. 203–51. Edited by Anthony King. Washington, D.C.: The AEI Press.

SALISBURY, ROBERT, JOHN HEINZ, EDWARD LAUMANN, AND ROBERT NELSON (1988). "Iron Triangles: Similarities and Differences among the Legs." Paper presented at the annual meeting of the American Political Science Association, Washington, D.C.

SHULL, STEVEN (1983). *Domestic Policy Formation: Presidential—Congressional Partnership?* Westport, CT: Greenwood Press.

SMITH, HEDRICK (1988). *The Policy Game.* New York: Random House.

THURBER, JAMES (1991). "Dynamics of Policy Subsystems in American Politics." In *Interest Group Politics,* 3d ed., pp. 319–43. Edited by Allan

Cigler and Burdett Loomis. Washington, D.C.: Congressional Quarterly Press.

USLANER, ERIC (1989). *Shale Barrel Politics*. Stanford, CA: Stanford University Press.

WAMSLEY, GARY (1985). "Policy Subsystems as a Unit of Analysis in Implementation Studies: A Struggle for Theoretical Synthesis." In *Policy Implementation in Federal and Unitary Systems*, pp. 71–96. Edited by Kenneth Hanf and Theo Toonen. Boston: Martinus Nijhoff.

WEAVER, PAUL (1978). "Regulation, Social Policy, and Class Conflict." *The Public Interest* 50 (Winter): 45–63.

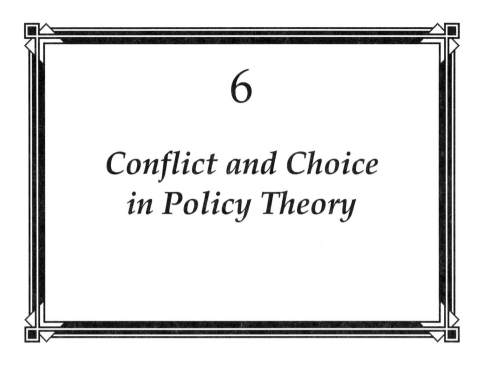

6

Conflict and Choice in Policy Theory

INTRODUCTION: THE AGE OF DEAD IDEAS?

Forty years ago Lasswell challenged us to develop a rigorous and "scientific" approach to policy science; since then progress has been, at best, erratic. Doron claims we are no closer to achieving the goals of policy science than when they were first enunciated in the 1950s (1992, 304). Many questions have been raised concerning the quality of published research on policy, especially regarding its theoretical content. The widespread assumption is that policy science has been a disappointment, but perhaps we are simply being unrealistic about what we can achieve. Early policy scholars may have created unrealistic expectations that virtually guaranteed disappointment.

Another perspective on this problem concerns the intellectual context in which policy science has developed. The social sciences seem to be enveloped in a kind of epistemological ennui generated by a perverse gap between our ability to *build* theory and *critique* theory. We are apparently much better at the latter than the former. Torgerson writes that "Current methodological departures. . .have not been kind to frameworks. . . . The tendency—or, if one wishes, fashion—is to question, not to establish or maintain or even revise frameworks" (1992, 228).

Indeed it seems that just about every ideational construct we have developed has now been debunked or discarded. This is the postindustrial/

postmodern/postpositivist era. We have read about the end of ideology, the end of liberalism, even the end of history. Much modern scholarly analysis focuses on "deconstructionism." One wonders: What is left? In such a climate of rejection should we be surprised that policy science has not lived up to initial expectations?

Although policy science has yet to save the world, there has been undeniable progress in the development of policy theory. It would be a serious mistake to conclude we do not have a rich theoretical tradition in policy science. However, this field of scholarly endeavor is still in a nascent stage compared to other, more developed areas of scientific inquiry.

Although it is impossible to assemble this disparate set of theoretical work into one cohesive construct, it may be instructive to combine some of the more prevalent theoretical features into a graphic composite. Figure 6-1, The Policy-Making Milieu, is a simple representation of the major concepts presented in this book. The term *milieu* was selected because the more commonly used terms, *system* and *process*, connote a degree of orderliness and unity that is lacking in actual policy making.

The periphery of the figure represents the general stages of policy making and the formal institutions of government. Rather than attempt to identify discrete policy types, such as Lowi's typology or incremental and nonincremental policy, I have merely indicated that many different types of policy result from the policy formulation stage.

In the center of Figure 6-1 I have placed *extragovernmental entities*, meaning those entities that are not part of the formal structure of government but play a role in policy making. These are not "external inputs." Rather, they are very much an integral part of the process. These sources of extragovernmental input are arranged in a hierarchy of inclusiveness; "elites" is the most exclusive entity, and "Voters/Public Opinion" the most inclusive. The placement of these entities in the center of the figure accurately portrays the centrality of these sources in the policy-making milieu.

Between the formal institutions of government and the nongovernmental entities is an area labeled "Exchange Medium," referring to the way in which policy-making participants interact. This model views policy making as an exchange process in which policy makers in the formal institutions of government—elected officials, bureaucrats and judges, and staff, interact with extragovernmental entities—and each other—in an effort to gain what they value. The model identifies both the substantive matter exchanged in this medium, and the nature or character of the exchange. The substance of exchanges in policy making include: information, power, rights, and resources. Each exchange is characterized by one or more of the following: cooperation, conflict, competition, bargaining, exploitation, and occasionally indifference. The exchange medium completely surrounds the extragovernmental entities; this is meant to show that these entities affect all stages of the policy-making process, but also recognizes that extragov-

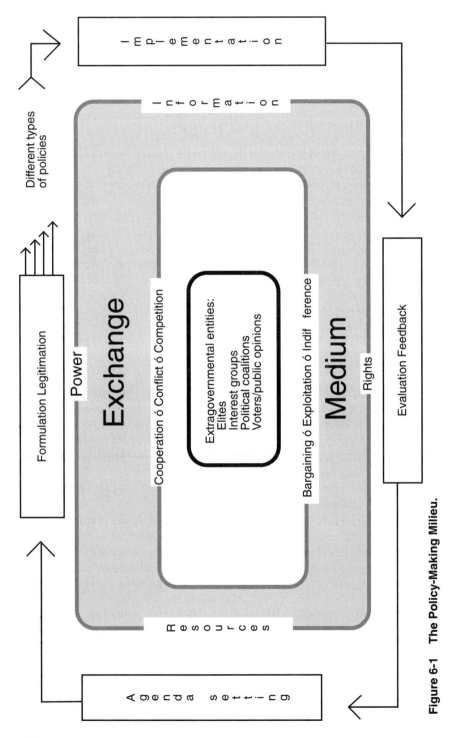

Figure 6-1   The Policy-Making Milieu.

ernmental entities are in turn influenced by the formal structures of government at every stage of the process.

This schematic of the policy-making milieu is sufficiently generic that most if not all of the concepts discussed in this book are represented. A pluralist theorist would focus on interest groups operating by way of bargaining; a public choice theorist would assume that self-serving exploitation is the principal modus operandi for all actors; a democratic theorist would concentrate on voters and public opinion influencing government by way of competition and conflict in the electoral arena. And a student of subsystems would be most interested in the cooperative exchanges that take place between governmental and nongovernmental entities.

This model, like all models, is a simplification and does not include every element in the milieu. For example, it would be more accurate to specifically indicate that every actor or institution in the policy-making milieu may engage in an exchange with every other actor in the milieu. Such a diagram would be more valid, but it would also be a mess. A model must be understandable to be useful.

Can it be said that we have no theory with which to work? The implication of this figure is clear: While we have rejected much of our conceptualization of reality, there is still a core of policy theory which can support future inquiry. Amid dead ideas there is life.

Figure 6-1 is a view to the past, of what we have already conceived. Building upon this, policy scholars continue to generate an impressive array of conceptual tools with which to analyze public policy. Despite the critics, policy scholars are engaged in a constructive theoretical dialogue. Hendrick and Nachmias perceptively argue, in essence, that what has been perceived as failure is actually a hallmark of progress: "The fact that so many more questions are being raised now is not an indicator of failure [of policy science] but rather a manifestation of progress and the increased awareness of complexity and its attendant uncertainty" (1992, 312).

THE FUTURE: THEORETICAL CHOICES

Students of public policy have much to work with; an astounding array of conceptual work is available, and only a small part of it has been presented in this book. The challenge before us now is to figure out how all these concepts, theories, and approaches relate to each other. So much theory has been developed without a full understanding of how it relates to other theories, that the field is beset by disparate and seemingly unconnected conceptualization. To a great extent the future success and direction of policy studies will be determined by the extent to which policy theorists investigate and resolve this balkanization of policy theory; the emphasis of future theoretical work must be directed toward the *relationships* between policy theories. The literature is aware of the problem (see, e.g., Brunner and Ascher 1992; Mesaros and Balfour 1993), but there is little coherence to the critique, and it has not produced a comprehensive and constructive understanding of theory relationships; it is a piecemeal attempt to overcome the disadvantages of piecemeal theory building.

There are many opinions regarding what is "wrong" with policy theory. These various perspectives and debates can be categorized into four basic and closely related issues: The scope of policy theory; the goals of policy theory, the underlying paradigm(s), which guide(s) policy theory building; and the role of values in policy theory. I explore each of these issues and propose a "contingent approach" to organize various theoretical perspectives into a more cohesive and coordinated body of theoretical work.

The Scope of Policy Theory

Twenty year ago Dror claimed that social science was characterized by an "oscillation between ideographic micro-studies and 'grand theory'" (1971, 9). In regard to public policy the former has received much more attention than the latter, even after decades of searching for Kuhn's paradigms (Ball 1976, 153). Thus far the one best paradigm has yet to be found, but policy theorists are still in open debate as to whether micro- or macro-theory should be the focus of theory-building efforts.

The question is whether a general theory is needed but simply has not yet been developed, or whether it is impossible to construct such a theory, and policy scholars would do well to spend their time on more "manageable tasks" (Anderson 1990, 262). Some scholars are prepared to sound the death-knell for general macro-theory (Bobrow and Dryzek 1987, 5). Anderson claims the ". . . quest for a general theory [of politics] has been consigned to the disciplinary dustbin" (1990, 262). DeLeon explains that attempts to develop an "all-encompassing metatheory" failed because policy science lacks the theoretical and conceptual foundation for it, and it contradicts the applied orientation (1988, 26).

Others advise that policy science needs less ambitious—and more realistic—theory. Anton argues that we need "middle-range generalizations" that are somewhere between macrotheory and the "bootleg conceptual frameworks" that characterize most policy case studies (1989, 20. See Lane's [1990] related discussion of *concrete theory*). Portis points out that, "Rather than the development of an elaborate general theory, the social scientist is primarily concerned with understanding specific situations in light of their relevance to his social commitments. . ." (1988, 234).

But can policy science ever escape from its theoretical "second-class status" without a theory (or theories) that provides some macrolevel theoretical coherence to the field? Indeed much of the criticism is precisely due to the absence of generalizable theory. Jenkins notes that "To some. . . a field with no integrated theory is weak and of little use in applied matters" (1978, 32).

A close look at the literature reveals that, while a grand general theory has yet to emerge, conceptual contributions have been made that are widely generalizable. Although there is no consensus on a general theory per se, there are some frameworks that permit diverse application. Jenkins-Smith (1990) and Goodin (1982, 18) point out the widespread use and application of utilitarianism. The "advocacy coalition" framework can be applied to an extremely diverse set of policy-making situations (Sabatier 1987, 1988). And the Easton systems model promised near-universal application; it has been widely criticized, not because of its lack of generalization, but because it worked so poorly as a "middle-range theory" in the "specific situations" alluded to previously. The point is policy scholars have not given up on developing widely generalizable theory. Indeed progress is being made, primarily because of an inherent realization that policy science will never attain scientific legitimacy without it. Policy science will never have a theory that explains everything, at least not at an acceptable level of detail. But theory that explains how other theories fit together may produce some similar advantages.

The disillusionment with general theory can be traced in part to a misapplication of such theories. Many policy analysts believe that general theory is of limited utility—that it cannot serve the interests of applied research. This derives from attempts to apply general theory to specific cases—and expecting theoretical guidance at the microlevel. Demanding detailed specificity in macrotheory will not lead us out of the theoretical thicket. Rather policy scholars must pick and choose carefully which theories are to be applied. This requires a better understanding of the relationship between macro- and microtheories, and their intended uses (the subject of the following section).

Much time and effort has been spent generating the ad hoc theories that Blair and Maser (1977) describe. And much effort, at least in the past, has been generated to produce general theory. The pressing task before us now is to develop better general theory and a greater understanding of how that theory relates to the microtheory favored by so many contemporary scholars.

In sum both micro- and macrotheory are needed if the policy sciences are to develop their full potential. In addition we need a much fuller understanding of how these two disparate sets of constructs fit together. This will reduce the tendency to misapply policy models. A micro–macro continuum of theoretical constructs would permit the selection of an appropriate level of generalization/specificity, depending upon its application. Thus the choice of theory dimension is contingent upon its application. This leads to the next concern in the literature: What are the goals and the purposes of policy theory?

The Goals of Policy Theory

Lasswell's seminal call for a policy science was based on the assumption that science could help policy-makers produce "good" policy. This was supposed to be the "instrumental end" of policy science (Graham 1988, 152). But in the ensuing forty years that goal has proven illusive as policy science continues to suffer from an "inability to translate existing theories into concrete policy guidance." (May 1986, 110. Also see Greenberger et al. 1976, 23). It may be that the goals of policy science have changed, or, that goal displacement has occurred.

One critique of policy theory holds that the goal of theory is to be practical—to be directly relevant to applied policy problems. Bobrow and Dryzek argue that ". . .policy analysis is above all a practical activity. . . . If we can determine the appropriate role of theory in relation to this practice, then we can go far toward determining how to make good use of the various frames" (1987, 16). DeLeon is even more fundamental: "The policy sciences will continue to be required to answer the following oldest and most insistent of political questions: What have you done for me lately? And what can you do for me tomorrow?" (1988, 111). At its most extreme the applied orientation creates a "technician posture" for the policy scientist (Heineman et al. 1990, 27). Thus to meet Lasswell's mandate for good policy guidance, theory becomes a management tool.

Not everyone is comfortable with this interpretation; Forcese and Richer consider theory to be "the object or goal of science, and therefore theory is the output and the result of cumulative research" (1973, 47). This of course turns the relationship around: Is theory a means or an end? It appears that most scholars are comfortable with the theory-as-tool prescription, but there is a concern that theory may simply get in the way of actually solving problems. These concerns fall into two camps. The first camp argues that theory interferes because it is too general, and the other camp argues that the quest for theoretically valid analysis has resulted in too narrow a focus.

Several scholars express concerns about theory being too general. "Theory is both incomplete and general, meaning that heavy reliance on it may divert attention away from important aspects of the particular case it does not cover" (Brewer and deLeon 1983, 10). From a British perspective Hogwood and Gunn write that "In the United States in particular, political science has been seen as straining after ever higher levels of generalization (as in systems theory) at the cost of remoteness from 'real' problems" (1984, 34).

At the other end of the spectrum, scholars worry that narrow theoretical and methodological imperatives threaten the problem-solving orientation of policy science (Graham 1988, 153). Majone suggests that the cumulative effect of an overly narrow "decisionist" approach is to "produce an overintellectualized version of policy analysis which gives undue emphasis to the more technical aspects of a subject. . ." (1989, 19. Also see Putt and Springer 1989, 16). Dror makes a similar accusation: "At present policy scientists usually deal with microissues which easily fit into available 'hard' methodologies. . ." (Dror 1984, 4). The net result is disappointing; Chelimsky asserts that ". . . in many cases the question that most needs a response is precisely the one that researchers cannot answer" (1991, 228).

In a very real sense both of these perspectives are correct; both macro- and micro-theory have their place, but when they are misapplied, things go wrong. The disparity in viewpoints on this issue points to this troublesome conclusion: policy science has the potential to be oxymoronic; if the emphasis is on the policy, then it becomes increasingly difficult to emphasize the science, and vice versa. Lasswell's call for a "fuller realization of human dignity" (1951, 10) can be mated with scientific methodology only with great care.

In essence what these scholars are telling us is that general macrotheory serves the science component, and particularistic microtheory serves the policy component. Thus both are very necessary, both are an integral part of policy science, but neither can substitute for the other. Again, it is the relationship between the two that becomes important. It is not an either/or choice, but rather a decision contingent upon the goals that are chosen. Theory serves us, but only if we can specify what we want it to do.

That is not easy. Policy scholars have identified a host of purposes and goals for various theoretical approaches (for some examples see: Frohock 1967, 7–11; Goggin 1987, 13–22; Hofferbert 1990, 11–12). The only way that policy can be successfully mated to science is if we have a better understanding of the gap between scientific macrotheory and applied policy microtheory. When we improve our ability to choose one in relationship to the other—when we make each contingent upon the other—then the debate as to whether theory is too broad or too narrow will become moot. The previous critiques are valid, but only because policy science has yet to perfect our understanding of the relationship between micro- and macrotheory, and how they relate to the goals of policy science.

The Epistemology of Policy Theory

All social science, but especially political science, has been affected by the debate over positivist science and its scion, behavioralism. Many scholars speak of the postpositivist era, but many others still value the traditional scientific paradigm. And even the detractors of positivism admit that it still dominates most research. This section looks at both sides of the debate over positivist policy science, proposed alternatives, and how they relate to one another.

In recent years policy science has gone through an era of soul-searching and self-doubt. The very foundations of its existence are being called into question, especially the reliance on the traditional positivist paradigm.[1] Yehezkel Dror has persistently argued for moving beyond the confines of traditional positivism in policy science: "The inadequacy of present normal sciences for the purposes of policymaking improvement is the result of their basic paradigms. Therefore, in order to produce the scientific inputs necessary for policymaking improvement, a scientific revolution is essential" (1971, 28. Also see Dror 1984, 6). Although a scientific revolution has yet to take place, it is commonplace to speak of the postpositivist/postbehavioralist era. Heineman et al. surmise that attacks on the positivist tradition, at least in regard to policy analysis, "have damaged its claims, probably irreparably" (1990, 23).

Many of these critiques conclude that the problem lies only with *positivist* science, and some other form of scientific enterprise would be acceptable. Others disparage the scientific approach in general, arguing that policy simply does not lend itself to scientific investigation.

> Conventional ideas and approaches regarding solutions may actually inhibit their attainment. . . . Science's success in framing and answering questions within the scientific realm is indisputable; but for many other problems that fall outside the bounds scientists delineate, the rational bias, tight discipline, and quantitative procedures erected to support the scientific edifice provide little help. (Brewer and de Leon 1983, 3)

Some scholars take issue with specific elements in the positivist science tradition. Spitzer argues that policy is not amenable to "law-like propositions" (1989, 530). Putt and Springer note that science requires "systematic clarification" and "standardized procedures," but argue that policy analysis must not "rest upon routinized approaches to policy problems" (1989, 22–23). House claims that policy models can never be validated in a technically scientific sense (1982, 125–27. Also see MacRae 1985: 87–89).

A somewhat different point is made by Dubin, who intimates that social science has gradually strayed from its positivist moorings. He accepts the basic philosophy of positivism, but charges that social science theory has developed into something that is far different from the "pure" positivism of the physical sciences:

> {S]ocial scientists have tended to accumulate theories and theoretical models. The social scientist funds theory and not data. It is not unusual for courses in the area of theory in a social science discipline to be a recital of what each notable historical figure in the field believed or said. The student typically learns a history of ideas about the empirical world that falls within the range of his particular social-science discipline. But he may be singularly ignorant of the

---

[1]For a discussion of the "post-empiricist" philosophy of science, see Roth (1987) and Bernstein (1976).

descriptive and factual character of that domain. The behavioral scientist tends to accumulate belief systems and call this the *theory* of his field. (1969, 238–39)

Others take a different tack and argue that traditional science is perfectly adequate but incorrectly applied, creating a hypocritical pseudo-science. Writing about systems analysis, Hoos concludes that

> The interesting paradox remains that techniques which have been bought and sold as "scientific" could continue to ignore so blatantly the rudimentary precepts of scientific procedure. Independent verification and validation are virtually nonexistent. . . (1983, xii)
>   . . .With such key concepts as *system* and *model* elusive of articulation and subject to marked latitude of interpretation and semantic sleight-of-hand, the ascription of "scientific precision" to the method built on them constitutes a striking paradox." (1983, 8)

House and Shull make a similar point when discussing how models have been misapplied in policy analysis "The heyday of model development in the 1960's and 1970's spawned a saying on the part of the user community regarding the technicians who proselytize a particular model or methodology as the way to address a policy issue: 'When all you have is a hammer, the whole world looks like a nail'" (1988, 163).

A number of authors have proposed alternatives to traditional positivism, some of which are specific to policy theory. De Leon proposes a "post-positivist policy science" that "would transform the Eastonian 'black box' of political decision-making into a more transparent 'glass box' in which decisions could be openly viewed and understood, if not always influenced" (1988, 112–18). Hawkesworth describes a set of "post-positivist presupposition theories" (1988, 190), and Paris and Reynolds identify an "agentistic perspective" that is "different from, and in some ways incongruous with, the deterministic outlook of science" (1983, 30). Other alternatives to traditional positivism include "interpretive social inquiry" (Jennings 1983: 3–35); "a value-oriented epistemology" (Fischer 1980); "social constructionism" (Guba and Lincoln 1989); and "valuative discourse" (MacRae 1976). At a more pragmatic level House lists experience, brainstorming, persuasion, and common sense as "alternatives" to formal policy modeling (1982, 286).

Another area of promising conceptual development consists of a growing literature on *design science* and policy analysis by design. Policy design is a contextually sensitive, iterative analytical process in which analyst and subject interact. This may mean that the researcher alters the research in response to changing inputs from the subject, or it may mean that the researcher attempts to create or control the subject to be studied. Linder and Peters define it as "a purposeful or goal-directed rearrangement of a problem's manipulable features" (1988, 739. Also see Goggin 1987; Dryzek and

Ripley 1988; Schneider and Ingram 1990; Weimer 1992). Bobrow and Dryzek note that policy design is a "move from the philosophy of inquiry to the philosophy of design," but that it is "more a shift in emphasis than a radical break. . ." (1987, 19). Miller's concept of design science focuses on interactive technique, dynamic models, and feedback. She admits it "does not exist as a coherent paradigm" (1984, 266), but argues that it "replaces the implicit assumptions of natural science with the explicit assumptions that are more consistent with the accumulated results of empirical research on social systems " (1984, 253).

Although the development of the design perspective is a promising contribution to our ability to apply theory to real problems, it is not entirely new; in the seminal book *The Policy Sciences* Lazarsfeld and Barton counseled us to adapt research to the "structure of the situation" and the "respondent's frame of reference" (1951, 157).

None of these approaches to theory building constitute a full-blown alternative to positivism. Indeed some of them can or should be used in conjunction with traditional empirical approaches. However, they contribute to an increasingly sophisticated application of science, or some alternative, to the study of policy; they help us tailor theory to specific research questions. Alternatives to positivism, along with traditional positivist approaches, provide an epistomological diversity that increases our ability to match theory to application. Thus I think the significance of alternative approaches is not as a replacement for positivism, but as a complement to positivism.

Much of the criticism of positivist science is aimed at its quantitative orientation—the crude empiricism that Lasswell warned about (1951, 4–5). In the ensuing years qualitative analysis has gained widespread acceptance (see Strauss 1987; Berg 1989; Marshall and Rossman 1989; King, Keohane, and Verba 1994), and other non-quantitative approaches are receiving increasing attention. Nevertheless it would seem that the abandonment of quantitative analysis would blind one eye of an endeavor that already suffers from less than 20/20 vision (see Simon 1985, 293–304).

Despite the enduring criticism positivist science is still the dominant force in social science as a whole—and probably still the dominant force in policy science. In the case of the latter, Amy claims that positivism's persistence is due to political reasons rather than its value as a useful paradigm.

> There are. . . important political forces at work in policy analysis. These forces not only discourage the use of critical, post-positivist approaches, but also help to explain why positivist methodologies continue to dominate in policy analysis, despite the fact their their intellectual foundations were undermined at least a decade ago. Positivism survives because it limits, in a way that is politically convenient, the kinds of questions that analysis can investigate. Moreover, the aura of science and objectivity that surrounds positivist policy analysis adds to the image of the policy analyst as an apolitical technocrat. (1984, 210–11 See also Agnew and Pyke 1994)

Others still regard positivism as a valid approach to policy science. Even some critics agree that basic scientific principles are still a necessary foundation to good research. Dror writes that, "Despite all innovativeness, policy science belongs to the scientific endeavor and must meet the basic tests of science in respect to verification and validation" (1971, 14). MacRae notes that policy models still must be "tested by scientific procedures" (1985, 87). And there are many unapologetic proponents of positivism that view it as a prescription for discovering truth.

> But how are we to determine whether or not a proposition is true? It is this concern with verification that defines social science and distinguishes it from other kinds of knowledge. . . . But social scientists, by profession, are skeptics . . . [they believe in] dispassionate inquiry and a willingness to suspend belief. Evidence becomes something of an obsession, for it is through evidence, systematically garnered in accordance with fixed procedures, that social scientists arrive at "truth." This insistence on evidence is the hallmark of social science—the single most important factor that distinguishes it from knowledge derived from other sources. (Friedman and Steinberg 1989, 2)

Rather than abandon positivism, or immediately dismiss the many new epistomological contributions, it is much more constructive to utilize all approaches, but to do so in a manner that maximizes their utility rather than exposes their limitations. This calls for a careful application of multiple techniques and theories contingent upon the task at hand.

The Role of Values in Policy Theory

Much of the debate over paradigms centers on the role of values in both building and applying theories.[2] A considerable literature argues that objective, value-free research is simply not possible, or, it is possible, but it greatly limits the usefulness of policy science.

There are many authors who directly reject the basic premise of value-free science. Brewer and deLeon maintain that theory and model building are inevitably value laden: "The construction and interpretation of formal models and theories about social structures and processes are basically judgmental matters" (1983, 135). Hogwood and Gunn attack the rational model that has played such a dominant role in policy science: "The main intellectual difficulty with rationality models. . . is the part played by values. . . . To see 'rationality' and politics as intrinsically incompatible is based on a fundamental misunderstanding of the role of values in rational models" (1984, 48). DeLeon goes even further and claims that values shape methodology as well as theory: ". . . there is no such thing as a 'value-free' study or even methodology" (deLeon 1988, 39). Stone claims all analytical reasoning

---

[2]This debate is treated at length in MacRae 1976; Rein 1976; Fischer 1980, 1993; Diesing 1982; Noble 1982.

is shaped by "political struggle" and "political argument" (1988, 306. Also see Goodin 1988).

If it is true that a traditional Lasswellian policy science is impossible, then the scientific legitimacy of the endeavor is called into question. Portis argues that the absence of an objective theory makes it impossible to establish a "professional certification" for policy analysis (1988, 234–35). Lindblom makes a similar point; he says social scientists lose their professional imprimatur when they venture into value conflicts: ". . . professional researchers or social scientists have no special competence even to advise on the reconciliation of interests in conflict" (1986, 349).

Many scholars have been especially critical of the notion that objective policy analysis can somehow replace political exchange. This in turn leads to concern over its impact on democratic processes.

> The fact/value dichotomy deployed by empirical policy analysts subtly sustains the displacement of politics by science. It does so by holding out a promise of incontrovertible truth, which is both impossible and distortive of the political process. By promising a proof which is impossible, the scientific rhetoric of policy analysis endorses the repudiation of all decision criteria that fall short of certainty; in cultivating a desire for the indubitable, it denies the rationality of deliberative choice; in confusing the question of proof with the question of political choice, it unduly constricts the sphere of political freedom. (Hawkesworth, 1988, 188)

Other observers argue that value-free empiricism has forced policy analysis to de-emphasize the role of values: "Unfortunately for the analysis of policy and the health of democratic processes, the move toward scientific objectivity spawned a denigration of the importance of values" (Heineman et al., 1990, 13. Also see Goodin 1982). In short, policy analysis threatens rather than serves democracy, as Lasswell envisioned.

Others are willing to perhaps concede that objective research is possible, but only under very limited conditions, and these limits dramatically reduce the utility of policy science: "Perhaps the largest impediment to useful policy research is the prescription of disinterestedness, or to use the more frequent expression—value neutrality" (Rogers 1989, 15).

Not everyone is prepared to forsake value-free policy science. Indeed, as one of the premier tenets of the positivist paradigm, it still finds favor in many circles. Forcese and Richer argue that, "if science employs some standardized techniques of inquiry, and more important, explicit canons of verification, then science may correct for extra-scientific influences relative to a given social environment. . ." (1973, 24). Furthermore it is not at all clear that we have the theoretical foundation for value-directed analysis. Dror long ago noted an "absence of a methodology for prescriptive and policy-oriented behavioral science endeavors. . . . (1971, 11). I think most policy scholars would agree that we have yet to solve this problem. As May points out, "The continuing challenge for the education of future analysts is to enhance the capacity for critical thinking about policy problems and ideas. This requires going much beyond technical analyses to provide insights about policy principles and their compatibility with dominant political ideologies" (1989, 211). This would certainly expand the utility of policy science, but most of the theory developed thus far cannot guide such inquiry.

It seems clear that the potential for value-based research is a function of the type of research being conducted. We should not ask policy scientists to make recommendations regarding major policy issues, and then charge them with failing to use "pure" science. Conversely a scientific model may provide the most appropriate guide to answering a question regarding causative agents operating in an empirically discrete setting. Jenkins-Smith argues convincingly that the ability of policy analysts to fulfill the role of "objective technician" is dependent on identifiable characteristics of the policy arena, especially its "analytical tractability" (1990, 97–109).

Furthermore the various stages of research and analysis vary in terms of the potential for value input; the selection of the research question is undoubtedly guided by the predilections of the analyst, as is the interpretation of the results. But analysts with a variety of normative perspectives can probably agree on appropriate statistical procedures for data analysis.

We can condemn analysis as being hopelessly biased. Or, we can insist that all policy science be shoe-horned into a positivist model. Perhaps a better approach is to first identify the extent of the potential for value input, and second, develop appropriate theoretical constructs and research procedures that are designed to accommodate value input in a constructive manner.

This would require the development of an "ethic of policy theory," in which the normative commitments of the analyst or theorist—and the extent to which such commitments may affect the research—be identified in the initial stage of research. This creates three advantages. First, it permits all theory and analysis to be interpreted in light of known normative perspectives. Second, it makes policy science more congruent with democratic processes; it will be much clearer whether analysis is merely contributing increased empirical understanding *to* the policy-making process, of whether it is an active player *in* the policy-making process. And last, declared biases permit analysis from a variety of viewpoints; a conscious decision can be made to employ competing frameworks, methodologies, and analysts. Hogwood and Gunn propose a similar idea that they call *the analysis of analysis*, which would include "both the appraisal of the assumptions about facts and values built into definitions of a problem and proposed solutions to it, and the ability to analyze critically the often implicit assumptions associated with particular techniques..." (1984, 268).

The debate over the role of values in policy science, like the conflicts over paradigms, the goals of policy theory, and the scope of policy theory, is often based on absolutist perspectives. Yet most of what policy science purports to do is relativistic in nature. None of the arguments expressed in these debates are "wrong," per se, but their application is contingent upon a complex set of factors. Rather than choose one viewpoint over another, I think it is much more fruitful to identify the conditions under which they can be utilized most effectively. This will require a much greater understanding of how the "plethora of theories" (Blair and Maser 1977, 282) relate to each other as well as the larger question of how to build appropriate policy theory.

THE CONTINGENT APPROACH

The four conflicts identified above are closely related; one cannot be considered without the others. It is this relationship that is the focus of the contingent approach to building policy theory. A starting point to understanding these relationships is to think in terms of continua rather than absolutes or dichotomies. In Figure 6-2 a two-by-two matrix is presented using two continua: (1) positivist/post-positivist theory, and (2) micro-/macrotheory.

On the first continua the positivist approach emphasizes objective, value-neutral theory as the dominant ethic, while the postpositivist approach emphasizes a subjective value-driven ethic. On the second continua microtheory concentrates on finite, discrete phenomena, while macrotheory attempts to explain larger, more complex phenomena.

These two continua permit us to divide policy research into four quadrants. In the upperleft-hand quadrant Decision Analysis relies upon a positivist theoretical framework and is based on microtheory pertaining to finite, discrete phenomena. This type of analysis is concerned with specific decisions, that is, they are relatively discrete phenomena with a discernable time frame and impact. Quite often the only way to achieve such specification is to narrow the research to a single decision.

Traditional Policy Analysis is in the upper-right-hand quadrant. The pure policy science as envisioned by Lasswell would fall into this category. It is empirical and value neutral, but is based on macrotheories concerning the most important and complex policy problems.

In the lower-right-hand quadrant is Interpretive Policy Studies, which includes policy research and analysis that is explicitly normative in approach and makes a conscientious effort to produce specific policy outcomes. This is a recognition that policy science often crosses the line from advising policy makers, to being an active participant in the policymaking process. The focus of this type of research is often an entire policy area, with an emphasis on prescriptive evaluations of policy outcomes.

In the lower-left-hand quadrant is research I have labeled Component Analysis. Policy making is a disjointed process that is divided into stages,

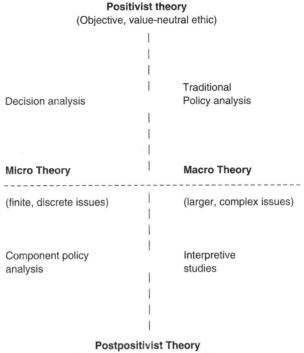

Figure 6-2   The Contingent Approach to Policy Theory.

different procedures or design features, substantive impacts, and policy tools. Many policy studies actually study just one or two of the components that comprise the entire policy-making milieu. Thus in contrast to the interpretive policy studies found in the lower-right-hand quadrant, component analysis focuses on one particular component of that process. Thus component analysis examines discrete elements in a policy-making area and, like interpretive policy studies, incorporates value-induced input into research with a conscientiously subjective orientation.[3]

Policy scholars have expended a great deal of effort attempting to create viable theory. And while no overarching grand theory has emerged, there is a considerable body of theory that displays a high degree of generality. In addition there are numerous microrange and middle-range theories that have made a contribution to our ability to understand public policy. The weakness in the literature is not the lack of theory, but our understanding of how all of the extent theoretical work fits together. The contingent approach advocated here is simply a beginning—a first step—designed to em-

---

[3]Concrete theory, as described by Ruth Lane (1990), may fit into this category.

phasize choices of theory. Additionally it could be argued that a contingent approach could be developed separately for theory, methods, and forms of knowledge acquisition. The point is that we must tailor our research tools to fit the task at hand; we must select the appropriate theories, concepts, and approaches depending upon the purpose of our research and what we hope to accomplish.

We often lapse into arguing various theoretical perspectives from an absolute rather than a relative perspective. As s result we fail to view our theoretical achievements as complementary. Rather we promote particular perspectives as mutually exclusive choices. This book began with a list of quotations deriding the quality of policy theory. The criticisms are valid, not because of the absence of theory, but because of our failure thus far to explain the contingent nature of that theory. When we have a better understanding of how to apply, connect, relate, and network various theoretical perspectives, the critics will have less to talk about.

CONCLUSION

In the last few years the amount of published research relevant to policy theory has ballooned. While I was writing this book I experienced considerable difficulty just keeping up with the new literature. I suspect that if I had waited fifteen or twenty years to publish this book, it would look quite different. This indicates that we may finally be moving beyond mere criticism of current theory and entering a new era of creative conceptualization and constructive theory building.

However, this view toward a brighter future should in no way distract from what has already been accomplished. Some of the readings in this book are now "classics" in scholarly writing. They have had a profound impact on the way we think about public policy. The relationship between these classics of the past and the flurry of new thinking is quite simply the scientific process in action: Theories are proposed, critiqued, modified or rejected, and they ultimately contribute to other theories that are proposed, critiqued, and modified or rejected.

No single theory will ever explain the totality of public policy making. We will always have multiple theories that are sometimes complementary, sometimes in competition. Our task is to evaluate each of them, choose the theories that are most appropriate to the task at hand, understand their relationship to other theories, and then judiciously apply them in a manner that increases our understanding. In addition we must perform these tasks in a manner that is ethical, professional, and enlightening, which is no small task, to be sure. If there is one point upon which nearly all scholars of public policy agree, it is the enormous difficulty of this undertaking. So the next time you read a new theory about how public policy is made, ask yourself,

Can I do better? If you think the answer is yes, then by all means make a contribution; we can use it.

REFERENCES

AGNEW, NEIL, AND SANDRA PYKE (1994). *The Science Game*, 6th ed. Englewood Cliffs, NJ: Prentice-Hall.

AMY, DOUGLAS (1984). "Toward a Post-Positivist Policy Analysis." *Policy Studies Journal* 13 (Sept.): 207-11.

ANDERSON, CHARLES (1988). "Political Judgment and Theory in Policy Analysis." In *Handbook of Political Theory and Policy Science*, pp. 184–98. Edited by Edward Portis and Michael Levy. New York: Greenwood Press.

ANDERSON, JAMES (1990). *Public Policymaking*. Boston: Houghton Mifflin Co..

ANTON, THOMAS (1989). *American Federalism and Public Policy*. New York: Random House.

BALL, TERENCE (1976). "From Paradigms to Research Programs: Toward a Post-Kuhnian Political Science." *American Journal of Political Science*. 20 (Feb.): 151–75.

BERG, BRUCE (1989). *Qualitative Research Methods*. Boston: Allyn & Bacon.

BERNSTEIN, RICHARD (1976). *The Restructuring of Social and Political Theory*. New York: Harcourt Brace Jovanovich.

BLAIR, JOHN, AND STEVEN MASER (1977). "Axiomatic versus Empirical Models in Policy Studies." *Policy Studies Journal* 5 (Spring): 282–89.

BLUHM, WILLIAM, ed. (1982). *The Paradigm Problem in Political Science*. Durham, NC: Carolina Academic Press.

BOBROW, DAVIS, AND JOHN DRYZEK (1987). *Policy Analysis by Design*. Pittsburgh: University of Pittsburgh Press.

BREWER, GARRY, AND PETER DELEON (1983). *The Foundations of Policy Analysis*. Homewood, IL: The Dorsey Press.

BRUNNER, RONALD, AND WILLIAM ASCHER (1992). "Science and Responsibility." *Policy Sciences* 25 (no. 3): 295–331.

CHELIMSKY, ELEANOR (1991). "On the Social Science Contribution to Governmental Decision-Making." *Science* 254 (Oct.): 226–331.

DEHAVEN-SMITH, LANCE, AND RANDALL RIPLEY (1988). "The Political-Theoretical Foundations of Public Policy." In *Handbook of Political Theory and Policy Science*, pp. 97–109. Edited by Edward Portis and Michael Levy. New York: Greenwood Press.

DELEON, PETER (1988). *Advice and Consent: The Development of the Policy Sciences*. New York: Russel Sage Foundation.

DIESING, PAUL (1982). *Science and Ideology in the Policy Sciences.* New York: Aldine Publishing.

DORON, GIDEON (1992). "Policy Sciences: The State of the Discipline." *Policy Studies Review* 11 (Autumn/Winter): 303–09.

DRESANG, DENNIS (1983). "Forward" to *The Logic of Policy Inquiry*, by David Paris and James Reynolds. New York: Longman.

DROR, YEHEZKEL (1968). *Public Policymaking Reexamined.* Scranton, PA: Chandler Publishing Co..

_____ (1971) *Design for Policy Sciences.* New York: American Elsevier.

_____ (1984) "On Becoming More of a Policy Scientist." *Policy Studies Review* 4 (Aug.): 13–21.

DRYZEK, JOHN, AND BRIAN RIPLEY (1988). "The Ambitions of Policy Design." *Policy Studies Review* 7 (Summer): 705–19.

DUBIN, ROBERT (1969). *Theory Building.* New York: The Free Press.

DUBNICK, MEL, AND BARBARA BARDES (1983). *Thinking About Public Policy.* New York: John Wiley.

DUNN, WILLIAM (1981). *Public Policy Analysis.* Englewood Cliffs, NJ: Prentice-Hall.

_____ (1988). "Methods of the Second Type: Coping with the Wilderness of Conventional Policy Analysis." *Policy Studies Review* 7 (Summer): 720–37.

EULAU, HEINZ (1977). "The Interventionist Synthesis," Workshop on "The Place of Policy Analysis in Political Science: Five Perspectives." *American Journal of Political Science* 21 (May): 419–23.

FISCHER, FRANK (1980). *Politics, Values, and Public Policy: The Problem of Methodology* . Boulder, CO: Westview Press.

_____ (1989). "Literature Review Essay: Beyond the Rationality Project: Policy Analysis and the Postpositivist Challenge." *Policy Studies Journal* 17 (Summer): 941–51.

_____ (1993). *Evaluating Public Policy.* Chicago: Nelson-Hall.

FORCESE, DENNIS, AND STEPHEN RICHER (1973). *Social Science Research Methods.* Englewood Cliffs, NJ: Prentice-Hall.

FRIEDMAN, SHARON, AND STEPHEN STEINBERG (1989). *Writing and Thinking in the Social Sciences.* Englewood Cliffs, NJ: Prentice-Hall.

FROHOCK, FRED (1967). *The Nature of Political Inquiry.* Homewood, IL: Dorsey Press.

GOGGIN, MALCOM (1987). *Policy Design and the Politics of Implementation.* Knoxville: University of Tennessee Press.

GOODIN, ROBERT (1982). *Political Theory and Public Policy.* Chicago: University of Chicago Press.

_____ (1988). "Political Theory as Policy Analysis—and Vice Versa." In *Handbook of Political Theory and Policy Science*, pp. 63–73. Edited by Edward Portis and Michael Levy. New York: Greenwood Press.

GORMLEY, WILLIAM (1987). " Institutional Policy Analysis: A Critical Review." *Journal of Policy Analysis and Management* 6 (Winter): 153–69.

GRAHAM, GEORGE (1988). "'The Policy Orientation' and the Theoretical Development of Political Science." In *Handbook of Political Theory and Policy Science*, pp. 150–61. Edited by Edward Portis and Michael Levy. New York: Greenwood Press.

GREENBERGER, MARTIN, MATTHEW CRENSON, AND BRIAN CRISSEY (1976). *Models in the Policy Process*. New York: Russel Sage Foundation.

HAM, CHRISTOPHER, AND MICHAEL HILL (1984). *The Policy Process in the Modern Capitalist State*. Brighton, Sussex, GB: Wheatsheaf Books.

HECLO, HUGH (1972). "Review Article: Policy Analysis." *British Journal of Political Science* 2 (Jan.): 83–108.

HEINEMAN, ROBERT, WILLIAM BLUHM, STEVEN PETERSON, AND EDWARD KEARNY (1990). *The World of the Policy Analyst*. Chatham, NJ: Chatham House Publishers.

HOFFERBERT, RICHARD (1990). *The Reach and Grasp of Policy Analysis*. Tuscaloosa, AL: University of Alabama Press.

HOGWOOD, BRIAN, AND LEWIS GUNN (1984). *Policy Analysis for the Real World*. London: Oxford University Press.

HOUSE, PETER (1982). *The Art of Public Policy Analysis*. Beverly Hills: Sage Publications.

HOUSE, PETER, AND ROGER SHULL (1988). *Rush To Policy*. New Brunswick: Transaction Books.

JENKINS, W. I. (1978). *Policy Analysis*. London: Martin Robertson.

JENKINS-SMITH, HANK (1990). *Democratic Politics and Policy Analysis*. Pacific Grove, Ca: Brooks/Cole.

JENNINGS, BRUCE (1983). "Interpretive Social Science and Policy Analysis." In *Ethics, The Social Sciences, and Policy Analysis*, pp. 3–35. Edited by Daniel Callahan and Bruce Jennings. New York: Plenum Press.

KING, GARY, ROBERT KEHANE, AND SIDNEY VERBA (1994). *Designing Social Inquiry: Scientific Inference in Qualitative Research*. Princeton, NJ: Princeton University Press.

LANE, RUTH (1990). "Concrete Theory: An Emerging Political Method." *American Political Science Review* 84 (Sept.): 927–40.

LASSWELL, HAROLD (1951). "The Policy Orientation." In *The Policy Sciences*, pp. 3–15. Edited by Daniel Lerner and Harold Lasswell. Stanford, CA: Stanford University Press.

_____. *A Pre-View of Policy Sciences* (1971). New York: American Elsevier.

LAVE, CHARLES, AND JAMES MARCH (1975). *An Introduction to Models in the Social Sciences.* New York: Harper and Row.

LEVY, MICHAEL (1988). "Political Theory and the Emergence of a Policy Science." In *Handbook of Political Theory and Policy Science*, pp.1–10. Edited by Edward Portis and Michael Levy. New York: Greenwood Press.

LINDBLOM, CHARLES (1986). "Who Needs What Social Research for Policy-making?" *Knowledge: Creation, Diffusion, Utilization* 7 (June): 345–66.

LINDER, STEPHEN, AND B. GUY PETERS (1988). "The Analysis of Design or the Design of Analysis?" *Policy Studies Review* 7 (Summer): 738–50.

MACRAE, DUNCAN JR. (1976). *The Social Function of Social Science.* New Haven: Yale University Press.

_____ (1985). *Policy Indicators.* Chapel Hill: The University of North Carolina Press.

MAJONE, GIANDOMENICO (1989). *Evidence, Argument and Persuasion in the Policy Process.* New Haven: Yale University Press.

MARSHALL, CATHERINE, AND GRETCHEN ROSSMAN (1989). *Designing Qualitative Research.* New York: Sage Publications.

MAY, PETER (1986). "Politics and Policy Analysis." *Political Science Quarterly* 101 (Spring): 109–25.

MAZMANIAN, DANIEL, AND PAUL SABATIER (1980). "A Multivariate Model of Public Policy-Making." *American Journal of Political Science* 24 (Aug.): 439–68.

MERRIAM, CHARLES (1921). "The Present State of the Study of Politics." *American Political Science Review* XV (May): 173–85.

MESAROS, WILLIAM, AND DANNY BALFOUR (1993). "Hermeneutics, Scientific Realism, and Social Research: Toward A Unifying Paradigm for Public Administration." *Administrative Theory and Praxis* 15 (no. 2): 25–36.

MILLER, JAMES G. (1956). "Toward a General Theory for the Behavioral Sciences." In *The State of the Social Sciences*, pp. 29–65. Edited by Leonard White. Chicago: University of Chicago Press.

MILLER, TRUDI C. (1984). "Conclusion: A Design Science Perspective." In *Public Sector Performance*, pp. 251–68. Edited by Trudi C. Miller. Baltimore: Johns Hopkins University Press.

MITCHELL, JERRY (1988). "The Limits of Positivism: Case Studies of Values in Science." *Policy Studies Journal* 17 (Fall): 215–20.

MUZZIO, DOUGLAS, AND GERALD DE MAIO (1988). "Formal Theory and the Prospects of a Policy Science." In *Handbook of Political Theory and Policy Science*, pp.127–45. Edited by Edward Portis and Michael Levy. New York: Greenwood Press.

NOBLE, JAMES B. (1982). "Social Structure and Paradigm Synthesis: Theoretical Commensurability and the Problem of Mannheim's Paradox." In *The Paradigm Problem in Political Science*, pp. 25–64. Edited by William T. Bluhm. Durham, NC: Carolina Academic Press.

PALUMBO, DENNIS (1981). "The State of Policy Studies Research and the Policy of the New *Policy Studies Review*." *Policy Studies Review* 1 (Aug.): 5–10.

_____ (1988). *Public Policy In America*. New York: Harcourt Brace Jovanovich.

PARIS, DAVID, AND JAMES REYNOLDS (1983). *The Logic of Policy Inquiry*. New York: Longman.

PORTIS, EDWARD (1988). "The Theoretical Illegitimacy of Social Scientific Expertise." In *Handbook of Political Theory and Policy Science*, pp. 231–42. Edited by Edward Portis and Michael Levy. New York: Greenwood Press.

PUTT, ALLEN, AND J. FRED SPRINGER (1989). *Policy Research*. Englewood Cliffs, NJ: Prentice-Hall.

QUADE, E. S. (1989). *Analysis for Public Decisions*, 3rd ed., revised by Grace Carter. New York: North Holland.

RANNEY, AUSTIN (1968). "The Study of Policy Content: A Framework for Choice." In *Political Science and Public Policy*, pp. 3–21. Edited by Austin Ranney. Chicago: Markham.

REIN, MARTIN (1976). *Social Science and Public Policy*. New York: Penguin Books.

RIPLEY, RANDALL (1985). *Policy Analysis in Political Science*. Chicago: Nelson-Hall.

ROBERTSON, DAVID, AND DENNIS JUDD (1989). *The Development of American Public Policy*. Glenview, IL: Scott-Foresman.

ROGERS, JAMES (1988). *The Impact of Policy Analysis*. Pittsburgh: The University of Pittsburgh Press.

_____ (1989). "Social Science Disciplines and Policy Research: The Case of Political Science." *Policy Studies Review* 9 (Autumn): 13–28.

ROTH, PAUL (1987). *Meaning and Method in the Social Sciences*. Ithaca: Cornell University Press.

RUDNER, RICHARD (1966). *Philosophy of Social Science*. Englewood Cliffs, NJ: Prentice-Hall.

SABATIER, PAUL (1989). "Political Science and Public Policy: An Assessment." Paper presented to the annual meeting of the American Political Science Association, Aug. 30– Sept. 2. 1989, Atlanta, GA.

_____ (1987). "Knowledge, Policy-oriented Learning, and Policy Change: An Advocacy Coalition Framework." *Knowledge: Creation, Diffusion, Utilization* 8 (June): 379–426.

_____ (1988). "An Advocacy Coalition Framework of Policy Change and the Role of Policy-oriented Learning Therein." *Policy Sciences* 21 (1988): 129–68.

SCHNEIDER, ANNE, AND HELEN INGRAM (1990). "Policy Design: Elements, Premises, and Strategies." In *Policy Theory and Policy Evaluation*, pp. 77–101. Edited by Stuart Nagel. New York: Greenwood Press.

SIMON, HERBERT (1985). "Human Nature in Politics: The Dialogue of Psychology with Political Science." *American Political Science Review* 79 (June): 293–304.

SPITZER, ROBERT (1989). "From Complexity to Simplicity: More on Policy Theory and the Arenas of Power." *Policy Studies Journal* 17 (Spring): 529–36.

STONE, DEBORAH (1988). *Policy Paradox and Political Reason*. Glenview, IL: Scott, Foresman.

STRAUSS, ANSELM (1987). *Qualitative Analysis for Social Scientists*. New York: Cambridge University Press.

TORGERSON, DOUGLAS (1992). "Priest and Jester in Policy Sciences: Developing the Focus of Inquiry." *Policy Sciences* 25 (no. 3): 225–35.

VAN MAANEN, JOHN, ed. (1983). *Qualitative Methodology*. Beverly Hills: Sage Publications.

WEIMER, DAVID (1992). "The Craft of Policy Design: Can it Be More than Art?" *Policy Studies Review* 11 (Autumn/Winter): 370–88.